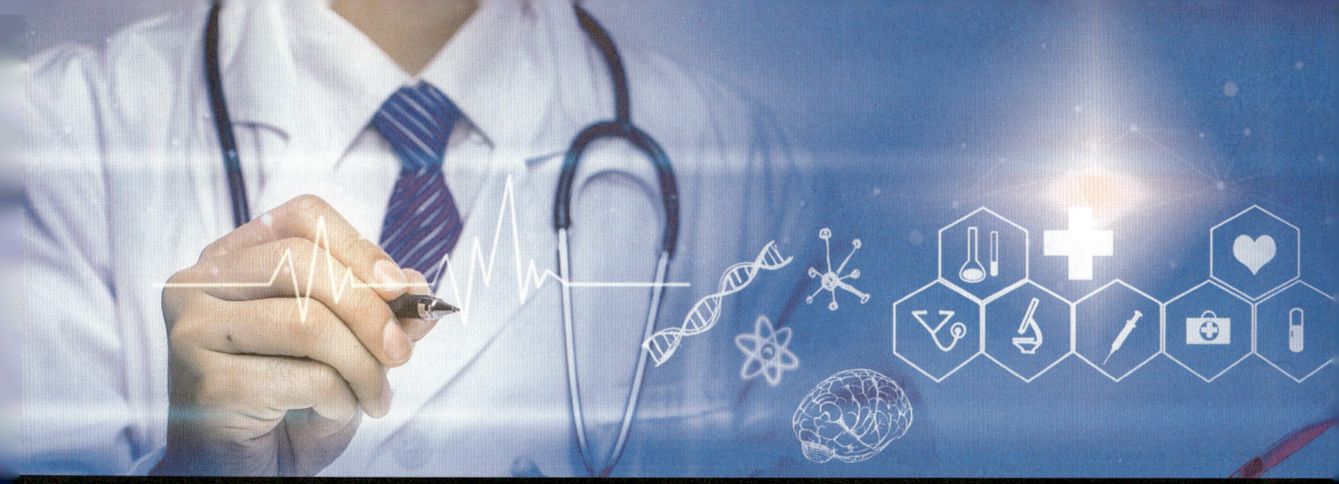

DIGITAL HEALTHCARE PLATFORM

A SOFTWARE ENGINEERING APPROACH

Sungyoung Lee

Professor,
Department of Computer Science and Engineering,
Kyung Hee University, Korea.

HONGREUNG PUBLISHING

DIGITAL HEALTHCARE PLATFORM

A Software Engineering Approach

by Sungyoung Lee

Sungyoung Lee

Professor
Department of Computer Science and Engineering,
Kyung Hee University, Korea

Publisher
HONGREUNG PUBLISHING COMPANY(August 14, 2020)

ISBN-13
979-11-5600-788-3

e-mail
hongpub@hongpub.co.kr

Web
http://www.hongpub.co.kr

Adress
10, Insubong-ro 50-gil, Gangbuk-gu, Seoul, Korea

TEL : (02) 999-2274~5, 903-7037 / **FAX** : (02) 905-6729

₩ 49,000

Contributors

Prof. Sungyoung Lee
Professor and Principal Investigator,
Mining Minds Platform,
Ubiquitous Computing Lab (UCLab),
Department of Computer Science and Engineering,
Kyung Hee University, South Korea

Prof. Byeong Ho Kang
Professor and HIT Lab Leader,
Computing and Information Systems,
University of Tasmania, Australia

Prof. Young-Tack Park
Professor and A.I. Lab Director,
School of Computer Science & Engineering,
Soongsil University, South Korea

Dr. Muhammad Bilal Amin
Project Lead,
Mining Minds Platform,
Research Professor,
Ubiquitous Computing Lab (UCLab),
Department of Computer Science and Engineering,
Kyung Hee University, South Korea

Dr. Oresti Banos
Assistant Professor,
Computational Behaviour Modelling,
University of Granada, Spain

Dr. Wajahat Ali Khan
Assistant Professor,
Department of Computer Science and Engineering,
Kyung Hee University, South Korea

Dr. Chunho Choi
Chief Researcher,
Human Convergence Technology Group,
Korea Institute of Industrial Technology,
South Korea

Dr. Maqbool Hussain
Assistant Professor,
Sejong University, South Korea

Dr. Muhammad Afzal
Assistant Professor,
Sejong University, South Korea

Dr. Mahmood Ahmad
Ubiquitous Computing Lab (UCLab),
Department of Computer Science and Engineering,
Kyung Hee University, South Korea

Dr. Asad Masood Khattak
Ubiquitous Computing Lab (UCLab),
Department of Computer Science and Engineering,
Kyung Hee University, South Korea

Dr. Muhammad Hameed Siddiqi
Ubiquitous Computing Lab (UCLab),
Department of Computer Science and Engineering,
Kyung Hee University, South Korea

Dr. Rahman Ali
Assistant Professor,
Quaid-e-Azam College of Commerce,
University of Peshawar, Pakistan

Dr. Thien Huynh-The
Ubiquitous Computing Lab (UCLab),
Department of Computer Science and Engineering,
Kyung Hee University, South Korea

Dr. Dinh-Mao Bui
Ubiquitous Computing Lab (UCLab),
Department of Computer Science and Engineering,
Kyung Hee University, South Korea

Dr. Claudia Villalonga
Research Center for Information and Communications Technologies,
University of Granada, Spain

Dr. Maqbool Ali
Ubiquitous Computing Lab (UCLab),
Department of Computer Science and Engineering,
Kyung Hee University, South Korea

Dr. Dohyeong Kim
Ubiquitous Computing Lab (UCLab),
Department of Computer Science and Engineering,
Kyung Hee University, South Korea

Dr. Taqdir Ali
Ubiquitous Computing Lab (UCLab),
Department of Computer Science and Engineering,
Kyung Hee University, South Korea

Dr. Jaehun Bang
Ubiquitous Computing Lab (UCLab),
Department of Computer Science and Engineering,
Kyung Hee University, South Korea

Dr. Jamil Hussain
Ubiquitous Computing Lab (UCLab),
Department of Computer Science and Engineering,
Kyung Hee University, South Korea

Seoungae Kim
Ubiquitous Computing Lab (UCLab),
Department of Computer Science and Engineering,
Kyung Hee University, South Korea

Hafiz Syed Muhammad Bilal
Ubiquitous Computing Lab (UCLab),
Department of Computer Science and Engineering,
Kyung Hee University, South Korea

Taeho Hur
Ubiquitous Computing Lab (UCLab),
Department of Computer Science and Engineering,
Kyung Hee University, South Korea

Shujaat Hussain
Ubiquitous Computing Lab (UCLab),
Department of Computer Science and Engineering,
Kyung Hee University, South Korea

Syed Imran Ali
Ubiquitous Computing Lab (UCLab),
Department of Computer Science and Engineering,
Kyung Hee University, South Korea

Dongwook Kang
Ubiquitous Computing Lab (UCLab),
Department of Computer Science and Engineering,
Kyung Hee University, South Korea

Muhammad Asif Razzaq
Ubiquitous Computing Lab (UCLab),
Department of Computer Science and Engineering,
Kyung Hee University, South Korea

Asim Abbas
Ubiquitous Computing Lab (UCLab),
Department of Computer Science and Engineering,
Kyung Hee University, South Korea

Muhammad Sadiq
Ubiquitous Computing Lab (UCLab),
Department of Computer Science and Engineering,
Kyung Hee University, South Korea

Usman Akhtar
Ubiquitous Computing Lab (UCLab),
Department of Computer Science and Engineering,
Kyung Hee University, South Korea

Jinhyuk Gong
Ubiquitous Computing Lab (UCLab),
Department of Computer Science and Engineering,
Kyung Hee University, South Korea

Soung Ho Cho
Ubiquitous Computing Lab (UCLab),
Department of Computer Science and Engineering,
Kyung Hee University, South Korea

Fahad Ahmed Satti
Ubiquitous Computing Lab (UCLab),
Department of Computer Science and Engineering,
Kyung Hee University, South Korea

Ubaid Ur Rehman
Ubiquitous Computing Lab (UCLab),
Department of Computer Science and Engineering,
Kyung Hee University, South Korea

Musarrat Hussain
Ubiquitous Computing Lab (UCLab),
Department of Computer Science and Engineering,
Kyung Hee University, South Korea

Cam-Hao Hua
Ubiquitous Computing Lab (UCLab),
Department of Computer Science and Engineering,
Kyung Hee University, South Korea

Anees Ul Hassan
Ubiquitous Computing Lab (UCLab),
Department of Computer Science and Engineering,
Kyung Hee University, South Korea

Sangbeom Park
Ubiquitous Computing Lab (UCLab),
Department of Computer Science and Engineering,
Kyung Hee University, South Korea

Muhammad Zaki Ansaar
Ubiquitous Computing Lab (UCLab),
Department of Computer Science and
Engineering,
Kyung Hee University, South Korea

Contents

Preface

The arrival of smart and personal devices has brought an opportunity for the healthcare providers and biomedical researchers to empower people for taking care of their health and wellness. Consequently, the influx of commercial fitness wearables with smartphone based timely, ubiquitous, and personalized services have taken the health and wellness market by storm. In parallel, research groups are also working on health and wellness systems that can alert of physical conditions or detect chronic illnesses. Despite this enormous effort by the industry and research, most of the current solutions are single device focused with limited scope and lack of interoperability and performance. Considering the limitations of existing efforts as an opportunity, we proposed and implemented Mining Minds as a comprehensive health and wellness platform.

Mining Minds is built on the core ideas of digital health and wellness paradigms to enable the provisioning of personalized support. It utilizes the prominent digital technologies such as real-time raw sensory data acquisition, big data, cloud computing, context-awareness, knowledge basis with analytics, and continuous investigation on people's lifestyle to provide a variety of smart coaching and support services.

Mining Minds platform is the collaborative effort of 20 researchers from various fields of computer sciences, healthcare, and wellness. The contributions of this effort have the potential to be reused, evolved, and adopted by other research teams and organizations working under the umbrella of healthcare and wellness. So far opensource community has mainly focused towards utility-based platforms with specific applications. There is a distinct lack of software related to the field of health and wellness. Among the available implementations, mostly are focused towards the healthcare management aspect including electronic health or medical record systems. This includes open source applications like FreeMedForms, FreeMED, OpenMRS, OpenVista, and WebEMS. Similarly, there are domain specific attempts like Caisis, which is a web-based information system for storage and analysis of data for cancer patients, and openMEDIS, which is a standardized web-based tool to collect and process information on health technology infrastructure in low and middle-income countries. IPath and ZephyrOpen are also open source platforms for telemedicine. Reviewing these attempts, it is evident that most of the implementations solely focus on the aspects of health and ignoring the wellness part. However, due to the influx of personal vital signs devices and their utilization for measuring individual's wellbeing has enforced the researchers to focus on attributes of wellness exclusively. Therefore, considering this absence as an opportunity, Mining Minds platform has been released as an open source health and wellness platform for researchers to evolve, reuse, and contribute.

This compilation presents the overview of Mining Minds platform and its core technologies. The primary motivation of this book is to introduce Mining Minds platform to the research and developer's community for its source code evolution, exposure, and utilization in various health and wellness platforms. Mining Minds version 2.5 has been released as Apache 2.0 license and is available for download at https://github.com/ubiquitous-computing-lab/Mining-Minds.

Mining Minds is a state-of-the-art health and wellness platform that is designed to be a layered architecture. Each layer pertains to the abstraction of raw sensory data acquired from multimodal data sources. Starting from the top, Service Curation Layer (SCL) is responsible for curating recommendation-based services based on user activity and nutrition-based scenarios. Knowledge Curation Layer (KCL) is responsible for curating data- and expert-driven knowledge that is further extracted as rules which play a decisive role in user lifelog monitoring and recommendation generation. Information Curation Layer (ICL) is responsible for context identification of the user based on the raw sensory data. The identified context is further classified into high- and low-level context. Data Curation Layer (DCL) is the foundation of Mining Minds platform, responsible for not only real-time data acquisition but also its non-volatile persistence. Furthermore, the user context identified by ICL is continuously monitored by DCL based on the rules provided by KCL for situation detection in which a user might require assistance in the form of recommendations via SCL. To provide utility-based support to the whole platform Supporting Layer (SL) is defined, which encapsulates concepts of distributed security and privacy, UI/UX, and visualization and analytics.

Current implementation of Mining Minds platform i.e., version 4.0 supports a 12-week service scenario for diabetes management based on user's activity and her nutrition. Moreover, it incorporates user educational and wellness awareness concept in its services; for example, providing exercise guidelines to its users with multimedia content. Current implementation integrates three data sources, i.e., smartwatch, smartphone, and a Kinect-based depth camera.

To support and contribute to the open source community, the components of the Mining Minds are designed with software engineering principles of reusability, and extensibility. Each component is built with the dual interfaces to support library and service like reusability. With the strength of reusability, Mining Minds platform can not only be reused as a whole platform but also at grainer level of layers; furthermore, a much finer level of individual components. For example, DCL is designed to operate independently as a core framework. Health and wellness platforms, which are device specific can accommodate more range of multimodal sensory devices by the raw sensory data acquisition of DCL. It can facilitate these platforms to communicate with a variety of multimodal data sources registered to a particular user for the sensory data acquisition. Thus, making these platforms compatible with an IoT-based health and wellness environment. Furthermore, DCL can curate the raw sensory data as user lifelog with continuous monitoring abilities, so that, it can identify any anomalies where a user might require automatic support or assistance from the health and wellness platform. Similar to DCL, KCL is designed to work as an independent knowledge gathering tool where it can acquire expert-driven knowledge by an authoring interface. This knowledge is formalized to be available for share-ability among many health and wellness platforms.

Another essential concept to support opensource is the extensibility of the platform by design. Bioinformatics researchers with the intention to extend the capabilities of current implementation require the components of the platform to be extensible and supportive towards evolution. Therefore, industry-proven object-oriented design patterns are incorporated in the implementation of Mining Minds. From example, to identify various types of context, Strategy pattern is used in the low-level context awareness component of ICL. This design enables bioinformatics researchers to extend the current implementation with additional and custom-made algorithms to support a larger set of activities to be identified as per their service scenarios.

Reliability of the source code is a necessity for the organic growth of any opensource platform. To support this, Mining Minds has been evaluated and tested at several levels utilizing software engineering practices. All the developed components implement black- and white-box testing techniques, including unit testing and integration testing. Furthermore, the implementation incorporates exception handling to support handsome recovery during failure cases.

The iterative process of Mining Minds development is tightly followed as per research and software industry practices. The platform is a composition of 15 loosely coupled and highly cohesive components. Each component is designed to execute as an independent library or a service. Construction of the components is regularly peer-reviewed for high quality of source code; furthermore, integrated under the supervision of a team lead and build engineer. For platform built, a two-step process has been adopted. For the first step, all the team build engineers compile layer-wise build and generate a local build with the help of a native-to-local build engineer. Continuous integration of layers and components supports local build. For the second step, the local build is replicated over publicly available opensource repository, which in our case is GitHub. This step is a periodic step, executed with the marking of a new platform build or a major release for the researchers and developers. Apart from continuous integration, this two-step build mechanism supports the large-scale heterogeneous codebase of Mining Minds platform. Furthermore, it facilitates the Mining Minds research team to build a pre- configured test virtual machine for open source community, saving their time from performing deployment settings and configurations for reuse.

Mining Minds is a mature implementation and a proof of concept with an outcome of production-level quality. It has a potential to evolve as a platform that can be reused and extended by the community. Therefore, for its organic growth, it requires proper exposure among the vital researchers and developers. Keeping these thoughts in perspective, this compilation of Mining Minds techniques and technologies is produced.

Prof. Sungyoung Lee

Part I

Mining Minds Overview

Chapter 1

Mining Minds

A Digital Health and Wellness Framework

Oresti Banos, Muhammad Bilal Amin,
Wajahat Ali Khan, Muhammad Afzal,
Maqbool Hussain, Byeong Ho Kang, and Sungyong Lee

The provision of health and wellness care is undergoing an enormous transformation. A key element of this revolution consists of prioritizing prevention and proactivity based on the analysis of people's conducts and the empowerment of individuals in their self-management. Digital technologies are unquestionably destined to be the main engine of this change, with an increasing number of domain-specific applications and devices commercialized every year; however, there is an apparent lack of frameworks capable of orchestrating and intelligently leveraging, all the data, information and knowledge generated through these systems.

This work presents Mining Minds, a novel framework that builds on the core ideas of the digital health and wellness paradigms to enable the provision of personalized support. Mining Minds embraces some of the most prominent digital technologies, ranging from Big Data and Cloud Computing to Wearables and Internet of Things, as well as modern concepts and methods, such as context-awareness, knowledge bases or analytics, to holistically and continuously investigate on people's lifestyles and provide a variety of smart coaching and support services.

This chapter comprehensively describes the efficient and rational combination and interoperation of these technologies and methods through Mining Minds, while meeting the essential requirements posed by a framework for personalized health and wellness support. Moreover, this work presents a realization of the key architectural components of Mining Minds, as well as various exemplary user applications and expert tools to illustrate some of the potential services supported by the proposed framework.

Mining Minds constitutes an innovative holistic means to inspect human behavior and provide personalized health and wellness support. The principles behind this framework uncover new research ideas and may serve as a reference for similar initiatives.

1.1 Introduction

Healthcare systems are facing unprecedented financial limitations at a time of rising demand for their services [1]. The magnitude of these constrains makes utterly necessary to change current care models in a bold manner, from late disease management to preventive personalized health, involving a major shift in when, where and how care and support is delivered to each particular patient and service user [2]. In fact, it is generally recognized that most prevalent diseases are partly caused or aggravated by lifestyle choices that people make in their everyday life. Unwholesome diets, tobacco use and sedentary conducts, among other unhealthy habits, potentially contribute to develop severe illnesses [3, 4] and also limit the effectiveness of medical treatments [5]. Thus, enabling people to make healthier choices, to be more resilient, and to deal more effectively with illness and disability when it arises, turns to be a fundamental part of this necessary new health perspective.

Information and communication technology is called upon to be a cornerstone of the new health era, playing a crucial role in empowering people to take charge of their own health and wellness, by providing them timely and ubiquitously with personalized information, support and control [6]. In fact, an extraordinary interest has been lately shown by the industry in the development of specific applications and systems for health and wellness management, particularly boomed by the growth of wearable and mobile technology [7]. The immediate targets of these solutions are healthy lifestyle services, especially oriented to the fitness domain, which primarily allow to track primitive user routines and provide simple motivational instructions. For example, mainstream commercial systems such as Withings Activite [8], Garmin Vivofit [9], Fitbit Surge [10] or Misfit Shine [11], which consist of sensorized bracelets and gadgets normally accompanied by mobile apps, provide some basic healthy recommendations based on the measured taken steps or slept hours. More prominent health and wellness systems have been shown at the research level, for example, to alert on physical conditions [12] or detect chronic illnesses [13], yet most of them are prototypes or work-in-progress. Some of these systems also provide educational modules and personal coaching for promoting healthier lifestyles and managing health conditions [14]. Despite their interest, main limitations of these solutions refer to misperformance, limited scope and lack of interoperability with other similar systems and applications.

To overcome the shortcomings of application-specific solutions and leverage the potential of health information systems in a wide sense, general frameworks capable of managing these resources are required. A few attempts are found in this respect in the literature, for example, in [15] a middleware framework integrating multiple interfaces and multiparameter monitoring of physiological measurement is presented. In [16], distributed signal processing algorithms for the analysis and classification of sensor data are provided as part of a framework for rapid prototyping of body sensor networks. A mobile platform to collect users' psychological, physiological and activity information for mental health research is presented in [17]. The authors of [18] propose a healthcare platform particularly devised for interfacing and processing data from body-worn physiological sensors and home appliances, with a proven utility in daily medication management. A novel framework that provides advanced functionalities for resource and communication abstraction, wearable health data acquisition and knowledge extraction is introduced in [19]. Most visible initiatives are especially being underpinned in the mobile health domain. That is the case of [20], an open mobile health project to help developers produce digital health data as useful and actionable as possible. Google Fit [21] by Google, SAMI [22] by Samsung or HealthKit [23] by Apple are examples of new commercial platforms also devised to integrate and share user's health data among diverse health and wellness applications.

Despite important contributions have been made through these platforms, there is still much room for improvement. For example, most mobile health frameworks are bound to the computational capabilities of the smartphone, require continuous maintenance and updates of end-user applications and normally trap data into their devices. Moreover, multiple systems and applications can generate similar health data and outcomes leading to unnecessary redundancy and over computation. These systems mostly operate on-demand; thus, determinants of health and wellness states can also be lost if not registered in a continuous manner. Platforms devised to share and integrate health and wellness data underutilize cloud resources while simply using them for storage. In the light of these limitations we present Mining Minds [24, 25], an innovative distributed framework that builds on some of the most prominent digital technologies to enable the provision of personalized healthcare and wellness support. This framework is particularly devised to seamlessly investigate on people's behavior and lifestyles in a holistic manner through mining human's daily living data generated through heterogeneous resources. Mining Minds aims to innovatively exploit the potential of cloud computing not only for storage but also for high performance computation supporting the discovery of personal and public health and wellness patterns, of primal necessity to facilitate proactive and preventive support.

1.2 Requirements of a digital health and wellness framework

Diverse types of data are normally required to neatly describe a person's health and wellness state, ranging from physical-sensory- and logical-personal profile and interests-, to social- human relations- and clinical-medical-data. Many technologies are increasingly available for the collection of these data, such as wearable devices, ambient sensors, social networks or advanced clinical systems. Thus, an important requirement of a digital health and well- ness framework is to provide a certain level of abstraction from heterogeneous resources to make their utilization transparent to the user. Health and wellness data go beyond standardized structured formats such as "traditional" electronic health records, particularly including other multimedia and unstructured data. Therefore, another primal requirement is to be capable of dealing with this dimension of heterogeneous data, as well as the underlying implications of the management of structured, semi-structured and unstructured data.

Not only data variety constitutes a key factor, but also data volume. Massive amounts of data are generated over time on and around the subject with the advent of new sensing and multimedia technologies. Accumulating and digesting these amounts of data are not trivial tasks and need to involve sophisticated processing and storage mechanisms to enable the persistence and availability of the data. Similarly, the rapid pace of data generation makes it necessary to also consider data velocity as a reference factor. This proves to be especially challenging when referred to data that represents real-time regular monitoring, such as continuous electrocardiogram measurements or body motion data. Another important concept that applies to health and wellness data is veracity. Different data types may represent similar concepts or contradict each other, or even be of little interest. There- fore, digital health and wellness frameworks should count on governance mechanisms to determine the consistency of the data, ensuring it is certain, meaningful, clean and precise.

Extracting the determinants of health and wellness is a very challenging task that requires more than simply collecting and persisting personal data. Accordingly, digital health and wellness frameworks must include automatic intelligent mechanisms to process person-centric data and extract interpretable information and insights for ensuring a personalized health and wellness support. Moreover, insights should not only be gained from individual users but from the collectivity. Thus, another important requirement consists in the application of advanced techniques to process information in "deidentified" form to enable population management and deeper insights into cause and effect. These insights can be particularly leveraged by health and wellness care systems to extend, adapt and evolve the knowledge provided by human domain experts.

Health and wellness information and knowledge are principally devoted to support advanced care services. Mechanisms such as alerts, recommendations or guidelines are particularly used as services to catalyze both information and knowledge to be delivered in a human-understandable fashion to users and stakeholders in general. However, most digital health and wellness systems only support general services that do not differentiate among people's particular needs or interests. Therefore, an important requirement is to provide services that operate on a person-centric manner. To do so, expert systems are required, for example, to precisely map user needs to the best possible recommendations, personalize the recommendations explanation or customize the mechanisms for the communication of these recommendations.

Users of health and wellness systems may be of a very diverse nature and play different roles. For example, busy patients may require getting a quick glimpse of their health conditions, fitness enthusiasts wish to observe a detailed description of their vitals and clinical experts be interested in an "in-depth" description of both health and wellness outcomes of multiple people. Accordingly, user interfaces need to be customized to the needs of each particular subject. Similarly, the user experience is of worth consideration. Users perceptions of system aspects such as utility, ease of use and efficiency should be considered to provide the most personalized experience. In fact, the user experience is dynamic as it is constantly modified over time due to the person changing circumstances. Thus, user responses and behavior need to be continuously tracked to support a sufficient level of personalization that helps guarantee adoption and engagement.

Finally, as it may be obvious, but unfortunately not often considered, all the afore- mentioned requirements need to be neatly accommodated to user security and privacy principles. The necessity of privacy and security is crucial for systems that build over sensitive information, and further augmented when data and services are shared by multiple entities in a distributed way. Data ownership, malicious data usage, as well as regulatory and legal policies are important hindrances in the widespread use and acceptance of health and wellness care systems. Therefore, it is of utmost importance to neatly adequate privacy, security, protection and risk management measures to all the processes concerned in a digital health and wellness framework.

1.3 Mining Minds Architecture

In the light of the aforementioned requirements we present here "Mining Minds", a novel framework aimed at comprehensively mining human's daily life data generated from heterogeneous resources for producing personalized health and wellness support.

Mining Minds philosophy revolves around the concepts of data, information, knowledge and service curation, which refer to the discovery, processing, adaptation and evolution of both contents and mechanisms for the provision of high-quality support services. Motivated by these concepts, a multilayer architecture is particularly devised for Mining Minds—Figure 1.1.

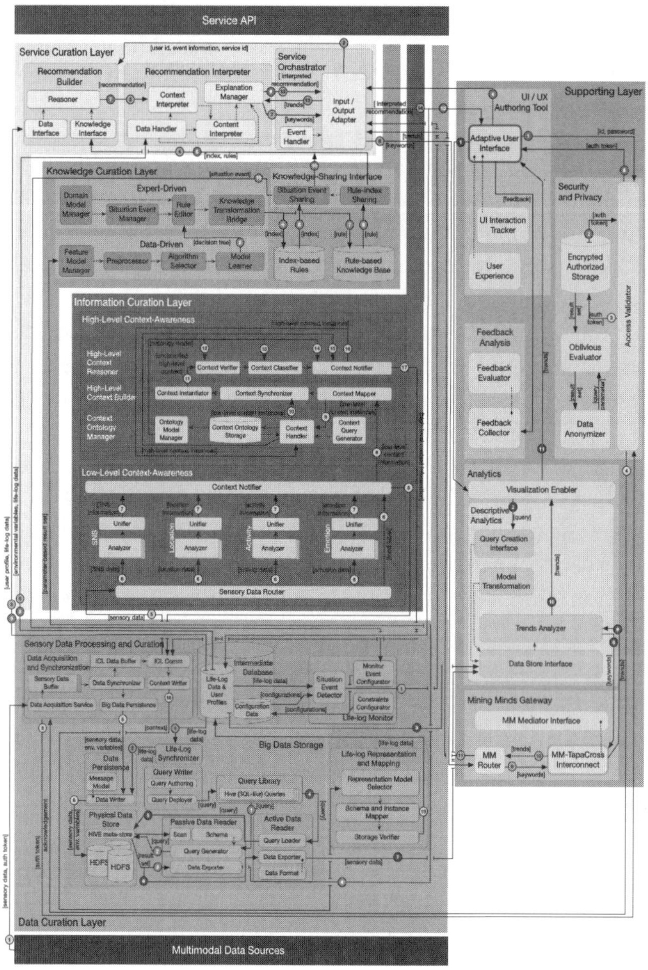

Figure 1.1 Mining Minds framework and functional diagram

In a nutshell, the data curation layer (DCL) is in charge of processing and persisting the data obtained from the multimodal data sources (MDS), which abstractly defines the possible sources of user health and wellness data. This includes, but is not limited to, data from social networks, questionnaires, wearable biomedical devices or ambient intelligence systems. The data processed by DCL is primarily used by the information curation layer (ICL) to infer low-level and high-level person-centric information. This information mainly describes the user context and behavior, and, to some extent, their physical, mental and social state. The information extracted by ICL is leveraged by the knowledge curation layer (KCL) to nurture and evolve the health and wellness knowledge primarily created by human experts. Data, information and knowledge are used by the service curation layer (SCL) to create intelligent health and wellness support services, mostly in the form of smart coaching and support recommendations. All the contents and processes are accommodated in terms of security and privacy by the supporting layer (SL), which also provides analysis of user experience, feedback and trends to guarantee the highest personalization.

1.3.1 Data Curation Layer

Data curation layer is responsible for acquiring, curating and persisting the data obtained from MDS so it can be processed for higher level understanding. To that end DCL relies on two main modules, Sensory Data Processing and Curation and Big Data Storage. Within the former, Data Acquisition supports the acquisition and synchronization of raw sensory data obtained from diverse sources, both in real-time and offline manner, as generic data streams. Due to the heterogeneous nature of the data, it is acquired asynchronously in real-time and temporarily cached in data buffers. These data buffers are initialized depending upon the number of data sources, i.e., each data source has a data buffer in the Data Acquisition component. All the data buffers are synchronized and communicated to ICL for the determination of the associated low and high-level contexts. In parallel, this synchronized data is stored in Big Data Storage for non-volatile persistence.

Upon receiving the context information determined by ICL, the context instances are curated by the Representation and Mapping component as a time-based log registering the detected human behaviors. This time-based log termed as lifelog is persisted in the Intermediate Database for shareability with other layers and applications. The stream of lifelog instances is analyzed by a monitoring component called lifelog monitor (LLM). The responsibility of the LLM is to perform time-based monitoring of the different attributes and variables hosted in the lifelog, and support trigger-based mechanisms to notify SCL for the occurrence of an abnormal or special event related to a given user. These abnormal events normally represent risky or unhealthy behaviors and are here defined as "situation events" or "situations" in general. These situations are described through diverse constraints, e.g., age, gender or medical conditions and monitorable variables, e.g., intensity of a particular activity or its duration. Situation events can be generated both statically at design-time and dynamically at run-time upon request from KCL.

The lifelog data persisted in the Intermediate Database is regularly synchronized with the Big Data Storage. Big Data Storage also provides read access to raw sensory and lifelog data. In case of historic data required by SL for analytics or KCL for data-driven rule generation, Big Data Storage provides queries for data streaming and intermediate data generation. These queries can be customized on request to return specific data based on the attributes selected by KCL and SL. Security and privacy components from SL are further involved in these processes to request authentication and data stream encryption before its persistence or sharing.

1.3.2 Information Curation Layer

Information curation layer represents the Mining Minds core for the inference and modeling of the user context [26]. ICL is composed by two main modules, namely, low level context awareness (LLCA) and high-level context awareness (HLCA). LLCA is in charge of converting the wide-spectrum of data obtained from the user interaction with the real and cyber-world, into abstract concepts or categories, such as physical activities, emotional states, locations and social patterns. These categories are intelligently combined and processed at HLCA in order to identify more meaningful semantic representations of the user context.

Low level context awareness is composed by four key components, respectively, Activity Recognizer, Emotion Recognizer, Location Detector and SNS Analyzer. The identification of the user physical actions is performed through the Activity Recognizer. This component may build on several sensing modalities as they happen to be available to the user, such as wearable inertial sensors, video and audio. The output of this component corresponds to elementary activity categories such as "sitting" or "walking". The Emotion Recognizer is defined to infer user emotional states, such as "surprise" or "sadness", by using video and audio data as well as more sophisticated sources exploring human physiological variations and responses. The user situation is determined by the Location Detector, which essentially builds on the data collected through indoor and outdoor positioning sensors, such as video and GPS, to specify the exact location of the user. The SNS Analyzer is in charge of processing the information generated by the user during their interactions in regular social networks, including posts, mentions, traces and even global social trends, in the form of both text and multimedia data. From here, personal and general interests, conducts and sentiments may be determined. All these components require compatible multimodal sensory data to operate. The provisioning of the necessary data is performed through the Input Adapter, which receives and routes the data curated by DCL to each LLCA component depending on its nature. Once new low- level context categories are identified after the analysis of this data, the Output Adapter serves them to DCL for persistence and to HLCA for further processing.

High level context awareness makes use of two components, namely, High-Level Context Builder and High-Level Context Reasoner, to represent, verify, classify and categorize the user high-level context. The context representation and verification is performed through ontologies, adopted in the past as a unified conceptual backbone for modeling context, while its classification and categorization is done through ontological inference and reasoning. Whenever new information is received from LLCA, a new ontological instance is created by the High-Level Context Builder and categorized into one of the considered high-level contexts by the High-Level Context Reasoner. Thus, for example, based on the actual time—e.g., midday; location—e.g., restaurant; and inferred activities—e.g., sitting; this component can determine the precise user context—e.g., lunch.

1.3.3 Knowledge Curation Layer

Knowledge curation layer is devised to enable the creation and evolution of both health and wellness knowledge. The knowledge is created either by the domain expert or knowledge engineer by using expert-driven or data-driven approaches. The Expert-Driven module provides a set of rule authoring components to allow specialists to describe in a logical form causes or premises and effects or conclusions, e.g., "if gender is male and age lower than 65 then activity level should be moderate". The authoring process is further supported through evidence materials and domain vocabularies to confirm the viability of the rules and facilitate their elaboration. The Data-Driven module leverages the contents of the lifelog for the automatic generation of rules. To that end, a data broker interface is defined to glean the contents of interest from the data persisted in DCL based on the features or attributes chosen by the expert, e.g., gender, emotional state and activity level. The process is automated by selecting and learning diverse mining models to discover and represent the underlying relationship among the considered health and wellness factors.

In both expert-driven and data-driven cases the generated rules are verified in terms of consistency and validated to avoid potential violations or redundancy with existing rules prior to be stored into the Knowledge Bases. KCL rules are not only persisted in traditional knowledge bases but also indexed according to salient conditions of these rules, also called "causes" or "situations". These situations refer to particular attributes of the rules than can be monitored by the platform and used for triggering the execution of specific rules. Accordingly, during the rule creation process the expert can select these condition attributes for their particular monitoring at DCL. The categorization of the knowledge bases through these indexes is particularly considered to enhance the performance of the reasoning processes hosted in SCL. In fact, once a situation is detected only its associated rules are shared with SCL through the Knowledge-Sharing Interface upon request of this layer.

The evolution of the knowledge is procured through two main mechanisms. On the one hand, the expert creation process can be considered as a sort of maintenance per se. In that view, rules may be dynamically updated or replaced based on new health and wellness findings from experts. On the other hand, rules can be added, replaced or modified through the data-driven approach while using new lifelog contents collected from different users.

1.3.4 Service Curation Layer

Service curation layer provides the means to transform the data, information and knowledge curated by DCL, ICL and KCL into actual health and wellness support services. The services are managed by the Service Orchestrator, in charge of attending the potential requests, invoking the necessary services and coordinating the processes involved in the curation of the services. The requests may be of various types, i.e., scheduled on time— e.g., "every day at 8 am"; triggered by direct user queries—e.g., "suggest me an exercise plan for today's workout"; or based on events—e.g., "user arrives at home". The last type of request particularly relates to the concept of situation, already described in previous sections. The idea is that the LLM component from DCL triggers SCL whenever a situation event is identified in order to generate a new recommendation for the user.

The services needed to satisfy a given request are invoked from an extensible catalog containing reference and auxiliary services. A major reference service is devised for this architecture for the generation of personalized health and wellness recommendations. This service consists of two parts. First, generalized recommendations are developed by the Recommendation Builder component through reasoning on the user profile and lifelog data provided by DCL and the knowledge facilitated by KCL for the specific domain of the service. In the case of handling a request derived from a situation detection the indexed rules hosted by KCL are particularly employed. Second, the recommendations undergo a personalization process through the Recommendation Interpreter in order to deliver the one that best fits the user interests and demands. Through this component all the potential recommendations are filtered based on the user preferences, conditions and possessions, as well as their actual context. Thus, for example, when the objective of the recommendation is to encourage the user to exercise, cycling would be avoided if the user does not own a bike, or a visit to the regular gym omitted in case the person is on a business trip. Similarly, this component can delay the delivery of a given recommendation when it is considered not to be a convenient moment for the user, e.g., if the person is in the middle of a meeting. Prior to be communicated to the user, the recommendation is refined to be easily interpreted by including multimedia contents to increase the interpretability and also incorporating motivational and engagement strategies to foster the user interest and attention.

1.3.5 Supporting Layer

The role of SL is to enrich the overall Mining Minds functionalities through advanced analytics, interactive and personalized UI/UX, implicit and explicit feedback analysis, and adequate privacy and security mechanisms.

The Analytics module is in charge of mining in a multi-dimensional and retrospective manner the data sets collected and curated from multiple users to reveal population health and wellness associations, patterns and trends. These trends may refer to current facts as well as expected or future tendencies. The exploration of present trends is per- formed through the Descriptive Analytics, which employs statistical techniques to relate explanatory variables of the persisted data. Thus, for example, based on the analysis of the inferred people lifestyles, it can be found that there is a growing use of hot beverages among adolescents, which further relates to a dramatic increase of stress patterns. The discovery of potential future facts is carried out by the Predictive Analytics, which develops on the outcomes of the Descriptive Analytics to make forecasts by using regression and machine learning models. Descriptive and predictive analytics contents are organized by the Visualization Enabler, which adjusts the style of the information to be communicated to the users based on their expertise and role.

Evaluating the services supported by Mining Minds requires feedback from the users, which is here powered by the Feedback Analysis component. The sources of feedback may be of a diverse nature, ranging from explicit feedback provided by the user, for example, through questionnaires, to implicit feedback obtained from the user behavioral responses. Analyzing implicit and explicit feedback from the users is motivated by the aspects of functionality, content, and presentation. Functionality-based feedback refers to the findings obtained while comparing, for example, the system recommendations and the behavioral reaction of the user to those recommendations. Content-based feedback measures the user satisfaction with respect to the specific information provided as part of the delivered services. Finally, presentation-based feedback measures the human- computer interaction with respect to the user interface (UI), which is of particular utility to understand the user experience (UX). All these types of feedback are devised to help assessing the level of interest and adherence of users to the services provided through Mining Minds as well as to evolve and maintain the internal contents and processes handled by the platform.

Considering user preferences, habits or mood, the UI/UX module enables the end- user applications interface to be adapted accordingly. This adaptation is needed to adjust the human-computer interaction experience with respect to font size, theme, or audio levels, among other characteristics. Two main components are involved in this process. First, the UI Interaction Tracker collects the data from the interaction between the person and the application to analyze the user's ability to understand and use the system, e.g., the readability of the contents or the perceptibility of the controls. Then, the UX component measures the satisfaction level based on the analysis of the collected data. The immediate result is a dynamic adaptation of the UI based on the measurements extracted from the evaluation of the UX.

Given the sensitivity of the collected user data, privacy and security need to be assured and exhibited, not only for storage, but also during the processing and delivery of services. To that end, state-of-the-art cryptographic primitives along with indigenous protocols are considered. For secure storage, the AES standard is particularly used, whereas for oblivious processing, homomorphic encryption and private matching is used. Considering the intensive data flow between end-user applications and Mining Minds, data randomization techniques are used to ensure a high entropy for minimal leakage of information. An authorized model ensures the legitimate disclosure of personal data and services with users. Slow processing of information is a common byproduct of the encryption; thus, to assist partial swiftness to Mining Minds, sensitive and non-sensitive information is decoupled where required. Anonymization procedures are also considered to enable the use of the collected and mined user's data by third party agents, e.g., for research purposes.

1.4 Mining Minds Implementation

An initial implementation of the proposed framework particularly oriented to promote healthy lifestyles and physical activity management is described here. Mining Minds is a distributed platform where the cloud environment plays a key role for supporting both persistence and limitless computational power. The Mining Minds implementation has been deployed over a hybrid cloud combining Microsoft Azure public cloud environment [27] and a Xen private cloud [28] for the big data storage, which runs over Hadoop File System with MapReduce [29]. For better scalability and performance each layer is deployed over a separate virtual instance on Microsoft Azure. DCL, ICL, KCL and SCL are hosted on standard Microsoft Azure instances with Windows Server 2012 R2 as guest operating system [30], while SL functionalities partake of the others. The cloud-based deployment of layers allows the encapsulation of their responsibilities as well as the re-usability of their features through an inter-layer communication. This communication is implemented by establishing service contracts among the layers, which communicate by means of RESTful web services [31] and high-performance sockets [32]. The communication between MDS and DCL is implemented through sockets given its real-time nature. Similarly, a high-performance socket-based implementation is particularly used for DCL-ICL communication for the transference of sensory data and context determination in real-time, and communication between DCL and the big data storage on private cloud. The most important service contracts with remaining layers are supported by DCL RESTful web services, which serve a data model with the structure of the Intermediate Database, here hosted by Microsoft SQL Server [33]. This data model is shared among the layers as an object model of ser- vice contract. The required data and information is populated by DCL and provided as responses to the upper layers.

To support active lifestyle services in this version ICL only implements the Activity Recognizer. This component consists of various steps that mainly combine signal processing and machine learning techniques to define a specific human activity recognition model capable of distinguishing among various commonplace activities [34]. The main input of this model is body motion data, namely, acceleration, which can be broadly obtained from smartphones and wearable inertial sensors. Acceleration is preferentially used here since it is the most prevalent sensor modality in standard activity recognition approaches [35]. A non-overlapping sliding window of three seconds is used for the data segmentation [36], and time and frequency features extracted for their discrimination potential [37]. The implemented model combines Support Vector Machines and Gaussian Mixture Models for the classification process, which have been demonstrated of particular utility in this domain [38, 39]. The developed Activity Recognizer further supports three operation modes depending on the avail- able data registered from the user. Specifically, a hierarchical approach is developed so that the model can determine the user activity based only on the inertial data collected through the smartphone, smartwatch or a combination of smartphone and smart- watch data if available.

Health and wellness knowledge is defined by medical experts and hosted in the Knowledge Bases of KCL. To that end, a simple rule authoring tool [40] is considered for the rule creation. Evidences and domain vocabularies are particularized to the definition of physical management and activity promotion plans [41]. SCL processes the contents generated by DCL, ICL and KCL for the generation of personalized physical activity recommendations. After a request is processed by the service orchestrator, generalized recommendations are produced by applying rule-based reasoning [42] on the existing knowledge and user data. User health and wellness data is transformed into a proper input query by using auxiliary services hosted in the service catalog. Similarly, auxiliary services are implemented for user goal discovery, e.g., ideal weight and calories to be burned per day [43]. During the reasoning, the interpreter analyzes each rule in the knowledge bases and fires the appropriate rules using a forward chaining procedure [44]. Recommendations are personalized by using content-based filtration techniques [45] employing user-centric information such as activity level and preferred physical activities.

Security and privacy components of SL are distributed among the different layers. Encryption techniques are employed to withstand any compromise on data storage facility or its unauthorized access, as well as to make health-related data processing and evaluation HIPAA compliant. Concretely, AES [46], private matching [47] and multi- dimensional anonymization [48] have been chosen to support the encryption and control access. Moreover, since the systems are deployed on public clouds, processing over direct encryption without losing accuracy is required. The indigenously proposed system of oblivious term matching [49] is considered here to that end.

1.4.1 Health and wellness promotion services

Various exemplary applications and tools have been developed to showcase some of the potential health and wellness services supported by Mining Minds—Figure 1.2. Personalized weight management is procured through an application that promotes activity routines customized to the user characteristics and preferences in order to attain a healthy weight. The app further provides the person with valuable information regarding their physical behavior, energy expenditure and weight loss patterns. Behavior change, and healthy lifestyle promotion is intended through a personal coaching application which delivers action recommendations and educational facts upon detection of unhealthy physical conducts. Conversely to other digital health and wellness systems and plat- forms, Mining Minds is not only devised to support regular users or patients but also specialists. Medical experts are facilitated with a comprehensive tool to inspect user's behavior, engagement and satisfaction in a continuous and retrospective manner. Apart from diverse statistics reporting personal goals, achievements and physical activity pat- terns, the tool allows the specialist to check the specific information and recommendations delivered by the platform to each particular user. Finally, an intuitive rule authoring tool has also been developed to enable the creation and management of the health and wellness knowledge exploited by Mining Minds. The main features and utilities of these applications and tools are described next.

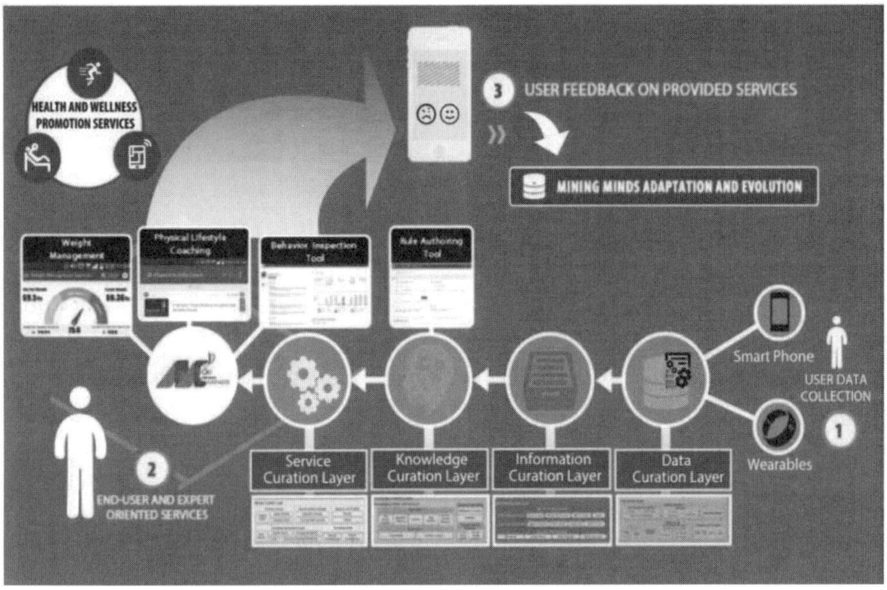

Figure 1.2 Mining Minds health and wellness service scenario

1.4.2 Personalized weight management app

A poor cstimation of calorics and activities as well as an unrealistic definition of mile- stones represent two of the most common reasons for failure in most weight loss programs. Accordingly, the main objective of this service is to empower people in the control of their weight through a continuous track of exercise and energy consumption and a personalized physical routine promotion to achieve the daily expenditure goals.

Users are initially requested to sign up into the application by entering their personal information such as demographics—age, gender, weight and height, preferences in terms of activities and exercise level—sedentary, moderate or intense. All this information is securely stored and processed by the Mining Minds platform to calculate the user physical state, ideal weight, as well as the calories to be burned every day, all displayed for simple access on the app main dashboard—Figure 1.3, top-left. The number of calories burned by the user in the present day is also displayed on this view. This value is estimated by the platform by analyzing the user activity patterns. To determine these patterns, Mining Minds elaborates on the acceleration data measured by the user smartphone, which is timely streamed through WiFi or 4G to the platform. To promote the user activity to achieve the daily calorie goal, exercise recommendations are given in an easy-to-understand manner.

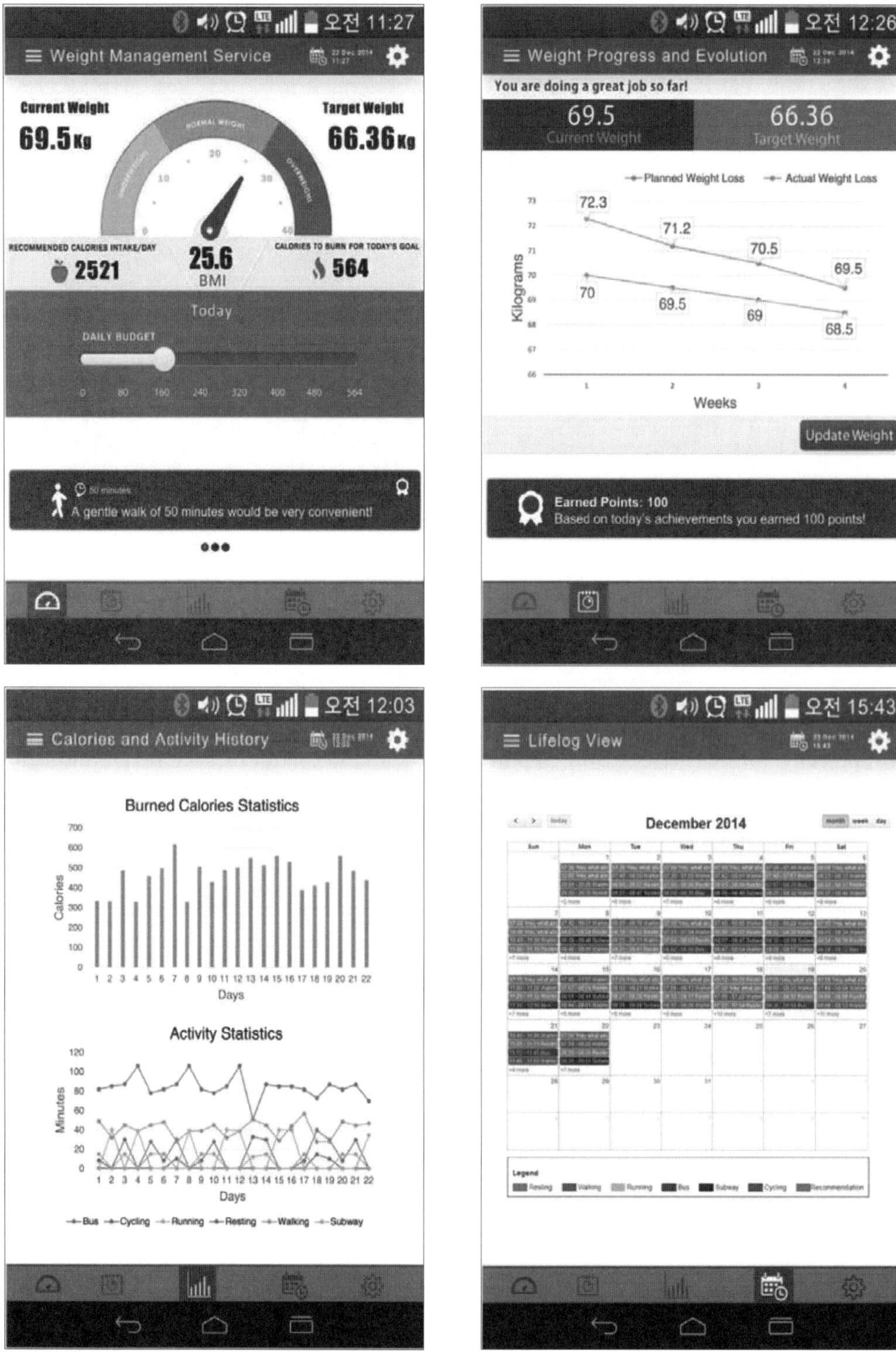

Figure 1.3 Personalized weight management app

The recommendations contain precise indications on the duration of the activity and its execution style as well as motivational statements for encouraging the user. The recommended activities, their duration and intensity are personalized to each individual based on their profile. The evolution of the user's actual weight with respect to the planned one is presented in a different frame—Figure 1.3, top-right. Here the user can easily self-report their current weight upon timely request of the platform. Other supportive features of the application provide the user with statistical analysis of burned calories and activity patterns —Figure 1.3, bottom-left, and a calendar view of the user comportment—Figure 1.3, bottom-right, specifically devised to support users in their self-monitoring and control.

1.4.3 Physical lifestyle coaching app

Behavior change, and healthy lifestyle promotion constitute central objectives in public health interventions. The service defined here explores sophisticated coaching mechanisms to raise people's health awareness while inducing wholesome activity habits, changing unhealthy routines and educating on healthier physical lifestyles. To that end the developed application continuously captures the user's body motion data registered through the inertial sensors of the smartwatch and smartphone. The data is then streamed to Mining Minds which processes it to infer the user's behavior and determine potential risk or unhealthy situations. After an unhealthy behavior is detected, e.g., "one hour of continuous sitting", the platform automatically generates a personalized physical recommendation or healthy educational fact, e.g., "stretch your legs, arms and back". Recommendations and facts are conveniently delivered according to the user context and availability and displayed on the application main screen in a timeline view—Figure 1.4.

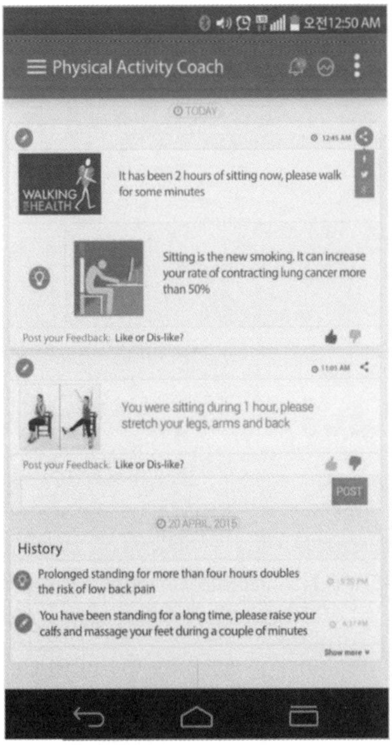

Figure 1.4 Physical lifestyle coaching app

Both recommendations and facts are also accompanied by multimedia contents—video, images and audio—to instruct the user on how to follow them as well as to attract and increase their interest and understanding. Moreover, users can value the delivered recommendations and facts according to their experience— "likes"/ "dislikes"— and also provide comments on them—e.g., "I cannot carry out the recommended stretching exercises" or "My back hurts when I bend my waist". This information constitutes a key source of feedback for experts and Mining Minds itself to realize the comprehensive- ness, applicability and impact of the services delivered by the platform.

1.4.4 Behavior Inspection Tool

Intelligent monitoring and smart coaching mechanisms are not planned to replace the role of specialists but rather complement it. In fact, the idea is that not only patients, but also medical experts can benefit from the data, information, knowledge and services handled by Mining Minds. The expert inspection tool developed here is particularly devised to facilitate and expedite the task of health and wellness counseling specialists. The tool— Figure 1.5—presents in an intuitive yet comprehensive fashion some of the most prominent user-centric information managed by the platform. On the left side of this expert view the specialist can check the recommendations and facts delivered by Mining Minds to the user, the reason behind these suggestions as well as the feedback provided on them.

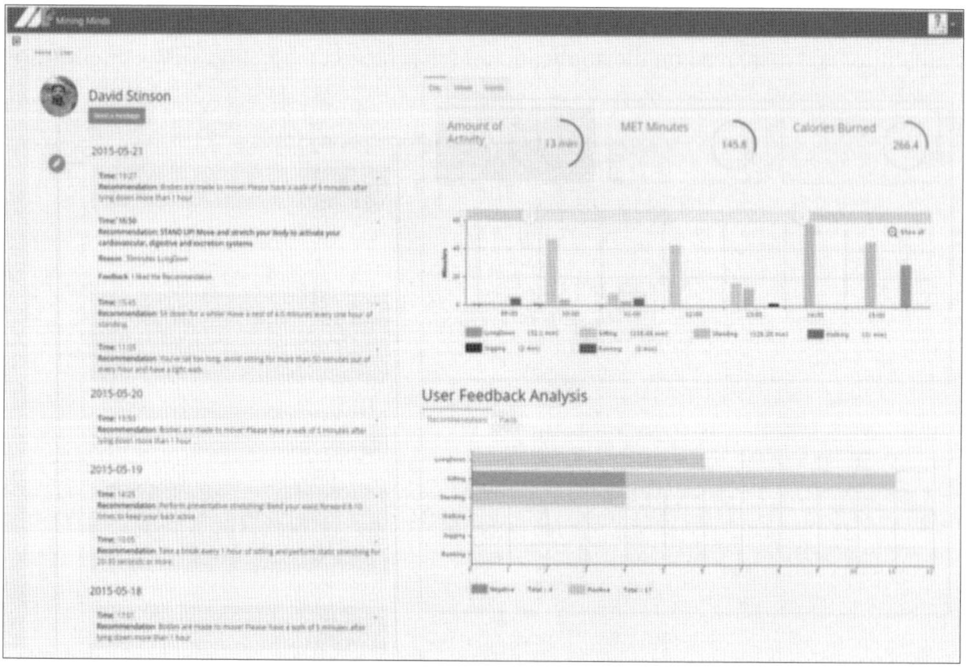

Figure 1.5 Behavior inspection tool

On the right side, diverse sort of analytics describing the physical achievements of the user, their behavioral patterns and their rating of recommendations and facts are shown. Energy expenditure achievements and physical activity patterns are displayed in a daily, weekly and monthly basis, thus providing the expert with a detailed view of the user past and present status. The user feedback analytics is of particular interest to help experts identify what kind of recommendations and facts are more positively valued and which ones may not be accepted. The tool is also incorporated with a feature that allows the specialist to directly communicate with the user through the developed apps by sending comments in the form of notifications. Through this tool, experts can in principle deal with more users while reducing the time required for the assessment of their progresses and evolution.

1.4.5 Rule Authoring Tool

Health and wellness experts are not only consumers of the services supported by Mining Minds but also content producers. The creation and management of Mining Minds health and wellness knowledge is handled by the specialists through an advanced rule authoring tool—Figure 1.6. This rule authoring tool is an adapted version of a prior one first introduced in [40]. The rule authoring tool provides domain experts with an easy to use dashboard to manage the existing rules, thus making possible their addition, update or deletion. An intuitive environment is provided for the creation of new rules and associated meta-information. The rule authoring tool incorporates a sophisticated physical activity wellness model which incorporates multiple domain concepts and vocabularies facilitating the rule creation task. The tool is also equipped with intelligent code completion technology to expedite the rule creation process and reduce the chance of errors. After the rule is created, the expert can simply save it, thus making it available for its use in Mining Minds.

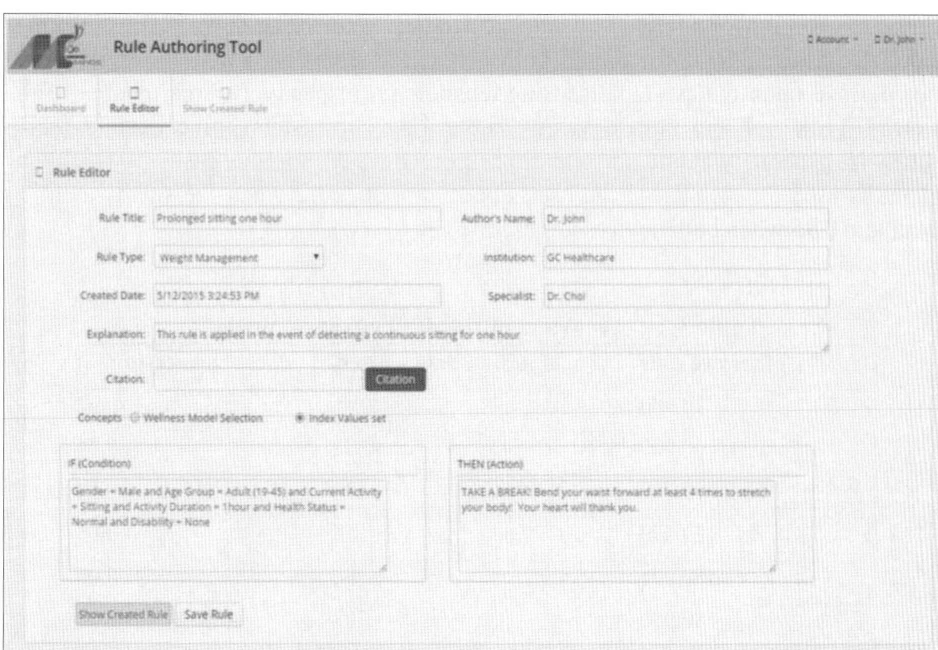

Figure 1.6 Rule authoring tool

1.5 Evaluation and discussion

A preliminary evaluation of the implemented version of the platform and services is per- formed here. An important asset of the platform refers to the curation and persistence of sensory data by DCL. Most health applications delete sensory data after processing it; however, persisting this information is of worth for generating datasets that can be used to evolve the knowledge models or learn new ones. To benchmark DCL capabilities, the accuracy and performance of the platform in the collection, processing and storage of the sensory data is measured. To that end, continuous data service calls over the period of 24 h are generated and evaluated. The accuracy is measured by the rate of missing data packets, here summarized in Table 1.1. The results show a very low error, 0.06 % in average, which means that practically all the sensory data sent to the platform is safely processed. The performance, presented in Table 1.2, measures the capacity of the system to store the data packets into the platform storage. The stress test shows a high consistency with the increasing usage of the system, which is capable of writing 2.2 requests or packets per second in average, each one composed by 7800 records of sensory data.

The capability of ICL for inferring user activities presents important advantages with respect to other wellness systems, which frequently rely on simple step counting for activity tracking. For example, it permits to derive more precisely the user energy expenditure based on the cost of each performed activity, especially for those that do not entail any ambulation. To evaluate the potential of the implemented activity recognition model ten volunteers aged from 23 to 37 years were requested to perform the supported activities, namely, “walking”, “jogging”, “running”, “stretching”, “sweeping”, “eating”, “sit- ting”, “standing” and “lying down”. The performance of the model is evaluated by com- paring both actual and detected activities for three different scenarios defined upon the available sensing technology, respectively, smartphone—Table 1.3, smartwatch—Table 1.4 and both devices—Table 1.5. The results prove notable recognition capabilities in general, yielding an overall F-score of 0.93 for the case in which only the smartphone is used for registering the user’s body motion, 0.92 when the smartwatch is solely employed, and 0.95 when both devices are used.

Table 1.1 Accuracy of the data curation process

No. of service calls	No. of missed data packets	Packet loss error (%)
30,000	6	0.02
60,000	22	0.04
90,000	39	0.04
120,000	55	0.05
150,000	96	0.06
180,000	308	0.17
Average		0.06

An initial user-centric analysis is also performed in terms of adherence to the provided recommendations. Ten independent volunteers between the ages of 26 and 38 years were asked to use the developed applications during a couple of weeks to measure the response time to the recommendations generated by the platform. This time accounts for the period elapsed since the user receives a recommendation and follows it. The average number of recommendations per day were 9, ranging from 5 to 14. The subject's response time varied from 1 min to 1 h, with average values shown in Table 1.6. These results may give some hints on the interest shown in the use of these services, although further analysis, including more subjects and longer time spans, is required to obtain solid conclusions.

Table 1.2 Performance of the data persistence process for different operation runs

Run duration (hr.)	2	4	6	8	10	12	14	16	18	20	22	24
Performance (avg. data writes/sec.)	2.20	2.21	2.20	2.20	2.10	2.21	2.21	2.21	2.20	2.20	2.20	2.20

Finally, the effectiveness and usability of the developed expert tools is also assessed. To that end, different aspects of the tools were evaluated by six medical experts two nutritionists, two fitness instructors and two nurses—from an independent health and wellness counseling company. The experts were instructed on how to use the tools and then provided with a set of questionnaires to evaluate their look and feel, interface layout complexity, time required to access a given resource or create a new rule and the understandability and correctness of the concepts and contents facilitated by these tools. The results of the evaluation prove a satisfaction level of 7.5 out of 10 in average. The aspects that were more highly rated correspond to the usefulness, organization and simple access to the displayed health and wellness information. For the behavior inspection tool, the experts particularly valued having a user-centric description of the behavioral patterns plus the possibility of identifying the acceptability of the delivered recommendations through the feedback analysis report. For the rule authoring tool, the specialists especially considered the benefits provided by the health and wellness models during the rule creation process, although they showed some concerns regarding the amount of time required to write a given rule. All the positive and negative feedback obtained through all these evaluations is being considered at the moment for evolution and improvement of the developed services.

Table 1.3 Activity recognition performance when operating on the smartphone data

Activity	SE	SP	PPV	NPV	F-score
Eating	0.87	0.99	0.86	0.99	0.86
Running	0.97	1.00	1.00	1.00	0.99
Sitting	0.94	0.98	0.93	0.98	0.94
Standing	0.88	0.99	0.95	0.98	0.91
Walking	0.99	0.99	0.98	1.00	0.99
Jogging	0.99	1.00	0.98	1.00	0.99
Stretching	0.96	0.99	0.91	1.00	0.93
Sweeping	0.93	0.99	0.90	0.99	0.91
Lying down	0.84	1.00	0.92	0.99	0.88

It is worth noting that all the developed apps and tools have been designed as end- user interfaces to the contents and services curated by Mining Minds, thus presenting important advantages for the customers, such as an effective reduction of the resources consumption—mainly in terms of storage, computation and battery, no need of regular updates of the client application, shareability of contents among diverse systems and applications, as well as a more dynamic and interactive experience. Despite these important advantages, there are some limitations that need especial consideration. Mining Minds builds on the assumption of having most mobile devices and systems of the Internet of Things fully and seamlessly connected soon. However, this condition is currently not always satisfied; therefore, the applications may require supporting temporary local storage and offline data transmission to overcome potential network disconnections. Another open issue refers to the cost of the communication between the apps and the platform. Applications such as the ones presented here operate over Wi-Fi and 4G interfaces. While the use of Wi-Fi presents no economic burden, some users could be concerned about using their data plans when huge amounts of data need to be transferred. For example, the developed user applications transmit around 500kB/min to communicate the sensory data to the platform, which translates into approximately 30GB/month when used non-stop. With the advent of 5G communications, flat-rate data plans are expected to become commonplace, thus helping to reduce the possible burden for the end-user. In either case, the utilization of compressed sensing techniques [50] is particularly envisioned for the future to make the data transmission more efficient. These mechanisms and other sophisticated strategies are also worth considering reducing battery consumption, for example, by interrupting the transmission of sensory data during periods of user inactivity.

Table 1.4 Activity recognition performance when operating on the smartwatch data

Activity	SE	SP	PPV	NPV	F-score
Eating	0.82	0.99	0.86	0.99	0.84
Running	0.96	1.00	0.94	1.00	0.95
Sitting	0.93	0.94	0.85	0.97	0.89
Standing	0.85	0.99	0.94	0.97	0.90
Walking	0.96	0.98	0.95	0.98	0.96
Jogging	0.92	1.00	0.97	1.00	0.95
Stretching	0.93	1.00	0.97	0.99	0.95
Sweeping	0.95	1.00	0.99	1.00	0.97
Lying down	0.85	1.00	0.93	0.99	0.89

Table 1.5 Activity recognition performance when operating on both smartphone and smartwatch data

Activity	SE	SP	PPV	NPV	F-score
Eating	0.89	1.00	0.88	1.00	0.88
Running	0.97	1.00	0.99	1.00	0.98
Sitting	0.95	0.98	0.94	0.98	0.95
Standing	0.91	0.99	0.95	0.98	0.93
Walking	0.99	0.99	0.98	1.00	0.99
Jogging	0.98	1.00	0.98	1.00	0.98
Stretching	0.97	0.99	0.92	1.00	0.94
Sweeping	0.94	1.00	0.94	1.00	0.94
Lying down	0.90	1.00	0.93	1.00	0.92

Table 1.6 Average user response time (in minutes) to recommendations

User	1	2	3	4	5	6	7	8	9	10
Avg. response time	24.47	34.44	3.42	5.38	40.44	7.21	28.29	13.99	8.56	36.84

1.6 Summary

This work has presented Mining Minds, a novel digital framework for personalized healthcare and wellness support. The framework has been neatly designed considering crucial requirements of digital health and wellness systems. This work has also described a unique architecture defined to provide the necessary functionality to enable curation and mining of data, information, knowledge and services for personalized health and wellness support. An initial realization of the key architectural components as well as various exemplary applications and tools showcasing some of the benefits provided by Mining Minds have also been presented and evaluated. The work is ongoing to complete the implementation of the devised architecture with new additional components, as well as to evaluate its services on a large-scale testbed.

Source Code

Mining Minds has been released as an opensource platform over GitHub for fellow researchers to reuse and extend our implementation for other use cases.
Source code can be downloaded from the following location:
https://github.com/ubiquitous-computing-lab/Mining-Minds

The contents of this chapter have been previously published in the following article:

Oresti Banos, Muhammad Bilal Amin, Wajahat Ali Khan, Muhammad Afzal, Maqbool Hussain, Byeong Ho Kang, and Sungyong Lee, "The Mining Minds Digital Health and Wellness Framework", BioMedical Engineering OnLine (SCIE, IF:1.43), DOI:10.1186/s12938-016-0179-9, 2016

References

[1] Hafner T, Shiffman J. The emergence of global attention to health systems strengthening. Health Policy Plan. 2013;28(1):41–50.
[2] Hood L, Flores M. A personal view on systems medicine and the emergence of proactive P4 medicine: predictive, preventive, personalized and participatory. N Biotechnol. 2012;29(6):613–24.
[3] Matheson EM, King DE, Everett CJ. Healthy lifestyle habits and mortality in overweight and obese individuals. J Am Board of Fam Med. 2012;25(1):9–15.
[4] Gillen MM, Markey CN, Markey PM. An examination of dieting behaviors among adults: links with depression. Eat Behav. 2012;13(2):88–93.
[5] Demark-Wahnefried W, Jones LW. Promoting a healthy lifestyle among cancer survivors. Hematol Oncol Clin North Am. 2008;22(2):319–42.
[6] Swan M. Health 2050: the realization of personalized medicine through crowdsourcing, the quantified self, and the participatory biocitizen. J Pers Med. 2012;2(3):93–118.

[7] Powell AC, Landman AB, Bates DW. In search of a few good apps. JAMA. 2014;311(18):1851–2.

[8] Withings Activité. http://www.withings.com/eu/en/products/activite. Accessed 29 Aug 2015.

[9] Garmin Vivofit. http://sites.garmin.com/en-US/vivo/vivofit/. Accessed 29 Aug 2015.

[10] Fitbit Surge. https://www.fitbit.com/surge. Accessed 29 Aug 2015.

[11] Misfit Shine. http://www.misfitwearables.com/products/shine. Accessed 29 Aug 2015.

[12] Banos O, Villalonga C, Damas M, Gloesekoetter P, Pomares H, Rojas I. Physiodroid: combining wearable health sensors and mobile devices for a ubiquitous, continuous, and personal monitoring. ScientificWorldJournal. 2014;2014(490824):1–11.

[13] Oresko JJ, Jin Z, Cheng J, Huang S, Sun Y, Duschl H, Cheng AC. A wearable smartphone-based platform for real-time cardiovascular disease detection via electrocardiogram processing. IEEE Trans Inf Technol Biomed. 2010;14(3):734–40.

[14] Hermens H, op den Akker H, Tabak M, Wijsman J, Vollenbroek M. Personalized coaching systems to support healthy behavior in people with chronic conditions. J Electromyogr Kinesiol. 2014;24(6):815–26.

[15] Chen P-H, Chen H-M. Framework design-integrating an android open platform with multi-interface biomedical modules for physiological measurement. J Converg Inf Technol. 2012;7(12):310–9.

[16] Fortino G, Giannantonio R, Gravina R, Kuryloski P, Jafari R. Enabling effective programming and flexible management of efficient body sensor network applications. IEEE Trans Hum Mach Syst. 2013;43(1):115–33.

[17] Gaggioli A, Pioggia G, Tartarisco G, Baldus G, Corda D, Cipresso P, Riva G. A mobile data collection platform for mental health research. Personal Ubiquitous Comput. 2013;17(2):241–51.

[18] Yang G, Xie L, Mantysalo M, Zhou X, Pang Z, Xu LD, Kao-Walter S, Chen Q, Zheng L-R. A health-iot platform based on the integration of intelligent packaging, unobtrusive bio-sensor, and intelligent medicine box. IEEE Trans Indus Inf. 2014;10(4):2180–91.

[19] Banos O, Villalonga C, Garcia R, Saez A, Damas M, Holgado JA, Lee S, Pomares H, Rojas I. Design, implementation and validation of a novel open framework for agile development of mobile health applications. Biomed Eng Online 2015;14(S2:S6),1–20.

[20] Estrin D, Sim I. Open mhealth architecture: an engine for health care innovation. Science. 2010;330(6005):759–60.

[21] Google Fit. https://developers.google.com/fit/overview. Accessed 29 Aug 2015.

[22] Sami S. https://developer.samsungsami.io/sami/sami-documentation/. Accessed 29 Aug 2015.

[23] Apple HealthKit. https://developer.apple.com/healthkit/. Accessed 29 Aug 2015.

[24] Banos O, Bilal-Amin M, Ali-Khan W, Afzel M, Ahmad M, Ali M, Ali T, Ali R, Bilal M, Han M, Hussain J, Hussain M, Hussain S, Hur TH, Bang JH, Huynh-The T, Idris M, Kang DW, Park SB, Siddiqui M, Vui L-B, Fahim M, Khattak A-M, Kang B-H, Lee S. An innovative platform for person-centric health and wellness support. In: Proceedings of the international work- conference on bioinformatics and biomedical engineering; 2015.

[25] Banos O, Bilal-Amin M, Ali-Khan W, Afzel M, Ali T, Kang B-H, Lee S. Mining minds: an innovative framework for per- sonalized health and wellness support. In: Proceedings of the 9th international conference on pervasive computing technologies for healthcare (PervasiveHealth 2015); 2015.

[26] Banos O, Bang JH, Hur TH, Siddiqui M, Huynh-The T, Vui L-B, Ali-Khan W, Ali T, Villalonga C, Lee S. Mining human behavior for health promotion. In: Proceedings of the 37th annual international conference of the IEEE engineering in medicine and biology society (EMBC 2015); 2015.
[27] Microsoft Azure. http://azure.microsoft.com. Accessed 29 August 2015.
[28] Barham P, Dragovic B, Fraser K, Hand S, Harris T, Ho A, Neugebauer R, Pratt I, Warfield A. Xen and the art of virtualiza- tion. ACM SIGOPS Oper Sys Rev. 2003;37(5):164–77.
[29] Padhy RP. Big data processing with hadoop-mapreduce in cloud systems. Int J Cloud Comput Serv Sci. 2012;2(1):16–27.
[30] Microsoft Windows Server. http://www.microsoft.com/en-us/server-cloud/products/windows-server-2012-r2/. Accessed 29 August 2015.
[31] Richardson L, Ruby S. RESTful web services. Sebastopol: O'Reilly Media Inc; 2008.
[32] Kim K, Kim C, Jung S-I, Shin H-S, Kim J-S. Inter-domain socket communications supporting high performance and full binary compatibility on xen. In: Proceedings of the Fourth ACM SIGPLAN/SIGOPS international conference on virtual execution environments; 2008. p. 11–20.
[33] Microsoft SQL Server. http://www.microsoft.com/en-us/server-cloud/products/sql-server/. Accessed on 29 Aug 2015.
[34] Banos O, Damas M, Pomares H, Rojas F, Delgado-Marquez B, Valenzuela O. Human activity recognition based on a sensor weighting hierarchical classifier. Soft Comput. 2013;17:333–43.
[35] Lara O, Labrador M. A survey on human activity recognition using wearable sensors. IEEE Commun Surv Tutor. 2012;99,1–18.
[36] Banos O, Galvez J-M, Damas M, Pomares H, Rojas I. Window size impact in human activity recognition. Sensors. 2014;14(4):6474–99.
[37] Preece SJ, Goulermas JY, Kenney LPJ, Howard D. A comparison of feature extraction methods for the classification of dynamic activities from accelerometer data. IEEE Trans Biomed Eng. 2009;56(3):871–9.
[38] Han M, Vinh LT, Lee Y-K, Lee S. Comprehensive context recognizer based on multimodal sensors in a smartphone. Sensors. 2012;12(9):12588–605.
[39] Banos O, Damas M, Pomares H, Prieto A, Rojas I. Daily living activity recognition based on statistical feature quality group selection. Expert Syst Appl. 2012;39(9):8013–21.
[40] Ali T, Hussain M, Ali Khan W, Afzal M, Lee S. Authoring tool: acquiring sharable knowledge for Smart CDSS. In: International conference of the IEEE engineering in medicine and biology society; 2013, p. 1278–81.
[41] Ainsworth BE, Haskell WL, Herrmann SD, Meckes N, Bassett DR, Tudor-Locke C, Greer JL, Vezina J, Whitt-Glover MC, Leon AS. 2011 compendium of physical activities: a second update of codes and met values. Med Sci Sports Exerc. 2011;43(8):1575–81.
[42] Forgy CL. Rete: A fast algorithm for the many pattern/many object pattern match problem. Artif Intell. 1982;19(1):17–37.
[43] Schofield W. Predicting basal metabolic rate, new standards and review of previous work. Hum Nutr Clin Nutr. 1984;39:5–41.
[44] Baget J-F. Improving the forward chaining algorithm for conceptual graphs rules. In: International conference on principles of knowledge representation and reasoning; 2004, p. 407–14.

[45] Gong S. Learning user interest model for content-based filtering in personalized recommendation system. Int J Digit Content Technol Appl. 2012;6(11):155–62.
[46] Daemen J, Rijmen V. The design of rijndael: AES—the advanced encryption standard. Heidelberg: Springer; 2002.
[47] Zhong S, Chen T. An efficient identity-based protocol for private matching. Int J Commun Syst. 2011;24(4):543–52.
[48] Ghinita G, Karras P, Kalnis P, Mamoulis N. A framework for efficient data anonymization under privacy and accuracy constraints. ACM Trans Database Syst. 2009;34(2):9.
[49] Pervez Z, Awan AA, Khattak AM, Lee S, Huh E-N. Privacy-aware searching with oblivious term matching for cloud storage. J Supercomput. 2013;63(2):538–60.
[50] Li S, Xu LD, Wang X. A continuous biomedical signal acquisition system based on compressed sensing in body sensor networks. IEEE Trans Indus Inf. 2013;9(3):1764–71.

Part II

Data Curation

Chapter 2

Data Curation Framework Overview

On Curating Multimodal Sensory Data for Health and Wellness Platforms

Muhammad Bilal Amin, Oresti Banos, Wajahat Ali Khan,
Hafiz Syed Muhammad Bilal, Jinhyuk Gong, Dinh-Mao Bui,
Soung Ho Cho, Shujaat Hussain, Taqdir Ali,
Usman Akhtar, and Sungyoung Lee

In recent years, the focus of healthcare and wellness technologies has shown a significant shift towards personal vital signs devices. The technology has evolved from smartphone-based wellness applications to fitness bands and smartwatches. The novelty of these devices is the accumulation of activity data as their users go about their daily life routine. However, these implementations are device specific and lack the ability to incorporate multimodal data sources. Data accumulated in their usage does not offer rich contextual information that is adequate for providing a holistic view of a user's lifelog. As a result, making decisions and generating recommendations based on this data are single dimensional.

In this chapter, we present our Data Curation Framework (DCF), which is device independent and accumulates a user's sensory data from multimodal data sources in real time. DCF curates the context of this accumulated data over the user's lifelog. DCF provides rule-based anomaly detection over this context-rich lifelog in real time. To provide computation and persistence over the large volume of sensory data, DCF utilizes the distributed and ubiquitous environment of the cloud platform. DCF has been evaluated for its performance, correctness, ability to detect complex anomalies, and management support for a large volume of sensory data.

2.1 Introduction

In recent years, there has been a shift in the way healthcare is handled and it is supporting systems. This change has made a drastic impact on the design of conventional healthcare models. Instead of late disease management and cure, these models are focusing on preventative-personalized health. Consequently, an opportunity is provided for healthcare providers to focus on when, where, and how; care and support are delivered to the particular patient and service consumer [1, 2]. The reason for this shift is the rising financial stress that healthcare systems have to face to support the growing demand for their services [3]. Therefore, service providers are pushing forward for wellness-based models and conducting research to investigate their effectiveness. The latest studies in biomedical healthcare have shown that the most prevalent diseases are partly caused or aggravated by poor lifestyle choices that people make in their daily routine. Unhealthy and fast food diets, use of tobacco, and sedentary routines with a lack of exercise are among the potential contributors to developing illnesses and limit the effectiveness of medical treatments [4–6].

With the advent of smart and personal devices, an opportunity has emerged for healthcare providers and biomedical researchers to empower people to take care of their health and wellness by providing them with timely, ubiquitous, and personalized support [7]. Consequently, the influx of fitness wearables with smartphone applications and systems supporting health and wellness has taken the market by storm [8]. For example, commercial systems and platforms such as Withings Activite [9], Garmin Vivofit [10], Fitbit Surge [11], Misfit Shine [12], Apple Watch [13] and HealthKit [14], Samsung

Gear [15], LG smartwatches [16], Google Fit [17], and Microsoft Band [18] with Microsoft Health [19], all primarily consist of sensor-based bracelets accompanied by mobile apps and provide some basic health recommendations based on the measured steps, calories, or hours of sleep. In parallel, research groups are also working on health and wellness systems that can alert of physical conditions [20] or detect chronic illnesses [21]. Despite this enormous effort by the industry and research, most current solutions are single-device focused and have a limited scope [1]. Therefore, they are unable to generate a context-rich user lifelog, which can provide a holistic view of user activity and behavior [22]. Such lifelogs are a necessity for the evolutionary wellness systems that support the self-quantification of its users [23]. Moreover, a context-rich lifelog is also a low-cost way to acquire valuable user information on which effective interventions from healthcare professionals can be based [24]. Considering the limitations of existing efforts as an opportunity, we have proposed and implemented a comprehensive cloud-based sensory data acquisition framework called Data Curation Framework or DCF.

The contribution of Data Curation Framework (DCF) is aligned with the definition of lifelog, meaning it is a black box of user life events [22]. Multidimensional insights into user activities and behaviors require a context-rich lifelog that can be developed by the accumulation of data from a larger set of multimodal data sources [22, 25]. Keeping this perspective as the primary motivation, DCF implements five core concepts in its design philosophy (illustrated in Figure 2.1). (i) The ability to continuously sense for raw sensory data from multimodal data sources in real time; (ii) the device-independent acquisition of raw sensory data. This concept contributes to the compatibility of DCF for IoT-based environments [26]. This property increases the ability of DCF to integrate a larger set of sensory devices; (iii) the induction of a larger set of sensory devices results in a richer context. DCF provides comprehensive curation of this context over a user lifelog. This context-rich lifelog can be used in multidimensional ways, e.g., data accumulated from a smartphone, a smartwatch, and a depth camera can accurately identify the context of a user posture in an environment. Therefore, a health and wellness platform using DCF can make recommendations not only pertaining to his activity but also the later on effect of that activity on his muscular health; (iv) DCF is equipped with a lifelog monitoring tool called LLM. In comparison with device-based activity recognition, lifelog monitoring looks for anomalies over richer context occurring over time. For reliability, expert-driven rules [27] provide intelligence to this monitoring (Rule creation is not part of the DCF scope); (v) DCF provides persistence to support the large volume of heterogeneous and multimodal raw sensory data associated with the lifelog. This property enables DCF to support the forthcoming concepts of data-driven knowledge generation [28], descriptive [29] and predictive analytics [30], and visualization [29].

DCF is a cloud-based implementation, as the cloud supports the infrastructure level DCF requirements. For continuous sensing, the ubiquitous nature of the cloud provides DCF with the ability to acquire sensory data in different contexts and environments. Similarly, for device independence, the cloud provides a central yet scalable computational resource that can accumulate sensory data from clients without being concerned with their computational abilities. For lifelog maintenance and monitoring, the cloud provides a hub for context curation and monitoring for anomalies detection. Lastly, to support the volume of data accumulated by DCF, the cloud provides a big data platform.

With the advent of smart and personal devices, an opportunity has emerged for healthcare providers and biomedical researchers to empower people to take care of their health and wellness by providing them with timely, ubiquitous, and personalized support [7]. Consequently, the influx of fitness wearables with smartphone applications and systems supporting health and wellness has taken the market by storm [8]. For example, commercial systems and platforms such as Withings Activite [9], Garmin Vivofit [10], Fitbit Surge [11], Misfit Shine [12], Apple Watch [13] and HealthKit [14], Samsung

Gear [15], LG smartwatches [16], Google Fit [17], and Microsoft Band [18] with Microsoft Health [19], all primarily consist of sensor-based bracelets accompanied by mobile apps, and provide some basic health recommendations based on the measured steps, calories, or hours of sleep. In parallel, research groups are also working on health and wellness systems that can alert of physical conditions [20] or detect chronic illnesses [21]. Despite this enormous effort by the industry and research, most current solutions are single-device focused and have a limited scope [1]. Therefore, they are unable to generate a context-rich user lifelog, which can provide a holistic view of user activity and behavior [22]. Such lifelogs are a necessity for the evolutionary wellness systems that support the self-quantification of its users [23]. Moreover, a context-rich lifelog is also a low-cost way to acquire valuable user information on which effective interventions from healthcare professionals can be based [24]. Considering the limitations of existing efforts as an opportunity, we have proposed and implemented a comprehensive cloud-based sensory data acquisition framework called Data Curation Framework or DCF.

The contribution of Data Curation Framework (DCF) is aligned with the definition of lifelog, meaning it is a black box of user life events [22]. Multidimensional insights into user activities and behaviors require a context-rich lifelog that can be developed by the accumulation of data from a larger set of multimodal data sources [22,25]. Keeping this perspective as the primary motivation, DCF implements five core concepts in its design philosophy (illustrated in Figure 2.1). (i) The ability to continuously sense for raw sensory data from multimodal data sources in real time; (ii) the device-independent acquisition of raw sensory data. This concept contributes to the compatibility of DCF for IoT-based environments [26]. This property increases the ability of DCF to integrate a larger set of sensory devices; (iii) the induction of a larger set of sensory devices results in a richer context. DCF provides comprehensive curation of this context over a user lifelog. This context-rich lifelog can be used in multidimensional ways, e.g., data accumulated from a smartphone, a smartwatch, and a depth camera can accurately identify the context of a user posture in an environment. Therefore, a health and wellness platform using DCF can make recommendations not only pertaining to his activity but also the later on effect of that activity on his muscular health; (iv) DCF is equipped with a lifelog monitoring tool called LLM. In comparison with device-based activity recognition, lifelog monitoring looks for anomalies over richer context occurring over time. For reliability, expert-driven rules [27] provide intelligence to this monitoring (Rule creation is not part of the DCF scope); (v) DCF provides persistence to support the large volume of heterogeneous and multimodal raw sensory data associated with the lifelog. This property enables DCF to support the forthcoming concepts of data-driven knowledge generation [28], descriptive [29] and predictive analytics [30], and visualization [29].

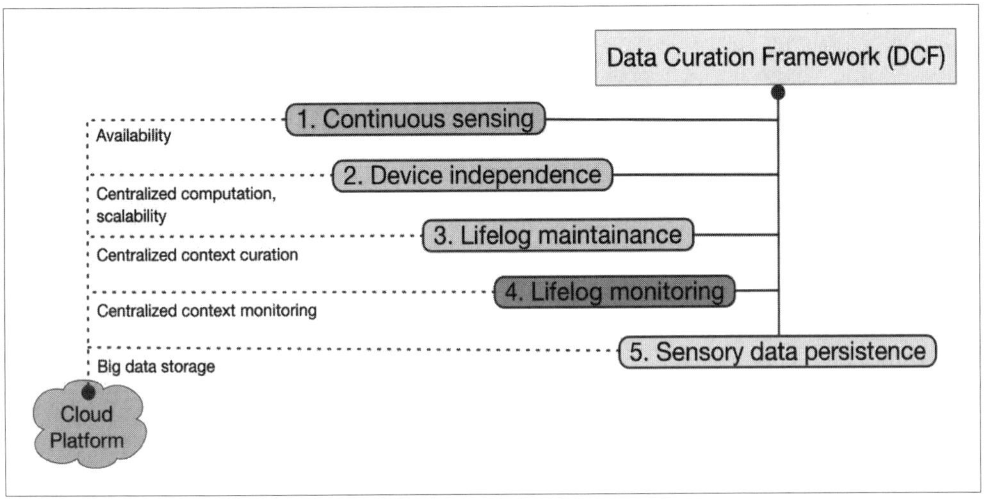

Figure 2.1 Data curation framework (DCF) philosophy

DCF is a cloud-based implementation, as the cloud supports the infrastructure level DCF requirements. For continuous sensing, the ubiquitous nature of the cloud provides DCF with the ability to acquire sensory data in different contexts and environments. Similarly, for device independence, the cloud provides a central yet scalable computational resource that can accumulate sensory data from clients without being concerned with their computational abilities. For lifelog maintenance and monitoring, the cloud provides a hub for context curation and monitoring for anomalies detection. Lastly, to support the volume of data accumulated by DCF, the cloud provides a big data platform.

DCF is currently part of the implementation of the Mining Minds platform [31]. DCF executes as a separate layer (Data Curation Layer or DCL) at the infrastructure level of the Mining Minds architecture [1]. It accumulates raw sensory data in real time from multimodal data sources and provides curation to the context identified on that data via the Mining Minds Information Curation Layer (ICL). DCL as the implementation of DCF monitors the context for anomalies based on the rules derived by the Mining Minds Knowledge Curation Layer (KCL). Furthermore, it preserves all of the sensory data in big data storage to support analytics and visualization provided by the Mining Minds Supporting Layer (SL). However, in this chapter, we only discuss data curation as a framework independent of the Mining Minds platform.

The contents of this chapter are as follows. Section 2.2 describes the related work with respect to DCF. Section 2.3 provides an overview of the methodology of DCF. Section 2.4 presents the details of the components participating in the implementation of DCF. Section 2.5 describes the execution scenarios of DCF in collaboration with a health and wellness platform. Section 2.6 evaluates various aspects of DCF including its accuracy, performance, scalability, its ability to perform reliable user lifelog monitoring and persistence. Section 2.7 concludes this chapter.

2.2 Related Work

Following the boom of health- and wellness-based systems, many systems for sensory data accumulation and analysis have been proposed for the people's healthcare and wellbeing. For analysis of these systems we have classified them into three different categories: (i) Mobile Health, where implementation is focused on the evolution of smartphones and their embedded sensors; (ii) Wearable Health, where implementation is incorporating wearable bands and smartwatches in combination with smartphone or gateways; and (iii) Data Accumulation and Curation, where the implementation focuses on the accumulated data from variety of sensors for analysis. The categories are discussed in the following subsections.

2.2.1 Mobile Health

In the last decade, the influx of smartphone usage in our daily lives has been enormous. These smartphones are equipment with various multimodal sensors like accelerometer, PPG, and GPS, which in fact used intelligently, can accumulate user activity data in real-time for further utilization. Therefore, the combination of smartphone devices and web services provides more opportunities for healthcare systems to evolve with reduced cost. Researchers have indicated that new requirements and trends are embedded SIM and mobile health platforms (mHealth) [32]. In [33], authors presented the capability of mobile devices (mobility, low-cost, remote, and equipped with sensors) in conjunction with web-service based approach, providing services relating to healthcare. Furthermore, the highlights of the proposed approach are listed and compared with existing remote health monitoring systems. Moreover, in the case of elderly, mobile phones are already participating in providing healthcare services [34]. In [35], the authors presented a mobile phone-based platform to collect the psychological, physiological, and activity information of the user for mental health research. In [36], a mobile version of a data processing toolbox originally devised for computer-based architectures and principally used for human behavior modeling was provided. In [37], a middleware integrating multiple interfaces for multi-parameter monitoring of physiological measurement is proposed. In [38], tools have been suggested for the analysis of the provenance of mobile health data. In [39], authors present a client-server life logging platform. It enables context capturing by the mobile phone and data processing at the server to extract meaningful high-level context.

In [40], the authors present a lightweight lifelogging framework called UbiqLog. This framework provides a configurable interface to enable and disable sensors within the smartphone. Although more sensors can be added due to the compatibility of the framework's data model; however, the sensors have to be embedded within the form factor of smartphone device. Authors in [40] acknowledge the fact that lifelog data tends to grow rapidly; therefore, an external server like storage is required for permanent persistence. Lifelog generated by UbiqLog is neither shareable nor reusable by external systems; furthermore, it does not support any monitoring on the data. Similarly, in [41], authors present an open-source toolkit for sensory data collection over smartphones called AWARE. For conducting small-scale studies, AWARE stores all the accumulated data locally on the smartphone; however, for larger scale, data is uploaded to the cloud. The toolkit provides a context plugin that can passively perform analysis on the accumulated data. In similarity with DCF, AWARE also implements a publish-subscribe model; however, it is only utilized for context sharing.

In [42], the DigMem system is proposed, which utilizes distributed mobile services, linked data, and machine learning to create rich and interactive HDMs (Human Digital Memory). An HDM, created by the data from the pervasive devices available in user's environment, produces a more dynamic and data-rich memory. Information such as how the user felt, where the user was, and the context of the environment can be established [42]. In contrast with DCF, the DigMem is a tri-component system with no service-based support for sharing its core asset data, i.e., memory boxes with health and wellness platforms. Although it collects data from multimodal sources, DigMem requires a compatible environment where its smartphone application can broadcast and look for information. Collected data is linked using semantic web technologies and presented as a memory box to its web application for visualization. DigMem's concept of linked data is conceptually similar to DCF's curation of user context; however, the focus of DigMem is on the visualization aspect of this data. Whereas in DCF, curated data is monitored for anomalies and its services provide lifelog as a user timeline for visualization. In [42], authors acknowledge the inclusion of big data in lifelogging systems and discusses the challenges involved in its incorporation in [43]. However, the implementation of big data in DigMem is not addressed.

2.2.2 Wearable Health

In the last decade, the usage of wearables has evolved from medical needs to a personalized accessory. Projects like SenseWare (SWA) [44] armband that collects physiological data using a bi-axial accelerometer, galvanic skin resistance (sweat rates), heat flux (heat dissipated from the body), and skin and near body temperature, have been utilized. In [45], the authors used SWA for the estimation of energy expenditure and step count during treadmill walking in cystic fibrosis patients, compared to healthy adults. In [46], the SWA has also been utilized for the monitoring of adherence in women with rheumatoid arthritis.

In the wearable health research, Microsoft's SenseCam [47] is considered a revolutionary pervasive device [48]. It is equipped with a digital camera and multiple sensors, including sensors to detect changes in light levels, an accelerometer, a thermometer for detecting ambient temperature, and a passive infrared sensor for detecting the presence of people. SenseCam has been used in various studies, for example, in [49], authors use the technology as a memory aid for capturing the user's daily routine. The images recorded are mapped as a lifelog and presented in a timeline format. In [50], the authors use SenseCam for the tracking of sedentary behavior. However, the focus of this utilization is about activity data accumulation and tracking.

In [51], authors present the InSense system. It utilizes acceleration, audio, and visual sensing, to perform real time context recognition. Conceptually InSense and DCF can be aligned and compared as they both work for real time data collection with a larger set of data sources to generate a context-rich lifelog. However, in InSense, data accumulation and its understanding are two separate activities. After the data is collected, it is manually annotated and rated by the user to create an interest operator. This process is completely offline and quite cumbersome for the user who has recorded an activity for few hours. Furthermore, the lifelog becomes rich therefore to annotation; thus, an effective monitoring in real time cannot be performed for the InSense users.

In more recent years, the utilization of multimodal sensor-based technologies has evolved to become personalized accessories (e.g., wearable bands and smartwatches such as Garmin Vivofit, Fitbit Surge, Misfit Shine, and Apple Watch). These technologies process independently of smartphones. The wearable wrist sensor stores and transfers the sensory data using a dongle device or a smartphone to a health management system. However, these systems are single data source-oriented, i.e., they only consider a wristband sensor; therefore, they cannot infer correct context about what a user is presently doing.

Regardless of the considerable research and development of healthcare and wellness systems, only a few implementations exist that execute as independent platforms for tackling complex and realistic scenarios. Highly funded commercial initiatives like Apple's HealthKit, Google Fit, and Microsoft Health have evolved the approach from an application to an ecosystem; however, these implementations are still single device or data integration-centric.

2.2.3 Data Accumulation and Curation

Considering lifelog data as an asset, some of the latest works have been focused on data accumulation and its extended utilization. In [52], the authors present the challenges of data accumulation in the Internet of Nano-Things [53] (IoNT) perspective. The challenges are discussed at communication protocol level, hardware level and software (middleware) level. Possible solutions and applications have been discussed as a proposed design.

In [54], authors present an energy efficient continuous sensing framework called Insight. The implementation of this framework focuses on small and wearable devices and has been demonstrated using a smartwatch. The data accumulation process is energy efficient, and this data is further used for prediction. Comparing the implementation of Insight with DCF, it is evident that the volume of data both the frameworks are concentration on is very different. Insight only uses wearable devices with small data footprint; furthermore, it does not use raw sensory data. If required, it leverages secondary application like Google Fit for the user activity data. Opportunistic (Event and interval driven) sensing [55] of Insight with stated sensing policy also contributes to limited size. This data is persisted in a folder like structure on the device's storage. On the other hand, DCF implements continuous accumulation in a device-independent mode; resulting in a much more scalable framework for a larger set of multimodal data sources. Consequently, the data generated in DCF is significant in volume, which requires big data storage, and the curated lifelog is context rich. DCF provides services on sharability of this data for knowledge generation, analytics, and visualization. As acknowledged by the authors in [54], computationally complex processes should be handled by devices with advanced computing abilities. Therefore, DCF utilizes the computational ability of the cloud to execute compute-intensive processes on the accumulated raw sensory data.

Some of the systems have a particular perspective on the accumulation and utilization of healthcare data originated at the clinical level. Instead of more real-time accumulation, these implementations are focused on evolutionary repositories with aggregation of historical and more recent clinical data available for utilization. Among these clinical data-oriented systems, NetBio [56] is a prominent implementation. It assembles vast amounts of curated and annotated, clinical and molecular data. This method enables NetBio clients to make unique discoveries that otherwise would be impossible with their own private datasets. NetBio uses big data technology for permanent persistence and core logic layers to make correlations between the billions of data points from the public domain with private genomic and clinical data sets. At a higher-level, NetBio provides a rich set of APIs that enable clients to integrate NetBio within their workflows and scenarios. Their current clients include pharmaceutical R&D and academic medical centers. The initial system was implemented for oncology; nevertheless, it is now expanding into metabolic and autoimmune diseases.

In contrast to all of the implementations discussed above, DCF is a novel attempt to implement a raw sensory data acquisition, curation, and monitoring framework. The sensory data acquisition services of DCF are independent of data sources. It is equipped to handle multimodal data sources directly communicating with the framework or via smartphone-like gateways. The acquired multimodal data is synchronized to represent an event of time for each user. With scalability in mind, numerous multimodal data sources can communicate in parallel with the DCF, making it a more IoT-oriented implementation. Furthermore, instead of being dependent on the computational ability of smartphones, DCF considers all of the communicating devices as a source of raw sensory data; thus, generating a context-rich user lifelog. The computation over the accumulated data and lifelog is performed over a cloud platform, keeping the framework compatible with data source with low computational abilities. From an evolutionary perspective, complex computational algorithms for context identification, data fusion, and mining can be implemented without disturbing client implementations. Moreover, the accumulated data can be used for concepts of data-driven knowledge generation, descriptive and predictive analytics, and visualization. Samsung SAMI [57] is also moving in a similar direction with an independent API and cloud support; however, their implementation is more data exchange-centric, and utilization for healthcare and wellness requires custom implementation and monitoring. Moreover, DCF curates the identified low- and high-level context on user-accumulated data as a comprehensive lifelog. The idea of lifelogging has already been presented in [22, 24, and 25]; however, DCF implements anomaly detection on lifelog instances based upon expert-driven rules in correlation with user profiles, keeping the monitoring vigilant as well as personalized.

2.3 Methodology

This section provides an overview of the proposed methodology of DCF. Participating components in the implementation of DCF are introduced in this section; however, technical details of these components are described in the following section.

DCF is intended to be incorporated as a foundation layer for health and wellness platforms where real-time multimodal sensory data acquisition, its curation as a lifelog, and monitoring for anomalies is essential. Furthermore, it provides permanent storage to acquired sensory data for extended usage (e.g., visualization, analytics, data-driven knowledge generation). For the independent execution of DCF, its implementation is encapsulated with interfaces for sensory data acquisition and its persistence. The curation of a lifelog and its monitoring is implemented as an implicit property of DCF with a separate interface to incorporate anomaly detection rules and publish-subscribe based response.

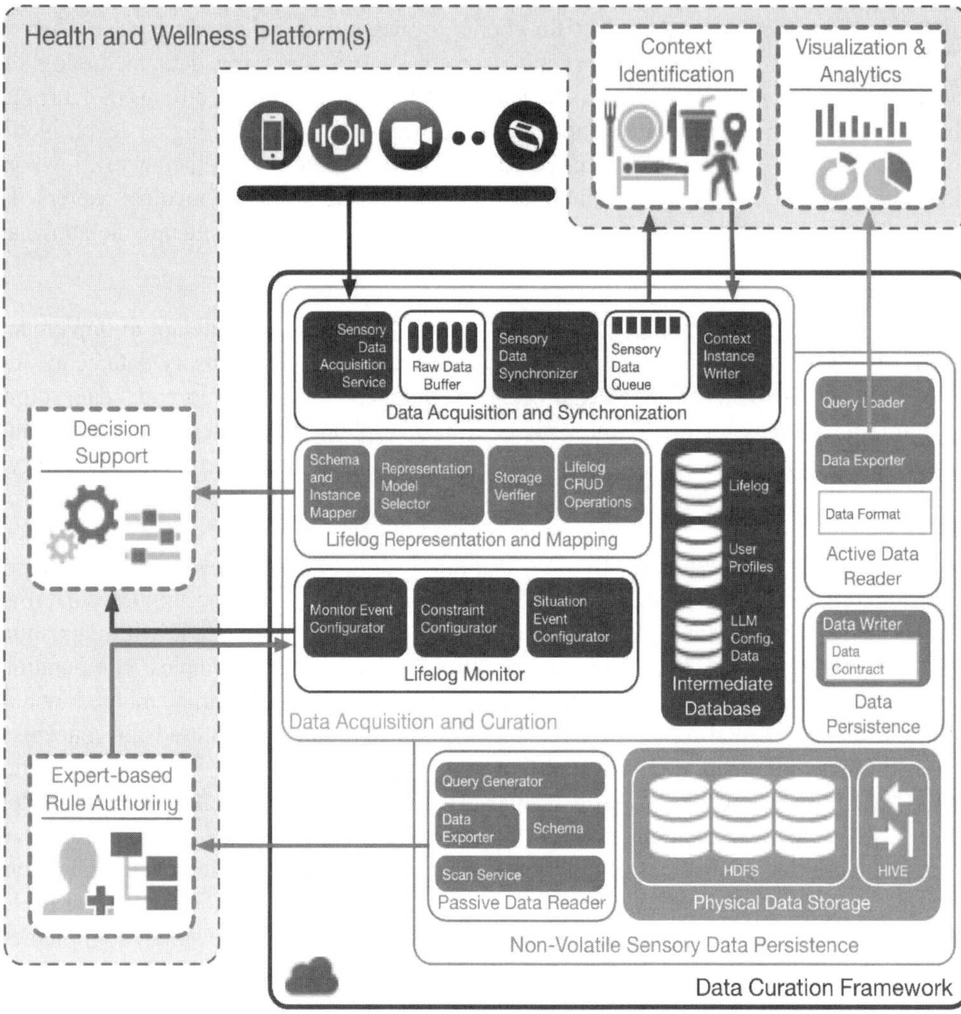

Figure 2.2 Data curation framework (DCF) architecture

As illustrated in Figure 2.2, DCF consists of two primary components, i.e., Sensory Data Processing and Curation, and Non-volatile Sensory Data Persistence. Within the former, the Sensory Data Acquisition and Synchronization subcomponent obtains the raw sensory data from multimodal data sources, both in a real-time (active) and offline (passive) manner. This data is synchronized based upon the user identification and the time stamp of the data generation, and subsequently, it is queued for the context determination. The definition and methodology of the identification of context vary in health and wellness platforms [58]; therefore, an interface to the synchronized sensory data residing in the queue is provided by DCF. This feature facilitates health and wellness platforms to plug-n-play their context identification engine without worrying about the real-time data acquisition from multimodal sources in a distributed environment. In response, these engines can feedback the DCF with identified context. The subcomponent of Lifelog Mapping and Representation receives the identified context and curates it by mapping the context instances to a time-based log registering the detected human activities and behaviors. The lifelog persists in the Intermediate Database for reuse. The stream of lifelog instances is analyzed by monitoring the subcomponent known as the Lifelog Monitor (LLM); it is responsible for performing customized unit-based (e.g., time-based, physical activity-based, nutrition-based) monitoring of user context available in the lifelog, cross-linked with the user profiles. LLM draws the association between the context available in the lifelog and implements anomaly detection based on expert-driven rules. Anomalies detected by LLM represent risky or unhealthy behavior and are described by various constraints (e.g., age, gender, medical conditions) and monitor-able variables (e.g., the intensity of a particular activity and its duration). LLM is equipped to provide a notification-based response to its client (a health and wellness platform or a user) with the help of a publish-subscribe mechanism.

The Non-volatile Sensory Data Persistence component is responsible for providing permanent and distributed big data persistence to the raw sensory data. It is termed non-volatile, as no update or delete operations are performed on the raw sensory data storage. The subcomponent of Data Persistence provides a data contract that is implemented by the clients of Physical Data Storage for permanent persistence of the data. Non-volatile Sensory Data Persistence also provides mechanisms to access this persisting data as a response to health and wellness platforms. This response can be of an online or offline type. For an online response, the Active Data Reader subcomponent is used. It provides a continuous stream of sensory data for extended data operations, including visualization and predictive analytics. For an offline response, the Passive Data Reader subcomponent is used. It provides a batch response that can be effectively used for training machine learning-based models and can provide data insights to experts for rule generation. To create periodic backups of lifelog data, the subcomponents of Data Persistence are again utilized. This method provides permanent storage of the lifelog data, which can be utilized in the future for user behavior analysis.

DCF is a hybrid cloud implementation with components distributed between a private and a public cloud. Therefore, privacy and security of user lifelog data has been given high importance. For its implementation, we have used custom built Health Fog framework [59], which provides Fog computing [60] as an intermediary layer between the client and DCF. Furthermore, it implements Cloud Access Security Broker (CASB) for data access policy. The modular design of Health Fog is capable of engaging data from multimodal data sources together with the adequate level of security and privacy using existing cryptographic primitives.

In the staging and production environments of DCF, the component of Sensory Data Processing and Curation is deployed over a public cloud (Microsoft Azure [61]) with compute-intensive instances to support scalability and high performance. However, the component of Non-volatile Sensory Data Persistence is deployed over a private cloud environment with distributed commodity machines, customized security [62], and large-space hard drives. Implementation details of these components are described in the following subsections.

2.4 Implementation Details

2.4.1 Raw Sensory Data Acquisition and Synchronization

Implementation of Raw Sensory Data Acquisition and Synchronization (DAS) consists of a REST [63] service that collects raw sensory data from multimodal data sources. The key in this acquisition is the association of accumulated data with their time of origination. All data sources subsist independently along with independent clocks; therefore, a logical clock is required for identifying the data origination at the same time from multiple sources. Consequently, DAS implements the time frame-based synchronization methods called Complete- and Incomplete-sync.

Complete-sync is the sunny day scenario in which all the data pertaining to an instance of time is accumulated within the specified period. It waits for the data accumulation from all the data sources at the DCF server within the duration of a three-second period. As soon as all the data is received, complete-sync encapsulates it as one message. Subsequently, the message is timestamped and enqueued in Sensory Data Queue for context determination by a health and wellness platform.

Algorithm 2.1 Time-based synchronization for raw-sensory data acquisition

Require: $buffer_{src}[1, ..., n]$: n is the total number of data sources

Ensure: $buffer_{dst}$: queue for time-synchronized data packets

```
procedure SYNC(buffer_dst)
    msg ← create_msg(NULL)
    while i ≤ No_of_datasources do
        buffer_src[i] ← Recv(data)                          d Complete-sync execution
        msg.add(create_msg(buffer_src[i]))
        if time_sec > time_window then
            if send_only = TRUE then                        d Incomplete-sync: Eager execution
                break
            end if
            while j ≤ No_of_datasources do   d Incomplete-sync: Rendezvous execution
                j ← i + 1
                if buffer_src[j].has_contents then
                    msg.add(create_msg(buffer_src[j])
                end if
            end while
            break
        end if
    end while
    msg.timestamp ← buffer_src[i].timestamp
    buffer_dst.enqueue(msg)
end procedure
```

In contrast to Complete-sync, Incomplete-sync executes when data from any of the sources is not received in the three-second time frame. This execution is further classified in two different modes, i.e., Eager and Rendezvous. In the Eager mode, the message is created with only the available data and buffered for context determination. In the Rendezvous mode, for the missing data, it associates the last sent data from the raw sensory buffer. Subsequently, a message is created and buffered for context determination. Implementation details of Complete-sync and Incomplete-sync with its dual modes are explained in Algorithm 2.1.

Due to the non-blocking (asynchronous) and scalable nature of data acquisition from multimodal data sources, DAS uses Node.js [64] for server-side implementation. Furthermore, it implements in-memory buffers for temporary storage of data that has arrived. Each buffer represents a particular type of multimodal data source. A buffer synchronizer is executed so that the accumulated data can be synchronized with the data that originated at the same time from all other data sources.

For communication from a multimodal data source to DAS, a JSON [65] object is defined. The contents of this object consist of four fields, i.e., a user id, a data source id, a timestamp of the data origination at a data source, and the payload. Due to service-based implementation, DAS is independent of the number of multimodal data sources.

2.4.2 Data Persistence

The asset of DCF is its persistence of a user's raw sensory data (from multimodal data sources) with the associated context as a lifelog. DCF defines two levels of abstraction on the data acquired. The first level is a higher-level abstraction referred to as an Intermediate Database hosted within a relational database (RDBMS). This database hosts three types of data, i.e., the user lifelog that represents user context over a period of time, the user profiles, and the knowledge base consisting of rules for anomaly detection required by LLM. The intermediate database is deployed over a public cloud instance.

The second level is a lower-level abstraction referred to as non-volatile distributed storage; it is hosted over Hadoop-based big data storage [66] on a private cloud instance. This storage also hosts three types of data; however, the granularity of data is at a finer scale. For example, this storage provides permanent persistence to all the raw sensory data acquired from the multimodal data sources; it maintains user-invoked backup of large-sized multimedia content, such as video data captured from a 3D camera and periodic backups of user lifelogs with associated user profiles.

The philosophy behind this two-level abstraction architecture of data storage is due to four main factors. (i) Performance, the user lifelog data is frequently accessed in soft-real time. Therefore, due to the inherent speed of the RDBMS, its storage is leveraged for lifelog persistence and access;

Data relationships, the user activities and behaviors are encapsulated as context by a comprehensive object-based relationship. For recommendation generation or high-level context determination by health and wellness platforms, relationships among entities of user profiles and their context are necessary. Thus, a tightly coupled structured data formation is held. Therefore, the schema-based approach of the RDBMS is leveraged for persistence instead of the unstructured data storage of big data;

Data volume, the magnitude of data generated by multimodal data sources, grows exponentially in a short period. Therefore, big data storage with its distributed non-volatile persistence is utilized for storing the raw sensory data as well as periodic backups of user profiles and lifelogs; (iv) The frequency of data updates, the user lifelog changes and evolves rapidly due to the continuous change in user context in real time. Due to the higher cost of data updates at the big data level, RDBMS is leveraged.

2.4.3 Lifelog Representation and Mapping

In DCF, the identified context is mapped over a timeline as a lifelog, providing a black box to user activities and behaviors over time. The lifelog is maintained in a relational database instance at the intermediate database of DCF. The maintenance of this lifelog including CRUD operations is the responsibility of the subcomponent of Lifelog Representation and Mapping (LLRM). The lifelog is represented as an object-oriented abstraction called a lifelog model in this mapping subcomponent. The lifelog model encapsulates attributes such as performed activities, preferred and visited locations, health and wellness goals to achieve, and recognized emotions of the users. For agility and extensibility, this object model is an implementation of Facade and Adapter design patterns [67]. The conceptual model of LLRM is illustrated in Figure 2.3.

The implementation of LLRM contains a mapper module that extracts objects, attributes, and relationships from input XML/JSON data as resources. It identifies and maps the classes for the extracted resources and places the instances accordingly using a deep copy method [68].

The Storage Verifier module validates the data according to the schema of the data tables in the intermediate database. Furthermore, it also validates the compatibility of data with the defined constraints (keys, values, primary keys, and foreign keys) on the data tables.

Depending upon the utilization, the lifelog model has higher-level abstractions, called representations, to customize the lifelog data access for health and wellness platforms. The current implementation provides four different representations: (i) The first representation provides an interface to internal DCF components for storing and retrieving lifelog data; (ii) the second representation provides an interface to external clients of DCF for retrieving lifelog data with user profiles; (iii) the third representation provides an interface to external clients of DCF for retrieving lifelog data and its associated raw sensory data from non-volatile storage; (iv) the fourth representation provides an interface to external clients of DCF for incorporating decisions made by health and wellness platforms as part of lifelog data. These representations are compatible with XML and JSON document formats.

2.4.4 Lifelog Monitoring

Lifelog Monitoring (LLM) is designed to perform continuous monitoring of the user context representing his activities and behavior in his lifelog. LLM itself does not recognize activities; however, it leverages the external activity recognition abilities of the health and wellness platforms to provide associated context, and it executes at a higher-level abstraction and draws associations between a user's low- and high-level contexts [69], then maps them to the anomaly detection rules built by an expert. As soon as this mapping is established, LLM registers them over the target user's lifelog and starts the monitoring process.

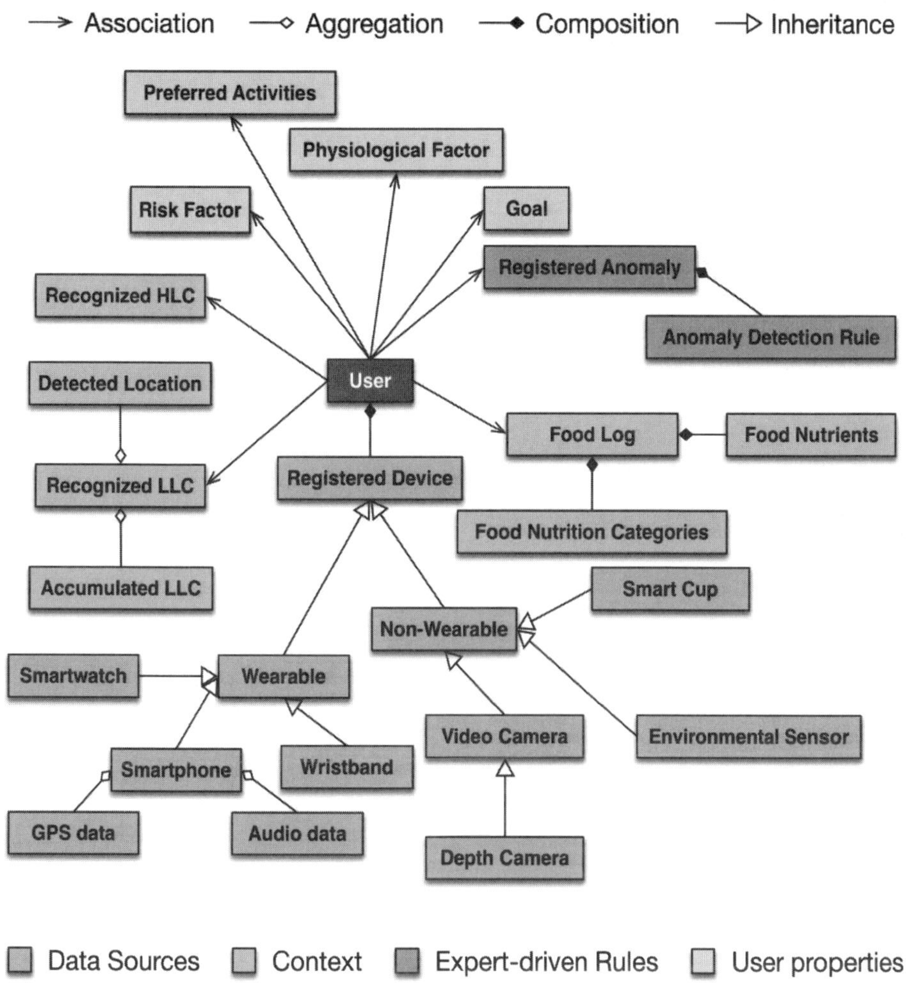

Figure 2.3 Lifelog model

To generate notification-based responses, LLM implements an observer pattern [67]. This mechanism facilitates LLM to host a subscriber list of clients for a particular user's lifelog. If an anomaly is detected, all of the subscribed clients are notified. This implementation is helpful for scenarios in which not only the user but also his care provider and a third-party wellness platform need to be alerted to a particular anomaly-related event.

LLM is designed to incorporate anomaly detection rules that are generated by the expert dynamically. This nature of the LLM requires a robust model to handle all of the anomalies to be detected in a particular domain. Therefore, LLM divides domains in terms of measuring quantities. The current implementation of DCF supports time as the measuring quantity for physical activities, as well as macronutrients (fat, carbohydrates, and proteins) and calories for food intake.

The overall complexity of the implementation of LLM is divided into three modules, i.e., the monitored event configurator, the constraint configurator, and the anomaly event detector.

Configurator modules are built to incorporate the anomaly detection rules. These rules are submitted to LLM using a JSON-based communication contract. This contract is described in the following listing:

```
{
    //Common communication format
    "AnomalyConditions":[
    {
    "ConditionKey"    :"Age",
    "ConditionType"     :"String",
    "ConditionValue"    :"Adult",
    "ConditionValueOperator" : "="},

    {
    "ConditionKey" :"Duration",
    "ConditionType"     :"String",
    "ConditionValue"    :"1h",
    "ConditionValueOperator" : "="},
     {
    "ConditionKey"  :"CurrentContext",
    "ConditionType"     :"String",
    "ConditionValue"    :"Sitting",
    "ConditionValueOperator":"="},
    "AnomalyID" : "1"
 ]
}
```

To uniquely identify dynamic anomalies in multi-situation scenarios, they are managed as key-value pairs. The output of the configurator modules is well-defined anomaly detection information, consisting of its monitored event and its target measuring quantity.

The anomaly detector module is responsible for monitoring the user lifelog for monitored events. For monitoring to occur, at least one respective anomaly associated with a particular monitored event must be registered for a user. As soon as the monitored event is detected, the anomaly detector registers the respective well-defined anomaly detection rule for that particular user. Lifelog data pertaining to these monitored events are filtered out from the stream of user context and managed in a monitorable log. This log has information related to the target measuring quantities. Different monitored events have different target quantities; therefore, the monitorable log facilitates the LLM to manage multiple monitored events for independent monitoring by persisting unique targets. The anomaly detector compares the difference of the measured quantities in regular intervals. Whenever the target is achieved, the anomaly detector publishes a notification to all the subscribers of the user's lifelog. The execution process of LLM is illustrated in the sequence diagrams of Figures 2.4 and 2.5.

2.4.5 Non-Volatile Sensory Data Persistence

The component of non-volatile sensory data persistence is responsible for providing permanent and distributed big data storage to raw sensory and lifelog data. Its subcomponents are designed to execute create and read operations as per the needs of the health and wellness platforms. These components primarily use Hive [70] queries over the Hadoop Distributed File System (HDFS).

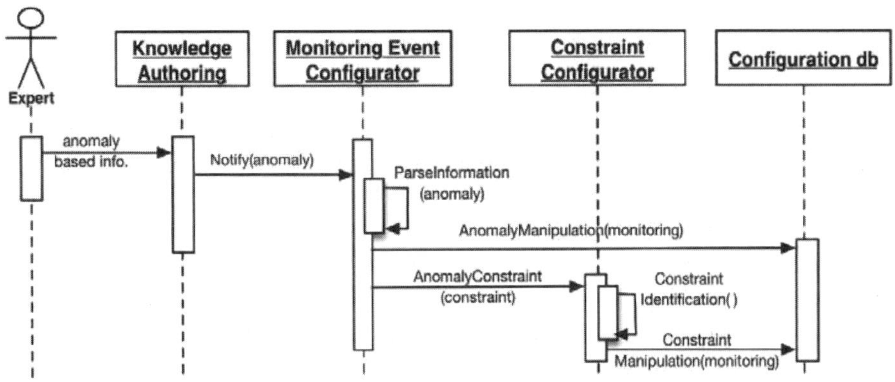

Figure 2.4 Sequence diagram of anomaly registration by the expert

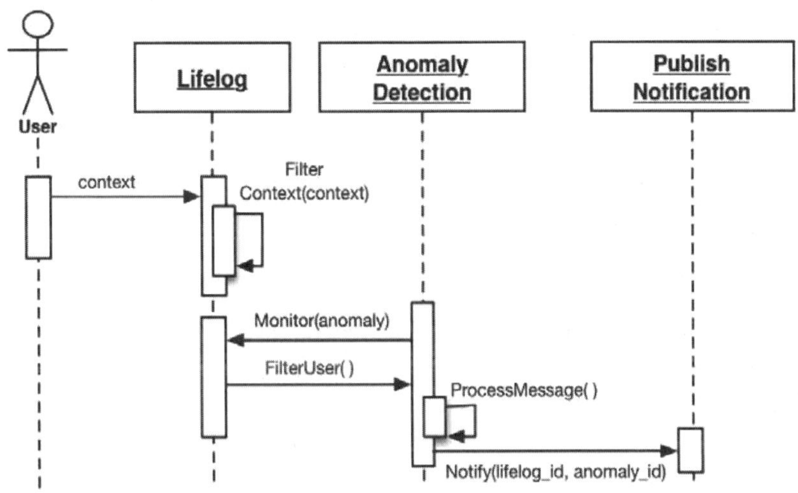

Figure 2.5 Sequence diagram of message flow in the lifelog monitoring

The subcomponent of Big Data Persistence is responsible for storing the raw sensory data communicated from the data acquisition and synchronization component every three seconds. This subcomponent is also used for user invoked periodic persistence of multimedia contents such as 3D depth videos.

There are two types of data reading subcomponents for access over distributed storage, i.e., Active Data Reader and Passive Data Reader. Active data reader (ADR) is primarily used to provide a continuous response to a real-time request for data visualization and analytics by a health and wellness platform. ADR hosts a repository of pre-defined Hive queries for a data read. An evolutionary repository grows with more usage and the addition of more clients. Upon receiving the request for data, ADR matches the request parameters with the available set of queries. In the case of a parameter match, the selected query is executed with a continuous stream-based response back to the client.

A passive data reader (PDR) is primarily designed from a machine learning perspective, as historical data persistence in the HDFS is useful for the training of models for data-driven knowledge generation. These models can support the expert to generate rules, which can be further utilized by LLM for anomaly detection. Execution of PDR is a two-step process: first, the schema of the data is sent to the client for parameter selection and request generation; second, after the selection is performed and sent to PDR with the request, it generates a query dynamically upon receiving the parameters. This query is executed over HDFS and the response is created and provided in a JSON format. The execution of PDR is an offline process and may take hours to complete.

2.5 Execution Scenarios

To understand the workings of DCF, we have incorporated its execution in the Mining Minds project as our client health and wellness platform. Depending on the needs of the platform and its participating layers (ICL, KCL, Service Curation Layer or SCL, and SL), DCF concurrently performs the online and offline execution. These executions are termed as active and passive execution flows. These execution flows are illustrated in Figure 2.6 and described in the following subsections.

2.5.1 Active Execution Scenario

The latest version of the Mining Minds platform supports the recognition of ten activities and three emotions (described in Table 2.1). They are recognized by ICL and returned as identified high- and low-level context. To facilitate ICL, DCF acquires four different types of raw sensory data (activity, location, audio, and 3D video) per user in an online manner. DCF communicates with three multimodal data sources for raw sensory data acquisition, i.e., a smartwatch, a smartphone, and a depth camera. The smartwatch accumulates accelerometer, gyroscope, magnetometer and PPG data, and synchronizes itself with the Mining Minds smartphone app. The smartphone itself collects accelerometer, gyroscope, magnetometer, GPS, speed, and audio bytes of three seconds for determining user activities, locations and emotions. The Mining Minds smartphone app communicates all this raw sensory data to the DCF.

For soft-real-time data acquisition, this non-blocking communication occurs every three seconds. In parallel, a depth camera (Kinect [71]) attached to a PC also communicates with the DCF for sending the semantics of the captured 3D video. These semantics provide activity and behavior-related information of the user to ICL. Inside DCF, the sensory data acquisition service receives this accumulated information asynchronously and buffers the data depending on its data source. These raw data buffers are initialized based on the number of data sources, i.e., each data source has a raw data buffer in the sensory data acquisition and synchronization subcomponent. All the buffer contents are synchronized and enqueued for determination of the associated low- and high-level context. From this point forward, the synchronized data is dequeued and then sent in parallel to ICL and distributed big data storage for context identification and non-volatile persistence respectively.

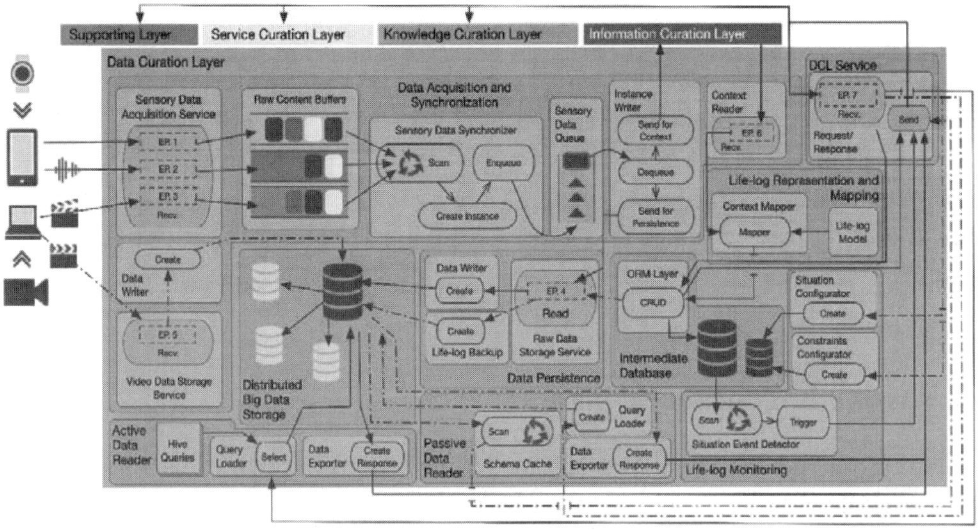

Figure 2.6 DCF execution flow

Upon receiving this synchronized data, ICL identifies the context and communicates it back to DCF. To reduce the ICL to DCF traffic, ICL only communicates if there is a change in context. For example, if a user has been sitting for more than one hour at work, ICL will identify the sitting activity at the office with its low- and high-level context identification. This context will not be communicated to DCF unless the user changes his activity to another. The received context from ICL is converted into a user lifelog instance and mapped to the object-oriented representation of the lifelog by the LLRM subcomponent. Furthermore, this subcomponent is also mandated for executing Create, Read, Update, and Delete (CRUD) operations regularly on lifelog data; therefore, it maintains the mapped data in the intermediate database.

The stream of incoming context is continuously monitored by LLM for anomalies described by well-defined rules. In the case of detection, LLM publishes a notification to SCL of the Mining Minds platform for a possible recommendation generation. Consequently, SCL gathers the required data, including the related context and user profile, and generates and pushes a recommendation to the user's smartphone. For a user request-based recommendation generation by SCL, DCF operates in a pull-based request response. LLRM receives the query generated by SCL via service. Required data, i.e., user profile and lifelog data, are extracted via a read operation and returned as a response to SCL for recommendation generation.

As mentioned earlier, in parallel to context determination, raw sensory data is also sent to non-volatile storage for persistence. SL of the Mining Minds platform for visualization and descriptive analytics requires this data. Following a request based on registered parameters, static queries are invoked by the active data reader subcomponent. It generates a stream-based response, as SL requires a continuous stream of data for visualization and analytics.

Table 2.1 Multimodal raw sensory data sources

Data Source	Sensor(s)	Context Type	Context Description
Smartwatch	Accelerometer, gyroscope, PPG.	activity	Climbing stairs, running, walking, cycling.
Smartphone	Accelerometer, gyroscope, longitude, latitude.	location	home, office, gym, school, restaurant, cafe
Smartphone	audio	emotion	anger, sadness, happiness
Depth camera	video	activity	Eating, sitting, standing, stretching, sweeping, and lying down.

2.5.2 Passive Execution Scenario

The passive execution flow of DCF pertains to the processes required for evolutionary support of not only DCF but also the overall Mining Minds platform. One of the primary processes that requires the passive execution of DCF is the provisioning of raw sensory data from non-volatile persistence for data-driven knowledge generation by KCL of the Mining Minds platform. This execution is based on a two-step process. First, KCL requests DCF for the schema of data maintained in the distributed by data storage. The passive data reader subcomponent processes this request by replying to KCL with the most recent version of the schema describing the data maintained in big data storage. Consequently, a domain expert at KCL's authoring tool selects the parameters based on the schema and generates the conditions for which data should be extracted from the big data storage. These parameters with conditions are returned to the passive data reader, which generates a dynamic query based upon the KCL provided parameters and executes it over big data storage. A response to this execution is returned to KCL in a pre-defined service contract. Extracted data from DCF assists KCL in the generation of rules that are used by LLM in the continuous monitoring of lifelog data during the active execution flow.

Another process that invokes the passive execution of DCF is the periodic backup and synchronization of the user's lifelog data persisted in the intermediate database with the associated raw sensory data maintained in the big data storage. The subcomponent of the lifelog sync performs this operation. SL of the Mining Minds platform uses this historic data for descriptive analytics.

Inside DCF, an instance of the data acquisition service also executes passively to copy the actual video contents from the user's PC to big data storage. This is also a periodic execution and exclusively authorized by the Mining Minds user.

2.6 Evaluation and Discussion

DCF has been evaluated from various aspects, e.g., from raw sensory data acquisition perspective, its accuracy of synchronization for sensory buffers, performance, and scalability has been evaluated. From context monitoring perspective, the ability of LLM to monitor upon user lifelog for existing anomalies, for dynamically added anomaly detection rules at runtime, and monitoring multiple users with various activities at runtime. From raw sensory data persistence perspective, its ability to read and write sensory data, and execution time of different queries with varying complexities. The results and discussion of these evaluations have been discussed in following subsections.

2.6.1 Accuracy

To evaluate the accuracy of the synchronization process, a smartphone (Samsung Galaxy S5 running Android 5.0 Lollipop, Samsung, Seoul, South Korea) and second-generation Kinect (rel. 2014) connected to a PC communicate with the DCF server running on a cloud instance with the 64-bit Windows 8.1 operating system, 16 GB of RAM, and a 3.10 GHz AMD A8-7600 Radeon R7, AMD, Sunnyvale, CA USA with 10 computing cores of 4C + 6G. Multiple requests from a single user from both clients (smartphone and PC), generated and synchronized at the server, are validated for accuracy. A time window of three seconds is allocated to temporarily hold the incoming data in memory buffers. For a conclusive evaluation, 100 data packets containing activity, location, voice, and 100 data packets containing video data are sent from the smartphone and the PC respectively. These communications occur randomly at different points in time during the defined three second window. The results from this evaluation reflect that the raw sensory data from both clients has been successfully synchronized at the server. The evaluation in Figure 2.7 illustrates the exact time in milliseconds of raw sensory data packets sent from both the smartphone and PC during ten different time windows. For example, for the first-time window, the smartphone communicated at 521ms; however, the PC communicated at 2545ms. The response synchronizer at DCF was able to identify both of these data packets as part of a single window of communication. As illustrated, all of the data packets have been successfully synchronized to the server, proving the correctness of our synchronization process over data acquisition of raw sensory data.

2.6.2 Performance

To evaluate the performance during raw sensory data acquisition and its synchronization we setup an environment of five multimodal data sources: (i) LG Watch R(TM), smartwatch connected with a Samsung Galaxy S5 smartphone running Android 5.0; (ii) Shimmer3 sensor connected with a Samsung Galaxy S5 smartphone running Android 5.0; (iii) Samsung Galaxy S6 Edge running Android 5.0 for audio data; (iv) Second-generation Kinect (rel. 2014) connected with a Samsung Notebook 9 running MS Windows 8.1; and (v) a PC emulating an environmental sensor. These sensors communicate with a DCF server (64-bit Windows 8.1 operating system, 16 GB of RAM, and a 3.10 GHz AMD A8-7600 Radeon R7 with 10 computing cores of 4C + 6G) in an asynchronous manner by sending sensory data packets with an increment from 10 to 10,000. The target timeout deadline given to the data acquisition and synchronization subcomponent is 5 seconds to accumulate, synchronize and queue the synchronized data in a memory buffer. The results of the performance testing are presented in Figure 2.8. From the results, it is quite evident that our implementation of the data acquisition and synchronization subcomponent is able to accumulate and synchronize 10,000 packets from the five sensors within the provided timeout deadline. Due to server warmup, our implementation initially took 3.5 s for 10 packets; however, the performance improved with subsequent executions. The fastest time was recorded for 800 packets with a total time of 3.15 s. The time to accumulate, synchronize and enqueue increased after 1800 packets and reached at 10,000 packets with a total time of 3.31 s, which is still 51% faster than the provided deadline of 5s.

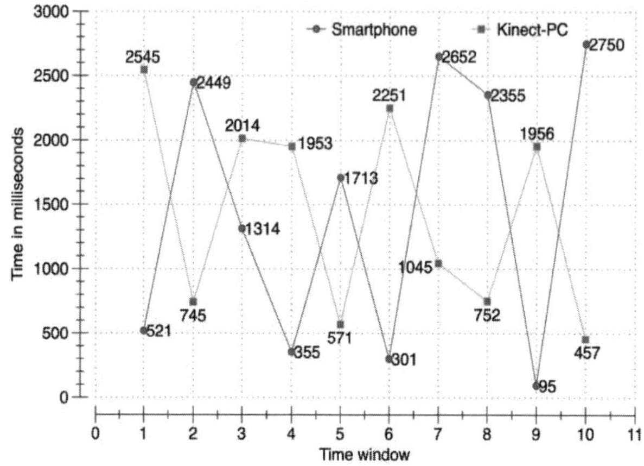

Figure 2.7 Data synchronization testing per time-window

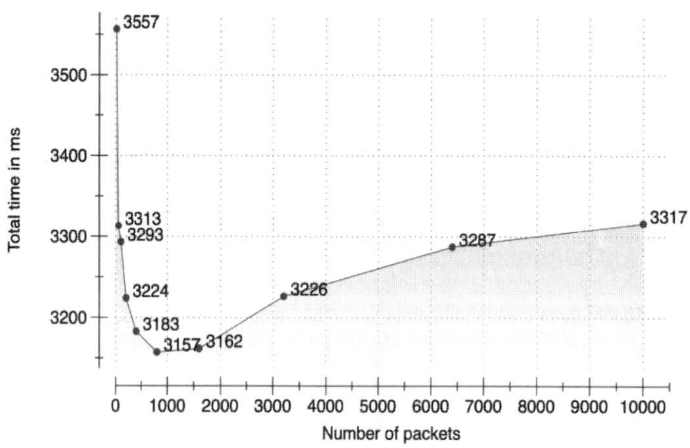

Figure 2.8 Performance testing

2.6.3 Scalability

To evaluate the ability of DCF to scale appropriately with the increase in number of multimodal data sources we setup an environment that simulates an incremental number of data sources (from 5 to 320). This test case stresses the data acquisition and synchronization subcomponent with a fixed packet size of 10,000 packets per data source with each packet containing a pre-accumulated sensory data of user activity for three seconds (30 kb) by using Samsung Galaxy S5 smartphone running Android 5.0. DCF server is running on a cloud instance with NodeJS v5.8, 64-bit Windows 7 Operating System, 4 GB of RAM, and 3.8 GHz AMD A10-5800K APU. Results of scalability testing are presented in Figure 2.9. From the results, it can be seen that our implementation was able to scale successfully from 5 multimodal data sources to 160. For 160 data sources with the maximum of 10,000 packets per data source, DCF was able to accumulate, synchronize and enqueue within 1.2min (=72,258.2ms). Therefore, our presented implementation can contribute significantly in environments where larger set of data sources will be added over time. As a response, DCF can accumulate, synchronize, and buffer the raw sensory data for these devices without any distinctive time delay. Although this evaluation depends on the size of the data packets; however, from our calculation user activity data accumulated over a duration of three seconds using a smartwatch and a smartphone is 24kb, which is smaller than the size of the packet used in this evaluation. To check the threshold of our implementation, we stress tested this evaluation with 320 data sources (illustrated in Figure 2.10). Consequently, the total time increased exponentially to 41 min (=2,470,064ms).

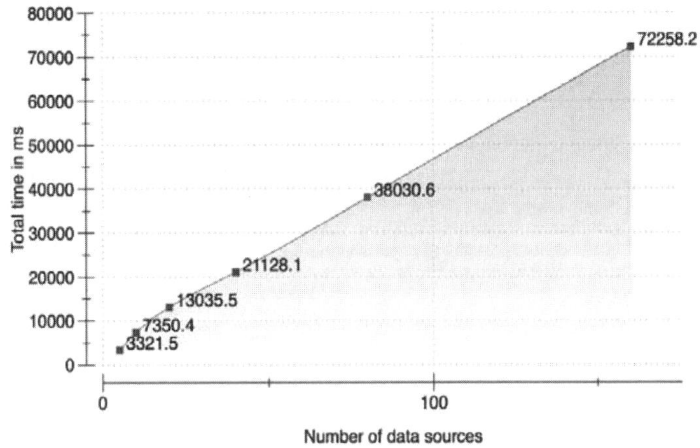

Figure 2.9 Scalability testing

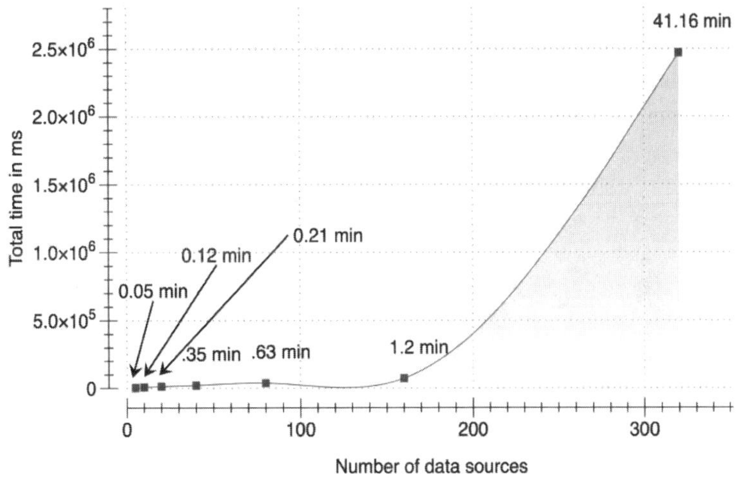

Figure 2.10 Stress testing of scalability

2.6.4 Lifelog Monitoring

The presence of an anomaly is a key-driving concept of lifelog monitoring. In the presence of registered anomaly detection rules, LLM provides monitoring for single or multiple users, over their lifelog.

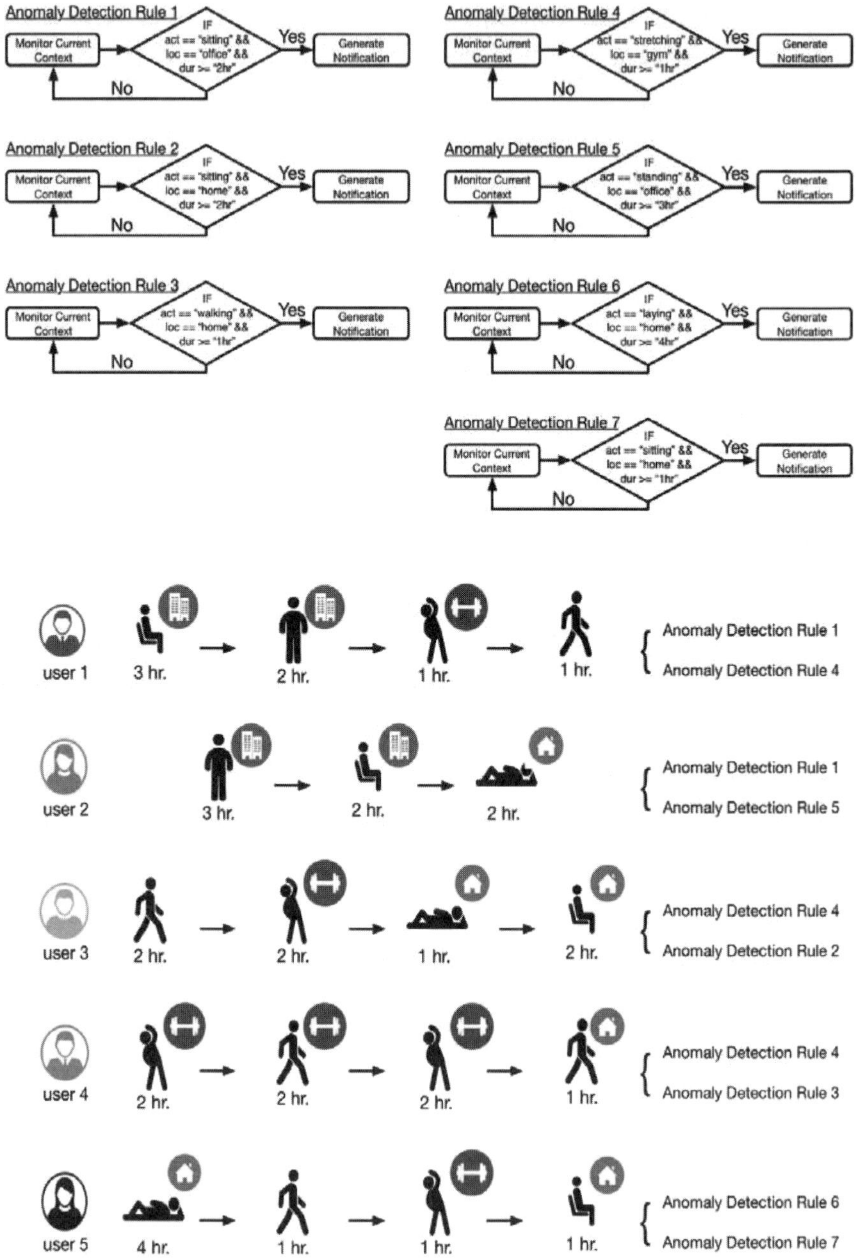

Figure 2.11 Anomaly detection rules and scenarios

For the evaluation of LLM, five users were selected to provide context information by performing various activities at user specified locations. Each user provided context using an LG Watch R(TM) for activity data (accelerometer, gyroscope, and PPG sensors were used), smartwatch connected with a Samsung Galaxy S5 smartphone running Android 5.0 for location data (GPS sensor was used) and a Second-generation Kinect (rel. 2014) connected with a Samsung Notebook 9 running

MS Windows 8.1 for indoor activity data using depth camera. Using the LLM interface, seven rules were dynamically incorporated in the execution of LLM. Definition of these rules and their correspondence with the users is illustrated in Figure 2.11. The monitoring was performed over a seven-hour snapshot of user lifelog; however, to save the time of the participants, the hour was scaled down to minutes. DCF accumulated 840 records of entries per user (= 4200 records in total); however, as lifelog only records when the context changes and marks the entries with starting and ending time, the number of records vary from user to user.

The monitored lifelog of the user 1 is shown in Figure 2.12. The context of the user is sitting at his workplace. After continuously monitoring for 2 h, LLM publishes a notification as he has been in a sedentary state according to the applied anomaly detection rule 1. The user continues his context for another hour then changes it to standing for 2 h and later on doing some exercise at the gym. According to another registered rule for his lifelog, as the user continues the exercise for 1 h, LLM publishes another notification.

Similar to the first user, the lifelog of user 2 is illustrated in Figure 2.13. As the lifelog of this user is registered with anomaly detection rules 1 and 5; therefore, the user has been notified twice in 7 h. Firstly, for standing at her workplace for 3 h; nevertheless, she continues her context for another hour. Secondly, for being sedentary and sitting at her workplace for continuous 2 h.

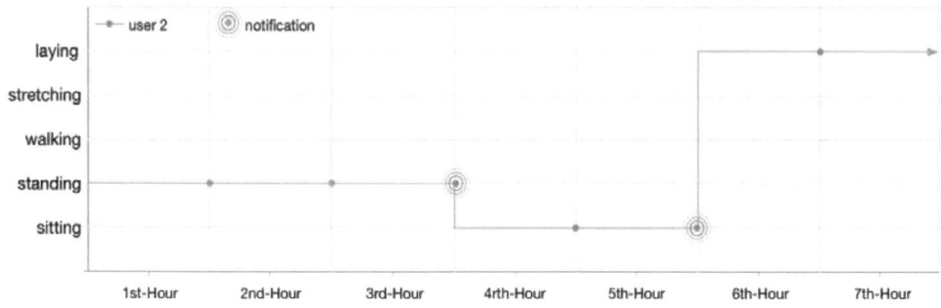

Figure 2.13 User 2, 7 h lifelog

The lifelog of user 3 is illustrated in Figure 2.14. As the lifelog of this user is registered with anomaly detection rules 4 and 2; therefore, the user has been notified twice in 7 h. Firstly, for doing exercise at the gym for continuous 1 h; nevertheless, the user continues his context for another hour. Secondly, for being sedentary and sitting at his home for continuous 2 h.

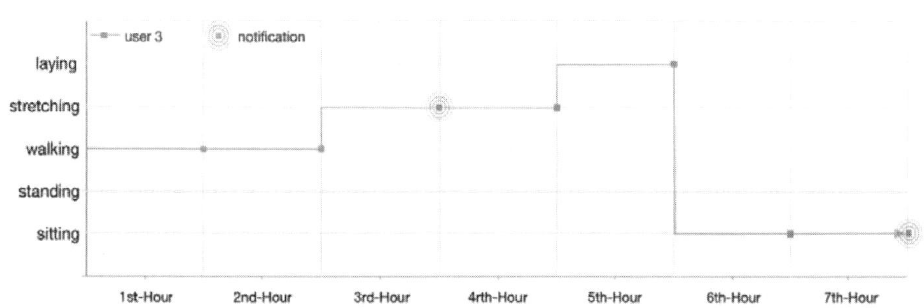

Figure 2.14 User 3, 7 h lifelog

User 4 gets notified thrice (illustrated in Figure 2.15) as his lifelog is registered for anomaly detection rules 3 and 4. These rules are invoked by LLM when the user performs exercise at the gym for continuously 1 h twice and walking at home for 1 h.

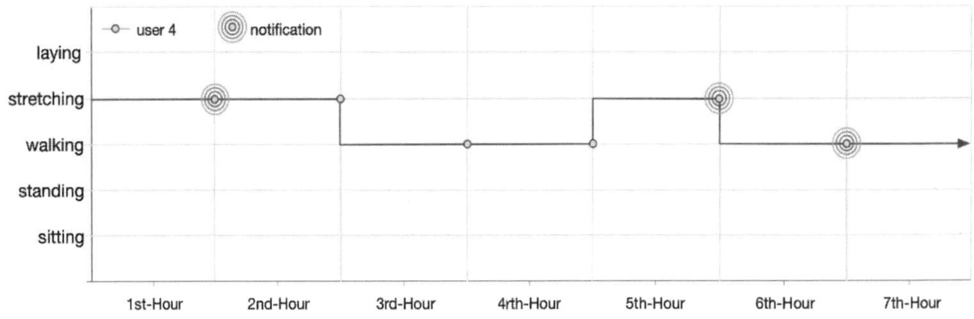

Figure 2.15 User 4, 7 h lifelog

User 5 gets notified twice (illustrated in Figure 2.16) as her lifelog is registered for anomaly detection rules 6 and 7. These rules are invoked by LLM when the user is laying at home for continuously 4 h and sitting at home for 1 h.

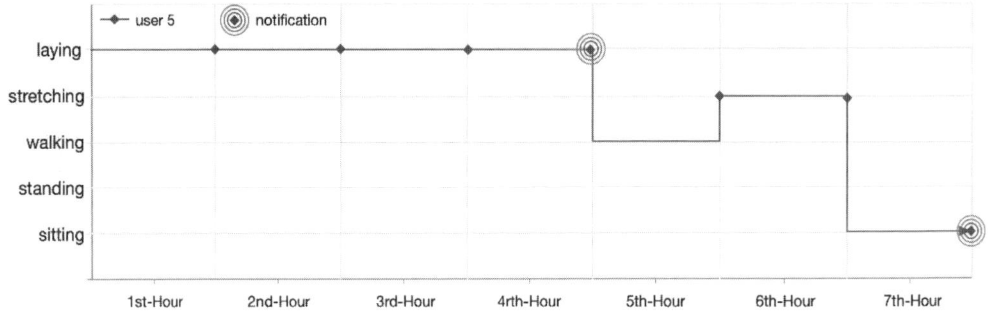

Figure 2.16 User 5, 7 h lifelog

The performance of the LLM is based on its timely generation of notifications for the health and wellness services of client frameworks. For its evaluation, the delay between the occurrence of anomaly and publication of notification is evaluated. The results are crosschecked with the help of anomaly log. LLM monitors the lifelog based on a cyclic monitoring interval defined in seconds. It publishes the subscribers with the maximum delay less than the interval of monitoring cycle.

For this evaluation 1000 requests were generated for each monitoring interval and DCF server hosting LLM is running on a cloud instance with 64-bit Windows 8.1 Operating System, 16GB of RAM, and 3.10 GHz AMD A8-7600 Radeon R7 with 10 computing cores of 4C + 6G. Results from this evaluation are shown in Figure 2.17. From these results it can be observed that the interval duration greater than 1s is appropriate for the evaluation environment, i.e., integrated execution with mining minds platform. Due to the distributed nature of mining minds platform, client communication overhead is introduced; therefore, leading a delay of little over the monitoring cycle interval in some cases. However, keeping the monitoring cycle interval at 3s, LLM publishes notifications with 96.97% efficiency. In the case of 5s, notification publication efficiency is 95.84%.

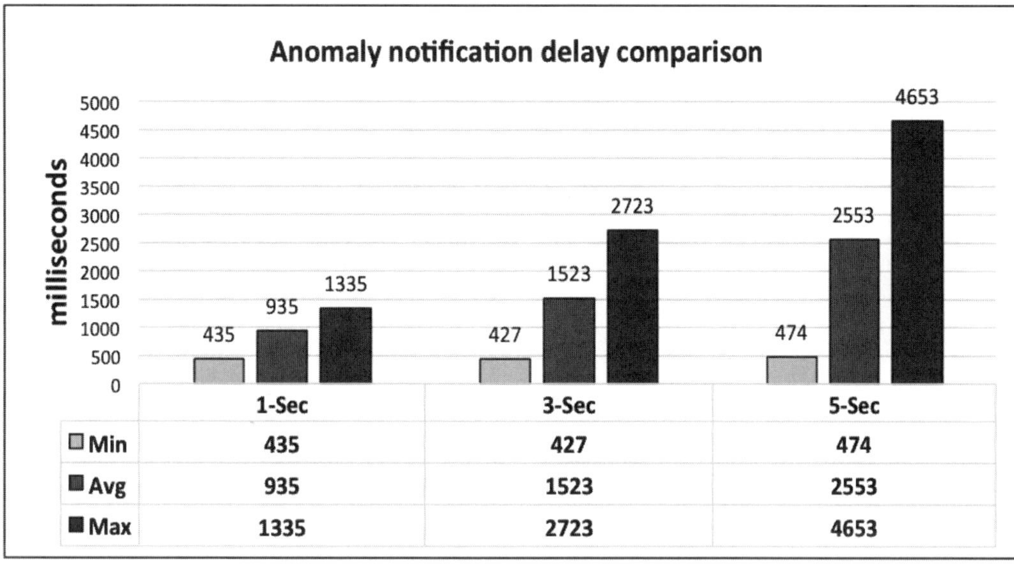

Figure 2.17 LLM performance evaluation

2.6.5 Non-Volatile Data Persistence

The big data storage is deployed over a private cloud instance at the Ubiquitous Computing Laboratory of Kyung Hee University, South Korea [72].

To evaluate the non-volatile data persistence components over HDFS, we have performed experimentation on read and write operations. These operations have been executed for three different raw sensory data sizes, i.e., 1 Gb, 5 Gb, and 9 Gb. This data is distributed over a private cloud infrastructure having four nodes with the following configurations: (i) Name-node, equipped with Intel Core i-5 3.3 GHz, 4 Gb of RAM; (ii) First data node, equipped with an AMD 2.7 GHz, 2 Gb of RAM; and (iii) 3rd and 4th data nodes are equipped with Intel Core i-5 3.3 GHz, 2 Gb of RAM.

In this evaluation (illustrated in Figure 2.18), the subcomponents of data persistence and the passive data reader are evaluated. As expected, the write operation is substantially faster than the read operation. The time difference for both read and write is proportional to the volume of raw sensory data in big data storage.

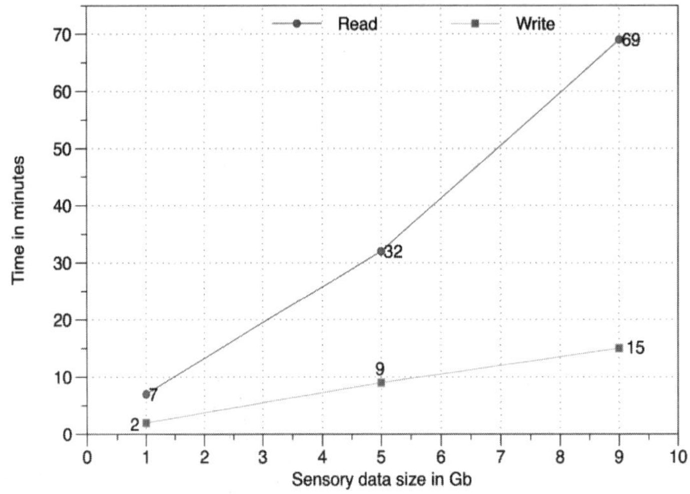

Figure 2.18 Read and write time over big data storage

To evaluate the execution and response time of the active data reader over HDFS, eight different SL-based queries are executed. These queries (described in Table 2.2) with varying complexities are performed over 1.7 Gb of lifelog data maintained over big data storage. The structure of this data consists of user detected locations, user recognized low- and high-level context, and record of published recommendations as a response to the anomaly detection. For the user recognized low-level context the data structure consists upon the duration (start and end time) associated with recognized high-level context from identified locations, i.e., Home, Office, Yard, Mall, Restaurant, Outdoors, and Transportation. To measure the response and execution time accurately, each query has been executed 50 times. The evaluation is illustrated in Figure 2.19. This execution is performed with a single mapper and its associated reducer; however, with an increase in mappers the execution time improves.

Table 2.2 Query execution scenarios

Scenario	Query
A	SELECT count(userid) FROM userrecognizedactivity WHERE userid = 39;
B	SELECT count(userid) FROM userrecognizedactivity;
C	SELECT count(userid) FROM detected location WHERE StartTime BETWEEN '1/29/2014' AND '12/10/2014';
D	SELECT count(userid) FROM detected location WHERE LocationLabel = 'Home';
E	SELECT count(userid) FROM tblUserRecognizedHLC WHERE StartTime BETWEEN '5/10/2015,2:45:01 AM' AND '12/9/2015,11:58:31 PM';

F	SELECT count(RecommendationID) FROM tfblrecommendation WHERE RecommendationDate BETWEEN '5/18/2015,10:01:59 AM' AND '12/15/2015,2:32:09 PM';
G	SELECT count(RecommendationFeedbackID) FROM ShetblRecommendationFeedbacket3 WHERE FeedbackDate BETWEEN '5/18/2015,10:01:59 AM' AND '7/29/2015,3:20:28 PM';
H	SELECT count(UserRecognizedEmotionID) FROM tblUserRecognizedEmotion WHERE StartTime BETWEEN '5/10/2015,2:30:01 AM' AND '12/14/2015,2:00:00 PM';

From this thorough evaluation, it is evident that DCF can accurately perform synchronization of raw sensory data from multimodal data sources. Its performance-oriented implementation has been validated by performance and load-testing. Its ability to monitor a lifelog has been tested and validated with simple to complex situations for multiple users. Furthermore, the execution-time over data maintained in big data storage has also been evaluated over real raw sensory data sets of large volumes. These evaluations are designed keeping the requirements and contributions of DCF in mind. Furthermore, the results reflect positively on the claimed novelty stated in earlier sections of this chapter.

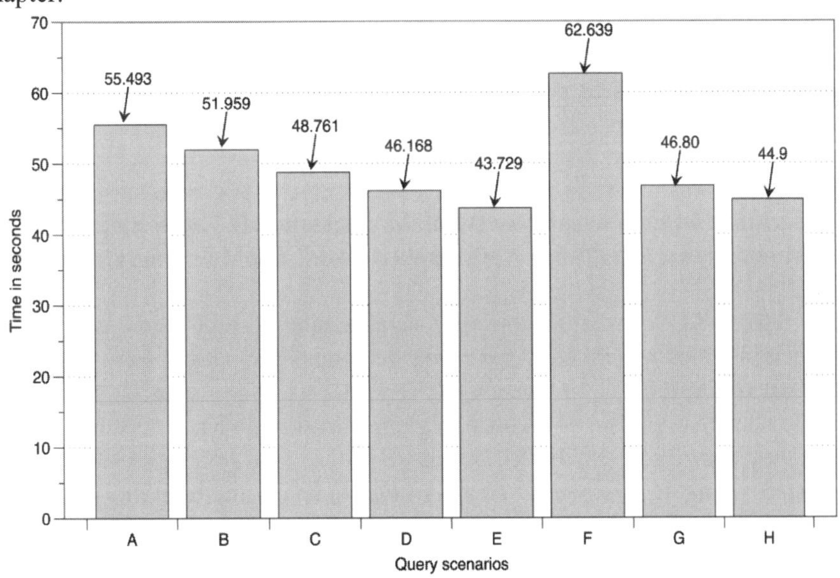

Figure 2.19 Query execution and response time over big data storage

2.7 Summary

In this chapter, we presented the Data Curation Framework (DCF). This framework focuses on curation of accumulated data from multimodal data sources in real time such that a context-rich user lifelog can be generated. This lifelog offers a holistic view on user activity and behavior which can further be utilized in multidimensional ways including effective interventions from healthcare professionals. The data source-independent implementation of DCF makes it more scalable and IoT compatible. Furthermore, it monitors this lifelog of registered users for the detection of anomalies. This monitoring is able to integrate static, dynamic, and complex created by the expert. DCF incorporates multi-level abstraction on the data, depending upon its usage and persistence. Frequently required user lifelogs, and profile data is maintained in an intermediate database; whereas, the historic and raw sensory data is maintained in non-volatile storage provided by big data technologies. This property enables DCF to support the forthcoming concepts of data-driven knowledge generation, descriptive and predictive analytics, and visualization.

Keeping the requirements of a data accumulation framework for health and wellness platforms, we have evaluated DCF for its performance, scalability, accuracy of the synchronization process of raw sensory data from multimodal data sources, monitoring of user lifelog, and data persistence. From the results, it is evident that DCF's implementation performs efficiently and effectively in realistic situations and scenarios while integrating with a health and wellness platform as the client.

Source Code

Source code can be downloaded from the following location:
https://github.com/ubiquitous-computing-lab/Mining-Minds/tree/master/data-curation-layer

The contents of this chapter have been previously published in the following article:

Muhammad Bilal Amin, Oresti Banos, Wajahat Ali Khan, Hafiz Syed Muhammad Bilal, Jinhyuk Gong, Dinh-Mao Bui, Soung Ho Cho, Shujaat Hussain, Taqdir Ali, Usman Akhtar, Tae Choong Chung, and Sungyoung Lee, "On Curating Multimodal Sensory Data for Health and Wellness Platforms", Sensors, vol. 16, no. 7, doi:10.3390/s16070980, 2016

References

[1] Banos, O.; Amin, M.B.; Khan, W.A.; Afzal, M.; Hussain, M.; Kang, B.H.; Lee, S.Y. The Mining Minds Digital Health and Wellness Framework. BioMed. Eng. OnLine 2016, in press.

[2] Hood, L.; Flores, M. A personal view on systems medicine and the emergence of proactive P4 medicine: Predictive, preventive, personalized and participatory. New Biotechnol. 2012, 29, 613–624.

[3] Hafner, T.; Shiffman, J. The emergence of global attention to health systems strengthening. Health Policy Plan. 2013, 28, 41–50.

[4] Matheson, E.; King, D.; Everett, C. Healthy lifestyle habits and mortality in overweight and obese individuals. J. Am. Board Family Med. 2012, 25, 9–15.

[5] Gillen, M.; Markey, C.; Markey, P. An examination of dieting behaviors among adults: Links with depression. Eat. Behav. 2012, 13, 88–93.

[6] Demark-Wahnefried, W.; Jones, L. Promoting a healthy lifestyle among cancer survivors. Hematol. /Oncol. Clin. N. Am. 2008, 22, 319–342.

[7] Swan, M. Health 2050: The realization of personalized medicine through crowdsourcing, the quantified self, and the participatory biocitizen. J. Personal. Med. 2012, 2, 93–118.

[8] Powell, A.C.; Landman, A.B.; Bates, D.W. In search of a few good apps. J. Am. Med. Assoc. 2014, 311, 1851–1852.

[9] Withings Activite. Available online: http://www.withings.com/eu/en/products/activite (accessed on 24 June 2016).
[10] Garmin Vivofit. Available online: http://sites.garmin.com/en-US/vivo/vivofit/ (accessed on 24 June 2016).
[11] Fitbit Surge. Available online: https://www.fitbit.com/surge (accessed on 24 June 2016).
[12] Misfit Shine. Available online: http://www.misfitwearables.com/products/shine (accessed on 24 June 2016).
[13] Apple Watch. Available online: http://www.apple.com/watch/ (accessed on 24 June 2016).
[14] Health Kit. Available online: http://www.apple.com/ios/health/ (accessed on 24 June 2016).
[15] Samsung Gear. Available online: http://www.samsung.com/us/mobile/wearable-tech (accessed on 24 June 2016).
[16] LG Smartwatches. Available online: http://www.lg.com/us/smart-watches (accessed on 24 June 2016).
[17] Google Fit. Available online: https://fit.google.com/fit/u/0/ (accessed on 24 June 2016).
[18] Microsoft Band. Available online: https://www.microsoft.com/microsoft-band/en-us (accessed on 24 June 2016).
[19] Microsoft Health. Available online: https://www.microsoft.com/microsoft-health/en-us (accessed on 24 June 2016).
[20] Banos, O.; Villalonga, C.; Damas, M.; Gloesekoetter, P.; Pomares, H.; Rojas, I. Physiodroid: Combining wearable health sensors and mobile devices for a ubiquitous, continuous, and personal monitoring. Sci. World J. 2014, 2014, 1–11.
[21] Oresko, J.J.; Jin, Z.; Cheng, J.; Huang, S.; Sun, Y.; Duschl, H.; Cheng, A.C. A Wearable Smartphone-Based Platform for Real-Time Cardiovascular Disease Detection Via Elcctrocardiogram Processing. IEEE Trans. Inf. Technol. Biomed. 2010, 14, 734–740.
[22] Gurrin, C.; Smeaton, A.F.; Doherty, A.R. LifeLogging: Personal Big Data. Found. Trends Inf. Retr. 2014, 8, 1–125.
[23] The Future of Lifelogging. Available online: http://blog.autographer.com/2013/05/the-future-of- lifelogging-interview-with-gordon-bell/ (accessed on 24 June 2016).
[24] Zini, F.; Reinstadler, M.; Ricci, F. Life-logs Aggregation for Quality of Life Monitoring. In Proceedings of the 5th International Conference on Digital Health 2015, Florence, Italy, 18–20 May 2015.
[25] Zhou, L.M.; Gurrin, C. A survey on life logging data capturing. SenseCam Symposium: Oxford, UK, 2012.
[26] Want, R.; Schilit, B.N.; Jenson, S. Enabling the Internet of Things. IEEE Comput. 2015, 48, 28–35.
[27] Ling, T.; Kang, B.H.; Johns, D.P.; Walls, J.; Bindoff, I. Expert-Driven Knowledge Discovery. In Proceedings of the Fifth International Conference on Information Technology: New Generations, 2008, ITNG 2008, Las Vegas, NV, USA, 7–9 April 2008; pp. 174–178.
[28] Hussain, M.; Afzal, M.; Ali, T.; Ali, R.; Khan, W.A.; Jamshed, A.; Lee, S.; Kang, B.H.; Latif, K. Data-driven knowledge acquisition, validation, and transformation into HL7 Arden Syntax. Artif. Intell. Med. 2015, in press.
[29] Hussain, S.; Lee, S. Visualization and descriptive analytics of wellness data through Big Data. In Proceedings of the 2015 Tenth International Conference on Digital Information Management (ICDIM), Jeju Island, South Korea, 21–23 October 2015; pp. 69–71.

[30] Budgaga, W.; Malensek, M.; Pallickara, S.; Harvey, N.; Breidt, F.J.; Pallickara, S. Predictive Analytics Using Statistical, Learning, and Ensemble Methods to Support Real-time Exploration of Discrete Event Simulations. Future Gener. Comput. Syst. 2016, 56, 360–374.

[31] Mining Minds Overview. Available online: http://www.miningminds.re.kr/english/ (accessed on 24 June 2016).

[32] Chen, H.; Jia, X. New requirements and trends of mHealth. In Proceedings of IEEE 14th International Conference on e-Health Networking, Applications and Services (Healthcom), Beijing, China, 10–13 October 2012; pp. 27–31.

[33] Elgazzar, K.; Aboelfotoh, M.; Martin, P.; Hassanein, H. Ubiquitous health monitoring using mobile web services. Procedia Comput. Sci. 2012, 10, 332–339.

[34] Kim, H.; Lee, K.; Kim, H.; Kim, J. Using mobile phones in healthcare management for the elderly. Maturitas 2014, 79, 381–388.

[35] Gaggioli, A.; Pioggia, G.; Tartarisco, G.; Baldus, G.; Corda, D.; Cipresso, P.; Riva, G. A Mobile Data Collection Platform for Mental Health Research. Pers. Ubiquitous Comput. 2013, 2, 241–251.

[36] Spina, G.; Roberts, F.; Weppner, J.; Lukowicz, P.; Amft, O. CRNTC+: A smartphone-based sensor processing framework for prototyping personal healthcare applications. In Proceedings of the 7th International Conference on Pervasive Computing Technologies for Healthcare, Venice, Italy, 5–8 May 2013.

[37] Chen, P.H.; Chen, H.M. Framework design-integrating an android open platform with multi-interface biomedical modules for physiological measurement. J. Converg. Inf. Technol. 2012, 7, 310–319.

[38] Prasad, A.; Peterson, R.; Mare, S.; Sorber, J.; Paul, K.; Kotz., D. Provenance framework for mHealth. In Proceedings of the 5th International Conference on Communication Systems and Networks, Bangalore, India, 7–10 January 2013; pp. 1–6.

[39] Belimpasakis, P.; Roimela, K.; You, Y. Experience Explorer: A Life-Logging Platform Based on Mobile Context Collection. In Proceedings of the 2009 Third International Conference on Next Generation Mobile Applications, Services and Technologies, Cardiff, UK, 15–18 September 2009; pp. 77–82.

[40] Rawassizadeh, R.; Tomitsch, M.; Wac, K.; Tjoa, A.M. UbiqLog: A generic mobile phone-based life-log framework. Pers. Ubiquitous Comput. 2013, 17, 621–637.

[41] Ferreira, D.; Kostakos, V.; Dey, A.K. AWARE: Mobile context instrumentation framework. Front. ICT 2015, 2, 1–9.

[42] Dobbins, C.; Merabti, M.; Fergus, P.; Jones, D. Creating human digital memories with the aid of pervasive mobile devices. Pervasive Mob. Comput. 2014, 12, 160–178.

[43] Dobbins, C.; Merabti, M.; Fergus, P.; Llewellyn-Jones, D. The Big Data Obstacle of Lifelogging. In Proceedings of the 28th International Conference on Advanced Information Networking and Applications Workshops, AINA 2014 Workshops, Victoria, BC, Canada, 13–16 May 2014; pp. 922–926.

[44] The SenseWear Armband. Available online: https://templehealthcare.wordpress.com/the-sensewear- armband (accessed on 24 June 2016).

[45] Dwyer, T.J.; Alison, J.A.; McKeough, Z.J.; Elkins, M.R.; Bye, P.T.P. Evaluation of the SenseWear activity monitor during exercise in cystic fibrosis and in health. Respir. Med. 2009, 103, 1511–1517.

[46] Almeida, G.J.; Wasko, M.C.M.; Jeong, K.; Moore, C.G.; Piva, S.R. Physical Activity Measured by the SenseWear Armband in Women with Rheumatoid Arthritis. Phys. Ther. 2011, 91, 1367–1376.
[47] Hodges, S.; Williams, L.; Berry, E.; Izadi, S.; Srinivasan, J.; Butler, A.; Smyth, G.; Kapur, N.; Wood, K. Chapter SenseCam: A Retrospective Memory Aid. Available online: https://www.microsoft.com/en-us/research/ publication/sensecam-a-retrospective-memory-aid/ (accessed on 24 June 2016).
[48] McCarthy, S.; McKevitt, P.; McTear, M.F.; Sayers, H.M. MemoryLane: An intelligent mobile companion for elderly users. In Proceedings of the Seventh Information Technology and Telecommunication Conference IT&T, Dublin, Ireland, 25–26 October 2007; pp. 72–82.
[49] Lee, H.; Smeaton, A.F.; Jones, G.; Blighe, M.; Byrne, D.; Doherty, A.; Gurrin, C. Constructing a SenseCam visual diary as a media process multimedia systems. Multimedia Syst. 2008, 14, 341–349.
[50] Kelly, P.; Doherty, A.; Berry, E.; Hodges, S.; Batterham, A.M.; Foster, C. Can we use digital life-log images to investigate active and sedentary travel behaviour? Results from a pilot study. Int. J. Behav. Nutr. Phys. Act. 2011, 8, 1–9.
[51] Blum, M.; Pentland, A.; Troster, G. InSense: Interest-Based Life Logging. IEEE Multimed. 2006, 13, 40–48.
[52] Balasubramaniam, S.; Kangasharju, J. Realizing the Internet of Nano Things: Challenges, Solutions, and Applications. Computer 2013, 46, 62–68.
[53] Akyildiz, I.F.; Jornet, J.M. The Internet of nano-things. IEEE Wirel. Commun. 2010, 17, 58–63.
[54] Rawassizadeh, R.; Tomitsch, M.; Nourizadeh, M.; Momeni, E.; Peery, A.; Ulanova, L.; Pazzani, M. Energy-Efficient Integration of Continuous Context Sensing and Prediction into Smartwatches. Sensors 2015, 15, 22616–22645.
[55] Kapadia, A.; Kotz, D.; Triandopoulos, N. Opportunistic sensing: Security challenges for the new paradigm. In Proceedings of the 2009 First International Communication Systems and Networks and Workshops, Athens, Greece, 5–10 January 2009; pp. 1–10.
[56] NetBio. Available online: http://netbio.com/ (accessed on 24 June 2016).
[57] Samsung SAMI IO. Available online: https://www.samsungsami.io (accessed on 24 June 2016).
[58] Bricon-Souf, N.; Newman, C.R. Context awareness in health care: A review. I. J. Med. Inform. 2007, 76, 2–12.
[59] Ahmad, M.; Amin, M.B.; Hussain, S.; Kang, B.; Cheong, T.; Lee, S. Health Fog: A novel framework for health and wellness applications. J. Supercomput. 2016, 1–19, doi:10.1007/s11227-016-1634-x.
[60] Fog Computing. Available online: http://internetofthingsagenda.techtarget.com/definition/fog- computing-fogging (accessed on 24 June 2016).
[61] Microsoft Azure. Available online: https://azure.microsoft.com (accessed on 24 June 2016).
[62] Pervez, Z.; Khattak, A.M.; Lee, S.; Lee, Y.K.; Huh, E.N. Oblivious access control policies for cloud based data sharing systems. Computing 2012, 94, 915–938.
[63] REST. Available online: https://en.wikipedia.org/wiki/Representational_state_transfer (accessed on 24 June 2016).

[64] Node.js. Available online: https://nodejs.org/en/ (accessed on 24 June 2016).
[65] JSON. Available online: http://www.json.org (accessed on 24 June 2016).
[66] Welcome to Apache Hadoop. Available online: https://hadoop.apache.org (accessed on 24 June 2016).
[67] Gamma, E.; Helm, R.; Johnson, R.; Vlissides, J. Design Patternsl: Elements of Reusable Object-Oriented Software; Addison-Wesley Professional: Boston, MA, USA, 1994.
[68] Object Copying. Available online: https://en.wikipedia.org/wiki/Object_copying (accessed on 24 June 2016).
[69] Villalonga, C.; Banos, O.; Khan, W.A.; Ali, T.; Razzaq, M.A.; Lee, S.; Pomares, H.; Rojas, I. Ambient Assisted Living. In 3rd Symposium of Ubiquitous Computing and Ambient Intelligence 2008 (pp. 86–94); Springer: Berlin, Germany, 2008; pp. 86–94.
[70] Apache Hive. Available online: https://hive.apache.org (accessed on 24 June 2016).
[71] Kinect. Available online: https://en.wikipedia.org/wiki/Kinect (accessed on 24 June 2016).
[72] Ubiquitous Computing Lab. Available online: http://uclab.khu.ac.kr/index.php (accessed on 24 June 2016).

Chapter 3

Data Acquisition & Synchronization

Muhammad Bilal Amin, Muhammad Sadiq, Wajahat Ali Khan, Usman Akhtar, and Sungyoung Lee

In the era of smart devices, the reliance of intelligence is the abundance of data. This data is heterogeneous in nature and generated by many small-scale sensory devices. With their task-specific nature, these sensory devices are energy efficient resources with limited computing and storage power. The effective utilization of these devices requires collaborative execution with remote storage and computing power. Internet of Things defines one such cluster formation of these devices which are single-task specific in themselves but achieves higher goals when executed in a collective environment. Data acquisition from these devices is accumulated at scalable resources like cloud where intelligent processes constitute the foundation of smart environments. However, the current implementations of data acquisition for cloud-centric IoT are driven by the APIs of the device manufacturers, resulting in platforms which are less dynamic and configurable for data acquisition. In this chapter, we propose our cloud-centric methodology with the focus on configurable data acquisition from IoT. Our methodology decouples communication of data from the strategical usage of the sensory device. Thus, making it more dynamic and applicable for evolutionary smart environments.

3.1 Introduction

The notion of a smart world has originated the concept of Internet of Things (IoT), where a cluster of devices works in coherence to achieve a particular goal [1]. The achievement of this goal heavily relies on the data accumulated by the sensory devices, as the intelligent processes can execute on this data for context derivation and decision making [2]. For continuous sensing of data from IoT, the ubiquitous nature of the cloud provides platforms with the ability to acquire sensory data in different contexts and environments [3], thus terms like Cloud-centric IoT [4], CloudIoT [5], Cloud-sensing, and Sensing as a Service [6] have emerged. Moreover, for device independence, the cloud provides a central yet scalable computational resource that can accumulate sensory data from a cluster of things without being concerned with their computational abilities. For the frameworks based on lifelogging [7] the cloud provides a hub for context curation and monitoring for anomalies. Furthermore, to support the volume of sensory data, cloud provides a big data platform [8].

In a computing environment like IoT, where a cluster of things is developed by several device manufacturers, it is unrealistic to inflict standards of data acquisition and make everyone comply [9]. A large-scale cluster of things with many associated spontaneous events along with cloud as a centralized hub of data, brings new challenges in formalizing techniques for data accumulation.

Current implementations of Cloud-centric IoT heavily depend on device's hardware and its embedded system. Thus, communication occurs with the protocols defined by the APIs of device manufacturer; consequently, keeping the data acquisition APIs, platforms and frameworks taking their lead and providing services that are less dynamic, device dependent, far less scalable and configurable.

Among them Aneka [10] is a platform implementation for cloud computing initially designed for High-Performance Computing (HPC); however, now exploited for IoT-centric deployment. With a very comprehensive implementation, authors of Aneka have provided real IoT-centric use cases [1]. Similarly, authors of [11] have combined the concept of Sensor Web with Service Oriented Architecture (SOA) and proposed a middleware called Open Sensor Web Architecture (OSWA) for sensor-based applications. Due to the lack of standardized data accumulation, a lot of implementations are focusing towards web-enabled interfaces with standard service descriptions and communications [12]. Consequently, few opensource research initiatives have emerged. This includes projects like OpenIoT [13], Kaa IoT1, Thinger.io2, DeviceHive3, and MainFlux4. Apart from providing cloud-centric IoT, these platforms profoundly focus on the connectivity with a larger set of devices for sensory data accumulation in different use cases. Furthermore, very large-scale research and development initiatives have also been taken in this regard including ClouT project5 (now BigClouT6), which leverages cloud computing as an enabler for IoT in larger smart spaces. Finally, there are service implementations like Xively7, ThingSpeak8, NetLab's CloudIn and CloudOut service9 CloudPlugs10, and Carriots11 with the sole focus on collecting data from things and storing over the cloud [5].

In this chapter, we present our proposed technique to cater the challenge of configurable data acquisition for cloud-centric IoT. Proposed methodology decouples the communication from data acquisition; such that, cloud sensing occurs based on the situation and environment. Furthermore, the sensory data is synchronized based on time-stamping to overcome the distributed clock challenges.

---

[1] http://devicehive.com
[2] https://thinger.io
[3] http://devicehive.com
[4] https://www.mainflux.com/index.html
[5] http://clout-project.eu
[6] http://bigclout.eu
[7] https://www.xively.com
[8] https://thingspeak.com
[9] http://www.netlabtoolkit.org
[10] https://cloudplugs.com
[11] https://www.carriots.com

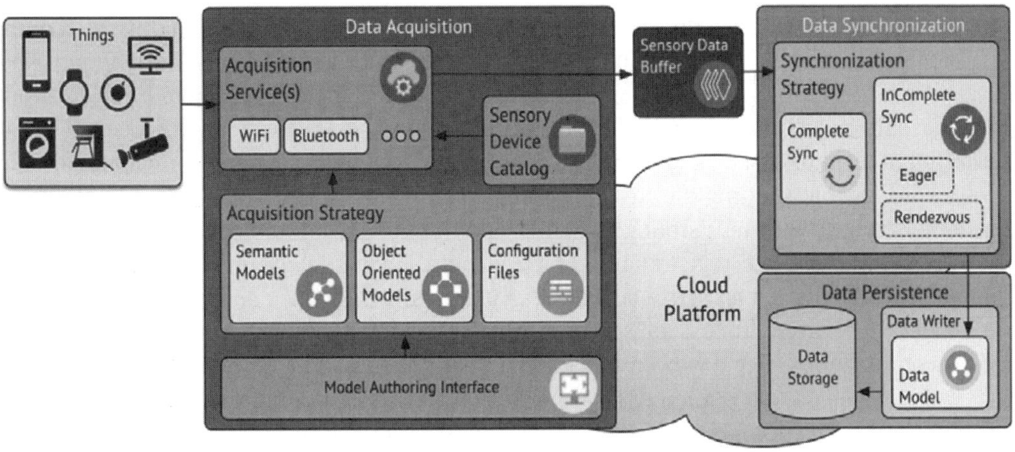

Figure 3.1 Cloud-centric IoT data acquisition architecture

3.2 Methodology

In this section, we provide the overview and implementation details of the proposed methodology. Figure 3.1 illustrates the high-level architecture for the configurable data acquisition in an IoT environment with cloud platform as the hub of sensory data accumulation. The overall process flow is described in three sequential stages, i.e., Data Acquisition, Data Synchronization, and Data Persistence.

Data acquisition stage provides the configurable communication by providing support to multimodal sensory devices from the cluster of things via agile acquisition strategy. Consequently, increasing the ability of cloud-centric IoT to scale further for acquiring data depending upon the needs and situations. Data synchronization stage synchronizes the multimodal sensory data pertaining to a single instance of time; albeit, received with a time difference. The key is the association of accumulated data with their time of origination. All data sources subsist independently along with independent clocks; therefore, a logical clock is required for identifying the data origination at the same time from multiple sources. Consequently, data synchronization implements the time frame-based methods called Complete- and Incomplete-sync. Data persistence stage provides storage to the synchronized sensory data as a timeline entry per user or environment.

For secure data in transit; all available sensory devices are registered in a Sensory Device Catalog. This catalog stores device names, types, and UUIDs for all the devices available in a smart environment. Prior to execution; data acquisition loads the respective IoT device's profile from sensory device catalog and reviews the available Acquisition Strategies. These strategies are described in static and dynamic models. A static model consists of Configuration files describing device registration, the protocol of data acquisition, the frequency of communication, and confidence level of the device. Static models can be configured at runtime; however, lacks extensibility. Therefore, suitable for less changing smart environments with a limited number of sensory devices.

Dynamic modeling consists upon Semantic and Object-oriented models describing similar device registration, the protocol of data acquisition, the frequency of communication and confidence level of the device. However, dynamic models offer extensibility with support to agility at runtime. These models are suitable for evolutionary and reusable smart environments. Furthermore, they can handle a larger set of sensory devices. Figure 3.2 illustrates the class diagram of object model illustrating data acquisition strategy. This implementation utilizes three object-oriented design patterns\footnote{http://www.oodesign.com}, including Singleton pattern for single instance utilization throughout the lifetime of execution, Strategy pattern for well-defined and reusable acquisition strategies with agile strategy selection and addition, and Composite pattern for dynamic sensor device addition and registration into the system. Each strategy in a model represents a situation provided by an expert via Model Authoring Interface. For example, in a smart environment where an environmental sensor checks the quality of air in the room can be configured for different situations. For newborn babies, the quality check will be more frequent. Thus, a strategy of data acquisition is authored by an expert which describes the sensors to communicate with, their communication protocol, their frequency of execution, data types, and in the case of redundant data, the confidence level of each sensory device. Depending upon this strategy sensing by the device to the cloud will occur. The same environment can be configured to react differently when adults are present in the room.

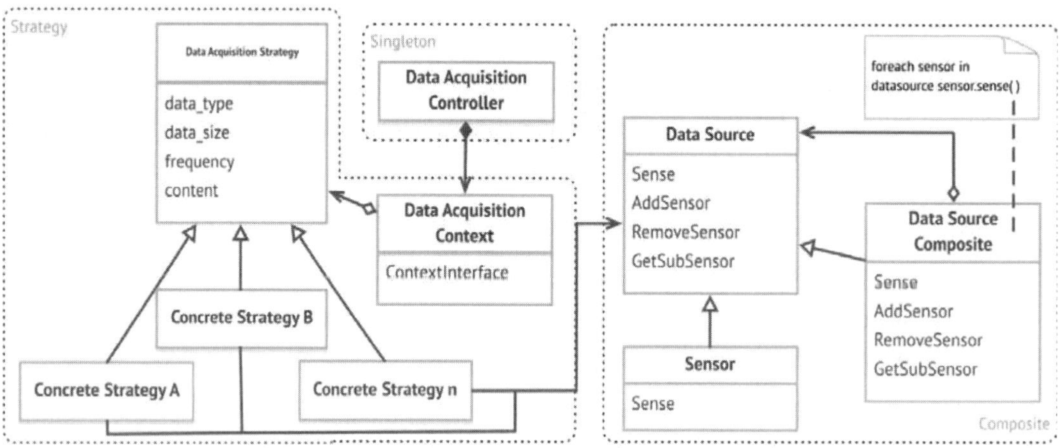

Figure 3.2 Data acquisition strategy dynamic object model

In a smart environment, multimodal sensory data from the cluster of Things is received by Data Acquisition Service depending upon the above-mentioned acquisition strategy. Data is received by this service via two widely used communication protocols, i.e., Wi-Fi and Bluetooth. Bluetooth is utilized when proximity is a concern. It is a recommended option when the proposed system is deployed on a private cloud or a localized server instance.

Accumulated data by the acquisition service is enqueued into the Sensory Data Buffer. Each communicating device in the cluster of things is allotted with its respected sensory buffer. For example, data from a CCTV camera will always be buffered into its designated sensory data buffer. Buffer size and its instances can scale dynamically to support a larger set of devices communicating in various situations.

Synchronization of sensory data is also implemented as strategies. Although configurable, the execution of these strategies depends upon data influx. These strategies are classified as Complete- and Incomplete Sync. Complete-sync is the sunny day scenario in which all the data concerning to an instance of time is received within the specified time frame. As soon as all the data is received, complete-sync encapsulates it with a timestamp and provides it to the Data Writer.

Incomplete-sync executes when data from any of the sources is not received in the pre-defined time frame. This execution is further classified in two finer modes, i.e., Eager and Rendezvous. In the Eager mode, the packet is created with only the available sensory data and sent to data writer. However, In the Rendezvous mode, for the missing data, it associates the last sent data from the sensory data buffer. Implementation and algorithmic details for these synchronization processes are described in [8]. Upon receiving the sensory data, data writer maps it to the data model; subsequently, writing it in the data Storage for volatile (RDBMS) or non-volatile (Big Data) persistence.

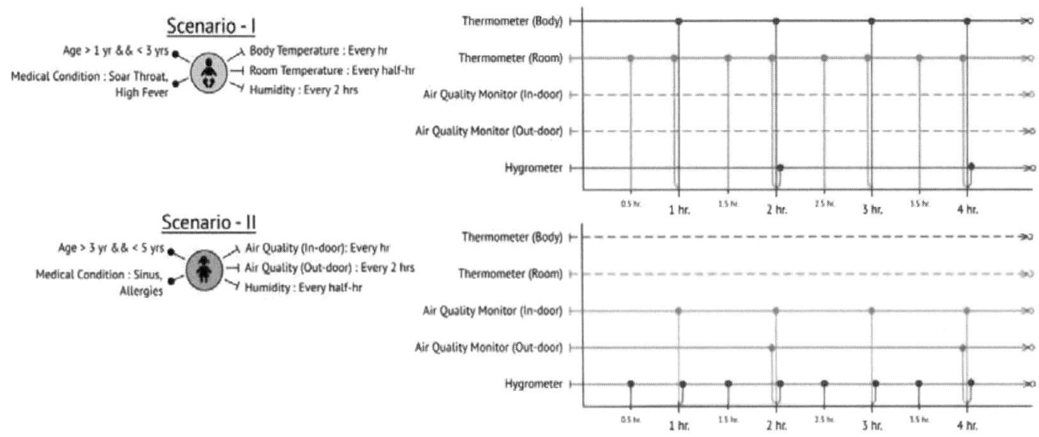

Figure 3.3 Execution scenarios

3.3 Evaluation

For evaluation, we configured the proposed system to execute in two different execution scenarios with five sensory devices emulating a smart space. For the first scenario, the system was configured for a baby having a medical condition to be monitored for the duration of 4 hrs. As per strategy, three among five different sensors accumulated the data. Figure 3.3 scenario-I illustrates the scenario with accumulated data correctly written as per configuration strategy. Similarly, for the second scenario, the same implementation was configured for a toddler with a medical condition to be monitored for 4 hrs. Three among five sensors accumulated data in different time frequencies as per strategy. Figure 3.3 scenario-II illustrates this scenario with accumulated data correctly written as per configuration strategy. The implementation is also evaluated for its synchronization strategies. Figure 3.4 illustrates the data being correctly synchronized in 5 different time windows although received from different sensors in a different yet close interval of time.

3.4 Summary

In this chapter, we have presented our cloud-centric data acquisition methodology for IoT. Our proposed methodology bridges the gap of configurable data acquisition from a sensor to the cloud. Thus, enabling cloud-centric IoT implementations to have more dynamic data acquisition.

Source Code

Source code can be downloaded from the following location:
https://github.com/ubiquitous-computing-lab/Mining-Minds/tree/master/data-curation-layer/data-acquisition-and-synchronization

The contents of this chapter have been previously published in the following article:

Muhammad Bilal Amin and Sadiq, Muhammad Sadiq Khan, Wajahat Ali Khan, Asad Masood Khattak, Usman Akhtar, and Sungyoung Lee "Configurable Data Acquisition for Cloud-centric IoT" Proceedings of the 12th International Conference on Ubiquitous Information Management and Communication, IMCOM '18 Langkawi, Malaysia, http://doi.acm.org/10.1145/3164541.3164594

References

[1] S. Marusic J. Gubbi, R. Buyya and M. Palaniswami, 2013. Internet of Things (IoT) - A vision, architecture elements, and future directions. Future Generation Comp. Syst.29, 7(2013), 1645–1660.

[2] Bo Hu Shanzhi Chen, Hui Xu and Hucheng Wang. 2014. A Vision of IoT: Applications, Challenges, and Opportunities With China Perspective. IEEE Internet Things J.1, 4(2014), 349–359.

[3] A. Pitsillides, A. Kamilaris and V. Trifa. 2011. The Smart Home meets the Web of Things. IJAHUC 7, 3(2011), 145.

[4] B. Kantarci and H.T. Mouftah. 2015. Sensing services in cloud-centric Internet of Things: A survey, taxonomy and challenges. In 2015 IEEE International Conference on Communication Workshop (ICCW). 1865– 1870.

[5] Alessio Botta, Walter de Donato, Valerio Persico, and Antonio Pescapé. 2016. Integration of Cloud Computing and Internet of Things. Future Gener. Comput. Syst.56, C (March 2016), 684–700.

[6] B. Kantarci and H.T. Mouftah. 2015. Sensing as a Service in Cloud-Centric Internet of Things Architecture. IGI Global.

[7] Cathal Gurrin, Alan F. Smeaton, and Aiden R. Doherty. 2014. LifeLogging: Personal Big Data. Foundations and Trends in Information Retrieval 8, 1(2014), 1–125.

[8] Muhammad Bilal Amin, Oresti Banos, Wajahat Ali Khan, Hafiz Syed Muhammad Bilal, Jinhyuk Gong, Dinh-Mao Bui, Soung Ho Cho, Shujaat Hussain, Taqdir Ali, Usman Akhtar, Tae Choong Chung, and Sungyoung Lee. On Curating Multimodal Sensory Data for Health and Wellness Platforms. Sensors16, 7(2016).

[9] J. A. Stankovic. 2014. Research Directions for the Internet of Things. IEEE Internet of Things Journal 1, 1(Feb2014), 3–9.

[10] Christian Vecchiola, Xingchen Chu, and Rajkumar Buyya. 2008. Aneka: a Software Platform for .NET based Cloud Computing. In High Performance Computing Workshop (Advances in Parallel Computing), Wolfgang Gentzsch, Lucio Grandinetti, and Gerhard R. Joubert (Eds.), Vol. 18. IOS Press, 267–295.

[11] Jue Yang, Chengyang Zhang, Xinrong Li, Yan Huang, Shengli Fu, and Miguel F. Acevedo. 2010. Integration of Wireless Sensor Networks in Environmental Monitoring Cyber Infrastructure. Wirel. Netw. 16, 4 (May 2010), 1091–1108.

[12] D. m. Han and J. h. Lim.2010. Smart home energy management system using IEEE 802.15.4 and zigbee. IEEE Transactions on Consumer Electronics 56, 3(Aug 2010), 1403–1410.

[13] John Soldatos, Nikos Kefalakis, Manfred Hauswirth, Martin Serrano, Jean-Paul Calbimonte, Mehdi Riahi, Karl Aberer, Prem Prakash Jayaraman, Arkady Zaslavsky, Ivana Podnar Žarko, Lea Skorin-Kapov, and Reinhard Herzog. 2015. OpenIoT: Open Source Internet-of-Things in the Cloud. Springer International Publishing, Cham, 13–25.

Chapter 4

Activity-focused Lifelog Monitoring

Context-based Lifelog Monitoring for Just-in-Time Wellness Intervention

Hafiz Syed Muhammad Bilal, Muhammad Asif Razzaq,
Muhammad Bilal Amin, and Sungyoung Lee

These days adoption of healthy behavior can be quantified through Ubiquitous computing and smart gadgets. This digital technology has revolutionized the self-quantification to monitor activities for improving lifestyle. Context based lifelog monitoring is among the processes of tracking individual's lifestyle in an effective manner. We have proposed a methodology for context-based monitoring of an individual's prolonged sedentary physical activity and unhealthy dietary behavior in the domain of wellness and give just-in-time intervention to adapt healthy behavior. It detects multiple unhealthy activities of its users and verifies the context for intervention generation. The results depict that the average response of the context-based just-in-time interventions is about 75%.

4.1 Introduction

Innovative and smart gadgets have supported the wellness domain to enhance individual health and improve socio-economic situations by quantifying the human activities and daily routine. In 1990s, wellness was introduced as *Wheel of Wellness* [1], [2] with categorization of nutritional knowledge, physical fitness, stress management, environmental and social awareness [4]. Today, wellness domain requires innovative user centric platforms which should digitize wellness and health parameters to provide precise recommendations and wellness services [3]. The change in behavior requires a just-in-time (JIT) intervention which meets the constraints and conditions of the environment. The intervention should adapt according to the individual's dynamic status, the goals to target and the changes required for improvement [5].

4.1.1 Behavior's Concerns and Wellness Applications

Wellness literature shows that unhealthy behavior includes smoking, sedentary lifestyle, higher alcohol intake, and unhealthy diet. The unhealthy diet may increase the risk of chronic diseases like cardiovascular disease, hypertension, diabetes, and premature mortality [6]. The mortality rate is the indication of population's health status which is linked with the higher risk of lifestyle-based diseases [13]. The unhealthy lifestyle is an influential cause of chronic diseases and premature death [9]. The regular interrupts in sedentary activities enhance metabolic profile of individual as compared to sedentary ones [8]. The design and development of wellness and health care applications are focusing to track the individual's activity log to identify lifestyle pattern [14].

The identified patterns support proactively to diagnose the cause of undesired fitness and health issues. There are multiple wellness applications are available [6] i.e. GoogleFit, Noom Coach, Apple Healthkit, Google Fit, and etc. These applications quantify user activities, step counts, calories consumption, and provide visualization of user status.

4.1.2 Context-based Adaptive Intervention

The design of intervention plays a vital role to adopt the changes in behavior. The retention or abandonment of intervention requires to consider the constraints, status and context of the user. The effectiveness of intervention needs to specify the extent and duration of engagement for targeted behavior. The JIT adaptive intervention is an emerging way to promote the healthy behavior adoption with the usage of powerful mobile and sensing technologies [5].

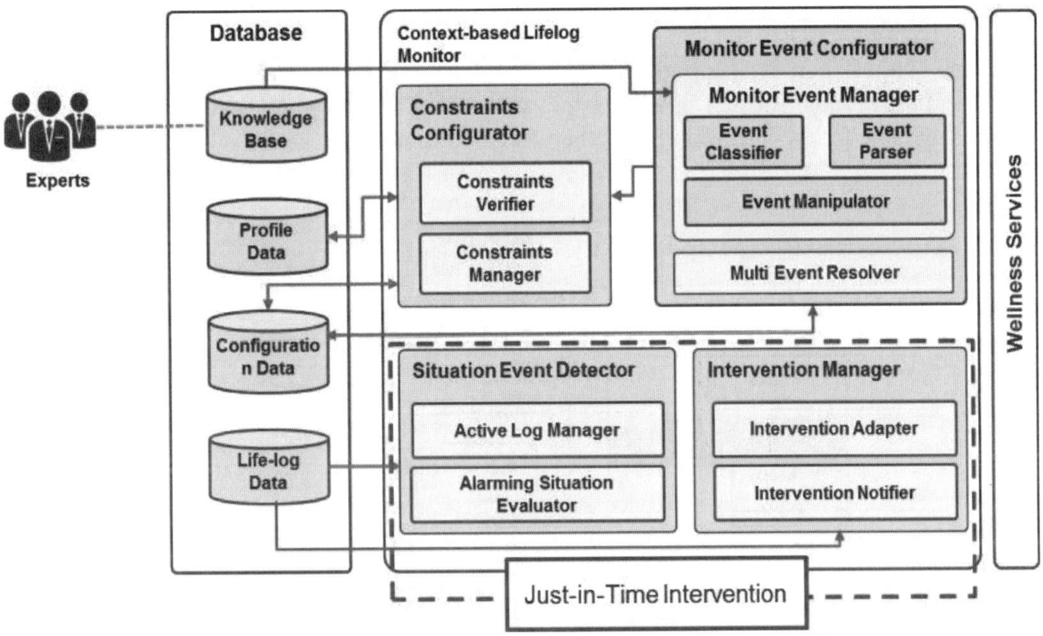

Figure 4.1 Architecture of context-based JIT lifelog monitor

4.2 Context-based Just-in-Time Lifelog Monitor Architecture

Most of the wellness applications recognizes the user activities and provide interactive visualization to the users on demands [14]. Self-quantification and managing log provide foundation to take proactive action to avoid bad impact of unhealthy lifestyle pattern. The proactive demands in wellness domain lead us to propose context-based JIT lifelog monitor for appropriate intervention generation. According to the JIT philosophy "produce right item, at the right time, in right quantity" [7] supports us to monitor the right person, at right time, for right behavior.

The proposed context-based JIT lifelog monitor as shown in Figure 4.1, consists of four components. These components manage the guidelines-based rules related to unhealthy patterns, monitor the lifelog, verify the context and constraints, and notify the wellness stakeholders instantly. The main components are Monitor Event Configurator, Constraints Configurator, Situation Event Detector, and Intervention Manager.

Monitor event manages the information of the monitor-able activities along with respective quantities in configuration database. The constraints define the situation of a specific monitor-able event and is responsible to manage the multiple constraint conditions related to the monitor-able events. Constraints configurator verifies the situation by checking all constraint conditions related to that monitor-able event. Situation event detector continuously monitors the event to verify the state where it crosses the threshold quantity defined by expert. The information of micro-nutrients is extracted from the food database of United States Department of Agriculture [17] and consumption of micro-nutrients are obtained with the help of serving quantity [18]. The physical activity behavior is categorized into sedentary or active on the basis of Canadian Physical Activity guidelines [16]. If context supports the intervention, then Intervention Notifier is activated otherwise Intervention Adapter modifies the intervention time by delaying until the context become favorable for the intervention or otherwise ignores it.

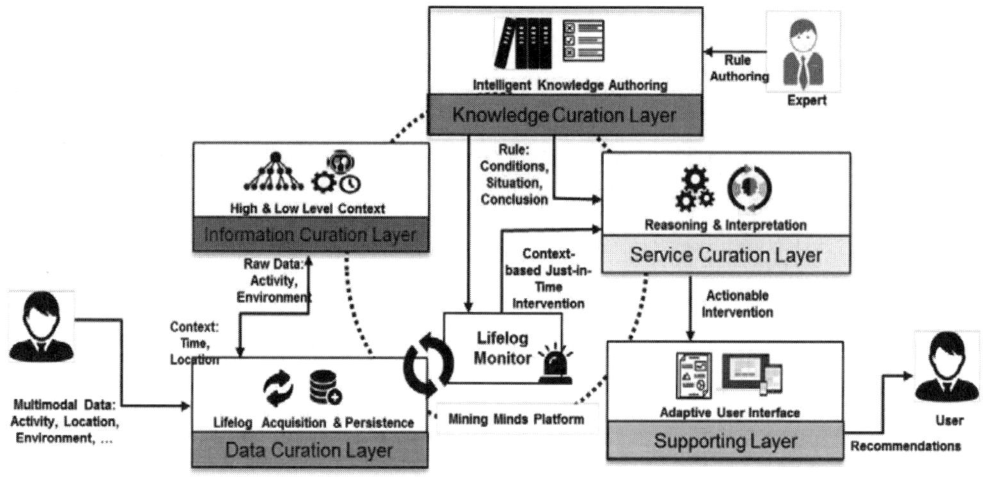

Figure 4.2 Integration of lifelog monitor with wellness platform

4.3 Integration of context-based lifelog monitor with Mining Minds

We have integrated the proposed lifelog monitor with Mining Minds (MM) platform [14], [11]. The individual's context is identified through key attributes location, time, physiological factors, preferences, and activity to generate personalized wellness recommendations [10]. The complexity of the platform is managed through Supporting Layer (SL), Knowledge Curation Layer (KCL), Information Curation Layer (ICL), Service Curation Layer (SCL), and Data Curation Layer (DCL) respectively as shown in Figure 4.2.

The SL provides multidimensional view of the activities' pattern and analytical reports. It classifies the stakeholders on the basis of access rights and demands [12]. The SCL manages personalized recommendation services to provide support either in push or pull mode on the basis of the user requirements [15]. The KCL helps an expert to express the knowledge into rules to define the unhealthy behavior using knowledge authoring environment [12].

The ICL recognizes individual's activities and context through sensory data of emotion, movement, and location. The lifestyle patterns are recognized through the low- and high-level contexts [11]. The DCL continuously gathers and manages the raw multimodal sensory data into lifelog and big data storage [3].

4.4 Experimental Setup

This work is focusing the unhealthy dietary habits and prolonged sedentary bouts. The context-based JIT intervention is provided to avoid the unhealthy habits of physical activities and dietary pattern. For this particular evaluation we have considered 12 volunteers with different gender and age. In order to assess the effectiveness of the JIT intervention, we have drawn the 12 scenarios on the basis of the profile information of our volunteers as shown in Table 4.1.

Table 4.1 Situations for Monitoring the Activities

Situation	Gender	Height (cm)	Weight (kg)	BMI	Activity Level	Calories Requirement	Recommended Fat (gm)
S1	Male	178	92	30.9	Sedentary	2075	57
S2	Male	173	73	24.4	Active	2312	51
S3	Female	168	72	25.5	Sedentary	2020	45
S4	Female	164	56	20.8	Active	1982	40
S5	Male	179	69	21.5	Sedentary	2033	52
S6	Male	176	78	25.2	Active	2112	54
S7	Male	165	48	17.5	Sedentary	1676	43
S8	Female	164	68	25.3	Active	1931	43
S9	Male	165	78	28.7	Active	2042	52
S10	Male	180	98	30.2	Active	2298	59
S11	Female	164	58	21.6	Sedentary	1793	40
S12	Male	168	90	31.9	Sedentary	2100	53

The wellness platform has recorded the volunteers' activities for 21 days with at-least 4 consecutive days for a user. The intimation is generated just-in-time on the basis of detected prolonged activities, location, and the food that they logged.

The context-based just-in-time lifelog monitor has monitored the activities of the user and generated interventions of the unhealthy lifestyle. The response of the volunteers increases when it considers the context of the volunteers while generating the intervention. After analysis of the lifelog, it is observed that the intimation for fats has improved the intake and consumption effectively as shown in Figure 4.3(a). The analysis of the log represents that about 42% of interventions are unattended in case of context-less intervention. The result shown in Figure 4.3(b) represents the impact of context-based intervention as compare to context-less intervention. The context-based intervention is about 17.5% more effective than context-less intervention.

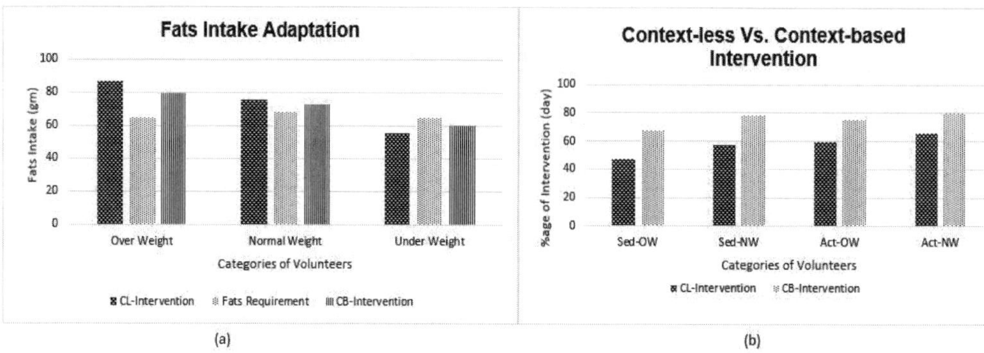

Abbreviation:

CL: Context Less
CB: Context Based
Sed: Sedentary
Act: Active
OW: Over Weight
NW: Normal Weight
Cal: Calories

Figure 4.3 Evaluation of intervention effectiveness on the basis of context

4.5 Summary

The designed context-based just-in-time lifelog monitor, monitors the activities and generates the interventions about the alarming situation on the basis of the context. The push-based indication to right person, at right time for alarming event helps the individual to change unhealthy behavior proactively. The novel approach of context-based monitoring and just-in-time intervention generation has not only improved the dietary habits but also reduced the number of prolonged sedentary bouts. This precautionary approach can support to avoid chronic diseases by reducing weight and adopting active lifestyle. In future we want to use behavior theory to adopt healthy behavior by identifying the behavior status of the user and generate behavior-based intervention.

Source Code

Source code can be downloaded from the following location:
https://github.com/ubiquitous-computing-lab/Mining-Minds/tree/master/data-curation-layer/lifelog-monitoring-system

The contents of this chapter have been previously published in the following article:

Hafiz Syed Muhammad Bilal, Muhammad Asif Razzaq, Muhammad Bilal Amin, and Sungyoung Lee, "Context-Based Lifelog Monitoring for Just-in-Time Wellness Intervention", 16th International Conference on Smart homes and health Telematics (ICOST 2018), Singapore, Singapore, July 10-12, 201

References

[1] Ali, R., Afzal, M., Hussain, M., Ali, M., Siddiqi, M.H., Lee, S. and Kang, B.H., 2016. Multimodal hybrid reasoning methodology for personalized wellbeing services. Computers in biology and medicine, 69, pp.10-28.

[2] Banos, O., Amin, M.B., Khan, W.A., Afzal, M., Hussain, M., Kang, B.H. and Lee, S., The Mining Minds Digital Health and Wellness Framework.

[3] Ardell, Donald B. High level wellness, an alternative to doctors, drugs, and disease. Bantam Books, 1979.

[4] Amin, M. B., Banos, O., Khan, W. A., Muhammad Bilal, H. S., Gong, J., Bui, D. M., ... & Chung, T. C. (2016). On curating multimodal sensory data for health and wellness platforms. Sensors, 16(7), 980.

[5] Banos, O., Amin, M. B., Ali Khan, W., Ali, T., Afzal, M., Kang, B. H., & Lee, S. (2015, May). Mining Minds: An innovative framework for personalized health and wellness support. In Pervasive Computing Technologies for Healthcare (PervasiveHealth), 2015 9th International Conference on (pp. 1-8). IEEE.

[6] Ahmad, M., Amin, M. B., Hussain, S., Kang, B. H., Cheong, T., & Lee, S. (2016). Health Fog: a novel framework for health and wellness applications. The Journal of Supercomputing, 1-19.

[7] Kvaavik, Elisabeth, et al. "Influence of individual and combined health behaviors on total and cause-specific mortality in men and women: the United Kingdom health and lifestyle survey." Archives of internal medicine170.8 (2010): 711-718

[8] Petersen, Kristina EN, et al. "The combined impact of adherence to five lifestyle factors on all-cause, cancer and cardiovascular mortality: a prospective cohort study among Danish men and women." British Journal of Nutrition 113.05 (2015): 849-858

[9] Katz, D. L., and S. Meller. "Can we say what diet is best for health?" Annual Review of Public Health 35 (2014): 83-103.

[10] Azumio(2015) Argus quantify your day-to-day. http://www.azumio.com/s/argus/index.html

[11] Thorp, A. A., Owen, N., Neuhaus, M., & Dunstan, D. W. (2011). Sedentary behaviors and subsequent health outcomes in adults: a systematic review of longitudinal studies, 1996–2011. American journal of preventive medicine,41(2), 207-215.

[12] Millennium Ecosystem Assessment, Ecosystems and Human Wellbeing: A Framework for Assessment (Island Press, Washington, DC, 2003)

[13] Khan, W.A., Amin, M.B., Banos, O., Ali, T., Hussain, M., Afzal, M., Hussain, S., Hussain, J., Ali, R., Ali, M. and Kang, D., Mining Minds: Journey of Evolutionary Platform for Ubiquitous Wellness.

[14] Sweeney, T. J., & Witmer, J. M. (1991). Beyond social interest: Striving toward optimum health and wellness. Individual Psychology, 47, 527-540.

[15] Witmer, J. M., & Sweeney, T. J. (1992). A holistic model for wellness and prevention over the lifespan. Journal of Counseling and Development, 71, 140-148

[16] CSEP(2017) Canadian Physical Activity guidelines. http://csep.ca/CMFiles/Guidelines/CSEP_PAGuidelines_adults_en.pdf

[17] USDA Food Composition Database. https://ndb.nal.usda.gov/ndb/

[18] Portions per person. https://www.cookipedia.co.uk/recipes_wiki/Portions_per_person

Chapter 5

Dietary-focused Lifelog Monitoring

Unhealthy Dietary Behavior-based user lifelog monitoring for wellness services

Hafiz Syed Muhammad Bilal, Wajahat Ali Khan, and Sungyoung Lee

Unhealthy behavior, constitutes of unhealthy diet, smoking, physical inactivity and alcohol intake, increases the risk of chronic diseases and premature mortality. These unhealthy behaviors can be avoided by little intention and guidance. Diet is an influential factor of healthcare. Healthy and balanced diet selection is related to the better life expectancy and decreases the chances of chronic diseases. The Ubiquitous computing revolutionized the wellness domain towards user centric preference-based health management. In this chapter we present a method for monitoring and indication of users' unhealthy nutrition consumption. We evaluated 3 different timings of indication to user for induction of healthy dietary pattern. The "location and time-based indication" depicts very promising result of 78% in the adoption of healthy diet pattern and has positive impact on the intake of fat nutrient in diet.

5.1 Introduction

Today in wellness domain, technology focuses to improve personal health and socio-economic conditions through self-quantification from innovative and smart gadgets. According to theoretical model, wellness was introduced in 1990s [1], [2] as Wheel of Wellness. The initial high-level wellness models were defined and categorized into nutrition knowledge, stress management, physical fitness and environmental & social awareness [3]. The wellness is a concerning target of healthcare domain to avoid and prevent the diseases with the development of innovative user centric platform. The platforms are capable to digitize health and wellness domain and provide wellbeing services and recommendations [4]. Good physical health, proper food, freedom to live, social interaction and safety define the human wellbeing [5]. So active routine, balanced diet, proper hydration, leisure and finance are ingredients of healthy lifestyle [6].

5.1.1 Consequences of Unhealthy Behavior

Multiple researches have shown that specific unhealthy behaviors, including smoking, physical inactivity, higher alcohol intake and, unbalanced diets are associated with an increased risk of cardiovascular disease, cancer and premature mortality [7]. Practicable improvements in lifestyle behaviors are likely to have a significant impact at both the individual and population level. The health status of the population can simply be measured from mortality rate, where unhealthy behaviors have been associated with a higher risk of lifestyle diseases [8]. Diet is an influential health agent and bad diet pattern is among the prominent causes of premature death and chronic disease [9]. The diet constitutes of multiple nutrients in different proportions. It is quite difficult to calculate multiple attribute to all variations in dietary pattern. According to the FSC (Australia New Zealand Standards Code) [16] the recommended balanced diet for an average adult is as shown in Table 5.1.

Table 5.1 Nutrition requirements of average adults

	Component	Quantity Per Day
Average Adult-Requirements	Energy	2000 Calories
	Protein	50 grams
	Fat	70 grams
	Carbohydrates	310 grams
	Sugars	90 grams
	Sodium (salt)	2.3 grams
	Dietary Fiber	30 grams

5.1.2 Wellness Applications for Human Activity Analysis

Currently, the designing trend of healthcare and wellness applications changes to manage and analyze the users' temporal activity data to identify healthy and unhealthy lifestyle pattern [11]. The identified patterns may help to understand and diagnose the root cause of any undesired health issues. Instead of reactive approach to cure and manage diseases, these applications are focusing on proactive personalized health approach. Multiple ubiquitous applications are available i.e. 7 Minute Workout, LoseIt, Noom Coach and etc. These applications are used to quantify and log user activities, and calories consumption to empower users for visualization. In the upcoming portions we have discussed Mining Minds platform, Nutrition focused lifelog monitor architecture and evaluation methodology.

5.2 Mining Minds & Dietary-focused Lifelog Monitoring

Context based health informatics is a fruit of technology revolution for community [14]. The emerging software technology has reshaped the world through big data infrastructure and deep learning techniques to analyze the buried pattern under pile of data. Our project, Mining Minds MM [11], [12] is providing a platform to educate, engage and trigger the users on the basis of preferences and context to support for leading long healthy lifestyle. It is possible because of the use of state-of-the-art technologies and emerging electronic gadgets. The concepts, from curation of raw sensory data to services orchestration, make the platform capable to manage the current requirements of user centric model in healthcare and wellness domains [13].

Mining Minds platform provides interface to communicate and gather multimodal data generated from different sensors to capture the temporal and spatial information along with activities (figure 4.1). The key attributes time, place and activity are used to understand the user context and support to generate context based personalized wellness recommendations [12].

The SL is in-charge of the interaction with users and providing analytical reports on the basis of customer's requirement in a graphical manner. The granularity of analytics depends on the access level permission of users. Comprehensive view of the habits, activities and classification is provided to wellness stakeholders on the demand base and access right to understand and make decision for improvement [14], [15].

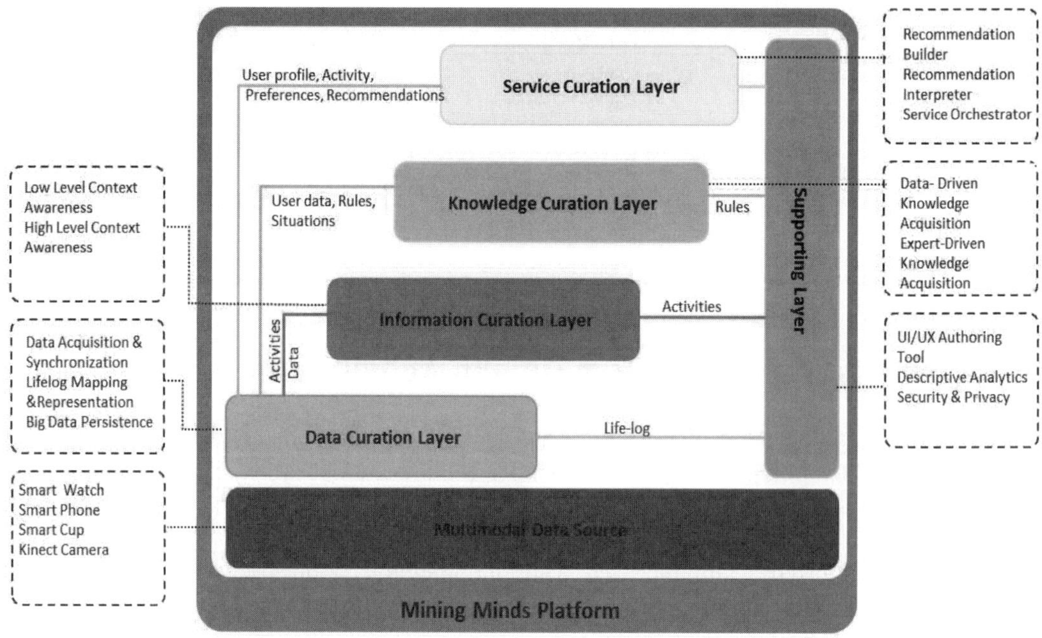

Figure 5.1 Mining Minds Platform

The SCL is the orchestrator of personalized recommendation services in push and pull mode. In push mode the indication for recommendation is generated by platform while in pull mode the user requests for recommendations. The knowledge based personalized recommendation are provided by exploring demographic, physiological, health status, context and preferences information [14].

The KCL provides a data driven and an expert driven knowledge acquisition authoring environment to expert. Experts can transform their experiences and wellness knowledge in to rules through authoring environment. These rules guide about the unhealthy context-based situation in the lifelog and provide remedies to avoid unhealthy patterns in term of actions [15]. So, the rules are then transformed into executable guidelines to highlight monitoring situations and the recommendation for action plan. Besides authoring environment, the experts are supported through data driven approach which consists of machine learning algorithm to facilitate through previous information and knowledge.

ICL recognize user's activities and context from multimodal sensory data through hierarchical models. It consists of multiple recognizers for activity, emotion and location respectively. These recognizers provide the low-level context awareness. The fusioning of low-level context supports to recognize various high-level context. It is the essential layer of MM platform to manage the activity context, e.g. sitting in office. These low levels and high-level contexts play an essential role for defining the lifestyle pattern [15].

DCL provides the ability to continuously sense and manage the raw sensory data from multimodal data sources. The data acquisition is device independent and can support large induction of sensors which helps to identify richer context [4]. It provides data curation through data acquisition and synchronization, data representation and mapping and big data storage processes [14].

Monitoring of lifelog is to find out the existence of an unhealthy situation in the current activities of user on the basis of expert provided situations. These situations are provided by expert using the rule authoring capabilities of KCL e.g. eating fats more than requirement. We proposed a monitoring architecture to search out real-time unhealthy situation. It has an ability to filter out the alarming situations based on the context and conditions defined by nutritionist, intimate the wellness service at real time and provide information for descriptive analytics.

5.3 Nutrition Focused Lifelog Monitor Architecture

Current wellness applications recognize the user activities, log them and represent in an interactive graphical manner [11]. In addition to present the user's activities logs, a range of applications also provides the impact of co-related activities on health and recommendations [10]. It is more beneficial to indicate the unhealthy nutritional habits to the healthcare stakeholders which may help them to avoid their bad impact. The proactive approach towards healthy lifestyle drive us to construct a nutrition focused Lifelog Monitor (LLM). The LLM, shown in Figure 5.2, constitutes of three major components. These components manage the rules related to unhealthy habits provided by experts, monitor the lifelog under the guidance of these rules and indicate the wellness services instantly. The three main components are Monitor Event Configurator, Constraints Configurator and Situation Event Detector.

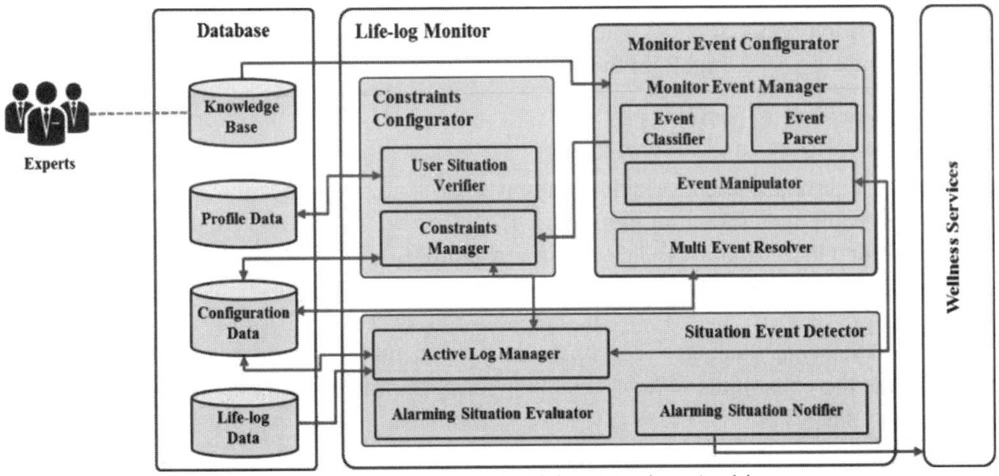

Figure 5.2 Nutrition focused Lifelog Monitor Architecture

5.3.1 Monitor Event Configurator

Nutritionists are the expert to provide guidelines for identification of the alarming micro nutrition intake with respect to the context of the user. These guidelines are authored through authoring environment and share in common configuration format. The monitor event configurator is responsible for extracting the monitoring situations from a common configuration format as shown in Figure 4.3. The situations are parsed and classified into monitoring situations and situation constraints. The monitoring situation constitutes of nutrition and its quantity for a particular day. The Event manipulator map the monitoring situation in configuration data for further access.

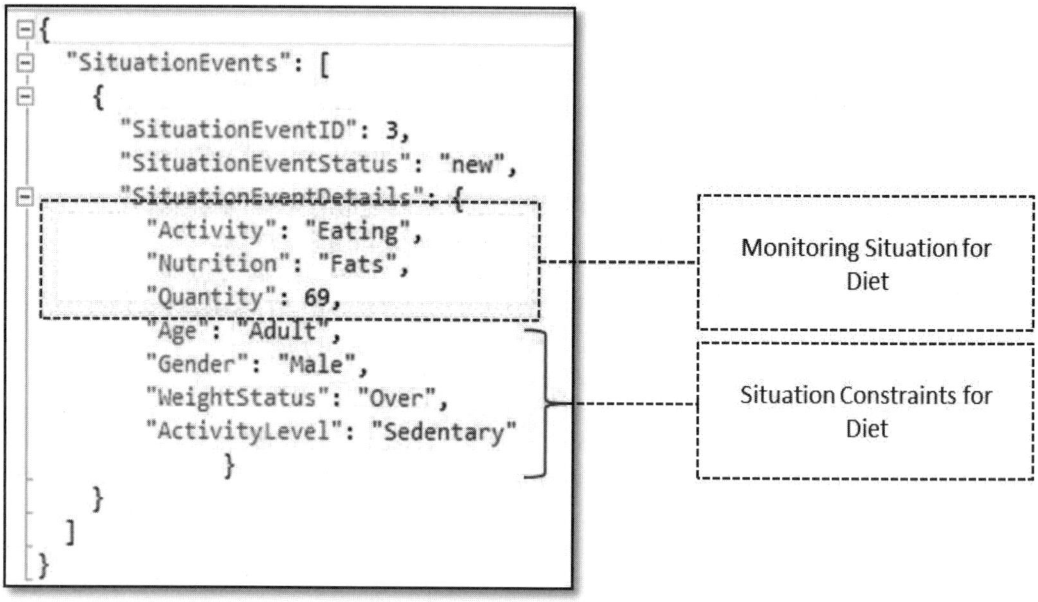

Figure 5.3 Common configuration format for complete Situation

Nutrition monitoring situation consist of information related to activity, type of nutrition and the quantity of nutrition required daily. The rest of the part defines the constraints that are related to the situation and support to highlight the context of the situation.

5.3.2 Constraint Configurator

Constraints of a particular monitor-able situation are essential to understand the context in which monitoring is required as shown in Figure 5.3. If the constraints are not satisfied, then there is no need to monitor those situations. The constraint configurator not only manages the constraint portion but also verifies the situation's constraint at real time.

The constraint manager manages the constraint portion into configuration database for further usage. It stores the constraints in key-value pair format to maintain the dynamicity for handling multiple constraints.

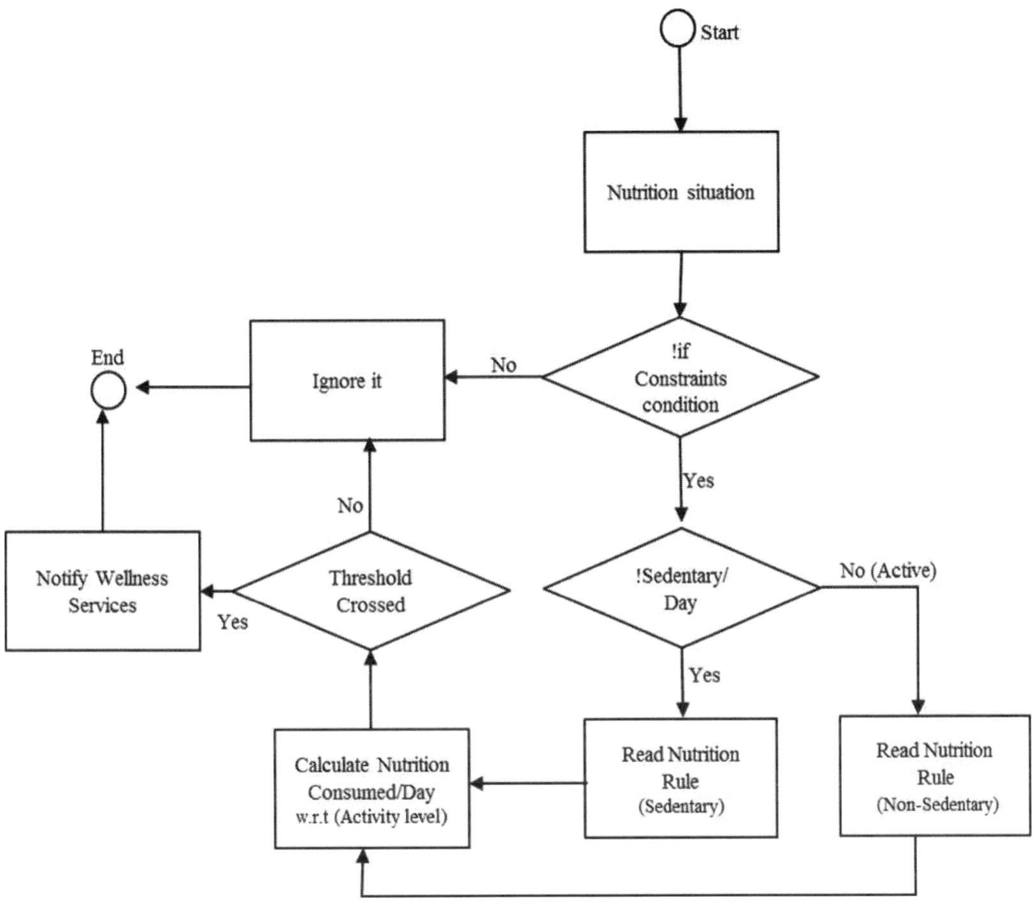

Figure 5.4 Flowchart of Lifelog monitoring

The User Constraint Verifier (UCV) is activated whenever a monitor-able activity is detected. It searches the user profile to verify the constraints to satisfy the context of the situation. It communicates all those situations whose context are matched for further detection and monitoring.

5.3.3 Situation Event Detector

The identification of an unhealthy diet depends on the intake of the amount of nutrients in a whole day till current time. Monitoring of such situation is performed by Situation Event Detector (SED), which is key component of the LLM. It identifies the situation when amount of nutrients crosses the threshold values with respect to some context. These situations are identified by the guidelines provided by the expert in the form of rules. The situation detection task is performed by Alarming Situation Evaluator (ASE) which map the intake nutrients with the defined target. While indication in a particular communication format is performed by the Alarming Situation Notifier (ASN).

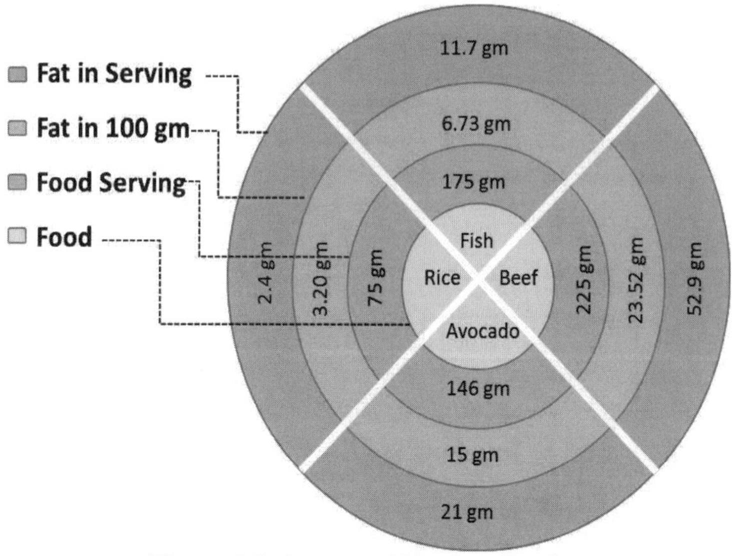

Figure 5.5 Amount of Nutrient Serving

ASE identify the abnormal nutrition situation by comparing the quantity of nutrition accumulated in the whole day as shown in Figure 5.4. For the accumulation of nutrients, we used the information extracted by the guidelines of United States Department of Agriculture [18]. It provides about the amount of nutrient per 100 gm of food. It converted nutrient amount into serving amount with the help of information extracted about serving [19] as shown in Figure 5.5.

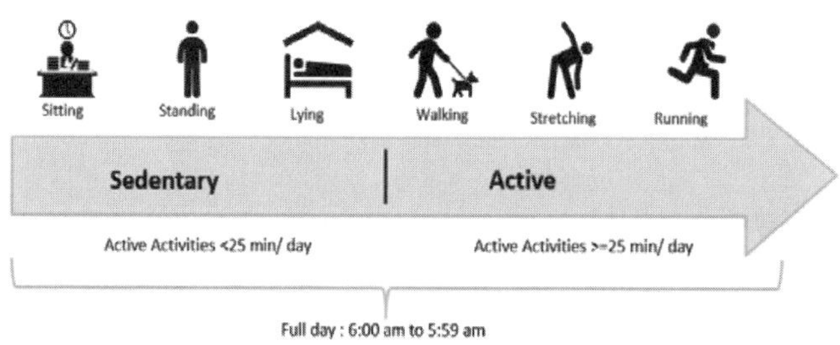

Figure 5.6 Activities for Behavior Identification

It also performs analysis of user behavior in-term of sedentary or active in a particular day as per the information extracted from Canadian Physical Activity guidelines [17] as shown in Figure 5.6. The ASE handover the unhealthy nutrition situation to ASN for the conversion of the nutrition and user information into common communication format and send it to the wellness services for indication and recommendations.

5.4 Evaluation of Dietary-focused Lifelog Monitoring

To evaluate the indication for nutrition in real environment, we enhanced our previous work of activity monitoring to nutrition monitoring and integrated it with Mining Minds platform. The MM platform has provided the service of logging food through picture and tag. The user can take food picture and sends to the mining minds platform with food tag. Our database contains 2055 food items with their serving amount of nutrients. In this evaluation we focused particularly on the amount of fat nutrient required by a person and intake of it. The nutrition monitoring component manipulate the food nutrient for maintaining the log and nutrient consumption in a particular day.

5.4.1 Experimental Setup

In this work we are considering the eating activity for nutrition monitoring along with physical activities, so that we can validate monitoring of nutrition quantity intake for two different kinds of user i.e. the sedentary and the active one. We have 10 adult volunteers of different ages and gender. All of them have different height and weight. Through BMI calculation we can see there are three main groups of people on the basis of weight, as shown in Table 5.2.

Table 5.2 Volunteers Detail involved in Experiment

Subject	Age	Gender	Height(cm)	Weight (kg)	BMI	Weight Status
S1	33	Male	178	92	29	Over
S2	27	Male	173	73	24.4	Normal
S3	28	Female	168	72	25.5	Over
S4	29	Female	164	56	20.8	Normal
S5	24	Male	179	69	21.5	Normal
S6	25	Male	176	75	24.2	Normal
S7	24	Male	165	48	17.5	Normal
S8	28	Female	165	64	23.5	Normal
S9	23	Male	165	66	24.2	Normal
S10	39	Male	180	86	26.5	Over

The Mining Minds platform has high accuracy to identify different activities: sitting, standing, lying, walking, stretching, running and eating [15]. Our nutrition expert provides the amount of nutrition required in different groups of people. The adults can be divided into 12 groups on the basis of gender, weight status, and activity level with the recommended fat amount (gm) per day as shown in Table 5.3.

We have recorded the activities of the volunteers as a whole for 3 weeks with minimum of 4 days in a week. The indication is provided on the basis of food that they logged and the location detection with respect to time.

Table 5.3 Situations for Monitoring the Activities

Sr.#	Age Group	Gender	Weight Status	Activity Level	Recommended Fat
1	Adult	Male	Over	Sedentary	69 gm
2	Adult	Male	Over	Active	72 gm
3	Adult	Male	Normal	Sedentary	70 gm
4	Adult	Male	Normal	Active	82 gm
5	Adult	Female	Over	Sedentary	60 gm
6	Adult	Female	Over	Active	70 gm
7	Adult	Female	Normal	Sedentary	66 gm
8	Adult	Female	Normal	Active	78 gm
9	Adult	Male	Under	Active	85 gm
10	Adult	Female	Under	Active	74 gm
11	Adult	Male	Under	Sedentary	69 gm
12	Adult	Female	Under	Sedentary	61 gm

5.4.2 Evaluation Criteria

The performance of the LLM is monitored on the basis of the feedback gathered from the volunteer as well as the log saved by them regarding the fat intake a whole day. These volunteers are students, about 30% enjoy their meals in the lab and rest take meal either at home or restaurant. The timing for the breakfast is between 7:00 am to 10:00 am, for lunch is 12:00 pm to 3:00 pm and for dinner is 6:00 pm to 10:00 pm.

In the 1st week duration MM platform only recorded the food log without creating any indication and recommendation of food. In this duration volunteers had recorded all the food stuff that they took in the whole day. The breakfast, lunch and dinner were recorded very well but there was issue regarding other supplementary food stuff (like chocolates, biscuits, chips). In next 2 weeks, LLM started monitoring and indicated the volunteers about the food on the basis of required fats and fats already consumed by them. The indication is produced to the wellness service whenever the amount of nutrient particularly fats crossed threshold value for a particular day i.e. 6:00 am to 5:59 am. Moreover, if the amount of nutrient crossed the threshold value with a particular meal then after that indication is also generated.

5.4.3 Experimental Result Analysis

LLM starts monitoring of the nutrients as soon as user logged the food. It manipulates the physical activity status of the user to identify the sedentary or active status. Then check for the threshold with respect to the category of user for nutrient. We have evaluated the effectiveness of indication in three different scenarios:

I. Start of Meal time,
II. Food logging time,
III. Location and Meal time based

After analysis of the food log, it is observed that the indication of nutrition on the basis of location and time is quite effective as shown in Figure 5.7. While the indication at the food logging time is the least effective. According to the volunteers' feedback, they have to remember about the food recommendation for long period of time. According to the analysis, we divided the volunteers into 3 categories which were overweight, normal weight and underweight groups and all of these were under the category of sedentary activity level. The result shows that there is an impact of indication that improved the intake of fats amount of all three categories, but the change in overweight category is little higher as shown in Figure 5.8.

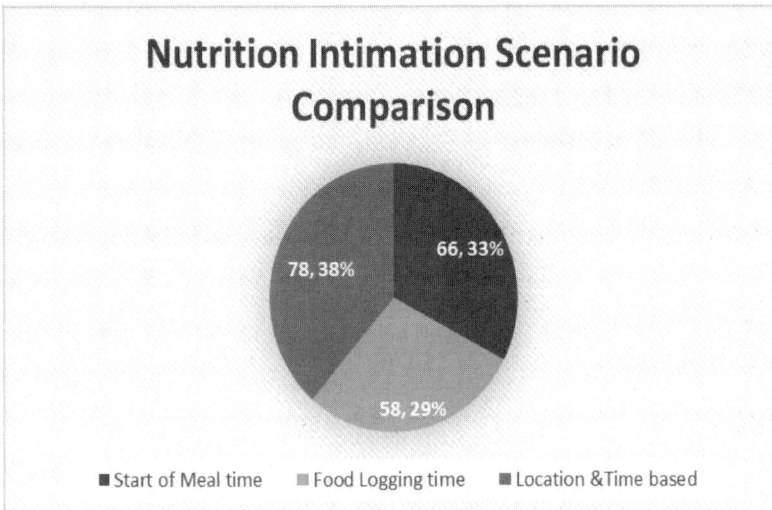

Figure 5.7 Nutrition Intimation Scenario Comparison

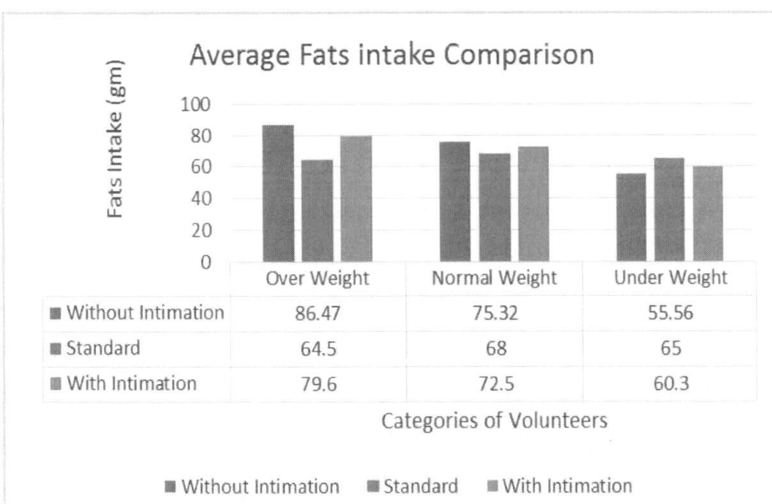

Figure 5.8 Fat Intake Comparison Chart

5.5 Summary

The designed LLM monitors the fat nutrient and indicate about the target values to the user recommended by the expert rules. The push-based methodology of indication supports the users to adopt healthy dietary behavior proactively. It is a new approach to monitor nutrition and push information instead of waiting for the user or expert to examine the daily diet. This technique can support the wellness applications to become proactive to avoid the bad impact of unhealthy behavior. The precautionary approach can be adopted for more effective way to reduce weight and maintain balanced diet for longer period. Currently, the LLM monitors diet for sedentary and active adult persons with respect to gender and weight status. In wellness domain the diet has a big influence on diabetic, cardiac and hypertensive patients. In future we will extend the LLM for monitoring and intimating the dietary pattern for chronic disease patients.

Source Code

Source code can be downloaded from the following location:
https://github.com/ubiquitous-computing-lab/Mining-Minds/tree/master/data-curation-layer/lifelog-monitoring-system

The contents of this chapter have been previously published in the following article:

Hafiz Syed Muhammad Bilal, Wajahat Ali Khan, and Sungyoung Lee, "Unhealthy dietary behavior-based user life-log monitoring for wellness services", 15th International Conference On Smart homes and health Telematics (ICOST 2017), Paris, France, Aug 29-31, 2017

References

[1] Sweeney, T. J., & Witmer, J. M. (1991). Beyond social interest: Striving toward optimum health and wellness. Individual Psychology, 47, 527-540.

[2] Witmer, J. M., & Sweeney, T. J. (1992). A holistic model for wellness and prevention over the lifespan. Journal of Counseling and Development, 71, 140-148

[3] Ardell, Donald B. High level wellness, an alternative to doctors, drugs, and disease. Bantam Books, 1979.

[4] Amin, M. B., Banos, O., Khan, W. A., Muhammad Bilal, H. S., Gong, J., Bui, D. M., ... & Chung, T. C. (2016). On curating multimodal sensory data for health and wellness platforms. Sensors, 16(7), 980.

[5] Millennium Ecosystem Assessment, Ecosystems and Human Wellbeing: A Framework for Assessment (Island Press, Washington, DC, 2003)

[6] Thorp, A. A., Owen, N., Neuhaus, M., & Dunstan, D. W. (2011). Sedentary behaviors and subsequent health outcomes in adults: a systematic review of longitudinal studies, 1996–2011. American journal of preventive medicine,41(2), 207-215.

[7] Kvaavik, Elisabeth, et al. "Influence of individual and combined health behaviors on total and cause-specific mortality in men and women: the United Kingdom health and lifestyle survey." Archives of internal medicine170.8 (2010): 711-718

[8] Petersen, Kristina EN, et al. "The combined impact of adherence to five lifestyle factors on all-cause, cancer and cardiovascular mortality: a prospective cohort study among Danish men and women." British Journal of Nutrition 113.05 (2015): 849-858

[9] Katz, D. L., and S. Meller. "Can we say what diet is best for health?." Annual Review of Public Health 35 (2014): 83-103.

[10] Azumio(2015) Argus quantify your day-to-day. http://www.azumio.com/s/argus/index.html

[11] Ahmad, M., Amin, M. B., Hussain, S., Kang, B. H., Cheong, T., & Lee, S. (2016). Health Fog: a novel framework for health and wellness applications.The Journal of Supercomputing, 1-19.

[12] Banos, O., Amin, M. B., Ali Khan, W., Ali, T., Afzal, M., Kang, B. H., & Lee, S. (2015, May). Mining Minds: An innovative framework for personalized health and wellness

[13] support. In Pervasive Computing Technologies for Healthcare (PervasiveHealth), 2015 9th International Conference on (pp. 1-8). IEEE.

[14] Khan, W.A., Amin, M.B., Banos, O., Ali, T., Hussain, M., Afzal, M., Hussain, S., Hussain, J., Ali, R., Ali, M. and Kang, D., Mining Minds: Journey of Evolutionary Platform for Ubiquitous Wellness.

[15] Ali, R., Afzal, M., Hussain, M., Ali, M., Siddiqi, M.H., Lee, S. and Kang, B.H., 2016. Multimodal hybrid reasoning methodology for personalized wellbeing services. Computers in biology and medicine, 69, pp.10-28.

[16] Banos, O., Amin, M.B., Khan, W.A., Afzal, M., Hussain, M., Kang, B.H. and Lee, S., The Mining Minds Digital Health and Wellness Framework.

[17] Australia New Zealand Food Standard Code (FSC). http://www.foodstandards.gov.au/code/Pages/default.aspx

[18] CSEP(2017) Canadian Physical Activity guidelines. http://csep.ca/CMFiles/Guidelines/CSEP_PAGuidelines_adults_en.pdf

[19] USDA Food Composition Database. https://ndb.nal.usda.gov/ndb/

[20] Portions per person. https://www.cookipedia.co.uk/recipes_wiki/Portions_per_person

Part III

Context-Awareness

Chapter 6

Low-level Context-Awareness

Smartphone Location-Independent Physical Activity Recognition Based on Transportation Natural Vibration Analysis

Taeho Hur, Jaehun Bang, Dohyeong Kim,
Oresti Banos, and Sungyoung Lee

Activity recognition through smartphones has been proposed for a variety of applications. The orientation of the smartphone has a significant effect on the recognition accuracy; thus, researchers generally propose using features invariant to orientation or displacement to achieve this goal. However, those features reduce the capability of the recognition system to differentiate among some specific commuting activities (e.g., bus and subway) that normally involve similar postures. In this chapter, we recognize those activities by analyzing the vibrations of the vehicle in which the user is traveling. We extract natural vibration features of buses and subways to distinguish between them and address the confusion that can arise because the activities are both static in terms of user movement. We use the gyroscope to fix the accelerometer to the direction of gravity to achieve an orientation-free use of the sensor. We also propose a correction algorithm to increase the accuracy when used in free living conditions and a battery saving algorithm to consume less power without reducing performance. Our experimental results show that the system can adequately recognize each activity, yielding better accuracy in the detection of bus and subway activities than existing methods.

6.1 Introduction

The goal of activity recognition (AR) is to recognize common human activities in real-life settings [1]. AR modules are based on data acquired from sensors such as an accelerometer, video, and GPS. Research on AR began in the 1980s and has become a core technology in the field of healthcare, life care, and wellness, which all require information about users' life patterns to provide personalized services. Many studies have suggested methods to recognize numerous activities with high accuracy [2–6]. In particular, accelerometers are a popular way to recognize users' activity. That line of research started by assuming that intrinsic energy would vary with motion, and thus uses accelerometers to measure those variations. Previous research tried to measure the change of motion precisely, so researchers attached many accelerometers to each part of the body and analyzed the resulting data [7–11].

AR methods building upon multiple sensors became less frequent after the introduction of smartphones. The methods devised from previous research required users to buy sensors of different types and attach them to different parts of their bodies. Each sensor is expensive, and the resulting systems are cumbersome to use in real life. However, smartphones are equipped with multi-modal sensors, and many people worldwide (and more people every year) carry one [12]. Therefore, AR research has significantly shifted direction in recent years, and now focuses more predominantly on the use of smartphones. Most AR research on smartphones uses the accelerometer and shows considerably high accuracy in recognizing ambulatory activities, such as staying, walking, and jogging [13–17]. However, it shows low accuracy in recognizing when a user is in a bus or subway [18–20]. That discrepancy in accuracy occurs because different physical activities involve certain significant physical differences that are indicated in the magnitude and pattern of acceleration signals. When people are inside a vehicle like a bus or subway, they either stand or sit, relatively motionless. However, it is quite difficult to distinguish between standing/sitting on a static floor or being in a vehicle; no large difference appears in the patterns of rare acceleration signals. This will be discussed further in Section 7.1.

In this chapter, we propose movement activity recognition while commuting using accelerometer and GPS data from a smartphone to recognize when a user is staying, walking, jogging, and in a bus or subway train. We do not distinguish between standing and sitting but combined them into staying because it is difficult to distinguish these two activities using only one device. For instance, when we use a smartphone while staying still, the acceleration signal will not show much variation, only the small movements involved in handling the phone. We cannot determine whether the current physical activity is standing or sitting because we do not consider the orientation and position, only the magnitude of the variation. We recognize these five activities (staying, walking, jogging, riding in a bus, and riding in a subway) as basic activities in daily life that occur frequently and can thus be used as source data for a lifelog. We use the accelerometer and gyroscope embedded in a smartphone to correct the acceleration data and obtain a fixed signal vector irrespective of the direction of the X, Y, and Z axes. We collected data and extracted features by carrying a smartphone in shirt and pants pockets, in a bag, and in the hand, which are the general positions in which users carry smartphones. We have proposed a correction algorithm to achieve higher accuracy. The purpose of the correction algorithm is to maintain the current activity result unless it is truly changed. For example, if the recognized activity shows walking and there was a misrecognition as jogging in the middle of walking, it compares the current recognized activity and previously recognized activity to conclude whether the final correct activity is walking or jogging. A battery-saving algorithm is also presented in this chapter. According to commute time statistics among OECD countries in 2016 [21], the average commute time takes no more than one hour, which means it will take about two hours a day for commuting considering turnaround time. According to our experiment, when the accelerometer and GPS is turned on all the time, the battery is drained within three hours. Applying the battery-saving algorithm will increase the battery depletion time up to five hours when the sensors are turned on continuously. Our purpose is to let the phone last for a day without recharging. As the application is intended to be used only in the commuting time, it is possible for the phone to last for a day. The contributions of this chapters are:

(1) Movement activity recognition with a smartphone without considering position or orientation. We use the Z-axis to extract natural vibration features from a bus and subway and use that information to distinguish staying, riding in a bus, and riding in a subway.

(2) Distinguishing bus riding from subway riding by extracting natural vibration features. Most research is conducted in a constrained environment and thus shows poor results when used in free living conditions.

(3) Correction and battery saving algorithm to increase accuracy and maintain longer battery usage in free living conditions. We propose a correction algorithm to increase accuracy by determining a user's current activity by referring to previously recognized activity. We also propose a battery-saving algorithm to consume less power while maintaining recognition accuracy.

The remainder of this chapter is structured as follows. Section 7.2 describes related AR works. Section 7.3 describes our proposed methodology to recognize activities, along with the correction and battery saving algorithms. Section 7.4 describes our experimental environment and results. Section 7.5 discusses some issues, and we present our final conclusion in Section 7.6.

6.2 Related Works

Research on AR using inertial sensors has long been undertaken, with various accomplishments. AR was initially achieved by attaching individual sensors to various body parts. The most remarkable research was conducted by Bao et al. [7]. They attached five 2D accelerometers on the forearm, wrist, pelvis, knee, and calf and recognized activities such as walking, running, standing, sitting, watching TV, cycling, eating, and reading. They showed an average of 84% accuracy independent of user. Banos et al. [22] dealt with sensor displacement problems, which is also a classic problem in the area of inertial sensor-based AR. They also proposed multi-sensor fusion-based asymmetric decision weighting method for robust activity recognition [23].

The challenges for smartphone-based AR are (1) determining whether to perform the processing in the phone or transmit the data to a server, (2) deciding what kind of smartphone sensors to use, (3) handling the position and orientation problem, and (4) recognizing complex activities rather than basic ambulatory activities. At the early stage of the research, the phone served merely as a data collection device [4]. The data were either transmitted directly to the server through online communication or connected to the server after data collection was complete. In both cases, the server performed the whole recognition process. As smartphone performance increased, the recognition process moved to the smartphone itself.

Most AR research uses only an accelerometer, but some studies have used other inertial sensors. For example, Shoaib et al. used an accelerometer, gyroscope, and magnetometer to evaluate recognition results using different combinations of sensors [24]. The accelerometer and gyroscope showed reasonable results even when used independently, but the magnetometer was not sufficient to use alone because of the device orientation problem. Khan et al. used a pressure sensor and microphone along with an accelerometer [25]. They used the microphone based on other research [20,26]. The pressure sensor was used to track altitude—particularly the relative altitude between different points, which could be helpful in recognizing activities that result in an increase or decrease in altitude, such as climbing or descending stairs.

Some researchers tried to achieve position- or orientation-independent recognition. Anjum et al. collected data with the phone in different orientations [27]. To solve the orientation problem, they rotated the three orthogonal reference axes to align with the three transformed axes with eigenvector corresponding to the axes in descending order of signal variation. Henpraserttae et al. proposed a projection-based method for device coordinate estimation to handle the device orientation problem [28]. They transformed all input signals into a single global reference coordinate system. Lu et al. used orientation-independent features, one-time device calibration (which can be perceived by the user), and classification techniques in which activities are modeled by splitting them into several sub-classes, each of which is associated with particular body positions [29].

Some of the research tried to identify vehicles, such as car, bus, or subway. They were to recognize more contexts including vehicles with a single phone with sensors in it. Wang et al. tried to recognize walking, cycling, and riding in a vehicle [18]. They used signal vector magnitude (accelerometer magnitude) to combine three axes of acceleration signals into one to try to recognize activity independent of the orientation of the smartphone, and then extracted vertical and horizontal features from that signal. Bus and subway showed low accuracy compared to the others because of their apparent similarity. The confusion between bus and subway seemed to be caused by extracting vertical and horizontal signals from the accelerometer magnitude signal. In other words, it is difficult to retrieve the original intact signal after the acceleration signal has been combined. Siirtola et al. also worked to recognize the activity of driving a car [19]. They used calibration- and orientation-independent features to achieve device-independent AR. They collected data from five different body locations to achieve position independence, and were able to distinguish activities into two main categories: active (running, walking, cycling) and inactive (sitting, standing, on a table, in a car). Driving a car was more poorly recognized than the others. Han et al. used additional sensors in the smartphone with a hierarchical structure [20]. They recognized staying, walking, running, and shaking using the accelerometer. Shaking indicates either a bus or a subway, and they used the microphone to distinguish between them.

Other research proposed energy-saving methods. Anguita et al. proposed the novel multi-class hardware-friendly support vector machine (MC-HF-SVM) approach, which uses fixed-point arithmetic to recognize activities instead of the conventionally used floating-point arithmetic algorithms to balance the trade-off between recognition accuracy and computational cost [30]. MC-HF-SVM can vary the fixed-point number representation (number of bits) to control accuracy and complexity, leading to improvements in both recognition accuracy and power requirements. Yan et al. tried to save energy by continually tracking the current/ongoing activity of the user and dynamically adjusting sampling frequency and classification features to maintain the optimal value of a specific activity [31]. Morillo et al. compared a series of smartphones and sensors with regard to battery consumption [32]. They then adopted a dynamic sampling rate and duty cycle to reduce the overall battery usage. Liang et al. [33] used a hierarchical recognition method. In order to reduce the computational workload in the feature extraction stage, they first used basic time domain features to measure similarities. Then, they adopted frequency domain feature extraction according to similarities. They also changed the sliding window size dynamically.

6.3 System Design

In this section, we introduce our methodology to recognize staying, walking, jogging, riding a bus, and riding a subway in real-life situations by using a single smartphone without considering any specific placement or orientation. For analysis of the problems, we have used the data collected by ourselves; details are shown in Section 7.2. Figure 6.1 shows the overall architecture of our proposed method. We collect accelerometer and GPS data from the smartphone. The preprocessor works to combine acceleration signals and remove the gravity. The feature extractor extracts feature of time domain, frequency domain, and linear predictive coding (LPC) features. We use a Gaussian mixture model (GMM) classifier for classification. A GPS manager validates the proper GPS signal reception and maps the beacon location. An AR verifier manages the sensor for battery saving and corrects the activity to determine the final activity.

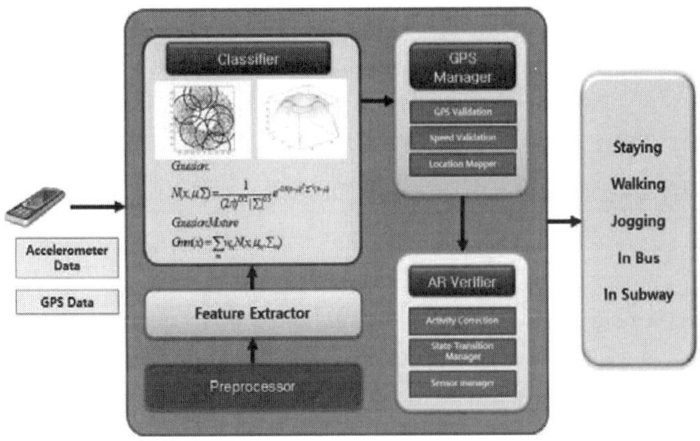

Figure 6.1 Overall architecture of the proposed methodology. AR: activity recognition

6.3.1 Accelerometer Data Preprocessing

Before the emergence of smartphones, AR researchers attached individual accelerometers to the body and extracted features based on the axis with the pattern most characteristic of an activity. However, this method is not applicable for smartphones because people do not carry their smartphones in a fixed position and do not consider the orientation. Thus, we use signal vector magnitude (accelerometer magnitude) to offset the direction information which combines three acceleration signals into one, as shown in Equation (1). If we extract features from the accelerometer magnitude signal, we can easily distinguish staying, walking, and jogging, which all show large differences in pattern and magnitude. Figure 6.2 illustrates this distinction using our collected data.

$$SignalVectorMagnitude = \sqrt{acc_{x_i}^2 + acc_{y_i}^2 + acc_{z_i}^2} \quad (1)$$

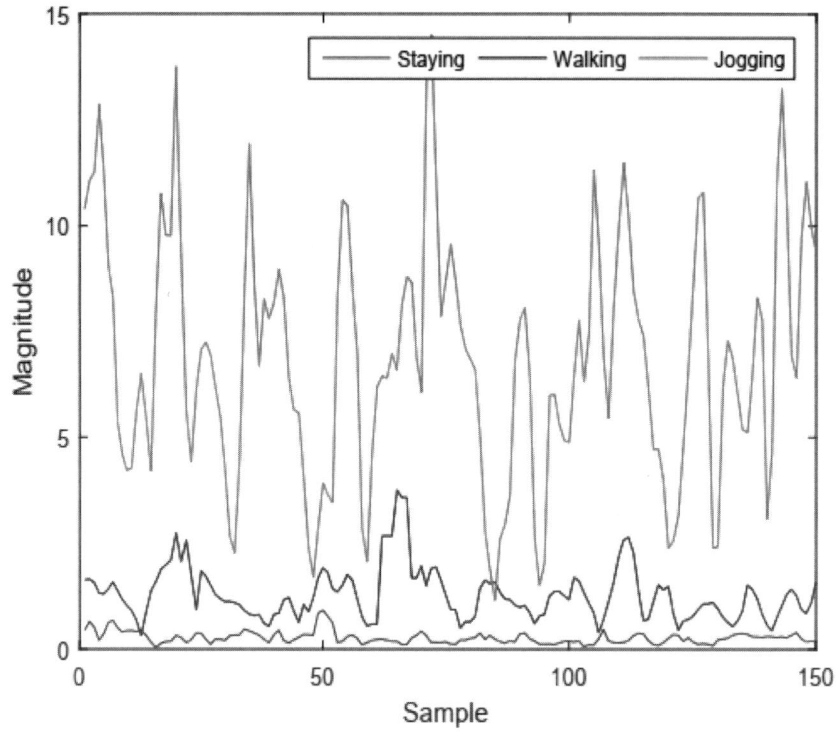

Figure 6.2 Comparison of staying, walking, and jogging using accelerometer magnitude signals

Although using accelerometer magnitude can distinguish staying, walking, and jogging well, it is hard to use this method to distinguish staying, riding a bus, and riding a subway (as shown in Figure 6.3). People usually stay still inside the vehicle, which means there is no large difference between staying and riding in a vehicle, and it is also hard to distinguish between bus and subway, as only a small amount of variation occurs while inside the vehicles. Our hypothesis is that each vehicle has a natural vibration that can be used to accurately determine the corresponding activity taking place. For this, we need to take a look into the gravity axis. Existing research used accelerometer magnitude for cases in which the direction of a smartphone was not fixed, because accelerometer magnitude offsets the effect of the axis. However, this method cannot reflect the natural features that occur in each axis. A method was proposed to solve that problem by extracting vertical and horizontal features from an accelerometer magnitude signal [18]. However, that method could not perfectly restore the original characteristics, which degraded the accuracy of vehicle recognition. Therefore, we use a method to fix the acceleration signal using a gyroscope. Thanks to the smartphone environment we are using, android API provides this function, getRotationMatrixFromVector [34,35]. In this way, all three axes of the accelerometer show zero value while placing still in any direction. This will lead us to gain the magnitude of gravity axis (Z-axis) when the phone is moved in up-and-down direction.

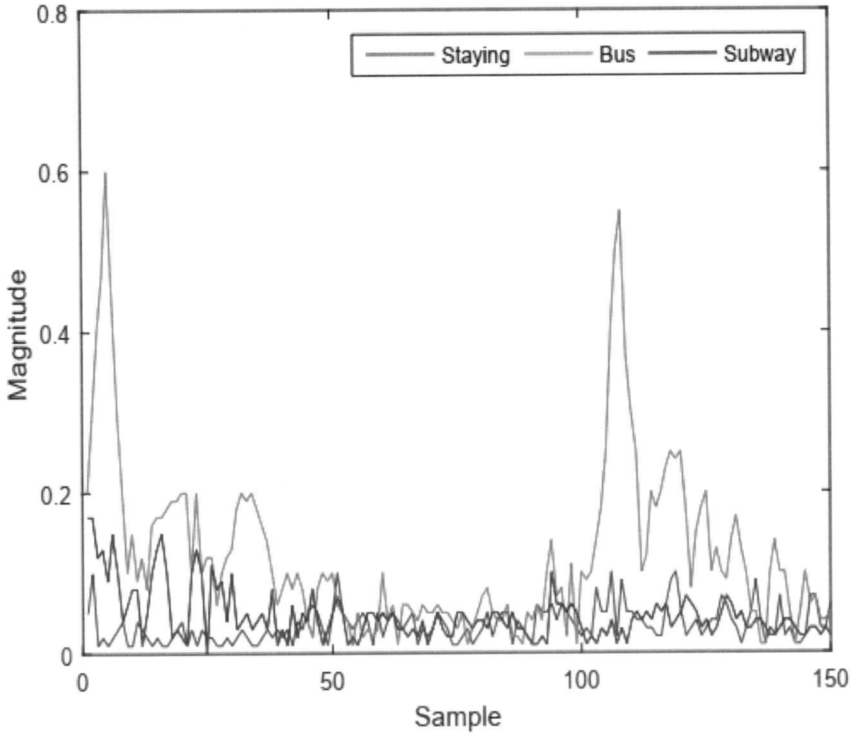

Figure 6.3 Comparison of staying, riding a bus, and riding a subway using accelerometer magnitude signals

6.3.2 Feature Extraction and Classification

For features we use to classify staying, walking, and jogging, we used 10 features from the accelerometer magnitude signal, including the fifth-degree linear predictive coding (LPC), one LPC estimation error, three one-second standard deviations (STD), and one mean crossing rate (MCR). These features are used in our previous work, and were already chosen to be best [20]. For classifying two vehicles, we use different features. As mentioned in Section 7.3.1, our hypothesis is that each vehicle will have its own natural vibration, and vehicles with similar characteristics (such as a car and a bus) will have similar natural vibrations. While inside the vehicles, people will be motionless and the smartphone with only the gravity axis will show large vibration. To observe the differences, we used a fast Fourier transform (FFT) to change the time domain signal into a frequency domain signal to consider a vehicle's natural vibration frequency. Figure 6.4 is a representative figure showing the signals for staying, riding a bus, and riding a subway in the frequency domain of our collected data.

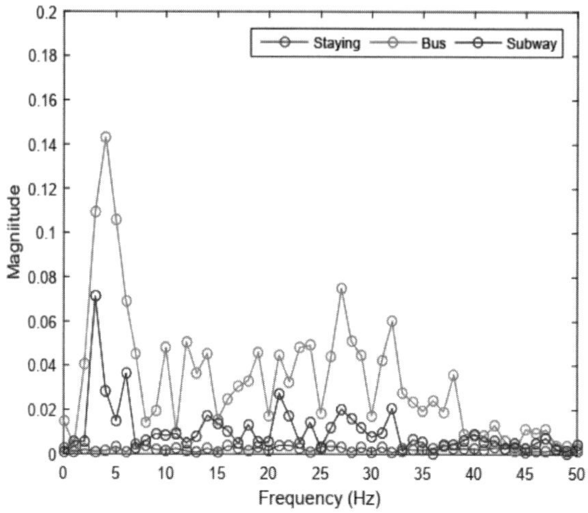

Figure 6.4 Z-axis signal in the frequency domain for staying, riding a bus, and riding a subway

The highest frequency shown in the bus is around 5.3 Hz and is distributed between 3 and 7 Hz. This seems to happen because of variance in the speed of the bus and road conditions. Another characteristic is that the bus shows higher magnitude than staying and the subway. The highest frequency in the subway is around 2.3 Hz and is distributed between 2 and 4 Hz. Another characteristic is that the subway shows a magnitude similar to staying except between 2 and 4 Hz. In staying, no particular frequency shows high magnitude; thus, staying does not appear to have a natural vibration, unlike the bus and subway. Based on this analysis, we use five kinds of features: mean and standard deviation for staying, bus, and subway; maximum magnitude between 3 and 4 Hz to distinguish bus from subway in the same frequency domain; frequency of maximum magnitude of bus and subway; ratio of 2–4 Hz to the whole frequency; and ratio of 3–7 Hz to the whole frequency. We also extract the same features on the X and Y axes. Even though the Z-axis reflects the natural vibration, the magnitude of the signal is very weak and could easily be contaminated with noise. Therefore, we enhance our accuracy by considering signal changes such as acceleration of the vehicle. For this, we do not need to consider the direction of the vehicle, only the variation in magnitude. Thus, we combine the X and Y signals and transform the result with FFT. We also use features of correlation between the XY and Z axes in both the time and frequency domains to determine the relation between the XY axis and the natural vibration from the Z axis.

There might be unnecessary features among what we have chosen. Therefore, we apply our own feature selection method which measures the feature based on the relevancy and the redundancy from the mutual information of the feature [36]. The relevancy is calculated as in Equation (2):

$$Rel(X) = \frac{I(C;X)}{log_2(|\Omega_c|)} \tag{2}$$

where X is a feature variable, C is a class variable, and Ω_c is the state space of C. $I(C; X)$ is the mutual information between C and X, which can be calculated by:

$$I(C;X) = \sum_{c\in\Omega_c} \sum_{x\in\Omega_X} p(c,x)\log_2(\frac{p(c,x)}{p(c)p(x)}) \quad (3)$$

where Ω_X is the state space of the variable X; $p(c, x)$, $p(c)$, and $p(x)$ are, respectively, the joint and marginal probability distributions. The redundancy is calculated as in Equation (4):

$$Red(X,Y) = \frac{I(X;Y)}{log_2(|\Omega_X|)} \quad (4)$$

The mutual information can be calculated by summing over the state space of the variable where the variables should be discretized first. The discretization algorithm is illustrated in Algorithm 7.1. Once the relevance and the redundancy have been calculated, we utilize the well-known searching mechanism called greedy forwarding to extend the selection of features. The whole selection process is illustrated in Algorithm 7.2.

After extracting and selecting features, let us assume that (X^C is a training data matrix $N \times K$ for class C, where each row is a training sample, and each column is a feature value. We have chosen a Gaussian Mixture Model for classification as it is suitable to use a mixture model to represent multiple distributions of collected data for multiple dimensions of features [20]. We determine the parametric probability density function of each class, denoted by $p(X^C \mid \lambda^c)$, where λ^c is the parameter set that includes the mixing weights and individual Gaussian mean vectors and covariance matrices:

$$p(X^c|\lambda^c) = \sum_{i=1}^{M} \omega_i N(X^c|\mu_i \sum_i) \quad (5)$$

where N is a Gaussian distribution and is given by:

$$N(x|\mu_i \sum_i) = \frac{1}{(2\pi)^{D/2}|\Sigma_i|^{1/2}} \exp\left\{-\frac{1}{2}(x-\mu_i)' \sum_i^{-1} (x-\mu_i)\right\} \quad (6)$$

The mixing weights must satisfy the following condition:

$$\sum_{i=1}^{M} \omega_i = 1 \quad (7)$$

During the training phase, the parameters $\lambda^c = (\omega, \mu, \Sigma)$ are determined to maximize the training data likelihood p(X^C | λ^c). In the inference phase, given all the class parameter sets $\lambda^{C1}, \lambda^{C2}, \ldots, \lambda^{Cm}$ and an input vector x, the class label is determined by:

$$c = \mathrm{argmax}_c (p(x|\lambda^c)) \quad (8)$$

Algorithm 6.1: Feature Quantization

```
Input : M—Total number of features
        X(1..M)—Training data
        Δ—The quantization error
     Output: N—Number of quantization levels
             Y(1..M)—Quantized data
  N = 2;
while 1 do
     MaxError = 1 × 10^16;
     for m = 1 to M do
        Upper = max(X(m));
        Lower = min(X(m));
        Step = (Upper Lower)/N; Partition = [Lower : Step : Upper];
        CodeBook = [Lower Step, Lower : Step : Upper];
        [Y(m), QError] = Quantiz(X(m), Partition, CodeBook);
        if QError > MaxError then
           MaxError = QError;
        end
     end
     if MaxError < Δ then
           break;
    end
    N = N + 1;
    end
```

Algorithm 6.2: Feature Selection with Greedy Forward Searching

```
Input : M-Total number of features
        N-Total number of data samples
        K-Number of features to be selected
        X-Training data matrix (M × N) C-Class labels (1 × N)
Output: S − The index vector of the selected features (1 × K) S = Φ;
for m=1 to M do
    Xm = Xm − μ(Xm);
    Xm = Xm/□(Xm);
end
    X = Quantiz(X);
    for k=1 to K do
        BestScore = −1e + 16;
        BestIndex = 0;
        for i=1 to M do
            if Xi not in S then
               f=0;
               c=0;
for Xj in S do
               c = c + 1;
   f = f + Red(Xi, Xj);
end
```

```
            f = Rel(X_i) − f / c;
            if f > BestScore then BestScore = f ; BestIndex = i;
        end
      end
      end
      S = S, BestIndex;
end
```

6.3.3 Adding GPS Data

So far, this study has focused on acceleration data for activity recognition. If we use GPS outdoors, we can distinguish buses from subways more easily. Therefore, we collect GPS data along with acceleration data to acquire location (latitude and longitude) and speed information. The acquired acceleration data are used for feature extraction and activity recognition. GPS data are used for correction to recognize buses and subways. The accuracy of GPS varies with surroundings and location. If the GPS signal is not received properly, both location and speed data will be incorrect. If the location data are significantly incorrect, the speed could appear higher than is accurate to compensate for the differences between accurate and inaccurate location points. This will cause a problem if the user is actually staying, but the recognized result shows vehicle because of the speed. To prevent that problem, we determine a threshold speed to distinguish staying from buses and subways. The basic idea is that staying will show zero speed, while in reality, this might not be true. We placed three smartphones outside on flat ground for 3 hours while recording latitude and longitude. When we analyzed the latitude and longitude values, they did not maintain linearity; some values showed unnaturalness, which means the value showed significant difference once in a series of similar values. This happened for all three phones, and more than five times respectively. Given that the formula for obtaining speed is distance divided by time, we averaged all of the values of differences and obtained 9.6 km/h. Therefore, we set the threshold speed as 9.6 km/h to differentiate ambulatory activities and vehicle activities. In other words, if the speed from GPS is greater than 9.6 km/h, we assume that the current activity is not staying, walking, or jogging, but either bus or subway. We also use GPS for ground-level sections of the subway. To distinguish between bus and subway on similar courses, we collected five beacons between two stations. Our experiments were conducted in Seoul, South Korea. We input the GPS address ofevery beacon for the subway stations using Google Maps. To use this method in a different context, the GPS address should be changed. In Korea, the time from one station to the next takes 2–3 min on average. Therefore, we set the time interval to 30 s among the beacons. Each beacon has its own latitude and longitude. If the subway passes from one beacon to another within 30 s, we determine that the user is on the subway. If the user does not pass from one beacon to another within 30 s or passes onlyone beacon, we determine that the user is on the bus. An illustration of this procedure is given in Figure 6.5.

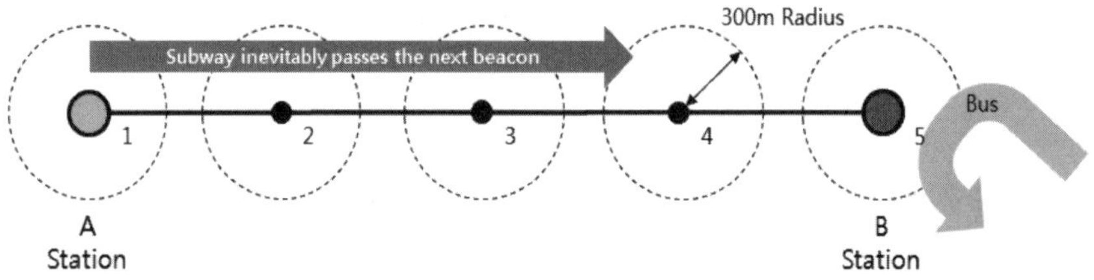

Figure 6.5 Distinguishing bus and subway on ground level using GPS location data

6.3.4 Correction Algorithm for Activity Recognition

Guaranteeing accurate recognition requires a correction mechanism. During any activity, the user might handle the phone in a way that will change the pattern of acceleration data and greatly affect the accuracy. Bus and subway recognition will also be affected if the GPS signal is not received properly or when the bus or subway train stops at a station. All of these occurrences constitute noise and could lead to incorrect results. To correct this problem, we make the final activity decision only if two sequential results (current and previous) are the same. If they are not the same, we maintain the activity as the last recognized activity. Figure 6.6 shows the flowchart for this process.

After the data is collected, we consider the speed first. A low speed could be any activity, but a speed greater than 9.6 km/h can only be the bus or subway. The first five data points (15 s) are an initializing stage. Therefore, the first recognized result will be shown at the 15th second. In this first recognition cycle, there will be no correction result in the previous stage, so the correction result will be the same as the recognized result. The correction flow starts from the next cycle. If the recognized result differs from the previously recognized result, the final result will show the same one as previously corrected result, and the current corrected result will be set as the same activity and terminate the flow. If the recognized result is same as the previously recognized result and it is not staying, then the final result is shown as the current activity. Then, it saves the current activity to correction result and terminates the flow. On the other hand, if the recognized activity is the same as the previously recognized activity and both are staying, we take a look into the previously corrected result. If the previously corrected result was not bus or subway, the current activity will be staying. However, if the previously corrected result was bus or subway, we take a look whether the previously recognized results maintained as staying for 3 min. Additionally, if the staying showed for 3 min, the final activity is concluded as staying. If the staying did not show 3 min of staying continuously, the activity will be concluded as the previously corrected result, which will be either bus or subway. The 3 min interval is set to prevent misrecognition as staying. When a bus and subway run on smooth road and rail, the recognition result will frequently show staying. When either vehicle is stopped at a station, it will also show staying due to the lack of movement. So, once the algorithm recognizes the activity as vehicle, and staying occurs in the middle, we disregard this result and force the algorithm to show the result as vehicle. However, we need a breakpoint or the activity will not be changed from vehicle. As mentioned above, the time from one station to another in Korea is 2–3 min for either bus and subway, and the longest traffic light standby time is about 3 min for the bus. So, we set the break time to 3 min. If the staying shows 3 min, now the algorithm determines that the user is actually staying and escapes from the recognition as vehicle.

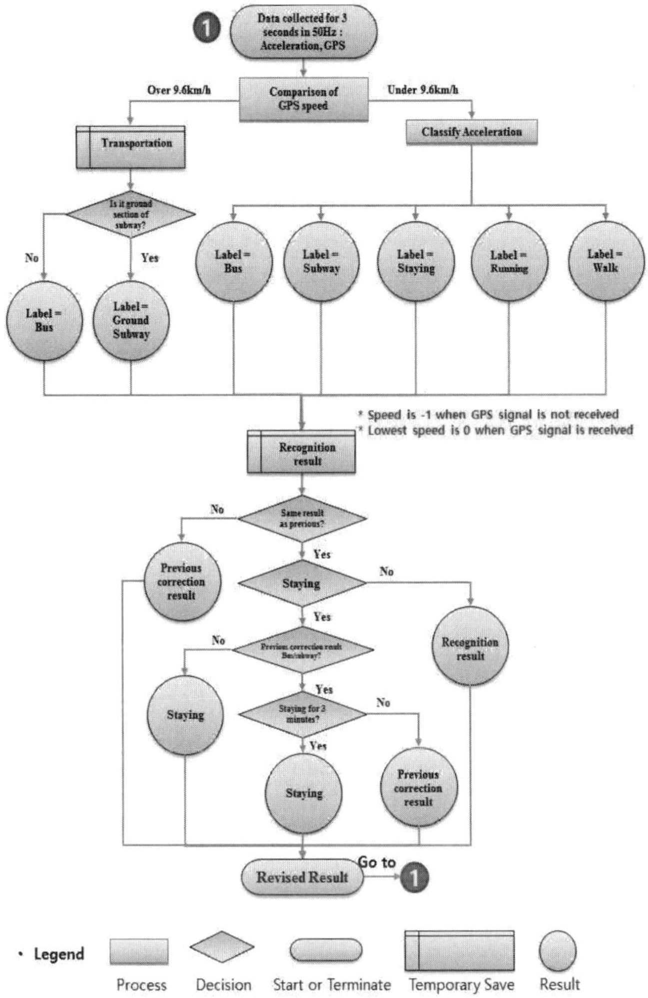

Figure 6.6 Flowchart of the proposed AR algorithm

Figure 6.7 shows an example operation of the correction algorithm. A total of 30 activities were recognized, and the correction was performed for each activity. Note that one activity label is concluded after 3 s and that we set the size of the window in this way. The first four correction results (12 s) are not shown because they are in initialization stage. The fifth result shows the same in both recognition and correction parts as there are no data to refer to from the previous. On the sixth result, the actual recognition changed from staying to walking. However, the previous correction result was walking, so the algorithm disregarded the recognition result and set the correction result as walking. This happened again on the 12th. On the other hand, the 13th recognition result was staying, which is the same as the previous (12th) recognition result. Although the correction result is different from walking, this is regarded as the ground truth activity and the correction result is changed to staying. Taking a look at the 23rd result, the recognition results of both 22nd and 23rd are staying. It seems that the correction result should be changed to staying even if the previous (22nd) correction result was bus. However, as mentioned above, we set a 3 min interval in the vehicle activity. So, the algorithm ignores the recognition result (staying) and concludes the correction result as bus.

Number	Recognition	Correction
1	Staying	Initializing
2	Staying	Initializing
3	Staying	Initializing
4	Walking	Initializing
5	Walking	Walking
6	Staying	Walking
7	Walking	Walking
8	Walking	Walking
9	Walking	Walking
10	Walking	Walking
11	Walking	Walking
12	Staying	Walking
13	Staying	Staying
14	Staying	Staying
15	Walking	Staying
16	Walking	Walking
17	Bus	Walking
18	Bus	Bus
19	Bus	Bus
20	Bus	Bus
21	Bus	Bus
22	Staying	Bus
23	Staying	Bus
24	Bus	Bus
25	Bus	Bus
26	Bus	Bus
27	Staying	Bus
28	Staying	Bus
29	Bus	Bus
30	Bus	Bus

1-4: Initialization stage – No output

5-6: Sequential recognition not same (5: Walking != 6: Staying)
-> Output previous correction result (6: Walking)

7-10: Sequential recognition same -> No change

11-12: Sequential recognition not same (11: Walking != 12: Staying)
-> Output previous correction result (12: Walking)

12-13: Sequential recognition same (12: Staying == 13: Staying)
-> Output recognition result (13: Staying)

14-15: Sequential recognition not same (14: Staying != 15: Walking)
-> Output previous correction result (15: Staying)

16-17: Sequential recognition not same (16: Walking != 17: Bus)
-> Output previous correction result (17: Walking)

17-18: Sequential recognition same (17: Bus == 18: Bus)
-> Output recognition result (18: Bus)

21-22: Sequential recognition not same (21: Bus != 22: Staying)
-> Output previous correction result (22: Bus)

22-23: Sequential recognition same (22: Staying == 22: Staying)
but staying was not recognized for 3 minutes
-> Output previous correction result (23: Bus)

26-27: Sequential recognition not same (26: Bus != 27: Staying)
-> Output previous correction result (27: Bus)

27-28: Sequential recognition same (27: Staying == 28: Staying)
but staying was not recognized for 3 minutes
-> Output previous correction result (28: Bus)

Figure 6.7 Example of the correction algorithm

Figure 6.8 shows another example of the correction algorithm's operation. Until the 140th result, it is similar to the previous example. After that, if the correction result changes to subway, it ignores the recognition result but keeps the correction result as subway. From the 149th, the recognition result turned to staying until the end. This means that the user actually got off the subway and was staying still. However, due to the 3-min interval problem, the correction result kept showing subway. After 3 min (which means 60 blocks after), the algorithm finally concluded the ground truth activity as staying. This case is the only disadvantage of our algorithm; however, we cannot eliminate this 3 min interval feature because it will lead to substantial error without it.

Number	Recognition	Correction
...		Walking
133	Walking	Walking
134	Staying	Walking
135	Staying	Staying
136	Staying	Staying
137	Staying	Staying
138	Subway	Staying
139	Subway	Subway
140	Staying	Subway
141	Staying	Subway
142	Walking	Subway
143	Subway	Subway
144	Staying	Subway
145	Subway	Subway
146	Staying	Subway
147	Staying	Subway
148	Subway	Subway
149	Staying	Subway
150	Staying	Subway
151	Staying	Subway
152	Staying	Subway
...		Subway
207	Staying	Subway
208	Staying	Subway
209	Staying	Staying

133-134: Sequential recognition not same (133: Walking != 134: Staying)
-> Output previous correction result (134: Walking)

134-135: Sequential recognition same (134: Staying == 135: Staying)
-> Output recognition result (135: Staying)

137-138: Sequential recognition not same (137: Staying != 138: Subway)
-> Output previous correction result (138: Staying)

138-139: Sequential recognition same (138: Subway == 139: Subway)
-> Output recognition result (139: Subway)

139-140: Sequential recognition not same (139: Subway != 140: Staying)
-> Output previous correction result (140: Subway)

140-141: Sequential recognition same (140: Staying == 141: Staying)
but staying was not recognized for 3 minutes
-> Output previous correction result (141: Subway)

141-142: Sequential recognition not same (141: Staying != 142: Walking)
-> Output previous correction result (142: Subway)

142-143: Sequential recognition not same (142: Walking != 143: Subway)
-> Output previous correction result (143: Subway)

150-151: Sequential recognition same (150: Staying == 151: Staying)
but staying was not recognized for 3 minutes
-> Output previous correction result (151: Subway)

⋮

208-209: Sequential recognition same (208: Staying == 209: Staying)
And staying was recognized for 3 minutes
-> Output recognition result (209: Staying)

Figure 6.8 Example of the correction algorithm

Figure 6.9 shows the state transition diagram. Staying, walking, and jogging can alternate, but bus and subway cannot be changed to each other due to the nature of reality. Normally, bus and subway cannot be changed to staying, except when staying was misrecognized as bus or subway for 3 min, as shown in the above example.

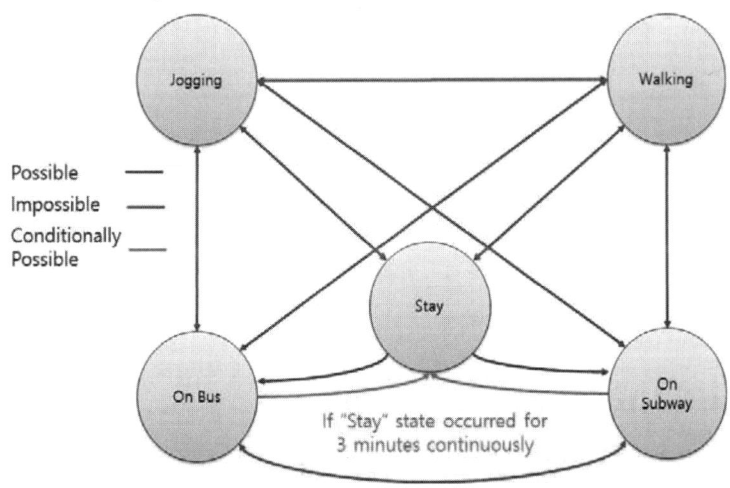

Figure 6.9 Transition state diagram between activities

6.3.5 Battery-Saving Algorithm

The method just explained constantly receives GPS and acceleration signals even when data from one sensor does not affect the recognition; this consumes unnecessary battery. To check for differences in sensor battery consumption, we used two phones and fully charged them before each experiment. We created a simple application that uses the accelerometer and GPS and repeated each experiment 10 times. The phone consumes an average of 2% of the battery for 2 h in idle state. However, it consumes 5% of the battery when it runs the accelerometer and 11% when concurrently using GPS. We therefore composed a battery-saving method to prevent rapid battery depletion and guarantee that our recognizer can be used for at least one day. Our algorithm dynamically turns the sensors on and off or changes the sampling frequency according to the activity. If the previous activity was bus and the current speed is more than 9.6 km/h, the recognizer turns off the accelerometer until the speed goes below 9.6 km/h. If the activity is recognized as staying, walking, jogging, or subway, GPS does not affect the recognition, so we extend the cycle for receiving a GPS signal from 1 s to 30 s. Figure 6.10 shows the battery-saving algorithm adjustment compared to the original algorithm.

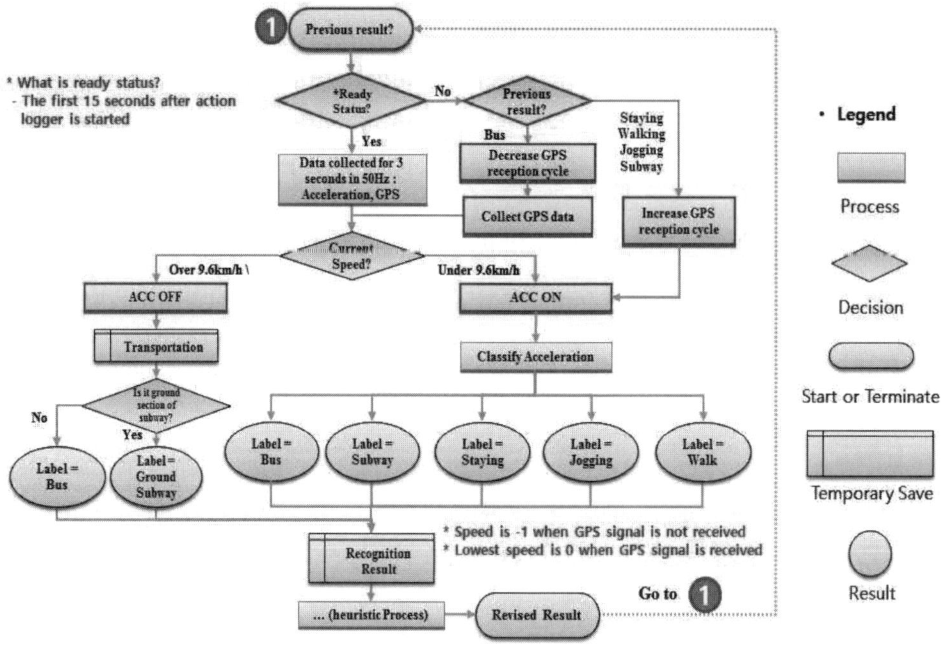

Figure 6.10 Flowchart of the proposed battery-saving algorithm. ACC: accelerometer

6.4 Experiment

In this section, we introduce our experimental environment. We describe the devices used, data collection environment, performance evaluation method, and results. We also describe an experiment conducted in the field.

6.4.1 Experimental Environment

We used a Samsung Galaxy S3 (SHW-E210K, SHW-M440S, GT-I9300T) for data collection and testing. One window contains 150 samples of acceleration data collected for 3 s on the X, Y, and Z axes at 50 Hz. We use the highest speed acquired during 3 s of GPS data. Detailed specifications for the device used in this research are shown in Table **1.**

Table 1. Specifications of the Samsung Galaxy S3.

Smartphone	Galaxy S3
OS	Android 4.1.2 (Jellybean)
CPU	Quad core 1.2 GHz
Memory	1 GHz DDR2
Sensors	Accelerometer, Gyroscope, GPS, etc.
Network	3G, WiFi

6.4.2 Data Collection Environment

We used four smartphones positioned in a shirt pocket, a pants pocket, a bag, and held in a hand for simultaneous data collection, as shown in Figure 6.11. Those four positions represent common ways people carry their smartphones.

Figure 6.11 Smartphone carried in four different positions

Ten subjects participated in data collection: two females and eight males between the ages of 24 and 28 years. We collected data while staying, walking, jogging, and riding in a bus and subway while carrying the smartphones. We collected both standing and sitting data while on a bus and a subway and while staying. We also used the smartphones while staying (e.g., browsing the internet) in order to prevent misrecognition of the activity because the phone was in use. The total length of datasets collected is shown in Table 6.2.

Table 6.2 Total length of the collected datasets

Activity	Bus	Subway	Jogging	Staying	Walking	Total
Number of Samples (s)	26,826	9996	3030	34,212	19,446	93,510

Collected data are distributed as shown in Table 6.3 for performance evaluation.

Table 6.3 Distribution of the collected dataset for training, validation, and testing

Activity	Training (80%)	Testing (20%)	Total
Bus	7153	1789	8942
Subway	2665	667	3332
Jogging	808	202	1010
Staying	9123	2281	11,404
Walking	5185	1297	6482
Total	24,934	6236	31,170

6.4.3 Performance Evaluation Result

In this section, we show the recognition results based on the accelerometer, along with the results of our proposed method. First, we performed an experiment using an existing method by processing the sensor data with accelerometer magnitude. Based on that, we extracted 10 features: the fifth degree LPC, LPC error, three STD, and one MCR. Table 6.4 shows the result confusion matrix.

Table 6.4 Confusion matrix for AR using 10 features (Average accuracy: 0.895)

Activity	Bus	Subway	Jogging	Staying	Walking
Bus	0.9214	0.0414	0.0001	0.0331	0.0040
Subway	0.0192	0.8619	0	0.1168	0.0021
Jogging	0	0	0.9713	0	0.0287
Staying	0.0452	0.1759	0	0.7714	0.0075
Walking	0	0.0004	0	0.0510	0.9486

Our proposed method additionally uses natural vibration features extracted from the XY-axis and Z-axis and correlations of the XY-axis and Z-axis, for a total of 44 features. Table 6.5 shows the confusion matrix of the result.

Table 6.5 Confusion matrix of AR using the proposed method with 44 features (Average accuracy: 0.9182)

Activity	Bus	Subway	Jogging	Staying	Walking
Bus	0.8912	0.0119	0	0.0924	0.0045
Subway	0.0114	0.8103	0	0.1783	0
Jogging	0	0	1	0	0
Staying	0.0100	0.0481	0	0.9411	0.0008
Walking	0	0.0004	0	0.0510	0.9486

The accuracy for bus and subway was 92.14% and 86.19%, respectively, using accelerometer magnitude—higher than that for our proposed method, which was 89.12% and 81.03%, respectively. However, the existing method had only 77.13% accuracy for staying, whereas our method was 94.10% accurate for the dominant activity in real life. This is a critical issue for any AR system to be used in the real field. Although our method showed lower accuracy in recognizing bus and subway, the confusion between them was only 1.2%, which is very low. Our method showed some delay in recognizing bus and subway, but it did not misrecognize staying as riding in a vehicle. The delay in recognizing a vehicle is fairly short, which might not be a big problem because it takes 2–3 min to move from one station to another.

6.4.4 Experiment for Battery Consumption

In this section, we show the results of our proposed battery-saving algorithm. We performed this experiment in the field. Figure 6.12 shows that our battery saving algorithm conserved energy compared with the normal way. On the bus, battery usage decreased by about 5%—from 9% to 4%—over 35 min, which means the efficiency increased by up to 55%. The bus spends more time running than stopping at bus stops or for traffic, and that turns off the acceleration data. The other activities saved about 2% of the battery from 9% to 7% over 30 min, which means the efficiency increased by up to 22%. Applying the battery-saving algorithm did not affect the recognition accuracy because we applied the correction algorithm.

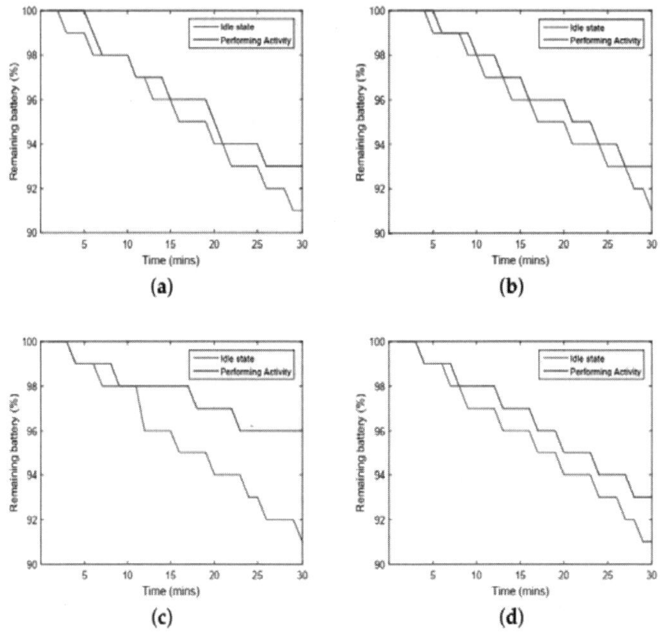

Figure 6.12 Comparison of the performance of the battery-saving algorithm during different activities. (**a**) Staying; (**b**) Walking; (**c**) Riding in a bus; and (**d**) Riding in a subway

6.4.5 Experiment in a Free-Living Condition

To determine the accuracy of our proposed method, we conducted an experiment in a free-living condition, applying both the correction and battery-saving algorithms. We chose five subjects who had not been data collectors in earlier experiments and asked them to carry the smartphone randomly in four different positions. They were told to perform the test list shown in Table 6.6 and note the result manually each time. We did not include walking or jogging because the accuracy of those activities is high.

As shown in the table below, our proposed activity recognition technique showed good results in free living conditions. Most of the tests were perfect, except for test numbers 1, 2, 5, and 6. For the misrecognized cases, the meaning of misrecognition applying the correction algorithm is that the activity is misrecognized during the whole activity cycle. For example, test number 5 was to check whether our application can recognize "staying" while the user is on board an escalator. It might misrecognize at the beginning to another activity, but it will soon recognize correctly as staying. It may also suddenly misrecognize to a different activity in the middle of boarding time, but this will be regarded as misrecognition and still the corrected result will show the proper activity, which is staying. Among a total of 48 attempts, three times were misrecognized. This means that for the whole time while on board the escalator, the corrected result did not show staying. It did recognize the activity properly as staying in the middle of boarding occasionally, but due to the correction algorithm, it disregarded this result and kept showing the corrected result, which is actually wrong. This misrecognition situation can be escaped when the user performs a different activity by breaking the correction. Other problems occurred when recognizing between staying and subway. Unlike a bus, a subway has small vibrations, which can cause confusion between staying and subway.

Table 6.6. Test list to test the performance of the proposed method in free living conditions

No.	Test List	Result (Correct Result/Total No. of Times)
1	Standing on a subway	33/34
2	Sitting on a subway	13/14
3	Standing on a bus	14/14
4	Sitting on a bus	33/33
5	Standing on an escalator (to see whether it misrecognizes escalator as a bus or subway)	45/48
6	Turning on the activity recognition application while on a subway	46/48
7	Turning on the activity recognition application while inside a bus (to see whether it misrecognizes the activity while receiving GPS signal)	8/8
8	Seeing whether it turns to a different activity while the bus is stopped for a traffic signal or a bus stop for a long time (2–3 min)	6/6
9	Riding on a bus for more than 2 h (to see whether it misrecognizes the bus as a subway)	14/14
10	Waiting for a bus or subway at the station for a long time (to see whether it misrecognizes the wait as a bus or subway)	52/52
11	Test all activities, including transferring to bus and subway, for at least 2 h	19/19

Table 6.7 shows the accuracy with and without applying the correction. The accuracy is based on the field test conducted in Table 6.6 as walking and jogging is excluded in this table. Accuracy is computed by calculating the correct result among the actual activity from all cases. While not applying the correction, the subway shows poor result, in that it frequently confuses with staying. On the other hand, bus shows reasonable result because it can get help from the GPS and reduce the error of classifying to other activities. Staying shows the best result, as no such factors affect that activity. When the correction method is applied, the accuracy greatly increases, because the function of the correction method is to maintain the current activity until it is surely changed. It is still not one hundred percent complete for several reasons, such as the lack of GPS signal reception, the maintenance of a false activity if it recognizes the activity incorrectly from the beginning, and the absence of movement for a long time inside of a vehicle (traffic jam, accident, etc.).

Table 6.7 Accuracy with and without applying the correction method from the field test

Activity	Accuracy without Applying Correction	Accuracy Applying Correction
Bus	81	97
Subway	63	95
Staying	93	98

6.5 Discussion

In addition to collecting the bus data, we also collected a small amount of data while inside a car. We analyzed the acceleration signal and found that the difference between a bus and a car is small. Applying natural vibration features has largely solved the confusion problem for staying, riding a bus, and riding a subway. Because people usually remain relatively motionless inside a vehicle, it is difficult to distinguish the difference among them with simple features, particularly on a subway. As shown in the experimental results in Section 7.4.4, staying is more confused with riding a subway than riding a bus. As a bus runs on the road, it faces many obstacles, such as an unpaved road or a speed bump and sudden stops from cars cutting in its path or a person on the road. Those changes produce large variations in acceleration signals, which makes it easier to determine that the current state is not staying. On the other hand, subways run smoothly on the rail and do not typically experience sudden interferences. Although the magnitude of natural vehicle vibration is low and difficult for a human to perceive, the sensors are delicate enough to detect this vibration. However, this is not enough. At the beginning, we started to make our work only to use the accelerometer. The offline test showed quite well, while it still showed many errors in the field test because no constant pattern could be found—especially on the bus. So, we decided to include the GPS even though it consumes a lot of battery. The GPS works as an assistant of the main detector and complements the misrecognition of riding a bus. A problem occurs when a user walks inside a subway. A bus is too short to walk for a long time, but a user can walk from the very front cabin to the very rear cabin of a subway, which would take some time. In that case, our recognizer will recognize the activity as walking even though the user is inside a vehicle. If the user stops walking and stays still again, the recognizer will eventually determine the activity to be subway, but confusion could occur between staying and riding a subway. We use a correction algorithm to overcome the practicality problem by referring to the previous activity to decide whether the current activity is well classified. We showed that this method is applicable in free living conditions, but our recognizer is currently limited to the capital city of Korea for exactness because the GPS addresses of the subway beacons are manually input. If this recognizer is to be used in other countries, it will be necessary to input different beacon addresses. We chose four general positions in which people carry smartphones, but many other positions are possible. We collected data from the trousers front pocket, but people also carry their phones in their hip pockets, inside pockets, and coat pockets. Likewise, we collected data using only backpacks, but people also carry their phones in purses, handbags, and briefcases. As we experimented with those different positions, our algorithm continued to perform well most of the time, but mistakes occurred occasionally. Finally, the number of activities is limited in this work because we wanted to reflect the position and orientation free concept and to maximize practicality. Smartphones are used by most people, so no one needs to buy additional sensors for a daily life activity recognizer. However, this single device can detect only overall body movements, not detailed movements performed by a hand or leg. To extend the recognizable activities, it is necessary to include more sensors or fix the position.

6.6 Summary

In this research, we proposed an activity recognition method using an accelerometer and GPS in a smartphone environment to be practical in free living conditions. We separated activities into two categories: ambulatory activities and vehicles. To detect vehicles, we assumed the natural vibrations of two different vehicles and extracted the features. To guarantee practicality, we applied orientation- and position-free concepts, a correction algorithm to increase accuracy in free living conditions, and a battery-saving algorithm with no accuracy degradation. The outcome of our research will greatly help to recognize user activity in daily living. There are some limitations to increasing recognizable activities using a single device with a free carrying environment. In future work, we will add additional activities while complying with minimum sensor device requirements, such as using a smartphone and smartwatch.

Source Code

Source code can be downloaded from the following location:

https://github.com/ubiquitous-computing-lab/Mining-Minds/tree/master/information-curation-layer#2-low-level-context-awareness

The contents of this chapter have been previously published in the following article:

Taeho Hur, Jaehun Bang, Dohyeong Kim, Oresti Banos, and Sungyoung Lee, "Smartphone Location-Independent Physical Activity Recognition Based on Transportation Natural Vibration Analysis", Sensors (SCIE, IF:2.033), Vol.17, Issue 4, 2017

References

[1] Kim, E.; Helal, S.; Cook, D. Human activity recognition and pattern discovery. IEEE Pervasive Comput. 2010, 9, 48–53.
[2] Lara, O.D.; Labrador, M.A. A survey on human activity recognition using wearable sensors. IEEE Commun. Surv. Tutor. 2013, 15, 1192–1209.
[3] Shoaib, M.; Bosch, S.; Incel, O.D.; Scholten, H.; Havinga, P.J. A survey of online activity recognition using mobile phones. Sensors 2015, 15, 2059–2085.
[4] Turaga, P.; Chellappa, R.; Subrahmanian, V.S.; Udrea, O. Machine recognition of human activities: A survey. IEEE Trans. Circ. Syst. Video Technol. 2008, 18, 1473–1488.
[5] Chen, L.; Hoey, J.; Nugent, C.D.; Cook, D.J.; Yu, Z. Sensor-based activity recognition. IEEE Trans. Syst. Man Cybern. Part C (Appl. Rev.) 2012, 42, 790–808.
[6] Banos, O.; Amin, M.B.; Khan, W.A.; Afzal, M.; Hussain, M.; Kang, B.H.; Lee, S. The Mining Minds digital health and wellness framework. Biomed. Eng. Online 2016, 15, 76.
[7] Bao, L.; Intille, S.S. Activity recognition from user-annotated acceleration data. In Proceedings of the International Conference on Pervasive Computing, Vienna, Austria, 21–23 April 2004; pp. 1–17.
[8] Ravi, N.; Dandekar, N.; Mysore, P.; Littman, M.L. Activity recognition from accelerometer data. In Proceedings of the Twentieth National Conference on Artificial Intelligence, Pittsburgh, PA, USA, 9–13 July 2005; Volume 5, pp. 1541–1546.
[9] Maurer, U.; Smailagic, A.; Siewiorek, D.P.; Deisher, M. Activity recognition and monitoring using multiple sensors on different body positions. In Proceedings of the International Workshop on Wearable and Implantable Body Sensor Networks, Cambridge, MA, USA, 3–5 April 2006.
[10] Banos, O.; Damas, M.; Pomares, H.; Prieto, A.; Rojas, I. Daily living activity recognition based on statistical feature quality group selection. Expert Syst. Appl. 2012, 39, 8013–8021.
[11] Banos, O.; Damas, M.; Pomares, H.; Rojas, F.; Delgado-Marquez, B.; Valenzuela, O. Human activity recognition based on a sensor weighting hierarchical classifier. Soft Comput. 2013, 17, 333–343.
[12] Smartphone Ownership and Internet Usage Continues to Climb in Emerging Economies, PewResearchCenter. Available online: http://www.pewglobal.org/2016/02/22/smartphone-ownership- and-internet-usage-continues-to-climb-in-emerging-economies (accessed on 2 February 2016).
[13] Banos, O.; Villalonga, C.; Garcia, R.; Saez, A.; Damas, M.; Holgado-Terriza, J.A.; Pomares H.; Lee, S.; Rojas, I. Design, implementation and validation of a novel open

[14] framework for agile development of mobile health applications. Biomed. Eng. Online 2015, 14, S6.
[15] Kaghyan, S.; Sarukhanyan, H. Activity recognition using K-nearest neighbor algorithm on smartphone with tri-axial accelerometer. Int. J. Inf. Models Anal. 2012, 1, 146–156.
[16] Berchtold, M.; Budde, M.; Gordon, D.; Schmidtke, H.R.; Beigl, M. Actiserv: Activity recognition service for mobile phones. In Proceedings of the 2010 International Symposium on Wearable Computers, Seoul, Korea, 10–13 October 2010; pp. 1–8.
[17] Ayu, M.A.; Mantoro, T.; Matin, A.F.A.; Basamh, S.S. Recognizing user activity based on accelerometer data from a mobile phone. In Proceedings of the 2011 IEEE Symposium on Computers & Informatics, Kuala Lumpur, Malaysia, 20–23 March 2011; pp. 617–621.
[18] Du, H.; Yu, Z.; Yi, F.; Wang, Z.; Han, Q.; Guo, B. Group mobility classification and structure recognition using mobile devices. In Proceedings of the 2016 IEEE International Conference on Pervasive Computing and Communications (PerCom), Sydney, Australia, 14–18 March 2016; pp. 1–9.
[19] Wang, S.; Chen, C.; Ma, J. Accelerometer Based Transportation Mode Recognition on Mobile Phones. In Proceedings of the 2010 Asia-Pacific Conference on Wearable Computing Systems, Shenzhen, China, 17–18 April 2010; pp. 44–46.
[20] Siirtola, P.; Röning, J. Ready-to-use activity recognition for smartphones. In Proceedings of the 2013 IEEE Symposium on Computational Intelligence and Data Mining, Singapore, 16–19 April 2013; pp. 59–64.
[21] Han, M.; Lee, Y.K.; Lee, S. Comprehensive context recognizer based on multimodal sensors in a smartphone. Sensors 2012, 12, 12588–12605.
[22] Average Minutes Per Day Spent Travelling to Paid Work or Study by Men and Women in OECD Countries Plus China, India and South Africa, as of 2016, Statista. Available online: https://www.statista.com/ statistics/521886/travel-time-spent-work-study-countries/ (accessed on 1 February 2017).
[23] Banos, O.; Toth, M.A.; Damas, M.; Pomares, H.; Rojas, I. Dealing with the effects of sensor displacement in wearable activity recognition. Sensors 2014, 14, 9995–10023.
[24] Banos, O.; Damas, M.; Guillen, A.; Herrera, L.J.; Pomares, H.; Rojas, I.; Villalonga, C. Multi-sensor fusion based on asymmetric decision weighting for robust activity recognition. Neural Process. Lett. 2015, 42, 5–26.
[25] Shoaib, M.; Scholten, H.; Havinga, P.J. Towards physical activity recognition using smartphone sensors. In Proceedings of the 2013 IEEE 10th International Conference on Ubiquitous Intelligence and Computing, Vietri sul Mare, Italy, 18–21 December 2013; pp. 80–87.
[26] Khan, A.M.; Tufail, A.; Khattak, A.M.; Laine, T.H. Activity recognition on smartphones via sensor-fusion and KDA-based SVMS. Int. J. Distrib. Sens. Netw. 2014, 10, doi:10.1155/2014/503291
[27] Ward, J.A.; Lukowicz, P.; Troster, G.; Starner, T.E. Activity recognition of assembly tasks using body-worn microphones and accelerometers. IEEE Trans. Pattern Anal. Mach. Intell. 2006, 28, 1553–1567.
[28] Anjum, A.; Ilyas, M.U. Activity recognition using smartphone sensors. In Proceedings of the 2013 IEEE 10th Consumer Communications and Networking Conference, Las Vegas, NV, USA, 11–14 January 2013; pp. 914–919.
[29] Henpraserttae, A.; Thiemjarus, S.; Marukatat, S. Accurate activity recognition using a mobile phone regardless of device orientation and location. In Proceedings of the 2011

International Conference on Body Sensor Networks, Dallas, TX, USA, 23–25 May 2011; pp. 41–46.
[30] Lu, H.; Yang, J.; Liu, Z.; Lane, N.D.; Choudhury, T.; Campbell, A.T. The Jigsaw continuous sensing engine for mobile phone applications. In Proceedings of the 8th ACM Conference on Embedded Networked Sensor Systems, Zurich, Switzerland, 3–5 November 2010; pp. 71–84.
[31] Anguita, D.; Ghio, A.; Oneto, L.; Parra, X.; Reyes-Ortiz, J.L. Energy Efficient Smartphone-Based Activity Recognition using Fixed-Point Arithmetic. J. UCS 2013, 19, 1295–1314.
[32] Yan, Z.; Subbaraju, V.; Chakraborty, D.; Misra, A.; Aberer, K. Energy-efficient continuous activity recognition on mobile phones: An activity-adaptive approach. In Proceedings of the 2012 16th International Symposium on Wearable Computers, Newcastle, UK, 18–22 June 2012; pp. 17–24.
[33] Morillo, L.M.S.; Gonzalez-Abril, L.; Ramirez, J.A.O.; de la Concepcion, M.A.A. Low energy physical activity recognition system on smartphones. Sensors 2015, 15, 5163–5196.
[34] Liang, Y.; Zhou, X.; Yu, Z.; Guo, B. Energy-efficient motion related activity recognition on mobile devices for pervasive healthcare. Mob. Netw. Appl. 2014, 19, 303–317.
[35] SensorManager, Android Developers. Available online: http://developer.android.com/reference/ android/hardware/SensorManager.html (accessed on 5 March 2016).
[36] SensorEvent, Android Developers. Available online: https://developer.android.com/reference/android/ hardware/SensorEvent.html#values (accessed on 5 March 2016).
[37] Vinh, L.; Lee, S.; Park, Y.; d'Auriol, B. A novel feature selection method based on normalized mutual information. Appl. Intell. 2012, 37, 100–120.

Chapter 7

High-level Context-Awareness

Ontology-based High-Level Context Inference for Human Behavior Identification

Claudia Villalonga, Muhammad Asif Razzaq, Wajahat Ali Khan, Sungyoung Lee, and Oresti Banos

Recent years have witnessed a huge progress in the automatic identification of individual primitives of human behavior, such as activities or locations. However, the complex nature of human behavior demands more abstract contextual information for its analysis. This work presents an ontology-based method that combines low-level primitives of behavior, namely activity, locations and emotions, unprecedented to date, to intelligently derive more meaningful high-level context information. The chapter contributes with a new open ontology describing both low-level and high-level context information, as well as their relationships. Furthermore, a framework building on the developed ontology and reasoning models is presented and evaluated. The proposed method proves to be robust while identifying high-level contexts even in the event of erroneously detected low-level contexts. Despite reasonable inference times being obtained for a relevant set of users and instances, additional work is required to scale to long-term scenarios with a large number of users.

7.1 Introduction

A revolutionary wave of smart systems has recently emerged to enable the automatic identification of human behavior. Proposed solutions are generally intended to recognize the primal dimensions of human behavior and context, including people's activities, emotions and locations. Video systems [1] and on-body sensors [2] have extensively been considered for the recognition of physical activity. Other works have used positioning technologies to track the user location and derive movement patterns [3]. Video, audio or a combination of both modalities have also been proposed for analyzing speech and facial expressions in order to recognize some emotional states [4,5]. Data-driven, knowledge-driven and hybrid methods are normally considered for processing these sensory data to identify human behavior. In data-driven approaches, machine learning techniques are used to detect patterns matching some known contexts describing behavior [6–8]. In knowledge-driven approaches, ontologies and rules are utilized to model and infer different contexts [9–11]. Both data-driven and knowledge-driven techniques are further combined in hybrid methods to determine various components of human behavior [12,13].

Despite the value of the contributions made for the automatic identification of human behavior, it is fair to say that most existing solutions tend to apply to a sole dimension of behavior. In other words, most systems are only capable of identifying activities, locations or emotions, but generally not a combination of them. While these primitives could be considered in isolation for a preliminary analysis of a person's behavior, their appropriate combination can lead to more meaningful and richer expressions of context for behavior understanding. Hence, there is a clear opportunity for developing new methods for the automatic identification of richer human behavior information.

This work presents an ontology-based method to intelligently combine cross-domain behavior primitives, also referred to as low-level contexts, in order to infer more abstract human context representations, hereafter high-level contexts. The proposed method particularly extends beyond the state-of-the-art while uniting emotion information as a novel behavioral component together with activity and location data to derive more meaningful contextual information. This chapter contributes with an open ontology, the so-called Mining Minds Context Ontology, integrating all of the contextual definitions to link both low and high-level context domains. This work further contributes with the design, implementation and evaluation of a framework, namely the Mining Minds High-Level Context Architecture, which builds on the Mining Minds Context Ontology and reasoning techniques to enable the inference of high-level context from low-level context primitives in real time. The Mining Minds High-Level Context Architecture constitutes the core engine for the inference of high-level behavioral information in the Mining Minds platform [14,15]. Despite the proposed framework being originally devised to serve this platform, the Mining Minds High-Level Context Architecture has been defined in a way so it can be used independently for determining high-level context information from other similar sources of low-level context data.

The rest of the chapter is organized as follows. Section 8.2 presents the related work. Section 8.3 describes the Mining Minds Context Ontology and presents some examples of context to illustrate the different modeling principles and the inference logic. Section 8.4 presents the Mining Minds High-Level Context Architecture and describes the inference method for the identification of the user context based on the Mining Minds Context Ontology. Section 8.5 describes the implementation of the Mining Minds High-Level Context Architecture and the results of its evaluation. Finally, the main conclusions and future steps are presented in Section 8.6.

7.2 Related Work

A number of surveys have reviewed the use and foundations of ontologies for context modeling. For example, a survey on context-aware systems [16] describes the basic design principles of context-aware architectures and depicts the different context models. Special focus is placed in this survey on the analysis and comparison of several approaches using ontologies. Another review of context modeling and reasoning techniques [17] discusses the requirements for modeling different context information and introduces the concept of high-level context abstractions. This survey describes and compares several ontology-based models of context information. Finally, a more recent survey on context-aware computing for the Internet of Things [18] evaluates 50 projects including the majority of research and commercial solutions proposed in the field of context-aware computing from 2001 to 2011. An extensive evaluation of research prototypes, systems and approaches building on ontology-based modeling and reasoning solutions is presented in this survey.

Many ontologies have been specifically proposed to model and recognize user context. The most well-known context ontologies and ontology-based context frameworks are described in the following. One of the most prominent ontologies for modeling context in pervasive environments is SOUPA (Standard Ontologies for Ubiquitous and Pervasive Applications) [19]. The core of the SOUPA ontology defines generic vocabularies for several domains: person, agent, belief-desire-intention, action, policy, time, space and event. Similarly, CONON (CONtext ONtology) [20] is a noticeable ontology for smart home environments. The CONON upper ontology captures the general features of different context entities: person, activity, computational entity and location. Both SOUPA and CONON ontologies are generic and can be extended to describe the context in the application-specific domain. For example, the Context Broker Architecture (CoBrA) [21] adopts the SOUPA ontology, whereas the SOCAM (Service-oriented Context-Aware Middleware) [22] builds on the CONON ontology. The CoBrA ontology describes places, agents and events in an intelligent meeting room. The ontology proposed in SOCAM models persons, activities, locations and devices for smart home and vehicle environments. Apart from these early well-known solutions, more recent context ontologies and ontology-based context frameworks have been proposed. The Pervasive Information Visualization Ontology (PIVOn) [23] is composed of four ontologies for the description of intelligent environments: user, device, environment and service. The user model describes the static characteristics of the users, their agenda and their situation, including the user location, the current task and goals. The mIO! ontology [24] models' context-related knowledge for the adaptation of applications in mobile environments. This ontology defines concepts like information on location and time, user information and its current or planned activities, as well as devices located in his or her surroundings. The Context Aggregation and REasoning (CARE) middleware [25] performs ontological and statistical reasoning to support the context-aware adaptation of Internet services in a mobile computing environment. The ontology, which models the user context within the CARE middleware, describes the user activities (actions and movements), interests, contacts, calendar items and places. For example, the context business meeting is defined as including any activity performed in a conference room within a company building and having at least two actors, each of which is an employee. Thus, the ontology in the CARE middleware models context based on activities and locations.

Some other works focus on the detection of a specific category of context, mainly activities, sometimes utilizing in their definition other types of contexts, such as locations. ActivO is the ontology used in COSAR [26], an activity recognition system that supports hybrid statistical and ontological reasoning. The ActivO ontology models a set of activities and the context data required to recognize them (the person performing the activity, the location of the activity and the time extent in which the activity takes place). The authors of the ActivO ontology have also proposed a very similar approach, but using OWL2 for modeling and reasoning [13]. Furthermore, some activities involve the interaction with objects. Thus, contextual information about the interaction (time and location) can be used to model and infer the activities. An ontology-based approach is used to model activities for smart homes in [9]. The proposed ontology models activities based on a sequence of user-object interactions and the location of the objects. For instance, the activity *making tea* is composed of the primitives *get cup*, *get tea*, *pour water*, *get milk* and *get sugar*, which take place in the *kitchen.* Composite activities in smart homes are modeled and recognized in [27]. Ontological and temporal knowledge modeling formalisms are combined to describe composite activities, like, for example, *make tea and then wash hands.* The work in [28] describes an ontology-based technique for multilevel activity recognition. The proposed ontology models atomic gestures (actions that cannot be decomposed), manipulative gestures (execution of simple atomic gestures), simple activities (temporal sequences of manipulative gestures) and complex activities (concurrent execution of simple activities). One example of a complex activity could be *clean up*, which is composed of the simple activities *put in dishwasher* and *clean table*. Finally, [29] proposes a fuzzy ontology for the representation of activity and the reasoning on vague, incomplete and uncertain knowledge. The ontology core models three domains: users, environment including locations and actions, activities and behaviors. Actions are atomic events, activities can be a single action or a composed set of actions, and behaviors are a sequence of activities and/or actions. For example, the behavior *coffee break* includes the action *exit office*, the activity *make coffee* or *take coffee* and the action *enter office*.

7.3 Mining Minds Context Ontology

There are multiple reasons supporting the choice of ontologies for context modeling and inference: ontologies surpass non-semantic models for context modeling in terms of flexibility, extensibility, generality, expressiveness and decoupling of the knowledge from the code [30–32]. More specifically, ontologies provide implicit semantics that enable the derivation of new information from existing ones, a key characteristic to procure interoperability among different systems. Moreover, the hierarchical structure of ontologies, with subclasses inheriting the properties from their ascendant classes, facilitates its evolvability and maintenance. In fact, new concepts can be easily added to the ontology and related to the existing ones, with multiple existing methods for the automatic validation of conflicts and semantic inconsistencies. Several reasoners are also available and can be used with the defined ontologies. Ontological reasoning can be inherently applied on ontology-based models; thus, simplifying the inference task and avoiding the need for the explicit definition of rules. Finally, using ontologies to infer context is also beneficial from the implementation perspective since no changes are required in the architecture and/or implementation whenever the model is extended; thus, only requiring the adaptation of the ontology itself.

The Mining Minds Context Ontology models context for human behavior identification in order to enable the provision of personalized health and wellness services in Mining Minds [14,15]. Since Dey proposed the first widely-accepted definition of context [33], many different interpretations of context have arisen. In Mining Minds, human context is defined as any information characterizing the physical, mental and social situation of a person that enables the identification of their behavior. Furthermore, human context is here categorized into two different levels of abstraction: low-level context and high-level context. Low-level context is defined as primitive context, i.e., contexts that can be directly identified from user data and do not require any other type of context information to be derived. Specifically, activities, locations and emotions are here considered as the three categories of low-level context. Activities can be normally identified from the body movement; locations can be directly derived from the user position; and emotions can be obtained from the user sentiments or physiological responses. High-level context is the context that requires several contexts of a diverse nature in order to be identified. This means that a high-level context builds on a combination of low-level contexts. Therefore, high-level contexts are more complex and abstract contexts.

The Mining Minds Context Ontology aims at comprehensively modeling the most commonplace and widely used contexts for health and wellness services, such as the ones supported by Mining

Minds. These contexts are typically observed for both sedentary and active lifestyles. Specifically, the high-level contexts include daily contexts like *office work*, *sleeping*, *housework*, *commuting*, *amusement*, *gardening*, *exercising*, *having meal* and *inactivity*. The low-level contexts required to compose the description of the high-level context have to be automatically recognizable. Thus, very simple low-level contexts in the domains of activities, locations and emotions are defined. Low-level contexts describing activities include sedentary activities associated with unhealthy habits, mild activities of daily living and some vigorous ones related to sport and fitness practices. Namely, the modeled activities are *lying down*, *standing*, *sitting*, *riding escalator*, *riding elevator*, *walking*, *running*, *jumping*, *hiking*, *climbing stairs*, *descending stairs*, *cycling*, *stretching*, *dancing*, *sweeping* and *eating*. Similarly, the low-level contexts describing the locations comprise the places where the user spends their daily life, i.e., *home*, *office*, *yard*, *gym*, *mall*, *restaurant*, *outdoors* and *transport*. The low-level contexts describing the emotions embrace the most prominent moods or states of mind, which are *anger*, *happiness*, *neutral*, *sadness*, *fear*, *disgust*, *surprise* and *boredom*. The specific combinations of low-level contexts that compose each high-level context are derived from the experience of the Mining Minds behavioral scientists. Figure 7.1 graphically represents these definitions of high-level context, which are modeled in the Mining Minds Context Ontology. The considered contexts are intended to represent a wide spectrum of situations and actions in a person's life; however, it must be noted that this list can certainly be extended in view of potential future applications while considering other less recurrent contexts.

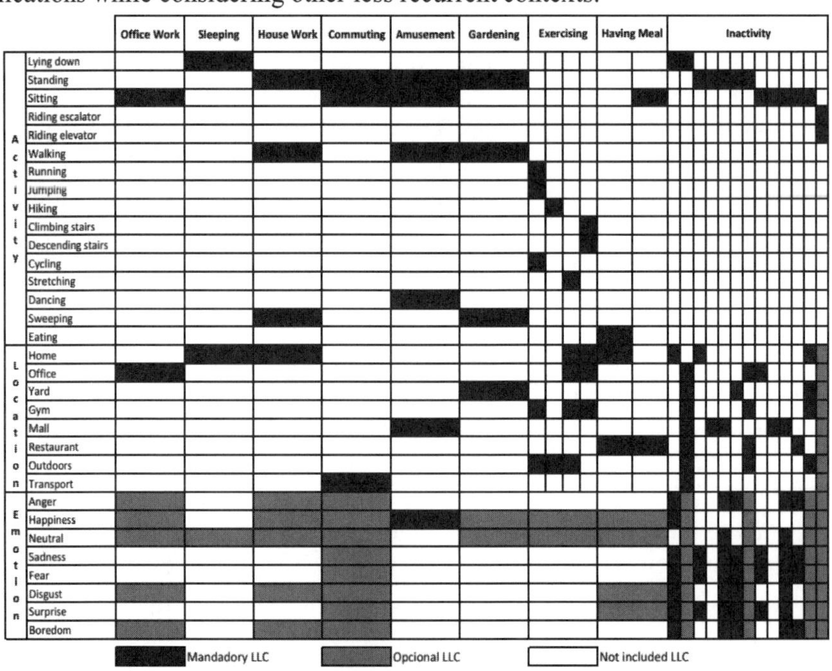

Figure 7.1 Graphical representation of the combination of low-level contexts that compose the high-level contexts modeled in the Mining Minds Context Ontology

In broad strokes, the main novelties of the Mining Minds Context Ontology are a more comprehensive description of context using a two-level model and the incorporation of emotion information to detect some high-level contexts. First, a layered approach is followed in which high-level contexts build on a combination of low-level contexts. Current approaches model context in different dimensions, for example the user is performing an activity, has a location and has a mood. However, in these models, there is no clear link between the different dimensions of context, neither are they used to derive other contexts. Thus, some valuable information for the identification of human behavior is lost when using a one-level model. Second, the emotions enable the definition of new high-level contexts, which can only be identified whenever a specific emotion takes place. This is the case of the high-level context *amusement*, which must imply that the person is happy and having fun. For this context, it is not enough to know that the person is *sitting* in the *mall*, but also that their emotion is *happiness* in order to infer that the context refers to *amusement*. Therefore, in some cases, the activity and the location might not be enough to detect the high-level context, and the emotion enables the identification of more diverse high-level contexts. The Mining Minds Context Ontology is an OWL 2 ontology [34] and is publicly available at [35].

7.3.1 Terminology for the Definition of Context

The Mining Minds Context Ontology defines the concept of user context. The context is associated with a given user and has a start and an end. While a context has necessarily a start referring to the time in which the context initiates, the finalization of the context is not strictly necessary. This is motivated by the fact that the context may be prolonged over time and be still valid at the present time. A given context can refer to either low or high-level context. Low-level contexts represent either activities, locations or emotions, which can further compose a high-level context. In some cases, only one category

of the low-level context is enough to determine the high-level context. This is the case of *inactivity*, where a sole sedentary activity like *sitting* defines this context. In some other cases, a specific category of low-level context is essential in order to identify the high-level context. For example, *amusement* can only be detected if the emotion is of type *happiness*. Accordingly, the ontology has been designed to support any combination of low-level contexts to define a specific high-level context. Given the seldom availability of emotion data, the ontology has been designed to procure the identification of some high-level contexts, even in the absence of emotion information. The modeling of this concept of context using the formal ontological description is presented in the following.

The main concept of the Mining Minds Context Ontology is the class *Context*, which represents the context of a user in an interval of time. Several necessary conditions are described for this class to model the concept of context (Figure 7.2). The existential and universal restrictions on the object property *isContextOf* ensure that any individual of the class *Context* is linked to an individual of the class *User* representing the user to which the context belongs. The existential and universal restrictions on the functional data property *hasStartTime* state that all of the individuals of the class *Context* must be related along this property to a unique *dateTime* data type of the W3C XML Schema Definition Language (XSD) [36] representing the instant of time in which the context starts. The universal restriction on the functional data property *hasEndTime* indicates that if there is a relationship of an individual of the class *Context* along the property *hasEndTime*, it has to be to a member of the XSD *dateTime* data type representing the end time of the interval in which the context is valid.

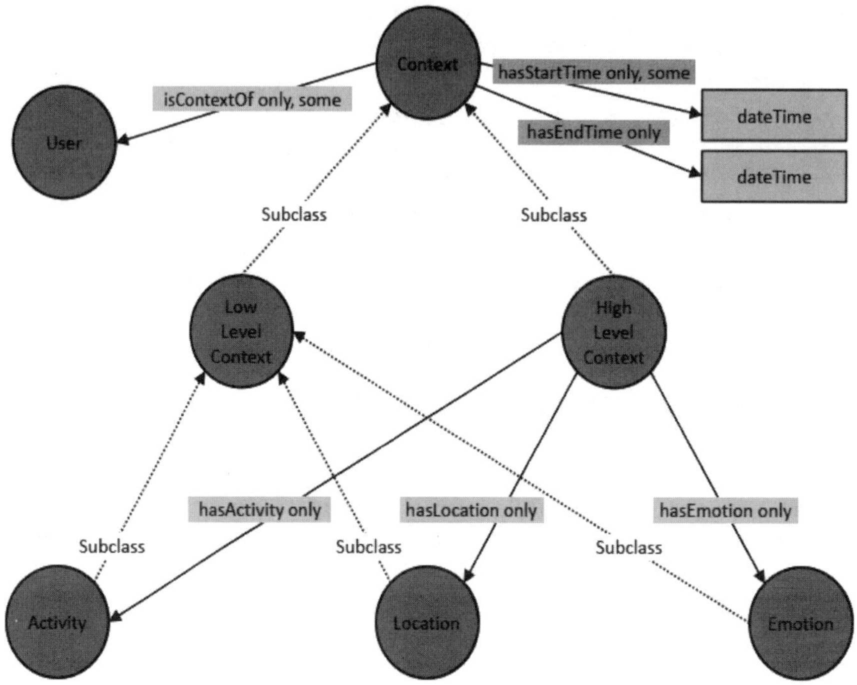

Figure 7.2 Mining minds context ontology: the class *Context*, its subclasses and the relations among them

The class *LowLevelContext* represents the basic categories of low-level contexts via the classes *Activity*, *Location* and *Emotion*. The class *HighLevelContext* models the concept of high-level context. The universal restrictions on the object properties *hasActivity*, *hasLocation* and *hasEmotion* model the relationship between the individuals of the class *HighLevelContext* and the individuals of the different subclasses of *LowLevelContext*, which compose the high-level context. The different types of high-level contexts are modeled via ten subclasses of the class *HighLevelContext*. Their equivalent anonymous classes as defined in Protégé [37] are presented in Figure 7.3.

```
HighLevelContext
  and (hasActivity some Sitting)
  and (hasLocation some Office)
  and (hasActivity only Sitting)
  and (hasEmotion only (Anger or Boredom or Disgust or Happiness or Neutral))
  and (hasLocation only Office)
```

(a)

```
HighLevelContext
  and (hasActivity some LyingDown)
  and (hasLocation some Home)
  and (hasActivity only LyingDown)
  and (hasEmotion only Neutral)
  and (hasLocation only Home)
```

(b)

```
HighLevelContext
  and (hasActivity some (Standing or Sweeping or Walking))
  and (hasLocation some Home)
  and (hasActivity only (Standing or Sweeping or Walking))
  and (hasEmotion only (Anger or Boredom or Disgust or Happiness or Neutral))
  and (hasLocation only Home)
```

(c)

```
HighLevelContext
  and (hasActivity some (Sitting or Standing))
  and (hasLocation some Transport)
  and (hasActivity only (Sitting or Standing))
  and (hasLocation only Transport)
```

(d)

```
HighLevelContext
  and (hasActivity some (Dancing or Sitting or Standing or Walking))
  and (hasEmotion some Happiness)
  and (hasLocation some Mall)
  and (hasActivity only (Dancing or Sitting or Standing or Walking))
  and (hasEmotion only Happiness)
  and (hasLocation only Mall)
```

(e)

```
HighLevelContext
  and (hasActivity some (Standing or Sweeping or Walking))
  and (hasLocation some Yard)
  and (hasActivity only (Standing or Sweeping or Walking))
  and (hasEmotion only (Happiness or Neutral))
  and (hasLocation only Yard)
```

(f)

```
HighLevelContext
  and
   (((hasActivity some Hiking)
     and (hasLocation some Outdoors)
     and (hasActivity only Hiking)
     and (hasLocation only Outdoors))
   or
   ((hasActivity some Stretching)
     and (hasLocation some (Gym or Home or Office or Outdoors))
     and (hasActivity only Stretching)
     and (hasLocation only (Gym or Home or Office or Outdoors)))
   or
   ((hasActivity some (ClimbingStairs or DescendingStairs))
     and (hasLocation some (Gym or Home or Office))
     and (hasActivity only (ClimbingStairs or DescendingStairs))
     and (hasLocation only (Gym or Home or Office)))
   or
   ((hasActivity some (Cycling or Jumping or Running))
     and (hasLocation some (Gym or Outdoors))
     and (hasActivity only (Cycling or Jumping or Running))
     and (hasLocation only (Gym or Outdoors))))
  and (hasEmotion only (Happiness or Neutral))
```

(g)

```
HighLevelContext
  and
   (((hasActivity some Eating)
     and (hasLocation some (Home or Restaurant))
     and (hasActivity only Eating)
     and (hasLocation only (Home or Restaurant)))
   or
   ((hasActivity some Sitting)
     and (hasLocation some Restaurant)
     and (hasActivity only Sitting)
     and (hasLocation only Restaurant)))
  and (hasEmotion only
        (Disgust or Happiness or Neutral or Surprise))
```

(h)

```
HighLevelContext
  and (not (Amusement or Commuting or Exercising or Gardening or HavingMeal
          or HouseWork or OfficeWork or Sleeping))
  and (hasActivity some
        (LyingDown or RidingElevator or RidingEscalator or Sitting or Standing))
  and (hasActivity only
        (LyingDown or RidingElevator or RidingEscalator or Sitting or Standing))
```

(i)

```
HighLevelContext
  and (not (hasActivity some Activity))
  and (not (hasEmotion some Emotion))
  and (not (hasLocation some Location))
```

(j)

Figure 7.3 Mining minds context ontology: definition of the ten subclasses of *HighLevelContext*. **(a)** *OfficeWork*; **(b)** *Sleeping*; **(c)** *HouseWork*; **(d)** *Commuting*; **(e)** *Amusement*; **(f)** *Gardening*; **(g)** *Exercising*; **(h)** *HavingMeal*; **(i)** *Inactivity*; **(j)** *NoHLC*.

In order to be a member of the defined class *OfficeWork* (Figure 7.3a), an individual of the class *HighLevelContext* must have a property of type *hasActivity* which relates to an individual of the class *Sitting*, and this property can only take as a value an individual of the class *Sitting*. Moreover, the individual of the class *HighLevelContext* must also have a property of type *hasLocation*, which relates to an individual of the class *Office* and only to an individual of the class *Office*. Finally, in case the individual of the class *HighLevelContext* has a property of type *hasEmotion*, this property must relate to an individual of the class *Anger*, the class *Boredom*, the class *Disgust*, the class *Happiness* or the class *Neutral*. This universal restriction does not specify that the relationship along the property *hasEmotion* must exist, but if it exists, it must link to the specified class members.

7.3.2 Instances of Context

An illustrative scenario is presented here to showcase the representation of instances of low-level contexts and high-level contexts in the Mining Minds Context Ontology (Figure 7.4). Let us imagine that it is 10 November 2015, and the user with identifier 9876 enters at 11:03:55 the office building of her or his working place. This event is detected by a location detector, a positioning system that interprets the coordinates of the user as the location of her or his office. Therefore, the low-level context of category location is identified as being of type *office* at 11:03:55. She or he starts talking on the phone, and a system capable of recognizing emotions detects from the tone of her or his voice that the user is bored. Thus, the low-level context of category emotion is identified as being of type *boredom* at 11:05:05. The phone call finalizes at 11:06:40, and then, no emotion is detected anymore. Meanwhile, at 11:05:25, the user sits down at her or his workplace. This event is detected by an activity recognizer that continuously measures her or his body motion. The low-level context of category activity is identified as being of type *sitting* at 11:05:25. It should be noted that every change in any of the low-level contexts may potentially lead to a new high-level context. For example, at 11:05:05, the combination of the activity *sitting*, the location *office* and the emotion *boredom* creates a high-level context that is classified as *office work*. At 11:06:40, when the emotion is no longer available, but the activity remains as *sitting* and the location as *office*, the high-level context for this user continues being identified as *office work*. Some combinations of low-level contexts do not constitute a known class of high-level context, based on the defined ontology. This is the case of the two high-level contexts at the beginning of this scenario. Namely, only location or the combination of the location *office* and the emotion *boredom* turn out to be not enough to identify a more abstract high-level context. Each context has associated a name, which serves as a unique identifier. These names are automatically created by the system whenever a new context is detected and are composed of the prefix *"llc_"* or *"hlc_"* and a sequential unique number. For the sake of simplicity, in this example, up to three digits are considered; however, large numbers are normally used by the system to procure unique identifiers. Furthermore, in order to make the example more understandable, for the low-level contexts, the membership of the instance to its name has been appended. For example, the context representing the activity *sitting* is named *llc_360_sitting*.

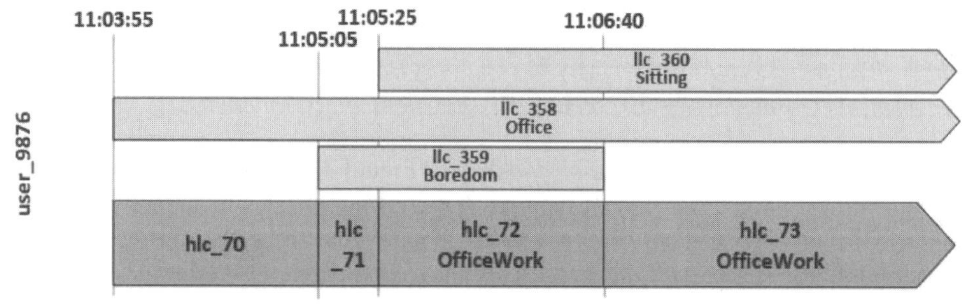

Figure 7.4 Exemplary scenario representing low-level contexts and high-level contexts

The terminology described in Section 8.3.1 is utilized at this point to generate the instances of context resulting from this scenario. The instances of low-level context are directly created from the information provided by the activity recognizer, location detector or emotion recognizer. In Section 8.3.2.1, the generation of the low-level contexts is presented. High-level contexts can be created from the information of the low-level contexts which are part of it and which triggered its occurrence. In Section 8.3.2.2, the generation of the high-level contexts is introduced. High-level contexts can also be classified, i.e., the membership of the high-level context or the class to which a high-level context belongs can be determined. In Section 8.3.2.3, the inference of the membership of the high-level contexts is described. Since the process of inferring the membership of a high-level context is also called classification, the high-level contexts for which their membership has been inferred are hereafter called *classified* high-level contexts. Conversely, the high-level contexts for which their membership has not been inferred are hereafter called *unclassified* high-level contexts. Finally, it is possible that the classification of an unclassified high-level context does not result in any inferred statement. In other words, the high-level context does not belong to any of the classes of high-level context defined in the terminology. In this case, the high-level context, which has been intended to be classified, but does not belong to any known class, is called *unidentified* high-level context.

7.3.2.1 Instances of Low-Level Context

The low-level contexts are modeled as members of the subclasses of *LowLevelContext*: *Activity*, *Location* and *Emotion*. Figure 7.5 shows how the low-level contexts for the presented scenario are described in Protégé. *llc_358_office*, *llc_359_boredom* and *llc_360_sitting* are members of the classes *Office*, *Boredom* and *Sitting*, respectively. These instances model the low-level context of the user with identifier 9876. Thus, *llc_358_office*, *llc_359_boredom* and *llc_360_sitting* are related along the property *isContextOf* to the individual *user_9876*, which is a member of the class *User*. All of the individuals representing the low-level contexts have a relationship along the property hasStartTime to a value in the form of XSD *dateTime*, which represents the start time of the interval in which the low-level context is valid. For example, for the individual *llc_359_boredom*, the property *hasStartTime* links to the value *"2015-11-10T11:05:05"^^dateTime*, which indicates that this context started at 11:05:05 on 10 November 2015. Moreover, for this very individual, the property *hasEndTime* relates to the value *"2015-11-10T11:06:40"^^dateTime*, which means that this low-level context only occurred until 11:06:40 on 10 November 2015. Therefore, the individual *llc_359_boredom* models a low-level context of the type *boredom* for the user with identifier 9876 and which was valid in the period of time comprising from 11:05:05 to 11:06:40 on 10 November 2015.

Figure 7.5 Representation of the instances of low-level context for the exemplary scenario by using the Mining Minds Context Ontology in Protégé. (**a**) *llc_358_office* is a member of the class *Office*; (**b**) *llc_359_boredom* is a member of the class *Boredom*; and (**c**) *llc_360_sitting* is a member of the class *Sitting*

7.3.2.2 Instances of Unclassified High-Level Context

The unclassified high-level contexts are modeled as members of the class *HighLevelContext* for which their properties and types are stated. Property assertions are used to define the low-level contexts that compose the unclassified high-level context. The properties *hasActivity*, *hasLocation* and *hasEmotion* relate to the individuals of the subclasses of the classes *Activity*, *Location* and *Emotion*, respectively. Reasoning in OWL is based on the Open World Assumption (OWA), which means that it cannot be assumed that something does not exist unless it is explicitly stated that it does not exist. Therefore, type assertions are used as closure axioms to indicate that an unclassified high-level context is composed of a unique and finite set of low-level contexts. Specifically, for each of the low-level context components of the high-level context, it is stated the type equivalent to the anonymous class represented by the universal restriction on the property *hasActivity*, *hasLocation* or *hasEmotion* where the value of the filler is the collection comprising only the low-level context. Furthermore, type assertions are also used as closure axioms to indicate that there is no low-level context of a specific category being part of the unclassified high-level context. In this case, for each of the categories of low-level context absent on the unclassified high-level context, it is stated that the type equivalent to the anonymous class is the negation class of the existential restriction on the property *hasActivity*, *hasLocation* or *hasEmotion* where the filler is the class representing the category of low-level context, *Activity*, *Location* or *Emotion*, respectively.

Figure 7.6 shows how the unclassified high-level contexts for the presented scenario are described in Protégé. *hlc_70*, *hlc_71*, *hlc_72* and *hlc_73* are members of the class *HighLevelContext*. Similarly, as for the low-level contexts, the individuals representing the unclassified high-level contexts have relationships along the properties *isContextOf*, *hasStartTime* and *hasEndTime*. For the individual *hlc_72*, the property *hasActivity* relates to the individual *llc_360_sitting*, the property *hasLocation* to the individual *llc_358_office* and the property *hasEmotion* to the individual *llc_359_boredom*. Due to the OWA, *hlc_72* has been asserted as the type *hasActivity only ({llc_360_sitting})*, the type *hasLocation only ({llc_358_office})* and the type *hasEmotion only ({llc_359_boredom})*. These statements indicate that the individual *hlc_72* only has a *hasActivity* relationship to *llc_360_sitting*, a *hasLocation* relationship to *llc_358_office* and a *hasEmotion* relationship to *llc_359_boredom*. The individual *hlc_73* is composed of the same activity and location as *hlc_72*; however, no emotion is part of this unclassified high-level context. Therefore, *hlc_73* has been asserted as the type *not (hasEmotion some Emotion)*. This statement indicates that the individual *hlc_73* does not have any property of type *hasEmotion* linking to an individual of the class *Emotion*, i.e., this unclassified high-level context does not contain any emotion.

7.3.2.3 Instances of Classified High-Level Context

The classified high-level contexts are obtained using a reasoner that infers the membership of the unclassified high-level contexts. Thus, a classified high-level context is an individual of the class *HighLevelContext*, which is determined to be also a member of one of the ten subclasses of *HighLevelContext*: *OfficeWork*, *Sleeping*, *HouseWork*, *Commuting*, *Amusement*, *Gardening*, *Exercising*, *HavingMeal*, *Inactivity* or *NoHLC*. Figure 7.7 shows the classified high-level contexts for the working scenario and that have been inferred in Protégé using the Pellet reasoner [38]. The individuals *hlc_70* and *hlc_71* are not presented in the figure since they do not belong to any known class of high-level context, i.e., they are unidentified high-level contexts.

(a)

(b)

(c)

(d)

Figure 7.6 Representation of the instances of unclassified high-level context for the exemplary scenario by using the Mining Minds Context Ontology in Protégé. (**a**) *hlc_70*; (**b**) *hlc_71*; (**c**) *hlc_72*; and (**d**) *hlc_73* are composed of some of the low-level contexts *llc_358_office* (member of the class *Office*), *llc_359_boredom* (member of the class *Boredom*) and *llc_360_sitting* (member of the class *Sitting*)

The individual hlc_72 is inferred by the reasoner to belong to the class OfficeWork (Figure 7.7a). Since this individual of the class HighLevelContext complies with the definition of the class OfficeWork, it is classified as being a member of this class. hlc_72 fulfills the existential and universal restrictions on the property hasActivity, which state that a member of the class OfficeWork must have some hasActivity relationship to an individual of the class Sitting and only to a member of this class. These restrictions are met since the property hasActivity only links the individual hlc_72 to the individual llc_360_sitting, which is a member of the class Sitting. Similarly, hlc_72 also fulfills the existential and universal restrictions on the property hasLocation. Furthermore, hlc_72 fulfills the universal restriction on the property hasEmotion, which states that in the case a member of the class OfficeWork has a hasEmotion relationship, it has to link to only an individual of the class Boredom. In fact, hlc_72 is only related along the property hasActivity to the individual llc_359_boredom, which is a member of the class Boredom.

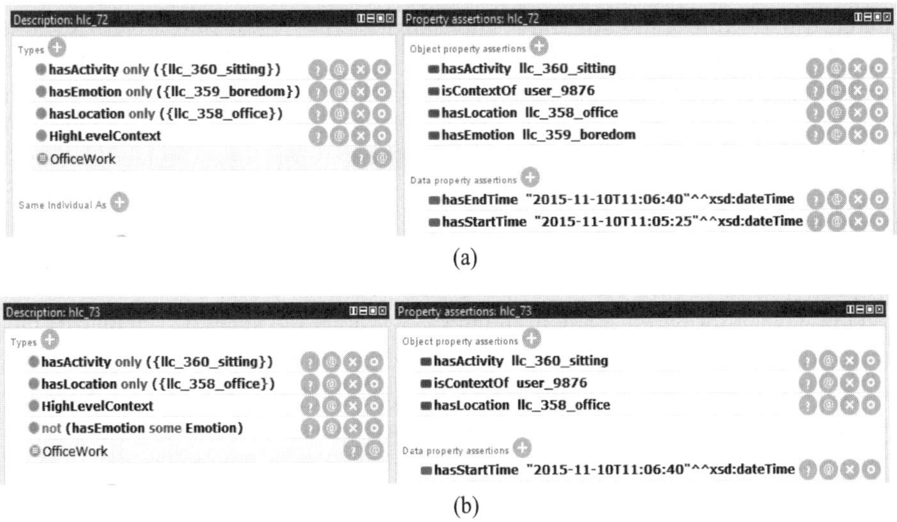

Figure 7.7 Representation of the instances of classified high-level context for the exemplary scenario by using the Mining Minds Context Ontology in Protégé. (**a**) *hlc_72*; and (**b**) *hlc_73*, which are both inferred to be members of the class *OfficeWork*, are composed of some of the low-level contexts *llc_358_office* (member of the class *Office*), *llc_359_boredom* (member of the class *Boredom*) and *llc_360_sitting* (member of the class *Sitting*)

The individual hlc_73 is also classified by the reasoner as being a member of the class OfficeWork (Figure 7.7b). Similar to the classified high-level context hlc_72, the individual hlc_73 also complies with the existential and universal restrictions on the properties hasActivity and hasLocation. However, the property hasEmotion about the individual hlc_73 is not asserted. The universal restriction on the property hasEmotion does not state that the relationship must exist. In fact, it may not exist at all and the restriction still be fulfilled, as is the case for hlc_73. Thus, the individual hlc_73 can be inferred as being a member of the class OfficeWork. The classification as members of the class OfficeWork of the two individuals of the class HighLevelContext, hlc_72 and hlc_73, one with a hasEmotion relationship and another without it, proves the flexibility of the Mining Minds Context Ontology, which enables the identification of high-level contexts, even if one of the pieces of low-level information is missing. This is considered to be helpful in real-life scenarios where emotion recognition systems are not always available or may generate detection events in a less regular basis than activity recognizers or location detectors.

7.4 Mining Minds High-Level Context Architecture

The Mining Minds High-Level Context Architecture (HLCA) is the system architecture devised for the identification of the user context in Mining Minds. Conversely to most similar approaches, the HLCA supports the instance-based identification of context. The HLCA infers abstract context representations based on categories, such as physical activities, emotional states and locations. These categories, which are derived from the wide-spectrum of multimodal data obtained from the user interaction with the real- and cyber-world, are intelligently combined and processed at the HLCA in order to determine and track the user context. The inferred user context can be utilized by the Mining Minds entities and any other third party to enable the provision of personalized health and wellness services. The HLCA relies on the Mining Minds Context Ontology (Section 8.3) and applies ontological inference to identify the user context. Furthermore, the ontology is utilized in the representation of the context shared between the components of the HLCA. The HLCA consists of four main components (Figure 7.8): High-Level Context Builder (Section 8.4.1), High-Level Context Reasoner (Section 8.4.2), High-Level Context Notifier (Section 8.4.3) and Context Manager (Section 8.4.4).

In a nutshell, the operation of the HLCA is as follows. The High-Level Context Builder receives unstructured low-level information, namely activities, emotions and locations, yielded by the Low-Level Context Architecture, an independent Mining Minds entity that is in charge of identifying the user low-level context using data driven-approaches. Then, based on the received low-level context information, the High-Level Context Builder generates the ontological concepts representing the user context. The Context Mapper is in charge of interpreting the received low-level information and transforming it into the corresponding ontological concepts. The Context Synchronizer seeks concurrent low-level contexts, identifying other user contexts valid at the same moment in time. The Context Instantiator generates a new instance of an unclassified high-level context linking to the low-level contexts that compose it. The High-Level Context Reasoner receives the unclassified high-level context for its verification and classification. The Context Verifier checks the semantic and syntactic consistency of the unclassified high-level context. The Context Classifier identifies the membership of the unclassified high-level by applying ontological inference. The High-Level Context Notifier makes available the newly-classified high-level context to any third-party application that registered for this type of information. During the context identification process, several components interact with the Context Manager, which provides the persistence of the Mining Minds Context Ontology, as well as supports the easy access to low-level context and high-level context information.

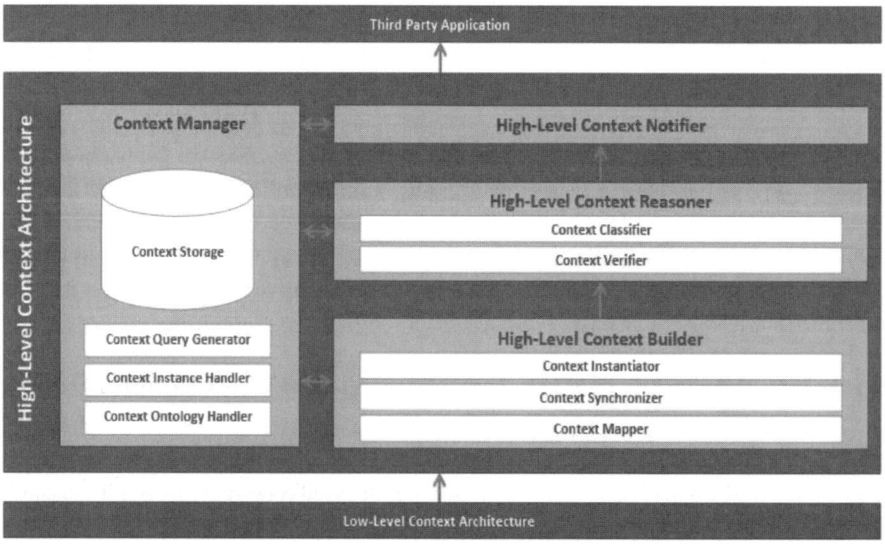

Figure 7.8 Mining Minds High-Level Context Architecture

In the following, the different components of the HLCA are described in detail. For the sake of understanding, an example from the scenario presented in Section 8.3.2 is here considered to illustrate the operation of each component of the HLCA. Namely, the inference of a new high-level context at 11:05:25 on 10 November 2015 is considered. At that moment, a new low-level context of the category *sitting* for the user with identifier 9876 is detected by the Low-Level Context Architecture. This event triggers the operation of the HLCA, which after the processing identifies a new high-level context of type *office work* and serves it to the registered third-party applications.

7.4.1 High-Level Context Builder

The High-Level Context Builder receives the low-level information, i.e., activities, emotions and locations, and generates the ontological concepts representing an unclassified high-level context associated with that information. The High-Level Context Builder has three subcomponents: the Context Mapper, the Context Synchronizer and the Context Instantiator.

7.4.1.1 Context Mapper

The Context Mapper interprets the received low-level information and transforms it into the corresponding ontological concepts. Specifically, it maps the labels plus metadata into ontological instances of low-level context. Whenever the Context Mapper gets a new label, it creates an instance of the subclass of the class *LowLevelContext* which represents the corresponding activity, location or emotion (as described in Section 8.3.2.1). The property *hasStartTime* is stated to relate this instance to the time in which the low-level context started and which is part of the received metadata. Furthermore, the user to which the context belongs is related along the property *isContextOf*. Once the low-level context instance has been created, it is stored in the Context Manager for its persistence (see Section 8.4.4.3) and it is notified to the Context Synchronizer.

For the working example, the Context Mapper receives at run-time the activity label "sitting" and several metadata, i.e., the identifier of the user "9876" and the time in which the context starts "2015-11-10T11:05:25". The Context Mapper generates an instance of low-level context and then asserts the properties about it. The instance *llc_360_sitting* of the class *Sitting* presented in Figure 7.5c is created. This instance has a *isContextOf* relationship to the individual *user_9876* and a *hasStartTime* relationship to the value *"2015-11-10T11:05:25"^^dateTime*.

7.4.1.2 Context Synchronizer

The Context Synchronizer searches for concurrent low-level contexts, whenever the Context Mapper has notified a newly detected low-level context instance. A change in the low-level context implies a new high-level context, comprising the new low-level context and the other low-level contexts still valid at the start of the new low-level context. The Context Synchronizer needs to determine the other low-level contexts of a given user which are valid the start time of the new low-level context instance created by the Context Mapper. Therefore, one of the most important roles of the Context Synchronizer is to align concurrent low-level contexts of the same user which might have been received in an unordered manner due to the diverse delays introduced by the different components of the Low-Level Context Architecture. In order to search for the concurrent low-level contexts, the Context Synchronizer requests information stored in the Context Manager and accesses it through the Context Instance Handler (see Section 8.4.4.3). Once the Context Synchronizer has determined the low-level contexts concurrent to the one that triggered the process, the Context Instantiator is invoked.

In the considered example, when the Context Synchronizer is notified by the Context Mapper about the identification of the new low-level context represented by the instance *llc_360_sitting*, it searches for concurrent low-level contexts by querying the information stored in the Context Manager. The instances *llc_358_office* and *llc_359_boredom*, presented in Figure 7.5a, b, are found to be concurrent to the low-level context *llc_360_sitting*. These two low-level contexts belong to the same user, i.e., user with identifier 9876, and they are still valid at 11:05:25 on 10 November 2015, when the new low-level context *sitting* starts.

7.4.1.3 Context Instantiator

The Context Instantiator creates a new instance of an unclassified high-level context linking to the constituent low-level contexts. Whenever the Context Synchronizer detects a set of low-level contexts which are concurrent to a newly detected one, the Context Instantiator creates a new instance of an unclassified high-level context containing these low-level contexts (as described in Section 8.3.2.2). Therefore, an instance of the class *HighLevelContext* is created and the different low-level contexts which compose the high-level context are related to it along the properties *hasActivity*, *hasLocation*, and *hasEmotion*. Moreover, the closure axioms are established via type assertions on these properties. In case there is a low-level context of a particular type, the Context Instantiator generates the axiom stating that the property can only link to that given low-level context. Otherwise, if no low-level context has been determined for one of the categories-activities, locations or emotions-, the Context Instantiator creates the axiom stating that there is no low-level context of that category. Furthermore, the Context Instantiator establishes a *hasStartTime* relationship to the time in which the high-level context change happened, i.e., the time in which the newly detected low-level context started and which triggered the creation of the new unclassified high-level context. Moreover, the user to which the high-level context belongs is related along the property *isContextOf*. The identifier of the user to which the high-level context belongs is the same than the one associated to the low-level contexts which compose the high-level context. Once the Context Instantiator has created the instance of an unclassified high-level context, this is served to the High-Level Context Reasoner (see Section 8.4.2) for its verification and classification.

For the working example, the Context Instantiator receives from the Context Synchronizer the newly detected low-level context represented by the instance *llc_360_sitting* and the concurrent low-level contexts *llc_358_office* and *llc_359_boredom*. The Context Instantiator creates the instance *hlc_72* of the class *HighLevelContext* (see Figure 7.6c) and links it to the low-level contexts which compose it. Therefore, the properties *hasActivity*, hasLocation, and *hasEmotion* relate, respectively, to the instances *llc_360_sitting*, *llc_358_office*, and *llc_359_boredom*. The closure axiom *hasActivity only ({llc_360_sitting})* indicates that the individual *hlc_72* only has a *hasActivity* relationship to the individual *llc_360_sitting*. Similarly, the other two closure axioms, *hasLocation only ({llc_358_office})* and *hasEmotion only ({llc_359_boredom})*, state the uniqueness of the relationships. The Context Instantiator also specifies that the instance *hlc_72* has a *isContextOf* relationship to the individual *user_9876* which is the owner of the different low-level contexts composing the high-level context. Finally, the Context Instantiator creates a relationship along the property *hasStartTime* to the moment in which the change in the low-level context triggered the identification of the new high-level context. The start time of the high-level context *hlc_72* is the start time of the low-level context *llc_360_sitting*. Thus, for the instance *hlc_72* the property *hasStartTime* links to the value *"2015-11-10T11:05:25"^^dateTime*.

7.4.2 High-Level Context Reasoner

The High-Level Context Reasoner performs a consistency check on the unclassified high-level context instance created by the High-Level Context Builder (see Section 8.4.1). In case the instance is valid, the High-Level Context Reasoner identifies the context type to which the high-level context belongs, i.e., it classifies the high-level context instance. In order to perform these tasks, the High-Level Context Reasoner applies ontological inference supported by the formal description of context in the Mining Minds Context Ontology (see Section 8.3.1). The High-Level Context Reasoner comprises two subcomponents: The Context Verifier and the Context Classifier.

7.4.2.1 Context Verifier

The Context Verifier checks the semantic and syntactic consistency of the unclassified high-level context provided by the High-Level Context Builder. Therefore, the instance of unclassified high-level context is validated and verified versus the Mining Minds Context Ontology, which s stored in the Context Manager and can be accessed through the Context Ontology Handler (see Section 8.4.4.2). During the consistency check, non-logical or malformed high-level contexts can be detected. For example, the high-level contexts which do not contain the necessary property *hasStartTime* or the ones composed from multiple different instances of low-level contexts of the same type. Once the Context Verifier has ensured that the unclassified high-level context is valid, this instance is provided to the Context Classifier for further processing.

In the described example, the Context Verifier receives from the Context Instantiator the newly created high-level context *hlc_72*. This instance is checked for its semantic and syntactic consistency, it is considered to be valid, and it is then served to the Context Classifier.

7.4.2.2 Context Classifier

The Context Classifier identifies the type of high-level context to which the unclassified high-level context belongs; thus, converting the unclassified instance into a classified high-level context. The classification of the unclassified high-level context instance into one of the defined high-level context classes is based on the inference functionalities provided by the Mining Minds Context Ontology. Specifically, one of the key features of this ontology is that it can be processed by a reasoner which can automatically perform the classification process. This means that the unclassified high-level context instance is compared versus the definitions of the different high-level context classes to determine whether it complies with the conditions that define the class. In case it complies, the instance is inferred to belong to that class. The classification process is triggered every time the Context Classifier receives a new valid instance of high-level context from the Context Verifier. After the membership of the unclassified high-level context instance has been determined, the Context Classifier adds to the unclassified high-level context instance the axiom stating that this instance belongs to a specific type of high-level context. Therefore, the instance of the class *HighLevelContext* which models the classified high-level context is related along the property *rdf:type* to the subclass of the class *HighLevelContext* representing the high-level context of which the instance is a member. It is possible that the unclassified high-level context does not belong to any of the known classes described in the Mining Minds Context Ontology. This means that no membership is inferred, and the unclassified high-level context is considered to belong to an unidentified type of high-level context. In this case, the classified high-level context has the same exact representation than the corresponding unclassified high-level context. Finally, the Context Classifier serves the classified high-level context to the High-Level Context Notifier (see Section 8.4.3).

For the working example, the Context Classifier receives from the Context Verifier the high-level context *hlc_72*. The Context Classifier applies the classification method to this unclassified high-level context in order to determine its membership. The individual *hlc_72* is inferred to belong to the class *OfficeWork* since it complies with the definition of the class *OfficeWork* (as described in Section 8.3.2.3). Therefore, the Context Classifier creates the axiom *hlc_72 rdf:type OfficeWork* which indicates that the individual *hlc_72* is a member of the class *OfficeWork*. The classified high-level context instance *hlc_72* is provided to the High-Level Context Notifier for its notification.

7.4.3 High-Level Context Notifier

The High-Level Context Notifier makes available to third party applications the newly identified high-level contexts. The High-Level Context Notifier receives from the High-Level Context Reasoner a classified high-level context instance and notifies the subscribed third parties about the detection of a new high-level context. This notification is only conducted if the new instance belongs to a high-level context type different than the previous one. Only changes in the high-level context type are notified, this means that differences in the low-level context composition which do not imply a change on the type of high-level context are not communicated to the third parties. Furthermore, the High-Level Context Notifier stores the new high-level context into the Context Manager for its persistence via the Context Instance Handler (see Section 8.4.4.3) and gets as an answer from this component the previous valid high-level context.

For the described example, the High-Level Context Notifier receives from the High-Level Context Reasoner the high-level context *hlc_72* which has been classified as *OfficeWork*. The High-Level Context Notifier contacts the Context Instance Handler for the persistence of the instance *hlc_72* into the Context Storage. Moreover, the High-Level Context Notifier receives from the Context Instance Handler the previous valid instance of high-level context *hlc_71*. The High-Level Context Notifier compares the membership of *hlc_72* to the membership of the previous valid high-level context *hlc_71*. The High-Level Context Notifier determines that there has been a change in the type of high-level context, the previous instance *hlc_71* was unidentified and the new instance *hlc_72* is *office work*. Therefore, the third parties are notified about the change in the high-level context modeled as the instance *hlc_72*.

7.4.4 Context Manager

The Context Manager persists the Mining Minds Context Ontology, including the terminology for the definition of context and the instances of context. Furthermore, this component eases the interactions with the persisted context information by facilitating the exchanges with the storage infrastructure. The Context Manager has four subcomponents: The Context Storage, the Context Ontology Handler, the Context Instance Handler and the Context Query Generator.

7.4.4.1 Context Storage

The Context Storage is a database which provides persistence for the storage of the Mining Minds Context Ontology, including both the context definition terminology and the context instances. Since the context is modeled via an ontology and the context instances are represented as ontological instances, this storage is devised to be a database of the type triple store. Moreover, the Context Storage also provides read and write functionalities for the Mining Minds Context Ontology. However, this storage cannot be directly accessed, and all the interactions are handled through the Context Ontology Handler and the Context Instance Handler.

7.4.4.2 Context Ontology Handler

The Context Ontology Handler provides the management functionalities to interact with the Mining Minds Context Ontology terminology stored in the Context Storage. This component enables loading the context ontology to the Context Storage at the system start time. The Context Ontology Handler also supports the retrieval of the context ontology which is stored in the Context Storage, so that the rest of components of the HLCA have access to the latest version of the ontological terminology. Furthermore, the Context Ontology Handler enables the extension at runtime of the context ontology. The extensibility is required to evolve the context ontology, therefore, including new types of low-level contexts and new definitions for the high-level contexts. Every time the ontology is updated, the rest of components of the HLCA making direct use of the context ontology are notified to obtain an updated version of the terminology.

7.4.4.3 Context Instance Handler

The Context Instance Handler deals with the retrieval and storage of context information in the Context Storage. The Context Instance Handler offers three different functionalities: storage of a newly mapped low-level context, retrieval of concurrent low-level contexts, and storage of a newly inferred high-level context while retrieving the previous valid high-level context. The Context Instance Handler poses to the Context Storage the SPARQL queries [39] created by the Context Query Generator in order to retrieve the persisted context information. Specifically, the logic of the Context Instance Handler for the storage of a newly inferred high-level context is as follows. The identification of a new high-level context implies that the previous context for the given user is not valid anymore. Therefore, the storage process includes the finalization of the previous valid high-level context instance. This operation entails to set the value of the end time of the previous valid high-level context stored in the Context Storage. In order to find the previous valid high-level context, the Context Instance Handler needs to pose the appropriate SPARQL queries to the Context Storage. The Context Query Generator is invoked to create the queries for the previous valid high-level context based on the newly inferred high-level context instance (see Section 8.4.4.4). Furthermore, it must be noted that an earlier new high-level context could be inferred after the classification of a posterior one. This scenario is not very common but could happen due to the different delays in the data-driven recognition process for the low-level contexts. If this situation occurs, the newly inferred high-level context is only valid until the start time of the posterior high-level context already stored in the Context Storage. Therefore, the storage process also includes the finalization of the newly inferred high-level context instance.

In the considered example, the High-Level Context Notifier interacts with the Context Instance Handler to persist the newly classified high-level context instance *hlc_72* and to retrieve the previously valid instance of high-level context. Therefore, the Context Instance Handler stores the instance *hlc_72* into the Context Storage. Moreover, the Context Instance Handler retrieves from the Context Storage the previously valid instance of high-level context. The previous high-level context is here an individual of the class *HighLevelContext* modeling the context of the user represented by the individual *user_9876* and which is valid at at 11:05:25 on 10 November 2015.

In order to retrieve the previous high-level context for the instance *hlc_72*, the Context Instance Handler invokes the Context Query Generator which creates the SPARQL queries presented in Listing 1. This query is posed to the Context Storage which returns as the matching result the high-level context *hlc_71*. Then, the Context Instance Handler finalizes the previous high-level context instance *hlc_71*. This means that the individual *hlc_71* is related along the property *hasEndTime* to the value *"2015-11-10T11:05:25"^^dateTime*, which is the value for the property *hasStartTime* of the newly identified high-level context *hlc_72*. In this exemplary scenario, it is assumed that there are no delays in the recognition of the low-level contexts and therefore, there are no high-level contexts posterior to *hlc_72* which had already been detected.

7.4.4.4 Context Query Generator

The Context Query Generator is the component which generates the SPARQL queries [39] required by the Context Instance Handler in order to find the matching context instances stored in the Context Storage. The SPARQL queries are automatically created based on some information derived from the context instance that the Context Instance Handler provides to the Context Query Generator. The Context Query Generator is capable of generating several different SPARQL queries depending on the expected outcome required for each specific use case scenario. The Context Query Generator creates SPARQL queries for the identification of a low-level context still valid at the start time of a newly recognized low-level context, which belongs to the very user and which is of the same context category. The Context Query Generator also creates SPARQL queries for the identification of the start time of the next posterior low-level context which belongs to the actual user and which is of the same context category. The Context Query Generator can also create SPARQL queries for the identification of low-level contexts of a given user which are concurrent at the start time of a newly recognized low-level context instance. In addition, the Context Query Generator creates SPARQL queries for the identification of a high-level context which is still valid at the start time of a new high-level context and which belongs to the same user. Finally, the Context Query Generator creates SPARQL queries for the identification of the start time of the next posterior high-level context belonging to the same user.

The logic for the creation of SPARQL queries for the identification of a high-level context which is still valid at the start time of a new high-level context and which belongs to the same user is the following. There are two cases in which the previous high-level context is still valid, either it does not have an end time or its end time is posterior to the start time of the new high-level context. In the first case, the SPARQL needs to match a high-level context for the same user which has a start time previous to the start time of the new high-level context but does not have an end time. In the second case, the SPARQL needs to match a high-level context for the same user which has a start time previous to the start time of the new high-level context and an end time posterior to the start of the new high-level context.

The specific SPARQL query to request the previous high-level context for the instance *hlc_72* is presented in Listing 8.1. In the considered example, the previous high-level context for *hlc_72* is an individual of the class *HighLevelContext* which belongs to the user represented by the individual *user_9876* and which is valid at 11:05:25 on 10 November 2015. Therefore, the matching individual has to be a member of the class *HighLevelContext*, must have a *isContextOf* relationship to the individual *user_9876*, must have a *hasStartTime* relationship to a value less than or equal to *"2015-11-10T11:05:25"^^dateTime*, and must not have any *hasEndTime* relationship.

```
SELECT ?hlc
WHERE
 { ?hlc rdf:type HighLevelContext ;
     isContextOf user_9876 ;
     hasStartTime ?starttime .
  FILTER NOT EXISTS ?hlc hasEndTime ?endtime .
  FILTER ( ?starttime <= "2015-11-10T11:05:25"^^xsd:dateTime )
 }
```

Listing 7.1 SPARQL query to request the previous high-level context for the instance *hlc_72*.

7.5 Evaluation

This section analyzes both the robustness and performance of the Mining Minds High-Level Context Ontology and Architecture. Section 8.5.1 explores the tolerance offered by the Mining Minds Context Ontology for the inference of high-level contexts under the presence of low-level context errors. Section 8.5.2 studies the performance of the Mining Minds High-Level Context Architecture with respect to processing time and management of context instances.

7.5.1 Robustness of the Mining Minds Context Ontology

The proposed Mining Minds Context Ontology has been evaluated to determine how robust the identification of high-level contexts can be in the event of having erroneously detected low-level contexts. In other words, this evaluation aims at measuring the level of resilience of the high-level context level against errors originated at the low-level context level. Pellet (v2.3.2) [38], an open source OWL DL reasoner for Java has been used in the evaluation test program. First, a set of 1800 instances representing all the possible combinations of low-level contexts, i.e., activities, locations and emotions, have been generated. Then, the instances have been posed to the reasoner and the corresponding high-level contexts have been inferred. The resulting array of high-level contexts represents the ground-truth for this evaluation. Subsequently, various scenarios with increasing levels of error in the low-level contexts have been defined. Namely, 5, 10, 20 and 50 per cent of errors have been respectively introduced in the 1800 instances as to emulate potentially erroneous low-level contexts. For example, in the case of having a 10% of affected instances a total of 180 randomly selected instances are deliberately modified. The error has been introduced by replacing the supposedly affected low-level context with a new value randomly selected from the remaining contexts in the affected category (activity, location or emotion). Thus, for example, if the original instance of high-level context is composed of the contexts *sitting*, *office* and *boredom*, and the affected context is the activity, the newly generated instance could contain the contexts *running*, *office* and *boredom*. Moreover, in order to evaluate the prominence of each specific context category or combination thereof, the analysis has been formulated for all the combinations of low-level categories, i.e., introducing errors in solely the activity, location, emotion, or combination of activity and location, activity and emotion, location and emotion, and all activity, location and emotion. The instances resulting from all these scenarios have been posed to the reasoner and the resulting high-level contexts have been compared against the ground truth to determine the accuracy of the model. Each of the experiments has been repeated one hundred times in order to ensure the statistical robustness. The average and standard deviation accuracy is presented in Table 7.1 for each corresponding study.

Table 7.1 Mean and standard deviation of the accuracy of the high-level context recognition under different levels of errors in the detected low-level contexts

	5%	10%	20%	50%
Activity	97.60 ±0.05	95.13 ±0.05	90.39 ±0.04	75.32 ±0.20
Location	99.45 ±0.02	98.82 ±0.05	97.61 ±0.15	93.93 ±0.02
Emotion	99.63 ±0.02	99.18 ±0.05	98.32 ±0.05	96.04 ±0.07
Act & Loc	97.08 ±0.10	94.27 ±0.16	88.48 ±0.11	72.63 ±0.10
Act & Emo	97.16 ±0.12	94.22 ±0.06	89.60 ±0.10	73.53 ±0.30
Loc & Emo	99.00 ±0.05	98.02 ±0.09	96.24 ±0.05	91.25 ±0.09
Act & Loc & Emo	96.56 ±0.06	93.10 ±0.30	87.52 ±0.11	71.60 ±0.13

From an overall analysis of the obtained results it can be concluded that the impact of the error introduced in the low-level context is generally lower at the high-level context. For example, in the case of introducing a 5% error, the accuracy drops approximately no more than 0.4% at best and 3.5% in the worst-case scenario. Similarly, for the 10%, 20% and 50% error cases the minimum and maximum accuracy drops are below the corresponding level of error. Experiencing a lesser impact is generally due to the fact that not all the misrecognitions at the low-level context lead to an inference error at the high-level context. For example, if the activity *running* is recognized instead as *climbing stairs*, and provided the rest of low-level contexts to be *gym* for the location and *neutral* for the emotion, the inferred high-level context remains to be *exercising*. Similar examples in which the error in the low-level context is not propagated to the high-level context can be found for the case of erroneous locations and emotions. It can also be observed that the activity is the most prevalent category in terms of error impact, which is certainly as a consequence of the importance given to the activity context in the definition of high-level contexts. Conversely, the location and especially the emotion tend to show a lower effect on the high-level context. In fact, the definition of some high-level contexts allows for a good level of resilience against errors in the locations and the emotions. This is the case of the high-level context *inactivity*, which is determined from a sole sedentary activity, like *lying down*, and nearly any location and emotional state. Therefore, even if the location is erroneously detected, the inferred high-level context would result in *inactivity*. The only exception to this case would happen if the location is misrecognized as *home*, since *lying down* at *home* and with a *neutral* emotional state is identified as the high-level context *sleeping*. Moreover, errors simultaneously present in various low-level contexts generally increase the chance of misidentification of the actual high-level context. Therefore, the combinations of errors in several low-level categories report a lower accuracy in the high-level context recognition than in the case of having only errors in a single category. As it was expected, the highest impact is observed when all three low-level contexts are subject to error. Either way, the error in the recognition of the high-level context remains below the level of error introduced in the considered low-level contexts. Finally, it must be noted that owing to the descriptive logic characteristic of ontologies, and conversely to probabilistic classification models, combinations of correct low-level contexts will always lead to a correctly inferred high-level context.

7.5.2 Performance of the Mining Minds High-Level Context Architecture

The HLCA has been implemented and benchmarked in order to assess its performance. The HLCA has been implemented in Java using available open source libraries. All the components of the HLCA build on Apache Jena (v2.11.2) [40], a semantic web framework which includes some APIs for handling RDF [41], OWL [34], and SPARQL [39]. In the implementation of the High-Level Context Reasoner, an off-the-shelf open source reasoner, namely Pellet (v2.3.2) [38], has been utilized in combination with Jena to enable the ontological inference functionalities. Furthermore, in the Context Manager, the Jena Triple Store (TDB) has been used as the Context Storage for the persistence of the Mining Minds Context Ontology. The communication between the Low-Level Context Architecture and the HLCA has been implemented by means of RESTful web services [42] and establishing service contracts among these two architectures. The same mechanism applies to the communication of the HLCA with the third-party applications registered to get access to the newly identified high-level contexts.

For the evaluation, this implementation of the HLCA has been executed on a laptop operating Windows 10 with a 1.80 GHz Intel Core i7 CPU, 8GB RAM, and a HDD with 5400-RPM spindle speed, I/O data-transfer rate up to 6 Gb/s and 16 MB buffer. Using a test Java application, the Low-Level Context Architecture has been emulated. The evaluation has consisted in the generation of 250,000 random low-level contexts belonging to 100 different users and which represented their context information for a time span of 16 days. First the category of the low-level context (activity, location or emotion) has been randomly selected and then one of the types for that category has also been randomly chosen. After that, the metadata associated to the low-level context label has been generated. The low-level context has been randomly assigned to one of the 100 users. The start time of each low-level context has also been randomly selected between 1 and 10 s after the start time of the previous low-level context. The generated low-level contexts, including the labels and the metadata, have been input one at a time to the HLCA for their mapping, synchronization, instantiation, verification, classification and notification. It is important to notice that the low-level contexts are served to the HLCA sequentially and at their simulated occurrence time. Thus, the HLCA works at real-time and processes each single instance on-the-fly right after receiving it. Concurrency is procured through user-based multithreading, thus supporting simultaneous processing of low-level contexts from different users taking place at the same time. Some resources such as the Context Storage are shared among threads (users). During the evaluation the time required for the context identification has been calculated and the volume of information generated and stored on the Context Storage has further been determined.

Figure 7.9 shows the time invested by each of the HLCA components and the system as a whole in the context identification process. The number of instances indicates the number of high-level contexts which have already been processed by the HLCA when the recognition process is triggered due to a change in the low-level context. Even if the context recognition process is performed instance-wise, the number of previously processed instances is important because of the volume of information generated by the system during the recognition process and persisted in the Context Storage. The processing times are further averaged to have an overall figure summarizing the time taken by each component of the HLCA. Table 7.2 presents the mean and standard deviation of these times as well as the percentage of these times devoted to the interaction of the component with the Context Manager. This interaction is particularly relevant because the Context Manager hosts the Context Storage, the shared resource which persists and loads the context information.

Table 7.2 Mean and standard deviation of the processing time invested by each of the HLCA components in the context identification, as well as the percentage of these times devoted to the interaction with the Context Manager

	Context Mapper	Context Synchronizer	Context Instantiator	Context Verifier	Context Classifier	Context Notifier
Mean (s)	0.986	2.188	0.001	0.032	0.046	1.012
Standard Deviation (s)	0.348	1.670	0.000	0.014	0.019	0.268
Context Manager (%)	99.53	99.97	0.00	0.00	0.00	99.99

One can observe the differences of scale in the processing times for each of the components of the HLCA and the disparate tendencies of these times when the number of recognized context instances increases. The processes in which the HLCA component does not have any interaction with the Context Storage take much less time than the ones involving it. Furthermore, in the cases where the Context Storage is not involved, the processing time does not increase with the number of identified context instances. The Context Classifier and the Context Verifier take only some milliseconds to verify and classify the high-level context instance. This time is quite small due to the architectural design principle for which each single instance of high-level context is reasoned separately on-the fly at run-time. The Context Instantiator does not access either the Context Storage, since the required interactions to find the concurrent low-level contexts are performed by the Context Synchronizer. Therefore, the Context Instantiator takes only one millisecond to create a new instance of high-level context and this time does not increase with the number of instances because of the independence of the process from any other high-level context.

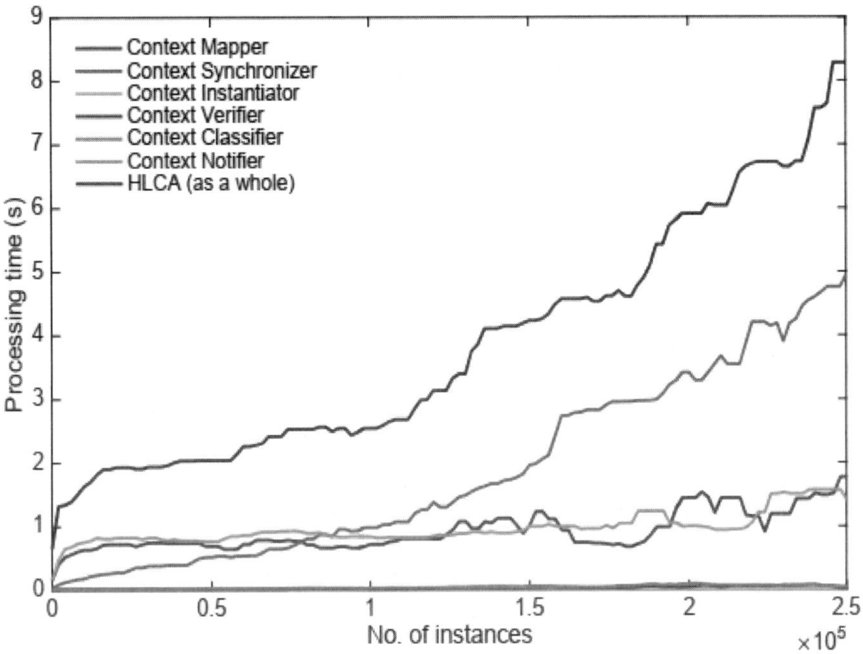

Figure 7.9 Processing time invested by each of the HLCA components in the context identification. The number of instances indicates the amount of previously processed high-level contexts when the recognition process is triggered

In case the components of the HLCA invoke the Context Storage, the processing times rise and the interactions with the Context Storage tend to represent most of the computational time, specifically more than 99%. This means that the actual component is relatively quick to perform its job but the context read and write processes which involve the Context Manager delay the complete process. The processing time for the Context Mapper and the High-Level Context Notifier follows a similar pattern. These processing times increase with the number of instances, at the beginning and with very few instances the times rocket, but then they stabilize and reach values around one second. The similarity in the evolution of the processing times for these two components is normal because their interactions with the Context Manager are of the same type. In the first case, the Context Mapper stores the new low-level context instance, retrieves the previous low-level context and after updating it, stores it again into the Context Manager. In the second case, the High-Level Context Notifier stores the new high-level context instance, retrieves the previous high-level context, compares them and after updating the previous instance, stores it again into the Context Manager. Therefore, the evolution of the processing time for operations that involve read and write to the Context Manager can be observed in the times for the Context Mapper and the High-Level Context Notifier. The processing performed by the Context Synchronizer in order to request concurrent low-level context instances is the most time demanding process of the HLCA. In this case, most of the time is devoted to the execution of the SPARQL queries and the retrieval of the matching solutions from the Context Manager. The processing time for the Context Synchronizer increases almost lineally with the number of instances. In fact, for few instances this time is below the processing time for the Context Mapper and High-Level Context Notifier, but then it becomes much higher. Therefore, the Context Synchronizer is the bottle neck of the HLCA, with a clear impact on the evolution of the time required for the context identification.

The relevance of the time invested by the HCLA to recognize a high-level context fairly depends on the application domain. Thus, for example, if an alert has to be sent right away or a prompt action be taken based on the detected high-level context, then this time might be arguably long. However, if the identified information is rather used for analyzing the trajectories of behavior over time, then this time turns to be hardly relevant. Under these considerations, the processing time for the recognition of high-level contexts could be the main limitation of the actual implementation of the HLCA and should be improved in future work. A potential solution could consist in introducing a cache system into the High-Level Context Builder to save temporarily only the latest instances of low-level context and periodically persist them into the Context Manager. With such a solution the Context Synchronizer would not need to interact with the Context Manager and could pose the SPARQL queries directly to the cache; thus, retrieving the low-level context instances from a much smaller store. The Context Mapper, also part of the High-Level Context Builder, could share this very cache with the Context Synchronizer and increase its performance as well. If the cache would prove to be a good solution, such a system could also be introduced in the Context Notifier. This component has a similar behavior than the Context Mapper and its processing time could be reduced as well. Alternate solutions for accelerating the processing time for the identification of high-level contexts could include parallelizing tasks, defining different levels of cache-memory or simply scaling the infrastructure through cloud-based services.

Finally, Figure 7.10 depicts the size of the Context Storage in the Context Manager increasing lineally with the number of stored high-level context instances. The initialization of the Context Storage, i.e., storing the terminology defining the Mining Minds Context Ontology, requires only 408.5 KB on disc. The storage of each new high-level context instance, which has associated the storage of the low-level context instance which triggered its creation, increases the size of the Context Storage in 17 KB, in average. Thus, for the previous simulation of 250,000 changes in the context, which leads to a total of 500,000 context instances on disc (i.e., 250,000 high-level context instances and 250,000 low-level contexts instances), the Context Storage reached a size of 4.06 GB. Despite the Context Manager proves to fairly handle this volume of data, the increasing time observed for I/O operations in long-term scenarios with several users demands for some of the aforementioned solutions.

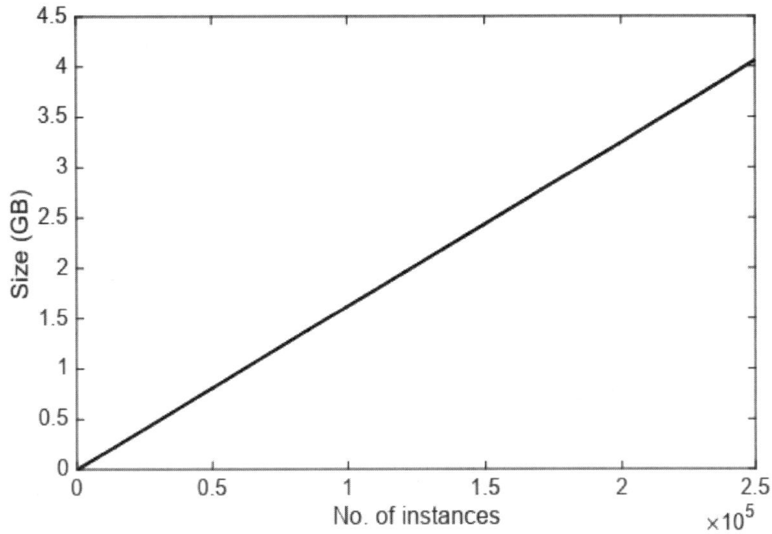

Figure 7.10 Size of the Context Storage depending on the number of persisted instances of high-level context. It must be noted that the storage of each high-level context instance has associated the storage of the low-level context instance which triggered its creation. Thus, for example, 250,000 instances in the X-axis represent 250,000 high-level contexts plus 250,000 low-level contexts stored on disc

7.6 Summary

This work has presented an ontology-based method for deriving high-level context information out of the combination of cross-domain low-level context primitives, namely activities, locations and emotions. The modeling of the low and high-level contexts is defined through the so-called Mining Minds Context Ontology, while the processing and inference of contexts is performed by the Mining Minds High-Level Context Architecture, both contributions of this work. The Mining Minds Context Ontology has been designed to support any combination of low-level contexts to define a specific high-level context. The unprecedented incorporation of emotions in the context definition enables the representation of new high-level contexts that can only be identified whenever a specific emotion takes place. The Mining Minds Context Ontology has also been designed to procure the identification of some high-level contexts even in the absence of emotion information. The Mining Minds High-Level Context Architecture builds on the Mining Minds Context Ontology and reasoning techniques to enable the inference of high-level context from low-level context primitives in real time. The evaluation of the implemented architecture proves the reasonably good robustness properties of the Mining Minds Context Ontology against potentially erroneous low-level contexts. In fact, the results have showed that the impact of the error introduced in the low-level context is always lower at the high-level and that the activity is the most prevalent category in terms of error impact, while the location and especially the emotion tend to show a lesser effect on the high-level context. The current prototype implementation of the Mining Minds High-Level Context Architecture has been proven to perform well with respect to processing time and management of context instances. However, in order to ensure the scalability of the Mining Minds High-Level Context Architecture, the synchronization and database transactions management needs to be improved. Future work includes modifications in the database management to accelerate the inference time, the evaluation of this architecture with real users and the evolution of the Mining Minds Context Ontology in order to include more types of low-level context and new identifiable high-level contexts.

Source Code

Source code can be downloaded from the following location:

https://github.com/ubiquitous-computing-lab/Mining-Minds/tree/master/information-curation-layer/high-level-context-awareness

The contents of this chapter have been previously published in the following article:

Claudia Villalonga, Muhammad Asif Razzaq, Wajahat Ali Khan, Hector Pomares, Ignacio Rojas, Sungyoung Lee, and Oresti Banos, "Ontology-Based High-Level Context Inference for Human Behavior Identification", Sensors (SCIE, IF: 2.033), Vol.16, Issue 10, doi:10.3390/s16101617, 2016

References

[1] Ke, S.R.; Thuc, H.L.U.; Lee, Y.J.; Hwang, J.N.; Yoo, J.H.; Choi, K.H. A review on video-based human activity recognition. Computers 2013, 2, 88–131.

[2] Lara, O.D.; Labrador, M.A. A survey on human activity recognition using wearable sensors. IEEE Commun. Surv. Tutor. 2013, 15, 1192–1209.

[3] Fallah, N.; Apostolopoulos, I.; Bekris, K.; Folmer, E. Indoor human navigation systems: A survey. Interact. Comput. 2013, 25, 21–33.

[4] Fasel, B.; Luettin, J. Automatic facial expression analysis: A survey. Pattern Recognit. 2003, 36, 259–275.

[5] Koolagudi, S.G.; Rao, K.S. Emotion recognition from speech: A review. Int. J. Speech Technol. 2012, 15, 99–117.

[6] Liao, L.; Fox, D.; Kautz, H. Extracting places and activities from gps traces using hierarchical conditional random fields. Int. J. Robot. Res. 2007, 26, 119–134.

[7] Banos, O.; Damas, M.; Pomares, H.; Prieto, A.; Rojas, I. Daily living activity recognition based on statistical feature quality group selection. Expert Syst. Appl. 2012, 39, 8013–8021.

[8] Pan, Y.; Shen, P.; Shen, L. Speech emotion recognition using support vector machine. Int. J. Smart Home 2012, 6, 101–108.

[9] Liming, C.; Nugent, C.; Okeyo, G. An Ontology-Based Hybrid Approach to Activity Modeling for Smart Homes. IEEE T. Hum. Mach. Syst. 2014, 44, 92–105.

[10] Khanna, P.; Sasikumar, M. Rule Based System for Recognizing Emotions Using Multimodal Approach. Int. J. Adv. Comput. Sci. Appl. 2013, 4, 7.

[11] Bae, I.H. An ontology-based approach to ADL recognition in smart homes. Future Gener. Comput. Syst. 2014, 33, 32–41.

[12] BakhshandehAbkenar, A.; Loke, S.W. MyActivity: Cloud-Hosted Continuous Activity Recognition Using Ontology-Based Stream Reasoning. In Proceedings of the IEEE International Conference on Mobile Cloud Computing, Services, and Engineering, Oxford, UK, 8–11 April 2014.

[13] Riboni, D.; Bettini, C. OWL 2 Modeling and Reasoning with Complex Human Activities. Pervasive Mob. Comput. 2011, 7, 379–395.
[14] Banos, O.; Bilal-Amin, M.; Ali-Khan, W.; Afzel, M.; Ali, T.; Kang, B.H.; Lee, S. The Mining Minds Platform: A Novel Person-Centered Digital Health and Wellness Framework. In Proceedings of the 9th International Conference on Pervasive Computing Technologies for Healthcare, Istanbul, Turkey, 20–23 May 2015.
[15] Banos, O.; Bilal Amin, M.; Ali Khan, W.; Afzal, M.; Hussain, M.; Kang, B.H.; Lee, S. The Mining Minds digital health and wellness framework. BioMed. Eng. OnLine 2016, 15, 165–186.
[16] Baldauf, M.; Dustdar, S.; Rosenberg, F. A survey on context-aware systems. Int. J. Ad Hoc Ubiquitous Comput. 2007, 2, 263–277.
[17] Bettini, C.; Brdiczka, O.; Henricksen, K.; Indulska, J.; Nicklas, D.; Ranganathan, A.; Riboni, D. A survey of context modelling and reasoning techniques. Pervasive Mob. Comput. 2010, 6, 161–180.
[18] Perera, C.; Zaslavsky, A.; Christen, P.; Georgakopoulos, D. Context Aware Computing for The Internet of Things: A Survey. IEEE Commun. Surv. Tutor. 2014, 16, 414–454.
[19] Chen, H.; Finin, T.; Joshi, A. The SOUPA Ontology for Pervasive Computing. In Ontologies for Agents: Theory and Experiences; Tamma, V., Cranefield, S., Finin, T., Willmott, S., Eds.; BirkHauser: Basel, Switzerland, 2005; pp. 233–258.
[20] Wang, X.H.; Zhang, D.Q.; Gu, T.; Pung, H.K. Ontology based context modeling and reasoning using OWL. In Proceedings of the Second IEEE Annual Conference on Pervasive Computing and Communications Workshops, Orlando, FL, USA, 14–17 March 2004; pp. 18–22.
[21] Chen, H.; Finin, T.; Joshi, A. An ontology for context-aware pervasive computing environments. Knowl. Eng. Rev. 2003, 18, 197–207.
[22] Gu, T.; Pung, H.K.; Zhang, D.Q. A Middleware for Building Context-Aware Mobile Services. In Proceedings of IEEE Vehicular Technology Conference (VTC), Milan, Italy, 17–19 May 2004.
[23] Hervás, R.; Bravo, J.; Fontecha, J. A Context Model based on Ontological Languages: A Proposal for Information Visualization. J. UCS 2010, 16, 1539–1555.
[24] Poveda Villalon, M.; Suárez-Figueroa, M.C.; García-Castro, R.; Gómez-Pérez, A. A context ontology for mobile environments. In Proceedings of the Workshop on Context, Information and Ontologies (CEUR-WS), Lisbon, Portugal, 11–15 October 2010.
[25] Agostini, A.; Bettini, C.; Riboni, D. Hybrid Reasoning in the CARE Middleware for Context Awareness. Int. J. Web Eng. Technol. 2009, 5, 3–23.
[26] Riboni, D.; Bettini, C. COSAR: Hybrid Reasoning for Context-aware Activity Recognition. Pers. Ubiquitous Comput. 2011, 15, 271–289.
[27] Okeyo, G.; Chen, L.; Wang, H.; Sterritt, R. Dynamic sensor data segmentation for real-time knowledge-driven activity recognition. Pervasive Mobile Comput. 2014, 10, 155–172.
[28] Helaoui, R.; Riboni, D.; Stuckenschmidt, H. A Probabilistic Ontological Framework for the Recognition of Multilevel Human Activities. In Proceedings of the 2013 ACM International Joint Conference on Pervasive and Ubiquitous Computing (UbiComp '13), Zurich, Switzerland, 8–12 September 2013; ACM: New York, NY, USA, 2013; pp. 345–354.

[29] Rodriguez, N.D.; Cuellar, M.P.; Lilius, J.; Calvo-Flores, M.D. A fuzzy ontology for semantic modelling and recognition of human behaviour. Knowl. Based Syst. 2014, 66, 46–60.
[30] Korpipaa, P.; Mantyjarvi, J.; Kela, J.; Keranen, H.; Malm, E.J. Managing context information in mobile devices. IEEE Pervasive Comput. 2003, 2, 42–51.
[31] Strang, T.; Linnhoff-Popien, C. A context modeling survey. In Proceedings of the Sixth International Conference on Ubiquitous Computing, Workshop on Advanced Context Modelling, Reasoning and Management, Nottingham, UK, 7–10 September 2004.
[32] Chen, H.; Finin, T.; Joshi, A.; Kagal, L.; Perich, F.; Chakraborty, D. Intelligent agents meet the semantic Web in smart spaces. IEEE Int. Comput. 2004, 8, 69–79.
[33] Dey, A.K. Understanding and Using Context. Pers. Ubiquitous Comput. 2001, 5, 4–7.
[34] W3C OWL Working Group. OWL 2 Web Ontology Language: Document Overview (Second Edition); W3C Recommendation, 11 December 2012. Available online: http://www.w3.org/TR/owl2-overview/ (accessed on 10 March 2016).
[35] Mining Minds Context Ontology Version 2. Available online: http://www.miningminds.re.kr/icl/context/ context-v2.owl (accessed on 10 March 2016).
[36] Peterson, D.; Gao, S.; Malhotra, A.; Sperberg-McQueen, C.M.; Thompson, H.S. W3C XML Schema Definition Language (XSD) 1.1 Part 2: Datatypes; W3C Recommendation, 5 April 2012. Available online: http:
[37] //www.w3.org/TR/xmlschema11-2/ (accessed on 10 March 2016).
[38] Protégé. Available online: http://protege.stanford.edu/ (accessed on 10 March 2016).
[39] Sirin, E.; Parsia, B.; Grau, B.C.; Kalyanpur, A.; Katz, Y. Pellet: A practical OWL-DL reasoner. J. Web Semant. 2007, 5, 51–53.
[40] Harris, S.; Seaborne, A. SPARQL 1.1 (SPARQL Query Language for RDF); W3C Recommendation, 21 March 2013. Available online: http://www.w3.org/TR/sparql11-query/ (accessed on 10 March 2016).
[41] Apache Jena. Available online: https://jena.apache.org/ (accessed on 10 March 2016).
[42] Brickley, D.; Guha, R.V. RDF Schema 1.1; W3C Recommendation, 25 February 2014. Available online: https://www.w3.org/TR/rdf-schema/ (accessed on 10 March 2016).
[43] Richardson, L.; Ruby, S. Restful Web Services. Available online: http://transform.ca.com/LAC-Creating- RESTful-web-services-restful-interface.html?mrm=508752&cid=NA-SEM-API-ACF-000011-00000946- 000000110 (accessed on 10 March 2016).

Chapter 8

Context Fusioning

mlCAF: Multi-Level Cross-Domain Semantic Context Fusioning for Behavior Identification

Muhammad Asif Razzaq, Claudia Villalonga, Usman Akhtar, Wajahat Ali Khan, Maqbool Ali, Asad Masood Khattak, Taeho Hur, Jaehun Bang, Dohyeong Kim, and Sungyoung Lee

The emerging research on automatic identification of user's contexts from the cross-domain environment in ubiquitous and pervasive computing systems has proved to be successful. Monitoring the diversified user's contexts and behaviors can help in controlling lifestyle associated to chronic diseases using context-aware applications. However, availability of cross-domain heterogeneous contexts provides a challenging opportunity for their fusion to obtain abstract information for further analysis. This work demonstrates extension of our previous work from a single domain (i.e., physical activity) to multiple domains (physical activity, nutrition and clinical) for context-awareness. We propose multi-level Context-aware Framework (mlCAF), which fuses the multi-level cross-domain contexts in order to arbitrate richer behavioral contexts. This work explicitly focuses on key challenges linked to multi-level context modeling, reasoning and fusioning based on the mlCAF open-source ontology. More specifically, it addresses the interpretation of contexts from three different domains, their fusioning conforming to richer contextual information. This chapter contributes in terms of ontology evolution with additional domains, context definitions, rules and inclusion of semantic queries. For the framework evaluation, multi-level cross-domain contexts collected from 20 users were used to ascertain abstract contexts, which served as basis for behavior modeling and lifestyle identification. The experimental results indicate a context recognition average accuracy of around 92.65% for the collected cross-domain contexts.

8.1 Introduction

Context-awareness (CA) is considered to be an essential element in the ubiquitous and pervasive computing systems [1] and is widely recognized by the research community. It is treated as a key technology for situation awareness applications such as [2,3]. Dey et al. [4] defined the context as *"context is any information that can be used to characterize the situation of an entity"*. In the last two decades, significant work has been performed by developing CA prototypes, middleware, and applications [5]. CA provides a good approximation to the people for their interactions with the environment. State-of-the-art technologies play a critical role in capturing those interactions using several sensing modalities such as accelerometers or GPS sensors embedded in wearables and subsequently interpreted as *contexts*. However, it is challenging in context-aware infrastructure to exploit, integrate, and culture to enrich the fused information in the changing environment. It is pertinent to mention that most existing context-aware solutions cater contextual information in various discrete domains [6,7] and are unable to handle it cohesively. This discreteness provides enough opportunity to develop a context-based cross-domain fusion framework to model entities, dynamic relationships and realize richer human behavior information through fused outputs.

Context fusioning (CF) is considered as an integral part of any context-aware system [8]. For cohesive contextual information, the CF is deemed as a key approach to fuse various contexts from multiple domains [9,10] as well as to increase the understandability of a user's context. CF helps to identify relevant actions, correlates their sequence in cross-domains [11]. It also handles the redundancy of contextual information for raising the context confidence [8]. Even though, the state-of-the-art CF approaches have gained much importance, however, they were unable to prove its deployment for real-world personalized user context in the health and wellness domain [8,12].

Keeping in mind the above-mentioned facts, our motivation was to design and develop an efficient framework to fuse the multi-levels cross-domain contexts for providing a richer contextual information. To achieve this goal, this study was undertaken with the following objectives: (1) extend the state-of-the-art context-awareness approaches from a single domain (i.e., physical activity) to cross-domains (i.e., physical activity, nutrition, and clinical), (2) infer a more abstract representation of cross-domain contexts (3) separate the ontology model (T-Box) and the application data (A-Box), and (4) provide an effective contextual state of the users in a real-time manner to boost health and wellness services.

The key contributions of this research are: (1) enhanced physical activity domain ontology [6] with inclusion of nutrition (57 food items) and clinical (6 blood glucose and 5 blood pressure levels) domains; (2) functional framework for administering the Web Ontology Language (OWL) reasoning paradigm comprising of constraint-based rules (real-time) and Semantic Query-Enhanced Web Rule Language (SQWRL) based queries (offline) for recognizing contexts and behavioral patterns; (3) proof of concept for ontology modeling, framework implementation, and evaluation in health and wellness domains.

In this study, an open source efficient framework *multi-level Context-Awareness Framework* (mlCAF) is proposed, which fuses the multi-levels cross-domain contexts efficiently to provide a richer context-awareness information to its users. This study is the extension of our previous work [6,13], which is illustrated in Figure 8.1. Figure 8.1a indicates our previous work, which relies only on a single domain consisting of physical activities whereas, Figure 8.1b presents the extended version, which addresses challenges related to context-aware behavioral representation accurately for users by introducing cross-domain (i.e., physical activity, nutrition, and clinical) to support the health as well as the wellness domain.

The proposed framework under discussion is designed and developed for the Ubiquitous Computing Lab., Kyung Hee University, Yongin (http://uclab.khu.ac.kr/) project named *Mining Minds* (http://www.miningminds.re.kr/) (for details see Section 10.3), however, it can also be deployed with other platforms. The current version of this proposed framework is available for downloading from the GitHub open source platform [14].

For the realization of mlCAF, this study has considered diabetes scenario, as it has a strong relationship between physical activity, and dietary habits [15]. Usually, physical activities are recommended to people who suffer from diabetes as a part of a glycemic control and overall health improvement [15]. *Global Report on Diabetes* [16] by *World Health Organization* (WHO) states physical inactivity and unhealthy dietary practices are the key risk factors for this chronic disease. However, these key risk factors are modifiable through environmental, behavioral and lifestyle changes but they require raising people's self-awareness.

The rest of the chapter is organized as follows: Section 10.2 presents the related work. Section 10.3 introduces short descriptions of the *Mining Minds* platform, the evolved ontology illustrated with examples and the extended architecture. Section 10.4 provides insights into ontology-based context reasoning, and usage of semantic rules. Section 10.5 discussed mlCAF with example scenarios for *Vertical Fusioning* and *Horizontal Fusioning* techniques. Section 10.6 introduces the details of experimental results and evaluation along with behavioral rule definitions. Finally, main conclusions are drawn jointly with future steps in Section 10.7.

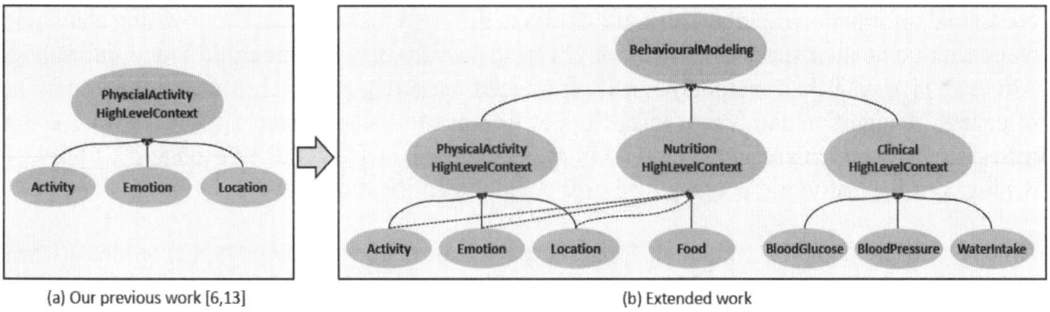

Figure 8.1 Extended Domains for Ontology evolution in mlCAF

8.2 Related Work

Nowadays, the most dominant context information consumers are mobile applications, which engage different capabilities of sensors in the shape of context [11]. Sensor-equipped smart devices are widely used for providing health monitoring services [17]. These devices provide intelligence for recognizing daily life activities performed by users like standing, walking, driving etc. Context-aware (CA) systems from an Internet of Things (IoT) perspective were also surveyed [5] as for how CA can play its role in aggregating contextual information rather than processing whole sensory data. The work [18] introduced details of context-aware systems and their role in developing applications for end users. The recent advancements in IoT identify that context-awareness has become an inevitable part of IoT applications. All the information related to sensors not only, from a specific domain but also from heterogeneous domains, comes under the definition of context-awareness.

The heterogeneous domains handle dynamic contexts in a smart environment, to represent daily life activities correctly and assist people well-being with technologies [19]. The cross-domain context management can also play the vital role in knowledge integration from different sources in even recommender systems [20]. The initial efforts on cross-domain context management in Feel@Home environment [21] addressed context producer-consumer patterns for intra-domain and cross-domain in home/office environment by using indoor applications and executing mobile applications on mobile devices. However, this framework supported distributed administration and processing of contexts. The challenges linked to the cross-domain context management were also addressed by [22], in which authors identified context patterns in the multi-domain environment and proposed iCROSS context management infrastructure. Lin et al. [23] developed a unified approach for mutual tagging of heterogeneous domains constituted by the people, their associated events at certain locations by integrating based on feature similarity and cross-domain relations.

Context act as a key binding element for integrating information at different levels [9] in multi-domains. For instance, context information can be a valuable input taken as a parameter for executing context-aware algorithms at different levels of healthcare tracking and monitoring applications. Events that occur in an environment can be recognized by identifying relevant actions and also by correlating sequences of actions [11] using fusioning across cross-domains. In [8], Khattak et al. discussed context representation and fusioning as an integral part of any context-aware system. It increases understandability, confidence and reduces redundancy. Contextual Information encompasses basic elements for situation awareness semantically [24]. The obtained contextual information can play substantial roles at different fusion levels by providing convincing clues with contextual spectrum which ranges from sensory data to human-provided information. Alti et al. [10] with their methodological centralized reasoning approach, showed the importance of context recognition and fusion regardless of its source. A three layered context-aware system infrastructure with inference functionality was proposed in [12], but was unable to prove its deployment for real-world personalized user context identification.

Amongst different context modeling approaches such as: (1) key-value pairs; (2) model-oriented; (3)logic-based; (4) ontologies [25], we are motivated for choosing ontology in context modeling and reasoning. Some of the prominent work using ontologies as a based model is discussed, which includes SOCAM, CoBrA, COSAR, etc. SOCAM [26] is a Service-oriented Context-Aware Middleware that works on server-based architecture style with underlying ontology. This provides context-aware services in smart home and vehicle environment. It supports information sensing, semantic representation, and reasoning of context using SOCAM ontology by modeling person, activities along with locations leaving out nutrition contextual aspects. At the same time, CoBrA [27] is also an agent-based centralized middleware architecture connecting context modeling, reasoning, knowledge sharing through context brokers in an intelligent meeting room for places, agents and events only. COSAR [28] recognizes human activities and reasons context-awareness through hybrid reasoning techniques, i.e., ontological/statistical using mobile network services. However, it also focuses only on performed activities and their location in an activity recognition system.

In order to increase the ontological expressiveness and query answering, Web Ontology Language (OWL) and Semantic Web Rule Language (SWRL) can be integrated to execute knowledge-base system. OWL can be used for problem-solving modeling in terms of ontological development and SWRL may be applied for effective knowledge inference. Using these technologies, Chi et al.

[29] constructed a system of chronic kidney disease dietary consultation and proved its effectiveness. In pervasive environments knowledge-driven approaches [30] provide an opportunity to knowledge engineers and domain experts for specifying domain models for capturing and reasoning over recognized activities. Using knowledge driven techniques, ontologies have proven their abilities in describing a service at a certain point of time in the form of abstract context. These abstract contexts assemble and desegregate knowledge relevant to the current situation, the work by Smirnov et al. [31] proposes a classification methodology related to their use in Decision Support Systems based on the fusion of context-based information. OWL knowledge-based systems and SWRL can infer new knowledge regarding habit associations of users in a smart home environment [32].

We have adopted context fusioning techniques in context-awareness with the support of the proposed framework called *Multi-level Context-aware Framework* (mlCAF). In order to obtain real-time abstract and richer context in cross-domains, fusioning can be incorporated to infer the abstract contexts in health and wellness domains. Moreover, our proposed framework enables CA platforms to provide better context to adopt behavior and life style.

8.3 Preliminaries on the Mining Minds Platform

Mining Minds, an innovative platform based on concepts of the digital health and wellness paradigm, provides personalized healthcare and wellness support. It is mainly the collection of innovative services, tools, and techniques applied collectively to monitor human's daily life data, generated from heterogeneous sources. To provide innovative services and utilize different tools, the *Mining Minds* platform architecture [33] is divided into five distinct layers: *Data Curation Layer*, *Information Curation Layer* (ICL), *Knowledge Curation Layer*, *Service Curation Layer* and *Supporting Layer* [34]. In a nutshell, *Data Curation Layer* is in charge of acquisition, processing and persisting the asynchronous, real time, multimodal sensory data obtained through heterogeneous sources like SNS, smart phone, Kinect, wearable biomedical devices etc. This processed sensory data is used by *ICL* [35] to model *Low-level Context* (LLC), and infer *High-level Context* (HLC). Health and wellness knowledge is maintained through domain experts or knowledge engineers in *Knowledge Curation Layer*, which contains rules used to determine personal contexts and behavior. *Service Curation Layer* caters users with personalized situation aware recommendations based on determined context and knowledge from Knowledge Curation Layer. Finally *supporting layer* is responsible for advanced analytics, feedback, privacy and security for the *Mining Minds* platform.

Mining Minds supports automatic behavior identification through inferring multimodal human context using heterogeneous sensory data. These contexts are identified at two granular layers namely *Low-level Context Awareness* (LLCA) and *High-level Context Awareness* (HLCA). LLCA comprises of physical activities, emotions, and location, which are obtained through machine learning classification techniques. These are applied over sensory data obtained through several devices, such as smart watches, smart phones or Kinect video devices [34]. Also, food items taken during meals are processed through user's specific tagged meal images, which are collected using the smart phone camera. This study also handles contexts for people with two different chronic diseases, diabetes and hypertension, by capturing blood glucose levels, blood pressure, and helps in determining health conditions with the help of clinical health contexts. This work portrays more comprehensive state of the user in which dietary habits are attached to physical activities and health conditions for better identification of human behavior using sensing modalities in the *Mining Minds* platform.

Mining Minds seamlessly supports people's lifestyles by intelligently fusing human's daily physical activities and nutrition information along with emotion and location. Behavioral patterns can be derived using diverse HLCs, modeled through inferring over LLCA. ICL layer utilizes the *Mining Minds Context Ontology* (MMCO), which is considered as conceptual backbone for modeling, representing, and inferring HLCs from LLCs. Existing framework [13] lack capability to capture ontological nutrition, health state LLCs and corresponding HLCs. Nutrition is, as important as, physical activities, these are considered most fundamental parts for human health and well-being. Any of unhealthy behavior relating to physical activity or diet may lead to chronic diseases and premature mortality. However, by managing the physical activities patterns and practical dietary risk for chronic diseases can be reduced.

8.3.1 Role of Physical Activities and Nutrition in Diabetes Management

There is a strong relationship between physical activity, dietary habits, and diabetes for people suffering from some chronic disease. Usually, exercises are recommended to all those people who suffer from diabetes as a part of a glycemic control and overall health [15]. In daily life activities, all such individuals are encouraged to decrease the sedentary activities and advised to get involved in healthy activities. These activities are performed by adapting behavior-change strategies, and technology-based strategies which enable people to promote the adoption and maintenance of physical activities. These physical activities help in blood glucose management and overall health maintenance for individuals with diabetes and prediabetes. There is an association between physical activities and the management of glycemia in the individuals having intermediate hyperglycemia or prediabetes [36]. This study provides a strong evidence regarding how an improvement in physical activities can result in lowering diabetes and cardiovascular risks. This lifestyle modification helps individuals in reversion to normoglycemia health conditions. Han et al. [37] proposed a layered healthcare framework for recognizing user's activities, identifying and providing unhealthy activity patterns to the caregiver. This study claims the possibility of predicting lifestyle diseases associated with an emotional state such as depression; chronic disease like diabetes using sensory data. It is mainly managed by monitoring long-term disease influenced activities such as like frequent eating, frequent drinking, sleeping disorder, less physical activities, etc. Our previous work handled only physical activities, whereas the presented work includes nutrition and chronic disease domains modeled in the ontology. Ontologies model domain-specific concepts and provide reasoning facilities, for this we evolved our previous ontology, only which handled physical activity contexts.

8.3.2 Mining Minds Context Ontology Evolution

In the context modeling world, ontologies outweigh non-semantic models in terms of knowledge sharing, flexibility, reusability, abstraction and validation [17]. Ontologies are, therefore, extensible, expressive, possess decoupling nature, as knowledge and code can co-exist. Additionally, and more specifically ontologies enable derivation of new information based on hierarchical structure from existing underlying concepts using class and properties inheritances. Ontologies are evolvable as they provide rich quality and expandable abstract model by including new concepts along with existing ones with handling support of inconsistencies. Besides semantic modeling, ontologies are also supported with the bunch of reasoners, which can be inherently applied for inference and reasoning tasks. Finally, inferring context using ontologies have several implementation benefits in the application development architecture, as these possess resilience and evolving features. These features make ontologies extendable and adaptation of ontology by the architecture itself. Keeping all the above-mentioned facts and benefits, we extended our previous ontology by incorporating all associated contextual features for the study under consideration. The open-source *Mining Minds Context Ontology* (MMCO) [38] models daily life contexts, used for human behavior identification which is inevitable for the provision of personalized health and wellness services. A comparative ontological metrics analysis is presented in Table 8.1, as how ontology evolution has resulted in an increase in ontology metrics, and axioms. Existing work [6] used around 45 classes to model physical activity contexts but in order to add concepts pertaining to nutrition and chronic disease, the classes count raised to 225 along with associated properties and expressivity which is discussed further in this section in detail.

Table 8.1 Ontology Metrics during Ontology Evolution

MMCO Metrics	Metrics Detail	MMCO V2.0 (Existing Work) [6]	MMCO V3.0 (Extended Work)
Metrics	Axioms	793	1092
	Logical Axioms	624	859
	Class count	45	225
	Object Property count	3	25
	Individual count	114	157
	DL Expressivity	ALCO	ALCHOF(D)
	Asserted Triples	0	3312
	Inferred Triples	0	6041
Class Axioms	SubClassOf	32	222
	Equivalent Classes	9	17
	Disjoint Classes	5	14
Individual Axioms	Class Assertion	360	58
	Object Property Assertion	212	27
	Data Property Assertion	0	1

In *Mining Minds*, human context is understood as any information characterizing the physical, nutritional, emotional, health and social situation of a person leading towards the better identification of human behavior. In the development of OWL2 ontologies, *Classes* act as a source of an abstraction mechanism for organizing resources with similar characteristics. Furthermore, *individuals*, also called instances, are members of the OWL Classes and can be related to others using *properties*. In *Mining Minds*, the *subClassOf* constraint is used for designing, assigning classes and individuals for LLC, and HLC. These HLCs are further categorized as *Physical Activity High-level Contexts* (PA-HLCs), *Nutrition High-level Contexts* (N-HLCs) and *Clinical High-level Contexts* (C-HLCs) *classes*. The main concept of MMCO ontology is the *HighLevelContext* class, which has three *subclasses* as *PhysicalActivityContext*, *NutritionContext* and *ClinicalContext* defining the different high-level contexts in the domains of physical activity, nutrition and clinical. The *Location*, *Emotion*, *Activity*, *Food*, *BloodPressure*, *BloodGlucose*, and *WaterIntake* classes have been described to model the different *Low-level Contexts* (LLCs). These classes are related to the class *HighLevelContext*, with the help of object properties *hasLocation*, *hasEmotion*, *hasActivity* [13], *hasFood*, *hasBloodPressure* and *hasBloodGlucose*.

The scalable MMCO comprehensively models' contexts at different abstraction levels. PA-HLC are modeled based on the LLC's belonging to the categories *Activity*, *Location*, and *Emotion*. PA-HLC includes contexts for sedentary and active physical activities such as *OfficeWork*, *HouseWork*, *Amusement*, *Gardening*, *Commuting*, *Sleeping*, *Exercising*, and *Inactivity* discussed in detail by Villalonga et al. [6]. The N-HLC are modeled based on LLCs of the category *Food* which is described in a 57 food-item list and further categorized into 10 broader groups. This categorization and major nutrient identifications are performed in accordance with guidance and suggestions provided by *United States Department of Agriculture* (http://www.usda.gov/wps/portal/usda/usdahome) on daily food consumptions. Specifically, the different recognized Foods are categorized using 10 disjoint subclasses of the *Food* class, namely *Grain*, *Meat*, *SeaFood*, *Eggs*, *MilkAndDairyProducts*, *Legumes*, *Nuts*, *Fruits*, *Vegetable*, and *Snacks*. The identified 57 food items are members of these classes, as can be visualized in MMCO [38]. N-HLC models major food nutrient like Carbohydrates, Protein, and Fats which can be determined using LLCs belonging to the category *Food*. The C-HLCs are modeled based on LLCs comprising of 6 LLCs categories for *BloodGlucose*, 5 LLCs for *BloodPressure* and 3 LLCs for *WaterIntake*. Table 8.2 shows these underlying LLCs and describes the value ranges for each LLC. These LLCs are assigned based on the *BloodGlucose* values obtained through smart glucose meter, BloodPressure values captured through smart blood pressure monitor, and accumulated water intake values obtained through smart cup. Finally, C-HLC reflects four major health states for diabetic patients, such as normal, moderate, high risk and very high-risk health state.

The *PhysicalActivityContext* comprises of eight disjoint subclasses as discussed in our previous work [6]. However, the new *NutritionContext* and *ClinicalContext* classes are further divided into disjoint subclasses. The *NutritionContext* class, which represent N-HLCs has three disjoint subclasses decided based on major nutrient in food items, they are named as *Carbohydrates*, *Protein*, and *Fats*. The *ClinicalContext* class, which represents C-HLC class, is further subdivided as *NormalHealthState*, *ModerateHealthState*, *HighRiskHealthState*, and *VeryHighRiskHealthState* also shown in Figure 8.2 as a partial part of MMCO. Each *NutritionContext* and *ClinicalContext* subclasses are defined through complement classes, existential and universal axioms. These axioms constitute the necessary conditions required for equivalent anonymous class definitions. The equivalent anonymous classes for these *NutritionContext* and *ClinicalContext* subclasses have been described in Protégé and are shown in Figure 8.3.

Table 8.2 Low-level Context labels assigned based on ranges of values

Category	Low-Level Context Labels	Value Ranges
Blood Glucose [39] (mg/dL)	DangerouslyHighBG	≥315
	HighBG	>215 & <280
	BorderlineBG	>120 & <180
	NormalBG	>70 & <108
	LowBG	>50 & <70
	DangerouslyLowBG	≤50
Blood Pressure (Systolic/Diastolic) [40]	HypertensionStageII	≥160/100
	HypertensionStageI	>140/90 & <159/99
	PreHypertension	>120/80 & <139/89
	NormalBP	≤120/80
	LowBP	<90/60
Water Intake (mL)	OverHydration	>2000 mL
	NormalIntake	approx. 2000 mL
	Dehydration	<2000 mL

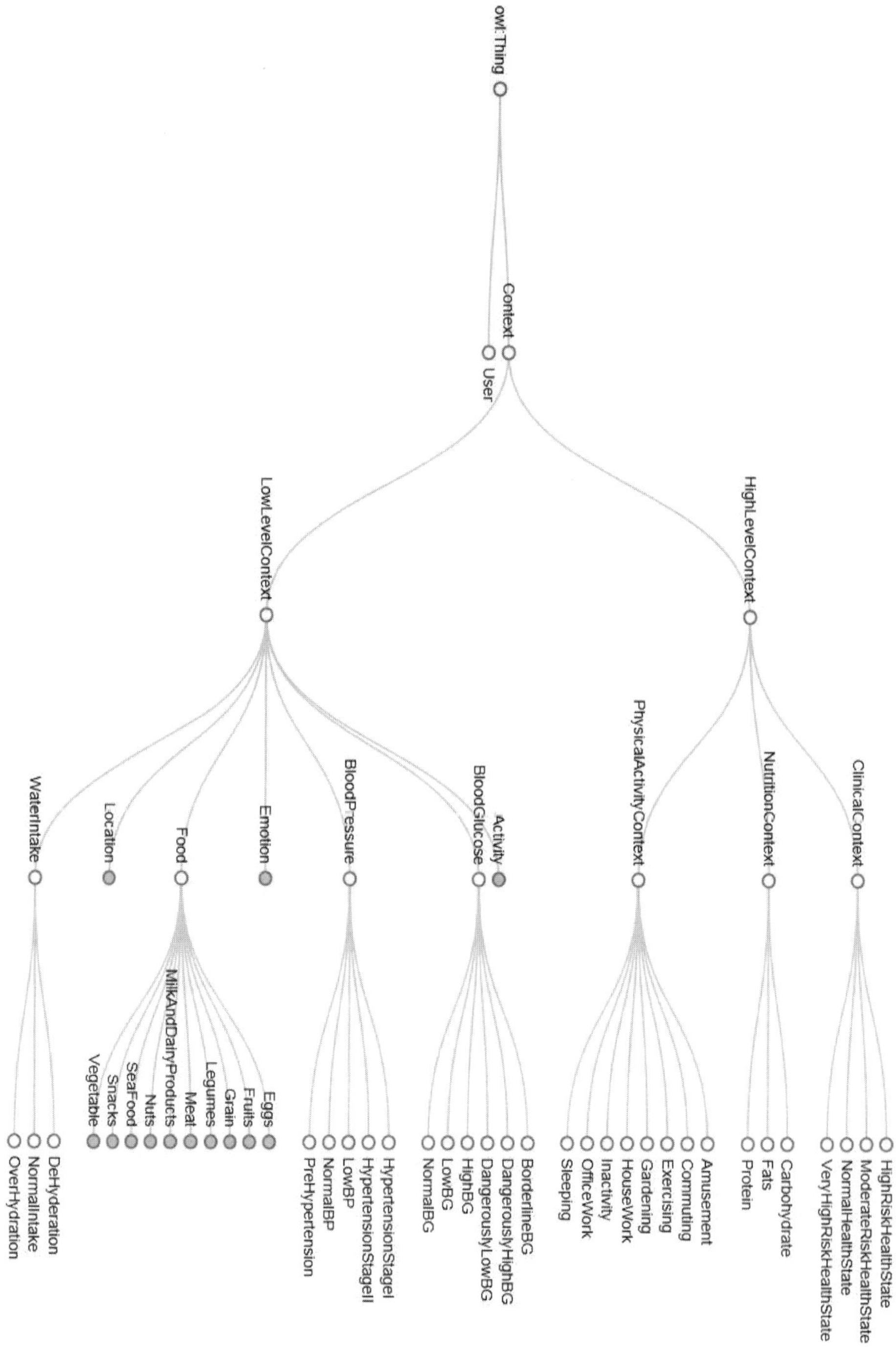

Figure 8.2 Partial view for extended MMCO: [38]: *LowLevelContext* class and 7 subclasses, *HighLevelContext* class with 3 subclasses, i.e., *PhysicalActivityContext* class with 8 subclasses, *NutritionContext* class with 3 subclasses and *ClinicalContext* class with 4 further subclasses

```
NutritionContext
  and ((hasActivity some Eating)
  and (hasLocation some
    (Home or Office or Restaurant))
  and (hasActivity only Eating)
  and (hasLocation only
    (Home or Office or Restaurant)))
  and (hasEmotion only
    (Boredom or Disgust or Fear or
Happiness or Neutral or Sadness or
Surprise))
  and (hasFood only
    (Beef or ChickenSnack or FriedFood
or Ham or Hamburger or IceCream or
Mackerel or Milk or Peanut or Pork))
```

(a) Fats

```
ClinicalContext
  and ((((hasBloodGlucose some BorderlineBG)
  and (hasBloodGlucose only BorderlineBG))
  and ((hasBloodPressure some HypertensionStageI)
  and (hasBloodPressure only HypertensionStageI)))
  or (((hasBloodGlucose some HighBG)
  and (hasBloodGlucose only HighBG))
  and ((hasBloodPressure some PreHypertension)
  and (hasBloodPressure only PreHypertension))))
```

(b) HighRiskHealthState

```
ClinicalContext
  and ((((hasBloodGlucose some BorderlineBG)
  and (hasBloodGlucose only BorderlineBG))
  and ((hasBloodPressure some NormalBP)
  and (hasBloodPressure only NormalBP)))
  or (((hasBloodGlucose some BorderlineBG)
  and (hasBloodGlucose only BorderlineBG))
  and ((hasBloodPressure some PreHypertension)
  and (hasBloodPressure only PreHypertension)))
  or (((hasBloodGlucose some NormalBG)
  and (hasBloodGlucose only NormalBG))
  and ((hasBloodPressure some PreHypertension)
  and (hasBloodPressure only PreHypertension))))
```

(c) ModerateRiskHealthState

```
ClinicalContext
  and ((hasBloodGlucose only NormalBG)
  and (hasBloodPressure only NormalBP))
```

(d) NormalHealthState

Figure 8.3 MMCO: Some of example for definitions of the *NutritionContext* and *ClinicalContext* are as (**a**) *Fats*; (**b**) *HighRiskHealthState*; (**c**) *ModerateRiskHealthState*; (**d**) *NormalHealthState*

In order to explain equivalent Class concepts, the N-HLC is modeled via the *Fats* class, Figure 8.3a, is considered as being equivalent to the anonymous class with certain constraints like *NutritionContext and (hasActivity some Eating) and (hasLocation some (Home or Office or Restaurant)) and (hasActivity only (eating) and (hasLocation only (Home or Office or Restaurant)) and (hasEmotion only (Happiness or Disgust or Boredom or Anger or Neutral)) and (hasFood only (Beef or ChickenSnack or FriedFood or Ham or HamBurger or IceCream or Mackerel or Milk or Peanut or Pork))*. This assures that to become instance of the defined class *Fats*, an individual of the *NutritionContext* class must have an object property of type *hasActivity*, which has to be associated with an instance of the *Eating* class, and this object property must take as only value an instance of the *Eating* class. Moreover, the instance of the *NutritionContext* class must also meet the condition for having a property of type *hasLocation* relating to an instance of the *Home or Office or Restaurant* class and only to an instance of the *Home or Office or Restaurant* class. The instance referring the *NutritionContext* class has an object property of type *hasEmotion*, this property must also relate to an instance of the *Happiness* class, the *Disgust* class, the *Boredom* class, the *Anger* class, or the *Neutral* class. Finally, the property of type *hasFood*, must relate to an instance of the *Beef* class, the *ChickenSnack* class, the *FriedFood* class, the *Ham* class, the *HamBurger* class, the *IceCream* class, the *Mackerel* class, the *Milk* class, the *Peanut* class, or the *Pork* class. In the definition and for inferring of *Fats* class the *hasFood* object property and *hasActivity some Eating* axioms are mandatory due to existential and universal restrictions on the involved object properties in addition to *hasLocation* and *hasEmotion* object properties. Similar class concept equivalence definitions are formulated for other N-HLCs, *Carbohydrates* and

Protein classes and C-HLC subclasses i.e., *NormalHealthState*, *ModerateHealthState*, *HighRiskHealthState*, and *VeryHighRiskHealthState*.

8.3.3 High-Level Context Awareness in Mining Minds

In *Mining Minds*, the core technologies devised for the inference and modeling of the user's context constitutes the *Information Curation Layer*, which is further subdivided to *Low-level Context Awareness* (LLCA) and *High-Level Context Awareness* (HLCA) as mentioned in Figure 8.4. The sensory data obtained through user is converted to *Low-level Context* (LLC) using machine learning approaches and it also becomes the basis for inferring in order to obtain *High-Level Contexts* (HLC) of three types i.e., *Physical Activity High-Level Context* (PA-HLC), *Nutrition High-Level Context* (N-HLC) and *Clinical High-Level Context* (C-HLC). The components drawn in by bold lines are the architectural perspective contributions to the existing work in order to improve context recognition and better behavioral modeling using nutritional and clinical information. LLCs contain seven main context categories *Activities*, *Locations*, *Emotions*, *Food*, *BloodSugar*, *BloodPressure*, and *WaterIntake*, which are recognized through respective recognizers. *Activity* LLC is identified from the body actions and mobility, positioning systems helps in identifying *Location* LLC, *Emotion* LLC is obtained from the user sentiments detected through voice recognizing systems [35]. *Food* LLC is obtained using labels of food items sent by users by capturing pictures of meals by using smart-phone. *BloodSugar* values are taken using a smart glucose meter, which communicates with the *Mining Minds* platform using API, *BloodPressure* is measured using the smart blood pressure monitor, and *WaterIntake* notifier gets input from the smart cup.

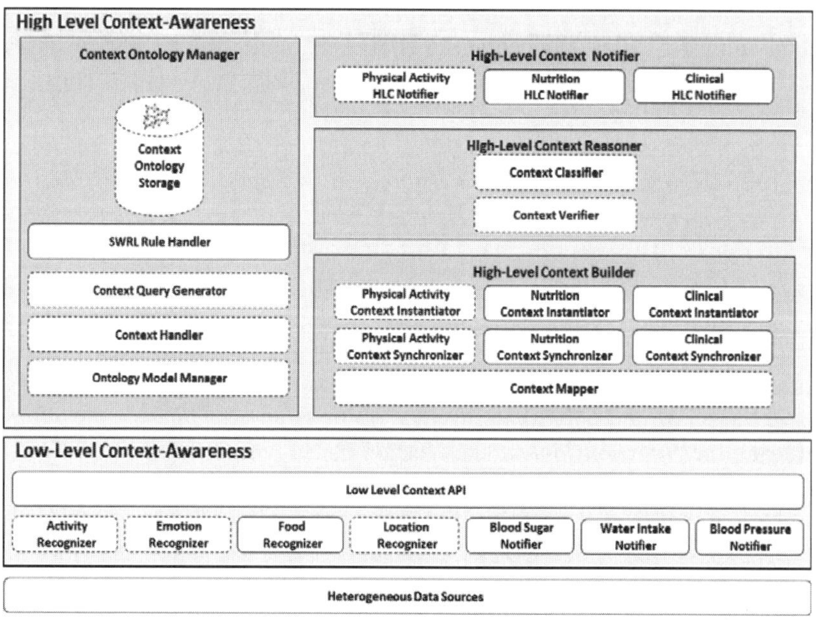

Figure 8.4 Mining Minds High-Level Context Awareness extended architecture

HLCA as shown in Figure 8.4 consists of four main components: *High-Level Context Builder*, *High-Level Context Reasoner*, *High-Level Context Notifier*, and *Context Ontology Manager*. The

HLC Builder receives the low-level information activities, emotions, locations, food, BloodSugar, BloodPressure and WaterIntake levels identified by LLCA and maps into ontological concepts named as unclassified context. The *Physical Activity Context Synchronizer* searches for concurrent LLC information related to activities, emotions, and locations whereas the *Nutrition Context Synchronizer* takes Food LLC into account additionally. Similarly, *Clinical Context Synchronizer* collects BloodGlucose and BloodSugar LLCs and synchronize them. The *Physical Activity, Nutrition and Clinical Context Instantiator* create a new instance of an *unclassified HLC* which links to the corresponding LLCs w.r.t. time. The unclassified PA-HLC, N-HLC and C-HLC are communicated to the *HLC Reasoner* for its validity and classification. The *Context Verifier* examines the syntactic and semantic consistency of the unclassified context. The *Context Classifier* administers ontological inference and classifies the unclassified context into one of the different PA-HLC, N-HLC or C-HLC. The *PA-HLC, N-HLC and C-HLC Notifier* notifies the newly identified PA-HLC, N-HLC and C-HLC to other *Mining Minds* layers for the creation of personalized health, wellness services [34] and necessary recommendations. The fourth component *Context Ontology Manager* is responsible for the persistence of MMCO, storage of LLC, PA-HLC, N-HLC, C-HLC and supports SPARQL/SQWRL queries for retrieval of LLCs, HLCs and behavioral contexts.

8.4 Context Reasoning

The main purpose of context reasoning is to check the consistency of contexts as well as deducing high-level implicit context information from low-level explicit contexts. In this study, ontology-based reasoning is performed with additional assistance for user-defined SWRL rules and SPARQL/SQWRL queries.

8.4.1 Ontology Based Reasoning

In Ontology-based reasoning, inferring is done based on ontological constraint-based rules exploiting *transitive property*, *subClassOf*, *subPropertyOf*, *disjointWith* and *inverseOf* properties. However, inclusion of complex rules increases the expressibility of ontological model, which enhances the ability of handling the multi-level context assertions.

8.4.2 SWRL Based Reasoning/SQWRL Based Retrieval

SWRL rules, an extension to OWL-DL is one of semantic rule representation for representing knowledge. These rules are designed to obtain the desired outcome based on already stored facts meeting several conditions and adds more power to OWL capabilities for deductive reasoning. Integration of SWRL to ontological based inferring systems have shown their importance for context-aware applications [41]. Ontological models have limitations for handling complex rules as in our case fusing multi-level cross-domain contexts, which are discussed in subsequent sections. SWRL adds flexibility in fusing Multilevel contexts thus resulting in inferring of additional contexts using already asserted facts. SQL like querying is human understandable, an introduction of *Semantic Query-Enhanced Web Rule Language* (SQWRL) on top of SWRL provides SQL-like operators for querying and extracting semantic information. SQWRL uses SQWRL Query API (https://github.com/ protegeproject/swrlapi/wiki/SQWRLQueryAPI) interface for executing the queries and accessing the results in a two-dimensional table.

8.5 Multi-Level Cross-Domain Context Fusioning

In the *Mining Minds*, we ideally focused on a solution catering contexts from multiple domains, as a proof of concept, we considered PA-HLC, N-HLC and C-HLC such that these are handled separately on one-level, fused together on another level and finally more concrete and abstract multi-level cross-domain contexts are obtained suggesting human behavior and lifestyle. This has helped in increasing the ability to apply our proposed solution to multi-domains, which initially was only composed of physical activity domain.

In Figure 8.5, a summarized overview is provided how the overall mechanism of mlCAF utilizing vertical fusioning and horizontal fusioning are performed at different levels, particularly with time constraints and reasoning periodicity. This horizontal fusioning is achieved using SWRLAPI (https://github.com/protegeproject/swrlapi) which works on top of OWL-based SWRL and SQWRL [42] query language discussed in the implementation Section 10.6. SQWRL uses SWRL's conjunctive semantic structure as its formal underpinning by providing novel set operators used to perform closure operations such as negation, additionally with counting, and aggregation.

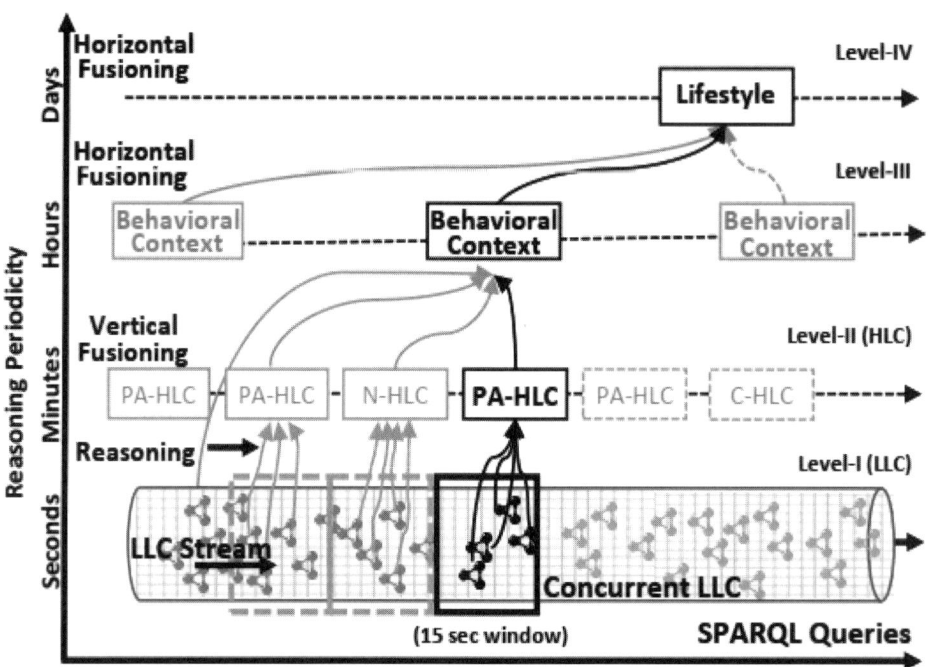

Figure 8.5 Exemplification of representation for mlCAF at different abstraction levels using Vertical and Horizontal Fusioning

8.5.1 Vertical Fusioning: Context Inferring in the Mining Minds

The MMCO is utilized to infer PA-HLC, N-HLC and C-HLC in a vertical fusioning manner utilizing ontological reasoning (Level-II). Using Pellet reasoner, an instance of the *PhysicalActivityContext* class, i.e., an unclassified PA-HLC, can be determined to be associated with one of the eight *PhysicalActivityContext* subclasses as mentioned in [13]. An instance of the *NutritionContext* class can be determined to be a member of one of the three *NutritionContext* subclasses: *Fats*, *Carbohydrates*, and *Protein*. Similarly, an instance of the *ClinicalContext* class, can be determined to be a member of one of the four *ClinicalContext* subclasses: *NormalHealthState*, *ModerateHealthState*, *HighRiskHealthState*, and *VeryHighRiskHealthState*. The instances of the *Food* class are asserted through the *hasFood* property, whereas instances of the *BloodGlucose* and *BloodPressure* classes are asserted using *hasBloodGlucose* and *BloodPressure* properties respectively. Reasoning in OWL is based on the *Open World Assumption* (OWA), which means that an assumption cannot be made for something if it does not exist until its nonexistence is declared explicitly. Following is an example discussed in order to illustrate the modeling principles and the inference logic through MMCO in the Protégé tool as shown in Figure 8.6. Figure 8.6a shows an instance of the *NutritionContext* class for which the object property *hasActivity* has been asserted to take the value *act_eating*, *hasEmotion* object property has been asserted to take the value *emo_happiness*, *hasFood* property has been asserted to take the value *food_fried_food*, *hasLocation* property has been asserted to take the value *loc_restaurant* and *hasUser* property has been asserted to take the value *Bob*; where *act_eating* is an instance of the *Eating* class, *emo_happiness* is an instance of the *Happiness* class *food_fried_food* is an instance of the *Fried_Food* class and *loc_restaurant* is an instance of the *Restaurant* class. Due to the OWA, the instance of the *NutritionContext* class has been asserted the type *(hasActivity only act_eating)* and the type *(hasEmotion only emo_happiness)* and *(hasFood only food_fried_food)* and the type *(hasLocation only loc_restaurant)* and the type *(hasUser only Bob)*. The reasoner is used to automatically classify this instance of the *NutritionContext* class. The instance complies with the *Fats* class definition; therefore, it is classified as being a member of the *Fats* class. The *Context Reasoner* infers *Fats* using vertical fusioning as LLC belongs to nutrition domain i.e., *Food* name and *Activity Eating* comes from physical activity domain as shown in Figure 8.6a. Similarly, vertical fusioning infers *Carbohydrates* and *Protein*. These contexts are concurrent, due to their overlapping temporal properties, we considered them as they are handled through vertical fusioning inferring. This process is scalable as we can fuse as many concurrent contexts depending on ontological modeling and service requirements.

An example scenario is plotted in Figure 8.7 explaining how vertical fusioning works on concurrent contexts i.e., Level-II fusioning as discussed previously in Section 10.5.1. These overlapping contexts are vertically fused to obtain abstract context form, using ontological based reasoning. Different vertically fused contexts are plotted based on overlapping low-level Activity, Emotion, Location and Food contexts.

(**a**) Fats

(**b**) VeryHighRiskHealthState

Figure 8.6 Instances of the *NutritionContext* and *ClinicalContext* classes which are classified as being members of the defined *NutritionContext* and *ClinicalContext* subclasses using the Pellet reasoner in Protégé. The inferred classes are highlighted in yellow: (**a**) *Fats* and (**b**) *VeryHighRiskHealthState* are inferred

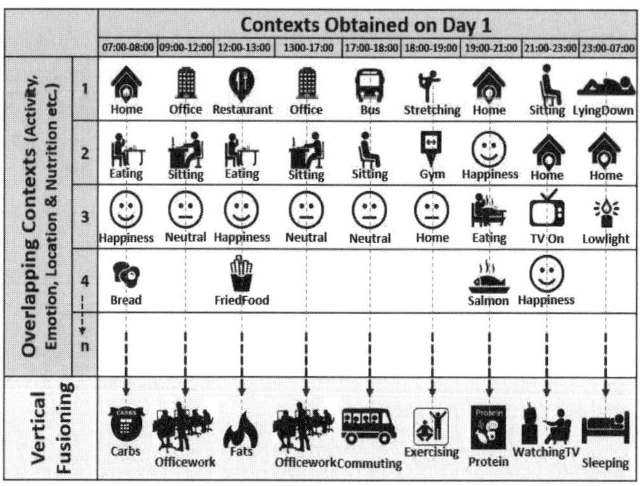

Figure 8.7 Example scenario explaining Vertical Fusioning using overlapping Low-level contexts

8.5.2 Horizontal Fusioning: Context Inferencing in the Mining Minds

The SWRL rules have been designed over and above with MMCO constraint-based rules, by keeping temporal characteristics of concurrent low-level contexts, inferred PA-HLC and N-HLC in view. SWRL combines these atomic dynamic contexts to provide a complete picture of highly interrelated atomic low-level contexts, PA-HLC and N-HLC. The general form of SWRL rule looks like as mentioned below.

$$\square_1 \wedge \square_2 \wedge \square_3 \ldots\ldots \wedge \square_n \square > \square_1 \wedge \square_2 \ldots\ldots\ldots \wedge \square_m \qquad (1)$$

where $\square_i$ symbolizes atomic low-level contexts (i.e., Activity, Location, Emotion, Food and clinical contexts), PA-HLCs, N-HLCs, C-HLCs and properties connecting these contexts whereas $\square_i$ represents outcomes of $\square_i$ in abstracted way named as behavioral contexts. These $\square_i$, $\square_i$ can be of the form C(x), P(x,y), etc., where C represents OWL concept description and P represents OWL property, and x, y are termed as Datalog variables. On both sides of arrows, these are connected using conjunctions. The resulting behavioral contexts are then utilized for lifestyle identification.

The contexts obtained using vertical fusioning do not provide enough evidence to establish human behavior as long as they belong to user's context at the point of time as shown in the example scenario, Figure 8.8. In order to get better picture, a mechanism is devised for fusing vertically fused contexts to a more abstract form, such that it can result into better behavior modeling. In this case, the time window will appear bigger rather than in seconds as in the case of VF. We obtained higher abstraction (Level-III, see Figure 8.5) for contexts spanning even more than a day, by fusing several vertically fused contexts using defined SWRL/SQWRL rules and queries. In order to prove the HF concept, considering these inferred PA-HLC, N-HLC and C-HLC along the time-line, they are reasoned at different point of time, means horizontally along with the timeline. With the introduction of SWRL/SQWRL rules additionally, as mentioned in Table 8.3 more multi-level contexts are obtained explained in next sections.

Using SWRL rules, retrieval through SQWRL, horizontal fusioning of cross-domain contexts from different levels is accomplished.

	Timings	07:00-08:00	09:00-12:00	12:00-13:00	1300-17:00	17:00-18:00	18:00-19:00	19:00-21:00	21:00-23:00	23:00-07:00	Horizontal Fusioning
Week 1	Day 1	Carbs	OfficeWork	Fats	OfficeWork	Commuting	Exercising	Protein	WathcingTV	Sleeping	Behavioral Context
	Day 2	Fats	OfficeWork	Carbs	OfficeWork	Commuting		Fats	Sleeping	Sleeping	Behavioral Context
	Day 3	Fats	OfficeWork	Fats	OfficeWork	Commuting		Fats	Sleeping	Sleeping	Behavioral Context
	Day 4	Protein	OfficeWork	Protien	OfficeWork	Commuting	Exercising	Fats	Sleeping	Sleeping	Behavioral Context
	Day 5	Fats	OfficeWork	Fats	OfficeWork	Commuting		Carbs	WathcingTV	Sleeping	Behavioral Context
	Day 6		Sleeping	Housework	Sleeping	Fats		Fats			Behavioral Context
	Day 7		HouseWork	Protein	HouseWork	Exercising	Amusement	Amusement	Fats	Sleeping	Behavioral Context

Figure 8.8 Illustration scenario explaining Horizontal Fusioning

Table 8.3 SWRL/SQWRL definitions: PA-HLC, N-HLC and LLC involved in Horizontal Fusioning for Behavior modeling

Rule	Behavioral Contexts	SWRL/SQWRL Horizontal Fusion Rules
1	Sedentary Behavior	User(?u) ∧ hasLocation(?u, Loc_Gym) ∧ isContextOf(?u, ?PAC-HLC) ∧ swrlb:equal(?PAC-HLC, "Exercising") ∧ hasStartTime(?PAC-HLC, ?starttime) ∧ hasEndTime(?PAC-HLC, ?endtime) ∧ temporal:duration(?h, ?starttime, ?endtime, "Hours") ∧ temporal:duration(?d, ?starttime, ?endtime, "Days") ∧ swrlb:lessThan (?h, 2) ∧ swrlb:lessThan(?d, 7) -> sqwrl:select(?u, ?h, ?d)
2	Lightly Active	User(?u) ∧ hasActivity(?u, Act_Walking) ∧ isContextOf(?u, ?PAC-HLC) ∧ swrlb:equal(?PAC-HLC, "Exercising") ∧ hasStartTime(?PAC-HLC, ?starttime) ∧ hasEndTime(?PAC-HLC, ?endtime) ∧ temporal:duration(?h, ?starttime, ?endtime, "Hours") ∧ temporal:duration(?d, ?starttime, ?endtime, "Days") ∧ swrlb:greaterThan(?h, 1) ∧ swrlb:lessThan(?h, 3) ∧ swrlb:equal(?d, 7) -> sqwrl:select(?u, ?h, ?d)
3	Moderately Active	User(?u) ∧ hasActivity(?u, Act_Running) ∧ isContextOf(?u, ?PAC-HLC) ∧ swrlb:equal(?PAC-HLC, "Exercising") ∧ hasStartTime(?PAC-HLC, ?starttime) ∧ hasEndTime(?PAC-HLC, ?endtime) ∧ temporal:duration(?h, ?starttime, ?endtime, "Hours") ∧ temporal:duration(?d, ?starttime, ?endtime, "Days") ∧ swrlb:greaterThan(?h, 3) ∧ swrlb:lessThan(?h, 5) ∧ swrlb:equal(?d, 7) -> sqwrl:select(?u, ?h, ?d)
4	Very Active	User(?u) ∧ isContextOf(?u, ?PAC-HLC) ∧ swrlb:equal(?PAC-HLC, "Exercising") ∧ hasStartTime(?PAC-HLC, ?starttime) ∧ hasEndTime(?PAC-HLC, ?endtime) ∧ temporal:duration(?h, ?starttime, ?endtime, "Hours") ∧ temporal:duration(?d, ?starttime, ?endtime, "Days") ∧ swrlb:greaterThan(?h, 1) ∧ swrlb:lessThan(?h, 3) ∧ sqwrl:makeSet(?s, ?d) ∧ sqwrl:groupBy(?s, ?d) ∧ sqwrl:size(?no_of_days, ?s) ∧ swrlb:equal(?no_of_days, 7) -> sqwrl:select(?u, ?h, ?no_of_days)
5	Extremely Active	User(?u) ∧ isContextOf(?u, ?PAC-HLC) ∧ swrlb:equal(?PAC-HLC, "Exercising") ∧ hasStartTime(?PAC-HLC, ?starttime) ∧ hasEndTime(?PAC-HLC, ?endtime) ∧ temporal:duration(?h, ?starttime, ?endtime, "Hours") ∧ temporal:duration(?d, ?starttime, ?endtime, "Days") ∧ swrlb:greaterThan(?h, 1) ∧ swrlb:lessThan(?h, 3) ∧ sqwrl:makeSet (?s, ?PA-HLC) ∧ sqwrl:groupBy(?s, ?PA-HLC) ∧ sqwrl:size(?Exercise_per_day, ?s) ∧ swrlb:equal(?Exercise_per_day, 2) -> sqwrl:select(?u, ?h, ?Exercise_per_day)
6	Meal Frequency	User(?u)∧ hasActivity(?u, ?Act) ∧ swrlb:equal(?Act, "Eating") ∧ hasStartTime(?Act, ?starttime) ∧ hasEndTime(?Act, ?endtime) ∧ temporal:duration(?d, ?starttime, ?endtime, "Days") ∧ sqwrl:makeSet(?s, ?d) ∧ sqwrl:groupBy(?s, ?d) ∧ sqwrl:size(?no_of_days, ?s) ∧ swrlb:equal(?no_of_days, 1) ∧ sqwrl:makeSet(?Actset, ?Act) ∧ sqwrl:groupBy(?Actset, ?p) ∧ sqwrl:size(?freq, ?Actset) ∧ swrlb:greaterThan(?freq, 2) -> sqwrl:select(?u, ?freq,?no_of_days)

8.6Implementation Details

The following sections discuss in detail about the implementation test environment, which was constructed using *Semantic Web APIs*. Furthermore, the evaluation for results and introduction of advanced queries along with detailed description are presented.

8.6.1 Test Environment

All experiments were performed on a single machine under 64bit Enterprise edition of *Microsoft Windows 7* on the top of AMD A10-5800K APU with 12 GB of RAM. Java engine was executed with Eclipse IDE Luna that ran using JRE 1.8.0_45-b15 64-bit version.

8.6.2 Semantic Web APIs Usage Details

The implementation [14] of HLCA in mlCAF is performed in Maven (https://maven.apache.org/)

based project management with Java along with available open source library, Apache Jena v2.11.2 (https://jena.apache.org/). The component *High-Level Context Builder* receives unstructured low-level information, namely locations, activities, emotions, food, BloodGlucose, and BloodPressure. The *Context Mapper* maps received low-level information in the form of the label for *Activity*, *Location*, *Emotions*, *Food*, *BloodGlucose*, and *BloodPressure* along with meta-data comprising of Start-time, user-info, etc., using semantic web framework including RDFS [43], OWL2 [44], and OWL-API (http://owlapi. sourceforge.net/).

It transforms this information into ontological triple format. The *Physical Activity Context Synchronizer* takes concurrent low-Level contexts like *Activity*, *Location* and *Emotion* valid at the same moment in time. Similarly, *Nutrition Context Synchronizer* processes whenever food low-level context has arrived. *Nutrition context synchronizer* takes the "Eating" activity low-level context along with Food low-level context in addition to emotion and location. The synchronized LLCs are obtained by SPARQL queries [45] using *Union* operators capable of combining two or more SELECT statements as mentioned in Figure 8.9 labeled as *Block 1 and Block 2*. *Block 1* retrieves results pertaining to underlying cross-domain LLCs whereas *Block 2* structure is designed to retrieve nutrition LLCs. The obtained synchronized LLCs are remodeled to *unclassified HLCs* depending on the concurrent LLCs. These different synchronized LLCs can be visualized in Figure 8.10 coupled w.r.t their timestamps in RDF format. The *High-Level Context Reasoner* receives either three types of *unclassified HLCs*, i.e., PA-HLC, N-HLC or C-HLC for their verification and classification. Firstly, the *Context Verifier* checks the semantic and syntactic consistency of the *unclassified HLCs* and then the *Context Classifier* performs the ontological inference and identifies the membership of the *unclassified HLCs* with the help of Pellet (https://www.w3.org/2001/sw/wiki/Pellet), an open source OWL-DL reasoner. All the contexts are stored in Jena TDB (https://jena.apache.org/documentation/tdb/). The *Physical Activity Context Notifier* or *Nutrition Context Notifier* makes the newly inferred HLCs Figure 8.11 to the *Mining Minds* or any third party entity for behavior analysis and recommendation generation.

```
SELECT ?llc
WHERE
 {
    { ?llc        rdf:type  ?type .
     ?type       subClassOf  ?category .                Block 1
     ?category  subClassOf  LowLevelContext .
     ?llc        hasStartTime  ?starttime .}

  UNION
   { ?llc        rdf:type  ?type .
     ?type       subClassOf  ?subcategory .
     ?type1      subClassOf  ?category .                Block 2
     ?category  subClassOf  LowLevelContext .
     ?llc        hasStartTime  ?starttime .}

  UNION
   { ?llc     isContextOf  user_20 .}

  FILTER NOT EXISTS ?llc  hasEndTime  ?endtime .
  FILTER ( ?starttime <= "2017-08-18T10:07:47+09:00"^^xsd:dateTime )
}
```

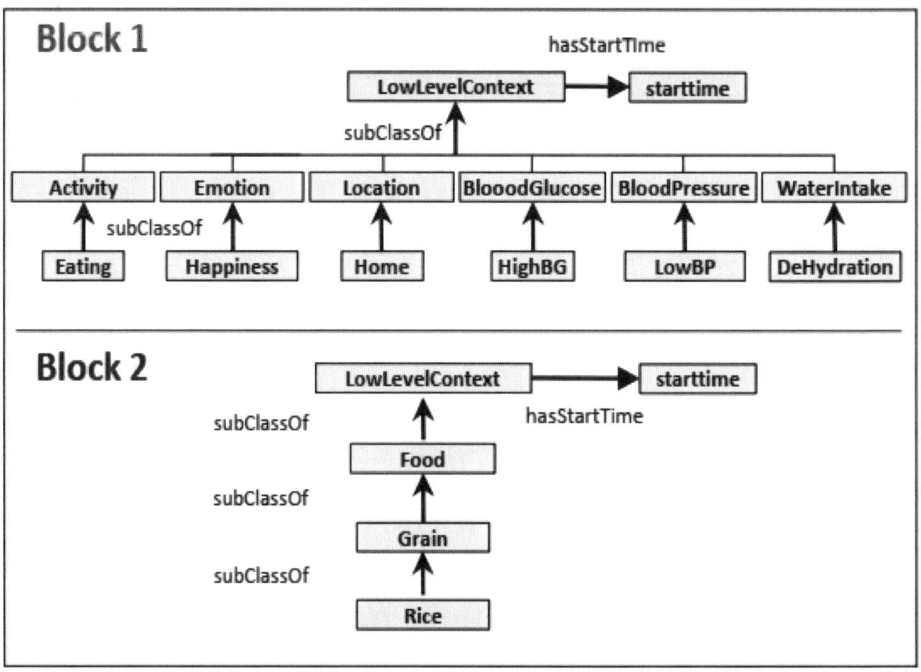

Figure 8.9 Evidential mappings of MMCO with SPARQL Query while retrieving Concurrent low-level Context w.r.t timestamps

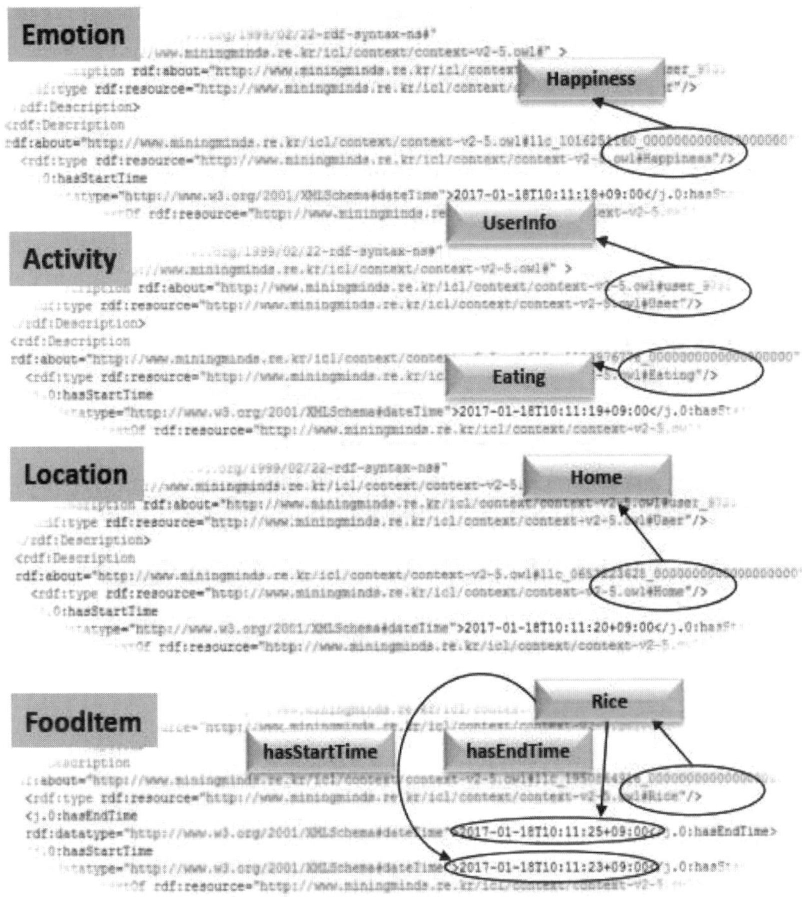

Figure 8.10 Context Synchronizer: Synchronizing low-level contexts w.r.t timestamps

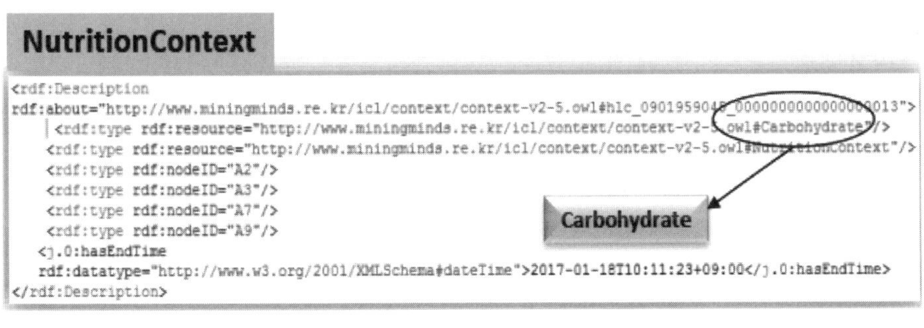

Figure 8.11 Inferred NutritionContext: Carbohydrate (Major Nutrient) in *Rice* Fooditem LLC

8.6.3 Experimental Results

The evaluation has consisted in the collection of around 141,872 *Low-Level Contexts* and 36,276 recognized *High-Level Contexts* belonging to 20 different adult volunteers in real environment using MM platform involving mlCAF framework. In example scenario, we considered user's LLC, PA-HLC and N-HLC spanning over-a-week as a case study to explain and provide enough evidence for vertical fusioning and horizontal fusioning, so that we can validate sedentary and active behaviors. The graphical representation mentioned in Figure 8.12 shows the HLCs inferred for different users with vertically fused PA-HLC and N-HLC. This representation gives intuition how vertical fusion helps in reducing huge volume of low-level contexts to PA-HLC and N-HLC. So instead of communicating all HLCs with third party entities, only whenever the change occurs, the respective vertically fused HLCs are delivered thus reducing network communication amongst entities. Out of 36,276 HLCs, only 4144 PA-HLC, N-HLC, and C-HLC were communicated behavior modeling APIs as shown in Figure 8.12

Heatmap confusion matrix representation shown in Figure 8.13 provides accuracies for recognized HLCs (i.e., PA-HLCs, N-HLCs and C-HLCs). Around 7.35% HLCs were not classified by the reasoner whereas 92.65% HLCs were realized correctly. It is evident that good accuracy results were achieved using cross-domain context fusioning, however, some missing LLCs lead to the declined accuracies for HLCs especially for N-HLCs. For a collected dataset, we evaluated how HLCA correctly inferred high-level contexts based on low-level contexts for the 15-s sliding window. We used the precision and recall measures to evaluate HLCA in mlCAF as shown in Figure 8.14 to address our performance challenges. The high inferring accuracy proved that HLCs are rarely misclassified but the problem arises when missing LLC leads to wrongly recognized HLC.

- Precision: Number of HLC correctly inferred by mlCAF divided by the total number of HLC defined in MMCO.

- Recall: Number of HLC correctly answered by the mlCAF divided by the total number of mlCAF in the dataset.

Uncertainty exists in ontological reasoning which leads to ambiguous results. By carefully analyzing *Unidentified PA-HLC* and *N-HLC*, it was realized that *Unclassified HLCs* are inferred to *Unidentified PA-HLC* and *N-HLC* with some missing or wrongly identified low-level contexts as shown in Figure 8.15.

In order to check disk space utilization, resources were examined by persisting RDF dataset pertaining to 20 different users. Figure 8.16 shows a linear relationship between Jena TDB resource utilization and increasing number of contexts.

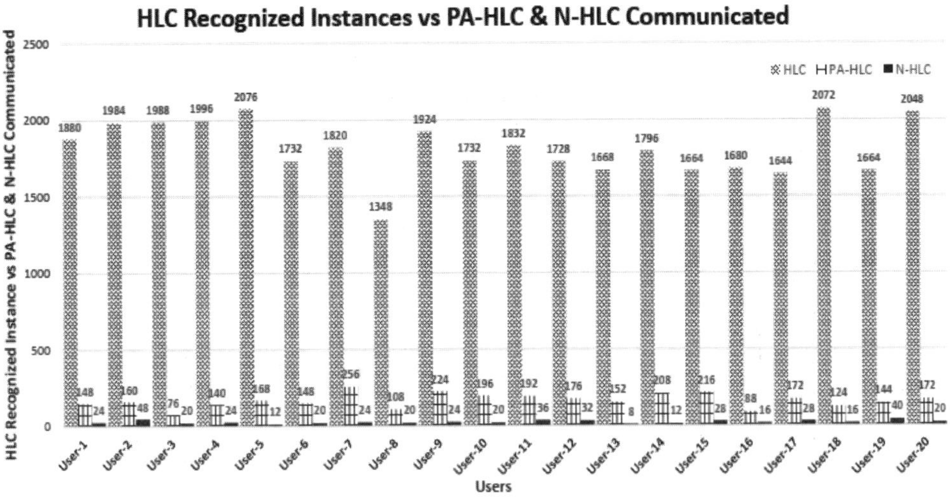

Figure 8.12 HLC Recognized Instances vs PA-HLC and N-HLC Communicated

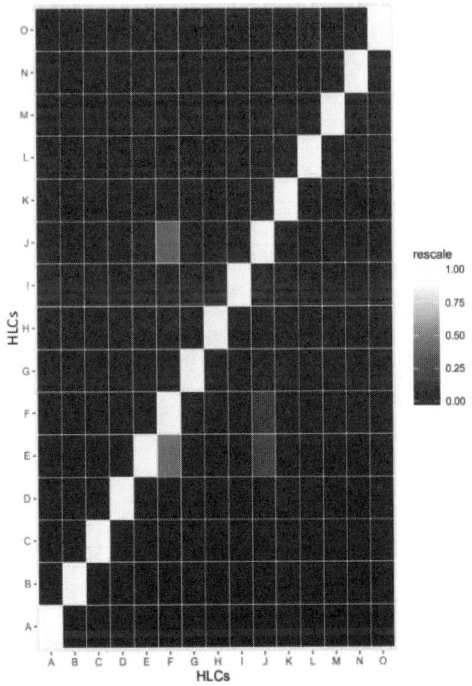

Figure 8.13 Confusion Matrix expressed as heat map for recognized HLCs (PA-HLC, N-HLC, and C-HLC). Legend: A = Amusement, B = Commuting, C = Exercising, D = Gardening, E = Carbohydrate, F = Fats, G = Housework, H = Inactivity, I = OfficeWork, J = Protein, K = Sleeping, L = HighRiskHealthState, M = ModerateRiskHealthState, N = NormalHealthState, O = VeryHighRiskHealthState

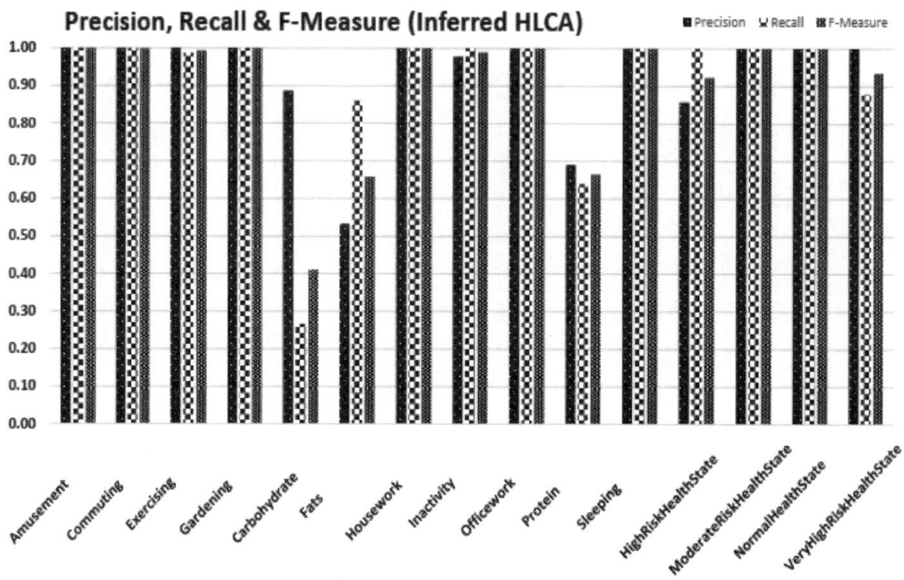

Figure 8.14 Precision, Recall and F-Measure for recognized PA-HLCs, N-HLCs and C-HLCs

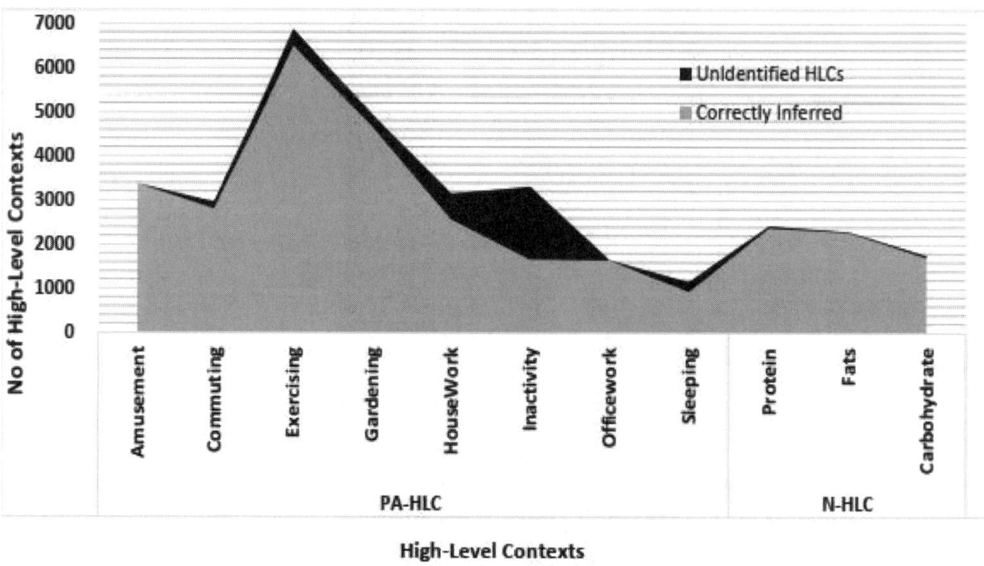

Figure 8.15 Unidentified PA-HLCs, and N-HLCs due to missing LLCs

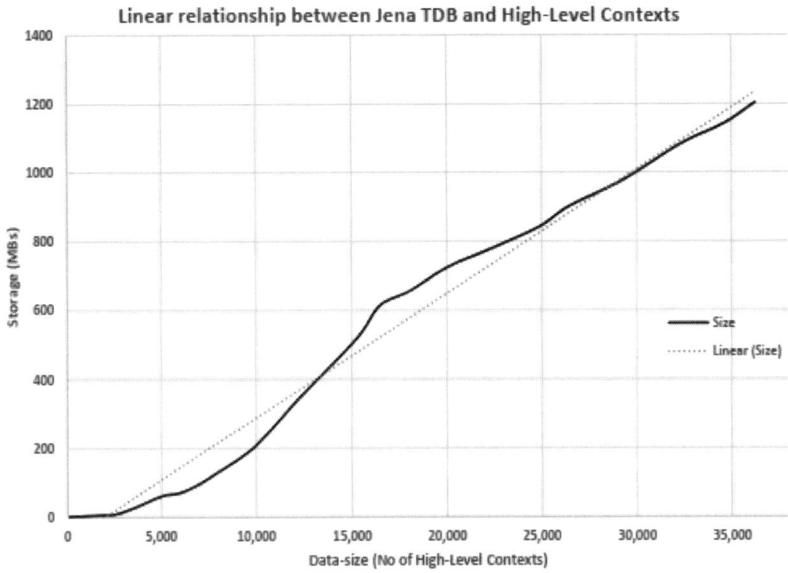

Figure 8.16 Impact of No of instances on Jena TDB

8.6.4 SQWRL based advanced Queries

In context-awareness for user personalization, SWRL/SQWRL queries were designed to aid horizontal fusioning to obtain human behavior. As mentioned in Table 8.3 the antecedent of each SWRL/SQWRL represents a conjunction (or union) of the user, LLC, PA-HLC, N-HLC and associated properties. These rules are constructed as per logic flow described in Figure 8.5. Daily physical activities, food intake and eating patterns can also have substantial effects on human health. Food intake frequency can induce healthy benefits and influences of the timing of meals and frequency on health may be large [46]. Healthy eating can be judged by identifying meal frequency and has a deep relationship with physical activities. In order to observe nutrition intake quantity *meal frequency* is also determined and queried. In this study, we presented SQWRL related to query constructions for behavior context based on user sedentary behaviors and also considered identification of meal frequency.

Rule 1. Sedentary Behavior

The meaning of the rule is as follows:

(i) If the user "u" has location "Loc_Gym".
(ii) The user "u" has PA-HLC as "Exercising" and it has some start time and end time.
(iii) The duration is less than two hours.
(iv) The difference in a number of days is less than seven days i.e., in a week.
(v) User "u" has "Sedentary Behavior" if "Exercising" PA-HLC is less than two hours in a week.

Rule 2. Lightly Active

(i) If the user "u" has a low intensity activity such as walking "Act_Walking" which is *subClassOf*

of PA-HLC.

(ii) The user "u" has PA-HLC as "Exercising" with start-time and end-time.
(iii) If the duration is between one hour and three hours.
(iv) If the difference in the number of days is less than seven days i.e., in a week.
(v) This SQWRL query selects the users "u" a "Lightly Active" if "Exercising" PA-HLC is between one hour and three hours but with LLC *Activity* as *Act_Walking* in a week.

Rule 3. Moderately Active

(i) If the user "u" has a moderately intensive activity such as Running with instance "Act_Running", which is *subClassOf* of PA-HLC.
(ii) The user "u" has PA-HLC as "Exercising" with start-time and end-time.
(iii) If the duration is between three hour and five hours.
(iv) If the difference in the number of days is less than seven days i.e., in a week.
(v) This SQWRL query selects the user's "u" a "Moderately Active" if "Exercising" PA-HLC is between three hours and five hours but with LLC *Activity* as *Act_Running* in a week.

Rule 4. Very Active

(i) If the user "u" has highly intensive "Exercising" with start-time and end-time as PA-HLC.
(ii) The duration of "Exercising" is between one hour and three hours.
(iii) The intensive "Exercising" is being performed daily.
(iv) This designed SQWRL query will retrieve a list of all users who perform highly intensive "Exercising" and they are termed as having *Very Active* behavioral context as they are regularly engaged in performing physical activities.

Rule 5. Extremely Active

(i) If the user "u" has vigorous-intensive "Exercising" with start-time and end-time as PA-HLC.
(ii) The duration of "Exercising" is between one hour and three hours.
(iii) The vigorous-intensive "Exercising" is being performed twice a day.
(iv) This SQWRL query will retrieve a list of all users who perform vigorous-intensive "Exercising" and the resultant users are considered to be of *Extremely Active* behavior, who perform intensive workouts twice a day having an overall duration of two hours or more.

Rule 6. Meal Frequency

(i) If the user "u" has some activity "Eating".
(ii) The user "u" has N-HLC as "Eating" and it has some start time and end time.
(iii) Count the activity "Eating" per day.
(iv) The presented SQWRL query calculates the frequency of an activity "Eating" in a day for the users and returns all users with given conjunctive conditions.

These captured human behaviors using VF and HF are transmitted to other Mining Minds platform layers for further support to user's health and wellbeing by monitoring physical activity, nutrition, and health-related states.

8.7 Summary

This chapter has presented the ontology-based modeling and cross-domain context fusioning, associated implementation using *multi-level Context-aware Framework* mlCAF, methods for transforming *Low-Level Contexts* (LLCs) into *Physical Activity High-Level Context* (PA-HLC), *Nutrition High-Level Context* (N-HLC) and *Clinical High-Level Context* (C-HLC). These PA-HLC, N-HLC and C-HLC are transformed using ontological based inference resulting in the vertical fusioning for cross-domain low-level contexts. In this work, the *Mining Minds Context Ontology* (MMCO) was extended to cater cross-domain contexts from physical activity, nutrition and clinical domains in order to identify major nutritional patterns and behaviors for users. It is pertinent to mention that a broader picture of human behavior modeling and lifestyle determination is obtained by using SWRL/SQWRL additionally as a horizontal fusioning, which keeps on creating associations amongst PA-HLC, N-HLC, C-HLC, and even LLCs at different levels. The main motivation behind this work lies in correctly identifying user's daily life contexts, behavior identification, as lifestyle, which lead to better community care and wellness. So the key direction that underpins our ongoing research in the *Mining Minds* involves real-time human behavior modeling and lifestyle prediction using cross-domain contexts. In this regard, experimental results indicate a context recognition average accuracy of around 92.65% for the inferred cross-domain contexts at different fusioning levels. Moreover, investigations are still underway for the identification for more efficient context fusioning mechanism through semantic technologies. it is confirmed that there is still a need for relevant data within in the referred time, which is to be used in the *Mining Minds* with MMCO for more accurate PA-HLC, N-HLC and C-HLC contexts situation analysis. In addition, creation and execution of more SWRL/SQWRL rules will have a significant impact on the overall platform in terms of better behavioral modeling and lifestyle identification. In future, we are planning to extend SWRL/SQWRL for lifestyle modeling and perform prediction analysis using inductive reasoning by applying data-driven approaches on gathered dataset i.e., A-Box assertions in the Jena Triple-store Database.

Abbreviations

The following abbreviations are used in this manuscript:

MMCO Mining Minds Context Ontology LLC Low-level Context
HLC High-level Context
PA-HLC Physical Activity High-level Context N-HLC Nutrition High-level Context
C-HLC Clinical High-level Context
BP Blood Pressure
BG Blood Glucose
VF Vertical Fusioning
HF Horizontal Fusioning

Source Code

Source code can be downloaded from the following location:

https://github.com/ubiquitous-computing-lab/Mining-Minds/tree/master/information-curation-layer/high-level-context-awareness

The contents of this chapter have been previously published in the following article:

Muhammad Asif Razzaq, Claudia Villalonga, Sungyoung Lee, Usman Akhtar, Maqbool Ali, Eun-Soo Kim, Asad Masood Khattak, Hyonwoo Seung, Taeho Hur, Jaehun Bang, Dohyeong Kim, and Wajahat Ali Khan, "mlCAF: Multi-Level Cross-Domain Semantic Context Fusioning for Behavior Identification", Sensors (SCIE, IF:2.677), Doi: 10.3390/s17102433., 2017

References

[1] Borges, V.; Jeberson, W. Survey of context information fusion for sensor networks based ubiquitous systems. arXiv 2013, arXiv:1309.0598.

[2] Meditskos, G.; Dasiopoulou, S.; Kompatsiaris, I. MetaQ: A knowledge-driven framework for context-aware activity recognition combining SPARQL and OWL 2 activity patterns. Pervasive Mob. Comput. 2016, 25, 104–124.

[3] Ni, Q.; Pau de la Cruz, I.; García Hernando, A.B. A foundational ontology-based model for human activity representation in smart homes. J. Ambient Intell. Smart Environ. 2016, 8, 47–61.

[4] Abowd, G.D.; Dey, A.K.; Brown, P.J.; Davies, N.; Smith, M.; Steggles, P. Towards a better understanding of context and context-awareness. In Proceedings of the 1st International Symposium on Handheld and Ubiquitous Computing (HUC '99), Karlsruhe, Germany, 27–29 September 1999; Springer: Berlin, Germany, 1999; pp. 304–307.

[5] Perera, C.; Zaslavsky, A.; Christen, P.; Georgakopoulos, D. Context aware computing for the internet of things: A survey. IEEE Commun. Surv. Tutor. 2014, 16, 414–454.

[6] Villalonga, C.; Razzaq, M.A.; Khan, W.A.; Pomares, H.; Rojas, I.; Lee, S.; Banos, O. Ontology-Based High-Level Context Inference for Human Behavior Identification. Sensors 2016, 16, 1617.

[7] Bae, I.H. An ontology-based approach to ADL recognition in smart homes. Future Gener. Comput. Syst. 2014, 33, 32–41.

[8] Khattak, A.M.; Akbar, N.; Aazam, M.; Ali, T.; Khan, A.M.; Jeon, S.; Hwang, M.; Lee, S. Context representation and fusion: Advancements and opportunities. Sensors 2014, 14, 9628–9668.

[9] Llinas, J.; Snidaro, L.; García, J.; Blasch, E. Context and fusion: Definitions, terminology. In Context-Enhanced Information Fusion; Springer: Cham, Switzerland, 2016; pp. 3–23.

[10] Alti, A.; Lakehal, A.; Laborie, S.; Roose, P. Autonomic Semantic-Based Context-Aware Platform for Mobile Applications in Pervasive Environments. Future Internet 2016, 8, 48.

[11] Wang, M.; Perera, C.; Jayaraman, P.P.; Zhang, M.; Strazdins, P.; Ranjan, R. City Data Fusion: Sensor Data Fusion in the Internet of Things. arXiv 2015, arXiv:1506.09118.

[12] Ni, Q.; García Hernando, A.B.; Pau de la Cruz, I. A Context-Aware System Infrastructure for Monitoring Activities of Daily Living in Smart Home. J. Sens. 2016, 2016, 9493047.

[13] Villalonga, C.; Banos, O.; Khan, W.A.; Ali, T.; Razzaq, M.A.; Lee, S.; Pomares, H.; Rojas, I. High-Level Context Inference for Human Behavior Identification. In Ambient Assisted Living. ICT-Based Solutions in Real Life Situations; Springer: Cham, Switzerland, 2015; pp. 164–175.

[14] HLCA at Github. Available online: https://github.com/ubiquitous-computing-lab/Mining-Minds/tree/ master/information-curation-layer/high-level-context-awareness (accessed on 20 September 2017).

[15] Colberg, S.R.; Sigal, R.J.; Yardley, J.E.; Riddell, M.C.; Dunstan, D.W.; Dempsey, P.C.; Horton, E.S.; Castorino, K.; Tate, D.F. Physical activity/exercise and diabetes: A position statement of the American Diabetes Association. Diabetes Care 2016, 39, 2065–2079.

[16] World Health Organization. Global Report on Diabetes; World Health Organization: Geneva, Switzerland, 2016.

[17] Yúrúr, Ó.; Liu, C.H.; Sheng, Z.; Leung, V.C.; Moreno, W.; Leung, K.K. Context-awareness for mobile sensing: A survey and future directions. IEEE Commun. Surv. Tutor. 2016, 18, 68–93.

[18] Baldauf, M.; Dustdar, S.; Rosenberg, F. A survey on context-aware systems. Int. J. Ad Hoc Ubiquitous Comput. 2007, 2, 263–277.

[19] Ponce, V.; Roy, P.; Abdulrazak, B. Dynamic Domain Model for Micro Context-Aware Adaptation of Applications. In Proceedings of the 2016 IEEE Intl IEEE Conferences Ubiquitous Intelligence & Computing, Advanced and Trusted Computing, Scalable Computing and Communications, Cloud and Big Data Computing, Internet of People, and Smart World Congress (UIC/ATC/ScalCom/CBDCom/IoP/SmartWorld), Toulouse, France, 18–21 July 2016; pp. 98–105.

[20] Zheng, Y.; Pan, W.; Sahebi, S.S.; Fernández, I. The 1st Workshop on Intelligent Recommender Systems by Knowledge Transfer & Learning (RecSysKTL). In Proceedings of the Eleventh ACM Conference on Recommender Systems, Como, Italy, 27–31 August 2017; ACM: New York, NY, USA, 2017; pp. 366–367.

[21] Guo, B.; Sun, L.; Zhang, D. The architecture design of a cross-domain context management system. In Proceedings of the 2010 8th IEEE International Conference on Pervasive Computing and Communications Workshops (PERCOM Workshops), Mannheim, Germany, 29 March–2 April 2010; pp. 499–504.

[22] Guo, B.; Zhang, D.; Sun, L.; Yu, Z.; Zhou, X. iCROSS: Toward a scalable infrastructure for cross-domain context management. Pers. Ubiquitous Comput. 2013, 17, 591–602.

[23] Lin, D.; Kapoor, A.; Hua, G.; Baker, S. Joint people, event, and location recognition in personal photo collections using cross-domain context. In Proceedings of the European Conference on Computer Vision–ECCV 2010, Crete, Greece, 5–11 September 2010; pp. 243–256.

[24] Snidaro, L.; García, J.; Llinas, J. Context-based information fusion: A survey and discussion. Inf. Fusion 2015, 25, 16–31.

[25] Tria, S.B.; Seridi-Bouchelaghem, H.; Mokhati, F. An Ontology-Based Context Model to Manage Users Preferences And Conflicts. Informatica 2016, 40, 71.

[26] Gu, T.; Pung, H.K.; Zhang, D.Q. A service-oriented middleware for building context-aware services. J. Netw. Comput. Appl. 2005, 28, 1–18.

[27] Chen, H.; Finin, T.; Joshi, A.; Kagal, L.; Perich, F.; Chakraborty, D. Intelligent agents meet the semantic web in smart spaces. IEEE Internet Comput. 2004, 8, 69–79.

[28] Riboni, D.; Bettini, C. COSAR: hybrid reasoning for context-aware activity recognition. Pers. Ubiquitous Comput. 2011, 15, 271–289.

[29] Chi, Y.L.; Chen, T.Y.; Tsai, W.T. A chronic disease dietary consultation system using OWL-based ontologies and semantic rules. J. Biomed. Inform. 2015, 53, 208–219.

[30] Okeyo, G.; Chen, L.; Wang, H. Combining ontological and temporal formalisms for composite activity modelling and recognition in smart homes. Future Gener. Comput. Syst. 2014, 39, 29–43.
[31] Smirnov, A.; Levashova, T.; Shilov, N. Patterns for context-based knowledge fusion in decision support systems. Inf. Fusion 2015, 21, 114–129.
[32] Wang, P.; Luo, H.; Sun, Y. A Habit-based SWRL Generation and Reasoning Approach in Smart Home. In Proceedings of the 2015 IEEE 21st International Conference on Parallel and Distributed Systems (ICPADS), Melbourne, Australia, 14–17 December 2015; pp. 770–775.
[33] Banos, O.; Amin, M.B.; Khan, W.A.; Afzal, M.; Hussain, M.; Kang, B.H.; Lee, S. The Mining Minds digital health and wellness framework. Biomed. Eng. OnLine 2016, 15, 76.
[34] Banos, O.; Bang, J.H.; Hur, T.H.; Siddiqui, M.; Huynh-The, T.; Vui, L.B.; Ali-Khan, W.; Ali, T.; Villalonga, C.; Lee, S. Mining Human Behavior for Health Promotion. In Proceedings of the 37th Annual International Conference of the IEEE Engineering in Medicine and Biology Society (EMBC 2015), Milan, Italy, 25–29 August 2015.
[35] Banos, O.; Villalonga, C.; Bang, J.H.; Hur, T.H.; Kang, D.; Park., S.B.; Hyunh-The, T.; Vui, L.B.; Amin, M.B.; Razzaq, M.A.; et al. Human Behavior Analysis by means of Multimodal Context Mining. Sensors 2016, 16, 1264.
[36] Færch, K.; Witte, D.R.; Brunner, E.; Kivimäki, M.; Tabak, A.; Jørgensen, M.E.; Ekelund, U.; Vistisen, D. Physical Activity and Improvement of Glycaemia in Pre-diabetes by Different Diagnostic Criteria. J. Clin. Endocrinol. Metab. 2017, 102, 3712–3721.
[37] Han, Y.; Han, M.; Lee, S.; Sarkar, A.; Lee, Y.K. A framework for supervising lifestyle diseases using long-term activity monitoring. Sensors 2012, 12, 5363–5379.
[38] Mining Minds Context Ontology. Available online: http://www.miningminds.rc.kr/lifelog/context/ context-v3.0.owl (accessed on 20 September 2017).
[39] American-Diabetes-Association. Available online: http://diabetes.org/ (accessed on 20 September 2017).
[40] Giles, T.D.; Berk, B.C.; Black, H.R.; Cohn, J.N.; Kostis, J.B.; Izzo, J.L.; Weber, M.A. Expanding the definition and classification of hypertension. J. Clin. Hypertens. 2005, 7, 505–512.
[41] Skillen, K.L.; Chen, L.; Burns, W. VIPR: A Visual Interface Tool for Programming Semantic Web Rules. In Proceedings of the 2016 Intl IEEE Conferences Ubiquitous Intelligence & Computing, Advanced and Trusted Computing, Scalable Computing and Communications, Cloud and Big Data Computing, Internet of People, and Smart World Congress (UIC/ATC/ScalCom/CBDCom/IoP/SmartWorld), Toulouse, France, 18–21 July 2016; pp. 277–284.
[42] O'Connor, M.; Das, A. SQWRL: A query language for OWL. In Proceedings of the 6th International Conference on OWL: Experiences and Directions, Chantilly, VA, USA, 23–24 October 2009; Volume 529, pp. 208–215.
[43] Brickley, D.; Guha, R.V. RDF Schema 1.1; W3C Recommendation. 25 February 2014. Available online: https://www.w3.org/TR/rdf-schema/ (accessed on 20 September 2017).
[44] W3C OWL Working Group. OWL 2 Web Ontology Language: Document Overview, 2nd ed.; W3C Recommendation.
[45] 11 December 2012. Available online: http://www.w3.org/TR/owl2-overview/ (accessed on 20 September 2017).

[46] Harris, S.; Seaborne, A. SPARQL 1.1 (SPARQL Query Language for RDF); W3C Recommendation, 21 March 2013. Available online: http://www.w3.org/TR/sparql11-query/ (accessed on 20 September 2017).

[47] Mattson, M.P.; Allison, D.B.; Fontana, L.; Harvie, M.; Longo, V.D.; Malaisse, W.J.; Mosley, M.; Notterpek, L.; Ravussin, E.; Scheer, F.A.; et al. Meal frequency and timing in health and disease. Proc. Natl. Acad. Sci. USA 2014, 111, 16647–16653.

Part IV

Knowledge Generation

Chapter 9

Wellness Model

Clinically Harmonized Wellness Concepts Model for Health and Wellness Services

Taqdir Ali, Maqbool Hussain, Muhammad Afzal, Wajahat Ali Khan, Taeho Hur, Dohyeong Kim, Jaehun Bang, Muhammad Bilal Amin, Sungyoung Lee, and Byeong Ho Kang

A considerable number of frameworks and platforms are available to model terminologies in the clinical domains, but wellness domain lacks a development framework. The objective of this chapter is to present a clinically influenced and harmonized wellness concepts model (WCM) in order to support diverse wellness applications and services. This model is supported by a novel framework in the wellness domain. In order to develop wellness concepts model, the proposed framework is divided into four processes; start-up and initiation process, WCM modeling and evolution process, WCM production process, and release process. The WCM modeling and evolution process extracts top level hierarchical concepts from the existing published literature using a systematic review process. The framework also extends its scope to evolution using the wellness recommendations guidelines. The evolution process is supported by clinical concepts harmonization with the help of terminology standard, SNOMED CT. We validated the top-level hierarchical concepts using a group of experts based on a decision-making method known as the nominal group technique (NGT). In the final decision of the NGT, 14.7% of the hierarchical concepts are eliminated from the model due to their voting score of less than 70% in the expert panel. The top-level concepts of the model are cross-validated using structured equation modeling (SEM). The chi-square ($\chi 2$) test and root mean square error of approximation test results demonstrated the acceptable goodness of fit indices for the WCM with respect to experts' and users' opinions. In order to fill the gap that existed in wellness and clinical domain, this chapter systematically investigated concepts for building a clinically harmonized model called the WCM. The proposed WCM development framework is validated through the NGT and SEM.

9.1 Introduction

9.1.1 Motivation

In the current wellbeing paradigm, individuals focus on positive aspects of health and wellness to protect themselves from illness based on the illness-health-wellness continuum [1], as shown in Figure 9.1. Health and wellness are often used interchangeably but their origins and meanings are different [2]. Health is state of complete physical, mental, and social wellbeing, and it is the absence of disease, while wellness refers to the state of living an optimally healthy lifestyle and wellness is more than healthcare [2], [3]. Researchers in health and social sciences proceeded their research directions towards abnormality, disease, sickness, and dysfunction, opposite to wellness based on pathogenic paradigm [4]. Wellness has been deliberated as a model for counseling and development for a healthier life and has a long history of counseling [5], [6]. According to Chini and Dorner from the Austrian Medical Association [7], Austria will face additional costs of 1.6 billion Euros in 2030, increasing to 3.7 billion Euros in 2050 [8], due to the high percentage of risky habits in youth. In Europe, about 60% of diseases are associated with the seven leading health risk factors, some of these are tobacco, alcohol, overweight, poor nutrition, and physical activity [9]. According to Branca et al. [10], 28-79% of adults are overweight in the World Health Organization (WHO) European Region and nearly 30% of adults are smokers [11].

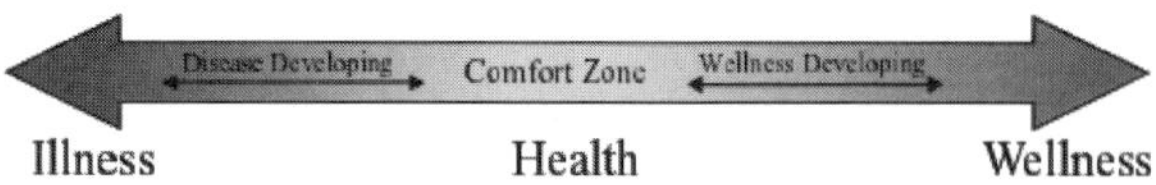

Figure 9.1 Illness-health-wellness continuum [1]

In current epoch of internet of things (IoT), a variety of healthcare and wellness applications are performing the role of counselor and recommender to change risky behaviors to healthy ones. The recommendation systems combine different healthcare and wellness knowledge with individual's data to provide personalized reminders, prompts, alerts, and guidance [12]. In knowledge-based recommendation systems, the shareability and integration of a knowledge base with many heterogeneous databases models is a challenging task [13]. In the clinical domain, knowledge shareability and interoperability can be achieved using standard terminologies (i.e., SNOMED CT, LOINC, and ICD10) and standard data models [14]. Unlike clinical domain, the wellness domain lacks such standard terminologies and data models. Therefore, knowledge integration and sharing are considerable barriers to the adoption of recommendation systems in the wellness domain. A holistic wellness concepts model (WCM) is needed to overcome the limitations of standard terminologies required for knowledge-related core functions such as knowledge acquisition, integration, and reusability. Moreover, the clinical terminology development processes (i.e. SNOMED CT, ICD-10, and LOINC) focus on the domain experts' knowledge and their validation only, because of the domain's sensitive nature [15]. The WCM development process amalgamates the domain experts' knowledge with concepts extraction from published articles and guidelines in the evolution process. This process validates the model through expert's opinion and statistical method.

9.1.2 WCM Importance in Knowledge-Based Systems and Services

The WCM plays a vital role in the creation of a reusable and integrable knowledge base. Usually, the recommendation systems generate recommendations based on users lifelog information. Whenever the schema and data of the lifelog repository for the different systems are heterogeneous, diverse, and do not follow standard terminologies, the integration of the systems with a knowledge base becomes challenging and is considered a critical issue in the adaption of decision and recommendation systems [16]. A unified concepts model and the representation of knowledge overcome the limitation of reusable and integrable knowledge base [17]. Therefore, a well-originated and holistic WCM can play a pivotal role in the initial breakthrough for the standard and unified concepts model in the wellness domain. This will result in reusability and easy integration of a knowledge base with heterogeneous legacy systems.

9.1.3 Synergy of Wellness with Clinical Modeling

Wellness terminologies have the same synergy as clinical terminologies with respect to utilization, such as the concepts usage in clinical and wellness notes, protocols, content, and knowledge of decision support and recommendation systems. For instance, the wellness applications used heterogeneous knowledge bases using diverse wellness concepts with the same synergy of clinical decision support systems (CDSS) [18]–[20].

In the clinical domain, there exist standard terminologies such as the International Classification of Diseases (ICD-9-CM), ICD-10 [21], [22], SNOMED CT [23], Read Codes Version 2, 3 [24], the Unified Medical Language System (UMLS) [25], Current Procedural Terminology (CPT) [48], and NANDA [49]. SNOMED CT is a comprehensive buildup of SNOMED RT and Clinical Terms Version 3 [45]. In numerous studies, it has been observed that SNOMED CT provides a large amount of coverage of clinical content in various domains such as diagnosis, treatment, laboratory tests, clinical statements, problems, and nursing. For instance, SNOMED CT covered 92.5% of the international classification for nursing practice (ICNP) nursing diagnosis and intervention catalogue concepts [26]. Similarly, SNOMED CT provided greater coverage of about 98.5% for the diagnosis and medical problems entered into a computerized physician order entry (CPOE) system [27]. Therefore, we considered SNOMED CT as a baseline for our proposed WCM and partially followed its design, development, and harmonization strategies and processes

9.1.4 Wellness Concepts Model (WCM) Overview

We designed a WCM development framework to develop, evolve, and validate the WCM. It includes start-up and initiation process, WCM modeling and evolution process, WCM production process, and a release process. In this study, we focus on the contributing process of WCM modeling and evolution, which consists following activities;

- Model Creation: The top-level hierarchical concepts model of the WCM is designed using extensive literature with a systematic review process.
- Model Evolution: The evolution process evolves the WCM using the wellness concepts used in published guidelines.
- Harmonization with standard terminology: We performed the harmonization activity to utilize the existing standard concepts, codes, and descriptions in the WCM.

- WCM Validation: We validated the top-level concepts of the WCM using the NGT process and cross-validated them using the statistical methods of structured equation modeling (SEM).

9.2 Related Works

Based on an extensive survey, Roscoe [28] stated in 2009 that researchers have failed to agree on a definition and the dimensional structure of wellness. Although several authors have proposed different definitions of wellness, a unified definition of wellness has not been crafted [28–31]. Authors mostly agree that wellness is a multidimensional and synergistic construct that is represented as a continuum and it has no end state [28], [29], [32]. Most of the authors have also come to an agreement and assume that wellness is more than the absence of illness [28]. According to the WHO definition of wellness, it is a state of complete physical, mental, and social well-being, and not merely the absence of disease or infirmity [28]. Many researchers have proposed different wellness models; one of the popular wellness models is Wheel of Wellness, introduced in the 1990s by Sweeney and Witmer [33], [34]. According to this model, the life forces that affect an individual's life are family, religion, education/industry, media, government, and community. In 2004, Myers and Sweeny [35] realized that the structure of the Wheel of Wellness should be re-examined due to the hypothesized relationships among its components and its complex structure. The Indivisible Self model was proposed as a higher-order wellness factor, which is based on Adler's [36] theory of holism, the indivisibility of self. Five main concepts are considered as second-order factors: Essential Self, Social Self, Creative Self, Physical Self, and Coping Self [35].Depken [37] described wellness as mainly comprising five dimensions: physical, intellectual, social, emotional, and spiritual. Authors mostly agree with these five dimensions; however, Hettler [32] mentioned an extended model with a sixth dimension: occupational. In 1997, Adams et al. [38] excluded the occupational dimension and included psychological in the wellness model. In the current years of IoT, wellness concepts have been used in many service applications worldwide. The most targeted components of wellness in service applications are physical, emotional, occupational, social, and psychological. One of the wellness ontologies, international classification of wellness (IWC) [39], has published by National Center for Biomedical Ontology (NCBO) on their BioPortal [40]. The wellness taxonomy of IWC comprises the emotional wellness, environmental wellness, financial wellness, intellectual wellness physical wellness, social wellness, spiritual wellness, vocational wellness, and wellness-NOS. Therefore, we included the IWC study in our survey with all mentioned concepts, but we used occupation and economic instead of vocational and finance of IWC, respectively, due to their use in many other studies [32], [41]–[44].Miller [42] provided a very intensive study on the wellness history and development of the concepts model.

The authors included important wellness factors such as physical, social, intellectual, demographics, mental, spiritual, emotional, occupation, and self-wroth in their proposed wellness model. Similarly, many research groups have designed and developed wellness models with distinct and overlapping concepts with each other. We included most of the wellness studies in our model creation using systematic review process. Therefore, our proposed model inspired by the amalgamation of all wellness models, discussed in the included studies, to produce a comprehensive wellness model. There are many knowledge elicitation methods have used to acquire concepts, knowledge, and requirements in literature. For instance, CommonKAD [45] is well-known a comprehensive methodology for KBS development, which pay attention to the expertise modeling in different phases of development life cycle of KBS and focus on different managerial aspects of KBS. Similarly, expert knowledge elicitation have used to estimate the parameters in health economic decision model [46]. All these methodologies have focused on some specific elicitation approach based on their requirements and experimental environment. Although these approaches lack the evolution from guidelines, harmonization with clinical standards, and cross-validation using empirical and statistical methods.

9.3 Methods and Materials

In this research, we emphasize the design, development, and evolution process of the concepts model in the wellness domain. It produces two artifacts in the form of a WCM development framework and the WCM terminology. In information technology research, real problems must be identified and conceptualized, appropriate techniques must be found for the solution, and these must be implemented and evaluated using appropriate methods and criteria [47]. Therefore, we followed a well-known and concise guideline of DSR [48] and its checklist [49], which provides a problem-solving paradigm to help develop artifacts and applications for actual business needs and problems [48]. We have designed a WCM development framework to develop the WCM, which comprises of start-up and initiation process, WCM modeling and evolution process, WCM production process, and the release process, as shown in Figure 9.2. In Start-up and initiation process of the WCM development, we performed the management tasks. a) We define the domain and scope of the wellness model such as physical, nutritional, environmental, clinical, and social aspects. b) We define the purpose and usage of wellness model such as wellness applications for physical activities, nutrition, and clinical recommendations and counseling systems. c) The team management activity is performed to manage domain personnel based on the domain's scope, purpose, and usage. d) After team organization, appropriate and scoped tasks are assigned to corresponding individuals with reasonable deadlines. e) In concepts source selection activity, credible resources are selected for developing a terminology model. We selected distinguished published research papers for the design and development of the WCM, while online published guidelines were selected as a source for the evolution of the model. The second WCM modeling and evolution process is an important and highly represents our contributions. Therefore, we focused on this process with more detail in following sub sections. This process comprises of domain analysis for the conceptual model creation and evolution, harmonization with standard terminology, and WCM validation.

In WCM Production Process, we transformed the conceptual model into an executable representation format. We selected an ontological representation for the WCM because it is a semantically rich representation of the knowledge [50]. Web Ontology Language (OWL) is used as a semantic web language to represent WCM ontology. The WCM Production Process has following sub-activities.

- In logical model transformation activity, the knowledge engineers and developers transform the conceptual model (harmonized and non-harmonized concepts) into a logical model representation, which is closer to the implementation.
- In concepts and relationships transformation activity, all the identified concepts and relationships are transformed to the desired executable representation.
- In consistency checking activity, we checked the syntactic and semantic consistency using Pellet [51] reasoner. WCM Ontology is validated using OntoClean framework [52]. The

metaproperties such as essence, rigidity, identity, unity, and dependency of OntoClean framework are applied to evaluate the ontology.

- In duplicate and conflict resolution activity, the knowledge engineers removed anomalies such as duplicate and conflicting concepts, which are identified in previous activity.

In Release process, we followed the steps to release and distribute the WCM to the end users. In plan release step, we decided the release version, included/excluded changes, the source of the release, the target community, the date and time, and the configuration of the release. In build release activity, the actual build is prepared from the source code of the WCM. After successful build, we tested the build and fixed the runtime errors and bugs. Finally, in distribute release activity, the release is distributed by the selected source. The recommended sources for WCM distribution are the Linked Open Data (LOD) using ''Linked Data Principles'' [53] and any community-accessible browser.

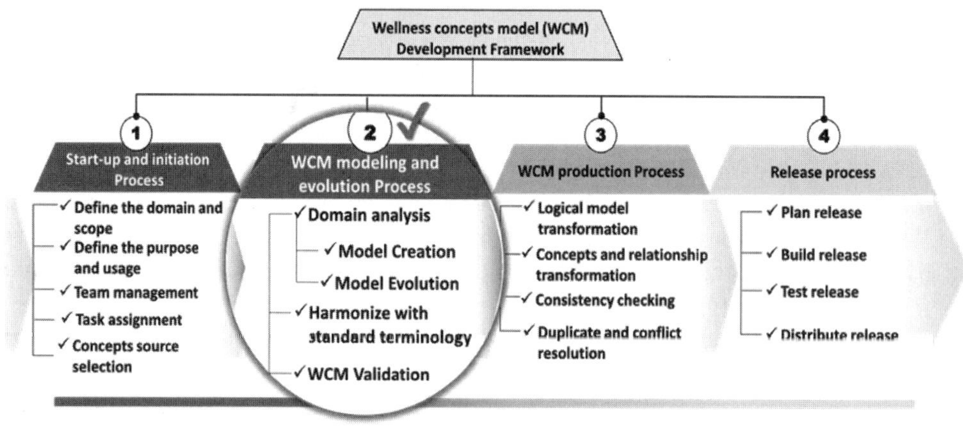

Figure 9.2 Wellness concepts model (WCM) development framework

9.3.1 WCM Modeling and Evolution Process

9.3.1.1 Domain Analysis

The domain analysis required extensive literature to find wellness concepts and relationships in order to build the top-level of the hierarchies. The identified hierarchies should be capable of arranging the subtypes of concepts under the top-level concepts. The whole process is iterative; therefore, we focused on wellness domain models and patterns, which have already been published in the literature, to initialize the conceptual model. In the evolution through subsequent iterations, different recommendation guidelines are used to extract concepts and their relationships, arranged under the initialized hierarchies of the conceptual model. Therefore, we performed modeling and evolution in two sub-activities: model creation and model evolution. In model creation, we modeled the top-level hierarchical concepts based on an extensive survey of wellness literature. In model evolution, we evolved the model by correlating concepts, used in recommendation guidelines, with top-level hierarchical concepts.

A. Model Creation

We performed the domain analysis literature based on the Preferred Reporting Items for Systematic Reviews and Meta Analyses (PRISMA) process followed in [54] with few changes, such as keywords, article types, and search engines. We searched for the potential keywords of wellness, wellbeing, wellness model, holistic wellness model, and healthcare and wellness in the range of the year 1920 to 2016. We searched these terms in Google Scholar, IEEE Xplore Digital Library, Machinery (ACM), PubMed, SpringerLink, and ScienceDirect with backward and forward citations. After removal of duplicate, unnecessary, unrelated titles, and abstracts in screening phase, we downloaded 117 different publications related to wellness models. We analyzed all the downloaded publications and identified 23 of the publications that discuss, design, and propose wellness concepts or models. Including the report characteristics of eligibility criteria, we considered four points in articles, a) discussed wellness concepts individually, b) designed or proposed new wellness model, c) evolved or modified the existing wellness model, and d) introduced or discussed the semantics of wellness concepts. The systematic review process followed is depicted in Figure 9.3. We analyzed the selected publications extensively to find candidate wellness concepts. We compared and summarized different wellness concepts and models from the selected publications, described in Table 9.1. In the selected publications, different authors have used diverse concepts for the same meaning but we categorized those diverse concepts under the common title of concept. The resultant wellness concepts, mentioned in Table 9.1, were documented and visualized using a mind map.

The mind map was selected because of its low level of difficulty, open extensibility, and medium to high memorability [55]. Additionally, most of the people are familiar and feel comfortable with the mind map technique using a simplified entity-relationship model (ERM) notation. The top-level concepts of the WCM were provided to a domain expert panel for validation. The validation process will be discussed in Section 11.3.2.

Table 9.1 Concepts identified in literature

Wellness Concepts		Study References
Physical	Exercise	[56], [57], [57], [32], [41], [35], [42], [58], [1], [38], [59], [60], [61], [62], [37], [63], [64], [44], [40]
	Nutrition	[56], [57], [57], [32], [41], [35], [42], [58], [1] [38], [59], [60], [61], [62], [37], [63], [64], [44], [40]
	Prevention	[38], [44], [40]
Social	Family	[32], [41], [35], [42], [58], [1], [38], [43], [59], [60], [61], [62], [37], [63], [64], [44], [40]
	Love	[32], [41], [35], [42], [58], [1], [38], [43], [59], [60], [61], [62], [37], [63], [64], [44], [40]
	Community	[32], [41], [35], [42], [58], [1], [38], [43], [59], [60], [61], [62], [37], [63], [64] [44], [40]
	Friendship	[32], [41], [35], [42], [58], [1], [38], [43], [59], [60], [61], [62], [37], [63], [64] [44], [40]
Intellectual	Problem Solving	[32], [41], [42], [1], [38], [59], [60], [61], [62], [37], [63], [64], [44], [40]
	Creativity	[32], [41], [42], [1], [38], [59], [60], [61], [62], [37], [63], [64] [44], [40]
Demographics	Gender Identity	[41], [35], [42], [44]
	Cultural Identity	[41], [35], [42], [43], [44]
Sense	Sense of Worth	[57], [41], [35]
	Sense of Control	[57], [41], [35]
	Sense of Humor	[57], [41], [35], [1]
Mental/Stress Management		[56], [57], [41], [35], [42], [58], [1], [43], [44]
Spiritual		[56], [57], [32], [41], [35], [42], [1], [38], [43], [59], [60], [61], [62], [37], [63], [40]
Emotional		[57], [57], [32], [41], [35], [42], [1], [38], [43], [59], [60], [61], [62], [37], [63], [44], [40]
Occupation		[32], [41], [42], [61], [62], [44], [40]
Self-care		[41], [35], [1], [43], [44]
Leisure		[41], [35], [1], [44]
Education		[41], [58], [43], [44]
Thinking		[57], [35], [44]
Self-worth		[35], [42], [44]
Media		[41], [44]
Government		[41], [44]
Local Safety		[1], [44]
Institutional Concern		[1],
Personal Attribution		[1],
Physiological		[38], [44]
Political		[43],
Economic		[43], [44], [40]
Healthcare		[58], [43], [44]
Environment		[58], [63], [44], [40]
Liberty		[57]

B. Model Evolution

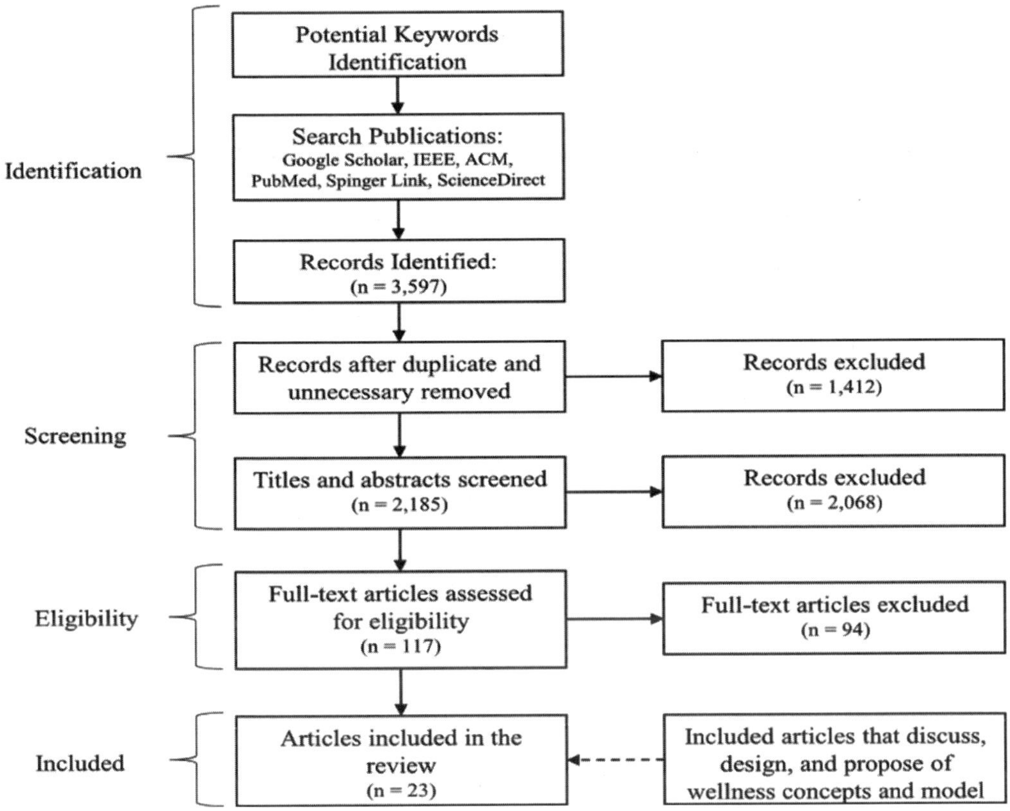

Figure 9.3 Systematic review process for survey literature

The WCM is evolved by finding the correlations between the concepts, which are extracted from related recommendation guidelines using an inspection method. The WCM evolution process consists of five steps as depicted in Figure 9.4. In the first step, a specific domain is selected based on the wellness requirements and field of interest. The wellness model covers different areas of healthcare and wellbeing such as obesity, diabetes, hypertension, mental disorders, dyslipidemia, and metabolic syndrome. In the second step, we defined the scope and objectives of the selected domain to evolve the WCM concepts in that particular domain. For instance, managing glucose and cholesterol levels, and handling cholesterol with other comorbidities are some of the important objectives and scopes for dealing with and managing diabetic patients.

In the third step, appropriate guidelines are selected based on the objectives and scope of the selected domain. Many healthcare and wellness institutions have designed and published recommendation guidelines to prevent unhealthy behaviors and to manage a healthier lifestyle.

In the fourth step, we identified the sections of the guidelines that describe recommendations pertaining to the selected objectives of the domain using an inspection method. In step five, the wellness concepts are identified from the recommendation text and represented in a conceptual graph [65]. After the wellness concepts are identified, concepts are searched in the current WCM to find duplicate concepts. The duplicate concepts are removed for placement in the WCM, while other identified concepts are connected to already existing concepts based on some appropriate relationship. The evolution process is explained in the following example scenario with each step of model evolution.

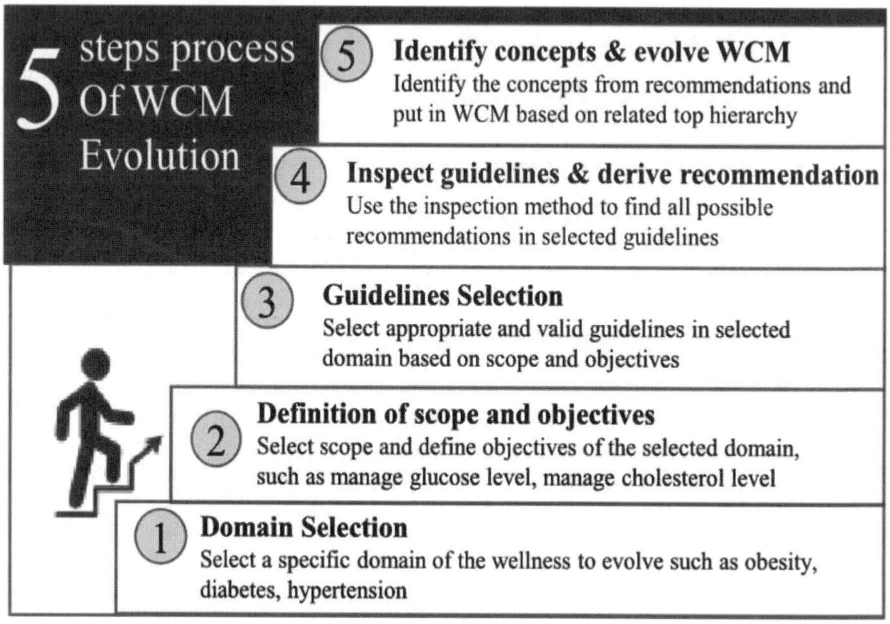

Figure 9.4 Five-step process of WCM evolution

Example Scenario:

Step 1: We selected diabetes domain to evolve the WCM for this scenario example.
Step 2: We selected the scope to manage the glucose and cholesterol levels of patients; we considered cholesterol with other comorbidities to be beyond the scope of this scenario.
Step 3: We selected recommendation guidelines for diabetes management along with related physical activities and nutrition guidelines because diabetes is greatly affected by healthier activities and diet. The title of selected guideline is ''Standards of medical care in *diabetes - 2016''* [66].
Step 4: The domain experts inspected the guideline, identified the recommendation parts, and derived the recommendation. For instance, one of the recommendations has to do with the assessment test of the risk factor for diabetes, shown in Table 9.2.

Step 5: After recommendation extraction, we extracted the concepts, identified the relationships among extracted concepts and built a conceptual graph as depicted in Figure 9.5, which is a formal representation of the aforementioned recommendation. The rectangles represent the concepts and circles represent the relationship between concepts based on semantics in the recommendation. The conceptual graph is used to evolve the WCM. Each concept of the conceptual graph is searched in the existing hierarchies of the WCM to avoid duplication. When the concept already exists, it is skipped, in other case the relationship of the concept is analyzed with concepts of WCM and added as a new concept. The "Is-A" relationship in the conceptual graph shows the generalization of the concept and that concept can be directly ''Is-A'' relationship, which already exists under the Physiological hierarchy, as shown in Figure 9.10. Similarly, relationships such as "has'', ''of'', and ''for'' show that the source and destination concepts belong to different hierarchies in the WCM. For example, there is an ''of'' relationship between Risk Factor and Diabetes. Therefore, Risk Factor is linked to the concept Habits-Behavior under the Self-care hierarchy while Diabetes is linked to the Disease under the Healthcare hierarchy of the WCM, as shown in Figure 9.10. The concept representation usually goes from generalization to specialization for each terminology. Therefore, the conceptual graph represents the concepts in the form of both specialization and generalization, and those concepts are easily integrate-able in terminologies. Similarly, the conceptual graph helps with analyzing the relationships among concepts during the evolution process.

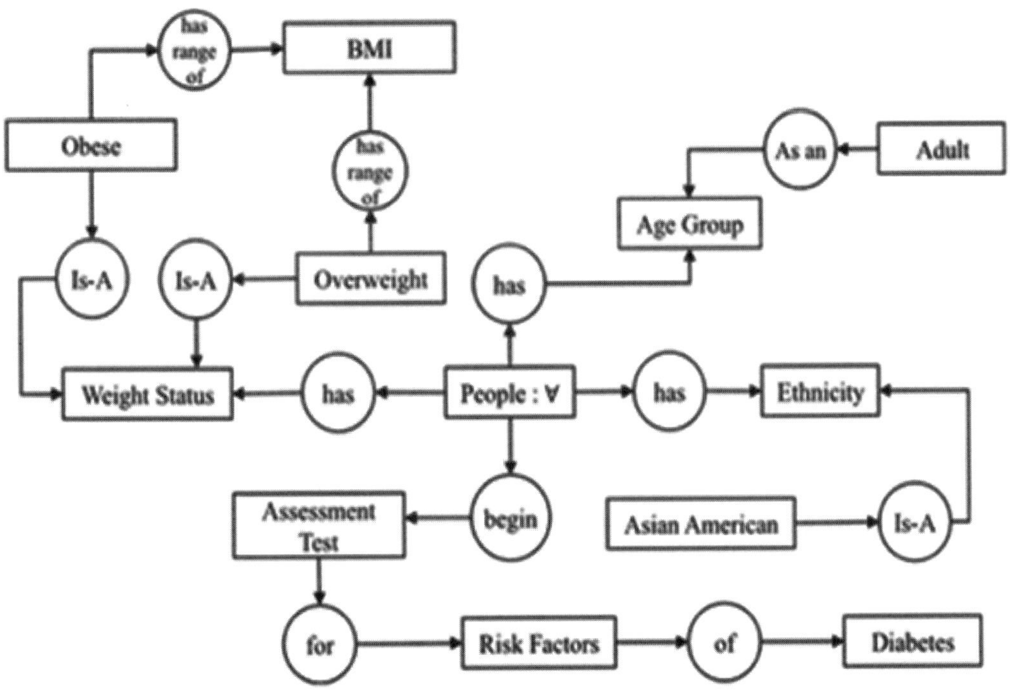

Figure 9.5 Conceptual graph created from recommendation

9.3.1.2 Harmonize with standard terminology

In order to make the WCM an align and compatible model, we performed a harmonization process with a clinical standard terminology system. In this activity, a standard terminology is searched for concepts and aligned WCM with standard concepts. Therefore, the harmonization process also helps in the evolution of WCM by adding the child hierarchies. The process of harmonization is depicted in Figure 9.6. In this process, each concept CW of the WCM is compared with concepts CS of standard terminology (ST). The concept is considered to be harmonized when the concepts or their children or their parents and siblings are matched. When a concept matched with multiple standard concepts then domain experts select the most appropriate one based on semantics. The description, code identifier and immediate children of the standard concept are placed in the WCM as a harmonized concept. The domain experts' intervention is necessary to select the immediate children of the standard concept during the addition process. When the immediate children are important in the wellness domain, then they are added to the WCM, otherwise, the children are ignored.

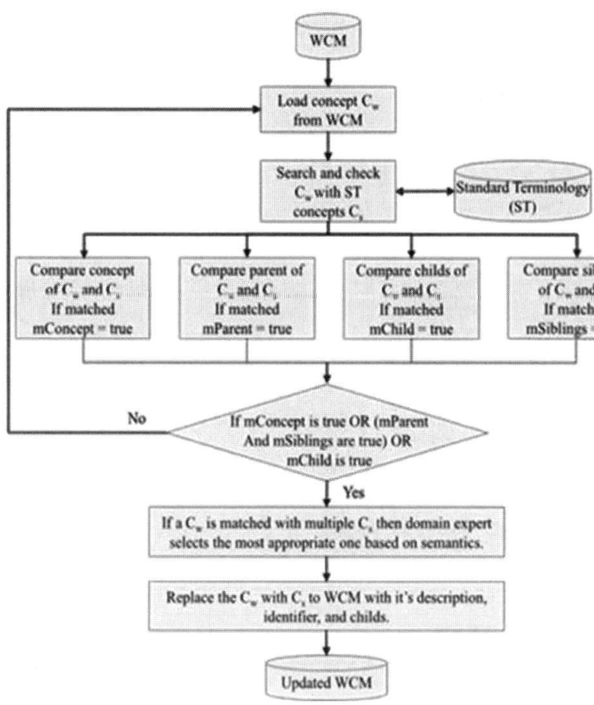

Figure 9.6 Wellness Concept Model Flow Chart

In this study, SNOMED CT is used as the standard terminology for harmonization. According to the aforementioned recommendation, the concept ''Weight Status'' is matched with standard concepts "Weights (code: 272102008, qualifier value), Body weight (code: 27113001, observable entity)''. According to the experts' decision, ''Weight Status'' is harmonized with ''Body weight (code: 27113001, observable entity)'' based on semantics types. Therefore, the ''Weight'' is replaced with ''Body weight (code: 27113001)'' and its children are added to the WCM. Table 9.3 shows some harmonized concepts, which are replaced in the WCM.

9.3.2 WCM Validation Process

A. Validation Process - Expert Opinion

In order to validate the top-level concepts of the WCM, we follow a formal expert group-based selection method, known as the nominal group technique (NGT) [67]. The NGT is selected because of its effectiveness in a multi-option decision-making process. A team of domain experts participated in a closed discussion to select appropriate concepts for the WCM. The following steps have been performed in the NGT method.

- Introduced the team members and selected a leader to handle the meeting cordially. In the panel, three physical instructors (PI-1, PI-2, and PI-3), three nutritionists (N-1, N-2, and N-3), and three clinicians (C-1, C-2, and C-3) are participated.
- The WCM model concepts are provided to the domain experts and the purpose and voting process are discussed.
- All domain experts analyzed the individual top-level concepts of the WCM silently without any discussion.
- At the end of the designated time period, the domain experts are requested to rank the concept by voting according to the defined ranking criteria. The range of the voting criteria was from 1 to 5. The domain experts voted for a concept and updated the evaluation matrix accordingly.

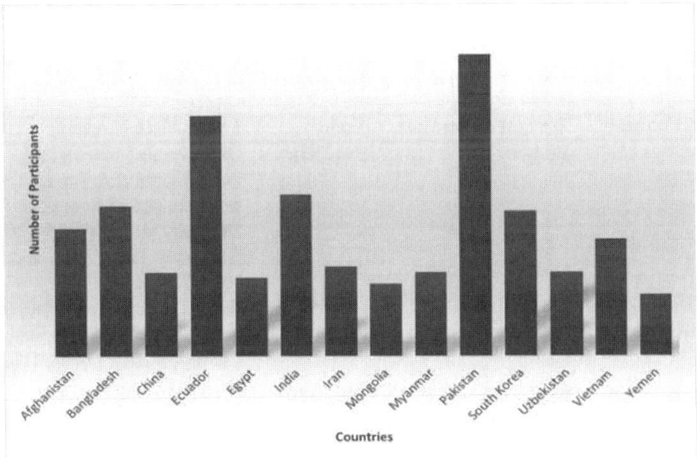

Figure 9.7 Number of participants with respect to countries

- With the consensus of the domain experts, a threshold value was defined for removing the lower ranked concepts from the WCM.
- The voting ranks of each concept, given by experts, are aggregated to find the total vote of that particular concept.
- The concepts with a lower accumulative rank than the threshold value are removed.

- The resultant model is considered to be a validated WCM.

Table 9.2 Recommendation extracted from guidelines

Recommendation: Categories of increased risk for diabetes
"Testing to assess risk for future diabetes in asymptomatic people should be considered in adults of any age who ar overweight or obese (BMI $\geq$ 25 kg/m^2 or $\geq$ 23 kg/m^2 in Asian Americans) and who have one or more additional risk factors for diabetes [66]."

B. Validation Process – User Opinion

In addition to expert opinion, we include user opinion for cross-checking of the WCM. We follow a well-known statistical method of structured equation modeling (SEM). SEM inspects the plausibility of complex models in terms of its significant constructs that domain experts and researchers have formulated for verification [1]. In this study, the population consisted of 322 including 146 graduate students, 94 researchers, and 82 employees from different organizations of fourteen different countries, as depicted in Figure 9.7. The participants are ensured with wellness field's job, research, and organization with experience of using any two wellness applications. The participants were aged between 24 and 59 years old.

Table 9.3 Examples of harmonized concepts

Harmonized Concepts	Standard Concepts	Code	Childs With [Codes]
Weight	Body weight	27113001	Birth weight [364589006] Body weight with shoes [424927000] Body weight without shoes [425024002] Dry body weight [445541000]
Obese	Obese	414915002	Body mass index 30+ - obesity [162864005] Body mass index 40+ - severely obese [408512008] On examination - obese [162690006]
Body Mass Index-BMI	Body mass index	60621009	Experts Decision: No need to add childs

We designed a questionnaire to measure and assess the top-level concepts of the WCM. We performed a statistical analysis to examine factors' structures using the SPSS Windows program [68]. We calculated the descriptive statistics to describe characteristics of the WCM concepts and to compare the results of experts' opinion and users' opinion.

We performed two important SEM tests, chi-square $\chi 2$ and root mean square error of approximation (RMSEA), to cross validate the NGT results and to find the goodness of fit of the model. The performed chi-square test observes the association between assumed and observed data, and it evaluates the assumed model against the observed data. Equation 1 calculates $\chi 2$ using the input data in Figure 9.7.

$$\chi 2 = \sum_{i=1}^{n} \frac{(O_i - E_i)^2}{E_i}$$

Where Oi represents the observed data, while Ei represents the expected value. In our study, the NGT processed data is assumed while the users' opinions are observed data. The null hypothesis H0 is that the users' opinions about the WCM model are close to the domain experts' opinions. Therefore, we performed RMSEA test to find the goodness of fit model based on the null hypothesis. Based on the expected and assumed values in $\chi 2$, we used Equation 2 to check goodness of file of users' opinion with experts' opinion.

$$RMSEA = \sqrt{max([((\chi^2/df) - 1)/(N - 1)], 0)}$$

9.4 Result and Evaluation

A. Validation Results – Expert Opinion

In the result of NGT process, the total number of votes are aggregated for each concept in the evaluation matrix as shown in the Total column of Table 9.4. A rounded threshold value of 31, which is 70% of the accumulative number of votes (45), was decided with the consensus of domain experts. We compared all the obtained votes of each concept with the threshold value. The concepts whose aggregated vote rank was less than the selected threshold value was removed. As a result of the NGT process, five concepts were removed from the top-level hierarchical concepts of the WCM, which is 14.7% of the top hierarchical concepts. The removed concepts are mentioned in Table 9.5 with corresponding vote values less than 31. Moreover, we cross-validated the WCM with a statistical method using structured equation modeling (SEM) for further verification by diverse and random communities' members.

Table 9.4 Evaluation matrix for nominal group technique (NGT)

Wellness Concepts		PI-1	PI-2	PI-3	N-1	N-2	N-3	C-1	C-2	C-3	Total
	Exercise	5	5	4	4	5	4	5	4	4	40
Physical	Nutrition	4	5	4	4	4	4	4	4	4	37
	Prevention	3	5	3	2	4	4	5	4	3	33
	Family	4	5	5	5	5	4	4	4	5	41
Social	Love	4	5	5	5	5	4	4	4	5	41
	Community	4	5	5	5	5	4	4	4	5	41
	Friendship	4	5	5	5	5	4	4	4	5	41
Intellectual	Problem Solving	4	4	4	4	4	3	4	4	4	35
	Creativity	4	4	4	4	4	3	4	4	4	35
Demographics	Gender Identity	5	5	4	5	4	5	5	4	4	41
	Cultural Identity	5	5	4	5	4	5	5	4	4	41
Sense	Sense of Worth	5	5	4	5	4	4	5	4	5	41
	Sense of Control	5	5	4	5	4	4	5	4	5	41
	Sense of Humor	5	5	4	5	4	4	5	4	5	41
Mental/Stress Management		5	5	5	5	5	5	5	4	5	44
Spiritual		4	4	5	3	4	4	4	3	4	35
Emotional		4	4	4	4	5	4	3	4	5	37
Occupation		5	5	5	4	4	5	5	4	5	42
Self-care		3	4	4	4	4	3	4	4	4	34
Leisure		4	5	5	3	4	4	4	4	4	37
Education		5	5	5	4	5	4	5	4	4	41
Thinking		3	3	3	3	3	4	2	3	3	27
Self-worth		4	5	4	5	4	4	4	4	4	38
Media		3	3	2	4	3	2	3	2	3	25
Government		2	3	3	4	3	3	2	3	2	25
Local Safety		5	5	4	4	4	4	4	4	4	38
Institutional Concern		4	4	4	4	3	4	4	4	3	34
Personal Attribution		4	3	3	3	3	3	3	4	3	29
Physiological		4	4	4	4	4	4	5	4	4	37
Political		2	3	1	2	2	2	2	3	1	18
Economic		4	4	5	4	2	3	3	3	3	31
Healthcare		4	4	5	4	4	4	4	4	4	37
Environment		4	4	5	5	4	4	5	4	4	39
Liberty		4	3	5	3	5	3	4	3	3	33

B. Validation Result – User Opinion

The descriptive statistics of users' opinions about the WCM such as mean, standard deviation, skewness, and kurtosis are illustrated in Table 9.6. The mean values in Table 9.6 infer that the users have little confidence in the lower mean values (e.g., less than 3.5). The concepts removed during the NGT process, shown in Table 9.5, have lower mean values than 3.5, which implies that users have similar opinions as experts concerning these concepts.

The standard deviation values infer that users' opinions have a low dispersive tendency; this shows that most of the users have the same opinion on WCM concepts. The skewness and kurtosis values are acceptable for proving a normal distribution, as most of the values are in an acceptable range (between +2 and −2) [69]. The calculated essential values to perform $\chi 2$ and RMSEA tests, are depicted in Table 9.7 and we used these to calculate $\chi 2$.

We obtained the $\chi 2$ value (2.01) using Equation 1. This value is acceptable because the recommended range for this statistical test is from a high of 5.0 [70] to a low of 2.0 [71]. The calculated statistical test value is tested against the chisquare distribution with $n - 1 = 34 - 1 = 33$ degrees of freedom. The critical value for the standard significance level $\alpha = 0.05$ is 47.400, which is greater than the calculated test value. Therefore, we do not reject the null hypothesis H0, which indicates that users' opinions about the WCM are very close to the experts' opinions. This statement is depicted in Figure 9.8 with respect to the values in the Expert Opinion and User Opinion columns of Table 9.7. Therefore, the overlapped and adjacent lines of the experts' and users' opinions in Figure 9.8 illustrate their closeness and agreement on the WCM concepts with a similar opinion. Furthermore, we calculated the RMSEA based on the obtained essential and chisquare values to evaluate the goodness of fit of the WCM.

In Equation 2, the calculated value of $\chi 2$ is 2.01, df is the degrees of freedom, and N is the sample size. Based on these values, we obtained a value of −0.0029, which is very close to zero. If a value is less than zero under the square root then the RSMEA is reported as zero [72]. Browne and Cudeck stated in [73] that an RMSEA value less than 0.07 indicates a good fit value and a reasonable error of approximation. Similarly, McQuitty mentioned the test of exact fit, which corresponds to the $\chi 2$ test of a model's goodness of fit and requires a confidence interval with a lower bound value of zero for the RMSEA statistic [74]. Therefore, the obtained value of -0.0029 of the RMSEA shows the goodness of fit of the WCM as a well-fit and exact fit model based on the comparison between experts' and users' opinions.

Table 9. 5 Removed concepts during NGT process

Concept	Political	Media	Government	Thinking	Attribution
Votes	18	25	25	27	29

C. WCM Evaluation

We evaluated our ontology using OntoClean with the help of three experts. The experts were provided with a sample of concepts (62 Concepts out of 442) from the ontology. They were also provided with the definitions of OntoClean meta properties such as rigidity, identity, unity, and dependency. The experts annotated the concepts and we compared the results for finding out the conflicting annotated concepts. The total number of annotations were $c * e * m$, where c is the sample of concepts to be annotated, e is the number of experts who annotated the sample, and m are the meta properties that are used for annotating the concepts. Therefore, the number of annotations were 768.

Table 9.6 Descriptive statistics of the top-level concepts of WCM

Wellness Concepts		Mean	Standard Deviation	Skewness	Kurtosis
Physical	Exercise	4.280	0.848	-1.154	0.807
	Nutrition	4.494	0.676	-1.472	2.664
	Prevention	4.239	0.766	-0.979	0.943
Social	Family	4.326	0.775	-1.164	1.212
	Love	4.326	0.775	-1.164	1.212
	Community	4.326	0.775	-1.164	1.212
	Friendship	4.326	0.775	-1.164	1.212
Intellectual	Problem Solving	4.050	0.677	-0.848	1.779
	Creativity	4.050	0.677	-0.848	1.779
Demographics	Gender Identity	3.680	0.941	-0.293	-0.776
	Cultural Identity	3.680	0.941	-0.293	-0.776
Sense	Sense of Worth	4.410	0.616	-0.537	-0.613
	Sense of Control	4.410	0.616	-0.537	-0.613
	Sense of Humor	4.410	0.616	-0.537	-0.613
Mental/Stress Management		4.693	0.475	-1.012	-0.526
Spiritual		3.935	0.896	-0.839	0.865
Emotional		4.267	0.663	-0.809	1.350
Occupation		4.124	0.738	-0.201	-1.143
Self-care		4.304	0.651	-0.810	1.319
Leisure		3.904	0.761	-0.647	0.484
Education		4.354	0.660	-0.793	0.674
Thinking		4.258	0.696	-0.732	0.576
Self-worth		3.994	0.832	-0.544	-0.218
Media		3.404	0.838	-0.204	-0.695
Government		3.062	1.021	0.034	-0.503
Local Safety		4.003	0.653	-0.610	1.253
Institutional Concern		4.102	0.650	-0.103	-0.643
Personal Attribution		3.484	0.840	0.033	-0.571
Physiological		3.634	0.932	-0.487	-0.236
Political		2.829	1.070	0.315	-0.675
Economic		3.885	0.958	-0.602	-0.521
Healthcare		4.174	0.622	-0.137	-0.519
Environment		4.503	0.638	-1.209	1.626
Liberty		4.317	0.748	-0.861	0.196

In cases where disagreement existed between experts, we applied majority voting strategy for selection of the meta-property. The metaproperties annotation for WCM is given in Table 9.8. Currently, the WCM contains 442 classes, 956 axioms (500 logical and 456 declaration axioms), and 15 properties. The object and data properties are represented as semantic relationships in domain and range triples. For instance, the domain Person has property hasNeed with ranges Civil Liberty, Political Liberty and others. Similarly, the domain Patient has the property of SuffersFrom with range Disease. Figure 9.9 illustrates partial semantic types of different WCM concepts. Figure 9.10 shows the partial resultant WCM ontology.

9.5 Discussion

Standard wellness terminologies help with obtaining interoperability, concepts consistency, and shareability features in documentation, information retrieval and knowledge management. There are a number of reasons for knowledgebase systems limited adaption by different stakeholders. WCM helps in resolving these limitations. The reasons include:

- The ease with which experts utilize and maintain the knowledge base using controlled vocabulary is an important factor for longer adaption of the system. WCM provides the controlled vocabulary to experts for engineering and evolving the knowledge base by hiding the complexities from him/her.
- An integrated health and wellness system is the vision of the research community. This is only possible if standards are used, resulting in shareable knowledge. Current wellness systems adaption of standards is very minimal, therefore sharable is an issue. WCM incorporates SNOMED CT terminology standard for resolving the sharable aspect.
- Wellness domain lacks a model that can be utilized for building wellness systems. WCM provides the roof to engineers for utilizing our model to develop wellness systems.

Table 9.7 Essential values for chi-square test and RMSEA

Wellness Concepts		Expert Opinion	User Opinion (O_i)	Expected Value (E_i)	χ^2 value
Physical	Exercise	4.444	4.280	4.514	0.012
	Nutrition	4.111	4.494	4.186	0.023
	Prevention	3.667	4.239	3.733	0.069
Social	Family	4.556	4.326	4.638	0.021
	Love	4.556	4.326	4.638	0.021
	Community	4.556	4.326	4.638	0.021
	Friendship	4.556	4.326	4.638	0.021
Intellectual	Problem Solving	3.889	4.050	3.959	0.002
	Creativity	3.889	4.050	3.959	0.002
Demographics	Gender Identity	4.556	3.680	4.638	0.198
	Cultural Identity	4.556	3.680	4.638	0.198
Sense	Sense of Worth	4.556	4.410	4.638	0.011
	Sense of Control	4.556	4.410	4.638	0.011
	Sense of Humor	4.556	4.410	4.638	0.011
Mental/Stress Management		4.889	4.693	4.978	0.016
Spiritual		3.889	3.935	3.959	0.000
Emotional		4.111	4.267	4.186	0.002
Occupation		4.667	4.124	4.751	0.083
Self-care		3.778	4.304	3.846	0.055
Leisure		4.111	3.904	4.186	0.019
Education		4.556	4.354	4.638	0.017
Thinking		3.000	4.258	3.054	0.474
Self-worth		4.222	3.994	4.299	0.022
Media		2.778	3.404	2.828	0.117
Government		2.778	3.062	2.828	0.019
Local Safety		4.222	4.003	4.299	0.020
Institutional Concern		3.778	4.102	3.846	0.017
Personal Attribution		3.222	3.484	3.281	0.013
Physiological		4.111	3.634	4.186	0.073
Political		2.000	2.829	2.036	0.309
Economic		3.444	3.885	3.507	0.041
Healthcare		4.111	4.174	4.186	0.000
Environment		4.333	4.503	4.412	0.002
Liberty		3.667	4.317	3.733	0.091

There also exist limitations in the implementation of WCM which is an on-going research area for the expansion of our system. These are described as follows:

Concepts can be categorized into two types, generalized and localized concepts. Normally, the generalized concepts mapping with the terminology standard (SNOMED CT) can be easily done with sufficient expertise or involvement of matching algorithms. On the other hand, localized concepts are part of WCM but are non-existent in SNOMED CT. Therefore, alignment of WCM localized concepts with SNOMED is our ongoing research as it has a direct effect on the sharable aspect.

The existing terminologies and model development methodologies usually focus on some specific elicitation approach according to their requirements. The evolution of the existing terminologies depends on the domain experts' knowledge and heuristics to add new contents. Similarly, they do not consider any standard terminology harmonization and validate the model through domain experts. On the other hand, our proposed methodology evolves the model using published articles and guidelines addition to domain experts' knowledge. We harmonize the model with clinical standard terminology to reuse the standard concepts of SNOMED CT.

We already described in section 11.1 that wellness is more than healthcare because health is state of physical, mental, and social well-being, while wellness is a state of living an optimal healthy lifestyle [2], [3]. The left side of the continuum in Figure 9.1, illness - health, is considered as the clinical aspect of the healthcare domain, because clinical aspect mainly focuses on disease, diagnosis, treatment, operations, and medicines [75], [76]. The clinical terminologies concern about the use of concepts in medical record or other clinical information systems [77]. However, clinical terminologies cover most of the clinical concepts and give less coverage to the non-clinical wellness concepts. One way to amalgamate wellness concepts with clinical terminology such as SNOMED CT is making Clinical Observations Recordings and Encoding (CORE) Problem List subset of SNOMED CT. There are well-known methodologies for encoding Problem Lists such as EMR based Problem List for general practice in British Columbia, Canada [78]. Similarly, a methodology for extracting intensive care unit (ICU) problem list have been proposed in the study [79]. The authors focused on the diagnosis concepts for admission to the ICU, anatomical locations and causes of diseases, and different relation types, which are used in Diagnoses for Intensive Care Evaluation (DICE) [79]. A Danish national subset for the nursing problem has developed to intend the standardized homecare nursing documentation for comparable reporting across the 98 Danish municipalities [80], Højen et al. included 80 concepts of "Clinical findings" into the resultant problem list. Mostly, the problem lists focused on the clinical aspect of concepts in recommended 4 hierarchies "Clinical findings, Procedure, Situation with explicit context, and Events" for building CORE problem lists [81]. As the scope of wellness domain is more than healthcare; therefore, some of the necessary concepts in wellness domain are not part of the SNOMED CT ontology. This restricted us from building SNOMED CT Problem List and compelled us for modeling a standalone WCM ontology. Some examples of concepts in WCM that cannot be enlisted as SNOMED CT Problem List includes Spiritual, Liberty, and Hospitality.

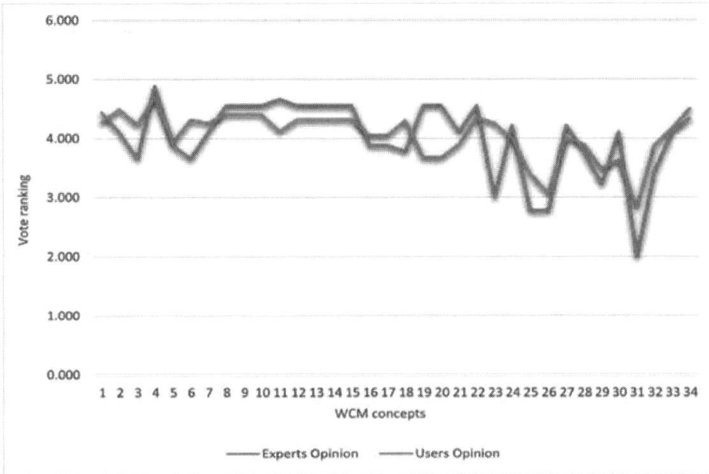

Figure 9.8 Experts and user opinions about WCM

Table 9. 8 OntoClean meta-properties information of WCM

	Rigidity				Identity				Unity				Dependence		
	+R	-R	~R	NA	+I	-I	+O	NA	+U	-U	~U	NA	+D	-D	NA
Expert 1	29	21	12	2	41	2	18	3	36	16	10	2	40	24	0
Expert 2	26	18	20	0	39	5	18	2	33	9	20	2	36	28	0
Expert 3	18	23	10	13	38	1	10	15	25	11	11	17	42	4	18
Total	73	62	42	15	118	8	46	20	94	36	41	21	118	56	18

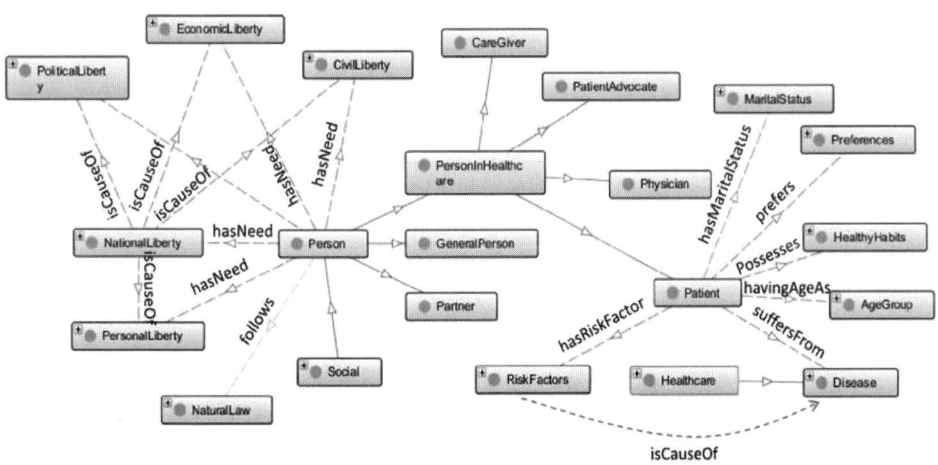

Figure 9.9 The partial semantic types of WCM concepts

Validation through the NGT method is an appropriate method to validate the holism of WCM hierarchical concepts. However, NGT validation is a very hectic and tedious task for domain experts to validate all the evolved concepts of the WCM in a single session. After evolution, the WCM has thousands of concepts, which cannot be validated by domain experts using a multi-voting process. Therefore, the statistical method of SEM is a suitable approach to validate the evolved WCM based on a large data set that covers all the evolved concepts.

The experts' and users' opinions on the hierarchical concepts of the WCM are very similar. Only one concept, Thinking, had conflicted values between the NGT and SEM. This concept had a vote of 27, which is less than the selected threshold value and it was removed during the NGT process. On the other hand, with SEM it has a mean of 4.258, which is greater than the threshold mean (mean = 3.5) and it is an acceptable concept according to users' opinions. In this conflicting situation, we preferred to use the experts' opinions. We discovered that the words Positive Thinking were used instead of Thinking in the questionnaire, which makes that question biased towards positive thinking. There are many published guideline resources for physical activities, nutrition, and healthcare that can easily be used in the evolution of the mentioned factors of the WCM. Some factors of the WCM may lack published guidelines. Therefore, some factors of the WCM evolved to a high level of depth and some factors evolved to a very low level of depth.

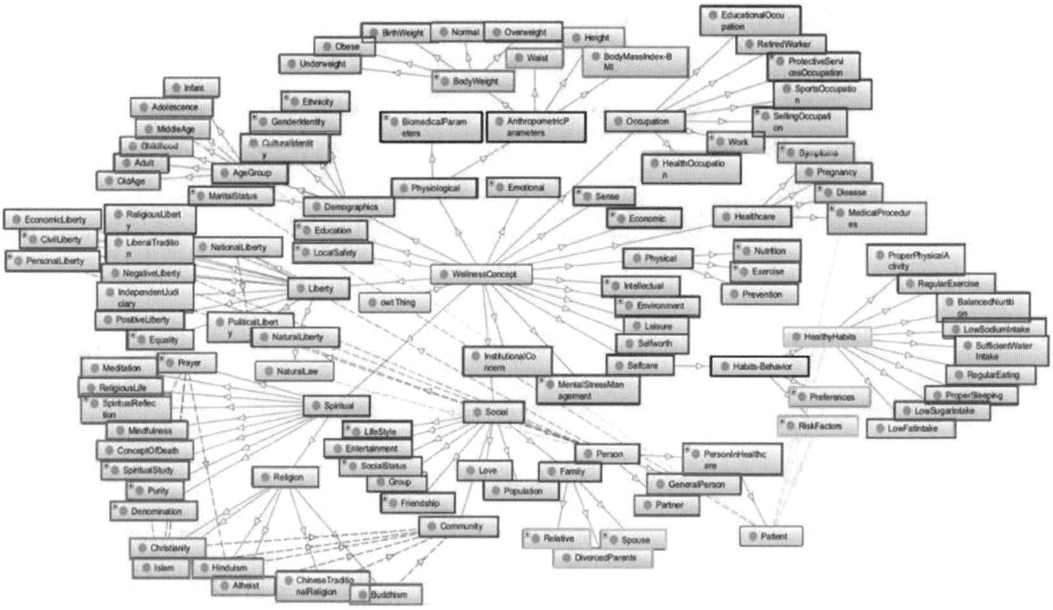

Figure 9.10 The partial resultant ontological representation of WCM

9.6 Summary

We have designed and developed a wellness concepts model (WCM) based on the proposed WCM development framework. The top-level hierarchical concepts model of the WCM is designed using extensive literature with a systematic review process, while we evolved the WCM using the wellness concepts used in published guidelines. We performed the harmonization activity to utilize the existing standard concepts, codes, and descriptions in the WCM. We validated the top-level concepts of the WCM using the NGT process and cross-validated them using the statistical methods of structured equation modeling (SEM).

In the future, we will extend this study to validate the evolved WCM with statistical methods on a large data set. We will integrate WCM in knowledge acquisition tool to create interoperable knowledge, and we will integrate it with heterogeneous data model systems to prove the applicability of the WCM with respect to knowledge acquisition.

Source Code

For source code please contact us at:

The contents of this chapter have been previously published in the following article:

Taqdir Ali, Maqbool Hussain, Muhammad Afzal, Wajahat Ali Khan, Taeho Hur, Muhammad Bilal Amin, Dohyeong Kim, Byeong Ho Kang, and Sungyoung Lee, "Clinically Harmonized Wellness Concepts Model for Health and Wellness Services", IEEE Access (SCIE, IF: 3.244), Vol.6, pp.26660-26674, 2018

References

[1] D. A. Els and R. De la Rey, ''Developing a holistic wellness model,'' SA J. Hum. Resour. Manage., vol. 4, no. 2, pp. 46–56, 2006.

[2] D. L. Stoewen, ''Health and wellness,'' Can. Veterinary J., vol. 56, no. 9, 983, 2015. (2017). Health and Wellness: Definition and Dimensions.

[3] Accessed: Dec. 2017. [Online]. Available: https://study.com/academy/ lesson/health-wellness-definition-and-dimensions.html

[4] D. J. W. Strümpfer, ''The origins of health and strength: From 'salutogenesis' to 'fortigenesis,''' South African J. Psychol., vol. 25, no. 2, pp. 81–89, 1995.

[5] J. E. Myers, ''Wellness as the paradigm for counseling and development: The possible future,'' Counselor Edu. Supervision, vol. 30, no. 3, pp. 183–193, 1991.

[6] J. E. Myers, ''Wellness, prevention, development: The cornerstone of the profession,'' J. Counseling Develop., vol. 71, no. 2, pp. 136–139, 1992.

[7] L. W. Chini and W. Dorner. (2017). Kranke Kinder, was Tun? Bessere Prävention Macht Auch Volkswirtschaft Gesünder. Accessed: Nov. 2017. [Online]. Available: http://www.aerztekammer.at

[8] A. Holzinger, S. Dorner, M. Födinger, A. C. Valdez, and M. Ziefle, ''Chances of increasing youth health awareness through mobile wellness applications,'' in HCI in Work and Learning, Life and Leisure. Berlin, Germany: Springer, 2010.

[9] E. Lungu, ''The European strategy for the prevention and control of noncommunicable diseases,'' J. Preventive Med., vol. 14, nos. 3–4, p. 6, 2006.

[10] F. Branca, H. Nikogosian, and T. Lobstein, The Challenge of Obesity in the WHO European Region and the Strategies for Response: Summary. Geneva, Switzerland: WHO, 2007.

[11] The European Tobacco Control Report 2007, WHO Regional Office Eur., Copenhagen, Denmark, 2007.

[12] J. Komulainen, I. Kunnamo, P. Nyberg, M. Kaila, T. Mäntyranta, and M. Korhonen, ''Developing an evidence based medicine decision support system integrated with EPRs

[13] utilizing standard data elements,'' in Proc. Eur. Conf. Artif. Intell. (ECAI), Riva del Garda, Italy, Aug./Sep. 2006.

[14] B. Johansson, N. Shahsavar, H. Åhlfeldt, and O. Wigertz, ''Database and knowledge base integration—A data mapping method for Arden syntax knowledge modules,'' Methods Inf. Med., vol. 35, nos. 4–5, pp. 302–308, 1996.

[15] J. A. Osheroff, J. M. Teich, B. Middleton, E. B. Steen, A. Wright, and D.E.Detmer,''Aroadmapfornationalactiononclinicaldecisionsupport,''

[16] J. Amer. Med. Inform. Assoc., vol. 14, no. 2, pp. 141–145, 2007. A. Y. Wang, J. H. Sable, and K. A. Spackman, ''The SNOMED clinical terms development process: Refinement and analysis of content,'' in Proc. AMIA Symp., Amer. Med. Inform. Assoc., 2002, p. 845.

[17] A. Wright and D. F. Sittig, ''A four-phase model of the evolution of clinical decision support architectures,'' Int. J. Med. Informat., vol. 77, no. 10, pp. 641–649, 2008.

[18] S.A.U.Nambi,C.Sarkar,R.V.Prasad,andA.Rahim,''Aunifiedsemantic knowledge base for IoT,'' in Proc. IEEE World Forum Internet Things (WF-IoT), Mar. 2014, pp. 575–580.

[19] E.Sanchezetal.,''Anarchitectureforthesemanticenhancementofclinical decision support systems,'' in Proc. Int. Conf. Knowl.-Based Intell. Inf. Eng. Syst., 2011, pp. 611–620.

[20] T. Ali, M. Hussain, W. A. Khan, M. Afzal, B. H. Kang, and S. Lee, ''Arden syntax studio: Creating medical logic module as shareable knowledge,'' in Proc. IEEE Int. Symp. Innov. Intell. Syst. Appl. (INISTA), Jun. 2014, pp. 266–272.

[21] S. L. Achour, M. Dojat, C. Rieux, P. Bierling, and E. Lepage, ''A UMLSbased knowledge acquisition tool for rule-based clinical decision support system development,'' J. Amer. Med. Inform. Assoc., vol. 8, no. 4, pp. 351–360, 2001.

[22] R. A. Deyo, D. C. Cherkin, and M. A. Ciol, ''Adapting a clinical comorbidity index for use with ICD-9-CM administrative databases,'' J. Clin. Epidemiol., vol. 45, no. 6, pp. 613–619, 1992.

[23] H. Quan et al., ''Coding algorithms for defining comorbidities in ICD9-CM and ICD-10 administrative data,'' Med. Care, vol. 43, no. 11, pp. 1130–1139, 2005.

[24] M. Q. Stearns, C. Price, K. A. Spackman, and A. Y. Wang, ''SNOMED clinical terms: Overview of the development process and project status,'' in Proc. AMIA Symp., Amer. Med. Inform. Assoc., 2001, p. 662.

[25] D. Robinson, E. Schulz, P. Brown, and C. Price, ''Updating the Read codes: User-interactive maintenance of a dynamic clinical vocabulary,'' J. Amer. Med. Inform. Assoc., vol. 4, no. 6, pp. 465–472, 1997.

[26] O. Bodenreider, ''The unified medical language system (UMLS): Integrating biomedical terminology,'' Nucl. Acids Res., vol. 32, pp. D267–D270, Jan. 2004.

[27] H.-A. Park, C. B. Lundberg, A. Coenen, and D. J. Konicek, ''Evaluation of the content coverage of SNOMED-CT to represent ICNP version 1 catalogues,'' in Nursing Informatics. Amsterdam, The Netherlands: IOS Press BV, 2009, pp. 303–307.

[28] H. Wasserman and J. Wang, ''An applied evaluation of SNOMED CT as a clinical vocabulary for the computerized diagnosis and problem list,'' in Proc. AMIA Annu. Symp., 2003, p. 699.

[29] L. J. Roscoe, ''Wellness: A review of theory and measurement for counselors,'' J. Counseling Develop., vol. 87, no. 2, pp. 216–226, 2009.

[30] D. B. Ardell, ''High level wellness strategies,'' Health Edu., vol. 8, no. 4, 2, 1977.

[31] C. C. Clark, Wellness Practitioner: Concepts, Research, and Strategies. New York, NY, USA: Springer, 1996.

[32] L. A. Jensen and M. N. Allen, ''A synthesis of qualitative research on wellness-illness,''QualitativeHealthRes.,vol.4,no.4,pp.349–369,1994.
[33] B. Hettler, ''Wellness promotion on a University Campus,'' Family Commun. Health, vol. 3, no. 1, pp. 77–95, 1980.
[34] T. J. Sweeney and J. M. Witmer, ''Beyond social interest: Striving toward optimum health and wellness,'' Individual Psychol., J. Adlerian Theory, Res. Pract., vol. 47, no. 4, pp. 527–540, 1991.
[35] J. M. Witmer and T. J. Sweeney, ''A holistic model for wellness and prevention over the life span,'' J. Counseling Develop., vol. 71, no. 2, pp. 140–148, 1992.
[36] J. E. Myers and T. J. Sweeney, ''The indivisible self: An evidence-based model of wellness,'' J. Individual Psychol., vol. 60, no. 3, pp. 234–244, 2004.
[37] A. Adler, Understanding Human Nature. New York, NY, USA: Routledge, 1927.
[38] D. Depken, ''Wellness through the lens of gender: A paradigm shift,'' Wellness Perspective, vol. 10, no. 2, pp. 54–69, 1994.
[39] T. Adams, J. Bezner, and M. Steinhardt, ''The conceptualization and measurement of perceived wellness: Integrating balance across and within dimensions,'' Amer. J. Health Promotion, vol. 11, no. 3, pp. 208–218, 1997.
[40] (2017). International Classification of Wellness. Accessed: Dec. 2017. [Online]. Available: http://bioportal.bioontology.org/ontologies/ICW
[41] P. L. Whetzel et al., ''BioPortal: Enhanced functionality via new Web services from the National Center for Biomedical Ontology to access and use ontologies in software applications,'' Nucl. Acids Res., vol. 39, no. 2, pp. W541–W545, 2011.
[42] J. M. Witmer, T. J. Sweeney, and J. E. Myers, ''The wheel of wellness counseling for wellness: A holistic model for treatment planning,'' J. Counseling Develop., vol. 78, no. 3, pp. 251–266, 2000.
[43] J. W. Miller, ''Wellness: The history and development of a concept,'' Spektrum Freizeit, vol. 27, no. 1, pp. 84–102, May 2005.
[44] T. G. Kirsten, H. J. Van der Walt, and C. T. Viljoen, ''Health, wellbeing and wellness: An anthropological eco-systemic approach,'' Health SA Gesondheid, vol. 14, no. 1, pp. 149–155, 2009.
[45] A. Seppälä, P. Nykänen, and P. Ruotsalainen, ''Development of personal wellness information model for pervasive healthcare,'' J. Comput. Netw. Commun., vol. 2012, Aug. 2012, Art. no. 596749.
[46] G. Schreiber, B. Wielinga, R. de Hoog, H. Akkermans, and W. Van de Velde, ''CommonKADS: A comprehensive methodology for KBS development,'' IEEE Expert, vol. 9, no. 6, pp. 28–37, Dec. 1994.
[47] D. Hadorn, G. Kvizhinadze, L. Collinson, and T. Blakely, ''Useof expert knowledge elicitation to estimate parameters in health economic decision models,'' Int. J. Technol. Assessment Health Care, vol. 30, no. 4, pp. 461–468, 2014.
[48] S. T. March and G. F. Smith, ''Design and natural science research on information technology,'' Decision Support Syst., vol. 15, no. 4, pp. 251–266, 1995.
[49] A. Hevner, S. T. March, J. Park, and S. Ram, ''Design science in information systems research,'' MIS Quart., vol. 28, no. 1, pp. 75–105, 2004.
[50] A. Hevner and S. Chatterjee, ''Design science research in information systems,'' in Design Research in Information Systems. New York, NY, USA: Springer, 2010, pp. 9–22.

[51] F.Ghazouani,W.Messaoudi,andI.R.Farah,''Towardsanontologicalconceptualization for understanding the dynamics of spatio-temporal objects,'' in Proc. 2nd Int. Conf. Adv. Technol. Signal Image Process. (ATSIP), Mar. 2016, pp. 543–548.
[52] M. Horridge and M. Musen, ''Snap-SPARQL: A java framework for working with SPARQL and OWL,'' in Proc. Int. Exper. Directions Workshop OWL, 2015, pp. 154–165.
[53] N. Guarino and C. Welty, ''Evaluating ontological decisions with OntoClean,'' Commun. ACM, vol. 45, no. 2, pp. 61–65, 2002.
[54] C. Bizer, T. Heath, and T. Berners-Lee, ''Linked data-the story so far,'' in Semantic Services, Interoperability and Web Applications: Emerging Concepts. Hershey, PA, USA: IGI Global, 2009, pp. 205–227, doi: 10.4018/jswis.2009081901.
[55] R. Q. Wolever et al., ''A systematic review of the literature on health and wellness coaching: Defining a key behavioral intervention in healthcare,'' Global Adv. Health Med., vol. 2, no. 4, pp. 38–57, 2013.
[56] M. J. Eppler, ''A comparison between concept maps, mind maps, conceptual diagrams, and visual metaphors as complementary tools for knowledge construction and sharing,'' Inf. Vis., vol. 5, no. 3, pp. 202–210, 2006.
[57] H. L. Dunn, ''High-level wellness for man and society,'' Amer. J. Public Health Nat. Health, vol. 49, no. 6, pp. 786–792, 1959.
[58] D. B. Ardell, High Level Wellness: An Alternative to Doctors, Drugs, and Disease. New York, NY, USA: Bantam Books, 1979.
[59] H. Mueller and E. L. Kaufmann, ''Wellness tourism: Market analysis of a special health tourism segment and implications for the hotel industry,'' J. Vacation Marketing, vol. 7, no. 1, pp. 5–17, 2001.
[60] J. Lafferty, ''A credo for wellness,'' Health Edu., vol. 10, no. 5, pp. 10–11, 1979.
[61] J. S. Greenberg, ''Health and wellness: A conceptual differentiation,'' J. School Health, vol. 55, no. 10, pp. 403–406, 1985.
[62] D. Moore and F. Leafgren, Problem Solving Strategies and Interventions for Men in Conflict. Alexandria, VA, USA: Springer, 1990.
[63] R. Crose, D. R. Nicholas, D. C. Gobble, and B. Frank, ''Gender and wellness: A multidimensional systems model for counseling,'' J. Counseling Develop., vol. 71, no. 2, pp. 149–156, 1992.
[64] R. F. Renger et al., ''Optimal living profile: An inventory to assess health and wellness,'' Amer. J. Health Behav., vol. 24, no. 6, pp. 403–412, 2000.
[65] J. Durlak, ''Health promotion as a strategy in primary prevention,'' in The Promotion of Wellness in Children and Adolescents. Washington, DC, USA: Child Welfare League America Press, 2000, pp. 221–241.
[66] J. F. Sowa, ''Conceptual graphs for a data base interface,'' IBM J. Res. Develop., vol. 20, no. 4, pp. 336–357, 1976.
[67] American Diabetes Association, ''Standards of medical care in diabetes— 2016,'' Diabetes Care, vol. 37, no. 1, pp. S1–S106, 2016.
[68] M. Gallagher, T. Hares, J. Spencer, C. Bradshaw, and I. Webb, ''The nominal group technique: A research tool for general practice?'' Family Pract., vol. 10, no. 1, pp. 76–81, 1993.
[69] G. A. Ferguson, Statistical Analysis in Psychology and Education. New York, NY, USA: McGraw-Hill, 1959.

[70] D. George and P. Mallery, IBM SPSS Statistics 23 Step by Step: A Simple Guide and Reference. Evanston, IL, USA: Routledge, 2016.
[71] B. Wheaton, B. Muthen, D. F. Alwin, and G. F. Summers, ''Assessing reliability and stability in panel models,'' Sociol. Methodol., vol. 8, pp. 84–136, Jan. 1977.
[72] B. G. Tabachnick, L. S. Fidell, and S. J. Osterlind, Using Multivariate Statistics. Boston, MA, USA: Allyn & Bacon, 2007.
[73] G. R. Hancock and R. O. Mueller, Structural Equation Modeling: A Second Course. Greenwich, CT, USA: Springer, 2013.
[74] M. W. Browne and R. Cudeck, ''Single sample cross-validation indices for covariance structures,'' Multivariate Behav. Res., vol. 24, no. 4, pp. 445–455, 1989.
[75] S. McQuitty, ''Statistical power and structural equation models in business research,'' J. Bus. Res., vol. 57, no. 2, pp. 175–183, 2004.
[76] M. Foucault, The Birth of the clinic. Evanston, IL, USA: Routledge, 2012.
[77] (2018). Clinical Terminology. Accessed: Jan. 2018. [Online]. Available: www.digitalhealth.gov.au/get-started-with-digital-health/what-is-digitalhealth/clinical-terminology
[78] A. L. Rector, ''Clinical terminology: Why is it so hard?'' Methods Inf. Med., vol. 38 nos. 4–5, pp. 239–252, 1999.
[79] F. Y. Lau, R. Simkus, and D. Lee, ''A methodology for encoding problem lists with SNOMED CT in general practice,'' in Proc. KR-MED, 2008, pp. 102–131.
[80] D. Arts, R. Cornet, E. De Jonge, and N. F. De Keizer, ''A literature review and a case study,'' Methods Inf. Med., vol. 44, no. 5, pp. 616–625, 2005.
[81] A. R. Højen, K. R. Gøeg, and P. B. Elberg, ''Re-use of SNOMED CT subset in development of the Danish national standard for home care nursing problems,'' in Proc. MIE, 2015, pp. 140–144.
[82] (2018). The CORE Problem List Subset of SNOMED CT. Accessed: Jan. 2018. [Online]. Available: www.nlm.nih.gov/research/ umls/Snomed/coresubset.html

Chapter 10

Expert-driven Knowledge Authoring

Wellness Concepts Model use and effectiveness in Intelligent Authoring Environment

Taqdir Ali and Sungyoung Lee

Intelligent recommendation systems have high impact on users to adopt healthy routines towards the optimal health and wellbeing. The wellbeing recommendation and decision support systems need up-to-date wellness knowledge for effective recommendations to the users. Lack of evolutionary knowledge base is the most prominent barrier in the effectiveness of wellness recommendation system and its applications for assisting in healthier life choices. Domain experts can transform their knowledge into the evolutionary knowledge base of intelligent recommendation system, when they have access to an intelligent and supportive knowledge authoring environment. We have proposed a system that provides an intelligent and supportive knowledge authoring environment with the help of scalable wellness concepts model (WCM). WCM helps in contextual selection of concepts and their values set using Intelli-sense approach during the rule creation. The use of WCM, in knowledge authoring environment, enhances experts' performance and decreases the chance of errors in wellness knowledge creation. It maximizes the concepts recall ratio of domain experts and provides guidance to some extent during rule creation process. We evaluated our system using user-centric evaluation by 6 domain experts. Each domain expert created 5 rules, containing 2 simple and 3 complexes using the proposed system. The results suggested that the proposed system has user-satisfaction level up to 80.42%.

10.1 Introduction

Wellness has broader scope than healthcare, health-care considered as part of the wellness domain. In illness-health-wellness continuum [1], individuals mainly focus on positive aspects of health and wellness sides to protect from illness. In the past few decades, the number of counseling approaches, in health and wellness domains, has grown exponentially [2, 3]. In current technological era, intelligent recommendation systems play very important role in recommending and counseling the users about healthier life. These systems depend on evolutionary knowledge base and which is considered as core component of the system [4, 5]. Knowledge acquisition is a challenging task and also a key barrier to adopt evolutionary knowledge base expert systems [6]. This is because of the cumbersome and unsystematic interaction between knowledge engineers and the domain experts.

Knowledge engineering "bottleneck" in expert systems adoption has encouraged the knowledge acquisition researchers to provide a controlled and assistive knowledge authoring environment to domain experts without doing extensive tasks [7]. In addition to interactive and easy to use features of authoring environment, the knowledge should be shareable, interoperable, and easily integrate-able to heterogeneous databases of the legacy systems [6]. All the three aspects of knowledge acquisition; easiness, shareability and interoperability, can be achieved by utilizing standard data models and standard terminologies [6, 8]. Domain experts feel comfort with standard terminologies in creating knowledge rules. Standard terminologies such as SNOMED CT [5, 10] and data model standards like Virtual Medical Record (vMR) [9] are designed for use in decision support systems. The list of standards in clinical domain is not limited to only these standards. Unlike clinical domain, wellness domain is lacking in standards and there exist neither the data models nor the terminological standards.

Without controlled vocabulary in authoring environment, domain experts utilize their own concepts that may differ from one expert to another. Therefore, inconsistency prevails in the knowledge rules created by different experts with their own terminologies. This lack of conceptual consistency leads to the interoperability issue of knowledge base with the legacy systems [6]. Additionally, the controlled vocabulary also helps the experts to maximize the recall of concepts during the rule creation. Experts feel comfort with controlled vocabulary and it enhances the performance of the experts. In similar way, the controlled vocabulary in the form of contextual selection of concepts [11] reduces the chance of errors during the rules creation. In current study, we take initiative to propose wellness concepts model (WCM), based on physical activities and nutrition domain, verified by the domain experts. This WCM is incorporated in Intelligent Knowledge Authoring Environment and used by the experts for rules creation. This WCM is a way towards standardization and controlled terminology in the wellness domain. In our proposed system, WCM facilitates domain experts to create knowledge rules using contextual selection of concepts.

Last two decades of 20th century, the wellness has been defined as a new paradigm in the health-care [12]. Many researchers have proposed different wellness models for different purposes; one of the popular wellness models is The Indivisible Self [3], which we have selected as a baseline for our proposed WCM. We have derived our WCM from the five second-order factors of The Indivisible Self. We extended the model in three basic areas Essential, Physical, and Nutrition. The main reason behind selecting these three components is the focus of evolutionary knowledge base for an innovative personalized health and wellness recommendation system called Mining Minds [13][14]. Mining Minds is a novel framework that focuses on digital health and wellness paradigms to enable the provision of personalized health and wellness support [13, 14, 15]. Therefore, our proposed knowledge authoring environment primarily focuses on the knowledge of users' physical activities, health status, and nutrition components in the wellness domain. Other components of wellness domain like mental health, spiritual and social life can easily be integrated with WCM for intelligent recommendations in corresponding domains.

The proposed knowledge authoring environment allows the domain experts to utilize the WCM concepts for keys as well as values in all facts of rules. The experts can easily select their desired concepts from the WCM tree in the rule editor, while the corresponding possible values set is shown in the immediate window as Intelli-sense. Therefore, the authoring environment provides the controlled vocabulary of wellness in two different ways like WCM tree and Intelli-sense window.

10.2 Related Work

10.2.1 Wellness Concept Model (WCM)

There are knowledge authoring tools available in clinical domain, while specifically wellness domain lacks Ardell, D. B. [16] have proposed definition of wellness and model for high level of wellness in nutrition knowledge, physical fitness, stress management and environmental awareness. In same way, Hettler B. [17] also categorized the wellness model in high level of concepts like physical, nutrition and social categories. Both of these high-level models are considered as pioneer models in wellness domain. A theoretical model based on counseling theory called Wheel of Wellness, was first introduced in early 1990s by Sweeney and Witmer [18][19]. The authors have identified a number of characteristics that are related to the healthy living, quality of life and longevity. They organized these characteristics according to life tasks, friendship and love. The original Wheel of Wellness model has seven sub-tasks in the life tasks. According to this model, the life forces that effect an individual's life are family, religion, education/industry, media, government, and community. After an extensive survey, Myers and Sweeney [3] have proposed an evidence- based model of wellness The Indivisible Self. The authors have realized that the structure of Wheel of Wellness should be re-examine due to hypothesized relationships among its components and the complex structure of it. The Indivisible Self has proposed a higher-order wellness factor, which is based on the Adler's [20] theory of holism, the indivisibility of self. Five main concepts are considered as second-order factors; Essential Self, Social Self, Creative Self, Physical Self, and Coping Self. These second-order factors are further categorized into 17 sub components. This model provides strong support for basic Adlerian concepts related to holism and the indivisibility of human existence is supported by this research findings. In our proposed WCM, we have considered this model as fundamental concepts in second-order of hierarchy. We enhanced wellness model by adding more concepts based on extensive literature with the help of a team of experts.

10.2.2 Knowledge Authoring Environment

There are knowledge authoring tools available in clinical domain, while specifically wellness domain lacks these tools. A multiple-method knowledge acquisition shell is proposed in [21] that generates knowledge acquisition tools without a specific model of problem solving. The system provides very generic environment to create knowledge for multiple domain, but domain expert needs help in technical aspects to formalize domain knowledge. In this case, the domain experts have dependency on knowledge engineers to build a domain knowledge base. A collaborative ontology editor and knowledge acquisition tool WebProtege is proposed by Tudorache, T et.al. in [22]. The system was built using the existing protégé infrastructure that supports collaboration on the backend side. The authors have developed a useful ontology editor for knowledge acquisition, but this editor is difficult to use for domain experts without semantic web knowledge to create domain knowledge. Dustin Dunsmuir et al. have proposed a system in [23], which enables clinicians to create knowledge rules without the help of knowledge engineers and programmers. The system is based on the "pattern and outcome" approach and works in the domain of anesthesia. However, its scope is limited and difficult to extend to other domains. This system creates rules directly in XML files; therefore, physicians are involved with XML files, which require the tedious extra task of XML training.

10.3 Methodology

10.3.1 Wellness Concepts Model (WCM) Paradigm

The focus of healthcare domain is transforming from disease to wellness, and wellness domain is shifting towards user centric model with innovative platforms [13]. The Mining Minds [13, 15] is an innovative platform that exploits digital health and wellness paradigms to the end users by providing wellbeing services and recommendations. Mining Minds mainly focuses on the health and wellness recommendations and guidelines. The structure of Mining Minds is divided into different layers and each layer is responsible to perform its related activities. Knowledge Curation Layer (KCL) [15] is one of these layers is designed to maintain the evolutionary knowledge base for the essential requirement for intelligent recommendation services. In KCL, our proposed Knowledge Acquisition Tool (KAT) facilitates expert to transform their knowledge and experience in to computer interpretable knowledge base. The KAT currently emphasizes on physical activities and nutrition knowledge for recommendations. Using KAT, the physical instructors and nutritionist transforms their knowledge utilizing the concepts of physical, nutrition, and user's essential information. These concepts are part of WCM and are related to each other through different relationships. Figure 10.1 illustrates the development and integration paradigm of WCM with KAT to evolve the wellness knowledge for Mining Minds.

A team of domain experts including 2 nutritionists and 3 physical instructors designed the conceptual model and provided the higher-level blueprint of WCM. A collaborative study between the teams of domain experts and knowledge engineers took place to initialize design and implementation of WCM. The knowledge engineers' team provided the identified relationships among the concepts represented the model in ontological format for computer interpretation. The domain experts' team validated the design and verified the WCM implementation. Eventually model is persisted in the repository. This WCM repository is integrated to KAT, which facilitates experts to evolve the knowledge base in user-friendly manner.

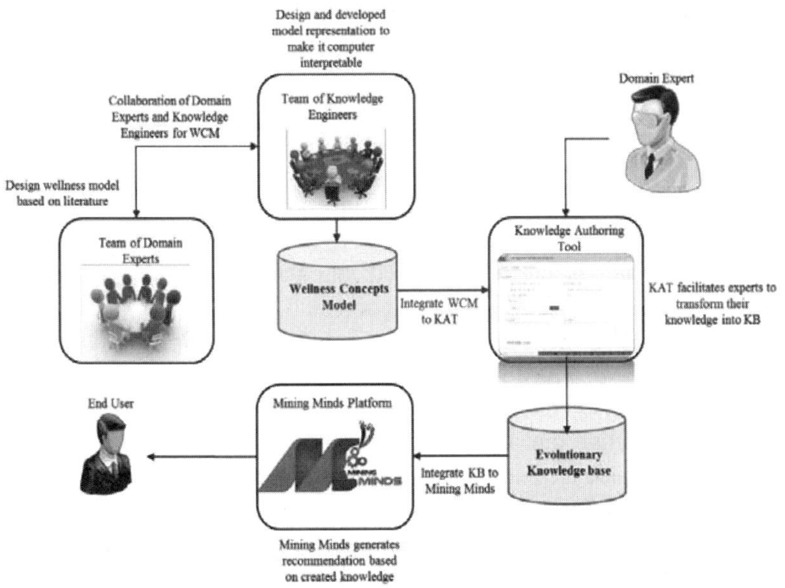

Figure 10.1 Integration of Wellness Concepts Model and Knowledge Acquisition Tool Paradigm

10.3.2 Wellness Concepts Model (WCM) Design

The Indivisible Self [3] provides very comprehensive evidence-based wellness model, which we selected as a core model for this study. We modified the model according to the health and wellness requirements of a recommendation system, specifically for physical activities and nutrition domains. The Indivisible Self model is composed of the second-order factors including Essential, Creative, Coping, Social, and Physical Self. The proposed WCM model extends the second-order

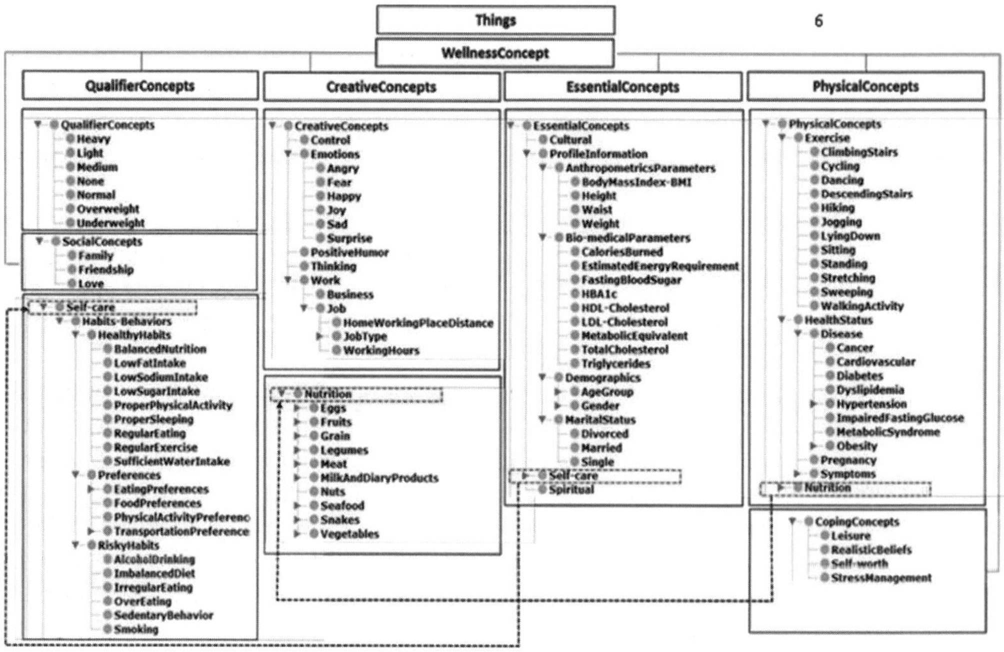

Figure 10.2 Partially represented Wellness Concepts Model (WCM)

hierarchy with multiple level of depth in Creative, Essential, and Physical components based on the nature of components. The Creative category contains Thinking, Emotions, Control, Positive Humor, and Work. Usually the wellness recommendation systems use emotion and work-related information of the users. Therefore, we extended the Emotion and Work categories under the Creative hierarchy. In same way, we have added many other concepts under the Essential category as shown in Figure 10.2. For instance, under the Profile Information, we put the demographic information, anthropometrics parameters, and bio-medical parameters. Under Self-care, which is subcategory of Essential, we have related all the behaviors and habits of users that play important role in self-care, like risky habits, healthy habits, preferences in food, activities, hobbies, and transportation. In Physical self, we added Health Status as subcategory and related it to diseases, symptoms, and other health related concepts. We put concepts that belong to physical activities under the exercise hierarchy while diet concepts under the nutrition hierarchy. Health status, physical activities, and nutrition are the main focus of wellness recommendation systems. We have introduced a new category qualifier concepts in second-order factors, which contains all the concepts that illustrate possible values set of other concepts. For instance, normal, heavy, light are some possible values set for dinner, lunch, and breakfast. We have provided maximum semantics in all these concepts that are usually use in wellness recommendations. For instance, each user has some preferences in food, physical activities, transportation, and eating time. New concepts can be plugged-in easily in a related hierarchy because of the flexible hierarchical structure of the model. Figure 10.2 shows wellness concepts model hierarchies partially, while figure 10.3 demonstrates the attribute relationships among some concepts. For instance, the three attribute relationships a) containsFoodOf b) containsActivitiesOf and c) foodIntake are used to connect different concepts. The a) relates food Preference with Nutrition, b) relates Physical Activities Preferences with Exercises, and c) relates Eating Preferences (Breakfast, Lunch, and Dinner) with Qualifier Concepts (Light, Medium, Heavy).

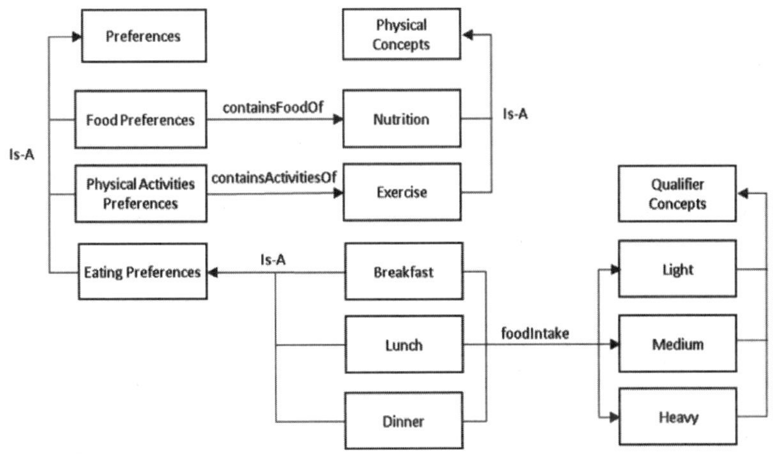

Figure 10.3 Attribute relationships in WCM

10.3.3 Implementation of WCFM Integrated KAT

In Figure 10.4, we present the implementation architecture of our proposed WCM integrated Knowledge Acquisition Tool (KAT). It consists of six sub-components Domain Model Manager, Rule Editor, Situation Event Manager, Knowledge Transformation Bridge, Knowledge Base and Knowledge Sharing Interfaces. Domain Model Manager: This component is responsible to manage the wellness model. It loads the WCM into the Rule Editor to use in rule editing activity. Rule Editor: As a core component of KAT, rule editor provides a user-friendly environment to domain expert to create knowledge rules. The knowledge rules represented in form of unordered production rules. The rule base reasoning (RBR) used to generate final recommendations to end users. It comprises of five further sub- components to perform distinct functionalities. Model Loader is in charge of loading WCM concepts into the rule's editor in tree structure for easy selection of desired concepts. This sub-component shows all the concepts in a single tree or sub-tree based on the top categories like Profile Information, Diseases, and Physical Activities. The Intelli-sense Manager provides a list of related concepts which are used to facilitate the experts to choose the desired value from the list. For instance, when expert wants to write Physical Activity = Sitting, the possible values set for Physical Activity are reflected to appear such as; Standing, Sitting, Walking, Jogging, and others. A separate inner Intelli-sense window is shown to reflect all possible values. Artifacts Controller fetches the operators into the Rule Editor and facilitate experts to select required operators from the list. The Rule Creator module creates the rule from all facts and conclusion created by experts in conditions and conclusion parts. It creates the hierarchy of conditions and conclusion in the created rules. The Rule Validator validates the rule and finds the duplications and conflicts of the new rule with the existing rules in the knowledge base. Situation Event Manager: Some rules may consist of some salient features that should monitor by the system as events, those features are called situation events. Whenever an abnormal situation occurs, the system generates recommendation and passes as an alert to the user. It facilitates expert to identify and select the desired facts as situation event. Knowledge Transformation Bridge: This module transforms plane rule into a computer executable format. We use relational schema representation for persisting rules in the knowledge base. Knowledge Base: In knowledge base, we have two repositories one for persisting the whole rules as Rule Base KB while the second repository as Index Based Rules for persisting the situations events in rules. These repositories are closely coupled to each other based on identifiers of situations and rules. Knowledge Sharing Interfaces: This component consists of two types of sharing interfaces. Situation Event Sharing interface shares the situation events with monitoring systems to observe the abnormal situations of the users. While Rule Index Sharing interface is responsible to share the knowledge rules with reasoning engine of the recommendation system.

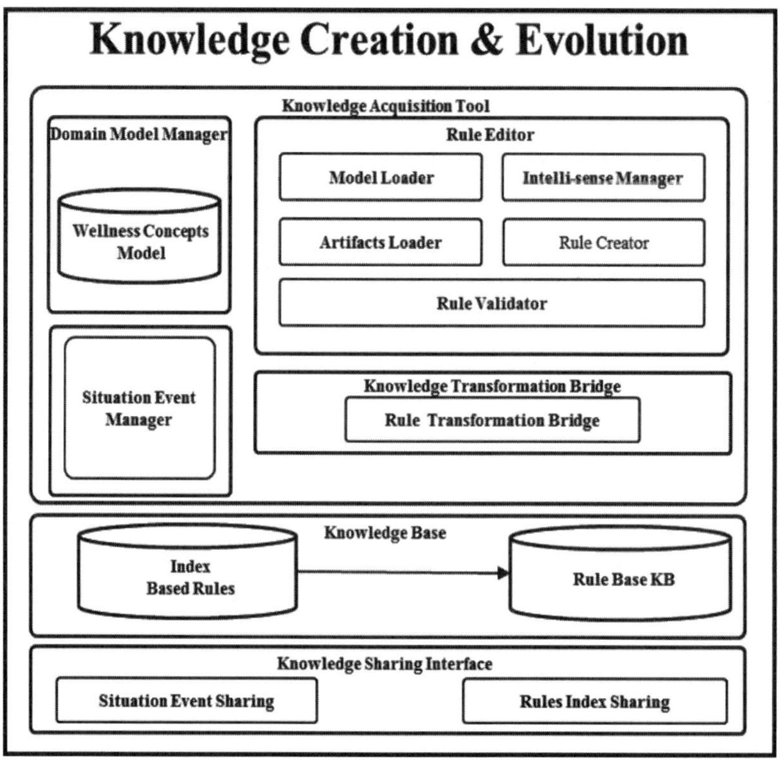

Figure 10.4 Architecture of WCM integrated KAT

10.4 Results and Evaluations

The main objective of WCM integration with knowledge acquisition tool is facilitating domain experts to transform and represent their knowledge to computer interpretable knowledge base. When domain experts are satisfied and comfortable in knowledge acquisition then adoption of wellness recommendation systems will be increase. Therefore, we evaluated the proposed WCM integrated KAT from domain experts to assess their satisfaction over the claimed facilitation of WCM augmented knowledge authoring environment experimental setup:

A) We provide the developed knowledge acquisition tool to the domain experts. Figure 10.5 shows the main Rule Editor of the system that we deployed on the web server.
B) In order to easily understand the usage of authoring environment, we also provided the system manual.
C) A visual representation of WCM is provided in a graphical format to understand the hierarchies of concepts. d) A set of questions is provided in a questionnaire form. Eight of the questions in the questionnaire are related to the; (i) organization of the information, (ii) concepts of WCM, (iii) performance and help of WCM in Rule Editor, (iv) coverage of desired concepts in WCM, and (v) user-friendliness of the system. e) Overall six domain experts are assigned including two physical instructors, two nutritionists, and two nurses to evaluate the system on the basis of questions.

During experiment session, each domain expert created five rules in corresponding fields using their experience and knowledge. After knowledge creation, each domain expert provided answers to the relevant questions in our provided questionnaire. Each question has 4 possible answers and we have assigned a weightage to each answer as shown in Table 10.1 based on the methods and protocols suggested in [24]. We evaluated the user satisfaction level based on the domain experts' feedback. And users' satisfaction level at average 80.42% has recorded. In Table 10.2, the domain experts' feedback (in percentage) is illustrated to each question. We first found out the average values for each question and then we calculated the system performance by determining the overall average value (80.42%) from the averages of individual questions.

Figure 10.5 Rule Editor

10.5 Summary

Every individual intends healthier life, which is possible with healthier physical activities and balanced diet. Wellness model is run by these categories. Without evolutionary knowledge base, a recommendation system is difficult to adopt. Our proposed intelligent knowledge authoring environment is beneficial to create evolutionary knowledge base with the use of a comprehensive wellness concepts model. It provides user-friendly environment to author wellness knowledge by domain experts without knowledge engineers intervention.

Table 10.1 Possible answers weightage

Question Evaluation Criteria	Weightage (%)
Highly Satisfied	100
Satisfied	80
Less Satisfied	60
Not satisfied	40

Table 10.2 Domain Experts feedback

	User Satisfaction (%)							
Evaluators	**Q1**	**Q2**	**Q3**	**Q4**	**Q5**	**Q6**	**Q7**	**Q8**
Physical Instructor - 1	80	60	100	80	80	80	80	60
Physical Instructor - 2	100	80	80	60	80	80	60	100
Nutritionist - 1	80	100	80	80	100	80	80	80
Nutritionist - 2	100	60	100	80	80	100	60	60
Nurse - 1	80	80	80	100	80	80	60	80
Nurse - 2	60	60	80	80	100	80	100	80
Average	**83.33**	**73.33**	**86.67**	**80.00**	**86.67**	**83.33**	**73.33**	**76.67**
Total Average	**80.42%**							

Currently, we have validated knowledge rules with respect to duplication and conflict of rules, but in future we will also focus on the semantic validation of rules that will enhance satisfaction level of domain experts.

Source Code

For source code please contact us at:

The contents of this chapter have been previously published in the following article:

Taqdir Ali and Sungyoung Lee, "Wellness Concepts Model use and effectiveness in intelligent knowledge authoring environment", 14th International Conference on Smart Homes and Health Telematics (ICOST). Inclusive Smart Cities and Digital Health, pp. 271-282, Wuhan, China, May 25-27, 2016

References

[1]. D. A. Els and R. P. De La Rey, "Developing a holistic wellness model," SA Journal of Human Resource Management, no. 2, pp. 46–56, 2006

[2]. Lenz, A. Stephen, and Robert L. Smith. "Integrating wellness concepts within a clinical supervision model." The Clinical Supervisor 29.2 (2010): 228-245.

[3]. Myers, Jane E., and Thomas J. Sweeney. "The indivisible self: An evidence-based model of wellness." Journal of Individual Psychology 60 (2004): 234-244.

[4]. K. Fehre, and K. P. Adlassnig. "Service-oriented Arden-syntax-based clinical decision support." Proceedings of eHealth2011. Vienna: Austrian Computer Society (2011): 123-8

[5]. Ali, T., Hussain, M., Khan, W. A., Afzal, M., Kang, B. H., & Lee, S. (2014, June). Arden syntax studio: Creating medical logic module as shareable knowledge. In Innovations in Intelligent Systems and Applications (INISTA) Proceedings, 2014 IEEE International Symposium on (pp. 266-272).IEEE.

[6]. Ali, T., Hussain, M., Ali Khan, W., Afzal, M., & Lee, S. (2013, July). Authoring tool: acquiring sharable knowledge for Smart CDSS. In Engineering in Medicine and Biology Society (EMBC), 2013 35th Annual International Conference of the IEEE (pp. 1278-1281). IEEE.

[7]. Shortliffe, E. H. (1986). Medical expert systems—knowledge tools for physicians. Western Journal of Medicine, 145(6), 830.

[8]. J. A. Osheroff, M. J. Teich, B. Middleton, E. B. Steen, A. Wright, and D. E. Detmer. "A roadmap for national action on clinical decision support." Journal of the American medical informatics association 14.2 (2007): 141-145

[9]. K. Kawamoto, G. Del Fiol, H. R. Starsberg, N. Hulse, C. Curtis, J. J. Cimino, H. R. Beatriz et al. "Multi-national, multi-institutional analysis of clinical decision support data needs to inform development of the HL7 virtual medical record standard." AMIA Annual Symposium Proceedings. Vol. 2010. American Medical Informatics Association, 2010

[10]. Summary of SNOMED CT Benefits, http://www.ihtsdo.org/snomedct/whysnomedct/benefits/ [Visited on February, 2016]

[11]. Ali, T., Hussain, M., Khan, W. A., Afzal, M., & Lee, S. (2014, January). Customized clinical domain ontology extraction for Knowledge Authoring Tool. In Proceedings of the 8th International Conference on Ubiquitous Information Management and Communication (p. 23). ACM.

[12]. Larson, J. S. (1999). The conceptualization of health. Medical Care Research and Review, 56(2), 123-136.

[13]. Banos, O., Amin, M. B., Ali Khan, W., Ali, T., Afzal, M., Kang, B. H., & Lee, S. (2015, May). Mining Minds: An innovative framework for personalized health and wellness support. In Pervasive Computing Technologies for Healthcare (PervasiveHealth), 2015 9th International Conference on (pp. 1-8). IEEE.

[14]. Mining Minds Overview, http://www.miningminds.re.kr/english/ [Visited on February, 2016]

[15]. Banos, O., Amin, M. B., Khan, W. A., Afzal, M., Hussain, M., Kang, B. H., & Lee, S. The Mining Minds Digital Health and Wellness Framework.

[16]. Ardell, Donald B. High level wellness, an alternative to doctors, drugs, and disease. Bantam Books, 1979.

[17]. Hettler, B. "Wellness: encouraging a lifetime pursuit of excellence." Health values 8.4 (1984): 13.

[18]. Sweeney, T. J., & Witmer, J. M. (1991). Beyond social interest: Striving toward optimum health and wellness. Individual Psychology, 47, 527-540.

[19]. Witmer, J. M., & Sweeney, T. J. (1992). A holistic model for wellness and prevention over the lifespan. Journal of Counseling and Development, 71, 140-148

[20]. Adler, A. (1954). Understanding human nature. New York: Fawcett. (Original work published 1927)

[21]. Puerta, A. R., Egar, J. W., Tu, S. W., & Musen, M. A. (1992). A multiple-method knowledge- acquisition shell for the automatic generation of knowledge-acquisition tools. Knowledge acquisition, 4(2), 171-196.

[22]. Tudorache, T., Nyulas, C., Noy, N. F., & Musen, M. A. (2013). WebProtégé: A collaborative ontology editor and knowledge acquisition tool for the web. Semantic web, 4(1), 89-99.

[23]. D. Dunsmuir, J. Daniels, C. Brouse, S. Ford, J. M. Ansermino, A knowledge authoring tool for clinical decision support, Journal of clinical monitoring and computing 22 (3) (2008) 189-198

[24]. Barua, A. (2013). Methods for decision-making in survey questionnaires based on Likert scale. Journal of Asian Scientific Research, 3(1), 35.

Chapter 11

Data-driven Knowledge Acquisition

An End-to-End Knowledge Engineering Process for Generating Production Rules

Maqbool Ali, Rahman Ali, Wajahat Ali Khan,
Jaehun Bang, Taeho Hur, Dohyeong Kim,
and Sungyoung Lee

Data-driven knowledge acquisition is one of the key research fields in data mining. Dealing with large amounts of data has received a lot of attention in the field recently, and a number of methodologies have been proposed to extract insights from data in an automated or semi-automated manner. However, these methodologies generally target a specific aspect of the data mining process, such as data acquisition, data preprocessing, or data classification. However, a comprehensive knowledge acquisition method is crucial to support the end-to-end knowledge engineering process. In this chapter, we introduce a knowledge acquisition system that covers all major phases of the cross-industry standard process for data mining. Acknowledging the importance of an end-to-end knowledge engineering process, we designed and developed an easy-to-use data-driven knowledge acquisition tool (DDKAT). The major features of the DDKAT are: (1) a novel unified features scoring approach for data selection; (2) a user-friendly data processing interface to improve the quality of the raw data; (3) an appropriate decision tree algorithm selection approach to build a classification model; and (4) the generation of production rules from various decision tree classification models in an automated manner. Furthermore, two diabetes studies were performed to assess the value of the DDKAT in terms of user experience. A total of 19 experts were involved in the first study and 102 students in the artificial intelligence domain were involved in the second study. The results showed that the overall user experience of the DDKAT was positive in terms of its attractiveness, as well as its pragmatic and hedonic quality factors.

11.1 Introduction

Knowledge systems have come a long way, from manual knowledge curation to automatic data-driven knowledge generation. The major drivers of this transition were the size and complexity of data. Since large datasets cannot be efficiently analyzed manually, the automation process is essential [2].

Initially in this process of knowledge automation, knowledge engineers followed ad-hoc procedures [3]. Later on, more systematic methodologies were devised, which can be referred to as data-driven knowledge acquisition systems.

Knowledge extraction from structured sources such as databases is an active area of research in the information systems community. To extract hidden knowledge or gain insights from structured or unstructured data, data science (DS) was created, supporting both automatic and semi-automatic data analysis [4]. Data science is similar to Knowledge Discovery in Databases and is intricately linked to data-driven decision-making concepts [5]. It employs techniques and theories drawn from many fields such as data mining (DM), machine learning, cluster analysis, classification, visualization, and databases [6]. Data mining plays an important role in exploring hidden patterns in data, lead- ing to insights that can be used to design decision support systems [7]. The CRoss-Industry Standard Process for Data Mining (CRISP-DM) is a widely used systematic methodology for DM and DS system development. According to a poll con- ducted in 2014, CRISP-DM was regarded as the leading methodology for data science projects, data mining, and analytics [8]. CRISP-DM consists of six well-defined phases: business understanding, data understanding, data preparation, modeling, evaluation, and deployment [9]. The major goal of developing CRISP-DM was to establish a data mining methodology and process model for end-to-end application execution. In this study, a data-driven knowledge acquisition system that covers all major phases of CRISP-DM is introduced to explain the end-to-end knowledge engineering process.

The data understanding phase of the data mining process involves collecting the data as well as inspecting it closely, which is crucial for the next phase, data preparation. In a dataset, instances represent data entities, which are further characterized by their properties. These properties can also be referred to as features or attributes, and they help to understand the characteristics of the data. Feature selection plays a crucial role in the procedure of 'knowledge discovery' [10]. Generally, a feature selection method evaluates the usefulness of the attributes (i.e., features) present in the dataset; a ranking methodology is considered the optimal way to score such features [11]. A substantial amount of research has been devoted to improving feature selection methodologies [11]–[15]. However, less attention is given to the development of a unified and comprehensive methodology for feature ranking. This study proposes an innovative feature ranking methodology called Unified Features Scoring (UFS). The primary ambition of UFS is to evaluate the feature set in a comprehensive manner dependent on several different feature selection measures, namely information gain (IG), gain ratio (GR), symmetric uncertainty (SU), chi-square (CS), and significance [12], [16]–[18]. UFS is a consensus methodology that assists the domain expert in selecting informative features for the data preparation phase of CRISP-DM.

Once a feature set is selected from a dataset and the data preparation phase is completed, a modeling phase (i.e. data classification) is initiated. Data classification is one of the most important data mining functions, and employs a number of features to predict a target variable [19] and produce a decision tree model. In the field of data mining, decision trees are one of the most well-known data classification methods for the representation of inductive knowledge [20]. However, the manual selection of an appropriate classifier (i.e., machine learning algorithm) from the available decision tree classifiers is a time-consuming exercise. To mitigate this, we adopted an accurate multi-criteria decision- making (AMD) methodology [21] to choose an appropriate classification algorithm for generating production rules. Acknowledging the importance of an end-to-end knowledge engineering process, we designed and developed an easy-to-use data-driven knowledge acquisition tool (DDKAT) to provide a data mining utility for both expert and non-expert data miners. An up-to-date version of this tool and its documentation can be downloaded from the GitHub open- source platform [1], [22]. This study is both an extension and a detailed study of previous work [23], [24]. The DDKAT is a web-based application that acquires health and wellness knowledge and shares the acquired knowledge in the form of production rules. All of the major phases of CRISP-DM are implemented and explained using a diabetes dataset as a case study (see Section 13.4.2). The DDKAT was designed for a UCLab project called Mining Minds (MM); however, other platforms can also utilize this tool for comprehensive knowledge acquisition purposes. Mining Minds2 provides personalized services to users to improve their quality of life (see Section 13.3.1 for more details). The major features of the DDKAT are the novel UFS methodology for data selection, easy-to-perform data preprocessing, integration of an AMD methodology for appropriate classifier selection, decision tree generation, and the translation of decision trees into production rules to share using an expert-driven approach. The motivation behind the DDKAT is to generate production rules in a comprehensive manner and to support the end- to-end knowledge engineering process. In order to achieve these goals, this study was undertaken with the following objectives:

1) To select suitable parameters from structured data to assist the domain expert in selecting informative features for the task at hand.
2) To select an appropriate decision tree algorithm for the creation of a classification model.
3) To generate production rules from various decision tree classification models in an automatic manner.
4) To design and develop an easy-to-use online web- based application for implementing the major phases of CRISP-DM.

The key contributions of this research are: (1) the UFS methodology for selecting suitable parameters, (2) Integration of an AMD methodology for selecting an appropriate decision tree algorithm (3) an automatic mechanism for generating production rules from various decision tree classification models, and (4) the data-driven knowledge acquisition tool.

The following are the highlights of this research:

1) This study introduces a knowledge acquisition system that covers all major phases of the CRISP-DM frame- work to provide a data mining utility for both expert and non-expert data miners.
2) We designed and developed an easy-to-use web-based data-driven knowledge acquisition tool for extracting shareable production rules from a dataset in a comprehensive manner to explain the end-to-end knowledge engineering process.
3) The DDKAT uses an innovative feature ranking methodology called Unified Features Scoring to comprehensively evaluate the feature set and assist the domain expert in selecting informative features for the data preparation phase of CRISP-DM.
4) The DDKAT uses an accurate multi-criteria decision- making (AMD) methodology to choose an appropriate decision tree classification algorithm.
5) The DDKAT uses an automatic approach to generate production rules from various decision tree classification models.

6) Two case studies were performed on a diabetes dataset to evaluate the DDKAT in terms of user experience.

7) Overall, the user experience of the DDKAT was positive with respect to its attractiveness as well as its pragmatic and hedonic quality factors.

The study is organized as follows. Section 13.2 describes related works, and Section 13.3 presents the architecture of the proposed system, functional mapping from the DDKAT to the phases of CRISP-DM, and detailed methodologies for the data understanding, data preparation, and modeling phases. Section 13.4 presents the results obtained in the data under- standing and data preparation phases. Section 13.5 evaluates the proposed system. Section 13.6 presents an overview of the DDKAT and describes the case study of a diabetes dataset to explain the phases of CRISP-DM. Section 13.7 discusses the significance, challenges, and limitations of this study. Finally, Section 13.8 concludes the chapter with a summary of the research findings and future directions.

11.2 Related Works

This research addresses important aspects of the data science process. This section briefly deals with: (1) DS background and the CRISP-DM methodology, (2) methodological studies of feature selection approaches used in the data understanding phase, (3) a discussion about knowledge representation and transformation techniques that require it, and (4) the overall limitations of existing systems. The term DS was used in the early 1960s to cover six processes [6]–problem identification, data collection, data preprocessing, data analysis, data modeling, and product evaluation–in order to extract knowledge for decision- making. Data mining is generally considered a sub-step of the DS process [6]. The main purpose of data mining techniques is to extract non-trivial knowledge from unprocessed data. The key benefits of the DM approach are (1) rapid growth of data, (2) reduced data storage cost, and (3) less data processing time [25]. CRISP-DM, published in the year 2000, is a widely-used systematic methodology for developing DM/DS projects. It is considered the de facto standard [26] for executing a DM project systematically. Gupta [25] dis- cussed software development and CRISP-DM, two different approaches to the data mining process. In the software development approach, the data mining process includes six steps: 'requirement analysis,' 'data selection and collection,' 'clean- ing and preparing data,' 'data mining exploration and validation,' 'implementation, evaluation, and monitoring,' and 'results visualization.' CRISP-DM is similar to the software development approach with the exception of steps 2, 3, and 6. The proposed knowledge acquisition system (DDKAT) includes the Unified Features Scoring methodology for selecting salient features from a dataset before the data preparation phase. This methodology is based on an empirical study of different feature selection measures, including information gain and the gain ratio. The following are some of the relevant feature ranking studies from a methodological point of view. Belanche and González [11] performed a thorough study of feature selection algorithms in synthetic problems to evaluate their performance. In this study, a scoring measure was devised to score the output of the feature selection methods, a solution that was considered to be optimal. Liu and Yu [27] proposed a categorizing framework to build an integrated system for automatic feature selection. This framework was based on a unifying platform and laid the important foundation for methodologically integrating differ- ent feature selection methods based on their shared characteristics. With respect to ensemble feature selection studies, Rokach et al. [13] investigated an ensemble approach that could enhance feature selection; however, the researchers only considered non-ranking filters. Similarly, Jong et al. [14] proposed an ensemble feature ranking methodology that integrated various feature rankings from the same and artificial datasets to improve the stability of feature ranking. In addition, Slavkov et al. [15] conducted a study on various aggregation approaches of the feature rankings of public neuroblastoma microarrays using multiple ranking algorithms and datasets. They showed that aggregating feature rankings produced favorable outcomes compared to the use of a single feature ranking method. Prati [12] also proposed a general framework for the use of ensemble feature ranking to improve the quality of feature rankings and was able to obtain bet- ter results than others. For such ensemble feature selection studies, various combinations of univariate filter methods are used in the literature, including (i) IG, GR, CS, and SU [16], [17], (ii) IG, CS, and SU [18], and (iii) IG, GR, SU, CS, and OneR [12]. This section also addresses knowledge representations and tree transformation techniques. In order to understand knowledge structures, most healthcare experts and knowledge engineers are interested in knowledge representation [28]. In the literature, comprehensive knowledge representation models such as decision graphs, production rules, and decision trees are extensively used by knowledge engineers to understand the complete structure of a classification scheme [28]. Different software has been developed for conveniently visualizing decision tree models [28]. In one study, a micromanagement design for group formations was presented in which an XML- encoded decision tree helped agents decide the tactics of a game using simple IF-THEN rules [29]. The Waikato Environment for Knowledge Analysis (WEKA) was used to automate the process of generating the decision tree. In a decision tree, a set of rules is dependent on the number of leaf nodes. All conditions encountered on the path from the root node to each leaf node are concatenated to construct production rules. The decision tree is traversed in a depth-first search (DFS) with a simple greedy solution to produce fairly good rule sets [30]. In [31], decision trees were first generated from a set of training cases, before transforming the trees from the same classification domain into production rules. The study also described the decision tree transformation technique used to construct the production rules. Platforms such as StarCraft: Brood War are available for converting decision trees into rules [29]. In addition, Holmes et al. [32] presented an algorithm that generated simple and accurate IF-THEN rules from models such as decision trees. In the literature, most decision trees are transformed using Weka text- To Xml [29], [33], in which only J48 classifier-based decision trees are converted into inter-operable XML files.

The rationale for transforming a decision tree into IF- THEN production rules is that these rules are (1) easy to understand and widely used in expert systems to represent knowledge [31], [34], (2) more compact and predictive than the decision tree from which they were generated [31], [32], and (3) used to construct a credible knowledge base from the same dataset to better support decision-making [24], [35]. Considering the above discussion and the rapid increase in data rates, it is almost impossible to extract hidden knowledge using manual approaches. The research community prefers to use data mining processes to resolve this problem. For the feature selection task of data mining, considerable research [11], [36] has focused on improving feature selection algorithms, yet less attention has been paid to developing a unified methodology for feature selection. In expert systems, production rules are commonly used as a formalism to express knowledge, and J48 classifier-based decision trees are generally used to generate rule sets from decision trees. To the best of our knowledge, there is no method to extract rule sets from multiple and different decision trees, e.g., classification and regression trees (CART).

11.3 Materials and Methods

With the goal of developing an end-to-end data-driven knowledge acquisition system for generating production rules, this section describes (1) the Mining Minds (MM) framework, (2) our proposed system architecture and component details, (3) functional mapping of the proposed system to the phases of CRISP-DM, and (4) detailed methodologies used for the data understanding, data preparation, and modeling phases of CRISP-DM. Each of these items is explained in the following subsections.

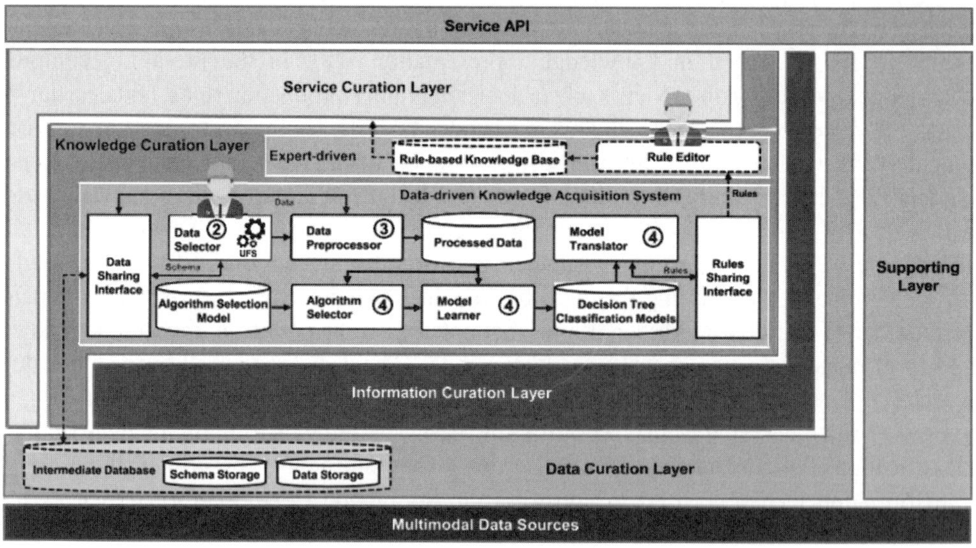

Figure 11.1 The Mining Minds frameworks layered architecture with a data-driven operational diagram. [23][38]

11.3.1 Architecture

The scope of this study is the data-driven module of the KCL, as shown in Figure 11.1; the components represented by dotted lines and their internal details are not covered in this study. This figure shows an abstract view of the end-to-end data-driven knowledge engineering process, whose work- flow is explained in the simulation section. Our proposed architecture consists of five major components, called the Data Selector, Data Preprocessor, Algorithm Selector, Model Learner, and Model Translator. In Figure 11.1, each component is labelled with a number to represent the corresponding phase of CRISP-DM. The functionality of each component is described as follows.

11.3.1.1 The functionality of the data selector component

This component acts as a data broker interface and corresponds to the data understanding phase of CRISP-DM. The Data Selector component obtains the required contents of the data stored in the DCL based on parameters or features established by the domain expert. It takes schema (i.e., feature information) as input from the Intermediate Database of the DCL through the Data Sharing Interface and displays it to the domain expert. In addition, to help the domain expert select suitable features, this component provides a feature scorecard, which is computed using our proposed UFS methodology.

11.3.1.2 The functionality of the data preprocessor component

Data preprocessing can play a major role in enhancing data quality. After loading the unprocessed data from the DCL through the Data Sharing Interface, this component performs basic data preprocessing tasks such as (1) the identification and replacement of missing values, (2) the detection and replacement of outlier values, and (3) data discretization corresponding to the data preparation phase of CRISP-DM. After performing these tasks, it stores the data into the Processed Data repository.

11.3.1.3 The functionality of the algorithm selector component

The Algorithm Selector component, part of the modeling phase of CRISP-DM, recommends an appropriate decision tree algorithm from the Algorithm Selection Model repository using an accurate multi-criteria decision-making (AMD) methodology [21].

11.3.1.4 The functionality of the model learner component

The Model Learner component, corresponding to the model- ing phase of CRISP-DM, loads the processed data from the Processed Data repository and the recommended algorithm from the Algorithm Selector component for data learning. After acquiring the data and the algorithm, this component generates the classification model and stores it in the Decision Tree Classification Models repository.

11.3.1.5 The functionality of the model translator component

The Model Translator component, also corresponding to the modeling phase of CRISP-DM, applies text preprocessing techniques to the generated classification model to prepare it for XML transformation. After text processing, this component transforms the processed classification model into an XML model. It then parses the resulting XML model to extract production rules that can be shared with the domain expert through the Rules Sharing Interface for validation. The Rule Editor component, represented by the dotted line in Figure 11.1, provides a user-friendly interface for knowledge experts to load the generated production rules and validate each rule before storing it into the Rule-based Knowledge Base.

Table 11.1 CRISP-DM phases and tasks performed in the DDKAT[26]

Business understandin	Data understanding	Data preparation	Modeling	Evaluation	Deployment
Understand application main	Select parameters	Convert data	Select classifier	Evaluate the results UFS method	Plan deployment
Identify application goa	Build query	Identify missing data	Build classification model	Evaluate the impact data preprocessing tas	Monitor applicati impact
Identify application o tives	Collect initial data	Replace missing data	Refine classification model	Evaluate u assessments	Maintain application
Analyze resource speci tion (software, hardwar	Compute feature scoring	Detect outliers	Convert to XML	Determine next steps	Prepare final repo
Prepare application d opment plan	Analyze attributes	Replace outliers	Extract production rules		Review applicatio
	Collect required data	Discretize data	Build rule sharing service		

11.3.2 Functional mapping of the proposed system with phases of the CRISP-DM

This section gives a description of the functional mapping of the DDKAT to the phases of CRISP-DM, as shown in Table 11.1, which details the tasks performed by the DDKAT for each phase. An understanding of the application domain is developed in the first phase of CRISP-DM, and parameter selection, query generation, feature scoring, and data collection are performed in the second phase. Data preprocessing (e.g., cleaning and discretization) and modeling (e.g., classifier selection, data learning, building of classification models, and translation into production rules) are covered in the third and fourth phases, respectively. In the fifth phase, the methodology and user assessments are evaluated. Finally, the sixth and final phase accounts for the deployment of the proposed system. Detailed methodologies for the data understanding, data preparation, and modeling phases of CRISP-DM are explained in the following subsections.

11.3.3 Methodology for the data understanding phase

To understand the data in this study, the parameters (i.e., features or variables) were selected and ranked in the data understanding phase. The following subsection describes the proposed Unified Features Scoring methodology for ranking and prioritizing the features.

UFS is an automatic feature ranking methodology that attempts to unify different feature selection measures in a comprehensive manner. It uses an intuitive approach to ensemble learning and produces a final ranked list by combining the results of various feature ranking techniques [16], [17].

The following is some rationale for the approaches used in UFS. Feature selection techniques are generally split into two categories: filters and wrappers [39], [40]. UFS focuses on filter-based methods, which allow for better generalization and are considered to be much faster and less computationally expensive than wrapper methods [39], [41]. UFS is based on five univariate filter-based measures to comprehensively evaluate the feature set–information gain, gain ratio, chi-square, symmetric uncertainty, and attribute significance (AS) [12], [16]–[18]. With each of these filter measures, the features are evaluated under various considerations. The rationale for choosing each is as follows:

- *Information gain*, one of the popular feature selection measures, measures how much information a feature provides about the target class [42].
- *Gain ratio* is a disparity measure that enhances information gain [42].
- *Symmetrical uncertainty* performs well for highly imbalanced feature sets [43].
- *CHI-square* is a statistical measure that determines the association of a feature with its target class [42].
- *Attribute significance* is a probabilistic measure that assesses an attribute's worth. It is a two-way function that computes the attribute's significance, or association with a class attribute [44].

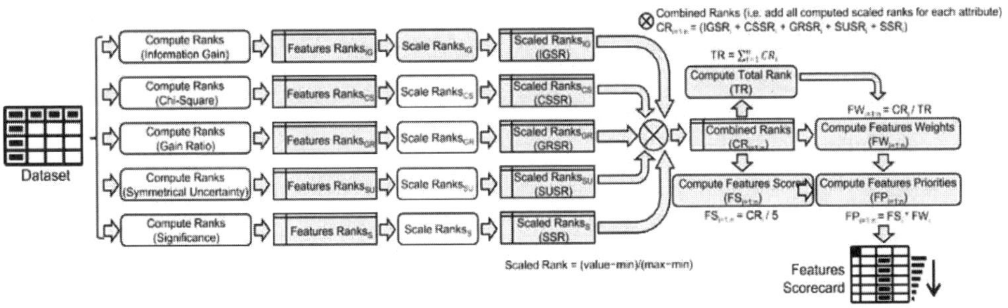

Figure 11.2 Unified features scoring workflow

UFS uses a ranking approach, which is attractive for features with empirical validity, simplicity, and scalability [16], [45]. Each filter measure has a different relative scale depending on its characteristics and biases. To account for these biases and avoid the impact of multiple relative scales (i.e., numerical instability), UFS bounds the values within small intervals and normalizes them to the same range (between 0 and 1) using min-max normalization (MMN), which is defined as follows:

$$MMN = \frac{\text{value} - \min}{\max - min}$$

Another key consideration in this process is limiting the effect of highly correlated features. In the rescaling process, UFS assigns rank 1 to the features with the highest feature index, in contrast to a previous study [16], which assigned rank 0 to the features with the highest feature index. After feature rescaling, UFS uses an order-based ranking aggregation approach, which is not only effective, but also easy to implement, scale insensitive, and elegant [12]. Finally, the UFS applies the arithmetic mean as an aggregating function to compute relative feature weights and ranking priorities. The workflow of the UFS methodology is illustrated in Figure 11.2.

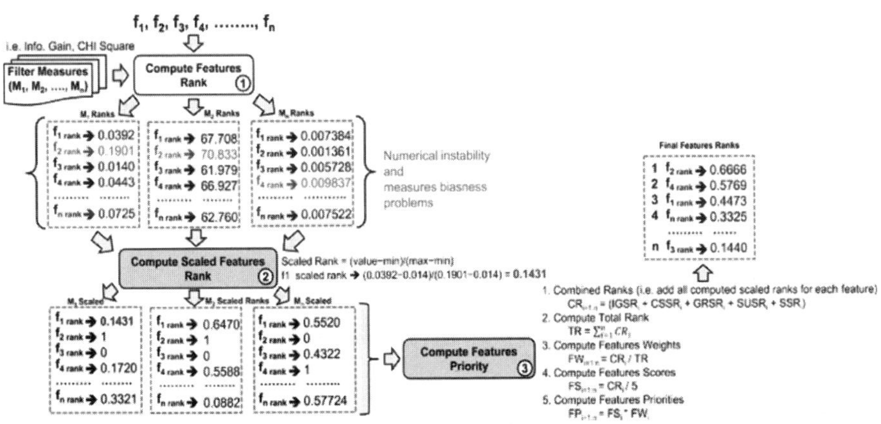

Figure 11.3 Diabetes dataset example for explaining UFS

UFS can also be explained using a benchmark diabetes dataset,[4] as shown in Figure 11.3. In Figure

13.3, $f_1, f_2, f_3, ..., f_n$ represent the features (such as *preg, plas, pres,...., age*) of the diabetes dataset, and $M_1, M_2, ..., _n$ represent the five aforementioned univariate filter-based measures. Ranks are computed using each filter measure. For example, using M_1 (information gain), the computed ranks of each feature are:

1, rank of @attribute *preg* 0.0392
2, rank of @attribute *plas* 0.1901
3, rank of @attribute *pres* 0.014
4, rank of @attribute *skin* 0.0443
.....
8, rank of @attribute *age* 0.0725

After calculating the information gain of each feature, min- max normalization is applied to each attribute. For example, the attribute preg is normalized to 0.1431. This process is then replicated for the other measures (M2, M3, M4, M5).

The different ranks of the feature are then combined; once each feature has been evaluated and scaled according to each filter measure, a comprehensive score of the individual feature is calculated, as shown in Figure 11.3. The attribute weight is also calculated based on the feature's individual score and the combined score of all the features present in the dataset. Finally, attribute priority is computed based on the contribution of a feature in terms of its individual measure score and its relative weight in a dataset; for example, here f2 had the highest priority. This can assist the domain expert in selecting high-priority features for the data preparation phase of CRISP-DM.

The purpose of the UFS approach is to (i) reduce the risk of selecting an irrelevant feature, (ii) yield more robust feature subsets, and (iii) improve classification performance [10], [16], [46], [47]. Although our proposed methodology has additional computational costs, it is worth it because it uses a preferable framework [48].

11.3.4 Methodology for the Data Preparation Phase

Data preprocessing tasks such as data cleaning and data transformation are typically performed in the data preparation phase to improve performance and knowledge accuracy. In real-world applications, missing values are filled in and outliers are removed in data cleaning, while data transformation involves data discretization. The discretization process simplifies the data, enables quick learning, improves the accuracy of the model, optimizes results, and removes outliers [49]. In this study, we used the mean/mode substitution approach to handle missing values, the interquartile range for outlier detection, and equal width binning for data discretization. We chose easy-to-use methods without considering the nature of the data; we do not claim that our selected data preparation methods will always produce excellent results because that is not the scope of our study. Our purpose is only to show the positive effects of various data preprocessing techniques on the predictive accuracy of a classifier.

11.3.5 Methodology for the Modeling Phase

This section covers the methodology used to perform model learning and model translation, which build the classification models and generate the production rules, respectively. The details of each method are explained in the following subsections.

To build the classification models, seven decision tree classifiers were considered for this study, namely BFTree, FT, J48, J48graft, RandomTree, REPTree, and SimpleCart. The characteristics of each classifier are shown in Table 11.2.

Table 11.2 Selected decision tree classifier characteristics

Decision Tree Classifier	Type of Classifier (Based-on)
BFTree	C4.5 and Cart
FT	Logistic regression function
J48	R. Quinlan C4.5 algorithm
J48graft	C4.5
RandomTree	Random selection of attributes
REPTree	C4.5 and regression
Simple-Cart	Cart

In order to select appropriate classifiers among these seven decision tree classifiers, a case-based meta-learning and reasoning framework (CB-MLR) [50] was used. CB-MLR internally uses a case-based reasoning methodology in which a case-base is first created from freely available data classification problems, where the features of each case are meta- characteristics of the datasets. These meta-characteristics include general, basic, and advanced statistical features as well as information-theoretic features of the datasets. Each of these categories of features represents a view of the dataset. The class label of each case is that found by the best classifier of the seven candidate classifiers, as defined by AMD [21]. This computation empirically evaluates and ranks these classifiers based on the accuracy and consistency of the classifier's performance. After ranking, the top three appropriate decision tree classifiers are recommended, and the top classifier is selected for the creation of a classification model.

The AMD methodology reduces the time and effort expended by the domain expert and enhances system performance [21]. An open source application of the algorithm selector is available on GitHub to support its theoretical value [51].

In this study, we used non-exhaustive k-fold cross- validation (i.e., rotation estimation) to measure and assess the performance of the machine learning methods in terms of predictive accuracy [28], [52]. More specifically, we selected 10-fold cross-validation (k 10) for computing the predictive accuracy [12], [53].

In k-fold cross-validation, the original dataset is randomly split into k equal-size sets. For example, for k 10, we randomly partitioned the original dataset into d0, d1, d2,. . . , d9. After partitioning, only one set (d0) is used as testing data while the remaining k 1 sets (d1, d2,. . . , d9) are used as training data. In the next iteration, d1 is used as testing data and d0, d2,. . . , d9 as training data. This process is repeated k times so that each set is used exactly once for validation. After completing k iterations, the k results are averaged to provide a single estimate, resulting in more accurate predictions [54], [55].

This technique estimates the quantitative measure of fit for the data as well as for the classification model. This fit is evaluated in terms of a statistical measure called the positive predictive value (PPV) [56]. Herein, the PPV is used as the measure of prediction accuracy.
The PPV is defined as:

$$PPV = \frac{\text{number of TPs}}{\text{number of TPs} + \text{number of FPs}}$$

where TPs are true positives and FPs are false positives. A true positive means there is a positive prediction and a positive result, while false positive means a positive prediction but a negative result [57]. Method for Model Translation

Production rules are easy to understand, widely used for knowledge representation, and more compact and predictive than decision trees. The translation process for converting multiple decision trees into production rules for automated use is explained in Algorithm 13.1. This algorithm takes input from the decision tree algorithm (DTA) and classification model (CM) and sequentially passes them through mandatory steps to generate production rules. The steps involved in the models are: (1) model preparation (line 4), (2) XML conversion (line 6), (3) XML parsing (lines 8 to 12), and (4) production rule generation from the Document Object Model (DOM) Tree object (lines 13 to 49).

In the first step, the model is prepared by performing a number of tasks such as text splitting, text trimming, and special character replacement. In the second step, XML conversion, indentation, comparison operator configuration, and file conversion tasks are performed [33]. In the third step, document parsing is performed using the DOM parser. Normally for a parsing task, the parser reads a XML document, extracts information, and exposes the document's current after validating the document with the W3C specification. The DOM parser maps the structure of an XML file to a DOM tree object and facilitates random access to the content of the XML document. In the final step, to generate the production rules, the attributes, operators, and values of each condition and the conclusions of each path are extracted by traversing the tree. For further details, please see our previous work [24].

Algorithm 11.1 Production Rule Generation from Decision Trees (D= DTA, CM)

Data: D = DTA, CM : Input dataset (decision tree algorithm, classification model)

Result: RS = Rule set

```
1.  PM ← preprocessModel(DTA, CM )
2.  XM← xmlConversion(PM )
3.  DTO← parseXML(XM )
4.  RootNode ← getRootNode(DTO) ;
5.  CurrentNode ← getFirstChild (RootNode) ;
6.  ruleID ← 0
7.  ruleList[]
8.  while CurrentNode null do
9.      if hasChildNode(CurrentNode) then
10.         currentNode = getFirstChild(CurrentNode)
11.     else
12.         If CurrentNode = LeafNode then
13.             ruleID++
```

```
                ruleConclusion ← getNodeValue(CurrentNode)
                ruleConditionsList[]
                PathNode ← CurrentNode
                While hasParentNode(PathNode) do
                    conditionAttribute ← getNodeAttribute(PathNode)
                    conditionOperator ←getNodeOperator(PathNode)
                    conditionValue ← getNodeValue(PathNode)
                    RuleCondition←ConditionAttribute∪ ConditionOperator∪ConditionValue
                    RuleConditionsList.add(RuleCondition)
                    PathNode ← getParentNode(PathNode)
                 End
                 RuleConditionsList ← reverse(RuleConditionsList)
                 Rule← ruleID ∪ ruleConditionsList ∪ RuleConclusion
                 RulesList.add(Rule)
            End
            While getNextSibling(CurrentNode) = null and CurerntNode != RootNode do
                currentNode ← getParentNode(currentNode)
            End
            CurrentNode ← getParentNode(CurrentNode)
        End
        currentNode ← getNextSibling(CurrentNode)
End
RS ← RuleList
Return RS: rule set
```

11.4 System Results

This section describes the evaluation of the proposed UFS methodology and data preprocessing phase. The purpose of this is to determine the impact of the proposed feature selection methodology on the predictive accuracy of the classification model in terms of feature ranking (data under- standing phase) and data preprocessing (data preparation phase).

11.4.1 Evaluation of the Unified Features Scoring Methodology

This section describes the evaluation setup and compares the proposed feature selection methodology with state-of-the-art feature selection methods.

Table 11.3 Selected dataset characteristics

Dataset	No. of Attributes	No. Instances	No. of Distinct Classes
Sonar	61	208	2
Cylinder-bands	40	540	2
Waveform	41	5000	3
Arrhythmia	280	452	13
Diabetes	9	768	2
Letter	17	20000	2
Glass	10	214	6

To evaluate our feature selection methodology, we chose seven datasets of varying complexity, as shown in Table 11.3. These benchmark datasets were acquired from the openML5 repository, and we selected those of small to medium size. Both binary and multi-class problems were considered for this study. We used five well-known classifiers in this study: J48, naive Bayes, support vector machine (SVM), k nearest neighbors (KNN) and JRIP. For comparison purposes, we utilized standard open-source implementations of these classifiers provided by WEKA.6 Using these open-source implementations, we wrote a method in Java that computes the predictive accuracy of these five classifiers in 10-fold cross-validation. Of the five classifiers, SVM and JRIP tended to perform best on the above-mentioned datasets. Figure 11.4 illustrates the experimental difference between the predictive accuracy of the classifiers, where the first part of the figure (with a white background) shows the results for only the datasets on which SVM performed best. Likewise, the second part of Figure 11.4 shows the three datasets on which JRIP performed better.

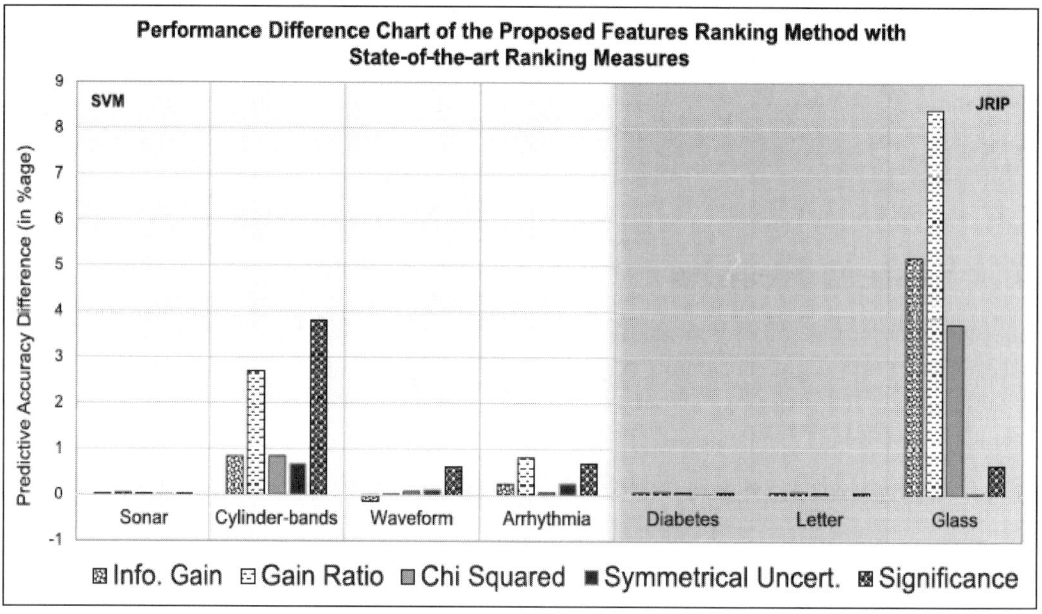

Figure 11.4 Performance difference for the proposed feature ranking method

We compared our proposed UFS methodology against five feature selection measures: information gain, gain ratio, symmetric uncertainty, chi-square, and significance. Figure 11.4 illustrates the difference in predictive accuracy between UFS and each feature selection measure. We can deduct from these results that our proposed methodology is competitive with state-of-the-art feature selection methods. We found that in 97.15% of cases, the UFS methodology had greater or equal predictive accuracy, while in the remaining 2.85% (1 out of 35; IG in the Waveform dataset) our method- ology had lower predictive accuracy.

11.4.2 Evaluation of the Data Preprocessing Tasks

This section describes the results of data preprocessing in terms of the predictive accuracy of classifiers on the Diabetes, Waveform, Glass, and Arrhythmia datasets. In data preprocessing, each data preparation step performs some modifications and stores the data for input to the next step, as well as for performance comparison purposes. We categorize these data as original data, filled data (obtained after replacing missing values), consistent data (obtained after replacing outliers), and finally discretized data (obtained after discretization). The results of this comparison are illustrated in Figure 11.5. Firstly, to determine the impact of the data preprocessing steps, the predictive accuracy against five decision tree algorithms (BFTree, J48, Random Tree, REPTree, and Simple Cart) was computed, as illustrated in Figure 11.5. These are the standard data preprocessing steps used to enhance the quality of data. For each dataset against each decision tree algorithm, the next data category from left to right had greater or equal predictive accuracy compared to the previous data category. These results were obtained for various datasets with different numbers of distinct classes, and we cannot claim generalization to other datasets. Nonetheless, these results demonstrate the positive effects of different data preprocessing techniques on the predictive accuracy of a classifier.

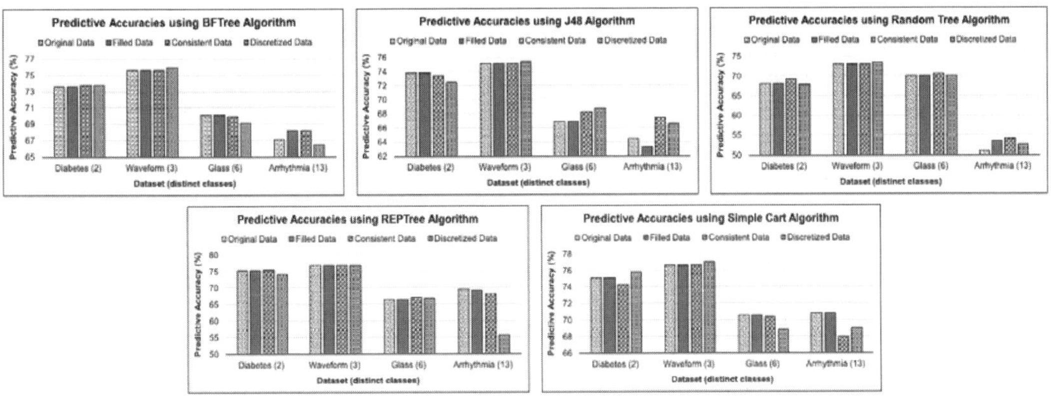

Figure 11.5 Comparative results of preprocessing steps in terms of predictive accuracy

11.5 System Evaluation

The evaluation phase of any proposed system is key in judging the worth of the system. This section evaluates the subjective perception of users towards the DDKAT product.

In this study, we considered user experience (UX) as the major criteria for evaluating the DDKAT. UX describes the quality of interaction between the participants and the com- puter system [58]. Normally, in a real-world situation, differ- ent users may have different feelings for the same product due to varying personal experiences. In order to mitigate this problem, the user experience is measured by collecting feedback from a large group of users [59]. To quantify a product's user experience, questionnaires are considered a highly efficient and cheap tool [59]–[61]. There are many research frameworks for state-of-the-art evaluation of user experience, such as the Questionnaire for User Interaction Satisfaction, System Usability Scale, Standardized User Experience Percentile Rank Questionnaire, Software Usability Measurement Inventory, AttrakDiff, and User Experience Questionnaire. Among these frameworks, the User Experience Questionnaire (UEQ) is the most widely used evaluation framework for interactive products for the following reasons: (1) it provides a thorough evaluation by accounting for both user experience and classical usability aspects, (2) it interprets results accurately, (3) it is free to use and has no fees, (4) it is reliable and easy to apply, (5) it requires low effort, and (6) it provides fast, direct, and valid quantitative measurements of UX [58]–[61]. The UEQ includes 26 items that are grouped into six scales: attractiveness, the appeal of the product; perspicuity, the ease of product use; efficiency, the speed with which it solves tasks; dependability, the user's control over product interaction; stimulation, the user's reactions to the product; and novelty, how innovative the product is [58] and [61]. These scales are further categorized into two quality measures, called pragmatic quality (PQ) for task-related quality aspects, and hedonic quality (HQ) for non-task related quality aspects. PQ accounts for perspicuity, efficiency, and depend- ability, while the HQ covers stimulation and novelty [58]. Each item in the UEQ comprises a pair of terms (adjectives) with opposite meanings and a 7-point Likert scale [61].

AttrakDiff is another established and popular online questionnaire designed to evaluate user experience. This questionnaire was designed and developed within the UEQ research framework and provides a limited free online interface (only 20 users) to investigate the attractiveness, pragmatic, and hedonic aspects of products [62]. Again, the pragmatic quality of a product is the ability for effective and efficient task completion, while the hedonic quality represents the joy and fun experienced by the user. Similarly, to the UEQ, it consists of 29 questions, where each question consists of a pair of contrasting adjective terms [63]. These are grouped into PQ, HQ (which is further divided into two sub-aspects: Identity (HQ-I) and Stimulation (HQ-S)), and Attractiveness (ATT) [64]. Due to the mobility of the participants and the short duration of the evaluation, a combination of AttrakDiff and UEQ can be used [63]. Regarding the correlation between the UEQ and AttrakDiff, the pair of terms used for ATT are nearly identical in both questionnaires. Similarly, it is expected that the perspicuity, efficiency, and dependability scales of the UEQ have a positive correlation with the PQ aspect of AttrakDiff, and the novelty and stimulation scales of the UEQ have a highly positive correlation with the stimulation scale of AttrakDiff [60]. In this study, we used both UEQ and AttrakDiff to assess the value of the DDKAT. In the following sections, we describe the design setup, evaluation process, and evaluation results.

11.5.1 Experimental Setup

For holistic evaluation of the DDKAT, we performed two studies involving multiple stakeholders and using quantitative methods such as surveys. In each study, we introduced and demonstrated the DDKAT before conducting the survey. The evaluation setup for both studies is shown in Table 11.4, where two types of users were considered for assessing the DDKAT. The first were experts with experience in using artificial intelligence (AI) domain applications, and the second were intermediate users who were studying or learning AI applications.

Table 11.4 Evaluations setup for the DDKAT

<table>
<tr><td colspan="2">Evaluation Criteria</td><td>Study I (Experts)</td><td>Study II (Intermediate Users)</td></tr>
<tr><td rowspan="4">Participant</td><td>Total</td><td>19</td><td>102</td></tr>
<tr><td>Distribution</td><td>• 11 academia professionals (6 lecturers, 4 assistant professors, 1 associate professor)
• 8 industry professionals (2 domain experts, 1 data analyst, 2 software developers, 3 software engineers)</td><td>• 22 graduate and postgraduate students of Expert System course
• 31 undergraduate and postgraduate students of Artificial Intelligence and Data Analytics course
• 49 graduate and postgraduate students of Machine learning course</td></tr>
<tr><td>Age</td><td>Between 20 and 60</td><td>Between 20 and 35</td></tr>
<tr><td>Education completion</td><td>Post-graduate and graduate</td><td>Under-graduate, graduate</td></tr>
<tr><td colspan="2">Conduct</td><td>Online</td><td>Paper</td></tr>
<tr><td colspan="2">Evaluation tool</td><td>AttrackDiff</td><td>UEQ</td></tr>
<tr><td colspan="2">Study type</td><td>Anonymous participants</td><td>Anonymous participants</td></tr>
<tr><td colspan="2">Project type</td><td>Individual evaluation</td><td>Individual evaluation</td></tr>
</table>

11.5.2 Experimental Execution

The procedure for conducting the evaluation was different in both studies. For Study I, an AttrakDiff project with the name Data-Driven Knowledge Acquisition Tool was created using the eSURVEY tool7 to measure the user experience of the DDKAT. After creating the project, the product was hosted on a web server and the URL was given to all participants. We sent an invitation email to the 19 participants and asked them to evaluate the DDKAT directly based on their judgments [65]. In the email, we mentioned all the features of the DDKAT, its usage instructions, the actual product's URL, and the eSURVEY URL for the AttrakDiff questionnaire. A demo session was conducted for the participants before they filled out the online AttrakDiff questionnaire. For Study II, a demonstration of all of the features of the DDKAT was given to students during class time of three different courses. After the demonstration, we answered all questions from the students. Finally, the UEQ survey form was distributed to all students to record their assessment.

11.5.3 Expert Evaluations

After the 19 knowledge experts evaluated the DDKAT and completed the online AttrakDiff questionnaire, the results were compiled using the eSURVEY tool as shown in Figures 11.6-8. Figure 11.6 shows a portfolio diagram, which summarizes the performance of the DDKAT in terms of PQ and HQ. This figure shows multiple confidence regions, such as too self- oriented, self-oriented, desired, neutral, task-oriented, too task-oriented, and superfluous. The values of HQ increased from bottom to top, while the values of PQ increased from left to right. For HQ, the top values were considered better than the bottom values, and for PQ, the right values were considered better than the left values. Based on the assessments of the 19 participants, the DDKAT was rated

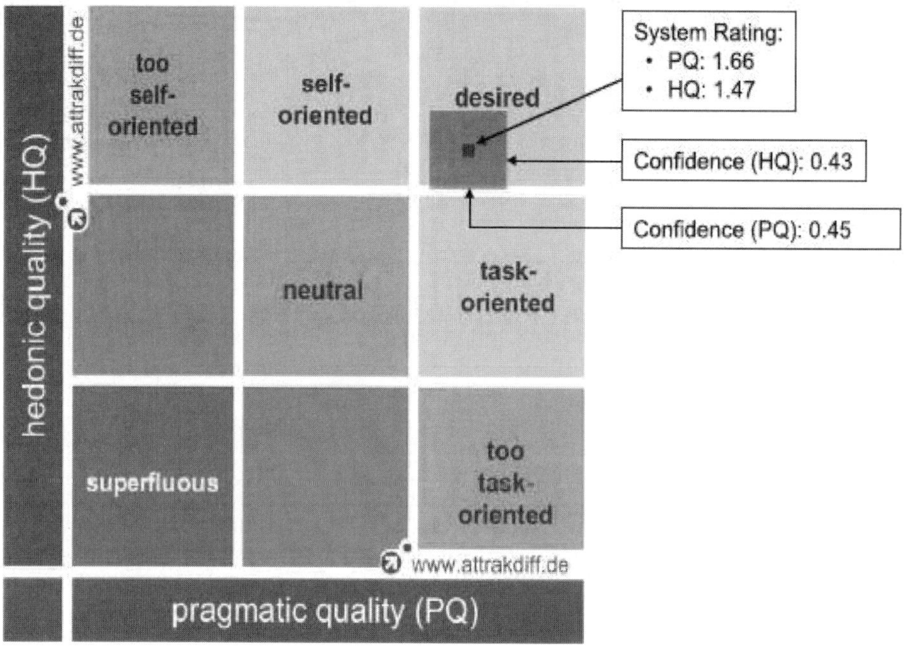

Figure 11.6 Portfolio diagram of the DDKAT with respect to PQ and HQ

''desired,'' as shown in Figure 11.6. Both PQ and HQ had a similar product confidence interval.

Another evaluation perspective is shown in Figure 11.7, in which PQ, HQ-I, HQ-S, and ATT were rated by computing their average scores, as shown on the y-axis. PQ represents the usability of the product and reveals how well users are accomplishing their objectives; HQ-S describes the supporting features of a system, such as its novelty, interesting and stimulating functions, contents, and presentation styles; HQ-I indicates the ability of users to identify with the system; and ATT represents the overall perceived quality of the system [65].]. The user assessments of all four dimensions fell between 1 and 2 for the DDKAT, which is in the ''above-average'' region. In particular, the attractiveness of the DDKAT gained more attention than the other three aspects, falling on the boundary of the ''good'' region. Figure 11.7 shows the average scores of the four AttrakDiff dimensions, while a detailed view of the ratings for these four dimensions is provided in Figure 11.8, which shows the AttrakDiff adjective-pair questions [65]. For the PQ and ATT dimensions of the DDKAT, the average score was 6 out of 7 for all adjective-pairs except ''technical human.'' Based on the results shown in Figures 11.6-8, the overall user experience was positive.

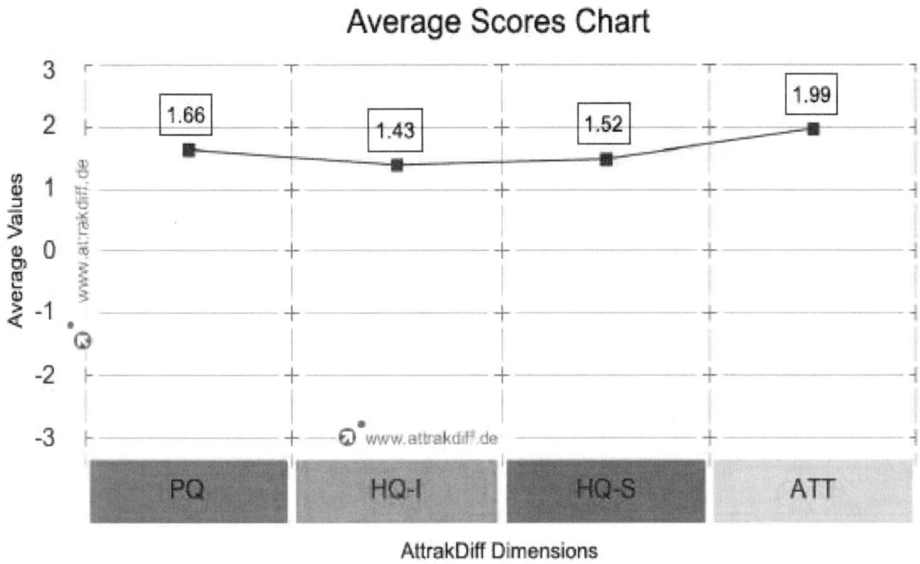

Figure 11.7 Average value of the four AttrackDiff dimensions for the DDKAT

11.5.4 Intermediate User Evaluations

The DDKAT was demonstrated to a number of artificial intelligence students, including all data mining processes and their features. The queries of the students were addressed after the demonstration. Finally, the UEQ survey was given to all students, and they were asked to fill it out based on their understanding [58]. After 102 intermediate users evaluated the DDKAT and completed the UEQ, the results were automatically generated using a data analysis tool8 [66]. Each item of the UEQ has answers ranging from 3 (strongly negative) to 3 (strongly positive) [61]. The compiled results are shown in Figures 11.9-11. As mentioned above, the UEQ evaluation survey consists of 26 items to determine the impact of the product under consideration. With the help of Cronbach's alpha coefficients, we could compute the mean value per item [58]. It was generally observed that participants did not choose extreme options, preferring to select those in the range of -2 to +2. For this reason, a value near +2 is considered to be a very positive impression [66]. Figure 11.9 shows that among the 26 items, the mean values of seven were greater than +2, demonstrating the good impact of the DDKAT. Figure 11.9 also shows that all mean values except that of item 17 fell between 1 and 2, which indicates that overall, all 102 AI domain students were satisfied with this product. To further analyze the UEQ, we calculated the means of six scales–attractiveness, perspicuity, efficiency, dependability, stimulation, and novelty [58], [61]–whose values were scaled in the range of 3 to 3 [59], as shown in Figure 11.10. It can be observed from Figure 11.10 that the values of all scales were greater than 1, indicating a positive response from the participants [59]. Attractiveness, efficiency, stimulation, and novelty fell between 1.5 and 2, demonstrating the very good quality of the DDKAT [59]. The perspicuity scale had a value close to 2, representing the very positive (near-optimal) feelings of the participants [59], while the dependability scale had a positive evaluation falling in the above-average region of user satisfaction.

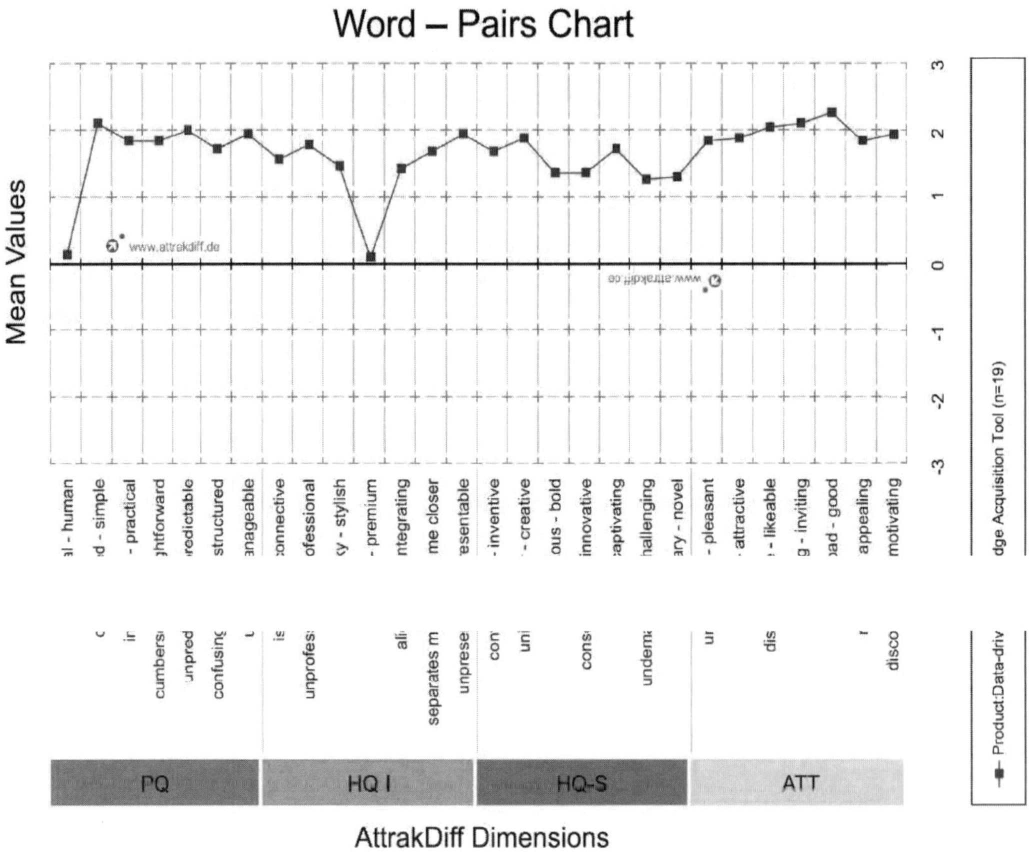

Figure 11.8 Mean values of AttrackDiff adjective-pairs for the DDKAT

To evaluate the precision of the mean estimates, we also computed 95% confidence intervals for each UEQ scale [67]. We found them to be small for all six scales, as shown in Figure 11.10. The smaller the width of the confidence interval the smaller the variation and the better the result In Figure 11.10, the error bars represent these confidence intervals. The confidence intervals for the DDKAT were 0.342 (1.791 to 2.133) for attractiveness, 0.327 (1.870 to 2.197) for perspicuity, 0.257 (1.776 to 2.033) for efficiency, 0.278 (1.294 to 1.572) for dependability, 0.345 (1.732 to 2.077) for stimulation and 0.311 (1.479 to 1.790) for novelty. To evaluate the consistency of the UEQ scales, we computed their reliability using the Cronbachs alpha coefficient, which was found greater than 0.7 for all six scales. The Cronbachs alpha coefficients for the DDKAT were 0.93 for attractiveness, 0.87 for perspicuity, 0.77 for efficiency, 0.71 for dependability, 0.89 for stimulation and 0.78 for novelty. The coefficient for dependability was slightly lower than that of the other scales, which could be due to an incorrect understanding of the items in this scale [59]. The UEQ scales are categorized into PQ, HQ, and ATT dimensions [61]. ATT is a pure valence dimension; PQ rep- resents the perspicuity, efficiency, and dependability; HQ expresses the stimulation and novelty. The UEQ evaluation tool found that PQ (1.79) and HQ (1.77) were good, with a mean value greater than 0.800 (see Figure 11.10) [59]. PQ represents the ease of use of the product [66], so the high PQ score of the DDKAT provides evidence that it is easy to use.

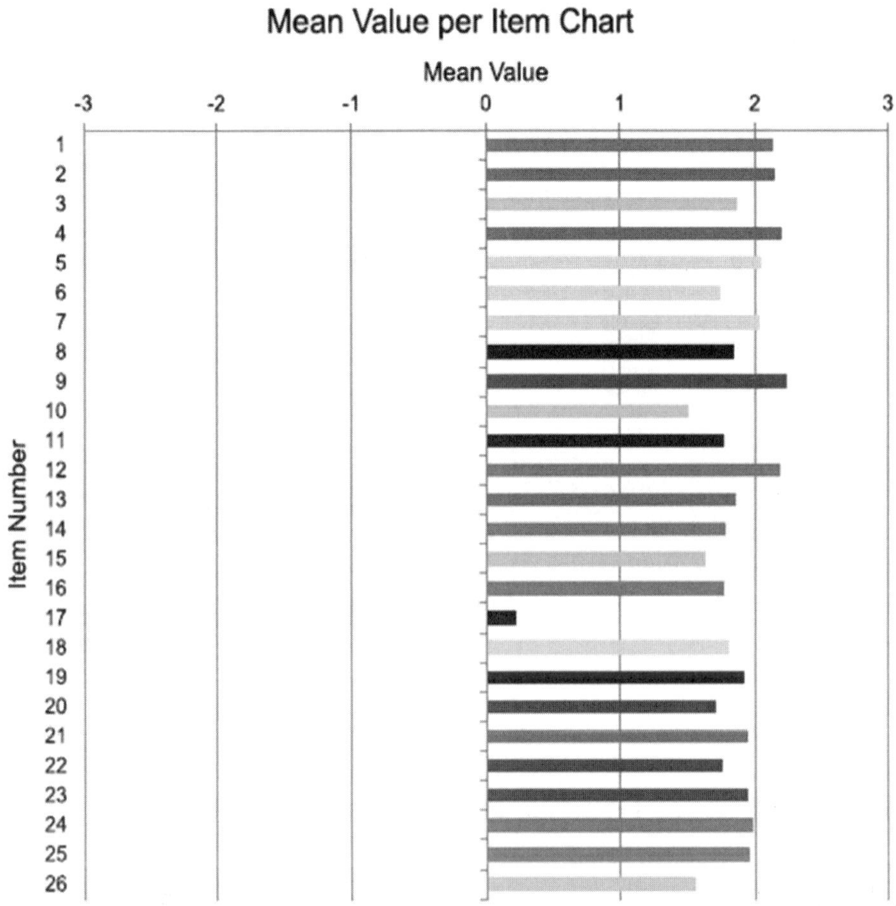

Figure 11.9 Mean value per item for the DDKAT product

In order to check the quality aspect of the DDKAT product, we have compared our results with other products as shown in Figure 11.11. For this purpose, the UEQ analysis tool provides a benchmark for the user experience [61]. Based on the available benchmark, the attractiveness, perspicuity, efficiency, stimulation, and novelty aspects of the DDKAT product are excellent, whereas the dependability aspect lies in the above average region. Here the term 'excellent' defines that the product under-consideration is among the best 10% of the result, while the term 'above average' defines that the evaluated product does not among the best 25% of the benchmark results and 50% of the benchmark results are worse than the evaluated product [61].

To confirm the quality of the DDKAT, we compared our results with those of other products, as shown in Figure 11.11. For this purpose, the UEQ analysis tool provides user experience benchmarks [61]. Based on the available benchmarks, the attractiveness, perspicuity, efficiency, stimulation, and novelty of the DDKAT product are excellent, while the dependability falls in the above average region. Here, the term 'excellent' means that the product is among the best 10%, while the term 'above average' means that the product is not among the best 25%, but is better than 50% of the benchmark results [61].

Based on the quantitative results obtained using the UEQ analysis tool and AttrakDiff, the overall user experience was evaluated as good in terms of the pragmatic, hedonic, and attractiveness features, and users were satisfied with the DDKAT. There is now only a need to improve security in order to increase the dependability of the product.

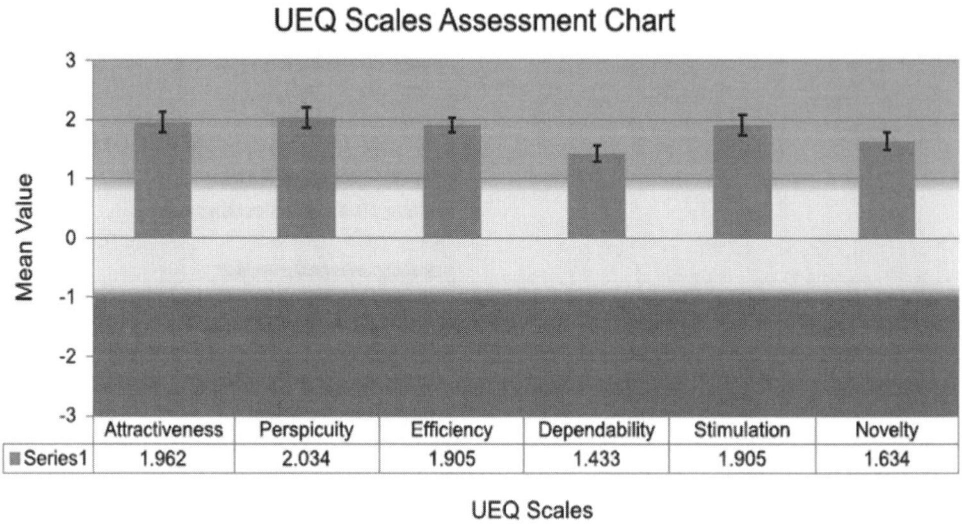

Figure 11.10 UEQ scale results for the DDKAT

11.6 Simulation of the DDKAT

This section describes an overview of the Data-Driven Knowledge Acquisition Tool, a case study to simulate the DDKAT for the end-to-end knowledge engineering process, and a mechanism for sharing the production rules.

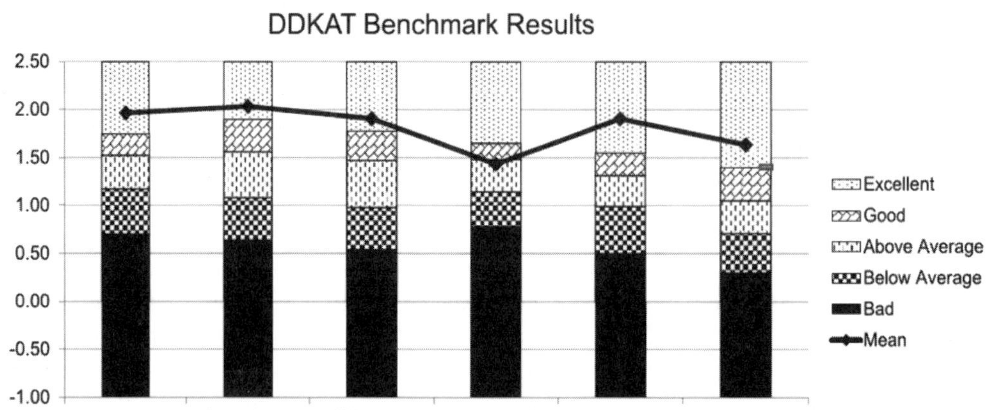

Figure 11.11 The benchmark results for the DDKAT

11.6.1 Data-Driven Knowledge Acquisition Tool Overview

We designed and developed the DDKAT, a tool for extracting hidden knowledge from structured data and converting it into production rules. This tool is a web-based application that covers almost all phases of CRISP-DM. It creates production rules using a data-driven approach to allow a domain expert to visualize hidden knowledge that is difficult to see with the naked eye. It was designed for our previously proposed Mining Minds platform [37], [38], and it acquires user profile and lifelog data from the Data Curation Layer and produces production rules to provide better services through the Service Curation Layer, as shown in Figure 11.1. The output of this tool is processed data, a classification model, and production rules.

The open-source implementation and documentation of this tool is beneficial for developers in the artificial intelligence domain and the healthcare community, who can use it to extract knowledge from raw data in a simple manner. Using this tool, a domain expert goes through the data science process, which applies data mining methods to extract knowledge from data. This process is well known in research communities such as artificial intelligence, machine learn- ing, statistics, and knowledge acquisition for expert systems. Moreover, the DDKAT helps the domain expert perform tasks such as:

- selecting salient features of the data based on personal knowledge and the machine's support.
- applying data mining methods in data preprocessing to enhance the predictive accuracy of the classification model.
- selecting an appropriate decision tree classifier to generate the classification model.
- translating the classification model into production rules to share with the expert for verification.

The DDKAT is an online, flexible, and loosely coupled software system that has been developed in Eclipse, Spring Web Model View Controller (MVC), JavaServer Pages (JSP), jQuery JavaScript library, Asynchronous JavaScript and XML (AJAX), and Bootstrap as front-end frameworks. For testing and validation purposes, Fiddler Web Debugger, JSONLint, and Apiary mock services have been used.

Some of the reasons for choosing the aforementioned technologies to develop DDKAT are:

- Spring Web MVC9 is an old and mature framework with
- excellent RESTful web service support.
- jQuery10 is a lightweight (write less, do more) library, which provides user-friendly functionality for JavaScript on your website.
- AJAX11 is an approach for developing fast and dynamic web pages that updates parts of the web page without reloading the entire page

11.6.2 Case study: Diabetes

This case study was used to illustrate aspects of development. It is helpful to perform an in-depth study and analysis of a real-world or an imagined scenario. As a case study to simulate the phases of CRISP-DM, the Pima Indians Diabetes Dataset12 was used in this work.

The simulation of the system is illustrated in Figure 11.12, where steps 1a to 1f belong to the data understanding phase of CRISP-DM, steps 2a to 2c belong to the data preparation phase, and steps 3(a,b,c) and 4(a,b,c) belong to the modeling phase.

1) Step -1

To start the end-to-end knowledge engineering process, the domain expert opens the DDKAT application by typing http://system-ip:8080/DDKAT/ into a browser. After loading the application, the domain expert clicks the Click to Start button to start the data understanding phase, which includes the following:

a. To view the available parameters (features) for a particular domain, the domain expert clicks the Load Schema button to send the schema request to the DCL.
b. The DDKAT parses the received schema and converts it into a tree structure using a jQuery plugin.
c. The domain expert first selects parameters based on his/her own experience and knowledge, then clicks the Visualize Features Scorecard button.
d. The DDKAT forwards the selected parameters query to the DCL to request the data.
e. The DDKAT receives data from the DCL and uses the UFS methodology to produce and display the Features Scorecard.
f. The domain expert analyzes/watches the features scorecard. In case of dissatisfaction, the domain expert reselects the parameters, repeating steps (c) to (f) until he/she is satisfied with the current parameter selection. When satisfied, the domain expert clicks the Data Preprocessor button to move into the data preparation phase.

2) Step -2

To start the data preparation phase, the domain expert clicks the Load Data and Save External Data buttons to load and store the selected data on the local machine.

a. The domain expert clicks the Fill Missing Values button. When this is clicked, the DDKAT first identifies all missing values from the loaded dataset, then fills them with appropriate values and stores the data in a processed data repository.
b. Similarly, the domain expert clicks the Remove Outliers button to detect and replace all outliers with appropriate values, and store that data in a processed data repository.
c. Finally, the domain expert clicks the Invoke Data Transformation button to discretize the loaded data and store that data in a processed data repository.

3) Step – 3

After completing the data preparation phase, the domain expert clicks the Model Learner button to start the modeling phase for building a classification model, which includes the following steps.

a. The domain expert clicks the Automatic Algorithm Selector button to view the best recommended algorithm by the DDKAT.
b. Based on this recommendation, the domain expert clicks the Choose Decision Tree Algorithm button to select the recommended algorithm or any other algorithm from the list to build the classification model.
c. After clicking the Learn Model button, the DDKAT learns and builds a classification model using the selected algorithm and processed dataset. It also computes and displays the classification accuracy of the original and processed datasets. In the classification model, each leaf represents one primitive production rule. For example, in Figure 11.12, there are

a total of 29 leaves, which indicates that 29 rules exist in this classification model (decision tree). The advantage of using decision trees is that each branch of the tree consists of only a small number of attributes rather than all of the attributes. Since the number of attributes directly affects the computational load, fewer attributes result in lower computational cost. For example, a total of nine attributes were used to describe each instance of the diabetes training data, but no path in the decision tree shown in Figure 11.12 uses more than seven attributes. Thus, the space of potential rules is reduced from 0(29) to 0(27) [31].

4) Step – 4

Once the classification model is built, the domain expert clicks the Translate Model button to generate production rules from the classification model, which involves the following steps.

a. The DDKAT performs text processing tasks to refine the classification model, including text trimming before and after the actual model, replacement of special characters, and text splitting.
b. The DDKAT applies an indentation and a comparison operator configuration, and converts this into an XML model.
c. The DDKAT parses the XML model and extracts: (1) the root node and (2) all child, sibling, and leaf nodes from the XML model. It also extracts all paths of leaf nodes. Finally, the DDKAT extracts the attributes, operators, and values of each condition and the conclusion from each path and converts them into production rules.

11.6.3 A Restful Web service for Sharing Production Rules

A RESTful Web service is a software service that is published on the Web and enables devices to communicate with each other [68]. To share production rules, a RESTful JavaScript Object Notation (JSON)-based web service was built on the Spring MVC framework. In this study, we built a flexible JSON object that contains an ArrayList. We named this object ruleList which then implemented the List interface, where each element of ruleList represents one complete rule. Since each rule can be composed of multiple conditions or multiple conclusions, each element of ruleList contained two ArrayLists (condition- List and conclusionList) and one name/value pair to represent ruleID, as shown in Figure 11.13. Furthermore, each condition- List of an element consisted of four name/value pairs to represent conditionID, conditionKey, conditionOperator, and conditionValue. Similarly, each conclusionList consisted of conclusionID, conclusionKey, conclusionOperator, and con- clusionValue. An online JSON editor13 was used to view and validate the JSON data. After JSON validation, a service was built with the title shareRules. This service creates a JSON object at runtime whenever it is called using http://system-ip:8080/DDKAT/shareRules. Fiddler,14 a free web debugging proxy for any browser, system, or platform, was used to test this web service. After successfully testing the service, a JSON object is created as shown in Figure 11.13. This figure shows the structure of the production rules, where one complete rule is highlighted. Each production rule has three parameters called conclusionLis nditionList, and ruleID, as discussed before.

11.7 Discussion of the significance, challenges, and limitations of this study

In every field, knowledge plays a vital role; all intelligent decisions are made based on knowledge. A data-driven approach is an effective way to improve business and society by extracting hidden knowledge from raw data.

This facilitates improved decision-making capabilities and helps extract production rules. The data-driven knowledge acquisition approach was conceived to support the creation of health and wellness knowledge, and provides a knowledge acquisition environment to domain experts to better sup- port decision-making. We developed a system that aims to automate the feature-ranking process to select and prepare the data, select an appropriate classifier, generate production rules, and finally share the knowledge to be validated by the domain expert.

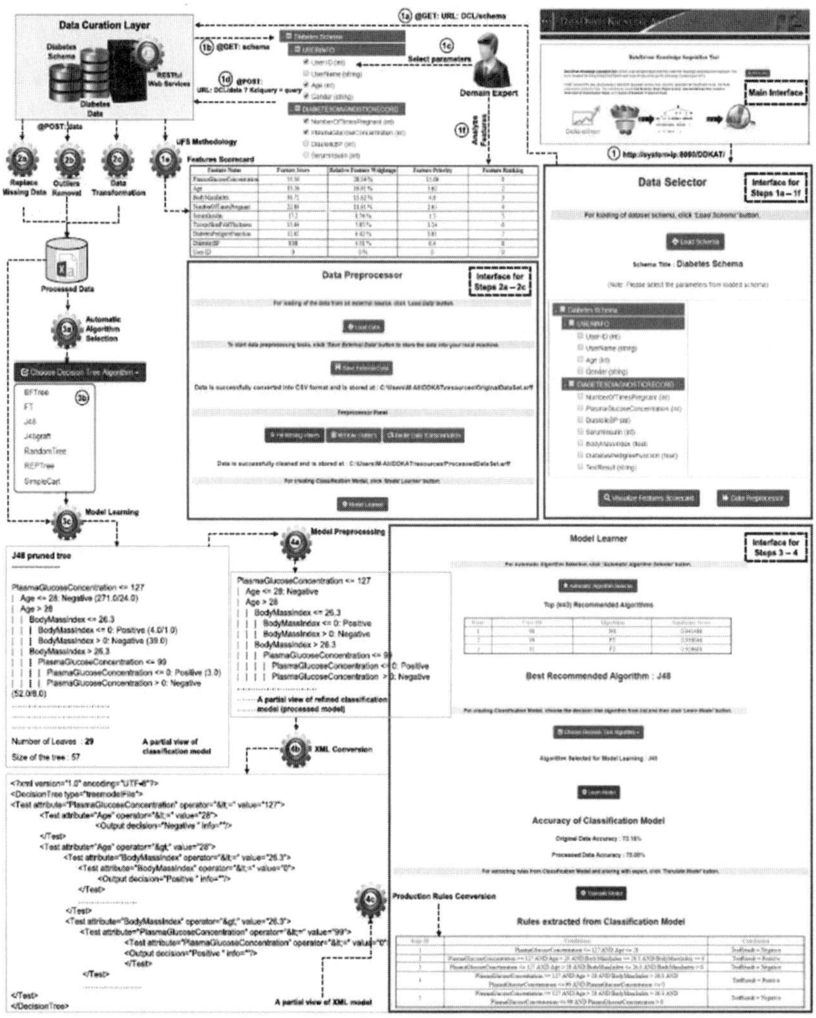

Figure 11.12 Simulation of the Data-Driven Knowledge Acquisition Tool

This system provides maximum availability (24/7) as well as an easy-to-use environment for extracting hidden knowledge in a systematic manner, which is required in most decision support and recommendation systems. Furthermore, this system is capable of extracting production rules from multiple decision trees. We used a depth-first search algorithm for this task, which is more suitable than a breadth-first search (BFS) due to its connectivity features and because it requires less space relative to the depth of the tree; BFS requires an exponential amount of space.15 Finally, the features of the developed tool were compared with the features of other well-known open-source data mining tools,16 as shown in Table 11.5.

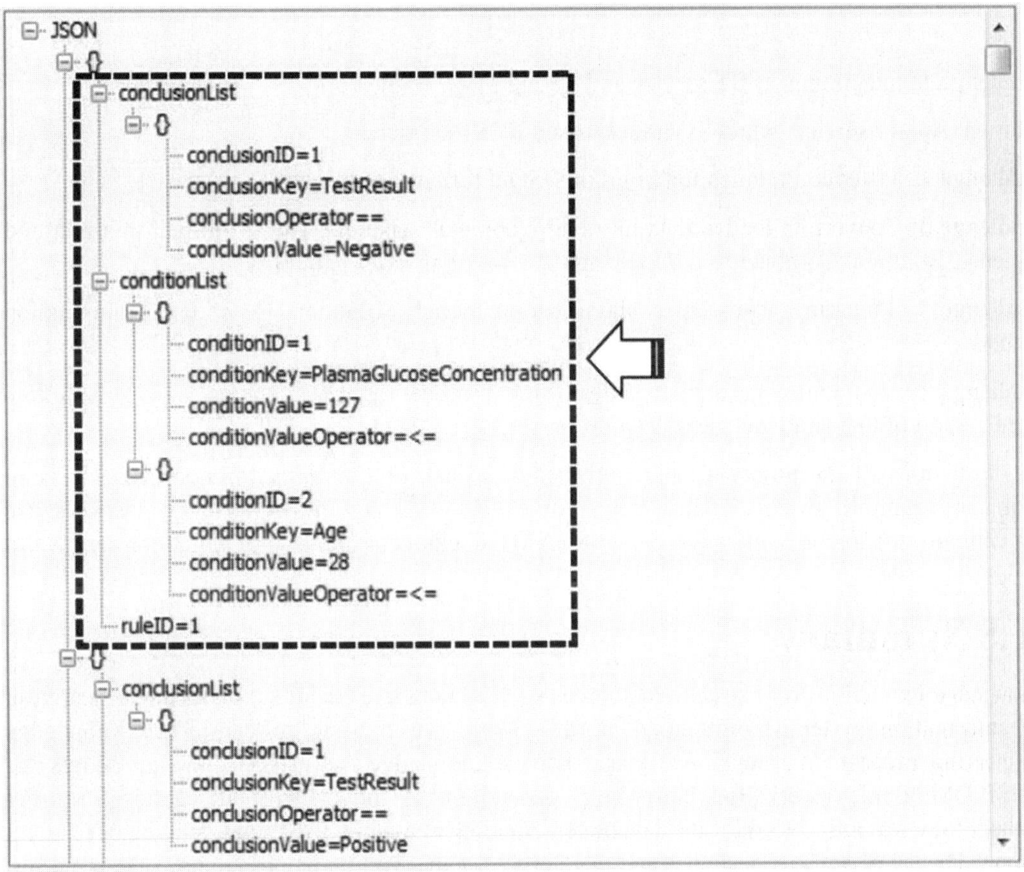

Figure 11.13 Structure of a shared production rule

During the development of the DDKAT, we encountered several challenges in implementing the UFS methodology and extracting production rules from the classification model. Some of the key challenges we attempted to resolve were the following:

Table 11.5 Comparison of the DDKAT with well-known open-source data mining

Data Mining Tool	Application	Programming Language	Category	DP[a] Support	UFS[b] Support	AMD[c] Support	PRG[d] Support
RapidMiner	Desktop, Web	Java	Predictive Analytics Software	Yes	No	No	Yes
WEKA	Desktop, Web	Java	Data Mining Software	Yes	No	No	Yes
RProgramming	Desktop, Web	C, Fortran, R	Predictive Analytics Software	Yes	No	No	Yes
Orange	Desktop	C++, Python	Data Mining Software	Yes	No	No	Yes
DDKAT	**Web**	**Java**	**Data Mining Software**	**Yes**	**Yes**	**Yes**	**Yes**

Challenge 1: Integrating REST service and Spring MVC framework

Solution: Apiary service, which is a mock-based REST service

Challenge 2: Faster communication Solution: JSON format

Challenge 3: Converting loaded data into CSV (comma- separated values) format in a required sequence. Solution: Combination of logic and the use of an exter nal utility

Challenge 4: Preparing a processed classification model. Solution: Use of text manipulation methods

Challenge 5: Extracting production rules from a processed classification model. Solution: Combination of logic and the use of a DOM parser.

The limitations of the proposed approach include a lack of flexibility to choose the decision attributes at runtime, absence of an administrative view to manage and authenticate users, the use of a complex and memory-intensive parser for XML documents, and lack of validation for invalid values.

11.8 Summary

Knowledge extraction from structured sources such as databases is an active area of research in the information systems community. In this work, we present an end-to-end knowledge engineering process. We developed a data-driven knowledge acquisition tool that adopts the CRISP-DM frame- work for knowledge generation. A novel Unified Features Scoring methodology was introduced for the data under- standing phase of CRISP-DM, making our system unique. The DDKAT was designed and developed for the Mining Minds framework; however, other service-enabled platforms can also utilize this product to extract production rules from a dataset. Two studies were performed in order to evaluate different aspects of the proposed knowledge acquisition system, and both found that the overall user experience of the DDKAT product was positive. The current version of this tool and its documentation is open-source and can be downloaded from GitHub [1], [22].

Source Code

For source code please contact us at:

The contents of this chapter have been previously published in the following article:

Maqbool Ali, Rahman Ali, Wajahat Ali Khan, Soyeon Caren Han, Jaehun Bang, Taeho Hur, Dohyeong Kim, Sungyoung Lee, and Byeong Ho Kang, "A data-driven knowledge acquisition system: An end-to-end knowledge engineering process for generating production rules", IEEE Access (SCIE, IF: 3.244), Vol.6, pp.15587-15607 , 2018

References

[1]. M. Ali. (2017). A Documentation of DDKAT for Knowledge Acquisition. Accessed: Dec. 4, 2017. [Online]. Available: https://github.com/ubiquitous-computing-lab/Mining-Minds/tree/gh-pages/doc/kcl- doc/DDKAT/doc17, http://imprc.cafe24.com/

[2]. M. Zorrilla and D. García-Saiz, ''A service oriented architecture to provide data mining services for non-expert data miners,'' Decision Support Syst., vol. 55, no. 1, pp. 399–411, 2013.

[3]. R. Ali, M. H. Siddiqi, and S. Lee, ''Rough set-based approaches for discretization: A compact review,'' Artif. Intell. Rev., vol. 44, no. 2, pp. 235–263, 2015.

[4]. V. Dhar, ''Data science and prediction,'' Commun. ACM, vol. 56, no. 12, pp. 64–73, 2013.

[5]. F. Provost and T. Fawcett, ''Data science and its relationship to big data and data-driven decision making,'' Big Data, vol. 1, no. 1, pp. 51–59, 2013.

[6]. I. Wikimedia Foundation. (2017). Data Science. Accessed: Feb. 18, 2017. [Online]. Available: https://en.wikipedia.org/wiki/Data_science

[7]. D. Tomar and S. Agarwal, ''A survey on data mining approaches for healthcare,'' Int. J. Bio-Sci. Bio-Technol., vol. 5, no. 5, pp. 241–266, 2013.

[8]. P.-S. Gregory. (2014). Kdnuggets Methodology Poll. Accessed: Jan. 12, 2017. [Online]. Available: http://www.kdnuggets.com/polls/ 2014/analytics-data-mining-data-science-methodology.html

[9]. C. Shearer, ''The CRISP-DM model: The new blueprint for data mining,''J. Data Warehousing, vol. 5, no. 4, pp. 13–22, 2000.

[10]. Y. Saeys, T. Abeel, and Y. Van de Peer, ''Robust feature selection using ensemble feature selection techniques,'' in Proc. Joint Eur. Conf. Mach. Learn. Knowl. Discovery Databases, 2008, pp. 313–325.

[11]. L. A. Belanche and F. F. González. (2011). ''Review and evaluation of feature selection algorithms in synthetic problems.'' [Online]. Available: https://arxiv.org/abs/1101.2320

[12]. R. C. Prati, ''Combining feature ranking algorithms through rank aggrega- tion,'' in Proc. Int. Joint Conf. Neural Netw. (IJCNN), 2012, pp. 1–8.

[13]. L. Rokach, B. Chizi, and O. Maimon, ''Feature selection by combin- ing multiple methods,'' in Proc. Adv. Web Intell. Data Mining, 2006, pp. 295–304.

[14]. K. Jong, J. Mary, A. Cornuéjols, E. Marchiori, and M. Sebag, ''Ensemble feature ranking,'' in Proc. Eur. Conf. Principles Data Mining Knowl. Discovery, 2004, pp. 267–278.

[15]. I. Slavkov, B. Zenko, and S. Dzeroski, ''Evaluation method for feature rankings and their aggregations for biomarker discovery,'' in Proc. MLSB, 2010, pp. 122–135.

[16]. W. Altidor, Stability Analysis of Feature Selection Approaches With Low Quality Data. Boca Raton, FL, USA: Florida Atlantic Univ., 2011.

[17]. W. Altidor, T. M. Khoshgoftaar, J. Van Hulse, and A. Napolitano, ''Ensem- ble feature ranking methods for data intensive computing applications,'' in Handbook of Data Intensive Computing. New York, NY, USA: Springer, 2011, pp. 349–376.

[18]. A. Kalousis, J. Prados, and M. Hilario, ''Stability of feature selection algo- rithms: A study on high-dimensional spaces,'' Knowl. Inf. Syst., vol. 12, no. 1, pp. 95–116, 2007.
[19]. R. Jensen and Q. Shen, Computational Intelligence and Feature Selection: Rough and Fuzzy Approaches, vol. 8. Hoboken, NJ, USA: Wiley, 2008.
[20]. J. R. Quinlan, ''Induction of decision trees,'' Mach. Learn., vol. 1, no. 1, pp. 81–106, 1986.
[21]. R. Ali, S. Lee, and T. C. Chung, ''Accurate multi-criteria decision making methodology for recommending machine learning algorithm,'' Expert Syst. Appl., vol. 71, pp. 257–278, Apr. 2017.
[22]. M. Ali. (2017). DDKAT—Data-Driven Knowledge Acquisition Tool, Version 1.0. Accessed: Dec. 04, 2017. [Online]. Available: https://github.com/ubiquitous-computing-lab/Mining-Minds/tree/master/ knowledge-curation-layer/DDKAT
[23]. M. Ali, M. Hussain, S. Lee, and B. H. Kang, ''SaKEM: A semi-automatic knowledge engineering methodology for building rule-based knowledge- base,'' in Proc. Int. Symp. Perception, Action, Cognit. Syst. (PACS), 2016, pp. 63–64.
[24]. M. Ali, S. Lee, and B. H. Kang, ''KEM-DT: A knowledge engineer- ing methodology to produce an integrated rules set using decision tree classifiers,'' in Proc. 12th Int. Conf. Ubiquitous Inf. Manage. Com- mun. (IMCOM), Langkawi, Malaysia, Jan. 2018, pp. 1–5.
[25]. G. Gupta, Introduction to Data Mining With Case Studies. Delhi, India: PHI Learning Pvt. Ltd., 2014.
[26]. Ó. Marbán, G. Mariscal, and J. Segovia, ''A data mining & knowledge discovery process model,'' in Proc. Data Mining Knowl. Discovery Real Life Appl., 2009, p. 8.
[27]. H. Liu and L. Yu, ''Toward integrating feature selection algorithms for classification and clustering,'' IEEE Trans. Knowl. Data Eng., vol. 17, no. 4, pp. 491–502, Apr. 2005.
[28]. M. Humphrey, S. J. Cunningham, and I. H. Witten, ''Knowledge visual- ization techniques for machine learning,'' Intell. Data Anal., vol. 2, no. 4, pp. 333–347, 1998.
[29]. D. Trevisani and L. Cecchi, ''Micromanagement basado en formaciones de grupo implementado con scripting dinámico—Micromanagement group formations based on dynamic scripting implemented,'' in Proc. 20th Argen- tine Congr. Comput. Sci., Buenos Aires, Argentina, 2014, pp. 1–10.
[30]. . H. Witten and E. Frank, Data Mining: Practical Machine Learning Tools and Techniques. San Mateo, CA, USA: Morgan Kaufmann, 2005.
[31]. J. R. Quinlan, ''Generating production rules from decision trees,'' in Proc. IJCAI, vol. 87. 1987, pp. 304–307.
[32]. G. Holmes, M. Hall, and E. Prank, Generating Rule Sets From Model Trees. Berlin, Germany: Springer, 1999.
[33]. S. Luc. (2015). WekaTextToXML: Convert Weka Decision Trees Into interoperable XML Files. Accessed: May 19, 2016. [Online]. Available: http://www.lucsorel.com/media/downloads/WekatextToXml.jar
[34]. P. Winston, Artificial Intelligence, 2nd ed. Reading, MA, USA: Addison-Wesley, 1984.
[35]. N. Caetano, P. Cortez, and R. M. Laureano, ''Using data mining for prediction of hospital length of stay: An application of the CRISP-DM methodology,'' in Enterprise Information Systems. Cham, Switzerland: Springer, 2014, pp. 149–166.
[36]. Y. Chen, Y. Li, X.-Q. Cheng, and L. Guo, ''Survey and taxonomy of feature selection algorithms in intrusion detection system,'' in Information Security and Cryptology. Berlin, Germany: Springer, 2006, pp. 153–167.

[37]. O. Banos et al., ''An innovative platform for person-centric health and wellness support,'' in Proc. Int. Conf. Bioinformat. Biomed. Eng., 2015, pp. 131–140.
[38]. W. A. Khan et al., ''Mining minds: Journey of evolutionary plat- form for ubiquitous wellness,'' in Proc. 12th Int. Conf. Ubiquitous Healthcare (u-Healthcare), 2015, pp. 1–3.
[39]. R. Stoean and F. Gorunescu, ''A survey on feature ranking by means of evolutionary computation,'' Ann. Univ. Craiova-Math. Comput. Sci. Ser., vol. 40, no. 1, pp. 100–105, 2013.
[40]. S. Whiteson, P. Stone, K. O. Stanley, R. Miikkulainen, and N. Kohl, ''Automatic feature selection in neuroevolution,'' in Proc. 7th Annu. Conf. Genetic Evol. Comput., 2005, pp. 1225–1232.
[41]. S. Doraisamy, S. Golzari, N. Mohd, M. N. Sulaiman, and N. I. Udzir, ''A study on feature selection and classification techniques for automatic genre classification of traditional malay music,'' in Proc. ISMIR, 2008, pp. 331–336.
[42]. A. Sharma and S. Dey, ''Performance investigation of feature selection methods and sentiment lexicons for sentiment analysis,'' IJCA Special Issue Adv. Comput. Commun. Technol. HPC Appl., vol. 3, pp. 15–20, Jun. 2012.
[43]. S. I. Ali and W. Shahzad, ''A feature subset selection method based on symmetric uncertainty and ant colony optimization,'' in Proc. Int. Conf. Emerg. Technol. (ICET), 2012, pp. 1–6.
[44]. A. Ahmad and L. Dey, ''A feature selection technique for classifi- catory analysis,'' Pattern Recognit. Lett., vol. 26, no. 1, pp. 43–56, 2005.
[45]. I. Guyon and A. Elisseeff, ''An introduction to variable and feature selec- tion,'' J. Mach. Learn. Res., vol. 3, pp. 1157–1182, Jan. 2003.
[46]. M. Attik, ''Using ensemble feature selection approach in selecting sub- set with relevant features,'' in Proc. Int. Symp. Neural Netw., 2006, pp. 1359–1366.
[47]. L. E. A. Santana, D. F. de Oliveira, A. M. Canuto, and M. C. de Souto, ''A comparative analysis of feature selection methods for ensembles with different combination methods,'' in Proc. Int. Joint Conf. Neural Netw., 2007, pp. 643–648.
[48]. Y. Saeys, I. Inza, and P. Larrañaga, ''A review of feature selec- tion techniques in bioinformatics,'' Bioinformatics, vol. 23, no. 19, pp. 2507–2517, 2007.
[49]. S. Garcia, J. Luengo, J. A. Sáez, V. Lopez, and F. Herrera, ''A survey of discretization techniques: Taxonomy and empirical analysis in supervised learning,'' IEEE Trans. Knowl. Data Eng., vol. 25, no. 4, pp. 734–750, Apr. 2013.
[50]. R. Ali, A. M. Khatak, F. Chow, and S. Lee, ''A case-based meta-learning and reasoning framework for classifiers selection,'' in Proc. 12th Int. Conf. Ubiquitous Inf. Manage. Commun. (IMCOM), Langkawi, Malaysia, Jan. 2018, pp. 1–7.
[51]. R. Ali and M. Sadiq. (2016). Automatic-Algorithm-Selector, Ver- sion 1.0. Accessed: Feb. 18, 2017. [Online]. Available: https://github. com/intelligent-decision-support-systems/automatic-algorithm-selector
[52]. G. Williams. (2010). Cross Validation, Data Mining, Desktop Sur- vival Guide, 2010. Accessed: Feb. 18, 2017. [Online]. Available: https://www.togaware.com/datamining/survivor/Cross_Validation.html
[53]. G. McLachlan, K.-A. Do, and C. Ambroise, Analyzing Microarray Gene Expression Data, vol. 422. Hoboken, NJ, USA: Wiley, 2005.
[54]. R. Kohavi et al., ''A study of cross-validation and bootstrap for accuracy estimation and model selection,'' in Proc. Int. Joint Conf. AI, Aug. 1995, vol. 14. no. 2, pp. 1137–1145.

[55]. G. Seni and J. F. Elder, ''Ensemble methods in data mining: Improving accuracy through combining predictions,'' Synth. Lectures Data Mining Knowl. Discovery, vol. 2, no. 1, pp. 1–126, 2010.

[56]. R. H. Fletcher and S. W. Fletcher, Clinical Epidemiology: The Essentials, 4th ed. Philadelphia, PA, USA: Lippincott Williams & Wilkins, 2005, p. 45.

[57]. A. K. Dubey, U. Gupta, and S. Jain, ''Analysis of k-means clustering approach on the breast cancer Wisconsin dataset,'' Int. J. Comput. Assist. Radiol. Surg., vol. 11, no. 11, pp. 2033–2047, 2016.

[58]. H. B. Santoso, S. Fadhilah, I. Nurrohmah, and W. H. Goodridge, ''The usability and user experience evaluation of Web-based online self- monitoring tool: Case study human-computer interaction course,'' in Proc. 4th Int. Conf. User Sci. Eng. (i-USEr), 2016, pp. 122–127.

[59]. H. B. Santoso, M. Schrepp, R. Isal, A. Y. Utomo, and B. Priyogi, ''Measuring user experience of the student-centered e-learning environ- ment,'' J. Educators Online, vol. 13, no. 1, pp. 58–79, 2016.

[60]. B. Laugwitz, T. Held, and M. Schrepp, ''Construction and evaluation of a user experience questionnaire,'' in Proc. Symp. Austrian HCI Usability Eng. Group, 2008, pp. 63–76.

[61]. M. Schrepp, A. Hinderks, and J. Thomaschewski, ''Construction of a benchmark for the user experience questionnaire (UEQ),'' Int. J. Interact. Multimedia Artif. Intell., vol. 4, no. 4, pp. 40–44, 2017.

[62]. M. Hashemi and J. Herbert, ''Baran: An interaction-centred user monitor- ing framework,'' in Proc. 2nd Int. Conf. Physiol. Comput. Syst. (ESEO), Angers, France, Feb. 2015, pp. 52–60.

[63]. K. Holl, C. Nass, K. Villela, and V. Vieira, ''Towards a lightweight approach for on-site interaction evaluation of safety-critical mobile sys- tems,'' Procedia Comput. Sci., vol. 94, pp. 41–48, 2016.

[64]. A. Heinicke, C. Liao, K. Walbaum, J. Bützler, and C. M. Schlick, ''User centered evaluation of interactive data visualization forms for document management systems,'' Procedia Manuf., vol. 3, pp. 5427–5434, Jan. 2015.

[65]. G. Desolda, C. Ardito, M. F. Costabile, and M. Matera, ''End-user com- position of interactive applications through actionable UI components,'' J. Vis. Lang. Comput., vol. 42, pp. 46–59, Oct. 2017.

[66]. M. Rauschenberger, M. Schrepp, M. P. Cota, S. Olschner, and J. Thomaschewski, ''Efficient measurement of the user experience of interactive products. How to use the user experience questionnaire (UEQ).Example: Spanish language version,'' Int. J. Artif. Intell. Interact. Multimedia, vol. 2, no. 1, pp. 39–45, 2013.

[67]. M. Schrepp, User Experience Questionnaire Handbook. All You Need to Know to Apply the UEQ Successfully in Your Project. Berlin, Germany: ResearchGate GmbH, 2015, doi: 10.13140/RG.2.1.2815.0245.

[68]. C. Pautasso, ''Restful Web services: Principles, patterns, emerging tech- nologies,'' in Web Services Foundations. New York, NY, USA: Springer, 2014, pp. 31–51.

Part V

Service Curation

Chapter 12

Personalized Recommendations

Personalization of Wellness Recommendations using Contextual Interpretation

Muhammad Afzal, Syed Imran Ali, Rahman Ali,
Maqbool Hussain, Taqdir Ali, Wajahat Ali Khan,
Muhammad Bilal Amin, Byeong Ho Kang, and Sungyoung Lee

A huge array of personalized healthcare and wellness systems are introduced into the portfolio of digital health and quantified-self movement in recent years. These systems share common capabilities including self-tracking/monitoring and self-quantifications, based on the raw sensory data. These capabilities provide solid ground for the users to be more aware of their health; however, such measures are inefficient for changing the unhealthy habits of the users. In order to induce healthy habits in the users, a system must be capable of generating context-aware personalized recommendations. The main obstacle in this regard is the contextual interpretation of recommendations based on user's current context and contextual preferences. To resolve these issues, we propose a methodology of cross-context interpretation of recommendations (CCIR) for personalized health and wellness services. The CCIR method adds additional capabilities to the traditional reasoning methods and builds advanced form of the reasoning with the incorporation of contextual factors in the process of interpretations of the recommendations. With CCIR, the self-quantification systems can be enhanced to generate personalized recommendations in addition to tracking, quantifying, and monitoring user activities. In order to validate the proposed CCIR methodology, a set of 40 contextual scenarios and corresponding recommendations are presented for the evaluation collected from 40 different end users and 10 domain experts. Using chi-square test evaluation, the results demonstrated acceptable "goodness of fit" indices for the system developed on proposed CCIR methodology with respect to the end users' opinion. Also, from the statistical observation, it is found that there exists a higher-level agreement towards the system between the participants of both end users and experts.

12.1 Introduction

The number of applications and systems for personalized healthcare and wellness management have rapidly grown during the recent years due to the increase in wearable and mobile technologies [3, 5, 11, 17, 18]. These systems and applications have augmented the portfolio of digital health and quantified-self movement. With advances in self-quantification applications, capturing and recording data of human health and fitness is now possible. With the availability of this data, systems and applications provide better understanding of users' health status and their relationship to the world around them [46]. Self-quantification systems and applications are of high importance to educate users of their health status; however, they solely cannot be considered sufficient to change unhealthy habits in the users. Changing unhealthy habits of the users, demands actionable recommendations. Existing systems such as Fitbit Flex [21] Jawbone Up [7], and Misfit Shine [32] are few examples of providing some basic recommendations based on the measured steps and slept hours. Samsung S Health [39] and Google Fit [23] are working as personal fitness coach and health-tracking platform respectively on the basis of capturing user steps counting. A large set of work exists in literature in the area of agent-based and social interactive healthcare monitoring and recommendations for aged population [14,12, 22] however, the scope of our study is focused on middle-aged adults' health and wellbeing recommendation services.

According to the research, contextual information such as location, time, activity, physical conditions, social interaction etc. are very important to generate trustworthy and accurate recommendations [9]. In traditional recommender systems only two types of entities; users and items, are utilized to provide recommendations [2, 9] However, accurate recommendations certainly depend upon the degree to which the recommender system has incorporated the relevant contextual information into the recommendations' generation method [4]). Interpretations of context may not be dealt equally in the approaches of different recommender systems. For instance, contextual modeling approach uses contextual information as an explicit predictor directly in the recommendation function; while in contextual pre-filtering approaches, information about the current context is used for the recommendation [1]. On the contrary, contextual post-filtering algorithm initially ignores the contextual information for the recommendation generation, then the resulting set of recommendations is refined for each user based on the contextual information [1, 4]. These three types of contextual approaches (context modeling, pre-filtering, and post-filtering) provide the opportunities to use contextual information in different kinds of recommender systems; collaborative, content, and knowledge-based recommender systems. In literature, different combinations of these approaches are associated with different types of recommender systems [25, 29, 40]. Regardless of the recommender systems' types and algorithmic approaches, involving context in recommendation poses a number of challenges:

A. How is the contextual knowledge acquired and represented in the system?
B. How is the context processed to evaluate the suitability of recommendations' forwardness?
C. How are the contextual preferences processed to evaluate the recommendations that are qualified in original or alternative form?

To cope with these challenges, we previously proposed an innovative digital health framework called Mining Minds [11] for personalized healthcare and wellness support. It provides personalized recommendations on the basis of expert knowledge and domain guidelines. In current status, the Mining Minds recommendations are generated based on the user's profile information and it does not handle to account for the user's current context, preferences, and environmental variables.

By not handling the contextual factors, the users of the Mining Minds are unable to get the final personalized recommendation services. The main objective of the proposed work is to solve the above-mentioned problem by adding the capability to the existing system to exploit not only the users' profile information but also their current context, preferences, and the environmental variables.

To achieve this objective, we proposed a cross-context interpretation of recommendations (CCIR) methodology to interpret the recommendations based on the user's contexts: physical context (low level and high-level contexts), environmental variables (weather), and preferences and interests. This method provides more insight about user's situation with respect to context and preferences thus leading to a higher level of personalization in health and wellness recommendations. The key contributions in this chapter to achieve the intended objectives are listed below.

- Mechanisms for contextual knowledge acquisition and representation.
- A rule-based matching method for context interpretation method to determine appropriateness of recommendation to be forwarded to the user.
- A contextual matrix aggregation method for contextual preference interpretation of recommendations.

For the evaluations of the proposed CCIR, a user-centric approach is followed to assess the validity of the methodology and acceptability of the system developed over CCIR methodology. All the experiments are performed on the basis of personalized physical activity recommendations. The rest of the chapter is structured as follows.

Section 14.2 provides explanation of related work and their difference with proposed work. Section 14.3 provides an overview of Mining Minds platform that provides a baseline for the proposed work. Section 14.4 describes the proposed CCIR methodology with technical details. Section 14.5 presents the experimental evaluation of the system (recommendation interpreter) that is developed based on the proposed CCIR methodology. Section 14.6 discusses the significance of the work and limitations. Section 14.7 concludes the work and provides a roadmap for the future work.

12.2 Related work

Recommender systems as an area of inquiry have been extensively researched in the past decade in a wide array of domains including healthcare and wellness promotion [43]. In this regard, key categorization of recommender systems includes content-based filtering, collaborative filtering, knowledge-based filtering and their hybridizations [43]. Over the years research interest has pivoted towards context-aware recommender systems [1]. These systems are capable of adapting to different situational needs of a user. Traditional recommender systems employed simple user models e.g., vector of item ratings. Later on, these models were extended to accommodate user preferences as well. But still earlier systems lacked the notion of "situated actions" [3]. Physical activity-based recommender systems belong to the category of systems which require adequate contextual information in order to provide reasonable recommendations to a user [19]. In healthcare and wellness domain cross-context information plays an important role where multiple contexts are aggregated to provide a holistic situational context. Most prevalent contextual factors considered in research literature include information such as time, location, current physical activity, weather, etc. [3] further categorized contextual factors into static and dynamic based on change over time. Most of the contexts in the purview of physical activity belong to dynamic contexts such as location, where new locations may be added later on. Following are some of the proposed recommender systems in the domain of healthcare and wellness promotion.

A physical activity recommender system designed by [38] provides leisure time physical activity to adults based on user with similar lifestyle and preferences. Moreover, ontologies are created to find distance among different physical activities. This system is lacking mechanism to dynamically evaluate user's current context to provide the most relevant recommendation at the given moment.

A mHealth application is proposed by [45] This system uses Body Mass Index, Basal Metabolic Rate, and required energy for performing predefined set of activities. This system also lacks mechanism to user's contextual information in order to provide more amenable set of recommendations based on the given situational settings.

Cypress [5] is a cyber-physical recommender system which is designed to discover smartphone exergame enjoyment. The key intent of this system is to induce healthy behavior by promoting exergames. The proposed system uses smart phone sensing capabilities in order to learn game preferences for a given user; moreover, the system can recommend similar games once the user's engagement level is reduced. This system is not geared to physical activity-based recommendations such as jogging, walking, swimming, stretching, etc.

A personalized therapy-based recommender system is proposed by [27]. A hybrid case-based reasoning technique is used to address user's current wellness problems by inferring information from past relevant cases. This system is primarily designed for general therapy recommendations and no such mechanisms are developed to address different contextual factors related to the user such as user's location.

A web-based wellness management system is proposed by [34]. This system caters for both physical activity and dietary requirements of a user. System is evaluated through the technology acceptance model at the end of a six-week longitudinal study. The proposed system lacks capabilities to acquire and process contextual information about the user. Wahidah Husain and Lim Thean Pheng developed a personalized wellness therapy recommender system using hybrid case-based reasoning [26]. This system also lacks capabilities for handling multiple contextual factors.

Faiz et al. [19] proposed an integrated approach of diet and exercise recommendation for diabetes patients. It is an ontology-based solution which integrates knowledge from different domains in order to provide a comprehensive recommendation. The proposed solution lacks capabilities to adapt to the changing user's context; hence, user has to sift through different recommendations to select the appropriate one.

A knowledge-based diet and physical exercise advisory system is developed by Charles et al. [16]. It is a web-based solution for diet and exercise recommendation based on expert system framework. This system employs information such as users' demographical data, religious information, health conditions, etc. Consequently, a set of recommendations are provided. Since, no sensory data is used; therefore, the proposed system is not capable of adapting to the contextual factors of the users.

PRO-Fit is a personalized fitness assistant framework which provides workout session recommendations [17]. It collects data from accelerometer and synchronizes it with the user's calendar in order to recommend personalized workout sessions. The proposed system also lacks capabilities of handling multi-context information.

The Runner [18] is a comprehensive recommender system for runners. It provides workout and nutrition recommendations to the users. Although the proposed system can process contextual information but its recommendations are limited to a single activity, i.e., running. Therefore, the system lacks mechanism for handling a wide array of popular physical activities such as stretching, cycling, dancing, etc.

Aforementioned are some of the recommendation systems in the domain of healthcare and wellness. Most of these systems are capable of handling static contextual factors but lack capabilities for adapting to changing user's contexts. Weather context is one of the important contexts for outdoor physical activity yet none of the aforementioned systems considered it. Moreover, a higher-level comparison of these systems with our system that is built on CCIR methodology is provided in Table 12.1.

12.3 Cross-context interpretation of recommendations (CCIR) methodology

The main motivation to develop a method for cross-context interpretations is to evaluate the recommendations on the basis of user context and contextual preferences. In case, the system generated recommendations are forwarded directly to the user without interpreting the contextual information, it may increase the chance for the users to not follow the recommendations and eventually tend to drop its use. Our proposed CCIR methodology considers the user current context to determine the appropriateness of delivery time and contents of the recommendations in order to make them more personalized according to the user situation. The abstract flow of information and processing is depicted in Figure 12.2, while in Figure 12.3, the complete functional flow diagram of CCIR methodology is shown to represent the data input and output of each component contributing to the personalized recommendations.

Service Orchestrator: Communication services are managed by the Service Orchestrator (SO). It takes care to handle the potential requests, invoking the necessary services, and coordinating the processes involved in the curation of the services. The requests may be of various types, i.e., scheduled on time (e.g., "every day at 8 am"), triggered by direct user queries ("suggest me an exercise plan for today's workout") or based on events (e.g., "sitting one hour"). In addition to service invocation, it handles the data requirements by communicating with data sources in other layers of the Mining Minds.

Table 12.1 High level comparison of existing systems with proposed system

System	Physiological factors	Rec. technique	Dynamic context	Multi-activity	Preferences
[38]	Ailments, gender, activity level, blood pressure, protein in urine, blood in urine, sleeping habits, etc	Ontology	Static (In-door/out-door, aerobic/non-aerobic, group/individual, winter sport)	Bicycling, Running, Swimming, Aikido, Horse Riding, Polo	Yes
[45]	BMI, BMR, energy, ailments, age, gender, weight, height	MET, RDR-Tree	No	Jogging, Swimming, Tennis, Walking, etc	Yes
[5]	Emotions	Regression and Classification	Dynamic (Game Enjoyment)	Exergame	Yes
[19]	BMI, BMR, age gender, weight, life style. ailments	MET, Ontology	Static (assumed user is available)	Run, Walk, Cycling	Yes
[15]	Ailments, pregnancy	Goal-driven backward	Static	Brisk walk, Jogging,	Yes
[17]	Life style, age, weight,	Content-based and	Dynamic (location and	Yoga, Jogging	Yes
[18]	Life style, age, weight,	Content-based and	Dynamic (location and	Yoga, Jogging	Yes
Proposed	BMI, age, gender, weight, life style, ailments, height	MET, Content-based Contextual Matrix	Dynamic (Location, High-level activity, Weather, Emotions)	Hiking, Running, Sitting, Stretching, Cycling, Walking	Yes

Recommendation Builder: Generalized recommendations are generated by the Recommendation Builder (RB) component through reasoning on the user profile and lifelog data provided by DCL, and the knowledge facilitated by KCL for the specific domain of the service. RB works on multimodal hybrid reasoning methodology expressed in our recent work [6]. RB follows a multimodal hybrid reasoning methodology which generates physical activity recommendations. This methodology integrates Rule-based Reasoning (RBR), Case-based Reasoning (CBR), and Preference-based Reasoning (PBR) in a linear combination which enables the system to generate personalized recommendations. The RBR part of the system uses explicit knowledge rules from physical activity guidelines and prepares new cases for the CBR methodology, whereas the CBR itself uses implicit knowledge in the form of physical activity guidelines as successful cases from expert's past experiences. The suggested recommendations of CBR methodology are either exactly similar to the requirements of the user's current situation or closed to the requirement. In case the recommendations are more than a preliminary level, personalization is implemented in the form of PBR which uses user's personal interests and preferences. However, the level of personalization achieved is trivial and cannot handle the user contextual situation; such as, what recommendation is more suitable in a particular location context, weather context, and other high-level activity contexts? Thus, RB provided recommendations are considered as an initial recommendation because of the fact that the recommendations are yet to be interpreted from the user's contextual perspective. These may result in forwarding the initial recommendation as-is or transforming it to a more amenable form. Moreover, user's availability status is not yet taken into account.

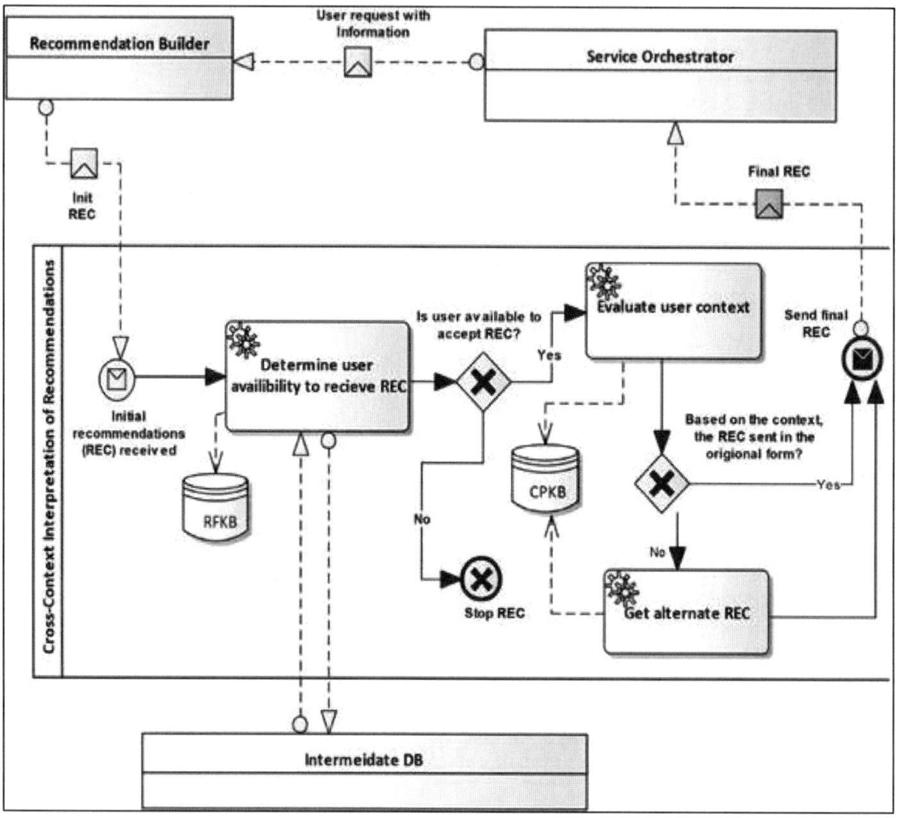

Figure 12.2 CCIR Methodology abstract flow of information and processing

Recommendation Interpreter: In Recommendation Interpreter (RI), the recommendations received from RB undergo a series of steps for personalization. The main personalization objective is to provide such recommendations as to best suit the user's requirements, interests, and demands. For achieving this goal, the CCIR methodology is activated and operated at the backend. First step of CCIR methodology is to consider user's availability status. Once a user is deemed available to comply with the physical activity-based recommendations, then current context of the user is evaluated. Current context of a user includes all the available contexts e.g., user's location, user's current activity, environmental conditions, and others. Moreover, user's preferences are incorporated on a priority basis by preference-based reasoner in the course of recommendation interpretation. There are two types of knowledge bases required for recommendation interpretations:

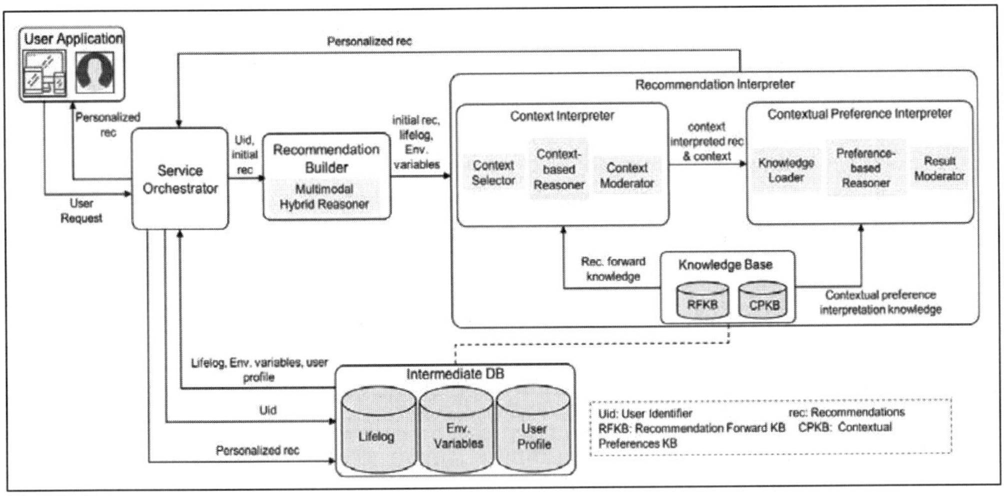

Figure 12.3 Cross-context interpretation of recommendations (CCIR) functional workflow

1. Recommendation Forward Knowledge Base (RFKB) is the knowledge base which consists of rules that account for user's context and specify the needed recommendations be forwarded based on current context of the user. For instance, the recommendations are not forwarded to the user if he/she is in the commuting context.
2. Contextual Preference Knowledge Base (CPKB) is the knowledge base that consists of rules for the evaluation of contextual preferences. The decisions are made on given rules whether the recommendation is appropriate in the original form or it needs to be fine-tuned based on the user's current context. For instance, if it is raining outside and the system generates an activity-oriented recommendation to be conducted outside, then the recommendation is changed to an alternative indoor activity.

Intermediate database: The data collected from wearable sensors and smart phone is curated and persisted in the intermediate database (IDB) with a logical division of user profile data, lifelog data, and environmental data. The user profile data include user demographics (gender, age), physiological factors (height and weight), and preference data. Contextual data is categorized into two type of contexts: low and high-level contexts. Low-level context includes location, emotion, and physical activities. High-level context includes more abstract representations of the user context which are determined from the low-level context, such as office-work, commuting, eating, and others. Environmental variables include weather context as rainy, sunny, and others. All these contextual parameters are constantly monitored by the information curation layer (ICL) as described in Section 14.3 about Mining Minds.

12.3.1 Contextual knowledge acquisition

The mode of data acquisition for RFKB is questionnaire based. The user is prompted to provide RFKB related information at the time of subscription to the Mining Minds services. Since this information is not incumbent on the user; therefore, he/she can opt out of this step. In which case, a survey is conducted to provide more common situations when a recommendation may be forwarded/blocked given different contexts. For example, as a default case when a user's location is "home" and high-level context is "sleeping", then any recommendation initiated by RB is stopped from being forwarded to the user. Hence, survey-based data serves as a default case until user provides his/her information for a given context. From surveying 40 users, we identified the common situations, where majority of the users agree on recommendation to forward or not. A partial list of these non-forwarding rules are described in Table 12.2 which shows if any of these rules matches for a given a context, the recommendation will not be forwarded.

12.3.2 Contextual preferences interpretation knowledge acquisition

CPKB is yet another important piece of knowledge about users' contextual preferences. This knowledge is instrumental for the "contextual preferences interpretation" task; discussed in detail in the coming sections. Its mode of acquisition is similar to that of RFKB. A comprehensive questionnaire is devised to acquire knowledge for contextually preferred recommendations. Items in the questionnaire are developed for commonly used contexts in physical activity recommendation domain [13, 28]. Each item was of dichotomous answer format (suitable = 1, not suitable = 0). For instance, if (location = home), the value for recommendations such as hiking and running are not suitable. Overall 40 users participated in the survey and answered to the questions in questionnaire. For computationally viable representation, we formulate the knowledge in a two-dimensional matrix for "contextually preferred recommendation". A majority vote method is utilized to set the final contextual matrix. As an example, in Table 12.3 we represent the location context with respective recommendations.

Preference information is stored in a two-dimensional matrix. In Table 12.3, there are 7 different location-based contexts including "Don't Care" as a default case. Each row is populated with 0 s and 1 s. For example, intersecting cell of "Gym" and "Hiking" contains It means that "Hiking" cannot be performed while location is "Gym". In case of "Gym" and "Running" the cell contains 1 which allows this activity for the given context. This contextual data matrix is populated through information provided by the user at the time of subscription to the Mining Minds services. In the absence of user specific data, a survey is conducted and majority vote is used to populate contextual matrices. Table 12.4 represents the majority vote results of a survey conducted from 40 different users for three different contexts (location, high level context, and weather).

Table 12.2 Partial list of context interpretation knowledge rules

Identifier	Rule Conclusion
R1	If (Location = Transport && HLC = Commuting && Weather = Don't Care)
R2	If (Location = Restaurant && HLC = HavingMeal && Weather = Don't Care)
R3	If (If (Location = Home && HLC = Sleeping && Weather = Don't Care))
***	***
Rn	If (If (Location = Office && HLC = OfficeWork && Weather = Don't Care))

12.3.3 Processing method of context interpretations

Processing of context interpretations play the key role in personalized recommendation. The rationale for the contextual interpretations is to model user's convenience and allow recommendations when user is in a more receptive mode. Current context of a user is required to model user's receptivity. Current context includes location information, high-level context and weather information; which is provided by Service Orchestrator. Moreover, user provided contextual knowledge is acquired through RFKB. RFKB stores user's information which accounts for his/her inclinations to receive physical activity-based recommendations. Knowledge stored in RFKB is in the form of production rules i.e., {Location = Transport, HLC = Commuting, Weather = Don't Care} → Recommendation Not Forwarded. RFKB only stores rules for blocking scenarios. As stated before, these blocking scenarios are provided either by the user or through a generalized survey-based response. RFKB can vary for different users as per their varied inclinations for receiving recommendations in different contexts.

Once a recommendation is generated by RB, it is received by Context Selector along with user_id. Based on the user_id, Context Selector fetches current context of the user from intermediate database (IDB) hosted in DCL. The recommendations along with the current context of the user are forwarded to the context-based reasoner for contextual interpretation. For this interpretation, the context-based reasoning requires rules, that are fetched from the RFKB. These rules specify such scenarios in which user is deemed unreceptive for a physical activity-based recommendation. Current context is evaluated/reasoned against the rules, using the rule-based reasoning approach with exact match strategy.

Table 12.3 Location context applicability with respect to recommended activity

Location Context	Recommendations					
	Hiking	**Running**	**Sitting**	**Stretching**	**Cycling**	**Walking**
Gym	0	1	1	1	1	0
Home	0	1	1	1	0	1
Office	0	0	0	1	0	1
Transport	0	1	1	0	1	0
Outdoors	1	1	0	1	0	1
Don't Care	0	1	0	1	0	1

If current context matches to any of the rules then initial recommendation, generated by RB, is blocked for further processing. Alternatively, initial recommendation along with the user_id and current context are forwarded to Contextual Preference Interpreter to assess the suitability of the recommendation within the scope of user's preferences.

12.3.4 Processing method of contextual preference interpretations

The main objective of contextual preference interpretations (CPI) is to evaluate the initial recommendation proposed by RB against user contextual preferences. There are three sub-components of CPI namely knowledge loader and preference-based reasoner, and result moderator. The knowledge loader acquires relevant knowledge from CPKB, while the preference-based reasoner performs reasoning on the user's specific preference-based data against the recommendations. Result moderator delivers the results to target entities. When context interpreter allows the initial recommendation to be further processed, then contextual preference interpreter is invoked. It receives the user_id, initial recommendations, and current context of the user from Context Interpreter. Based on the user_id, relevant contextual data is fetched from IDB through service orchestrator. CPKB stores users' physical activity preferences against different contexts, i.e., location, high level context and weather. If user has not provided his/her preferences, then CPKB is populated through generalized behavior patterns conducted on a public survey. Once user relevant context data is prepared then it is consolidated into contextual matrices similar in structure as shown in Figure 12.4.

Table 12.4 Knowledge for contextually preferred recommendations

What recommendation do you think is more appropriate to be acted upon at which location point?

Location Context	Recommendations					
	Hiking	Running	Siting	Stretching	Cycling	Walking
Gym	0	1	1	1	1	0
Home	0	1	1	1	0	1
Office	0	0	0	1	0	1
Transport	0	1	1	0	1	0
Outdoors	1	1	0	1	0	1
Don't Care	1	1	1	1	1	1

What recommendation do you think is more appropriate to be acted upon at which situation (high level context)?

Location Context	Recommendations					
	Hiking	Running	Siting	Stretching	Cycling	Walking
Amusement	0	1	1	1	1	0
Commuting	0	0	1	1	0	1
Exercising	1	1	0	1	1	1
Gardening	0	0	1	0	1	0
HavingMeal	0	1	0	1	1	1
Inactivity	1	1	0	1	1	1
Don't Care	1	1	1	1	1	1

What recommendation do you think is more appropriate to be acted upon in which weather condition?

Location Context	Recommendations					
	Hiking	Running	Siting	Stretching	Cycling	Walking
Rainy	0	1	1	1	0	1
Sunny	0	0	1	1	0	1
Windy	1	1	0	1	1	1
Cloudy	0	0	1	1	0	0
Don't Care	1	1	1	1	1	1

In Figure 12.4, the two-dimensional contextual matrix stores user's preferences for physical activities against different contexts. For example, a case is depicted in Figure 12.4, i.e., a user is in his/her office, in an inactivity mode, and weather is rainy outside. All this information is combined by taking the complete row of each occurring context and put it into the aggregate contextual matrix. This aggregate contextual matrix may have different values for another user based on his/her preferences. Once matrix is generated an aggregate vector is computed to summarize matrix results. The aggregate vector is computed by taking an "AND" operation on each column of the aggregate contextual matrix, i.e., putting the resultant bit 1, if all the bit values are 1 in a given column, 0 otherwise.

Preference-based reasoner first interprets the aggregate vector. Each bit in the vector represents a physical activity in a pre-specified order e.g., first bit represents "Hiking", second bit represents "Running", and so on. The activities that are marked 1 are applicable given the current context of the user, while others are not applicable. Hence, in the aforementioned case only Stretching and Walking are applicable recommendations in the given user context. The contextual interpretations of original recommendations on the basis of contextual preferences are given in Algorithm 14.1.

Location	Recommendations					
Context	*Hiking*	*Running*	*Sitting*	*Stretching*	*Cycling*	*Walking*
Gym	0	1	1	1	1	0
Home	0	1	1	1	0	1
Office	0	0	0	1	0	1
Transport	0	1	1	0	1	0
Outdoors	1	1	0	1	0	1
Don't Care	0	1	0	1	0	1

HLC	Recommendations					
Context	Hiking	Jogging	Sitting	Stretching	Cyclng	Walking
Amusement	0	1	1	1	1	0
Commuting	0	0	1	1	0	1
Exercising	1	1	0	1	1	1
Gardening	0	0	1	0	1	0
HavingMeal	0	1	0	1	1	1
Inactivity	1	1	0	1	1	1
Don't Care	1	1	1	1	1	1

Weather	Recommendations					
Context	Hiking	Jogging	Sitting	Stretching	Cyclng	Walking
Rainy	0	1	1	1	0	1
Sunny	0	0	1	1	0	1
Windy	1	1	0	1	1	1
Cloudy	0	0	1	0	1	0
Don't Care	1	1	1	1	1	1

Aggregate Contextual Matrix						
Context/Rec	*Hiking*	*Running*	*Sitting*	*Stretching*	*Cycling*	*Walking*
Location= Office	0	0	0	1	0	0
HLC= Inactivity	1	1	0	1	1	1
Weather= Rainy	0	1	1	1	0	1

Figure 12.4. Aggregate contextual matrix preparation

Algorithm 14.1 requires two inputs; original recommendation and current context of the user. Original recommendation is received from context interpreter component. Current context is comprised of three sub-contexts. Location and high-level context are provided by the user lifelog while weather related information is provided by environmental variables. LoadCurrentContext function takes userID and returns current location, high-level context and weather conditions in the vicinity of the user. This information is temporarily stored in cContext for further processing. It iterates over all the original recommendations oRec and for each recommendation r in oRec all the contexts are evaluated to generate context evaluation vector contextEvalVector. In Figure 12.4, for instance, there is value 1 for "stretching" recommendation against office location in the Location Contextual Matrix, in this case, 1 value is picked up and added at the corresponding index of context evaluation vector (contextEvalVector). Each contextEvalVector is added to the list of context evaluation vectors (contextEvalVectorList). On the basis of context evaluation vectors, an aggregate vector (aggregateVector) is computed with computeAggregateValues. Aggregate values computation is described in Algorithm 14.2.

Algorithm 12.1 Contextual interpretations of recommendations.

Input: oRec = {r1, r2, …, rn} //list of original recommendations
cContext = {c1, c2, …, cn} //list of current context
userID;
Output: iRec = {ir1, ir2, …, irn} // list of interpreted recommendations
LET
contextEvalVector = {v1, v2, …, vn} // list of values (0, 1)
contextEvalVectorList = {cv1, cv2, …, cvn}
aggregateVector = {v1, v2, …, vn} // list of values (0, 1)
Start
cContext = loadCurrentContext(userID)
foreach r in oRec

```
Begin
  foreach c in cContext
    Begin
      contextValue = evaluateContext(r, c);
     AddContextValue(contextEvalVector, contextValue);
    End
    contextEvalVectorList.add(contextEvalVector);
    aggregateVector = computeAggregateValues(contextEvalVectorList);//Algorithm 14.2
 End
 foreach v in aggregateVector
   Begin
    if (!(v) = = 0)
      Begin
        AddRecommendation(iRec, r); // add original recommendation r to iRec list
      End
    End
   IF (isEmpty(iRec))
      Begin
        iRec = Contextual Evaluation of Alternative Recommendations;
      End
   Return iRec;
Stop
```

Algorithm 14.2 receives the list of context evaluation vectors (contextEvalVectorList) as an input and returns the aggregate vector as an output. Each of vectors in the list is processed through logical AND operation. Logical_Anding_Operation function applies logical AND operation to all the elements of a vector and assigns the resulting value in aggregateVector list. Hence, first element of aggregateVector corresponds to the first vector in contextEvalVectorList, and so on. As shown in Figure 12.4, there are six context evaluation vectors corresponding to each recommendation namely, hiking, running, stretching, sitting, cycling, and walking. Each of these vectors are evaluated with logical_Anding_Operation in order to generate true (1) or false (0) value. For instance, the hiking context evaluation vector consists of 1, 1, and 0 values. When these valued are ANDed, we get false (0) value and it is added to the aggregate vector at first index. Similarly, running context evaluation vector is composed by 0, 1, and 1 values, when they are ANDed, they yield false (0) value and it is added to the aggregate vector at index 2. The process continues till the end of the context evaluation vector list and the resultant values of logical_Anding_Operation are added to the corresponding indexes of aggregateVector.

Aggregate vector is composed of 0 s and 1 s, since it is computed by bitwise ANDing operation. It checks each index value (0, 1), if the index value in the vector is 1, it means the corresponding original recommendation is in compliance with the current context of the user and the recommendation is added to the list of interpreted recommendations iRec. In case all the values are returned as 0 means false value, the algorithm will check for the possibilities of alternative recommendations.

Algorithm 12.2 Aggregate values computation.

```
Input: contextEvalVectorList //list of context evaluation vectors
Output: aggregateVector // list of values [0,1]
Start
    foreach vector in contextEvalVectorList
      Begin
        result = logical_Anding_Operation(vector)
        AddAggregateVector(aggregateVector, result)
      End
    Return aggregateVector
Stop
```

Definition 1 Alternative Recommendations

Let Rec be the set of all recommendations in the scope, and oRec be the set of original recommendations where, oRec ⊆ Rec; and iRec is the set of alternative recommendations where, altRec = Rec − oRec

The algorithm for contextual evaluation of alternative recommendations is similar to evaluations of original recommendations in Algorithm 14.1 with the exception that the input is the list of alternative recommendations rather the original recommendations. The definition of Alternative recommendation is given in Definition 1.

12.4 Experimental evaluation

12.4.1 Knowledge acquisition case study

For evaluation, we use a weight management scenario implemented in Mining Minds for healthy individuals, who live sedentary life. Sedentary lifestyle refers to one of these situations; either no physical activity, or with irregular pattern, or in an insufficient amount [41]. It includes the activities such as; sitting, reading, watching television, playing video games, and computer use for much of the day with little or no vigorous physical exercise [34].

12.4.1.1 Sedentary behaviors' recommendations translated from guidelines

Based on the monitoring capabilities of Mining Minds, we choose recommendations generated against multiple sedentary situations categorized in three categories; prolong sitting, prolong standing, and prolong lying down. In Table 12.5, a list of respective recommendations for selected sedentary situations is provided.

12.4.1.2 User current context collection

In Mining Minds, different type of context is recognized including low-level (LLC) & high-level context (HLC), location context (LC), emotion context (EC), weather context (WC), and others. The LLC, EC, and LC are used to identify the HLC using ontological reasoning using context ontology [44]. In Table 12.6, a partial list of different contexts is represented.

12.4.1.3 Knowledge rules for contextual interpretations

As mentioned previously, every recommendation that is generated by RB may not be appropriate for forwarding to the user unless contextual information is not aptly considered. From surveying users, we identified the common situations where majority of the users agree on recommendation to forward or not. A partial list of these non-forwarding rules is described in Table 12.2 that shows if any of these rules matches for a given context, the recommendation will not be forwarded.

12.4.1.4 Knowledge rules for contextual interpretations

In order to interpret the appropriateness of recommendations to be forwarded in their original state or in the alternative form, we investigate to find the knowledge for contextually preferred recommendations. This knowledge is collected through questionnaires composed of items related to three contexts: LC, HLC, and WC. Responses of surveyed users are recorded through the questionnaire. Through majority voting mechanism as explained in Section 14.3, the final answers are populated in a two-dimensional matrix for each context, as shown in Table 12.3.

12.4.2 Implementation scenario

A prototype implementation of the proposed CCIR method is implemented as a part of Mining Minds. Mining Minds is a distributed platform where the implementation is deployed over a hybrid cloud combining Microsoft Azure public cloud environment [10]. All of the layers of Mining Minds work independently, however, they are interrelated for the data and knowledge communication in order to perform their tasks. SCL layer is dependent on DCL for data communication while on KCL for knowledge communication. The resulting recommendations are communicated to SL layer for presentation. This communication is implemented by establishing service contracts among the layers, which communicate by means of RESTful web services [37].

12.4.2.1 Implementation workflow

The implementation diagram shown in Figure 12.5, describes the communication pattern between different layers and components. First, the recommendation request is received to SCL service orchestrator (SO) components either through user directly or from DCL. Service orchestrator passes the request to recommendation builder (RB). RB connects to KCL in order to find the rules against the triggered situation event. KCL returns all the candidates knowledge rules to take part in recommendation generation. RB determines the data requirement from the rules and make a data request to SO. SO connects to DCL's intermediate database and fetches all the required data (user profile data) for recommendations and forward to RB. In RB, multimodal hybrid reasoner performs reasoning over the rules and data, and builds the initial set of recommendations which is then passed to recommendation interpreter (RI). The recommendation received to RI from RB in JSON format have two parts: structured and unstructured. The structured part is for the computer interpretability while the unstructured part is for the explanation purpose. RI interprets the structured part according to the algorithms discussed in Section 14.3 of this chapter. The final contextualized recommendations are first sent to DCL to persist in the lifelog of the user and then sent to the SL for the user presentations.

12.4.2.2 End-to-end example scenario

Consider "John" as a user of the CCIR system with his current context described as follows. On a busy working day, John stays for longer hours in his office in an inactive state while the outside weather is sunny. In this scenario, location is office, high-level context is inactivity, and weather is sunny. The CCIR component receives original recommendation as input for the stated context

Table 12.5 Partial list of recommendations for prolong sitting, standing and lying down

Sedentary	Criterion	Recommendations	Identifier
Prolonged Sitting	• 15–20m sitting • 1h sitting in chair for non-obese adults	• TAKE A BREAK! Get out of your chair or couch every 15 min and merely stand up and then sit back down, or do some stretching for 20–30 s. • Take a five-minute walk for every hour you spend in your chair	• Rec 1 • Rec 2
Prolonged Standing	• 2h standing in workplace • 1 h standing for males	• TAKE A SITTING BREAK! Have a rest of 4–5 min, 2–3 times per hour of standing. • PERFORM PREVENTATIVE STRETCHING! Relax your legs every after 30 min	• Rec 3 • Rec 4
Prolonged Lying Down	• 1h lying down as a bed rest	• BODIES ARE MADE TO MOVE! Please have a walk of 5 min, 2–3 times every after 1 h of inactive lying down period	• Rec 5

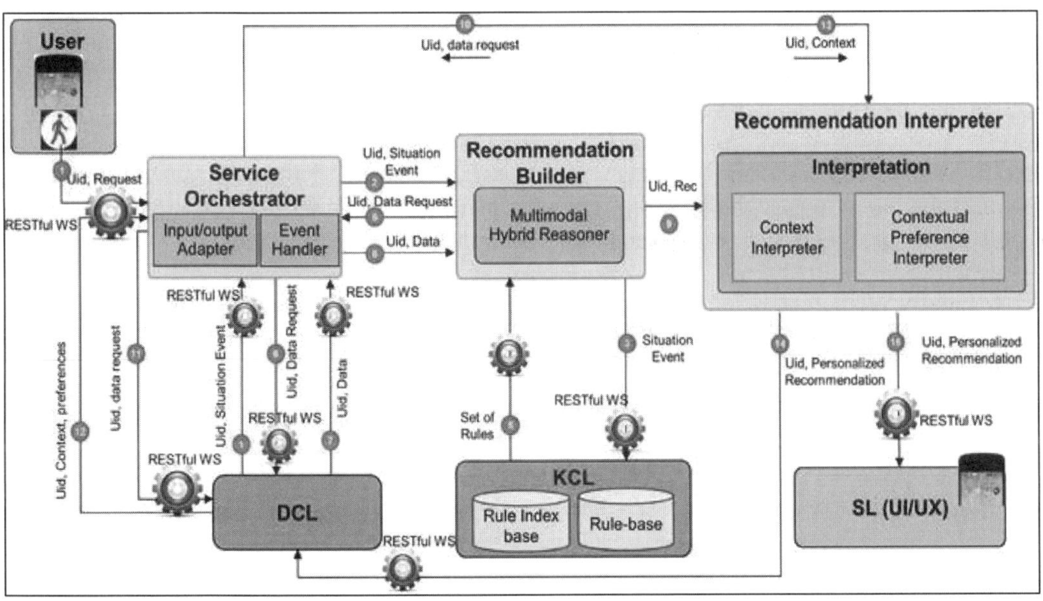

Figure 12.5. Intra and inter layer communications of CCIR of service curation layer with components and layers of mining minds

Table 12.6 Partial list of contextual scenarios consist of location, high level, and weather context

Context				Identifier
LLC	**LC**	**HCL**	**WC**	
Sitting	Home	Inactivity	Sunny	S1
Standing	Home	Inactivity	Sunny	S2
Stretching	Office	Officework	Windy	S3
Walking	Office	Exercising	Windy	S4
***	***	***	***	***
Sweeping	Outdoor	UnIdentifiedHLC	Rainy	S39
Running	Outdoor	Exercising	Rainy	S40

as "running". To generate interpreted recommendation for this scenario, the stepwise CCIR methodology is described as follows.
Step 1: Recommendation Interpreter (RI) receives "running" recommendation and user identifier (user_id) from recommendation builder (RB).

Step 2: RI fetches the current context (office, inactivity, and sunny) from the lifelog through service orchestrator.

Step 3: RI loads the rules of RFKB to check the appropriateness of user current context to determine whether the recommendation should be allowed and forwarded or stopped at this stage. Since John is "inactive" in office, so the system allows the recommendation to be forwarded because no such rule is available (see Table 12.2) to stop the recommendation.

Step 4: RI checks the recommendation "running" is applicable in the given context or not. Using the knowledge in contextual preference knowledge base (CPKB), RI finds that "running" recommendation is not applicable because of the "office" context.

Step 5: As recommendation "running" is blocked; therefore, RI searches for alternative recommendations to replace the "running" recommendation. We can see from the aggregate matrix (Figure 12.4), two alternative recommendations are applicable i.e., "walking" and "stretching".

Step 6: Finally, recommendation "walking/stretching" is forwarded to the user to follow and break the inactive state of the day.

Name:

Recommendation Evaluation

Guidelines: You are given physical activity based recommendations by two recommender systems i.e. System 1 (S1) and System 2 (S2). You are requested to assume yourself in a given context; in terms of location, high level context, weather and emotion.
Please tick (✓) mark each suitable recommendation of System 2. You may tick 1 or more recommendations of System 2. Cross (X) those recommendations of System 2 which are not suitable in the given context.
Note: Recommendations labeled "Not-to-Interrupt" indicate that the respective system decided to withhold the recommendation for that particular user's scenario.

No.	System 1	User's Context (Location, High Level Context, Weather, Emotion)	System 2
1	Running	Office, Office Work, Sunny, Neutral	Walking or Stretching
2	Stretching	Office, Inactivity, Sunny, Neutral	Stretching
3	Cycling	Home, House Work, Windy, Happiness	Walking or Stretching
4	Walking	Home, Inactivity, Rainy, Neutral	Walking
5	Walking	Home, Having Meal, Cloudy, Sadness	Not-to-Interrupt (because HLC context)

Figure 12.6. Questionnaire for recommendation evaluation

12.4.3 Experimental setup

In order to assess the effectiveness of the proposed system developed on CCIR methodology, we have conducted a questionnaire-based evaluation. A questionnaire is prepared with 40 scenario items collected in a week long activities of different users. Each scenario item has a context and a recommendation from two systems. A snapshot of the questionnaire is depicted in Figure 12.6 where **System 1** and **System 2** denote recommendation builder (RB) and recommendation interpreter (RI) respectively. Context and recommendation values are taken from the lifelog of the users stored in IDB. Because of the relational structure of lifelog, each recommendation is easily back tracked to corresponding contextual information. It is pertinent to mention here that the recommendations are generated on the basis of the contextual preferences stored initially in CPKB because none of the user provide their preferences during subscription time. As we mentioned in section 14.3.2, CPKB is considered as a default if user fails to provide his/her preferences during subscription time.

Questionnaire is distributed among 50 participants to observe the given context and respond to the recommendations. Among 50 participants, 40 were end users and 10 were domain experts who were having certain level of knowledge of the wellness domain and recommender systems. The portfolio of the end user participants includes 30 males and 10 females in the middle-aged group (25– 49 years). These participants belong to 10 different nationalities including South Korea, Pakistan, Vietnam, Spain, Myanmar, Ecuador, India, China, Bangladesh, and Uzbekistan. The distribution of participants based on gender and ethnicity are shown in Table 12.7.

While, the expert users were belonging from South Korea (3), Pakistan (2), Bangladesh (1), Iran (2), and Vietnam (2) in the range of middle-age (25–49 years). There are few assumptions which were considered for the proposed system evaluations.

- User's current context is available and is accurate.
- Acquired general activity preference trend from a user base (through a questionnaire) is representative of the target population.
- User is physically able to perform recommended activities.

Table 12.7 Gender and Ethnicity wise participant distribution

Ethnicity	Gender		Total
	Male	Female	
South Korea	9	1	10
Pakistan	8	1	9
Vietnam	3	2	5
India	1	1	2
China	2	0	2
Spain	1	1	2
Uzbekistan	0	2	2
Yemen	2	0	2
Ecuador	0	2	2
Bangladesh	4	0	4
Total	30	10	40

12.4.4 Evaluation of the system

All the results of the study are collected and analyzed in a tabular form. In case of multiple physical activity recommendations, if one of the physical activities is deemed appropriate then the entire recommendation is considered reasonable. Appropriate recommendations are labelled "Yes" while inappropriate recommendations are labelled "No". If a participant selects RI's results as more reasonable than RB's results will be deemed inappropriate.

Three kinds of analysis are performed on the data acquired from end users and expert users. Firstly, each user response is evaluated to find out the "goodness of fit" of the system. Secondly, statistical observations are recorded on the collected data using descriptive statistical analysis parameters including mean, standard deviation, and skewness. Thirdly, a comparison graph is drawn of end users and experts to find out mutual relationship in their response to the system.

12.4.4.1 Chi-Square goodness of fit test

We calculated the Chi-Square (X^2) value using Eq. (1) to check the "goodness of fit" of the system on the basis of end user's observation and expected values as shown in Table 12.8. In Eq. (1), O represents the observed value and E represents the expected value.

Table 12.8 Essential values for chi-square (X^2) test

Scenarios	Observed values		Total	Expected values		Chi Stat (X^2)	
	Yes	No		Yes	No	Yes	No
S1	38	2	40	34.675	5.325	0.319	2.076
S2	37	3	40	34.675	5.325	0.156	1.015
S3	38	2	40	34.675	5.325	0.319	2.076
S4	25	15	40	34.675	5.325	2.700	17.579
S5	33	7	40	34.675	5.325	0.081	0.527

S6	33	7	40	34.675	5.325	0.081	0.527
S7	35	5	40	34.675	5.325	0.003	0.020
S8	36	4	40	34.675	5.325	0.051	0.330
S9	38	2	40	34.675	5.325	0.319	2.076
S10	27	13	40	34.675	5.325	1.699	11.062
S11	36	4	40	34.675	5.325	0.051	0.330
S12	32	8	40	34.675	5.325	0.206	1.344
S13	38	2	40	34.675	5.325	0.319	2.076
S14	33	7	40	34.675	5.325	0.081	0.527
S15	36	4	40	34.675	5.325	0.051	0.330
S16	37	3	40	34.675	5.325	0.156	1.015
S17	37	3	40	34.675	5.325	0.156	1.015
S18	37	3	40	34.675	5.325	0.156	1.015
S19	36	4	40	34.675	5.325	0.051	0.330
S20	36	4	40	34.675	5.325	0.051	0.330
S21	37	3	40	34.675	5.325	0.156	1.015
S22	38	2	40	34.675	5.325	0.319	2.076
S23	28	12	40	34.675	5.325	1.285	8.367
S24	37	3	40	34.675	5.325	0.156	1.015
S25	36	4	40	34.675	5.325	0.051	0.330
S26	34	6	40	34.675	5.325	0.013	0.086
S27	35	5	40	34.675	5.325	0.003	0.020
S28	36	4	40	34.675	5.325	0.051	0.330
S29	35	5	40	34.675	5.325	0.003	0.020
S30	34	6	40	34.675	5.325	0.013	0.086
S31	36	4	40	34.675	5.325	0.051	0.330
S32	24	16	40	34.675	5.325	3.286	21.400
S33	33	7	40	34.675	5.325	0.081	0.527
S34	37	3	40	34.675	5.325	0.156	1.015
S35	37	3	40	34.675	5.325	0.156	1.015
S36	38	2	40	34.675	5.325	0.319	2.076
S37	38	2	40	34.675	5.325	0.319	2.076
S38	32	8	40	34.675	5.325	0.206	1.344
S39	32	8	40	34.675	5.325	0.206	1.344
S40	32	8	40	34.675	5.325	0.206	1.344

For our experiment, the null and alternative hypothesis are set as follows:

Null Hypothesis (H_0): There is no significant difference between the observed and expected values.

Alternative Hypothesis (H_1): There is a significant difference between the observed and expected values.

Based on the essential values as described in Table 12.8, we calculated the value of x^2 (105.491) with a degree of freedom value 39 [(r −1) (c-1) = (40–1) (2–1)]. The x^2 value is tested against the chi-square distribution for the standard level $\alpha = 0.05$ to find the critical (chi crit) value (54.572). Since the calculated chi-stat value is greater than the standard chi-crit value; thus, we reject the null hypothesis H_0, and accept the alternative hypothesis H_1. It shows that there exists significant difference between the observed values and the expected values regarding the system that is developed on the basis of our proposed CCIR methodology.

$$x^2 = \sum_{i=1} \frac{(O_i - E_i)^2}{E_i} \qquad (1)$$

12.4.4.2 Statistical observations

We compared the results of opinions by the experts and users for the 40 context scenarios using the descriptive statistics. We performed a statistical analysis to examine factors using the SPSS Windows program [20]. Using descriptive statistics, the arithmetic mean (M), standard deviation (SD), and skewness were calculated for both datasets of users and experts to observe their response's tendencies. The descriptive statistics are illustrated in Table 12.9, where the higher M value 34.625 shows that the majority of end users agree with the recommendations generated based on the given context scenarios.

Table 12.9 Mean, standard deviation, and skewness

Metric\User type	User	Expert
Arithmetic mean	34.675	8.850
Standard deviation	3.533	1.145
Skewness	−1.586	−1.419

Similarly, the standard deviation 3.533 infers that the end users have very small deviation in their agreement on different context scenarios. The skewness value −1.58 is acceptable for a normal distribution, because most of the values are in an acceptable range (between + 2 and −2) [21]. On the other hand, the standard deviation of the expert users has even a smaller deviation of 1.145 in their agreement on different scenarios. Also, the experts' skewness value −1.419 is in the range of acceptable values. From these statistical analyses, we infer that the participants of both the groups are in agreement and have a higher level of central tendency and a lesser level of variability in their responses to the system.

Table 12.10 Comparison of participants' response to the system

Scenarios	Observed values		Observed values (%)	
	Users	Expert	Users	Expert
S1	38	10	95	100
S2	37	8	92.5	80
S3	38	9	95	90
***	***	***	***	***
S38	32	9	80	90
S39	32	10	80	100
S40	32	10	80	100

12.4.4.3 Participants' response to the system

Finally, we record the response from both end-users and experts to find out the mutual relationships in their responses. Because of the unequal number of participants in each group, we converted the response values to the percentage response values as shown in Table 12.10. The average value (%) for the end-users is recorded as 86.688, which is very close to the average value (%) 88.500 of the expert users, means the participants of both the groups have almost similar opinion about the system. Also, a value-by-value comparison of the values in Table 12.10 is depicted in Figure 12.7. It can be seen from the figure that there exists a very close relationship in the response of the participants from both the groups. It leads us to the conclusion that both the groups are agreed in their opinion with respect to the positive response, thus the system is considered to be acceptable.

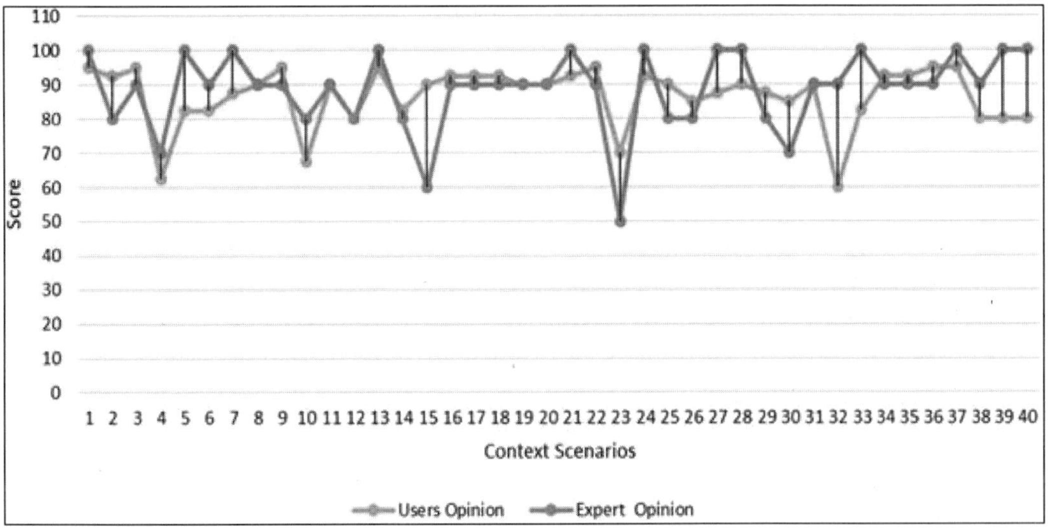

Figure 12.7. Score for different context scenarios showing opinion of experts and users about the system

In order to segregate the contexts, we have selected 34 (user) and 8.5 (expert) as a cutoff point. Hence cutoff point of 34 and 8.5 indicates that a particular context has gained over 85% acceptance from the participants. These contexts are a subset of daily activities performed by a user. Since the Mining Minds platform recognizes contexts such as location, high-level context, weather, and emotion, therefore selected scenarios belong to these particular contexts only. The main purpose of the aforementioned experimentation is to evaluate participants' response variability against different contexts and cross validation from the expert users. Analysis of participants' response helped us categorized these contexts in two clusters, i.e., acceptable performance and non-acceptable performance scenarios.

Table 12.11 Contexts with score less than the cutoff point

S. No.	Scenario item	**Contexts (Location, HLC, Weather, Emotion)**	**RB**	**RI**
1	4	Home, Inactivity, Rainy, Neutral	Walking	Walking
2	5	Home, HavingMeal, Cloudy, Sadness	Walking	N/I
3	6	Home, Sleeping, Windy, Neutral	Stretching	N/I
4	10	Outdoors, Commuting, Cloudy, Neutral	Walking	N/I
5	12	Gym, Exercising, Cloudy, Neutral	Running	Running
6	14	Mall, UnidentifiedHLC, UnidentifiedWeather, Sadness	Running	Walking

7	23	UnidentifiedLocation, Anger, Rainy, Inactivity	Cycling	Walking
8	26	Gym, Sleeping, UnidentifiedWeather, Neutral	Running	N/I
9	31	Restaurant, Sleeping, Windy, Sadness	Running	N/I
10	32	Home, Inactivity, Rainy, Sadness	Cycling	Walking
11	33	Yard, Sleeping, Sunny, Happiness	Walking	N/I
12	38	Office, OfficeWork, Sunny, Neutral	Walking / Running	Walking
13	39	Yard, UnidentifiedHLC, Cloudy, Sadness	Running /Stretching	Walking/ Cycling
14	40	Home, Exercising, Sunny, UnidentifiedEmotion	Walking	Walking

For end users, a total of 14 such contexts are identified which scored less than the cutoff point. These contexts are listed in Table 12.11. Both RB and RI have same recommendations for 4 out of 14 aforementioned contexts. Hence, in only 10 out of 14 contexts most participants marked RI's recommendations "unreasonable". Varied personal preferences could be one of the reasons since some of these contexts are rather rare e.g. "outdoors, commuting", "gym, sleeping", and "yard, sleeping", etc. This analysis necessitates acquiring of personal preferences of the user.

Two ways to address the issue of infrequent scenarios where the user have marked RI recommendations unreasonable: (i) Through acquiring user specific preferences data from the users themselves through a feedback mechanism, (ii) revising the validity of the contexts recognized by the system as it seems that some of the recognized contexts are not valid thus lead to generate un-reasonable recommendations.

12.5 Discussion

Recommendation systems tend to be very complex. These systems not only perform information filtering but also take into account different preferences of the users. Task of the recommender systems becomes more challenging in the wake of scarcity of the data. One of the main problems in recommendation systems is the cold start which is pertinent to mention along with the interpretation of recommendation with respect to user preferences. Cold start problem occurs in most of the systems that requires data to draw any inferences for users or items about which sufficient amount of information is not yet gathered. Therefore, system is unable to provide any useful recommendations to the user in the wake of cold start problem. In order to circumvent this issue, we have relied on a questionnaire-based data gathering technique which provides sufficient data to extract general patterns of human behavior under different conditions. These global patterns of human behavior are used to make initial recommendations to the user. These resulting patterns are stored in CPKB for each user and a generic level of personalization is achieved. This approach is evaluated with an experiment which examined the users with 40 different everyday scenarios and assess the viability of recommendations for each case. As per the experiment results most of the users showed inclination towards the provided recommendations. Their generalized response is depicted in Figure 12.7. It indicates that our system, in its early stages, is able to handle most of the everyday scenarios and successfully avoid cold start problem. But these generic patterns may not capture idiosyncrasies of different users. Hence, inferring preferences of users on the basis of general patterns can be very tricky. Therefore, in order to avoid such issues, each user is prompted to provide his/her preferences across multiple contexts customization of the recommender system.

Another important aspect of this experiment is to assess behavior of the recommender for infrequent scenarios. Since the proposed method is able to respond to different everyday scenarios, it is interesting to study its recommendations for rare events. Figure 12.7 provides item scores across different users. Each item denotes a specific scenario. Most of the scenarios capture everyday aspects while in some of the items rare or infrequent contexts are also incorporated. It is observed that the system's response to such events as rare or infrequent is not adequate. Some of these events are highlighted in Table 12.11. For infrequent events survey participants had provided varied responses and to approximate a generalized response required a much greater number of survey participants. In this regard a small subset of the users may be affected by the imprecise approximation of our system. In order to address the issue, more data is required for such cases to pinpoint a response which is applicable to a greater population. Moreover, this issue will not hinder those users who would have provided their preferences, explicitly.

With all positives, the proposed methodology has a room to improve by address the following major limitations:

- Contextual matrices are composed of binary values which may further be enhanced to reflect probabilistic decisions
- Current system lacks a feedback process which may enable the system to fine tune its recommendations

12.6 Summary

In recent years personalized healthcare and wellness systems have acquired a pivotal role in the quantified self-movement. These systems share some common characteristics such as self-tracking, self-monitoring, and self-quantification. In order to perform these tasks raw sensory data is acquired and processed for providing intelligent recommendations to the users. Most of these systems focus on valid recommendations, i.e., recommendations which are consistent with domain knowledge or guidelines. While contextual information about the user is not fully exploited. We have proposed cross-context interpretation of recommendation (CCIR), a mechanism in which contextual information about the user is seamlessly incorporated with the knowledge-based recommendation system. The key assertion of the proposed system is that contextual information should also be taken into account along with domain relevant recommendations. An empirical study is performed which validated our assertion and most of the users preferred context interpreted recommendations. Proposed system produced encouraging results in terms of user's acceptability. This system is in its early stages therefore more research is required in terms of identifying key contexts for user behavior modeling, ethnicity traits, and reduction the chances of infrequent scenarios. It will require to consider either increasing number of surveyed members for knowledge acquisition or explicitly obtained user preferences from the users themselves.

As a future work, we intend to incorporate the feedback mechanism for improving the quality of personalized recommendations. We also plan to investigate implicit and explicit data gathering mechanism for user experience quantification. This will enable us to measure the user satisfaction level for modifications in the services provision. Lastly, continuously evolution of knowledge bases (using expert and data driven approaches) will result in adapting recommendations that takes into account the trends as well.

Source Code

Source code can be downloaded from the following location:
https://github.com/ubiquitous-computing-lab/Mining-Minds/tree/master/service-curation-layer/recommendation-interpreter

The contents of this chapter have been previously published in the following article:

Muhammad Afzal, Syed Imran Ali, Rahman Ali, Maqbool Hussain, Taqdir Ali, Wajahat Ali Khan, Muhammad Bilal Amin, Byeong Ho Kang, and Sungyoung Lee, "Personalization of Wellness Recommendations Using Contextual Interpretation", Expert Systems with Applications (SCIE, IF: 3.928), Vol.96, pp.506-521, 2018

References

[1] Adomavicius, Gediminas, et al. "Incorporating contextual information in recommender systems using a multidimensional approach." ACM Transactions on Information Systems (TOIS)23.1 (2005): 103-145.
[2] Adomavicius, Gediminas, and Alexander Tuzhilin. "Toward the next generation of recommender systems: A survey of the state-of-the-art and possible extensions." IEEE Transactions on Knowledge & Data Engineering 6 (2005): 734-749.
[3] Adomavicius, Gediminas, and Alexander Tuzhilin. "Context-aware recommender systems." Recommender systems handbook. Springer, Boston, MA, 2011. 217-253.
[4] Adomavicius, Gediminas, and Alexander Tuzhilin. "Context-aware recommender systems." Recommender systems handbook. Springer, Boston, MA, 2011. 217-253.
[5] Agu, Emmanuel, and Mark Claypool. "Cypress: A cyber-physical recommender system to discover smartphone exergame enjoyment." Proceedings of the ACM workshop on engendering health with recommender systems. 2016.
[6] Ali, Rahman, et al. "Multimodal hybrid reasoning methodology for personalized wellbeing services." Computers in biology and medicine 69 (2016): 10-28.
[7] AliphCom dba Jawbone. (2014). Jawbone UP Retrieved June 6, 2017, from https://jawbone.com/up.
[8] Amin, Muhammad, et al. "On curating multimodal sensory data for health and wellness platforms." Sensors 16.7 (2016): 980.
[9] Asabere, Nana Yaw. "Towards a viewpoint of context-aware recommender systems (CARS) and services." International Journal of Computer Science and Telecommunications 4.1 (2013): 10-29.
[10] Banos, Oresti, et al. "The Mining Minds digital health and wellness framework." Biomedical engineering online 15.1 (2016): 76.
[11] Banos, Oresti, et al. "Human behavior analysis by means of multimodal context mining." Sensors 16.8 (2016): 1264.
[12] MORENO, Cristian BARRUEa Atia CORTESb Jonatan, and Miguel PEREZ-PASALODOSa Ulises CORTES. "Using multi-agent systems to mediate in an assistive social network for elder population." Artificial intelligence research and development:

Proceedings of the 18th international conference of the Catalan association for artificial intelligence. Vol. 277. IOS Press, 2015.
[13] Bull, Fiona C., Tahlia S. Maslin, and Timothy Armstrong. "Global physical activity questionnaire (GPAQ): nine country reliability and validity study." Journal of Physical Activity and health 6.6 (2009): 790-804.

[14] Chan, Victor, Pradeep Ray, and Nandan Parameswaran. "Mobile e-Health monitoring: an agent-based approach." IET communications 2.2 (2008): 223-230.
[15] Charles, E., D. Stanley, and E. Agbaeze. "Knowledge-based diet and physical exercise advisory system." International Journal of Science and Research (IJSR) 14.7 (2013): 2319-7064.

[16] Convertino, VICTOR A., SUSAN A. Bloomfield, and JOHN E. Greenleaf. "An overview of the issues: physiological effects of bed rest and restricted physical activity." Medicine and science in sports and exercise 29.2 (1997): 187-190.

[17] Dharia, Saumil, et al. "PRO-Fit: A personalized fitness assistant framework." SEKE. 2016.

[18] Donciu, Mihnea, et al. "The Runner--Recommender System of Workout and Nutrition for Runners." 2011 13th international symposium on symbolic and numeric algorithms for scientific computing. IEEE, 2011.
[19] Faiz, Irshad, Hamid Mukhtar, and Sharifullah Khan. "An integrated approach of diet and exercise recommendations for diabetes patients." 2014 IEEE 16th International Conference on e-Health Networking, Applications and Services (Healthcom). IEEE, 2014.
[20] Afzal, Muhammad, et al. "Personalization of wellness recommendations using contextual interpretation." Expert Systems with Applications 96 (2018): 506-521.

[21] Fitbit. (2017). Retrieved May 19, 2017, from https://www.fitbit.com/kr/home. George, D., & Mallery, P. (2016). IBM SPSS statistics 23 step by step: A simple guide and reference
[22] Gómez-Sebastià, Ignasi, et al. "Situated agents and humans in social interaction for elderly healthcare: From Coaalas to AVICENA." Journal of medical systems 40.2 (2016): 38.
[23] Google Inc. (2016). Google fit Retrieved from https://fit.google.com/u/0/.

[24] Gregory, Diane E., and Jack P. Callaghan. "Prolonged standing as a precursor for the development of low back discomfort: an investigation of possible mechanisms." Gait & posture 28.1 (2008): 86-92.
[25] Herlocker, Jonathan L., et al. "Evaluating collaborative filtering recommender systems." ACM Transactions on Information Systems (TOIS) 22.1 (2004): 5-53.

[26] Husain, Wahidah, and Lim Thean Pheng. "The development of personalized wellness therapy recommender system using hybrid case-based reasoning." 2010 2nd International Conference on Computer Technology and Development. IEEE, 2010.

[27] Lim, Thean Pheng, Wahidah Husain, and Nasriah Zakaria. "Recommender system for personalised wellness therapy." International Journal of Advanced Computer Science and Applications 4 (2013).

[28] Lin, Yuzhong, et al. "Motivate: Towards context-aware recommendation mobile system for healthy living." 2011 5th International Conference on Pervasive Computing Technologies for Healthcare (PervasiveHealth) and Workshops. IEEE, 2011.

[29] Martínez, Ana Belén Barragáns, et al. "What's on TV tonight? An efficient and effective personalized recommender system of TV programs." IEEE Transactions on Consumer Electronics55.1 (2009): 286-294.

[30] Mercola. (2014). Ten minutes of intermittent movement for every hour of sitting may counteract ill health effects of prolonged sitting. Fitness peak Retrieved from http://fitness.mercola.com/sites/fitness/archive/2014/09/19/intermittent-movement-prolonged-sitting.aspx.

[31] Microsoft. (2016). Microsoft azure: Cloud computing platform & services Retrieved June 6, 2017, from https://azure.microsoft.com/en-us/.

[32] Misfit: Fitness Trackers & Wearable Technology – Misfit.com. Retrieved June 6, 2017, from https://misfit.com/.

[33] Omar, A., et al. "Wellness management through Web-based programmes." Journal of telemedicine and telecare 11.1_suppl (2005): 8-11.

[34] Owen, Neville, et al. "Too much sitting: the population-health science of sedentary behavior." Exercise and sport sciences reviews 38.3 (2010): 105.

[35] Powell, Adam C., Adam B. Landman, and David W. Bates. "In search of a few good apps." Jama 311.18 (2014): 1851-1852.

[36] Preventing Work-related Injuries: Standing on the Job. (2016). Retrieved from http://www.cwhn.ca/node/40808.

[37] Richardson, Leonard, and Sam Ruby. RESTful web services. " O'Reilly Media, Inc.", 2008.

[38] Sami, Ashkan, et al. "Design of Physical Activity Recommendation System." IADIS European Conf. Data Mining. 2008.

[39] Samsung. (2015). Start a health challenge Retrieved June 6, 2017, from http://health.apps.samsung.com/.

[40] Su, Xiaoyuan, and Taghi M. Khoshgoftaar. "A survey of collaborative filtering techniques." Advances in artificial intelligence 2009 (2009).

[41] Thorp, Alicia A., et al. "Sedentary behaviors and subsequent health outcomes in adults: a systematic review of longitudinal studies, 1996–2011." American journal of preventive medicine41.2 (2011): 207-215.

[42] Thosar, Saurabh S., et al. "Effect of prolonged sitting and breaks in sitting time on endothelial function." (2015).

[43] Verbert, Katrien, et al. "Context-aware recommender systems for learning: a survey and future challenges." IEEE Transactions on Learning Technologies 5.4 (2012): 318-335.

[44] Villalonga, Claudia, et al. "High-level context inference for human behavior identification." International Work-Conference on Ambient Assisted Living. Springer, Cham, 2015.

[45] WUTTIDITTACHOTTI, Pongpisit, Sineerat ROBMEECHAI, and Therdpong DAENGSI. "mHealth: A design of an exercise recommendation system for the android operating system." Walailak Journal of Science and Technology (WJST) 12.1 (2014): 63-82.

[46] Almalki, Manal, Fernando Martin-Sanchez, and Kathleen Gray. "Self-quantification: the informatics of personal data management for health and fitness." (2013).

Chapter 13

Recommendation Generation

A Hybrid Framework for a Comprehensive Physical Activity and Diet Recommendation System

Syed Imran Ali, Muhammad Bilal Amin, Seoungae Kim, and Sungyoung Lee

The quantified self-movement has gained a lot of traction, recently. In this regard, research in personalized wellness support systems has increased. Most of the recommender systems focus on either calorie-burn or calorie-in take objectives. The achievement of calorie-burn objective is through physical activity recommendations while diet recommendations geared towards calorie-in take objectives. A very limited research is performed which track and optimize objectives for both calorie-burn and calorie-in-take, simultaneously based on well-known wellness support guidelines. In this regard, we propose a hybrid recommendation framework, which provides recommendations for physical activity as well as diet recommendation in order to support wellness requirements of a user in a comprehensive manner.

13.1 Introduction

Over the years, there has been a huge surge in wellness support systems. These systems have varied capabilities from a relatively simple step count feature to a more complex wellness regiment-management [1]. Another reason for this renewed interest is due to availability of wearable and mobile technologies. These technologies assist not only in innovative application development but also do so in research such as in development of hybrid frameworks and subsequent field studies for their efficacy evaluation [2].

In order to induce a sustainable healthy behavior a number of aspects related to wellness require consideration. These aspects relate to the comprehensibility of the recommendation regimen and personalization of the recommendations. Existing popular wellness management systems such as Misfit shine [3] Jawbone Up [4] Fitbit Flex [5] provide recommendations based on very limited set of parameters e.g. steps count and slept hours, hence there is a room for a more comprehensive and personalized recommendation framework, which is capable of providing actionable recommendations, based on a number of personalized parameters. The scope of our research is limited to providing wellness support services focused on middle-age users through a knowledge-based recommendation framework.

13.1.1 Expert-in-the Loop

Expert-in-the loop framework is yet another important consideration, which is under-researched in recommendation systems dealing with wellness support. This aspect of the recommender system deals with incorporating the domain expert curated information e.g. curated educational contents, for enhancing the general awareness of the user related to his/her peculiar fewer desirable habits. Moreover, domain experts e.g. nutritionists, can provide valuable input in menu construction for dietary recommendations. In this regard, our proposed framework deals with three key aspects of a wellness support regimen i.e. educational recommendation, physical activity recommendation, and dietary recommendation within the purview of enhancing the wellness of a target user pool.

Educational Recommendation: Educational recommendations assist in enhancing the awareness level of the user regarding the wellness domain. Moreover, factual nuggets embedded in the recommendation note also provide a rationale for adopting a balanced and active lifestyle that is elaborated by providing activity and dietary recommendations.

Physical Activity Recommendation: The physical activity recommendation is targeted to meet objectives stipulated in the calorie-burn goal. Whereas, the estimated calorie-burn goal is computed based on wellness guidelines in an automated manner. In this regard, the personalization element of the recommendation is also incorporated by assessing the contextual situation of the user at a given time of recommendation [6].

Dietary Recommendation: Dietary recommendation caters for the specific needs of a user in terms of calorie-in take requirements, as estimated from wellness guidelines, and health conditions e.g. diabetic patients are recommended low-glycemic food items. Another important factor of dietary recommendation regimen is the incorporation of local/territorial food information regarding the unsuitability of certain food items for consumption due to seasonal or viral containments. Expert(s) constructs menu-sets for each goal category and the system after multi-factor filtration provides the final recommendation [7].

13.2 Related Work

The There has been an extensive research performed in the area of wellness related recommender systems. These systems are geared towards either physical activity-based recommendation or dietary recommendation. Comprehensive systems, as an area of inquiry, the recommendation systems targeting both physical activity and dietary recommendation, are under-researched. In this section, we will provide an overview of an array of recommender systems. Our main focus is on the comprehensive recommender systems.

Recommendation systems, which provide recommendations regarding physical activity normally, employ user's contextual information. Contextual information based on different parameters such as location, current activity, weather information, etc. is poised to provide a holistic situational context. Such a situational context may be explored to determine various important factors such as user interpretability and suitability of a recommended physical activity for the given user context.

Dietary recommender systems specifically focus on the calorie-in-take goal. Moreover, these systems provide user with recommendation, which includes food items that collectively contribute in achieving the stated goal. Goal maybe user defined or expert recommended based on health condition and suitability constraints. In this regard, both expert's advised menu-sets and system generated menu-sets maybe used. Our proposed framework has adopted the former approach.

Acquiring an elaborate contextual user information is not straightforward. Moreover, it necessitates the inclusion of supporting modules which can provide accurate and timely contextual information about a user e.g. location, current activity, emotional state, etc. Although, the inclusion of such supporting modules may add to the complexity of the system, it is a requisite step towards the comprehensibility of the recommender system. Hence, when available the recommendation framework should be able to utilize such contexts as aforementioned. Following are some of the existing systems for physical activity recommendation.

PRO-Fit is a personalized physical activity recommender. It provides personalized workout session recommendations. Contextual data is collected through accelerometer. This data is later synchronized with user's weekly plans [8].

The Runner [9] is another popular recommender system for users who prefer running activity, geared towards the wellness needs of a specific group of users. It provides both physical activity and nutritional recommendations to users. Although it processes an array of contextual parameters, its physical activity recommendation is primarily oriented towards running.

A web based compressive recommender system is proposed by [10]. The proposed system is capable of processing a wide array of contextual parameters such as demographic information, health conditions, religious information, etc. Since sensory data is not taken into account, therefore system falls short of dynamically adapting to contextual requirements of the user.

Faiz et al. [11] proposed a comprehensive wellness support system for patients suffering from diabetic ailments. Semantic technologies such as ontology engineering is investigated in this work in order to provide wellness related recommendations.

A comprehensive web-based recommendation system and a six-week evaluation study is performed by [12]. This system is evaluated based on technology acceptance model. Although system is capable enough to cater for the basic needs of its targeted user group, it lacks comprehensibility in terms of handling a wide array of contextual factors e.g. user's location.

Aforementioned are a sample of studies, which addressed wellness support through designing comprehensive recommender systems/frameworks. Although most of the studied systems in this research are capable enough to address basic user needs, their comprehensibility in terms of processing multi-factor contextual information and assisting user in adopting healthy habituation (e.g. user awareness towards wellness through educational nuggets) is lacking.

In the subsequent section, we propose a comprehensive wellness support system which caters for educational, active-lifestyle and nutritional needs of a targeted user group.

13.3 Framework

Our proposed system is composed of a number of modules. These modules are divided into two categories i.e. main module and supporting modules. Main module represents the main working engine of the framework while the supporting modules provide services to the main module. Hence, the main business logic of the recommender resides in the multi-stage recommender system module as depicted in Figure 13.1.

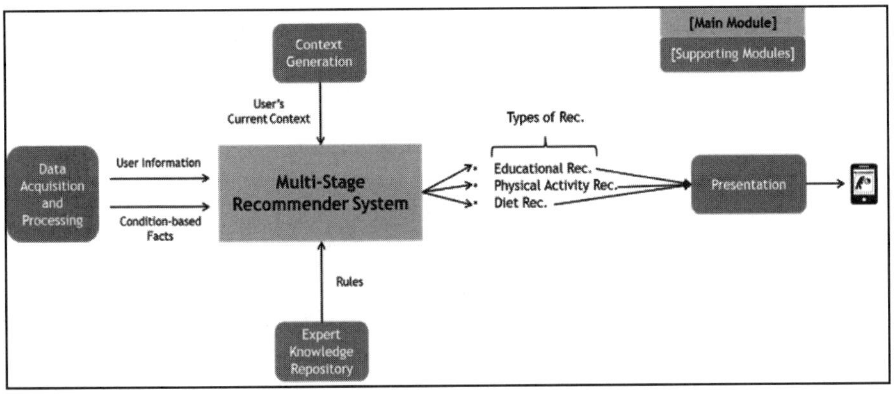

Figure 13.1 Abstract level overview of the main and supporting components of the proposed framework

Data Acquisition and Processing module acquires data from the sensory devices e.g. mobile phone, processes the required information and persists it. Moreover, this module is also tasked with storing personal information about the user i.e. demographic information, preferences related information, etc. A monitoring application resides in this module which tracks user's activities, food consumption (entered manually) and calculates a multi-factor vector regarding user's food consumption so far and activity-level. Each factor vector corresponds to a particular "situation". Context Generation module processes sensory raw data into meaningful user contexts such as user's current activity, location of the user, weather conditions, user's emotional state, etc. This information is very valuable for providing context-aware physical activity-based recommendation.

Expert Knowledge Repository module stores expert knowledge in terms of production rules. These rules are based on fact vectors. Against different situations there are different kinds of recommendations. These generic recommendations are stored in IF-THEN form i.e. IF clause of the rule captures the situation part while THEN clause denotes recommendation given by an expert in the given situation.

Presentation module deals with interfacing with the user's device i.e. mobile phone. A recommendation package is sent to the Presentation module. Presentation module presents the generated recommendation in a user-friendly manner.

Multi-Stage Recommender System is the main module which deals with processing the provided contextual information along with user profile, and situational information in order to provide a comprehensive recommendation. Stage-I of the module deals with calculating user's calorie-burn, in-take goals and a generic set of physical activity recommendation. It also has a case-based reasoning mechanism through which it infers the most appropriate rule from the knowledge base. Stage-II deals with refining the recommendation in a more personalized manner. For physical activity recommendation, Stage-II recommender creates a context matrix through which it infers which of the activities can be recommended to a user at a given time. Moreover, it is tasked with selecting the most appropriate menu-set based on goal, situational-fact vector, and user preferences. Providing educational recommendation is also the task of this component.

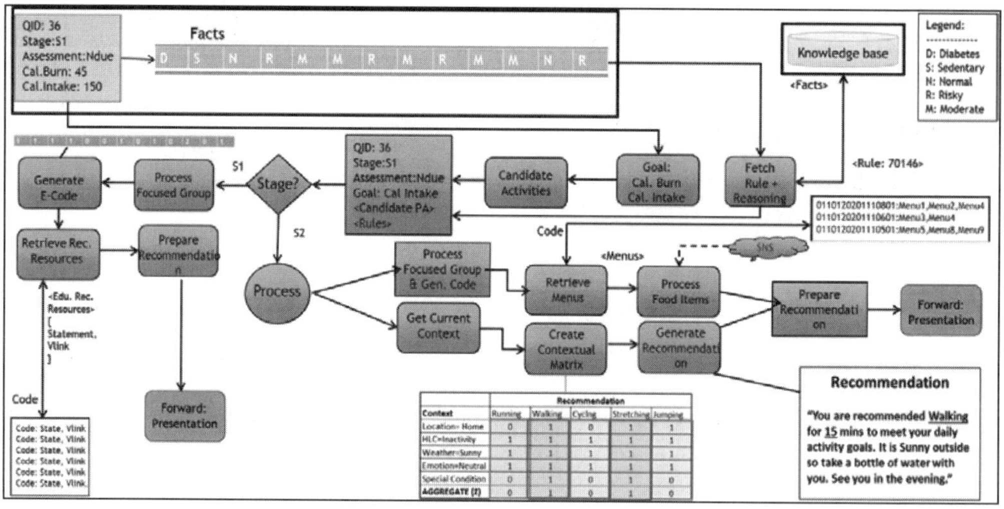

Figure 13.2 Execution Scenario for Educational, Physical activity and Dietary Recommendation

In Figure 13.2, a working scenario of the recommender system is depicted. Where S1 and S2 correspond to users in two different stages. S1 users are only provided Educational Recommendation for the first week. Educational recommendation is in the form of a text message, along with curated educational material in terms of web links, pictures, and video links, etc. Users in S2 category are provided with physical activity and dietary recommendation.

13.3.1 Rule-Structure for Interpretation and Recommendation generation

Knowledge base contains rules which are used for generating recommendations. Rule has components i.e. condition part, recommendation part, and an optional description part. Condition part corresponds to the situational vector which encapsulates a user's current situation in terms of physical activity, health status, weight status, fat consumption level, salt and sugar consumption level, protein consumption and food and vegetables consumption, etc. Recommendation component of the vector deals with the subset of the conditions in the situation which are risky and require a recommendation for improvement.

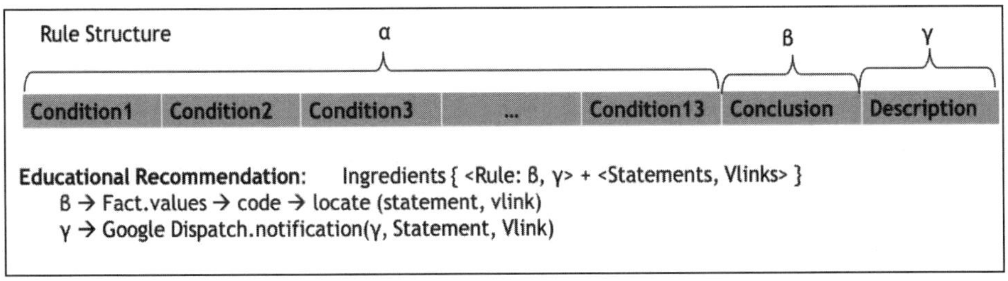

Figure 13.3 Rule utilization for educational recommendation

For example, if fat consumption and BMI of the user are abnormal then these two conditions would be part of Recommendation component. Description part of the rule accommodates a free text observation by the domain expert. Figure 13.3 and Figure 13.4 depicts how a rule is utilized a different kind of recommendation i.e. educational, physical activity, and dietary. It is important to note that an index mechanism is used to locate menu-sets for dietary recommendation. A code is generated based on conditions values augmented with the category of the calorie-in-take goal. Category of the goal is divided into four groups i.e. A, B, C, D, having mutually exclusive ranges.

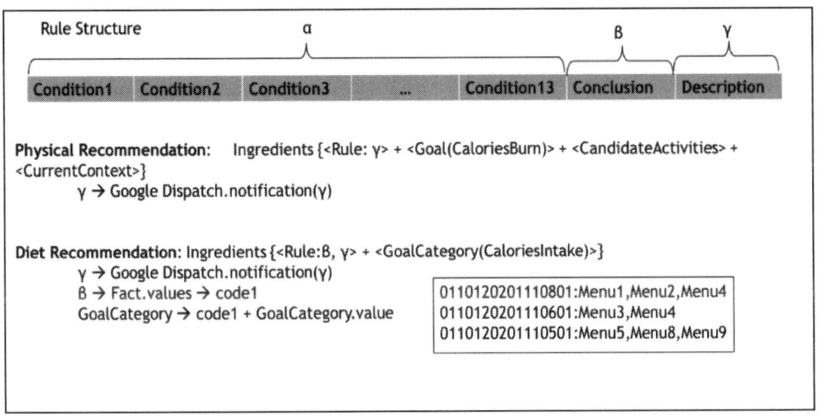

Figure 13.4 Rule utilization for both physical and dietary recommendation

13.3.2 Two-Stage Context-aware Physical Activity Recommender

Multi-stage recommendation module has two sub-components i.e. Stage-I and Stage-II recommenders. In order to generate a physical activity recommendation first goal is computed for the given user. This goal is based on the formulae provided in wellness guidelines. Subsequently, MET based formula is used to calculate different physical activities and their durations which can meet the stipulated goal. This generic information along with contextual information is fed to Stage-II recommender. This component generates a contextual matrix. This contextual matrix is computed based on surveyed results in which users were asked to provide their input regarding the suitability of a particular physical activity in different contexts. For example, Running was deemed not suitable when user is in Home while Stretching was deemed a reasonable recommendation in this context. Once a recommended activity is determined then it is conveyed in a user-friendly way. This process is depicted in Figure 13.5.

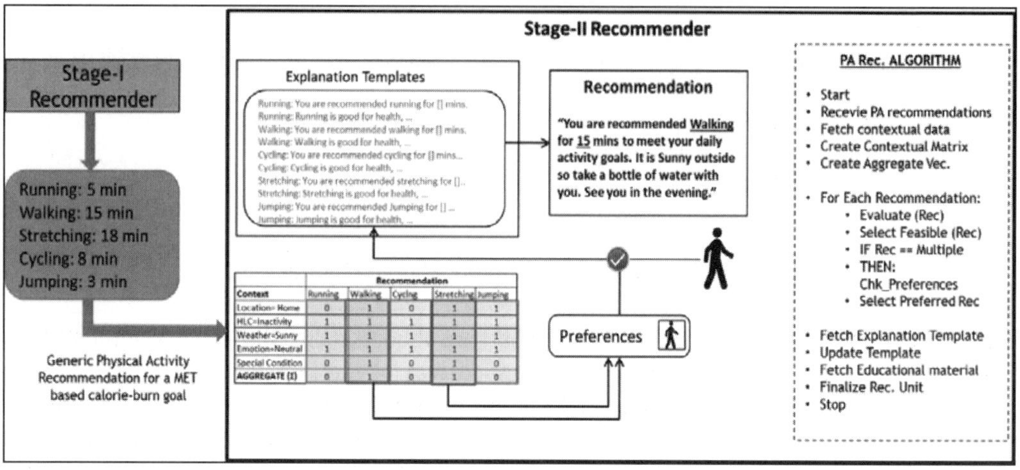

Figure 13.5 Scenario for a physical activity recommendation

A similar recommendation mechanism is used for diet recommendation. Stage-I recommender computed the calorie-in-take goal of a user. Category of the goal is determined, and all the expert curated menu-sets associated with the category are retrieved. If there are multiple menu-sets then in order to select one menu-set a filtration process is invoked. This filtration process takes into account the user disliked food items in each candidate menu-set and those food items which are tainted and have a government advisory for abstinence. The menu-set which has the least such food items as aforementioned is selected for a final recommendation. The process of dietary recommendation is depicted in Figure 13.6.

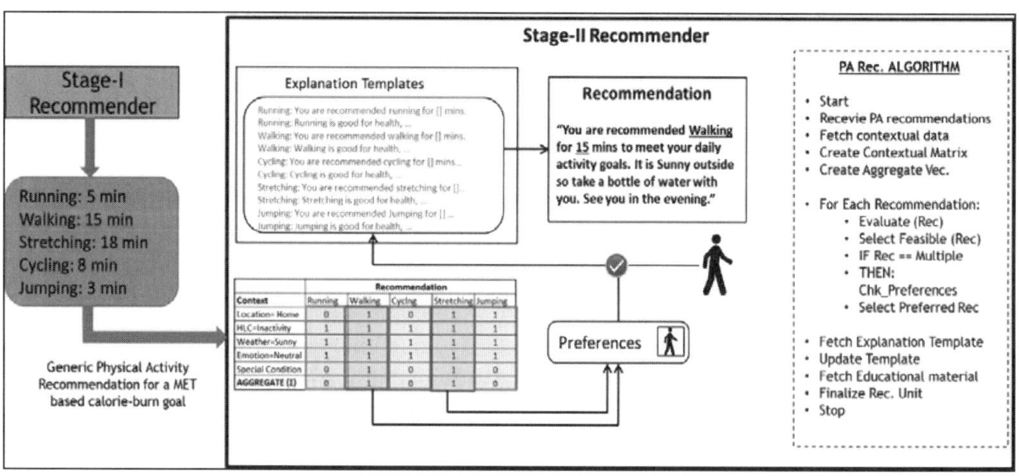

Figure 13.6 Scenario for dietary recommendation

13.4 Summary

In this research work we have proposed a hybrid framework for a comprehensive wellness support framework. Our proposed framework is capable of providing physical activity-based recommendation, dietary recommendation as well as educational recommendations to a selected targeted user group. Moreover, we have also catered for personalization aspects of the recommender system as well. Through expert-in-the loop mechanism, our framework is capable of providing educational recommendations to the user base. A multi-factor menu-set recommendation is also geared towards the specific nutritional needs of the users. The proposed approach combines different facets of wellness support systems in a holistic manner in order to provide a more comprehensive treatment to the specific needs of the users.

In future, we would like to extend our work in a number of directions. Educational contents can be pre-curated automatically for the expert and later domain expert can sift through the pre-curated recommendations. A feedback mechanism maybe introduced which monitors whether user has acted upon the given recommendation or not and record user's opinion regarding the generated recommendation. In terms of menu-set selection, a more automated approach may be investigated which can generate reasonable menu-sets under certain constraints.

Source Code

For Source code please email us at:

The contents of this chapter have been previously published in the following article:

Syed Imran Ali, Muhammad Bilal Amin, Seoungae Kim, and Sungyoung Lee, "A hybrid framework for a comprehensive physical activity and diet recommendation system", 16th International Conference On Smart homes and health Telematics (ICOST 2018), Singapore, Singapore, July 10-12, 2018

References

[1] Chan, Victor, Pradeep Ray, and Nandan Parameswaran. "Mobile e-Health monitoring: an agent-based approach." IET communications 2.2 (2008): 223-230.

[2] Asabere, Nana Yaw. "Towards a viewpoint of context-aware recommender systems (CARS) and services." International Journal of Computer Science and Telecommunications 4.1 (2013): 10-29.

[3] Misfit: Fitness Trackers & Wearable Technology –Misfit.com. Retrieved March 6, 2018, from https://misfit.com/.

[4] AliphCom dba Jawbone. (2014). Jawbone UP Retrieved March 6, 2018, from https://jawbone.com/up

[5] Fitbit. (2018). Retrieved March 6, 2018, from https://www.fitbit.com/kr/home

[6] Verbert, Katrien, et al. "Context-aware recommender systems for learning: a survey and future challenges." IEEE Transactions on Learning Technologies 5.4 (2012): 318-335.

[7] Gómez-Sebastià, Ignasi, et al. "Situated agents and humans in social interaction for elderly healthcare: From Coaalas to AVICENA." Journal of medical systems 40.2 (2016): 38.

[8] Dharia, Saumil, et al. "PRO-Fit: A personalized fitness assistant framework." SEKE. 2016.

[9] Donciu, Mihnea, et al. "The Runner--Recommender System of Workout and Nutrition for Runners." 2011 13th international symposium on symbolic and numeric algorithms for scientific computing. IEEE, 2011.

[10] Charles, E., D. Stanley, and E. Agbaeze. "Knowledge-based diet and physical exercise advisory system." International Journal of Science and Research (IJSR) 14.7 (2013): 2319-7064.

[11] Faiz, Irshad, Hamid Mukhtar, and Sharifullah Khan. "An integrated approach of diet and exercise recommendations for diabetes patients." 2014 IEEE 16th International Conference on e-Health Networking, Applications and Services (Healthcom). IEEE, 2014.

[12] Omar, A., et al. "Wellness management through Web-based programmes." Journal of telemedicine and telecare 11.1_suppl (2005): 8-11.

Chapter 14

Hybrid Reasoning

Multimodal hybrid reasoning methodology for personalized wellbeing services

Rahman Ali, Muhammad Afzal, Maqbool Hussain, Muhammad Hameed Siddiqi, Byeong Ho Kang, and Sungyoung Lee

A wellness system provides wellbeing recommendations to support experts in promoting a healthier lifestyle and inducing individuals to adopt healthy habits. Adopting physical activity effectively promotes a healthier lifestyle. A physical activity recommendation system assists users to adopt daily routines to form a best practice of life by involving themselves in healthy physical activities. Traditional physical activity recommendation systems focus on general recommendations applicable to a community of users rather than specific individuals. These recommendations are general in nature and are fit for the com-munity at a certain level, but they are not relevant to every individual based on specific requirements and personal interests. To cover this aspect, we propose a multimodal hybrid reasoning methodology (HRM) that generates personalized physical activity recommendations according to the user's specific needs and personal interests. The methodology integrates the rule-based reasoning (RBR), case-based reasoning (CBR), and preference-based reasoning (PBR) approaches in a linear combination that enables personalization of recommendations. RBR uses explicit knowledge rules from physical activity guidelines, CBR uses implicit knowledge from experts' past experiences, and PBR uses users' personal interests and preferences. To validate the methodology, a weight management scenario is considered and experimented with. The RBR part of the methodology generates goal, weight status, and plan recommendations, the CBR part suggests the top three relevant physical activities for executing the recommended plan, and the PBR part filters out irrelevant recommendations from the suggested ones using the user's personal preferences and interests. To evaluate the methodology, a baseline-RBR system is developed, which is improved first using ranged rules and ultimately using a hybrid-CBR. A comparison of the results of these systems shows that hybrid-CBR outperforms the modified-RBR and baseline-RBR systems. Hybrid-CBR yields a 0.94% recall, a 0.97% precision, a 0.95% f-score, and low Type I and Type II errors.

14.1 Introduction

An individual's healthy lifestyle impacts the overall health of a population and results in a healthier society [1]. Without a healthy lifestyle, i.e., proper diet, exercise, and controlled body mass index, individuals are prone to various diseases [2] that include lifestyle as an important cofactor [3]. Adopting physical activity is one of the key responses of individuals that helps in promoting a healthier lifestyle [4]. Similarly, wellness guidelines and automatic wellness recommendation systems play roles in public health promotion. These systems provide support for wellness experts in recommending the appropriate physical activity to individuals according to their personal requirements [5]. A healthier lifestyle involves a balanced combination of physical activity, mental behavior, and social interaction with other community members [6–8]. In this study, we focus on the physical activity aspect of a healthier lifestyle. We also focus on the development of a physical activity recommendation system to motivate users to keep their life active by involving themselves in various types of physical activities. Traditional physical activity recommendation systems provide general guidelines in the form of recommendations, which do not provide user-centric recommendations. To fulfill the personal needs of different users, a personalized physical activity recommendation system is required.

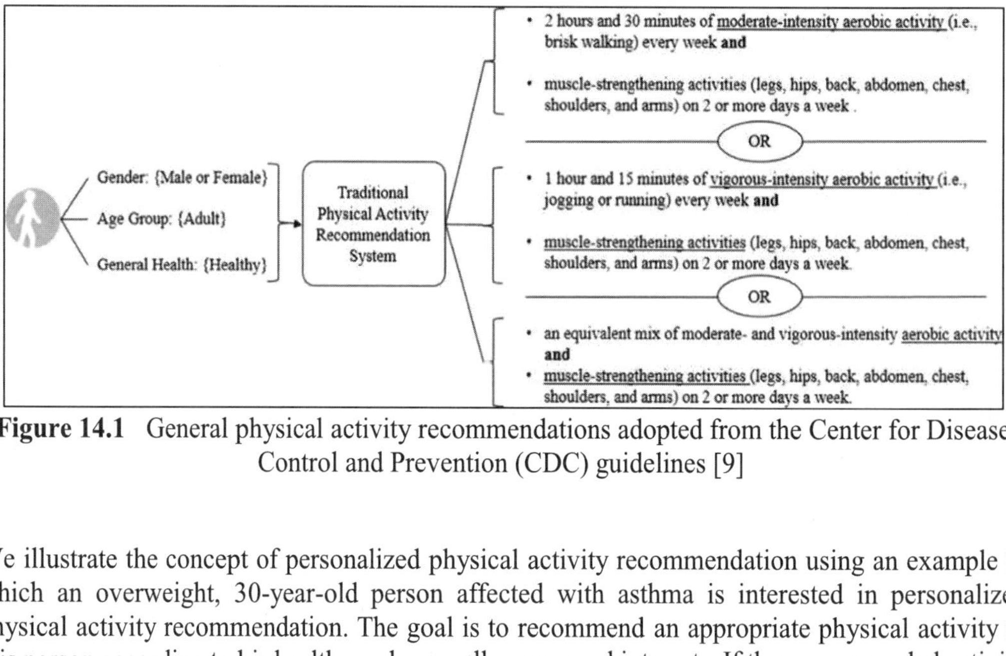

Figure 14.1 General physical activity recommendations adopted from the Center for Disease Control and Prevention (CDC) guidelines [9]

We illustrate the concept of personalized physical activity recommendation using an example in which an overweight, 30-year-old person affected with asthma is interested in personalized physical activity recommendation. The goal is to recommend an appropriate physical activity to this person according to his health needs as well as personal interests. If the recommended activity reflects his requirements, then it will be accepted; otherwise, it will be rejected. Existing physical activity recommendations, pro-posed by CDC [9], WHO [10], AHA [7], among others, recommend general physical activity for the whole community of users. These recommendations are abstract and exploit limited personal information of the users. An example of the CDC recommendations is shown in Figure 16.1.

Figure 16.1 shows that gender, age and health conditions are taken into consideration while suggesting options of physical activities. The following important questions arise:

A. Are the suggested recommendations appropriate for the person considered in the example?

B. Are the provided recommendations based on the user personal information (e.g., BMI), health, physical activities routines and preference list?

The answers to these questions are 'no', which mean that the system provides general guidelines and the user must investigate his personal information, daily routines, and preferences and choose appropriate physical activity for himself. Generally, this should not be the case and the recommendations shall reflect the person's specific needs. The system needs to be intelligent enough to first reason on the user personal profile information and calculate the user's weight status, target weight (goal status), and plan to achieve the goal. Based on these assessments, appropriate physical activity should be recommended according to the user current and past routines of activities and preference list.

To achieve the above stated goal, we are working on a personalized wellness platform called Mining Minds1 [11] (see Section 3.3). Mining Minds is a collection of services, tools, and techniques for collaboratively investigating and analyzing the user's personal profile and daily routines for providing personalized wellbeing services. These services are generated by executing knowledge rules using the Mining Minds (MM) reasoning engine. This study focuses on the reasoning methodology adopted by the reasoning engine to generate daily physical activity recommendations. A multimodal hybrid reasoning methodology (HRM) is proposed, which plays an important role in interpreting the user's profile, physical activity routines, and personal preferences for generating personalized physical activity recommendations. HRM integrates the rule-based reasoning (RBR), case-based reasoning (CBR), and preference-based reasoning (PBR) methodologies for enabling the reasoning engine to personalize the recommendations. RBR of the proposed HRM exploits domain knowledge rules extracted from guidelines, CBR exploits implicit knowledge obtained from experts' experience (successful cases), and PBR exploits users' personal preferences and interests to ensure accurate and personalized recommendations. The key ideas of HRM include the following: (i) exploitation of the diverse knowledge sources for personalized wellbeing recommendations using the integration of multiple reasoning methodologies, such as RBR, CBR and PBR in a linear combination to form HRM, (ii) reducing the bottlenecks of traditional single reasoning methodologies, which exploit only single knowledge sources for generating a single service at a time and (iii) enabling the generation of specific, relevant and personalized physical activity recommendations according to the user's specific requirements.

To validate the proposed HRM, a weight management scenario is considered, and a set of experiments are performed. The use of HRM for weight management is an innovative idea that guarantees specific and precise personalized physical activity recommendations. It is important to mention that our prescription of physical activities only focuses on healthy adults and not on people with disabilities, women who are pregnant and people who have medical complications.

The rest of the chapter is structured as follows. Previous research is summarized in Section 16.2. In Section 16.3, an overview of the MM platform is provided. In Section 16.4, the proposed HRM is discussed from architectural, knowledge acquisition and reasoning perspectives. In Section 16.5, the experiments are performed, and the system is evaluated based on a weight management scenario. In Section 16.6, a discussion on the methodological aspects of the chapter, different challenges faced, and limitations of the approach is provided. Section 16.7 concludes the work performed and outlines some possible future extensions. Section 16.8 acknowledges the contributors and financial sponsors.

14.2 Related work

Human experts are limited in number and expensive in terms of healthcare and wellness services provided. Healthcare decision support systems play effective roles in overcoming the shortage of human experts and improving quality of life with better services [12]. Decision support systems rely on automatic reasoning methodology for their decisions. Most of these systems are based on a single methodology for reasoning, such as CBR or RBR [13], among others. Nevertheless, a few uses multiple reasoning app-roaches with a certain integration strategy. The integration of multiple reasoning methodologies in a single system has attracted increased attention in the research community due to the improved performance with respect to accuracy. The analogy of integration of reasoning methodologies is adopted from the decisions made by domain experts, who rely on multiple knowledge sources rather than a single source. Domain experts use information from general guidelines, clinical trials, and past successful cases to arrive at a final decision. In automatic reasoning systems, the concept of multimodal reasoning methodology evolved from the use of heterogeneous knowledge sources to generate the final decision [13]. The knowledge source, such as guidelines and past successful cases are modeled as knowledge rules and case bases that require RBR and CBR for their executions.

The integration of reasoning approaches can follow any set of strategies, such as RBR followed by CBR, CBR followed by RBR and RBR and CBR in parallel [13,14]. In the first strategy, RBR is used as the main methodology for making the decision. If RBR fails, CBR is used [15]. In the second strategy, CBR is used for the master reasoning process and RBR is used to refine the decision [16]. An example of this strategy is reasoning system for diabetes management [17]. The CBR refines the rules for the outcome, specific to the patient's requirements. In other combinations, CBR and RBR are used in parallel, where either both outcomes are simply displayed or the best one is displayed based on some criteria. An example of parallel integration is the WHAT system [18,19], which is used for training beginning sports medicine students to design exercise regimens for patients with cardiac or pulmonary disorders. The regimens are produced by RBR and CBR in parallel and presented to the experts for choosing the best one. Other methodologies exist that closely cooperate with each other for generating final decisions [20,21]. Apart from RBR and CBR, filtration-based approaches, such as content-based filtration [22] and collaborative filtration [23,24] are also popular in the area of recommender systems for online shopping, product selection, and healthcare services. Preference-based recommender systems are used in e-applications such as e-commerce to offer alternative or cross-selling products to customers [25].

In the healthcare domain, hybrid reasoning approaches have been frequently used. In treatment planning for adolescent early intervention, hybrid CBR that uses RBR and fuzzy theory has been implemented [26]. For supporting physicians for the management of diabetes mellitus, integration of CBR, RBR and model-based reasoning (MBR) [27] and web-based CBR [28] has been proposed. For cancer decision support services, CBR has been integrated with RBR. The CBR part is used to adapt the production rules for decision making [21]. A recent study [29] integrates rough set theory and correlation analysis in a hybrid model, called H2RM, that predicts the diabetes type and manages patient observations for future trend analyses. Other similar studies can be found that focus on heart disease [12] and oncology [13], among others.

In the wellness field, the knowledge acquisition and reasoning engine (KARE) [5] is used in activity awareness for human-engaged wellness applications (ATHENA) [6] to promote active lifestyles. KARE uses the hybrid reasoning methodology by integrating the Random Forest, Naïve Bayes, and IB1 approaches. KARE generates food, physical activity, and music therapy recommendations for ATHENA users. For the elderly, an intelligent personalized exercise recommendations system is proposed [30] that utilizes the user's health status, goals and preference information. Similarly, a hybrid CBR/RBR approach has successfully been used for designing nutritional menus [31].

All these methodologies have the common basis of being used in an exclusive manner. They do not guarantee a minimization of the shortcomings of RBR and CBR, which are discussed as follows:

Conventional RBR systems lack the capability of specializing recommendations for individuals. In general, to deal with specific requirements of users and provide user-centric specialized recommendations, it is necessary to gradually increase the number of rules in the knowledge base. This approach not only results in knowledge base intractability problem, but also causes maintenance and combinatorial explosion issues [32].

Standard CBR systems provide solutions for new problems using a large and unbiased case base as implicit knowledge. However, the requirement of a large case base is a difficult task and associated with several other issues, such as physical storage, proper indexing and computational complexities [33]. The preparation of the query cases to feed the CBR cycle for generating physical activity recommendations is a challenging task.

There have been significant improvements in the integration of these methodologies in hybrid systems [34]; however, several challenging issues still need to be resolved for applying integration in the wellness domain.

The proposed HRM mitigates these problems by integrating RBR, CBR, and PBR in a sequential manner that exploits guideline rules, past successful experience cases and the personal preferences of users to enable personalization of recommendations.

14.3 Reasoning in Mining Minds platform

Advancement in technology greatly impacts the means of service provisioning to the community by employing innovative and state-of-the-art techniques. This includes handling real-time data streaming by utilizing a big data infrastructure with cloud data storage and processing abilities. Our indigenously developed MM platform [11,35] provides a comprehensive picture of the usage of these technologies for monitoring users and collecting information that can facilitate the use of healthcare applications on a global scale. An abstract design view of the MM healthcare platform is shown in Figure 14.2.

A multimodal hybrid reasoner is a key component of MM and plays the role of an intelligent service provisioning agent. It per-forms execution on the server side of the SCL and enables personalization of physical activity recommendations by integrating data and knowledge from diverse sources. The focus of this chapter is on the reasoning methodology and its usefulness in MM for generating personalized physical activity recommendations.

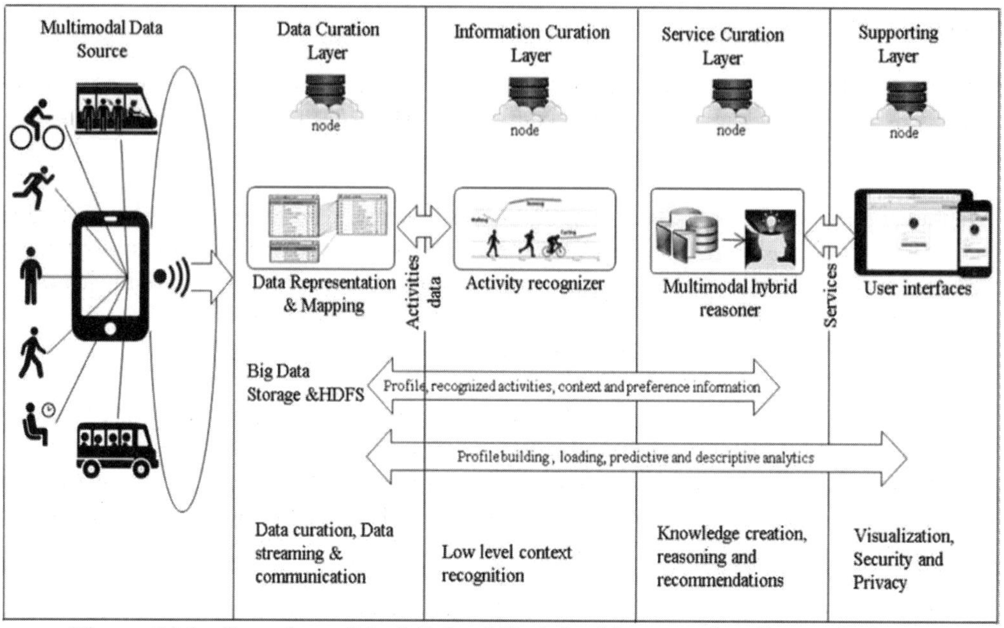

Figure 14.2 Overview of the Mining Minds healthcare and wellness platform

14.4 Multimodal hybrid reasoning methodology (HRM)

For building an intelligent physical activity recommendation system, we moved beyond the traditional single reasoning methodology systems to a multiple reasoning methodology system. Our work integrates RBR and CBR with PBR into a single methodology called multimodal hybrid reasoning methodology (HRM). HRM forms the basis of multimodal hybrid reasoner for the MM platform, which is the focus of this study. In HRM, these methodologies can be integrated in any of the following design strategies, shown in Figure 14.3.

In Figure 14.3 (a–c), the sequence of the design strategy of baseline-RBR is as follows: level-1 RBR is followed by level-2 RBR, which is followed by level-3 RBR and PBR. The design strategy of the modified-RBR follows the same strategy as the baseline-RBR, except for the ranged-METs2 rules, which are used at the level-3 RBR. The strategy of hybrid-CBR differs from those of the first two strategies at level-3, where CBR is used instead of RBR. In our study, we use the first strategy for building a baseline system to compare the results of the other strategies. The second strategy is the improved version of strategy 1, which is implemented in MM system (v1.0) but has its own limitations. To eradicate the shortcomings of the first two strategies, the third strategy of hybrid-CBR is used, which integrates RBR, CBR, and PBR. This strategy is experimented and realized outside the MM platform on a local set up in our lab.

Based on the idea illustrated above, we have defined the core components of the proposed multimodal hybrid reasoner and depicted them in the functional flow diagram shown in Figure 14.4.

Figure 14.4 shows high-level interactions of the different components of the reasoner along with the methodology used in each component. Like any other reasoning system, the core components of the proposed reasoner include the following: input/output interfaces, input data sources, knowledge bases, reasoning methodology and outputs. They are explained below as follows.

Input/output interfaces: user's smart phone that runs the MM application works as the input/output interface for the reasoner.

Input data sources: inputs of the reasoner include user requests, personal profile data, and daily physical activity data. The input data, except for the user requests, are stored in an intermediate database. The request for recommendation is received from the user's mobile application.

Knowledge base: knowledge of the reasoner is composed of rules created from physical activity guidelines and past successful cases obtained from the implicit experience of the domain experts. The rules are stored in the rule base, while the past successful cases (METs index) are stored in the METs case base (METCB).

Reasoning methodology: the reasoning methodologies include RBR, CBR, and PBR, which are integrated in a linear combination. The RBR methodology is applied at multiple levels: level-1, level-2, and level-3. At level-3, RBR is either used with distinct-METs rules or with ranged-METs rules. At the same level, CBR can also be used (using METs cases) as a counterpart of RBR for improved services. At the end, the multi-level filtration mechanism is applied in PBR to filter out irrelevant recommendations by utilizing the user's preferences and interests.

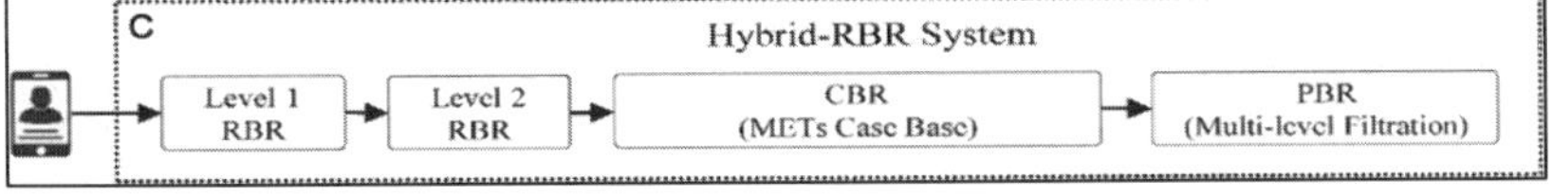

Figure 14.3 Multiple design views of the proposed hybrid reasoning methodology based on integration of different reasoning methodologies

Outputs: outputs of the reasoner include wellbeing recommendations for users, weight status, weight management plans, personalized physical activity recommendations and personalized filtered physical activity recommendations. These recommendations are aggregated and prepared by Results Propagator and then delivered to the end user and intermediate database. In the intermediate database, it is stored for future use as a successful case.

In the subsequent sub-sections, a detailed description of the architectural design of the proposed HRM is provided, and then, the process of knowledge creation is discussed; finally, the reasoning methodology is described in detail.

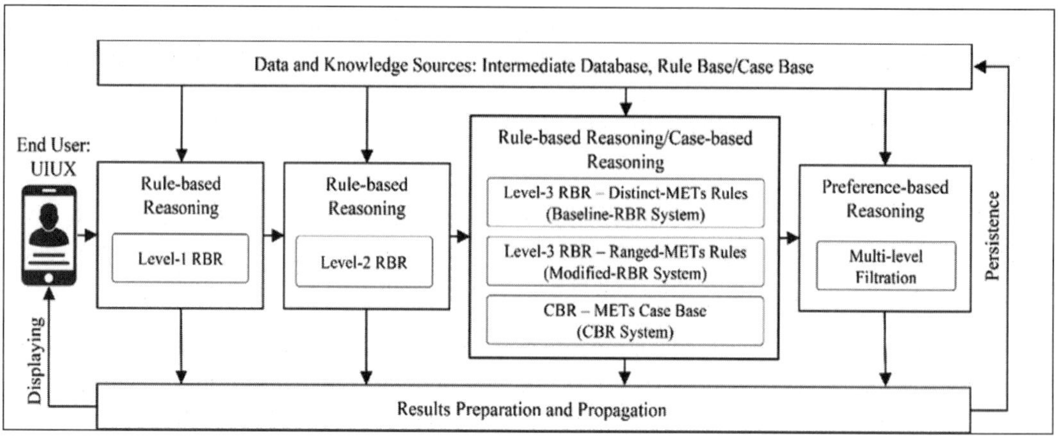

Figure 14.4 Functional flow diagram of the proposed multimodal hybrid reasoning engine

14.4.1 Architectural design and workflow

A detailed data flow diagram of the multimodal hybrid reasoning engine illustrating communication is shown in Figure 14.5.

The key components of the HRM are service request handler (SRH), data loader and manipulator (DLM), knowledge base (KB), knowledge loader (KL), hybrid reasoner (HR) and result preparator and propagator (RP). The hybrid reasoner consists of RBR, CBR, and PBR modules along with the PR module. The RBR, CBR, and PBR modules work cooperatively in a linear combination for enhancing recommendations. CBR is the key reasoning methodology that is activated by the output of RBR. The output of CBR in turn activates the PBR methodology to personalize the recommended physical activity.

From the service execution perspective, when a user requests service, the SRH analyzes the request and activates the appropriate module of the reasoner. SRH supports the MM platform for multiple service generation. SRH forwards the request to HR, where the RBR (level-1, level-2), level-3 RBR/CBR, and PBR methodologies are sequentially executed. Outputs of the HR are forwarded to the RP module for final preparation and forwarded to the user mobile application interface (UIUX) for being displayed to the users.

For the weight management scenario, the multimodal hybrid reasoning methodology operates in the following flow.

First, level-1 RBR is applied, which loads the weight status rules (WSR) (see Section 16.4.2) from the KB and the required personal profile data from the intermediate database (IDB) using the data loader (DL) component. The necessary computation on the personal data, e.g., BMI calculation from height and weight information, is performed using the data manipulator (DM) and passed to the level-1 RBR. The level-1 RBR uses RBR methodology to recommend weight status recommendations (normal, overweight, underweight) as a service to the user and to level-2 RBR for further processing.

Level-2 RBR receives the output of the level-1 RBR as input and performs the same reasoning procedure as level-1 RBR for recommending the goal state and associated calorie consumption plan and weight management plans. The level-2 RBR uses the goal and plan recommendation rules (GPR) loaded by KL from the KB and the personal profile data loaded by the DL from the IDB. The purpose is to generate goal and plan recommendations, which are provided to the users as a service and to level-3 RBR/ CBR for further processing.

Level-3 RBR/CBR receives the output of the level-2 RBR as input and further generates physical activity recommendations. Level-3 RBR/CBR supports both the RBR and CBR methodologies. The RBR results in baseline-RBR and modified-RBR systems. The baseline-RBR uses distinct-METs rules, while the modified-RBR uses ranged-METs rules that are loaded from the KB during the activity recommendation generation. The CBR methodology uses the METCB of the historical successful physical activity recommendations. In our case, we use the 2011 compendium of physical activity guidelines [36] as our key physical activity case base, which has physical activity recommendations associated with METs values. In either case (i.e., baseline- RBR, modified-RBR or hybrid-CBR), the list of all the performed physical activities is loaded from the IDB and commutated for the duration, number of consumed calories, remaining calories and corresponding metabolic equivalent (METs) value. The corresponding physical activities for the METs value are recommended and provided to the users. These physical activities are not filtered according to the preferences and interests of the users; therefore, they are forwarded to the PBR module for further personalization.

PBR first receives the physical activities recommended by level-3 RBR/CBR and then loads the personal preferences and interest's information from the IDB. The associated preference-based rules (PR) are loaded from the KB to apply multi-level filtration for filtering out irrelevant recommendations. The final filtered recommendations are personalized according to the user's personal preferences.
The personalized recommendations are passed to the RP for proper preparation and packaging to be forwarded to the user application to be displayed on the user's mobile application.

The user query, intermediate recommendations, and final personalized recommendations are stored in the future case base (FCB) for future use.

14.4.2 Knowledge acquisition

Knowledge is one of the most important ingredients of a reasoning system. This section describes how the knowledge used by the HRM is created. The key methodologies of HRM are RBR and CBR; therefore, we first need to create knowledge in the form of rules and cases. The process of knowledge acquisition is discussed below.

14.4.2.1 Rules base creation

Wellness guidelines are the key source of information for improving the quality of life. Translating guidelines into computer processable rules is a challenging task because it requires the involvement of knowledge engineers and domain experts [37]. In our study, knowledge from the unstructured guidelines of a weight management scenario is translated to rules with the help of three knowledge engineers and two domain experts. Based on the design of our study, the knowledge engineers first studied the weight management scenario, surveyed the weight management guidelines, indexed them, and categorized them into two groups:

(a) standard equations to compute standard values and

(b) indexes to be used in rule creation. An example of the first category is the calculation of calories burned/day, while an example of the second category is the BMI index. These rules are used by the RBR to generate physical activity recommendations. The process of guideline translation is described below.

14.4.2.2 Personal profile assessment

To classify users into under-weight, normal or overweight states, personal profile assessment based on the standard BMI index is required [38]. The BMI index and personal profile information are combined to form rules, which are shown in Table 14.1. For the BMI calculation, the standard BMI formula is used.

These rules are applicable for adults and used by level-1 RBR for finding the weight status of the users.

14.4.2.3 Goal setting and plan management

A weight management system requires goals and the associated plans to achieve the goals. A goal can be either a local goal or global goal (gloGoal). A global goal is the final objective of the user to be achieved, while the local goal refers to a set of sub-goals to reach the global goal. For example, the total weight to be lost is considered a global goal, while weekly targets are considered local goals. To set a global goal in the context of the weight management scenario, first, an estimation of the ideal body weight (idlWgt) is required, which can be obtained using the Robinson JD [39] equation. The difference between the current weight (curWgt) and ideal weight yields the best estimation for the target goal in terms of the number of kg to be lost. The ideal body weight and global goal are computed using Eqs. 1 and 2.

Table 14.1 Weight status rules (WSR) based on the standard Body Mass Index (BMI)

Gender	Age	BMI value	Weight status
M or F	>20	<18.5 kg/m^2	Underweight
M or F	>20	> 18.5 and < 25 kg/m^2	Normal
M or F	>20	> 25 and < 30 kg/m^2	Overweight

Table 14.2 Goals and weight management Plan Rules (GPR) for recommending the goal status and an appropriate plan

Gender Male (M)/Female (F)	Global Goal (gloGoal) - kg	Weight status (WS)	Plan prescription (PP)
M or F	0 (+ive)	Normal or Overweight	Weight Loss Plan (WLP): lose gloGoal(kg)
M or F	= 0 (neutral)	Normal	Weight Maintenance Plan (WMP): motivational statements
M or F	< 0 (-ive)	Underweight	Weight Gain Plan (WGP): gain gloGoal(kg)

$$idlWgt = 51.65\,kg + 1.85\,kg/inch\ over\ 5\,feet\ (man)$$
$$idlWgt = 48.67\,kg + 1.65\,kg/inch\ over\ 5\,feet\ (woman) \qquad (1)$$

The ideal body weight is a debatable topic but has successfully been used in healthcare systems, such as drug dosage estimation [39]and cell transplantation [40]. Therefore, we have adopted it for the estimation of the global goal in our study.

$$gloGoal\,(kg) = curWgt(kg) - idlWgt(kg) \qquad (2)$$

In our system, gloGoal by itself is a user service, but it is aimed towards devising plans for achieving the global goal. The rules defined for identifying appropriate plans, such as a weight loss plan, weight gain plan and weight maintenance plan (GPR), are shown in Table 14.2.
In Table 14.2, we only focus on the first two cases.
Details of the suggested plan, i.e., duration for achieving the global goal, can be computed using Eq. 3.

$$wghRedPlan(days) = roundup\,\left(\frac{7(days)*gloGoal(Kg)}{0.5\,(Kg)}\right) \qquad (3)$$

In Eq. 3, a constant value of 0.5 represents the weight to be lost for one week. From this equation, local goals for weeks and months can be determined by subtracting a weight of 0.5 kg from the weight of the previous week (weekly plan). These plans can also be estimated in terms of the calories burnt (per day, per week, per month, etc.) using Eq. 4.

$$calToBurDay = \frac{gloGoal(kg)*Cal(1kgfat)}{wghRedPlan(days)} \qquad (4)$$

In Eq. 4, Cal represents the number of calories equivalent to burning 1 kg of body fat. All these rules are used for setting the goal, devising plans, and managing weight and are used by level-2 RBR.

14.4.2.4 Physical activities assessment

Once a weight management plan is assessed, monitoring and recognition of the user's physical activities are required. Based on monitoring the previous day's activities, using the accelerometer sensor of the smartphone, the next day recommendations are planned. This process is performed in terms of the duration spent in each activity and the estimated number of calories burnt. The amount of each activity (amtAct) is calculated by taking sum of all the time slots (timSlot) during which the user performed that activity (Act), computed using Eq. 5.

$$amtAct_i = \sum_{j=1}^{t} Act_i timSlot_j \qquad (5)$$

The estimation of calories (Cal) for a specific activity (Acti) in a specific time duration, amtActi, can be estimated by the product of the METs of that activity with the amount of activity and current weight of the subject. This calculation is shown in Eq. 6, which is adapted from the compendium of physical activities [36].

$$Act_i.Cal = Act_i.METs * amtAct_i(h) * weight(kg) \quad (6)$$

METs estimates the capacity and tolerance level of an individual to exercise in which he/she may participate safely without hurting him/herself [41]. We use it in our system to estimate calories from the physical activities and vice versa. In our calorie estimation process, we use the average METs rather than the exact value. The average METs for an activity (e.g., walking) is calculated by considering all types of walking included in the METs guidelines [36] and taking the average. The same procedure is used for other activities that we consider (i.e., running, jogging, transportation, sitting, and standing). The rationale behind the average METs is the limitation of our current activity recognition system in recognizing the exact intensity of every sub-type of activity, for example, walking.
After applying Eq. 6, for all the activities, Eq. 7 is used to sum all the estimated calories.

$$totalBurnedCal = \sum_{i=1}^{a} Act_iCal \quad (7)$$

The remaining calories (remCalToBurn) for the rest of the day (in a daily calorie consumption plan) are computed using Eq. 8.

$$remCalToBurn = calToBurDay - totalBurnedCal \quad (8)$$

The aim of estimating the remaining calories is to recommend the appropriate physical activity using our reasoning system to meet the goals of the day. This recommendation requires the METs value computed from the remCalToBurn using Eq. 9 [36].

$$METs = \frac{remCalToBurn}{(amtAct=1h)*weight(kg)} \quad (9)$$

We use the METs value in both RBR and CBR to recommend the appropriate physical activity. For RBR, rules need to be created using the user's personal information and the required METs value. For CBR, a case base is to be prepared.

14.4.2.5 Rules creations

Based on the estimated METs value and the user's personal information (e.g., age), two types of rules are created. The first type is based on distinct-METs values, and the second type is based on ranged-METs value. The distinct-METs rules are used to build the baseline-RBR system, while the ranged-METs rules are used for building the modified-RBR system. When we considered distinct-METs and age together, we created a total of 122 rules for the 48 distinct-METs values. The distribution of the rules is as follows: 22 rules belong to the Young age group, 33 rules belong to the Older Adults group, and 47 belong to the Adults group. In the context of physical activity recommendation, age plays an important role; therefore, it is considered an essential part of the rules. The transformation of age to different age groups is supported by the guidelines from WHO [10] and UK [42]. These guidelines categorize users into three major age groups: Young (age 5–17), Adults (age 18–64), and Older Adults (age Z65). A partial list of the distinct-METs rules is shown in Table 14.3.

In the MM implementation, we use ranged-METs rules; there-fore, we first define ranges for the METs values used in these rules. According to the well-known physical activity guidelines from the center for disease control and prevention (CDC), American College of Sports Medicine (ACSM) [7], WHO [10], US [43] and UK [42], physical activities can be grouped into three categories: light (<3.0 METs), moderate (3.0–6.0 METs) and vigorous (46.0 METs). According to these guidelines, moderate to vigorous-intensity physical activities are recommended to Young, Adults and Older Adults, but with slightly changed doses and patterns. For example, the Young group is recommended a physical activity of METsZ 3–7, and the Adults and Older Adults groups are recommended a physical activity of METsZ3. However, the Older Adults group is recommended the same physical activities in the range of METs values for the Adult group but with lower intensity and dose due to their lower capabilities for exercise and physical activities. We have formulated these guidelines by considering the threshold value of METs r10.25 for Older Adults, METs r7 for Young and METs r23 for Adults. The light-intensity activities (i.e., METs o3) are appropriate for all age groups because they do not lead to injuries. Based on this grouping of the METs values by the age groups, the ranged-METs rules are defined and summarized in Table 14.4.

14.4.2.6 Case base creation

The CBR part of HRM operates based on well-established past successful cases to generate physical activity recommendations. The cases in the case base are adapted from the 2011 compendium of physical activity guidelines [36]. These guidelines contain a list of physical activities associated with METs values. We used the METs values and the associated physical activities as the two key attributes of our case base. We named this case base the METs case base (METCB). Based on the discussion made in Section 16.4, we extended the number of attributes of the METCB to include an additional attribute, age group. The relationship between age group and METs ranges is represented in Eq. 10 and depicted in Figure 14.6.

$$AgeGroup = AllAge \subseteq Young \subseteq OlderAdults \subseteq Adults \quad (10)$$

In the above Eq. 10 and Figure 14.6, it can be seen that we have added a fourth age group named 'All Age' (METs o3). It is a subset of all of the other age groups because activities of this intensity are not injurious and can equally be recommended to any age group. The current METCB contains 119 instances, which may increase in the future. Table 14.5 presents the detailed characteristics of the METCB.

14.4.3 Hybrid reasoning

Hybrid reasoning is the key methodology implemented in the proposed reasoning engine that generates personalized physical activity recommendations in the MM system. It is composed of RBR, CBR, and PBR and is discussed in the subsequent sub-sections.

Table 14.3 Distinct-METs rules for recommending physical activity in the baseline rule-based reasoning system (baseline-RBR)

Rule ID	Age group	METs	Activity prescription
R#1	Young	2	Walking, household
R#2	Older adults	6.5	Climbing hills with 0–9 lb load; Race walking; rock or mountain climbing
R#3	Young	7.8	Backpacking; hiking or organized walking with a day pack
--	--	--	--
R#122	Adult	15	Running; stairs up

Table 14.4 Ranged-METs rules for recommending personalized physical activity

Rule ID	Age group	METs value	Activity prescription
R#1	Young, Adults, Older adults	<3	Light activity
R#2	Adults	<= 23	Moderate – vigorous-intensity
R#3	Older adults	<= 10.25	Moderate – vigorous (lower intensity level)
R#4	Young	<= 7	Moderate

14.4.3.1 Multi-level rule-based reasoning (Multi-level-RBR)

In HRM, the RBR methodology works at three levels (level-1, level-2, and level-3). Its objectives include the following:

(1) assessment of personal information and recommendation for weight status, (2) assessment of the ideal body weight and recommendations for goals and plans and (3) assessment of the performed physical activities and recommendations for appropriate physical activity. The recommendations of each level are provided to the user, on one end, and to the next level, on the other. For example, the first level of recommendations is provided to the user and to the level-2 RBR. This process involves a sequential flow, and finally, recommendations are generated, which are provided to the users on their mobile applications. The idea of provisioning intermediate results to the users is motivated from the fact that MM system supports the PULL service model, where users can subscribe either to a single service or a combination of services. Using this approach, some of the user's subscribe only for weight status recommendations, while others subscribe

for goal and plan recommendations and physical activity recommendations. If the MM system is constrained only to support the PUSH service model, then it may be enough for the users who require services on the subscription basis but will not support users who require customized subscription-based services.

Algorithm 14.1 Rule-based reasoning for the recommendations of weight status.

```
Input: UID:uid
Output: Weight Status(WS): List Weight Status
Begin
Let SID: sid =Weight Status Service Id
 WSR: Set of Weight Status Rules, WSR =∅
KB: Knowledge Base
Foreach RULERinKB
If (R A sid)
WSR:=WSR [ R;
End If
End
for
Foreach
RULE RinWSR WS : =ExecuteWSRuleR;
uidÞ IfWS=Underweight"
PropgatWSResultsToUIUX(uid;WS);
InvokeLevel2RBRuid;WSðÞ;
Go tostep3
 Else PropgatWSResultsToUIUX uid;
End If
End
for
 FCB:=AddWStatus(uid;WS);
 Exit; End
```

Level-1 RBR.

Once the user query arrives at the HRM, level- 1 RBR gets activated, loads personal profile information, performs the necessary computations, retrieves the WSR (Table 14.1) and starts the rule-based reasoning process [44]. The outputs are provided to the end user and to the level-2 RBR. The steps of the level-1 RBR are listed in Algorithm 14.1.

Function 1 Rulesexecutionfortheweightstatusrecommendations.

```
ExecuteWSRule(RULER, UIDuid)
Let WS =WeightStatus,showing BMI status oftheuser
IDB: IntermediateDatabase
PPROF:PersonalProfile
BMI: BodyMassIndex
RHS: RightHandSide
LHS: LeftHandSide
```

```
Load PPROFofuidfromIDB;
Compute BMI;
IfR:LHS:values=(PPROF and BMI)
WS:=RHS ofR;
EndIf
 Return(WS)
```

In first step of Algorithm 14.1, WSR are loaded from the knowledge base using an iterative loop process. The design of the knowledge base is based on the types of services, and rules are stored accordingly. Therefore, the type of service identifies the type of rules to be loaded. The type of service can be identified by the service Id (sid, in this case). Once the rules are loaded, the execution commences. The definition of ExecuteSWRule() is given in Function 1, and it loads the personal profile data of the user from the IDB and performs the necessary computations. The data loading process of the IDB uses a simple object access protocol (SOAP)-based service, defined in the SCL. Finally, the pattern matching process starts, and when a rule is matched, it is fired, and its corresponding weight status recommendations are generated. The results of this function are returned to Algorithm 14.1 for further processing.

Table 14.5 Goals and weight management Plan Rules (GPR) for recommending the goal status and an appropriate plan

Attribute	Data type	Possible value	Description
Age group	Symbol	{All age, Young, Adults,	Age of the subject
		Older adults}	
METs	Float	Min=1.3, Max=23.0	Metabolic Equivalents of Tasks one hour
Recommendations	String	Physical activities {running, walking, cycling, traveling-bus and sub ways, standing, sitting}	Physical activities

When the weight status recommendations are received by Algorithm 14.1, they are forwarded to the user mobile application interface (UIUX) and to the level-2 RBR. The function PropgatWSResultsToUIUX is responsible for providing the recommendations to the user while the function InvokeLevel2RBR is used to invoke the level-2 RBR. The propagation function first communicates with the user's mobile application and then provides the generated intermediate recommendations along with some metadata for display purposes. In case the intermediate result of the level-1 RBR is the underweight status, then the system propagates motivational and educational statements using the PropgatWSResultsToUIUX() function.

Level-2 RBR.

Level-2 RBR is activated by level-1 RBR for setting goals and prescribing the associated weight loss and calorie consumption plan recommendations. In level-2 RBR, the goal and plan rules (GPR) specified in Table 14.2 are used along with Eqs. 1–4. The algorithmic steps of level-2 RBR are given in Algorithm 14.2.

Algorithm 14.2 Rule-based reasoning algorithm for goals and plans prescription recommendations.

```
Input: UID:uid,WS
Output: WeightLossPlan(WLP)
Begin
Let SID:sid =WeightLossServiceld
GPR: GoalandPlanRules,GPR=0
PP: PlanPrescription
Foreach RULERinKB//KB:KnowledgeBase
If (R A sid)
GPR=GPR;
End If
End for
Foreach RULE R in GPR
PP:=ExecuteGPRRule(RULER,UIDuid)
If PP="WLP"
Let wlPlan:= List oWLPlan4;
wl Plan=ComputeWLPlansInKgAndCalories(); //use Eq. 3
and 4
PropgatWLPResultsToUIUX(uid,wlPlan);
FCB:=AddRecommendedPlan(uid,wlPlan);//See discussion
InvokeLevel3RBR-CBR (uid,wlPlan["caloriesPlan");// See
Algorithm 14.3
Go to step3;
Else
PropgatWMPResultsToUIUX(uid,educational &
motivational statements for Weight Maintenance)
Go to step3;
End if
End for
Exit;
End
```

In Algorithm 14.2, the rules are loaded from the KB on the basis of service type (sid). The service is goal and plan recommendations, and the associated rules are the GPR. After the rules are loaded, Algorithm 14.2 executes ExecuteGPRRule to generate the plan prescription (PP) recommendations. The definition of this function is shown in Function 2, which takes each rule from the GPR and retrieves the required personal profile data from IDB and computes the ideal body weight (idlWgt) and global goal (gloGoal). The pattern matching process then starts, and each attribute of the left-hand side (LHS) of the rule R is checked against the loaded and computed values. When a match is found, rule R is fired, and its right-hand side (RHS) is provided as the PP recommendation. These recommendations are returned to Algorithm 14.2 for further processing. Function 2. Execution of the goal and plan rules for goal and plan recommendations.

Function 2 Execution of the goal and plan rules for goal and plan recommendations.

```
ExecuteWMPPlanRule (RULER; UIDuid)
Let IDB:IntermediateDatabase
gloGoal: globalGoal
idlWgt:idealWeight
PPROF:PersonalProfile
LHS: LeftHandSide
RHS: RightHandSide
PP: PlanPrescription
1. Load PPROFofuidfromIDB;
2. ComputeIdealWeight(idlWgt); //use Eq. 1
3. ComputeGlobalGoal(gloGoal); //useEq. 2
4. IfR:LHS:values =(PPROF; gloGoal)
PP:=RHS of R;
End if
5. Return(PP);
```

If the output retained in PP is weight loss plan (WLP), then the Compute WL plans in kg and calories function is activated for computing daily, weekly, and monthly plans in terms of the number kg to lose and the associated calorie consumption plans. These plans are forwarded to the users and are displayed on their mobile application interface (UIUX) and are also forwarded to level-3 RBR–CBR. The functions responsible for these tasks are Propgat WLP Results To UIUX() and Invoke Level 2RBR — CBR(), respectively. In case the PP value is the weight maintenance plan (WMP), then educational and motivational statements are provided to the users using the PropgatWMPResultsToUIUX() function.

Level-3 RBR–CBR.

In HRM, level-3 RBR–CBR uses either baseline-RBR or modified-RBR or CBR methodology. For these methodologies, an assessment of the performed physical activities is required in terms of the burned calories, remaining calories, and equivalent METs value. This assessment and the computations are performed using Eqs. 5–9. In the baseline-RBR, distinct-METs rules (Table 14.3) are used, while in the modified-RBR, ranged-METs rules (Table 14.4) are used to generate personalized physical activity recommendations. The algorithmic steps for both the baseline-RBR and modified-RBR are given in Algorithm 14.3 and are the same from the methodology perspective but different based on the nature of rules they use.

Algorithm 14.3 Assessment of physical activities and prescription of physical activity recommendations using rule-based reasoning.

```
Input: UID:uid,wlPlan
```

```
Output: PersonalizedPhysicalActivityRecommendations
(PAR):List oRecommendations4
Begin
Let SID:sid = Personalized PhysicalActivityRecommendation
Service APR:activityprescriptionrulesandAPR = ∅
Foreach RULERinKB//KB:KnowledgeBase
If (R A sid)
APR:=APR [ R;
End if
End for
Foreach RULERinAPR
PAR : = ExecuteActPrescRule(RULER; UIDuid)
If PAR=∅
Break;
End If
End for
PropgatPARResultsToUIUX(uid; PAR);
FCB:=AddRBRPAR(uid; PAR); //See discussion
InvokePBR(uid; PAR); //See Algorithm 14.5
Exit;
End
```

Algorithm 14.3 first loads the activity prescription rules (ARP) from the KB based on the service id, specified in the service request. For generating appropriate personalized physical activity recommendations (PAR), the ExecuteActPrescRule() function is used, the details of which are given in Function 3. The physical activities are recommended on the basis of the final computed METs values and the user's personal profile information. The METs value represents the intensity level of a physical activity. Within the same physical activity type, for example, walking, different intensity values exist that range from a METs value of 2.3 to a METs value of 12 [36]. Similar ranges exist for other activities as well, such as running, cycling, transportation, standing, and sitting. In the METs guidelines, a large number of distinct METs values are available, which makes it hard to define distinct METs rules. One of the solutions to this issue is to define range-based METs rules. In the MM implementation for the weight management scenario, METs range-based rules are used.

Function 3 Execution of distinct-METs and ranged-METs rules for physical activity recommendations.

```
ExecuteActPrescRule(RULER; UIDuid)
Let IDB:IntermediateDatabase
METs: MetabolicEquivalentofTask
PPROF:PersonalProfile
AMTACT:AmountofPhysicalActivityPerformed
PAR:PersonalizedPhysicalActivityRecommendations:List
Recommendations
LHS: LeftHandSide
RHS: RightHandSide
```

```
Load PPROF; AMTACT ofuidfromIDB;
Compute
AMOUNTOFPHYSICALACTIVITYperformedsofar;
//use Eq. 5
Compute CALORIESforeachACTIVITY;//useEq. 6
Compute TOTALBURNEDCALORIES;//useEq. 7
Compute REMAININGCALORIES;//useEq. 8
Compute METsvalue;//useEq. 9
If R:LHS:values=(PPROF; METs)
PAR:=RHS ofRULE;
End if
Return (PAR)
```

Once PAR are generated, they are provided to the end users on their mobile application interface (UIUX) using the Propgat PAR Results To UIUX() function. The output of Algorithm 14.3 can be a list of physical activities that are generated either on the basis of ranged-METs rules or multiple physical activities against a single METs value in a rule. To filter this list of recommendations and personalize them to another level, they are provided to the PBR methodology by using the Invoke PBR() function call of Algorithm 14.3.

When the weight status recommendations are received by Algorithm 14.1, they are forwarded to the user mobile application interface (UIUX) and to the level-2 RBR. The function PropgatWSResultsToUIUX() is responsible for providing the recommendations to the user while the function InvokeLevel2RBRðÞ is used to invoke the level-2 RBR. The propagation function first communicates with the user's mobile application and then provides the generated intermediate recommendations along with some metadata for display purposes. In case the intermediate result of the level-1 RBR is the underweight status, then the system propagates motivational and educational statements using the PropgatWSResults To UIUX() function. PBR methodology by using the Invoke PBR() function call of Algorithm 14.3.

Table 14.6 Local similarity values of the attribute 'age group' in the form of similarity matrix

Age group	All age	Young	Older adults	Adults
All age	1	1	1	1
Young	1	1	0	0
Older adults	1	1	1	0
Adults	1	1	1	1

14.4.3.2 Case-based reasoning (CBR)

To overcome the limitations of level-3 RBR implemented in the MM platform, we use CBR for generating more personalized recommendations. The CBR implementation is performed outside the MM implementation in our lab with the aim of enhancing the performance of HRM. The CBR methodology helps in recommending specific physical activity to users based on their gender information and required intensity for physical activity i.e., METs value. The CBR methodology is selected due to its capabilities of (1) recommending specific and precise physical activities to the user, (2) providing a list of top relevant physical activities as recommendations (e.g., walking) with multiple similar alternatives (e.g., running or cycling) and (3) refining the suggested recommendations based on the user's feedback for enhancing recommendation accuracy and specificity. CBR execution follows the standard CBR cycle (retrieve, reuse, revise and retain) to complete the process of suggesting and refining recommendations along with an incremental learning approach. In our study, we are unable to perform the revise step in HRM due to the limitation of the MM system in being unable to handle user feedback. This phase is left as future work.

Retrieve and reuse steps

In our CBR model, the case query contains two attributes, age group and METs value. The age value is retrieved from the personal profile of the user, which is transformed to the predefined age group. The value of the METs attribute is computed from the user's personal profile information and the physical activities the user performed so far. For this purpose, steps 1–6 of Function 3 are used. These values are provided to the retrieve step of the CBR, which starts retrieving similar cases from the METCB. For the retrieval of age group and METs values, two local similarity functions are defined, which are shown in Eqs. 11 and

$$METSim_l(nC, eC) = \frac{d_g(Max_{MET}, Min_{MET}) - d_l(nC_{MET}, eC_{MET}) - 1}{d_g(Max_{MET}, Min_{MET})} \quad (11)$$

Here, METSiml calculates the similarity of the METs between the new query case (nC) and existing cases (eC) in the METCB. Similarly, dg is the global distance function that calculates the distance between MaxMET (maximum METs value in the METCB, i.e., 23 for running) and MinMET (minimum METs value in the METCB, i.e., 1.3 for resting). Here, dl is the most important local similarity function that computes the distance between the METs values of nC and eC.

$$AGSim_l(nC, eC) = \left\{ \begin{matrix} AG_{ij} = 1 & for \forall (i \geq j) \text{ OR } (i = 0 \text{ OR } j = 1) \\ 0 & otherwise \end{matrix} \right\} \quad (12)$$

In Eq. 12, AGSiml is the local similarity function that matches the METs values of eC with nC. The similarity criterion used in the equation is the exact match, which is denoted as value 1. The interpretation of this value is that if the age group of the query case is similar to that of the existing case (i.e.,AGnC =AGeC), then this value will be 1; otherwise, it will be 0. The symmetric view of the local similarity function of this attribute is represented in a confusion matrix shown in Table 14.6.

In the above confusion matrix, the diagonal value of each age group is equal to 1, which shows the exact match relationship of each age group with itself. The age group, labeled as All Age, represents the list of METs values (less than 3) that can be equally recommended to the rest of the age groups; therefore, its value is 1 for all of the other age groups. Similarly, the METs values of the age group Young (less or equal to 7) are also a subset of the METs values of the Older Adults and Adults age groups; therefore, its value is 1 for all these age groups. This makes both the columns identical in the similarity matrix table.

After computing the local similarities, we use the weighted sum global similarity function, Simg, to compute the global distance between nC and eC, as shown in Eq. 13

$$Sim_g(nC, eC) = \beta(AGSim_l(nC, eC)) + \gamma(METSim_l(nC, eC)) \quad (13)$$

Here, β denotes the weight value assigned to the attribute age group and γ denotes the weight value assigned to the METs attribute. The value of β is 0.1 (i.e., β = 0:1), and the value of γ is 0.9 (i.e., γ 0:9). The higher value of γ represents the importance and contribution of the METs attribute in the final decision. For the selection of similar cases, we use k-NN [45] with k 3 to select the top three similar cases and reuse them as the suggested recommendations. In the MM system, the selection of the top three cases provides choices to the users for following any of the proposed recommendations based on their personal preferences and interests. The top recommended activities are of the same intensity or close to each other in intensity and have similar impacts on an individual's health. The acceptance of the top three recommendations is based on the threshold value (confidence), denoted by symbol m. We set the threshold value to be greater than or equal to 95 (i.e., m Z95). If a single case satisfies the threshold, only one recommendation is provided as the final physical activity recommendation. If more than 1 case is retrieved, then PBR is activated for further filtration and personalization of the suggested physical activity recommendations (see Section 16.4.2.4). The confidence value for the acceptance of recommendations is the threshold value, which is computed using Eq. 13. It is the aggregate score obtained from the local similarity values of Eqs. 11 and 12. The method used for aggregation is the weighted sum, which has a higher weight γ = 0:9 for the METs attribute and lower weight β = 0:1 for the Age Group attribute. To set the confidence/threshold value as m Z95 0:05 threshold, we were motivated by the well- known work [46–48] in the statistical community. The authors considered a 95% confidence interval or 0.05 threshold value as the acceptable value for accepting a hypothesis. The detailed working methodology of the proposed CBR is presented in Algorithm 14.4.

Algorithm 14.4 Case-based reasoning methodology for generating personalized physical activity recommendations.

Input: UID:uid,METCBurl, nC:= new Case, where nC∈
PPROF; METs and nC is computedusingEqs. 5–9
Output: PersonalizedPhysicalActivityRecommendations
(PAR)):List oRecommendations4
Begin
Let PAR:= A set of top 3 relevant existing cases as the proposed recommendations
Sim_g[] :=Array of global similarities of existing cases
$METCB_r$:= ReteriveCaseBaseFromKB(METCBurl),Where
$METCB_r$ is thematrix eCmAn, eCm is the set of existing cases,
i.e., eC=eC1,eC2,eC3,...,eCm. Similarly, An is the set of attributes,
i.e., An=A1,A2,A3,...,An
For i=1 toSizeOfCases(METCBr)
Let Siml []:=Array of local similarities of attributes of individual cases
For j=1 toSizeOfAttributes(METCBr)
Siml [Aj]:=ComputeLocSim(nC.Aj,METCBr [i,j]); //use Eqs. 11 and 12
End for

```
Simg [eCi]:=ComputeGlobSim (Siml); //weighted sum method (Eq. 13)
End for
PAR:=ApplyKNN(Simg]); //where k=3
PropgateCBRResultsToUIUX(uid,PAR);
FCB:=RetainCBRPAR(uid,PAR);//See discussion
InvokePBR(uid,PAR);//See Algorithm 14.5
Exit;
End
```

Algorithm 14.4 begins execution when nC is input to the CBR algorithm. In the first step, the ReteriveCaseBaseFromKB() function is used to load the existing cases from KB to the METCBr. For this purpose, the URL of METCB, METCBurl, is used. Each eC is matched against nC, and the distance is calculated using the local and global similarity functions (i.e., Eqs. 11 and 12). k-NN with k ¼ 3 is used to obtain the top three similar cases as the suggested physical activity recommendations. These recommendations are specific and precise compared with the results of the baseline-RBR and modified- RBR systems. The retrieved case(s) is/are passed to the end users as the proposed personalized physical activity recommendations with the help of the PropgateCBRResults() function. Similarly, this/ these recommendations(s) is/are also forwarded to PBR using the InvokePBR() function to filter them according to the user's preferences and interests.

Retain steps.

Once the reuse step suggests recommendation (s), the whole case needs to be retained in the case base as a new case. In the proposed HRM, we add this new case to a data store, called the future case base (FCB). If the retrieve step ends with a single recommendation, the whole case, including the user's personal profile and suggested activity, is stored in the FCB. However, if more recommendations are generated, the new case is stored in the FCB after applying the PBR methodology.

14.4.3.3 Preference-based reasoning (PBR)

The recommendations generated by the RBR and CBR methodologies are based on the knowledge created based on general guidelines, which are unable to reflect the user's personal interests and preferences. These recommendations are not personalized from the perspective of the user's personal interests and preferences; to satisfy them, another level of refinement and filtration of the suggested recommendations is required that is performed by the PBR methodology. The PBR mechanism exploits the user model, built on top of the user profile. A user model contains the user's personalized requirements, such as preferences and interests. This information is initially acquired from the user, during the registration process and updated thereafter. The recommendations provided by the RBR and CBR exploit data only from the user's personal profile and physical activity behaviors and do not take into account the preferences. When recommendations are pro- vided on the basis of these methodologies, multiple interpretations can be made. For example, consider a scenario where a user U requires X METs of physical activity to burn an amount Y of calories. The RBR or CBR can generate the following set of recommendations for the mentioned scenario.

Walking M1 minutes OR Running M2 minutes OR Cycling M3 minutes OR Hiking M4 minutes, etc.

These recommendations are equivalent and can meet the user's requirement mentioned in the scenario' however some of them may not fit the user's personal interests and preferences adequately. It may be that the user is interested in walking and cycling but not in running and hiking. Therefore, the final recommendations should only include walking and cycling.
To obtain the user's final preference-based personalized recommendations, we propose a multi-filter approach implemented as part of the PBR. According to this approach, filtered personalized physical activity recommendations (FPAR) are obtained from the list of generated personalized physical activity recommendations using the user preferences (UPrefrences). This process of filtration is shown in Algorithm 14.5.

Algorithm 14.5 Filtration of the personalized physical activity recommendations using user preferences.

```
Input: UID:uid,PAR
Output:
FilteredPersonalizedPhysicalActivityRecommendations(FPAR):List
ofilteredRecommendations4
Begin
Let UPrefrences[]=List ofuserpreferences
FCB:=FutureCaseBase
FPAR : = Ø
UPrefrences[]= loadUserPrefences(uid);//Load user presences from
userprofile inIDB
Foreach RecommendationRecinPAR
If (Rec A UPrefrences)
FPAR:= FPAR [ Rec];
End if
End for
PropgatFilteredPARToUIUX(uid; FPAR);
FCB:=AddFPAR(uid; FPAR); //see discussion
Exit
End
```

Table 14.7 Personal profile information of the volunteers, WHO participated in the evaluation of Mining Minds platform

User ID	Gender: Male (M), Female (F)	Age (Years)	Height (Feet)	Weight (Kg)	Preferred activities
1	M	26	6.2	84.5	Running, walking
2	M	28	5.7	72.5	Running, walking, cycling
3	M	28	5.8	70.1	Walking
4	M	31	5.4	68	Running, cycling

5	M	31	5.6	71.9	Walking, traveling
6	M	32	6	85.9	Running
7	F	32	5.2	65	Walking, jogging
8	M	37	5.8	75	Walking, cycling
9	F	30	5.2	75	Walking running, cycling
10	M	38	5.8	71	Running, cycling

Table 14.8 Distribution of the physical activities in the METs Case Base

S.No.	Type of activity	Distribution
1	Running	25
2	Walking	56
3	Cycling	18
4	Standing	5
5	Sitting	4
6	Transportation	4
7	Volunteer	7
Total instances		119

The process of preference-based reasoning starts by loading the user's list of preferences, denoted by UPrefrences, from the inter- mediate database. The filtration process is performed in step 2 by taking each recommendation from the PAR and checking it against the preference list of the user. If the recommendation does not satisfy the user's preference, it is filtered out; otherwise, it is added to the filtered list FPAR. This process is continued till all of the recommendations in PAR are checked. Finally, the filtered personalized recommendations are provided to the user on his mobile application interface using the PropgatFilteredPARToUIUX() function. At the same time, the final FPAR are retained in the FCB as the recommended physical activity. This incrementally grows the FCB, which can be best used in future for successful cases of physical activity recommendations.

14.5 Experiments and Evaluation

For evaluating the performance of the proposed HRM, we per-formed the following set of tasks. Initially, we defined a weight management scenario, then set up a set of experiments, and finally performed the experiments and analyzed the results.

14.5.1 Case-study: weight management

We considered and implemented a weight management scenario for healthy individuals who are overweight or tend to overweight. After implementation of the methodology, we asked ten volunteers (ages 26–38 years) to use the system for a couple of weeks. The basic personal information of these individuals is shown in Table 14.7.

The individuals were asked to use the application during the specified period of time and follow the recommendations pro-vided. During the user's physical activity, the mobile application collected the user's daily physical activity data using the accelerometer sensor of the smartphone. These activities included sit-ting, standing, moving in a bus, moving in a subway, walking, running and cycling, which are recognized by the activity recognizer module (in the ICL) of the Mining Minds platform (Figure 14.2). For the detailed methodological process of recognition of these activities and the support of ICL, refer to the work of Han et al. [49], and Banos et al., [50]. The data are stored in the DCL, from where they are recognized by the ICL and provided to the SCL for recommending the appropriate physical activity for the remaining targets.

14.5.2 Experimental setup

To perform the experiments, we first set up the required environment, then specified the data and knowledge used for the experiments and finally defined the evaluation criteria.

14.5.2.1 Environment

The implementation of HRM was performed on a distributed framework in the Microsoft Azure public cloud environment. As described in Section 16.3, the MM platform is composed of four layers, and each layer is deployed on an individual virtual instance. The proposed HRM is part of SCL, which was hosted on a standard A3 MS Azure instance with Microsoft Windows Server 2012 R2 as the guest Operating System (OS). HRM communicates with DCL and SL and communicates with DCL to load data for reasoning and storing final recommendations. With SL, HRM provides a recommendation service on the request and response model. The services in SCL are implemented as SOAP-based web services, and their accessibility is defined using service contracts between layers. Web services are implemented in Java and deployed on Glassfish server on virtual machine (VM).

For implementation of the third experiment, hybrid-CBR, which operates on METCB, we used myCBR3, which is an open-source similarity-based retrieval tool. We used the Windows environment on a PC with an Intel Pentium Dual-Core^{TM} (2.5 GHz) with 4 GB of memory.

14.5.2.2 Data and knowledge (rules/case base)

As we evaluate our proposed hybrid-CBR methodology in terms of the performance of the baseline-RBR and modified-RBR systems, we therefore require data and knowledge on all of these systems. For the baseline-RBR and modified-RBR experiments, we used the user's personal profile, physical activity data and knowledge rules created based on the guidelines (Tables 14.3 and 16.4). For the hybrid-CBR experiments, we use METCB, prepared from METs guidelines [36]. The size of our 'METCB' is 119 instances. It contains the activities we focus on in the MM platform. The distribution of these activities in METCB is shown in Table 14.8.

In the compendium of physical activity guidelines [36], "standing" and "sitting" are the sub-categories of volunteer physical activity. More details on the structure of METCB are given in Table 14.5. For the offline testing and evaluation of the methodology, we designed a Test Case Base (TCB) that contains 64 test instances. We prepared these test cases from the original METCB. The method used for defining the value of the METs attribute of the TCB was random value computation. The random value is computed from the METs attribute of the original METCB using Microsoft Excel [51]. The function used for the random value generation is shown in Eq. 14.

$$METs.value = randbetween\,(bottom, top) \qquad (14)$$

Here, bottom represents the minimum value of the METs and top represents the maximum value of METs for the new test cases. We used bottom = 1:3 and top =23. The values 1.3 and 23 are the minimum and maximum values, respectively, of the METs attribute in the original METCB.

14.5.2.3 Evaluation criteria

To evaluate the proposed reasoning methodology, a group of system-centric evaluation criteria are used [52]. We evaluated the system using Type I (False positive-FP) and Type II (False negative-FN) errors, precision, recall, accuracy, and f-score criteria. We do not focus on a user-centric evaluation that addresses the user's satisfaction because in the current implementation, only a proto-type of the MM platform is implemented. The hybrid-CBR experiments were performed in a closed environment in our lab; therefore, we leave user-centric evaluation as future work when the MM platform will be fully implemented with the feedback mechanism.

Table 14.9 Weight status and goal and plan recommendations generated by level-1- and level-2 rule-based reasoning of the proposed multimodal reasoning methodology

User ID	Level-1 RBR (Algorithm 14.1) Results		Level-2 RBR (Algorithm 14.2) results				
	BMI	Weight status	Ideal body weight	Goal (# of Kg to Weight management plan	Duration plan	Calories burning plan	Ideal body weight
1	23.9	Normal	78.0	6.5	weight loss	13	550
2	25.02	Overweight	64.8	7.7	weight loss	15	550
3	23.5	Normal	66.6	3.5	weight loss	7	550
4	25.7	Overweight	59.1	8.9	weight loss	18	550
5	25.8	Overweight	62.9	9.0	weight loss	18	550
6	25.7	Overweight	74.2	11.7	weight loss	23	550
7	26.2	Overweight	52.0	13.0	weight loss	26	550
8	25.14	Overweight	66.6	8.4	weight loss	17	550
9	30.24	Obese	52.0	23.0	weight loss	46	550
10	23.8	Normal	62.1	8.9	weight loss	18	550

14.5.3 Experiments and analysis of the results

As the design of HRM is based on RBR-first followed by the CBR strategy, we therefore first evaluate the RBR and then tailor its results to CBR. During the RBR execution, the level-1 RBR is first executed for reasoning the weight status of all of the subjects using Algorithm 14.1 and presenting the output as recommendations to the users, as shown in Table 14.9. If the weight status is not underweight, the output is fed to level-2 RBR for setting goals and recommending weight loss and calorie consumption plans using Algorithm 14.2. The resulting recommendations of the level-2 RBR are also shown in Table 14.9.

These recommendations include the goal in terms of kg to lose, weight management plan, number of weeks to successfully execute the plan and daily calorie consumption plan. The volunteers were asked to follow these plan recommendations. The objective of HRM is to recommend appropriate physical activities for these plans. The HRM estimates METs values to materialize the plans. The METs estimation is required in two cases:

- At the start of plan, when HRM initially recommends the physical activity for starting the plan.
- During the plan, i.e., the subject follows the plan and the system makes further recommendations.

In the first case, the METs estimation is performed only for the recommended 'daily calorie consumption plan', which is the output of the level-2 RBR. In the second case, the METs estimation is based on the remaining calories (see Eq. 8). Once the METs value is computed, the corresponding physical activity recommendations are generated. These recommendations can be generated using the baseline-RBR, modified-RBR and hybrid-CBR systems; therefore, we perform three different sets of experiments, which are discussed below.

Table 14.10 Physical activity recommendations generated by the baseline rule-based reasoning system

User ID	METs	Personalized physical activity recommendations
1	6.5	i. Climbing hills with 0–9 lb load. ii. Race walking; rock or mountain climbing
2	7.6	X
3	7.8	i. backpacking; hiking or organized walking with a daypack
4	8.1	X
5	7.6	X
6	6.4	X
7	8.5	i. bicycling; BMX ii. bicycling; mountain; general iii bicycling; 12 mph; seated; hands on brake hoods or bar drops; 80 rpm
8	7.3	i. climbing hills with 10–20 lb load
9	7.3	i. climbing hills with 10–20 lb load
10	7.7	X

14.5.3.1 Experiment 1: baseline-RBR system

The purpose of this experiment is to build the initial baseline-RBR system for comparing the results of the systems. The results of this experiment were generated prior to the implementation of the proposed idea in the MM platform. In level-3 RBR, distinct-METs rules, shown in Table 14.3, are used to generate physical activity recommendations using Algorithm 14.3 with exact match criteria. A few examples of the prescribed recommendations are shown in Table 14.10. These are based on the initial calorie consumption plan of the 10 volunteers.

While generating these recommendations, the first METs values for all volunteers are computed based on their calorie plans and then combined with the attribute age group to prepare the data for the rules. The symbol 'X' in Table 14.10 denotes that no recommendation is generated for these query cases. From Table 14.10, it is clear that five out of ten queries cases are unsuccessful and that recommendations could not be generated for them. These include the queries of users 2, 4, 5, 6 and 10. The reasons for the empty recommendations are that these queries do not match any rule described in Table 14.3. The distinct rules used in this experiment use METs values adopted from the METs guideline for physical activity, which does not include the values 7.6, 8.1, 7.6, 6.4, and 7.7. Therefore, no rule with these values exists in Table 14.3, and hence, no match is found during the reasoning process for the specified input query cases. For the detailed evaluation of the baseline-RBR system, the whole 'TCB' is used as a test case. The results are calculated and presented in Figures 14.7 and 14.8, which show that the recall of the baseline-RBR is very low (45%) and that the Type II errors are very high (54.5%). The limitations of this experiment are summarized as follows: (1) creation of distinct rules for each value of METs is a difficult task that results in a rule intractability problem, (2) the closest similar recommendations are overlooked if an exact match is not found, and (3) a high Type II error rate is observed.

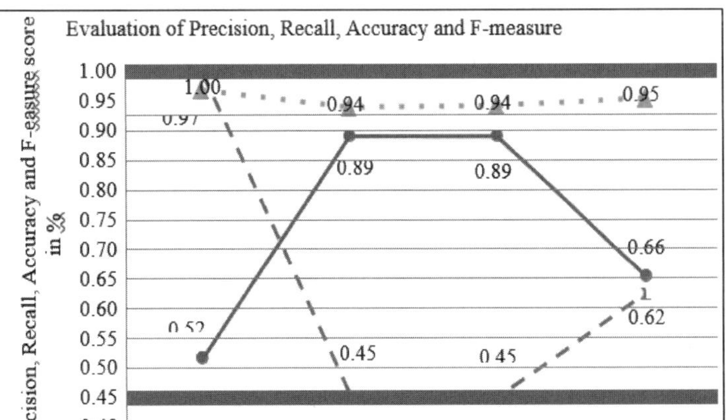

	Precision	Recall	Accuracy	F-measure
Baseline-RBR	1.00	0.45	0.45	0.62
Modified-RBR	0.52	0.89	0.89	0.66
Hybrid-CBR	0.97	0.94	0.94	0.95

Figure 14.7 Comparison of baseline-RBR, modified-RBR and hybrid-CBR system on the basis of precision, recall, accuracy, and f-measure

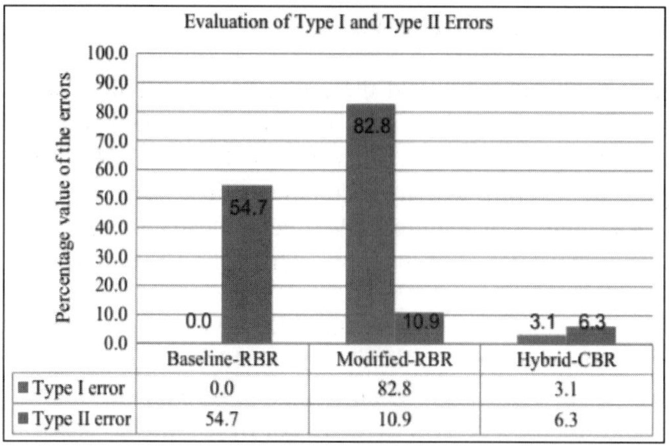

Figure 14.8 Comparison of baseline-RBR, modified-RBR and hybrid-CBR for Type I and Type II errors

14.5.3.2 Experiment 2: modified-RBR system

Based on the lesson learnt from the baseline-RBR system, level- 3 RBR is implemented with ranged-METs rules (Table 14.4) in the MM platform. Algorithm 14.3 is used to execute these rules. To demonstrate the effectiveness of this experiment, we consider an example query for volunteer 4 (Table 14.7) with age group = adults and METs = 8.1 (see Table 14.10). The modified-RBR generates multiple recommendations for this query, though baseline-RBR fails to do so. To fully evaluate Algorithm 14.3, the whole 'TCB' is applied, and the results produced are shown in Figures 14.7 and 3.8. The recall and accuracy are increased from 0.45 to 0.89 and the f-score is increased from 0.62 to 0.66, while the Type II error rate is reduced from 54.7 to 10.9. The advantage of the modified-RBR system is that all queries are served, and no query is returned with empty recommendation results. For example, when the query case with 'age group' = All Age and METs = 2.7 is processed, a total of 17 recommendations are generated, as shown in Table 14.11. When the baseline-RBR is used for this query, no recommendation is generated because the METs value of the query case has no match with the METs values of the distinct rules. However, in the modified-RBR, the ranged-METs rule with a METs value less than 3 is satisfied, and hence, all of the associated recommendations are generated.

Similarly, all of the queries yield results, and no query is unsuccessful. The limitation of the system is its high False Alarm rate (i.e., Type I error), as shown in Table 14.11. From this table, we see that a list of 17) recommendations is generated for a single query.

A summary of the Type I error for this experiment is shown in Figure 14.8. The high False Alarm rate results in a wide scope of recommendations that may not fit well with the user's required physical activity. This effect is normalized in PBR when multiple filters are applied for filtering unnecessary and irrelevant recommendations.

14.5.3.3 Experiment 3: CBR system

The objective of using CBR is to minimize limitations of the baseline-RBR and modified-RBR systems. To overcome these problems, we performed the CBR experiment in a local set up without involving the MM setup. The outputs of level-1 RBR and level-2 RBR and the estimated METs value generate a query case for the CBR methodology. Algorithm 14.4 uses the local similarity function, global similarity function, k-NN with k = 3 and a threshold m 4 = 95 to generate appropriate physical activity recommendations. The CBR methodology has significantly improved Type I and Type II errors, as shown in Figure 14.8. CBR offers the following advantages:

- Type I errors are reduced – k-NN with k 3 retrieves the top cases that are most relevant to the query case and specific to the user's requirement. Hence, the False Alarm rate is significantly reduced.
- Type II errors are reduced, and recall is improved – the global similarity function of CBR with threshold m 4 = 95 has reduced Type II errors. The retrieval of most similar recommendations minimized the False Negative cases and improved recall.
- Relevant and specific recommendations – the retrieve phase of CBR retrieves the top three recommendations that are either exactly the same as required by the user or close to the user's specific requirements for physical activity. Hence, the number of recommendations is reduced to an optimum level on the one hand and is closer to the user's specific requirements on the other.

Table 14.11 Physical activity recommendations generated for a single query case using the modified rule-based reasoning system

Recommendation	# METs	Suggested physical activity recommendations
1	1.3	Riding in a car or truck
2	1.3	Riding in a bus or train
3	1.5	Sitting; meeting; general; and/or with talking involved
4	1.5	Sitting; light office work; in general,
5	2.0	Walking; household
6	2.0	Walking; less than 2.0 mph; level; strolling; very slow
7	2	Sitting; child care; only active periods
8	2	Walking; less than 2.0 mph; very slow
9	2.3	Carrying 15 lb child; slow walking
10	2.3	Standing; light work (filing; talking; assembling)
11	2.5	Bird watching; slow walk
12	2.5	Walking from house to car or bus; from car or bus to go places; from car or bus to and from the worksite
13	2.5	Walking to neighbor's house or family's house for social reasons
14	2.5	Walking; to and from an outhouse
15	2.2	Sitting; moderate work
16	2.5	Automobile or light truck driving
17	2.8	Walking; 2.0 mph

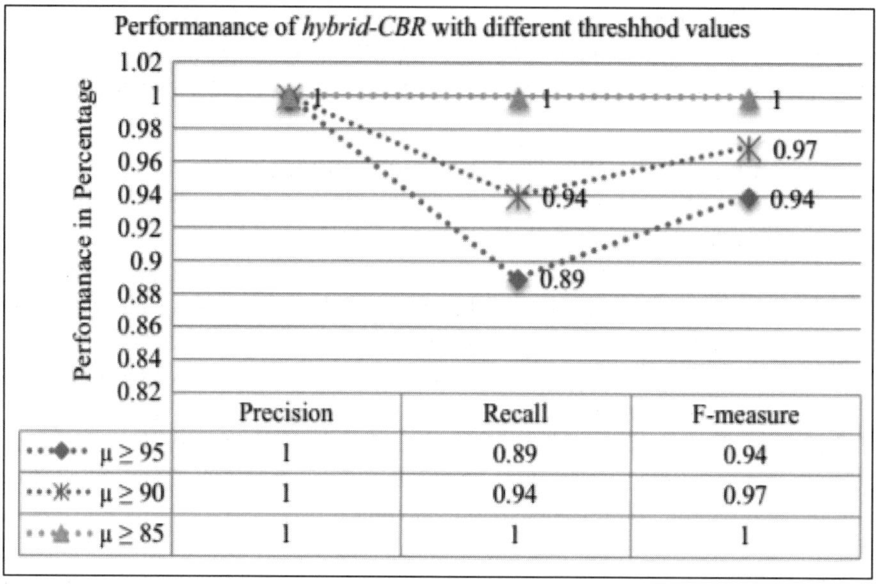

Figure 14.9 Performance of baseline-RBR, modified-RBR and hybrid-CBR with different threshold values

To demonstrate the effectiveness of the CBR methodology for these objectives, we consider the case of 10 volunteers of the MM evaluation team and their estimated METs values (Table 14.10). The initial recommendations for the calculated METs values and age group adults are shown in Table 14.12.

Table 14.12 shows that for each query case, the top three most relevant physical activity recommendations are provided, which fulfills the user's specific requirements. For the query age group = Adults and METs =8.1, baseline-RBR failed to generate recommendations (see Table 14.10) and modified-RBR produced 59 possible recommendation options, but CBR produced only three recommendations (Table 14.12). The difference between the required METs values of the query case and the one using the rules is only 0.1, which is negligible; however, baseline-RBR fails to generate recommendations. This clearly shows the effectiveness of the proposed CBR methodology in HRM.

Table 14.12 Physical activity recommendations generated using case-based reasoning methodology

User ID	New case (METs value)	Retrieved cases (METs value)	Suggested physical activity recommendations
1	6.5	6.5	i. climbing hills with 0–9 lb load.
		6.5	ii. race walking; rock or mountain climbing
		6.3	iii. climbing hills; no load
2	7.6	7.3	i. climbing hills with 10–20 lb load
		7.5	ii. bicycling; general
		7.8	iii. backpacking; hiking or organized walking with a daypack

3	7.8	7.8	i. backpacking; hiking or organized walking with a daypack
			ii. running; training; pushing a wheelchair or baby carrier
			iii. running; marathon
4	8.1	8	i. running; training; pushing a wheelchair or baby carrier
		8	ii. running; marathon
		8	iii. carrying 25 to 49 lb load; upstairs
5	7.6	7.3	i. climbing hills with 10 to 20 lb load
		7.5	ii. bicycling; general
		7.8	iii. backpacking; hiking or organized walking with a daypack
6	6.4	6.3	i. climbing hills; no load
		6.5	ii. climbing hills with 0–9 lb load
		6.5	iii. race walking; rock or mountain climbing
7	8.5	8.5	i. bicycling;
		8.5	ii. bicycling; mountain; general
		8.5	iii. bicycling; 12 mph; seated; hands on brake hoods or bar drops; 80 rpm
8	7.3	7	i. walking; 4.5 mph; level; firm surface; very; very brisk
		7.3	ii. climbing hills with 10–20 lb load
		7.5	iii. bicycling; general
9	7.3	7	i. walking; 4.5 mph; level; firm surface; very; very brisk
		7.3	ii. climbing hills with 10–20 lb load
		7.5	iii. bicycling; general
10	7.7	7.5	i. bicycling; general
		7.8	ii. backpacking; hiking or organized walking with a daypack
		8	iii. bicycling; 12–13.9 mph; leisure; moderate effort

Moreover, to fully evaluate the CBR methodology, we apply the whole 'TCB' to generate recommendations. The results are shown in Figures. 14.7 and 14.8. These results are significantly improved compared with those of the baseline-RBR and modified-RBR methodologies. The green line at the top of the graph in Figure 14.7 shows the performance of hybrid-CBR, which is superior to the other two approaches. Figure 14.8 pictorially shows that hybrid RBR/CBR has improved Type I and Type II error results compared with the other experiments. To present the results of hybrid-CBR with different threshold values i.e., m Z 95, m Z 90 and m Z 85, we applied the 'TCB' and calculated the results, which are shown in Figure 14.9. Figure 14.9 shows that the proposed hybrid-CBR model produces 100% results for precision, recall, and F-score when the threshold m is taken as 85.

Table 14.13 Physical activity recommendations for volunteer no. 8, generated using hybrid case-based reasoning methodology

User ID	Physical activity recommendations based on hybrid-CBR
8	i. walking; 4.5 mph; level; firm surface; very; very brisk
	ii. climbing hills with 10–20 lb load
	iii. bicycling; general

Table 14.14 Personalized filtered recommendations refined using the user's personal preferences	
User ID	**Personalized filtered recommendations**
8	i. To be healthy with normal body weight, you can take a very brisk walk on firm surface with a speed of 4.5 mph
	ii. To achieve today's goal for your required calories consumption, you can perform physical activity of bicycling

14.5.3.4 PBR (preference-based reasoning) results

We evaluated the PBR methodology results using an example and examined the filtration process, which filters the physical activity recommendations generated by level-3 RBR/CBR. Consider the physical activity recommendations, shown in Table 14.13, for volunteer no. 8.

As the preferences of volunteer no. 8 are walking and cycling (Table 14.7), PBR filters out the climbing hills recommendation. Similarly, all recommendations are filtered one by one, and the final filtered recommendations are sent to the result propagator, which forwards the recommendations in descriptive form to the end user. Table 14.14 shows the filtered recommendations in descriptive form.

14.6 Discussion

Physical activity recommendations help users adopt an active pattern of life. In this regard, the 2011 compendium of physical activities guidelines [36] suggests a wide range of activities with different intensity levels that are measured in terms of METs values. The study has described a hybrid multimodal reasoning methodology that has integrated RBR, CBR, and PBR. The RBR methodology is based on domain expert knowledge created from online guidelines for generating intermediate recommendations of goal setting, weight status and goal achieving plans that serve CBR to generate final physical activity recommendations. The goal of hybrid reasoning methodology is to ensure accurate and precise personalization of physical activity recommendations. A number of experiments are performed to demonstrate that the methodology achieves this goal. The results show that the hybrid-CBR system outperformed the baseline-RBR and modified-RBR systems and had significantly improved precision, recall, accuracy, f-measure, and Type I and Type II errors. The baseline-RBR system was tested with 122 distinct-METs rules, and it exhibited specificity with exact match criteria, but suffered from a high False Negative rate, low accuracy and the rule intractability problem. The modified-RBR system was tested with a reduced number of ranged- METs rules and implemented in the MM platform and exhibited improved accuracy, but at the cost of low precision. A large number of recommendations were generated, with the majority being irrelevant to the user requirements. In the results, the correctness of recommendations was compromised by the False Alarm rate, which is generally unsuitable in the context of a personalized recommendation system. For minimizing the Type I and Type II errors and increasing the accuracy, hybrid-CBR was tested, and it outperformed the other two systems.

The challenging issue associated with hybrid-CBR was the design and preparation of the case base. We resolved this issue by creating a case base, METCB, from the compendium of physical activities guidelines [36], user personal profile information. A CBR methodology has a complete cycle starting from retrieval to reuse, revise and retain; however, we did not focus on the revise step. The rational is that revise should be activated once any of the following conditions are obtained: (1) no existing case with confidence (nC, rC) Z95 is found in METCB or (2) the MM feedback mechanism returns user remarks indicating dissatisfaction. As the MM feedback mechanism is not yet built, we did not focus on these options and have planned them for future work. Furthermore, the current 'METCB' consists of only three attributes: age group, required METs value and recommended physical activity. This imposes the constraint of using multi-level RBR prior to applying CBR. The RBR refines the required high-level information from the basic profile and physical activity information to serve the CBR cycle for generating personalized physical activity recommendations. The RBR part of this methodology can be excluded and the complexity can be reduced if a case base with all of the required data, starting from the user's personal profile to the intermediate recommendations and final physical activity recommendations, are prepared and stored in a single case base. This case base will contain the user's personal profile, weight status, recommended plans for weight loss, required METs value, list of recommended physical activities, personal preference list and final filtered list of physical activities. To obtain a case base with the specified schema, we created a case base, named FCB, which incrementally adds new solved cases as successful cases for future use. For this purpose, in Algorithms 14.1–4, we added a statement that populates the respective attributes in the FCB. In the future, this case base will help in directly generating personalized physical activity recommendations. It will also help in validating results of other similar systems.

Regarding the scope of this study, using the weight management scenario, we only focused on a weight loss plan and did not address underweight and normal body weight cases. Therefore, the focus of recommendations is on weight loss plan rather than weight gain plan and weight maintenance plan. To smoothly tackle underweight and normal body weight cases, in Algorithm 14.1 and Algorithm 14.1, we display messages describing educational and motivational statements. However, we have not added details of these educational and motivational statements. In this study, we simply provide statements such as "eat high-fat foods or use protein powders to intake more calories", "maintain a reasonable amount of the exercise routine", and "you are doing good, keep it up" Furthermore, we also provide links to known online resources to educate the user about weight gain and weight maintenance.

We have partially implemented PBR with only a preference- based reasoning technique. The personalized recommendations are filtered one by one on the basis of the user's personal preferences and interests. A PBR system can provide more features; however, our interest lay only in filtering out irrelevant and unnecessary recommendations, and we therefore partially implemented the system in HRM. In the future, a complete user model may add more features to the system in terms of more personalized recommendations.

In the current technologically advanced era, a number of technologies (such as CCTV cameras etc.) can be used to monitor individuals' behaviors, specifically those of the elderly, to provide surveillance services [53]. This reduces the risk of a number of unobserved incidents that mostly occur among the elderly. The traditional surveillance mechanism can be avoided if "personal big data" are introduced to record the recognized daily physical activities of individuals and if analysis operations are enabled for them.

14.7 Summary

This chapter has presented HRM that effectively integrates multiple reasoning methodologies, such as RBR, CBR, and PBR, facilitating adoption and extension for different wellness services. The hybrid- CBR methodology achieves the objective of precise and specific personalized recommendation generation according to the user's specific needs. The application of HRM in a weight management scenario has proved that the precision, recall, accuracy, and f-score of personalized physical activity recommendations can be significantly improved if the integration of these methodologies is performed correctly. Hybrid-CBR achieves 0.97% precision, 0.94% recall, 0.94% accuracy, and a 0.95% f-score on the TCB with 64 test instance cases. Similarly, the Type I and Type II errors are significantly reduced. The significance of the proposed methodology is its preciseness in the recommendations made, which ensures personalization. Furthermore, the proposed methodology can be easily extended to other application areas, which will increase its worth.

In future, we plan to design and prepare an extended case base to host all the relevant information required for generation of personalized recommendations. This will enhance performance of CBR and RBR in HRM. Furthermore, it will reduce the complexity of the HRM. Moreover, the current personalized recommendations are merely based on mode and intensity features that lake 'amount' and 'frequency' characteristics. Hence, we plan to include these aspects in the future extensions. We also plan to extend HRM for recommending physical activity plans in dynamic way, using the user calendar and personal schedule information. Finally, we also plan to extend PBR part of the model by exploiting user model in comprehensive way to ensure more personalization.

Source Code

Mining Minds has been released as an opensource platform over GitHub for fellow researchers to reuse and extend our implementation for other use cases.
Source code can be downloaded from the following location:
https://github.com/ubiquitous-computing-lab/Mining-Minds/tree/master/service-curation-layer/recommendation-builder

The contents of this chapter have been previously published in the following article:

Rahman Ali, MuhammadAfzal, MaqboolHussain, MaqboolAli, Muhammad Hameed Siddiqi, Sungyoung Lee, and Byeong Ho Kang, "Multimodal Hybrid Reasoning Methodology for Personalized Wellbeing Services", Computers in Biology and Medicine (SCI, IF:1.24), Vol.69, pp.10-28, 2016

References

[1] O. Pakholok, The idea of healthy lifestyle and its transformation into health- oriented lifestyle in contemporary society, SAGE Open 3 (2013) 2158244013500281.

[2] M. Sharma, P.K. Majumdar, Occupational lifestyle diseases: an emerging issue, Indian J. Occup. Environ. Med. 13 (2009) 109.

[3] G.E. Fraser, D.J. Shavlik, Ten years of life: is it a matter of choice? Arch. Intern. Med. 161 (2001) 1645–1652.
[4] D.E.R. Warburton, C.W. Nicol, S.S.D. Bredin, Health benefits of physical activity: the evidence, Can. Med. Assoc. J. 174 (2006) 801–809.
[5] R. Ali, M.H. Siddiqi, S. Lee, B.H. Kang, KARE: A hybrid reasoning approach for promoting active lifestyle, in: Proceedings of the 9th International Conference of Ubiquitious Information Managment and Communication ICUIMC (IMCOM) Bali, Indonesia, 2015.
[6] M. Fahim, M. Idris, R. Ali, C. Nugent, B. Kang, E.-N. Huh, S. Lee, ATHENA: a personalized platform promote an active lifestyle wellbeing based physical, mental social health primitives, Sensors 14 (2014) 9313–9329.
[7] W.L. Haskell, I.M. Lee, R.R. Pate, K.E. Powell, S.N. Blair, B.A. Franklin, C.A. Macera, G.W. Heath, P.D. Thompson, A. Bauman, Physical activity and public health: updated recommendation for adults from the American College of Sports Medicine and the American Heart Association, Circulation 116 (2007) 1081.
[8] E. Verhagen, L. Engbers, The physical therapist's role in physical activity pro- motion, Br. J. Sport. Med. 43 (2009) 99–101.
[9] C. Centers for Disease, Prevention, Division of Nutrition, Physical Activity and Obesity, National Center for Chronic Disease Prevention and Health Promo- tion. Healthy weight, 2011.
[10] World Health, Organization, Global recommendations on physical activity for health, 2010.
[11] O. Banos, M. Bilal Amin, W. Ali Khan, M. Afzal, M. Ahmad, M. Ali, T. Ali, R. Ali, M. Bilal, m Han, J. Hussain, M. Hussain, S. Hussain, T.H. Hur, J.H. Bang, T. Huynh-The, M. Idris, D.W. Kang, S.B. Park, M. Siddiqui, L.B. Vui, M. Fahim, A.M. Khattak, B.H. Kang, S. Lee, An Innovative Platform for Person-Centric Health and Wellness Support, in: F. Ortuño, I. Rojas (Eds.), Bioinformatics and Biomedical Engineering, Springer International Publishing, Granada, Spain, 2015, pp. 131–140.
[12] J. Shen, J. Xing, M. Xu, Research on CBR-RBR fusion reasoning model and its application in medical treatment, in: Proceedings of the 21st International Conference on Industrial Engineering and Engineering Management Springer, 2014, pp. 431–434.
[13] D. Rossille, J.-Fo Laurent, A. Burgun, Modelling a decision-support system for oncology using rule-based and case-based reasoning methodologies, Int. J. Med. Inform. 74 (2005) 299–306.
[14] K. Khandelwal, D.P. Sharma, Hybrid Reasoning Model for Strengthening the problem solving capability of expert systems, Int. J. Adv. Comput. Sci. Appl. (IJACSA) 4 (2013).
[15] H.-J. Park, J.-S. Oh, D.-U. Jeong, K.-S. Park, Automated sleep stage scoring using hybrid rule-and case-based reasoning, Comput. Biomed. Res. 33 (2000) 330–349.
[16] G.J. Petot, C. Marling, L. Sterling, An artificial intelligence system for computer- assisted menu planning, J. Am. Diet. Assoc. 98 (1998) 1009–1014.
[17] S. Montani, R. Bellazzi, Supporting decisions in medical applications: the knowledge management perspective, Int. J. Med. Inform. 68 (2002) 79–90.
[18] K. Evans-Romaine, C. Marling, Prescribing exercise regimens for cardiac and pulmonary disease patients with CBR, in: Proceedings of the Workshop on CBR in

the Health Sciences at 5th International Conference on Case-based Reasoning (ICCBR-03), Citeseer, 2003, pp. 45–62.

[19] P. Berka, NEST: a compositional approach to rule-based and case-based rea- soning, Adv. Artif. Intell. 2011 (2011) 4.

[20] I. Bichindaritz, M.F. Siadak, J. Jocom, C. Moinpour, E. Kansu, G. Donaldson, N. Bush, M. Chapko, J.M. Bradshaw, K.M. Sullivan, CARE-PARTNER: a compu- terized knowledge-support system for stem-cell post-transplant long-term follow-up on the World-Wide-Web, in: Proceedings of the AMIA Symposium, American Medical Informatics Association, 1998, p. 386.

[21] J. Lieber, M. D'Aquin, P. Bey, B. Bresson, O. Croissant, P. Falzon, A. Lesur, Julien, V. Mollo, A. Napoli, The kasimir project: knowledge management in cancer- ology, in: Proceedings of the 4th International Workshop on Enterprise Net- working and Computing in Health Care Industry-HealthCom, 2002, pp.125–127.

[22] R. Van Meteren, M. Van Someren, Using content-based filtering for recom- mendation, in: Proceedings of the Machine Learning in the New Information Age: MLnet/ECML2000 Workshop, 2000, pp. 47–56.

[23] D.A. Davis, N.V. Chawla, N.A. Christakis, A.-Ls BarabÃ¡si, Time to CARE: a col- laborative engine for practical disease prediction, Data Min. Knowl. Discov. 20 (2010) 388–415.

[24] S. Hasan, G.T. Duncan, D.B. Neill, R. Padman, Towards a collaborative filtering approach to medication reconciliation, AMIA Annu. Symp. Proc. (2008) 288–292.

[25] B. Satzger, M. Endres, W. KieÃŸling, A preference-based recommender system, in: K. Bauknecht, et al., (Eds.), E-Commerce and Web Technologies, Springer- Verlag Berlin, Heidelberg, 2006, pp. 31–40.

[26] W.M. Wang, C.F. Cheung, W.B. Lee, S.K. Kwok, Knowledge based treatment planning for adolescent early intervention of mental healthcare: a hybrid case based reasoning approach, Exp. Syst. 24 (2007) 232–251.

[27] S. Montani, P. Magni, R. Bellazzi, C. Larizza, A.V. Roudsari, E.R. Carson, Integrating model-based decision support in a multi-modal reasoning system for managing type 1 diabetic patients, Artif. Intell. Med. 29 (2003) 131–151.

[28] L. Nguyen, Z. Sun, A. Stranieri, S. Firmin, CWDM: A case-based diabetes management web system, in Proceedings of the 24th Australasian Conference on Information Systems (ACIS), RMIT University, 2013, pp. 1–11.

[29] R. Ali, J. Hussain, M.H. Siddiqi, M. Hussain, S. Lee, H2RM: A hybrid rough set reasoning model for prediction and management of diabetes mellitus, Sensors 15 (2015) 15921–15951.

[30] M.H. Nassabi H. op den Akker M. Vollenbroek. An ontology-based recom- mender system to promote physical activity for pre-frail elderly, in: Pro- ceedings of the Mensch & Computer Walter De. Gruyter GmbH Co. KG, 2014, pp. 181–184.

[31] C. Marling G. Petot L. Sterling A CBR/RBR hybrid for designing nutritional menus, Multimodal Reasoning: Papers from them 1998 AAAI Spring Sympo- sium 1998, AAAI Press, Menlo Park.

[32] D. Wang, M. Yu, C.B. Low, S. Arogeti, Model-Based Health Monitoring of Hybrid Systems, Springer Science+Business Media, New York, 2013.

[33] A. Aamodt, E. Plaza, Case-based reasoning: foundational issues, methodolo- gical variations, and system approaches, AI Commun. 7 (1994) 39–59.

[34] C. Marling, E. Rissland, A. Aamodt, Integrations with case-based reasoning, Knowl. Eng. Rev. 20 (2005) 241–245.

[35] O. Banos, M. Bilal Amin, W. Ali Khan, M. Afzal, T. Ali, Kang, B. H., S. Lee, The mining minds platform: a novel person-centered digital health and wellness.

[36] B.E. Ainsworth, W.L. Haskell, S.D. Herrmann, N. Meckes, D.R. Bassett Jr, C. Tudor-Locke, J.L. Greer, J. Vezina, M.C. Whitt-Glover, A.S. Leon, Compendium of physical activities: a second update of codes and MET values, Med. Sci. Sport. Exerc. 43 (2011) (2011) 1575–1581.

[37] D. Nassim, J. Marie-Christine, Clinical practice guidelines formalization for personalized medicine, Int. J. Appl. Evol. Comput. 4 (2013) 26–33.

[38] World Health Organization, BMI classification World Health Organization. URL: ⟨http://apps.who.int/BMI/index.jsp⟩, (2013).

[39] J.D. Robinson, S.M. Lupkiewicz, L. Palenik, L.M. Lopez, M. Ariet, Determination of ideal body weight for drug dosage calculations, Am. J. Health -Syst. Pharm. 40 (1983) 1016–1019.

[40] S. Singhal, L.I. Gordon, M.S. Tallman, J.N. Winter, A.O. Evens, O. Frankfurt, S.F. Williams, D. Grinblatt, L. Kaminer, R. Meagher, Ideal rather than actual body weight should be used to calculate cell dose in allogeneic hematopoietic stem cell transplantation, Bone Marrow Transplant. 37 (2006) 553–557.

[41] M. Jette, K. Sidney, G. Blümchen, Metabolic equivalents (METS) in exercise testing, exercise prescription, and evaluation of functional capacity, Clin. Cardiol. 13 (1990) 555–565.

[42] UK, Guidlines, Technical Report: Physical Activity Guidelines in the UK: Review and Recommendations, 2010.

[43] US, Guidelines, Physical activity guidelines advisory committee report, 2008, Washington, DC: US Department of Health and Human Services, 2008, pp. A1–H14.

[44] J.-F. Baget, Improving the forward chaining algorithm for conceptual graphs rules, in: Proceeding of the International Conference on Principles of Knowl- edge Representation and Reasoning, 2004, pp. 407–414.

[45] T. Cover, P. Hart, Nearest neighbor pattern classification, Inform. Theory IEEE Trans. 13 (1967) 21–27.

[46] J. Neyman, Outline of a theory of statistical estimation based on the classical theory sof probability, Philosophical Transactions of the Royal Society of London, Ser. A, Math. Phys. Sci. 236 (1937) 333–380.

[47] D.G. Altman, S.M. Gore, M.J. Gardner, S.J. Pocock, Statistical guidelines for contributors to medical journals, Br. Med. J. (Clin. Res. Ed.) 286 (1983) 1489–1493.

[48] R.A. Fisher, Statistical Methods for Research Workers, Genesis Publishing Pvt Ltd, Edinburgh, Tweeddale Court London, 1925.

[49] M. Han, Y.-K. Lee, S. Lee, Comprehensive context recognizer based on multi- modal sensors in a smartphone, Sensors 12 (2012) 12588–12605.

[50] O. Banos, J. Bang, T. Hur, M.H. Siddiqi, T. Hyunh-The, L.B. Vui, A. Khan, A.T. W., C. Villalonga, S. Lee, Mining Human Behavior for Health Promotion, in: Pro- ceedings of the 37th Annual International Conference of the IEEE Engineering in Medicine and Biology Society (EMBC 2015) Milano, Italy, 2015.

[51] Microsoft, Microsoft Excel 2010 [computer software], Version 14.0.4760.1000 (32-bit), Microsoft Corporation, 2010.

[52] P. Pu, L. Chen, R. Hu, Evaluating recommender systems from the user's perspective: survey of the state of the art, User Model. User -Adapt. Interact. 22 (2012) 317–355.

[53] S.C. Mukhopadhyay, N.K. Suryadevara, R.K. Rayudu, Are Technologies Assisted Homes, Safer for the elderly? Pervasive Mob. Sens. Comput. Healthc. 2 (2012).

Part VI

Security, Privacy, and UI/UX

Chapter 15

Security & Privacy

Health Fog: A Novel Framework for Health and Wellness Application

Mahmood Ahmad, Muhammad Bilal Amin, Shujaat Hussain, Byeong Ho Kang, and Sungyoung Lee

In the past few years the role of e-health applications has taken a remarkable lead in terms of services and features inviting millions of people with higher motivation and confidence to achieve a healthier lifestyle. Induction of smart gadgetries, people lifestyle equipped with wearables, and development of IoT has revitalized the feature scale of these applications. The landscape of health applications encountering big data need to be replotted on cloud instead of solely relying on limited storage and computational resources of handheld devices. With this transformation, the out-come from certain health applications is significant where precise, user-centric, and personalized recommendations mimic like a personal care-giver round the clock. To maximize the services spectrum from these applications over cloud, certain challenges like data privacy and communication cost need serious attention. Following the existing trend together with an ambition to promote and assist users with healthy lifestyle we propose a framework of Health Fog where Fog computing is used as an intermediary layer between the cloud and end users. The design feature of Health Fog successfully reduces the extra communication cost that is usually found high in similar systems. For enhanced and flexible control of data privacy and security, we also introduce the cloud access security broker (CASB) as an integral component of Health Fog where certain polices can be implemented accordingly. The modular framework design of Health Fog is capable of engaging data from multiple resources together with adequate level of security and privacy using existing cryptographic primitives.

15.1 Introduction

In the past few years, health and wellness applications have emerged as a fast-growing category of mobile applications. This increasing trend is considered as a prompt and useful resource for collecting users' data which are used for generating recommendations for a healthy lifestyle. Using smart phone features, applications like Microsoft Health, Apple HealthKit, Samsung S Health, and Google Fit collect user's data by monitoring their daily activities, e.g., eating habits, sleeping patterns, and workout routines to generate certain recommendations which are helpful in maintaining a healthy lifestyle. To expand the spectrum of these recommendations, the data acquired from smart phones can be further synergized with other data resources like wearable sensors and a smart home environment. The processing on this integrated data acquired from various resources encompasses comprehension towards overall recommendations, thus creating the favorable environment to further engage other possible data resources including, but not limited to, social media and personal health records too. This expansion on data intake from various resources enables health and wellness applications to advise personalized and user-specific recommendations rather than giving general tips for a healthy lifestyle. Due to this reason the adaptation rate of such applications is on the rise with downloads in millions [1–4]. These applications offer a variety of features and plans like weight-loss, calorie-counter, women-health, and activity-recognition. To maximize the feature space of an application there is another trend of data-cross-sharing in which one application can share its data with the other, e.g., Fitocracy [5] can share its data with the RunKeeper [1].

The amount of data generated by smart phones and supportive need to include data from other resources make data volume enormous and its structure more complex. Although smart phones are sufficiently equipped with large memory size and computational resources for on-device storage and processing ability, however, to achieve increased battery life, data backup, centralized data storage, and to fulfill data-cross-sharing, there is another approach gaining momentum in a majority of applications which is the adoption of cloud services. Applications that used to store data locally are swiftly moving towards centralized data storage through the cloud. Using cloud services, applications can conveniently afford inclusion of data from multiple resources and subsequent execution of substantial and complex computations. In addition, the application access also become more flexible and ubiquitous in comparison to the legacy approach where only a single device has the privilege to exploit application features on which it is installed. A user can now access these applications more seamlessly on a range of devices from mobile devices to fixed terminals and even across various applications. The problems of data loss in case of malfunctioning or stolen device is an allied advantage of using cloud services for convenient recovery.

Mobile health applications are being designed to promote fitness and track beneficial health metrics aiding healthy living. To monitor and track daily activities there is a huge rack of applications with variety of services. After selecting few of them, we organize and very briefly explain their features in certain groups to analyze growth and trend of offered services as shown in Figure 15.1.

15.1.1 Data Source

The integrated sensors within a smart phone are the initial and foremost sources for data acquisition. For personalized recommendations the sensory information is fused together with user profile like her age, gender, BMI index, weight, food preferences, and disability information. In addition, many applications also acquire and utilize data generated by physical devices including wearables and IoT (internet of things) like pedometer, heart rate monitor, surveillance camera, and smoke detector. The social media and clinical data are a gradual and influential addition being considered while generating the user-centric recommendations.

15.1.2 Storage and Security

The data generated by health applications are usually stored on the user device. While opting for on-device storage, majority of applications lacks backup strategy of data and also do not employ encrypted data storage, thus considering physical possession of a device sufficient against data protection. This assumption of protection fails when a user is deprived of her device and loses it due to some reason. In this situation the device offers same privileged data access to any unauthorized user having the device possession. Also, the same situation leaves no alternate option for data recovery as well. Due to these reasons and realizing the necessity of protecting the applications data, its storage is deemed essential with encrypted storage along with opting for a storage location where data can be restored conveniently. Realization of these facts introduce the pivotal role of cloud computing as a growing trend amongst health applications. With ever increasing sophistication and integrated sensors in smart phones, health applications create enormous amount of data that are now more convenient to store and process with the induction of cloud. With this convenience, health applications can easily afford to engage and process data which are generated by other devices (IoT), wearables and third-party applications along with the data that are generated indigenously. This homogenization expands and evolves data into big data as current era of health applications deals with more volume, variety, and velocity of data used ever before. With this transformation, the data-driven health applications can now generate more realistic and personalized recommendations in comparison to legacy approach of generating general recommendation due to limited input of available data.

Features / Systems	ata Source						Storage & Security				U /UX			ervices						Inf rmation Sharing			owledge Maintenance		
	Sensory Data	User profile	IOT	Other apps	Clinical data	Soc al media	User dev ce	Cloud storage	B g data storage	Encrypted storage	User Experience	User Modelling	Adaptation of UI	Activ ty Recogn tion	Expert Svc	Wellness svc	Personal recommendation	Clinical svc	SDK/API	W th other apps	Soc al media	Other users	Open Knowledge	Knowledge acquis tion	Knowledge evolution
Google Fit	☑	☑	☑	☑	☒	☒	☑	☑	☑	☑	☒	☑	☒	☑	☑	☑	☒	☒	☑	☑	☑	☑	☑	☑	☒
Samsung S health	☑	☑	☑	☑	☒	☒	☑	☑	☑	☑	☒	☑	☒	☑	☒	☑	☑	☑	☑	☑	☑	☑	☑	☑	☒
M crosoft health	☑	☑	☑	☑	☑	☑	☑	☑	☑	☑	☒	☑	☒	☑	☑	☑	☑	☑	☑	☑	☑	☑	☑	☑	☑
Apple healthkit	☑	☑	☑	☑	☒	☒	☑	☑	☒	☑	☒	☑	☒	☑	☑	☑	☑	☒	☑	☑	☑	☑	☒	☑	☒
Open m ealt	☑	☑	☑	☑	☒	☒	☑	☑	☒	☒	☒	☑	☒	☑	☑	☑	☑	☒	☑	☒	☑	☑	☒	☑	☒
NoomCoac	☑	☑	☑	☑	☒	☒	☑	☑	☒	☒	☒	☑	☒	☑	☑	☑	☑	☒	☒	☑	☑	☒	☒	☑	☒
Argus	☑	☑	☑	☒	☒	☒	☑	☑	☒	☑	☒	☑	☒	☑	☑	☑	☒	☒	☒	☒	☑	☒	☒	☑	☒
Runtastic	☑	☑	☑	☑	☒	☒	☑	☑	☑	☑	☒	☑	☒	☑	☑	☑	☑	☒	☑	☑	☑	☒	☑	☑	☒
Runkeeper	☑	☑	☑	☑	☒	☒	☑	☑	☑	☑	☒	☑	☒	☑	☑	☑	☒	☒	☑	☑	☑	☒	☑	☑	☒
Zomb e Run	☑	☑	☒	☒	☒	☑	☑	☑	☒	☒	☒	☑	☒	☑	☒	☑	☒	☒	☒	☒	☑	☒	☒	☑	☒
M ning M nd	☑	☑	☑	☒	☑	☑	☑	☑	☑	☑	☑	☑	☑	☑	☑	☑	☑	☑	☒	☒	☑	☑	☑	☑	☑

Figure 15.1 Health and wellness applications: features survey and their categorization

15.1.3 User Interface (UI)/User Experience (UX)

The user interface (UI) has an important and profound role between the application and its user. The information on user interaction can be collected through user interface to maximize user experience. The importance of this aspect in modern applications is due to the fact that static interface lacks the ability to reflect user needs and satisfaction. In certain situations, the interface has to be redesigned and adjusted with respect to specific needs of its users, e.g., increased font size for a user with week eyesight. In this regard, the information from user profile data (age, gender, week eyesight or any other disability) together with the contextual information (mode, time of the day, weather, etc.) can be used for customizing the application interface. The application designed on these features adapts itself according to the situation and makes user experience more comfortable while interacting with the application. In addition, involving user feedback through continuous monitoring of how she interacts with the application adds more refinement and perfection for enhanced user experience.

User experience is an evolutionary process to adapt and personalize the user interface. The personalization aspect is the most important factor and is achievable with user involvement where interface is dynamic and subject to user experience. The adaptive UI is managed by the UX, user feedbacks, and movement in the application which is then fused with the user profile data. The user movements encompass number of clicks, color schemes, text size, brightness and navigation within the application. All these parameters can be used in a user satisfaction module where suitable weight assignment is done for the collected parameters. The accumulated weight along with certain bounds in terms of threshold can be shared and further verified with domain expert. A similar system has been proposed by Hussain et al. [30] in which user feedback, web monitoring, and contextual information are used for adaptive UI with the help of UX.

15.1.4 Services

Majority of applications are capable of recognizing user activities (walking, jogging, running, sleeping) and present this information visually at the end of the day or when-ever required by the user. Other than presenting the activities individually and their time duration, few applications also present the impact of one activity over the other, e.g., sleep efficiency with number of steps taken or changing heart rate due to running [3]. To promote the healthy lifestyle this information is also used to predict and anticipate certain trends, e.g., weight, calories deposit, or sleep efficiency. Sharing this information with health experts adds more comprehension and perfection towards user wellness with personalized recommendations. Clinical services and provisioning of SDK/API are also potential and growing features offered by few applications.

15.1.5 Information Sharing

The data-driven landscape for health and wellness applications has revolutionized their core operations by expanding the boundaries for data/information sharing across various applications. Instead of making data silos as an independent island of information, its sharing is now more frequent involving other applications, devices, social media, and domain experts. The application of Fitcoracy [5] can sync with RunKeeper [1], DigifitIcardio [6] can use data generated by a heart-rate monitoring device Mio [7]. Similarly, users can share their data through social media within a community of their peers [4]and also with domain experts, e.g., clinicians, personal care-givers, and dietitians.

15.1.6 Knowledge Maintenance

The knowledge which is derived from the personalized recommendations, user satisfaction level, and feedback analysis is preserved for later use as well as shared as an open knowledge. The discussion about knowledge acquisition, maintenance, and evolution in health applications is beyond the scope of this chapter; therefore, it is just highlighted as a feature alone.

Figure 15.1 represents growing trend within health and wellness applications with respect to data and their utility. The importance of diverse data sources and induction of public cloud is obvious; however, it also introduces significant challenges of data heterogeneity resolution, implications associated with personal data on public cloud, and secure sharing of user data and information with other entities. With the ambition of promoting healthy living and considering the aforementioned challenges, we propose a framework aiming swift and secure services. The proposed framework employs the Fog Computing as a mediator layer between the system entities used for data acquisition and system consumers over public cloud. The rationale behind using the Fog Computing is to bring computational resources close to data generating entities and preserving privacy aspect of user's data during heterogeneity resolution of multivariate data. Considering data preprocessing as a demanding task with respect to computation and energy, it is not feasible to perform it on the user device; also, executing the same on public cloud can expose individual identity thus compromising individual identity with information exposure. These end-to-end limitations can be resolved with data preprocessing within Fog. At the same time, only relevant and useful information is uploaded into the public cloud after preprocessing, thus avoiding unnecessary communication overhead due to entire upload of data. In this chapter we make following contributions:

- computational task for data heterogeneity resolution is done through Fog Computing instead of public cloud, thus minimizing the information leakage during this process,
- services pool and data access policies and guidelines are staked in Health Fog giving more flexibility in terms of management and autonomous control,
- The processed and encrypted data are made available to authorized users obliviously using existing cryptographic standards.

15.2 Definitions and technical Preliminaries

Before describing the Health Fog framework, we present some definitions and technical preliminaries.

15.2.1 Fog Computing

Fog computing, a Micro Datacenter paradigm, is a highly virtualized platform, which provides computation, storage, and networking services between the end nodes in an internet of things (IoT) and traditional clouds [8]. In contrast to the cloud, which is more centralized, Fog computing targets the services and applications with widely distributed deployments. Fog is aimed to deliver high-quality streaming to mobile nodes, like moving vehicles, through proxies and access points positioned accordingly, like, along highways and tracks. Fog suits applications with low latency requirements, emergency and healthcare-related services, video streaming, gaming, augmented reality, etc.

15.2.2 Cloud Access Security Broker

Cloud Access Security Brokers (CASB) are quickly emerging as a must-have security solution for organizations looking to adopt cloud-based applications. CASBs are either on-premise, or cloud-based (or both) security policy enforcement points which are placed between end users and the various cloud service providers. CASBs can inspect traffic, alert on anomalous behavior, and in most cases provide some level of data loss prevention (DLP) enforcement. Cloud Access Security Brokers can also consolidate multiple types of security policy enforcement, e.g., user authentication, single sign-on, authorization, credential mapping, device profiling, encryption, tokenization, logging, alerting, and malware detection/prevention [9,10].

15.2.3 Homomorphic Encryption

Homomorphic encryption *HE* is a form of encryption where a specific algebraic operation performed on the plaintext is equivalent to another (possibly different) algebraic operation performed on the ciphertext. An encryption scheme is said to be additive homomorphic if and only if

$$E_H(m_1) \odot E_H(m_2) = E_H(m_1 + m_2),$$

where $\odot$ is an operator. Pascal Paillier cryptosystem [23] possesses the property of additive *HE* which is as follows:

– Key generation: Let $N = pq$ be the RSA-modulus and g be an integer of order αN module N^2 for some integer α. The public key is (N, g) and the private key is $\lambda(N = lcm((p-1)(q-1))$

– Encryption: The encryption of message $m \in ZN$ is $E_h(m) = g^m r^N mod\ mod N^2$, where $r \in_R Z_N^*$

– Decryption: For ciphertext c, the message is computed from

$$m = \frac{L(c^{\lambda(N)} mod N^2)}{L(g^{\lambda(N)} mod N^2)}$$

A scheme is said to be multiplicative homomorphic if and only if

$$E_H(m_1) \odot E_H(m_2) = E_H(m_1 \times m_2)$$

The Goldwasser-Micali (GM) cryptosystem is a semantically secure scheme based on the quadratic residuosity problem. It has XOR homomorphic properties, in the sense that

$E_H(b).E_H(b') = E(b \oplus b')modN$, where $b$and b' are bits and N is the public key. A homomorphic encryption is said to be semantically secure if $E(H)$ reveals no information about m_1 and m_2; hence it is computationally infeasible to distinguish between the cases $m_1 = m_2$ and $m_1 \neq m_2$[22].

Here is an example of how a homomorphic encryption scheme might work in cloud computing.

Example:

Let us assume that a sensitive information comprising number 5and 10 is encrypted and uploaded in the public cloud. For simplicity and understanding purpose, the corresponding ciphertext of 5 and 10 appears as 10 and 20 after applying the homomorphic encryption, i.e., the algorithm multiplies original values with 2. To perform any operation on these encrypted values the cloud will use 10 and 20, without knowing the original values. To utilize the computational services of cloud for addition purpose, it will use the features of homomorphic encryption and return the answer 30. On receiving end, the value of 30 will be decrypted as 15 using the decryption key.

15.2.4 Private Comparison

Yaos classical millionaire's problem involves two millionaires who wish to know who is richer. However, they do not want to find out inadvertently any additional information about each other's wealth. More formally, given two input values x and y, which are held as private inputs by two parties Alice and Bob, respectively. the problem is to securely evaluate the Greater Than (GT) condition through a predicate function f such that $f(x, y) = 1$ if and only if $x > y$, without exposing inputs. We used Fischlin protocol [11] for the private comparison because it allows comparing two ciphertexts encrypted with the GM cryptosystem using the same public key. Fischlin uses theGM encryption scheme to construct a two-round GT protocol. The GM encryption scheme has the XOR, NOT, and re-randomization properties. They modified the scheme to get an AND property, which can be performed only once. The computation cost $O(n)$ for the server side is very efficient. Nevertheless, the overall computation cost for both the client and server sides are $O(nlogN)$, where N is the modulus. The scheme is as follows:

- Key generation: Let $N = pq$ be the RSA-modulus and z be a quadratic non-residue of $Z_n^*$with Jacobi symbol +1. The public key is (N, z) and the secret key is (p, q).

- Encryption: For a bit b, the encryption is $E(b) = z^r r^2 mod\ N$, where $r \in_R Z_N^*$.

- Decryption: For a ciphertext c, its plaintext is 1 if and only if c is a quadratic non-residue. If c is a quadratic residue in Z_N, c is quadratic residue in both Z_p^* and Z_q^*.

- xor-property: $E(b_1)E(b_2) = E(b_1 \oplus b_2)$.

- Not-property: $E(b) \times z = E(b \oplus 1 = E(b)$.

- Re-randomization: Randomization of ciphertext c can be done by multiplying an encryption of 0.

15.3 System Overview

The proposed system is designed in a layered architecture comprising data generating entities *DGE*, Fog computing and end users. Hospitals and clinical institutes, smart home environment, and users equipped with wearables and smart-phone are main entities of *DGE*. For brevity, the following discussion is with respect to a single user 'Alice' who is a member in *DGE* and formally expressed as DGE_{Alice}. Alice is living in a smart home environment and using few wearables to monitor her daily activities as shown in Figure 15.2. Her passion to achieve a healthy lifestyle is triggered due to a recent discovery on her weight gain during a visit to a nearby hospital. The preliminary diagnosis highlights the sedentary life style caused by irregular routines for diet and sleep along with inadequate physical workout. The doctor advises her to change monotonous routines causing weight abnormality by inducing sufficient workout and that too with regular feedback and careful monitoring round the clock. Considering the high tendency of weight gain in her family tree, she also decides to avail expert services from a nutritionist for appropriate diet selection. To apprise the doctor on her lifestyle and to seek specialized advice from a domain expert, a mechanized system is required that should support data shareability with adequate security and high availability. With these requirements, Alice joins the Health Fog where hospitals, domain experts, and other people like her are already registered, collaboratively pursuing a healthy lifestyle.

15.4 Data Outsourcing

Hospital and a user are two main data generating entities referred as DGE_H and DGE_U. A user living in a smart home environment using various devices d_i is represented as $DGE_U \prec d_1, d_2, \ldots, d_n \succ$.For any device d_i that is required to be used as an active member of DGE_U is commissioned with Health Fog through Health Fog client stub. A client stub is an application running on a smart phone responsible for data uploads, activation or deactivation of a particular device, i.e.,$d_i \epsilon DGE$.Provisioning of activation and deactivation of a commissioned device is meant to control data uploads from user's side as per individual needs and concerns of privacy. The client stub is also responsible for providing end to end user services through personalized recommendations, alerts, statistical analysis on daily activities, and expert advice. Other than this independent link established between the client stub and the Health Fog, DGE_H also deposits its data byits own and separate link with the Health Fog. The data which are uploaded by the DGE_H are assumed to be preprocessed with the removal of identifiable information of a patient/visitor of that hospital.

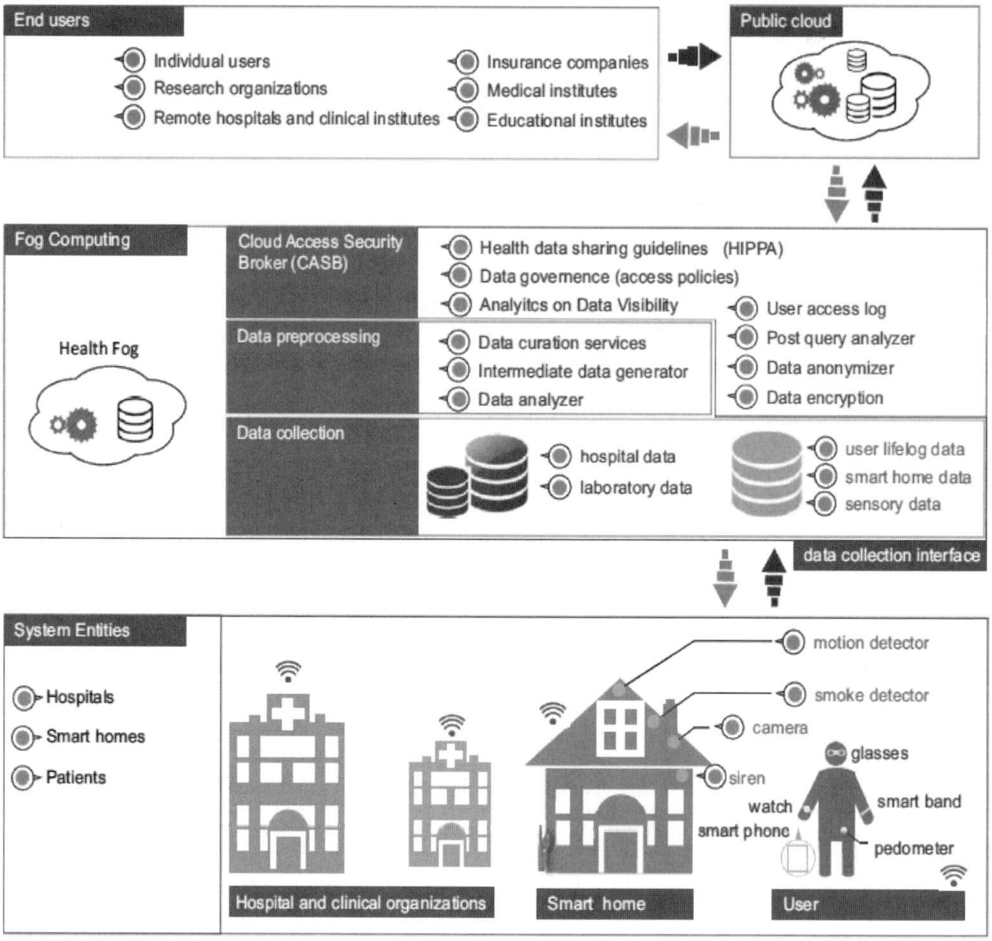

Figure 15.2 Health Fog: system architecture

15.5 Health Fog

The data arriving at the data collection layer of Health Fog are preserved under defined categories for user $DGE_U^{\circledast}$ and hospital $DGE_H^{\circledast}$. The data are then preprocessed for any missing value, noise reduction, erroneous values, duplicates, correct data labeling, and reduced as $DGE_U^{\odot}$ and $DGE_H^{\odot}$. The process Δ of data transformation for DGE_U and DGE_H is defined as

$$DGE_U^{\circledast} \circledast \overset{\Delta_{\sqcup}^{\theta}}{\rightarrow} DGE_U^{\odot}$$

$$DGE_H^{\circledast} \circledast \overset{\Delta_{\sqcup}^{\theta}}{\rightarrow} DGE_H^{\odot} \tag{1}$$

Through process Δ, we claim two advantages of data reduction and privacy gain represented as $\Delta_{\sqcup}$ and Δ^{θ}, respectively. Collectively these two operations are represented as $\Delta_{\sqcup}^{\theta}$ in Eq. 1. With data reduction we mean the transformation of raw data into useful information, whereas the privacy gain is the information exposure of knowing individual identity while processing the raw data.

Since these two operations are performed within Health Fog, communication overhead and information exposure for a curious cloud are marginally reduced which could appear otherwise.

The role of Cloud Access Security Brokers (CASB) is aimed to improve Health Fog security features by placing it in-between the public cloud and its consumers. CASB helps Health Fog to improve its monitoring, visibility, and control of user and data activity on public cloud. It also ensures that unauthorized parties do not gain access to corporate resources in the cloud by unification of consolidated polices ensuring their consistency and effectiveness at all operational frontiers. With CASB we propose following services.

15.5.1 Cloud Access Security Broker (CASB)

The personal data which have to be shared through public cloud need to be in compliance with certain rules and regulations. The statutory body of these rules and regulations is accommodated within the CASB. For this purpose, we refer to HIPPA as one of the policy guidelines while making data availability for the sharing purpose. Besides, polices that are defined at an organizational level can also be made part of CASB to further meet local needs for data sharing and its access. Through CASB the visibility into user data and access is also provisioned through analytic and data visibility sub component. For each access that passes through CASB, itis logged for post analysis for anomaly detection in user query or data access pattern. The query log for post query analysis is used for discovering the data access trends. The access trends help to improve data provisioning both in terms of refinement and improved security. To protect the individual identity from outsourced data without encryption, the anonymization is an option that can be used instead. With anonymization that involves techniques like generalization, suppression, and perturbation, to hide individual's identity is an option for data sharing without encryption, thus making data utility aspect more flexible with large number of users requiring no authentication. Although with anonymization the utility aspect on data becomes relatively minimal, however, it saves the cost of encryption/decryption and user management. For more details on anonymization readers may refer to [12,13].

The security and privacy issues on outsourced data in public cloud are not limited with the nature of data alone but also involve encryption techniques and access model as well. While achieving desirable security and privacy features on outsourced data, encrypted outsourcing in public cloud is highly recommended [14–16]. For this reason, the data outsourcing from Health Fog into the public cloud is provisioned with encryption. Addressing the general issues while interacting with the encrypted data over cloud mainly includes user management and how the data are accessed or explored. With exploration, we refer retrieving the desired results from encrypted data against user query parameters. In this regard, the user access is controlled with the help of authorized credentials and a decryption key. In Health Fog, the process of user verification is done through CASB followed by request routing to public cloud where data are outsourced. The request arriving at cloud is then processed against the request parameters over encrypted data. Besides protecting the outsourced public data, protecting request parameters is equally important and emphasized. After processing the user query, the result is sent back to the user where itis decrypted with authorized key. This whole process for data outsourcing, user accession, and response extraction is given in the following subsections.

15.5.1.1 Setup

Let $DGE_U^{\circledast}$ and $DGE_H^{\circledast}$ be the raw data collected from the user and hospital, respectively. After going through the process of Δ, these data are collectively represented as $D_*^{\odot}$.

$$DGE_U^{\odot} + DGE_H^{\odot} = D_*^{\odot} \tag{2}$$

For quick data exploration on $D_*^{\odot}$, an index ζ is also created for all unique keywords against the outsourced data. Once ζ is generated, Health Fog initializes proxy re-encryption by generating Health Fog key (ω_0) ,user key (ω_u) , and transformation key $(\omega_0 \to u)$. The owner key (ω_0) ensures the privacy of keywords within ζ, whereas keyword frequencies are concealed with CASBs secret key(sk). The Health Fog key (ω_0) ensures the privacy of keywords within ζ. The user key (ω_u) is used by the user to encrypt search criteria. The Health Fog only shares (ω_0) with the authorized users. The transformation key $(\omega_0 \to u)$. is used by the cloud server to transform ciphertext (encrypted inverted index). Transformation of ciphertext ensures that the Health Fog does not need to outsource separate encrypted index for each authorized user. Each user is also provided with authorized credentials, i.e., user id and password that are used each time a user forwards her request through Health Fog.

15.5.1.2 Data Outsourcing

For privacy aware data processing and oblivious request evaluation of user query on cloud, Health Fog encodes $\zeta_{k\omega_0 \ldots n}$ using a publicly known encoding function denoted as $\mathcal{H}$, i.e., $\mathcal{H}(\zeta_{k\omega_0 \ldots n}) \to \zeta^{\wedge}{}_{k\omega_0 \ldots n}$. The encoded keywords $(\zeta^{\wedge}{}_{k\omega_0 \ldots n})$ are then encrypted with proxy reencryption algorithm using $\varepsilon_p(\zeta^{\wedge}{}_{k\omega_0 \ldots n}) \to I^{\wedge^{\omega_0}}{}_{k\omega_0,\ldots n}$. To ensure that the cloud server cannot learn any information from the inverted index, Health Fog encrypts $\zeta_{f_{0,\ldots,n}}$ with CASB secret key, i.e., $\varepsilon(\zeta_{f_{0,\ldots,n}}, sk) \to \zeta^{sk}_{f_{0,\ldots,n}}$. After that, Health Fog encrypts (ω_u) with the public key of the user to whom it wants to grant searching capabilities over the outsourced data, i.e. $\varepsilon(\omega_u, k_{pub}) \to \omega_u^{k_{pub}}$. In a cloud storage system, outsourced data can be shared with multiple users each having its own access privileges over the outsourced data. With proxy reencryption Health Fog does not need to encrypt $\zeta_{k\omega_0 \ldots n}$ separately to permit each authorized user to query $\zeta^{\wedge^{\omega_0}}{}_{k\omega_0,\ldots n}$. An authorized user can submit its query encrypted with its proxy reencryption secret key (ω_{u_i}) . Cloud server then transforms $\zeta^{\wedge^{\omega_0}}{}_{k\omega_0,\ldots n}$ to $\zeta^{\wedge^{\omega u_i}}{}_{k\omega_0,\ldots n}$ using an appropriate transformation key $(\omega_0 \to u_i)$ provided by the Health Fog. Thus, the Health Fog only needs to encrypt $\zeta^{\wedge^{\omega_0}}{}_{k\omega_0,\ldots n}$ once, and *n* authorized users can query it, without compromising privacy of the outsourced data.

15.5.1.3 Query Generation

In order to privately search the cloud storage, a user obtains its proxy reencryption secret key from the Health Fog and deciphers it using the private key, i.e.$D(\omega_u^{pub}, k_{pri}) = \omega_u$. The user then defines a search criterion $(C_{k\omega_0,\ldots l})$ that consist of a list of keywords $k_{\omega_0,\ldots,k_{\omega_1}}$. Then $C_{k\omega_0,\ldots l}$ is encoded using a publicly known encoding function, i.e.$\mathcal{H}(C_{k\omega_0,\ldots l}) \to C^{\wedge}_{k\omega_0,\ldots l}$, where $\mathcal{H}$ is the same as used by the Health Fog during data outsourcing. To ensure confidentiality of the keywords,

$C^{\wedge}_{k\omega_{0,\ldots l}}$ is encrypted with proxy reencryption using the proxy reencryption secret key, i.e. $\mathcal{E}_p\left(C^{\wedge}_{k\omega_{0,\ldots l}}, \omega_u\right) = C^{\wedge\omega_u}_{k\omega_{0,\ldots l}}$.

Once privacy of the search criteria is assured, it is send to CASB who uses it to model oblivious search query. On receiving $C^{\wedge\omega_u}_{k\omega_{0,\ldots l}}$ the CASB defines a polynomial (P(x)), such that each element of $C^{\wedge\omega_u}_{k\omega_{0,\ldots l}}$ is a root of *P(x)* , i.e. $P\left(x \in C^{\wedge\omega_u}_{k\omega_{0,\ldots l}}\right) = \Sigma^{l}_{i=0}\alpha_i x^i = 0$.

Once *P(x)* is defined in accordance with $C^{\wedge\omega_u}_{k\omega_{0,\ldots l}}$, the CASB then initializes homo-morphic encryption by generating a public key (σ_{pk}) and secret key (σ_{sk}). The CASB encrypts the coefficients ($\alpha_{0,\ldots l}$) of *P(x)* with homomorphic encryption algorithm using (σ_{sk}) , i.e. $\mathcal{E}_H(\alpha_{0,\ldots l}, \sigma_{sk}) = \alpha^{\sigma_{sk}}_{0,\ldots l}$. Subsequently $\alpha^{\sigma_{sk}}_{0,\ldots l}$ and σ_{pk} are transferred to the cloud server. Encrypted coefficients $\alpha^{\sigma_{sk}}_{0,\ldots l}$ are used to execute search query over encrypted inverted index ($\zeta^{\wedge\omega_0}_{k\omega_{0,\ldots n}}$) . In the context of search over encrypted data, set intersection can be used to execute search query by matching search criteria with the inverted index.

15.5.1.4 Searching

Cloud server hosts the encrypted inverted index as encrypted keywords ($\zeta^{\wedge\omega_0}_{k\omega_{0,\ldots n}}$) and their concealed frequencies $\zeta^{sk}_{f_{0,\ldots n}}$ along with the outsourced data $\mathcal{F}$. Encrypted query $\alpha_{0,\ldots l}$ submitted by the CASB is evaluated against $\zeta^{\wedge\omega_0}_{k\omega_{0,\ldots n}}$. On receiving $\alpha^{sk}_{0,\ldots l}$, cloud server transforms $\zeta^{\wedge\omega_0}_{k\omega_{0,\ldots n}}$ with the respective users transformation key $\omega_0 \rightarrow u$, provided by the Health Fog, i.e. $\zeta_p(\zeta^{\wedge\omega_0}_{k\omega_{0,\ldots n}}, \omega_0 \rightarrow u) \rightarrow \zeta^{\wedge\omega_0}_{k\omega_{0,\ldots n}}$.

Once the encrypted index is transformed, cloud server defines a polynomial *P(y)* , using each element of $alpha_{0,\ldots l}$ as a coefficient of *P(y)* . It then computes oblivious value (Δ_{y_i}) by evaluating *r. P(yi)*, where $y_i \epsilon \zeta^{\wedge\omega_u}_{k\omega_{0,\ldots n}}$ and *r* is a random number, i.e. $\Delta_{y_i} = r.P(yi)$.

As the query is concealed using homomorphic encryption, cloud server cannot learn any information from $P(y_i \in \zeta^{\wedge\omega_u}_{k\omega_{0,\ldots n}})$. Once the cloud server has evaluated $P\left(y_{0,\ldots,n} \in \zeta^{\wedge\omega_u}_{k\omega_{0,\ldots n}}\right) = \Delta_{y_{0,\ldots,n}}$, it replies back the query evaluation result list of oblivious values along with the concealed keyword frequencies to the CASB, i.e. $\Delta_{y_{0,\ldots,n}}, \zeta^{sk}_{f_{0,\ldots n}}$.

15.5.1.5 Response Extraction

On receiving the cloud server response $\Delta_{y_{0,\ldots,n}}, \zeta^{sk}_{f_{0,\ldots n}}$, CASB decrypts the oblivious values using the homomorphic secret key, i.e.$D_H\left(\Delta_{y_i}, \sigma_{sk}\right) = \psi_i$, where ψ_i can be zero or a random number. As the search query was modeled as a polynomial having roots equal to the concealed search criteria, i.e. $P(x \epsilon C^{\wedge\omega_u}_{k\omega_{0,\ldots l}} = \Sigma^{l}_{i=0}\alpha_i x^i$, query evaluation at cloud server can result either in a zero or a non-zero value shown in Eq. 3.

$$P(y_i) = \frac{\psi_i = 0 \; if \; \{ y_i | y_i \, \epsilon \zeta^{\wedge\omega_u}_{k\omega_{0,\ldots n}} \wedge y_i \epsilon C^{\wedge\omega_u}_{k\omega_{0,\ldots l}} \}}{\psi_i = 0 \; if \; \{ y_i | y_i \, \epsilon \zeta^{\wedge\omega_u}_{k\omega_{0,\ldots n}} \wedge y_i \notin C^{\wedge\omega_u}_{k\omega_{0,\ldots l}}} \qquad (3)$$

Zero value reveals that inverted index contains keyword that matches with the concealed search criteria specified by the user, i.e. $C^{\wedge\omega_u}_{k\omega_{i,\ldots l}} \in \zeta^{\wedge\omega_u}_{k\omega_{0,\ldots n}}$, whereas non-zero reveals that concealed search criteria do not match with any of the keyword in inverted index; consequently, CASB recovers r. Once encrypted keywords are identified, CASB deciphers the corresponding frequency index using the secret key, i.e. $D_S(\zeta^{sk}_{f_i}, sk) \to \zeta_{f_i}$. After sorting the encrypted keywords based on their frequency count, CASB replies oblivious results to the user. On receiving the CASBs response, a user deciphers the search criteria using its proxy reencryption secret key. Through decryption the user learns the keyword that matches with the encrypted index, i.e. $D_P\left(C^{\wedge\omega_u}_{k\omega_{0,\ldots k}}, \omega_u\right) = C^{\wedge}_{k\omega_{0,\ldots k}}$, where k is the number terms that are identical between $C^{\wedge}_{k\omega_{0,\ldots l}}$ and $\zeta^{\wedge\omega_u}_{k\omega_{0,\ldots n}}$. During the query evaluation cloud server learns nothing about the inverted index or the search criteria, however; it accurately evaluates the search query and replies back the oblivious response.

15.6 Evaluation and Results

For experiment purpose we have used the Samsung Galaxy S-III smart phone. The sensory input of accelerometer and GPS has been used for activity detection and subsequent recommendations by the domain experts, i.e., doctor and the nutritionist. The data generated by these sensors of smart phone are retrieved on a 3-s interval. For optimal communication between the client stub and Health Fog, the 3-s interval data are batched over a minute and sent to the Health Fog after 60 s. For activity detection, these data are deposited on Health Fog through client stub along with other sensory inputs collected from the smart home environment. The user data generated within the hospital like history, prescriptions, etc., are also centralized into the Health Fog. After collecting all data resources, it is preprocessed and curated for activity detection and appear as intermediate data. This intermediate data is then shared with the doctor and the nutritionist or as preferred by the user. The calorie meter, activity detection, activity detail, and personalized recommendations are also shared with the users. The data acquired from accelerometer and GPS followed by the detected activity against this data are shown in Figure 15.3. Due to space limit the visibility of raw data has been restricted with fewer rows only followed by their transformation into useful information of activity on Health Fog. Depending upon the activity detection, the burned calories are calculated and logged. The final data for activity detection and calories is then deposited on the cloud and shared with the Hospital and nutritionist. The authorized entities can monitor the selected data as required. Figure 15.4 shows the total activities performed during a day to the user along with recommendations by the doctor and the nutritionist. The total amount of calorie intake is shown as 2200, whereas calorie consumption by each activity is shown separately. The number of times an activity is performed during a day is shown from *(T1, T2, Tn)*. The activities performed along with the food intake are then shared with the doctor on regular basis for appropriate advice and cure. The data input resources can be selected as per user's own preferences. Likewise, the control of sharing user's personal data (without disclosing her identity) with other entities is also under the discretion of user. The daily breakup of information comprising calories' break down, activity detection, duration, and recommendations by the doctors and nutritionist is shown to the user as appearing in Figure 15.5. The information which is uploaded from the Health Fog to the cloud is evaluated on local machine and Google App Engine [17] as cloud server. The local machine specification comprises on Intel(R) Core (TM) i3 processor and 4GB of RAM, whereas Microsoft(R) Windows7(TM) X 64bit is the OS installed.

Accelerometer Data				
User Device ID	X-coordinate	Y-coordinate	Z-coordinate	timestamp
25	16	14	14	11/26/2014 8:16
25	16	14	15	11/27/2014 8:16
25	16	14	15	11/28/2014 8:16
25	16	14	17	11/29/2014 8:16
25	16	14	18	11/30/2014 8:16
25	16	14	21	12/1/2014 8:16
25	16	14	22	12/2/2014 8:16
25	16	14	24	12/3/2014 8:16
25	16	14	25	12/4/2014 8:16
25	16	14	27	12/5/2014 8:16
25	16	14	28	12/6/2014 8:16
25	16	14	29	12/7/2014 8:16
25	16	14	29	12/8/2014 8:16
25	16	14	32	12/ /2014 8:16

Data				
User Device ID	latitude	longitude	speed	timestamp
25	12	16	16	11/26/2014 8:16
25	12	16	18	11/27/2014 8:16
25	12	16	18	11/28/2014 8:16
25	12	16	19	11/29/2014 8:16
25	12	16	19	11/30/2014 8:16
25	12	16	21	12/1/2014 8:16
25	12	16	22	12/2/2014 8:16
25	12	16	23	12/3/2014 8:16
25	12	16	23	12/4/2014 8:16
25	12	16	24	12/5/2014 8:16
25	12	16	25	12/6/2014 8:16
25	12	16	25	12/7/2014 8:16
25	12	16	26	12/8/2014 8:16
25	12	16	26	12/ /2014 8:16

Activity Recognition			
User Device ID	Ac tivity	Start Time	End Time
25	Cycling	11/26/2014 8:16	11/26/2014 8:20
25	Jogg ng	11/26/2014 8:35	11/26/2014 8:55
25	Running	11/26/2014 9:35	11/26/2014 9:40
25	Jogg ng	11/26/2014 10:00	11/26/2014 10:10
25	Walking	11/26/2014 10:20	11/26/2014 10:25
25	Walking	11/27/2014 9:35	11/27/2014 9:50
25	Cycling	11/27/2014 10:00	11/27/2014 10:20

Figure 15.3 Raw data for accelerometer and GPS along with activity recognition data

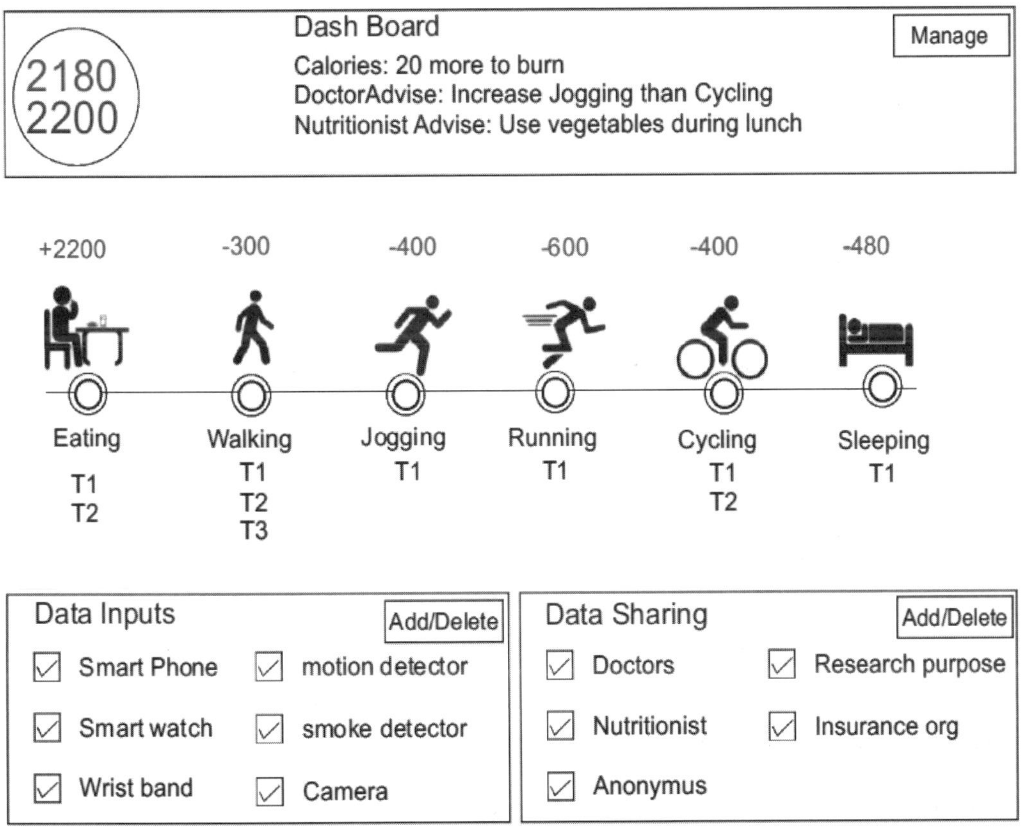

Figure 15.4 Health Fog: user interaction

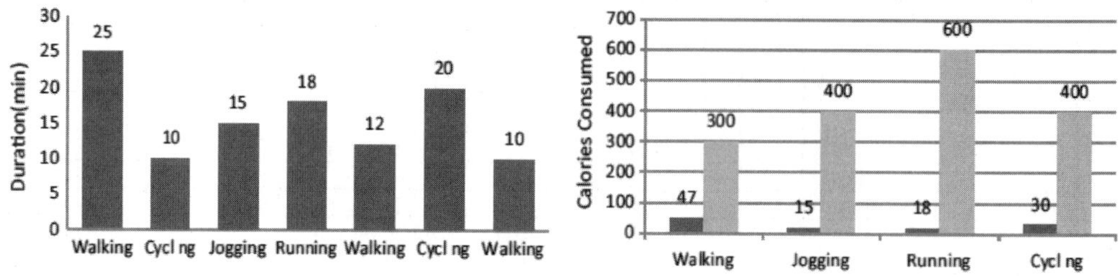

Figure 15.5 Calories' consumption

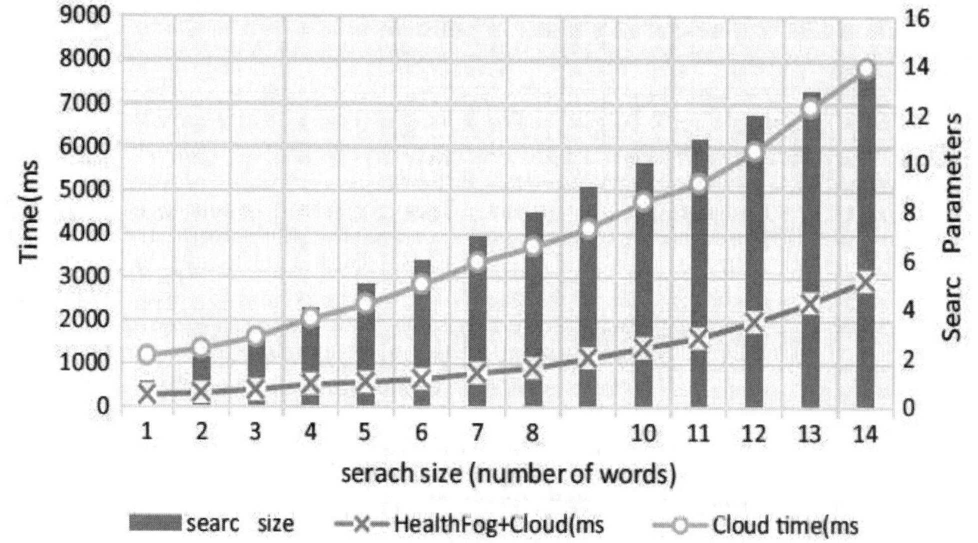

Figure 15.6 Comparison: execution time

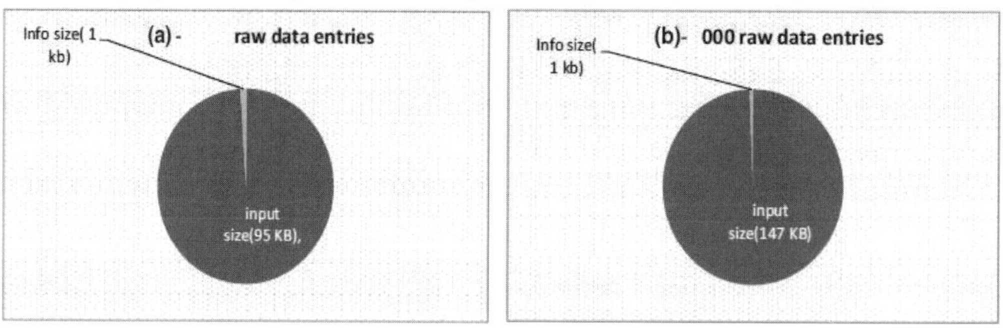

Figure 15.7 Data reduction

The performance gain with respect to execution time on the information which is preprocessed through Health Fog and without its preprocessing is shown in Figure 15.6. Here different selection parameters like user age, gender, BMI index have been used for the test purpose. This performance gain is achieved due to the transformation of raw data into required information thus eliminating unnecessary communication. The data reduction is shown in Figure 15.7 where 4000 raw data entries occupying 95 Kb of space are replaced with only 1 Kb of actual information. Similarly, 147 Kb of space for 6000 Kb raw data entries is again transformed into 1 Kb of actual information thus saving notable communication overhead due to unnecessary movement of raw data.

15.7 Discussion

The ever-growing demand for ubiquitous healthcare systems to improve human health and well-being has suitably engaged advanced technologies, namely cloud computing, IoT, sensory devices, and wearables. With this adoption, the opportunity of including multivariate data in healthcare applications has been made possible for personalized and patient centric services. For real-time provisioning of data from this technology, their omnipresence has been made available through smart phones and wearables for continuous monitoring. With the development of internet of things (IoT) and smart devices the data nodes are increasing at an exponential rate inviting big data to be stored and processed on cloud [18] due to certain reasons. These reasons primarily address the issues for central storage, complex computation, and information sharing. In an effort to optimize the whole process, Fog computing, which is an evolving paradigm shift, can facilitate such systems as a gateway between the end user and cloud. The constructive control of Fog computing effectively minimizes the unnecessary communication from data generating nodes to cloud. In addition, certain policies and rules can be integrated within the Fog to ensure data privacy and security. In conventional applications that are solely dependent on cloud, the latency increases and required quality of services degrades. For this purpose, Fog computing as an intermediary layer between the cloud and end user plays its pivotal role for low latency, better visualization, and context awareness [8,19]. Fog computing can also increase the security in the public cloud. A trustworthy cloud provider is necessary, but accidents still tend to happen and information gets lost. The exposure risk for information leakage can be limited which is sent to the cloud by initial processing on the fog [20]. Complex security challenges are being faced by big data and cloud computing. The most promising way to deal with these challenges is fog computing [21]. In recent years Cloud and Fog computing have drawn profound attention in e-health related systems and applications. In [24], authors present a cloud computing solution for patient data collection in health care institutions. The proposed system uses sensors attached to medical equipment to collect patient data and sends the data to cloud for providing ubiquitous access. Introducing smart gateways Chen et al. [25] introduce a smart gateway for health care system using wireless sensor network. The proposed gateway acting as a bridge between wireless sensor network and public communication networks has a data decision system. In [26], authors propose a mobile gateway for ubiquitous health care system using ZigBee and Bluetooth. The gateway presents various services such as alarms and analysis of medical data. Yang et al. present a personal health monitoring gateway based on smartphone [27]. The proposed gateway uses a Bluetooth interface to upload gathered data to remote servers. In [28] mobile fog is introduced for future internet applications which will be geographically distributed and are latency sensitive. Mobile fog consists of different devices like smartphones, smart watches, tablets, and even drones. A case study given by Tuan et al. [29] high-lights the feasibility of IoT to monitor human health in real-time using ubiquitous health monitoring systems. Their proposed health monitoring system exploit the concept of Fog computing at smart gateways providing advanced techniques and services such as embedded data mining, distributed storage, and notification service at the edge of network.

15.8 Summary

In this chapter, we have proposed a framework of Health Fog for sharing and processing health-related information based on data acquired from multiple resources. We have used Fog computing features as an intermediary layer between the cloud server and end user to avoid unnecessary flow of information and better control over data privacy and security while processing and sharing the information. In future extension to Health Fog, we will incorporate the social media as an input data resource and also, we will build the knowledge reservoir accrued over single instances of Health Fog users. With this addition the feature scale of Health Fog will be equipped with more usability and shareability.

Source Code

For Source code please contact us at:

The contents of this chapter have been previously published in the following article:

Mahmood Ahmad, Muhammad Bilal Amin, Shujaat Hussain, Byeong Ho Kang, Taechoong Cheong and Sungyoung Lee, "Health Fog: a novel framework for health and wellness applications", Journal of Supercomputing, (SCI, IF:0.858), Vol.72, Issue 10, pp.3677-3695, 2016

References

[1] FitnessKeeper (2015) Runkeeper everyone every run. http://runkeeper.com/
[2] Noom (2015) Noom help you to make a change. https://www.noom.com/
[3] Azumio (2015) Argus quantify your day-to-day. http://www.azumio.com/s/argus/index.html
[4] myfitnesspal (2015) Lose weight with myfitnesspal. https://www.myfitnesspal.com/
[5] Fitocracy(2015) Fitocracy. https://www.fitocracy.com/
[6] Digifit (2015) Digifit personal engagement solution. http://www.digifit.com/personal-solutions.html
[7] MIOLink (2015) Mio train with hcart. http://www.mioglobal.com
[8] Bonomi F, Milito R, Zhu J, Addepalli S(2012) Fog computing and its role in the internet of things. In: Proceedings of the first edition of the MCC workshop on Mobile cloud computing, ACM, pp 13–16
[9] Firstbrook P, MacDonald N (2015) The growing importance of cloud access security brokers. https:// www.gartner.com/doc/2032015/growing-importance-cloud-access-security
[10] HP cloud access security protection platform. Business white chapter: Case for a cloud access security brokers. hp.com/go/CloudAccessSecurity, (2015)
[11] Fischlin M (2001) A cost-effective pay-per-multiplication comparison method for millionaires. In: Topics in Cryptology CT-RSA 2001, Springer. pp 457–471
[12] Sweeney Latanya (2002) Achieving k-anonymity privacy protection using generalization and suppression. Int J Uncertain Fuzziness Knowl Based Syst 10(05):571–588
[13] Sweeney Latanya (2002) k-anonymity: a model for protecting privacy. Int J Uncertain Fuzziness Knowl Based Syst 10(05):557–570 1
[14] Evdokimov S, Günther O(2007) Encryption techniques for secure database outsourcing. In: Computer Security–ESORICS 2007, Springer, pp 327–342
[15] De Capitani S, Di Vimercati FS, Jajodia S, Paraboschi S, Samarati P (2007) A data outsourcing architecture combining cryptography and access control. In: Proceedings of the 2007 ACM workshop on Computer security architecture, ACM, pp63–69
[16] Curino C, Jones EPC, Popa RA, Malviya N, Wu E, Madden S, Balakrishnan H, Zeldovich N (2011) Relational cloud: a database-as-a-service for the cloud
[17] Google (2013) Google app engine. https://cloud.google.com/ products/app-engine

[18] Shi Y, Ding G, Wang H, Roman HE, Lu S(2015) The fog computing service for healthcare. In: 2015 2nd International Symposium on Future Information and Communication Technologies for Ubiquitous HealthCare (Ubi-HealthTech), IEEE, pp 1–5

[19] Stojmenovic I, Wen S(2014) The fog computing paradigm: Scenarios and security issues. In: 2014 Federated Conference on Computer Science and Information Systems (FedCSIS), IEEE, pp 1–8

[20] Stolfo SJ, Salem MB, Keromytis AD (2012) Fog computing: mitigating insider data theft attacks in the cloud. In: 2012 IEEE Symposium on Security and PrivacyWorkshops (SPW), IEEE, pp 125–128

[21] Yannuzzi M, Milito R, Serral-Gracia R, Montero D, Nemirovsky M (2014) Key ingredients in an iot recipe: fog computing, cloud computing, and more fog computing. In: 2014 IEEE 19th International Workshop on Computer Aided Modeling and Design of Communication Links and Networks (CAMAD), pp325–329

[22] Paillier P (2000) Trapdooring discrete logarithms on elliptic curves over rings. In: Okamoto T (ed) Advances in CryptologyASI—ACRYPT 2000. Springer, Berlin, Heidelberg, pp 573–584

[23] Paillier P (1999) Public key cryptosystems based on composite degree residuosity classes. In: Proceedings of the 17th international conference on Theory and application of cryptographic techniques, EUROCRYPT'99, Springer-Verlag, Berlin, Heidelberg, pp 223–238

[24] Rolim CO, Koch FL, Westphall CB, Werner J, Fracalossi A, Salvador GS (2010) A cloud computing solution for patient's data collection in health care institutions. In: Second International Conference on eHealth, Telemedicine, and Social Medicine, 2010. ETELEMED'10, IEEE, pp. 95–99

[25] Chen Y, Shen W, Huo H, Xu Y(2010) A smart gateway for health care system using wireless sensor network. In: 2010 Fourth International Conference on Sensor Technologies and Applications (SEN-SORCOMM), IEEE, pp 545–550

[26] Laine TH, Lee C, Suk H(2014) Mobile gateway for ubiquitous health care system using zigbee and bluetooth. In: 014 Eighth International Conference on Innovative Mobile and Internet Services in Ubiquitous Computing (IMIS), 2. IEEE, pp 139–145

[27] Yang S, Gerla M (2011) Personal gateway in mobile health monitoring. In: 011 IEEE International Conference on Pervasive Computing and Communications Workshops (PERCOM Workshops), 2IEEE, pp 636–641

[28] Hong K, Lillethun D, Ramachandran U, Ottenwälder B, Koldehofe B (2013) Mobile fog: a programming model for large-scale applications on the internet of things. In: Proceedings of the second ACM SIGCOMM workshop on Mobile cloud computing. ACM, pp 15–20

[29] Gia TN, Rahmani MJAM, Westerlund T, LiljebergP, Tenhunen H(2015) Fog computing in healthcare internet-of-things: a case study on ecg feature extraction

[30] Hussain J, Khan WA, Afzal M, Hussain M, Kang BH, Lee S(2014) Adaptive user interface and user experience based authoring tool for recommendation systems. In: Ubiquitous Computing and Ambient Intelligence. Personalisation and User Adapted Services. Springer, pp 136–142

Chapter 16

UI/UX

Model-based Adaptive User Interface based on Context and User Experience Evaluation

Jamil Hussain, Anees Ul Hassan, Hafiz Syed Muhammad Bilal, Rahman Ali, Muhammad Afzal, Shujaat Hussain, Jaehun Bang, Orest Banos, and Sungyoung Lee

Personalized services have greater impact on user experience to affect the level of user satisfaction. Many approaches provide personalized services in the form of an adaptive user interface. The focus of these approaches is limited to specific domains rather than a generalized approach applicable to every domain. In this chapter, we proposed a domain and device-independent model-based adaptive user interfacing methodology. Unlike state-of-the-art approaches, the proposed methodology is dependent on the evaluation of user context and user experience (UX). The proposed methodology is implemented as an adaptive UI/UX authoring (A-UI/UX-A) tool; a system capable of adapting user interface based on the utilization of contextual factors, such as user disabilities, environmental factors (e.g. light level, noise level, and location) and device use, at runtime using the adaptation rules devised for rendering the adapted interface. To validate effectiveness of the proposed A-UI/UX-A tool and methodology, user-centric and statistical evaluation methods are used. The results show that the proposed methodology outperforms the existing approaches in adapting user inter-faces by utilizing the user's context and experience.

16.1 Introduction

The user interface (UI) is a dominant part of interactive systems that directly connected to end user to access the functionalities of a system. In most of the well-engineered applications, users use a small portion of the offered functionality and major part goes underutilized due to poor UI [2]. Furthermore, the UI element usage are differing among different users. UI designers face a number of challenges while designing a UI for interactive systems [7] due to the heterogeneity issue [33]. The heterogeneity can broadly be defined as a multiplicity of end users, computing platforms, input/output capabilities, interaction modalities, markup languages, toolkits, user working environments, and contextual variability. The multiplicity of end users is based on their diverse nature of bio-psycho-social characteristics. Similarly, end-users use different computing platforms (i.e., mobile, tablet, computer etc.), which have different input/output capabilities (i.e., mouse, keyboard, HUD, HMD, touch, sensory input, eye-gauze, etc.) using their different interaction modalities (i.e., graphics, speech, haptic, gesture, EEG, ECG etc.) [33].

One way to overcome these differences is adaptive UI called model-based user interface (MBUID) [2,33] as com-pare to the one-size-fits-all design such as universal design, inclusive design, and design for all [2]. The one-size-fits-all approach cannot handle the context variability that leads to bad user experience (UX). Additionally, building multiple UI for same functionality for handling the context variability is difficult which incur high cost and also not know all context at design time. A main goal of adaptive UIs is *plasticity* [17], the ability of UIs to preserve usability across various of context of use [14].

The context-of-use triplet consists of user, platform, and environment aspects that could support adaptive UI behavior [7,14]. The user aspects include user profiles, demographics, cognition, physical characteristics, sensory abilities, user activities and task. User cognition is all about the user attention, learning ability, concentration, and user perceptions. Physical characteristics are user mobility and abilities or disabilities that effect the user interaction with the system, such as hand or finger precision. User sensory information are user sight, hearing, and touch sensitivity that also have direct impact on user interaction with the system.

The platform aspects include both physical devices (e.g. desktop, laptop, tablet, phone etc.), software (e.g. operating systems, application platforms, etc.) [2] are essential for the efficient adaptation of a UI. For example, smart phone and tablet require different adaptations at the user interface. Additionally, the user preferred input modality is also required for the UI adaptation. The environment aspects include spatiotemporal attributes, tasks, and situation where the interaction take place such as light and noise level, and user location and timing (e.g. where the user is right now or where user was at a particular time).

Although context-of-use is mainly defined based on information about users, platforms, and environments, other dimensions such as application domain, adaptation type, multimodal data source and user feedback that could be related to describe context and to appropriately adapt an interactive system.

In state-of-the-art MBUID adaptive user interface design research [3,15,19,20,27,41], researchers have focused on the development of adaptation rules. These rules are either created with the help of UX experts or system designers that use their own knowledge in the assistive authoring tools [21,41] or by the automatic deduction process of mining relevant rules from the users interaction data with the system. The automatic deduction process is performed using various machine learning techniques and algorithms [28]. These methods considered different adaptation dimensions such as culture, user characteristics, user disabilities like sight, hearing, physical, and user cognition for design the adaptation rules [18,36]. For example, UI adaptation can auto change the color according to culture by considering the cultural meanings of color and color symbolism, increase the font-size for vision impairment users, simplify the UI for novice users, hide/show widgets, and swap the widgets according to the user usage behaviors. However, adaptive UI requires more concrete and practical framework, which cover different adaptation dimensions such as user capabilities, preferences, needs, and user context. The adaptation that covers a diverse set of aspect requires a huge amount of knowledge along with complex adaptation algorithms.

In this chapter, we propose a model based adaptive UI methodology and implement an A-UI/UX-A tool that caters the adaptive UI based on the evaluation of user context and user experience. The main objective of the proposed solution is to deal with the personalized approach for building and managing the user interfaces by considering different adaptation dimensions such as context-of-use, multimodal data source, different adaptation aspect, and user in loop. We mainly deal with a user capability, preferences, needs, context-of-use, user interaction deep log, and user feedback for the generating an adaptive UI using adaptation rules created through A-UI/UX-A tool. This eventually leads to the evolution of information in the models and incorporation of personalized aspects in the user interface.

The rest of the chapter is structured as follow. In Sect. 2, adaptive user interface related work is described. In Sect. 3, a brief overview of Mining Minds platform is briefly described. In Sect. 4, the proposed adaptive user Interface framework is abstractly described. In Sect. 5, overall proposed framework is presented from architectural perspective, knowledge creation for adaptive UI perspective and runtime UI rendering based on user experience and context perspective. In Sect. 6, implementation of the A-UI-UX-A tool, experiments, and user-based evaluation is presented. Section 18.7 discusses the significance, challenges and limitations of the A-UI/UX-A tool and Sect. 8 concludes the work.

16.2 Related Work

Adaptive user interface design is a hot area of research since long. Numerous tools and reference architectures has been developed and proposed for creating the adaptive UI. This section briefly explores the proposed reference architectures, adaptation techniques and available tools along with their limitations.

For adaptive smart environment, a 3-layer architecture [31] was proposed that is based on the executable models for generation of an adaptive UI. However, the resulting model of the 3-layer architecture is unable to produce a granular level of adaptation due to generative runtime nature of the model. Furthermore, the proposed model ignores user feedback for improving quality of the UI in an incremental way.

CAMELEON-RT [7] is another reference architecture model for generating the migratable and plastic user inter-face. It provides the feature of adding adaptive behavior at runtime due to excellent conceptual depict of extensibility of adaptive behavior. However, they suggested the primary heuristics for the practical deployment of run time UI rendering.

TRIPLET: a computational framework for context-aware adaptation [38] consists meta model, reference frame-work and adaptation aspects for adaptive UI. Based on the extensive systematic review of existing work, they proposed context-aware adaptation (CAA) framework that covered different aspects such as continuous update (e.g. adaptation technique), platform heterogeneity, and different scenarios consideration. However, it hard to apply in broad perspective.

Malai [12] provides the UI development environment based on model-driven approach. They considered actions, interactions, instruments, presentations, and user interfaces as first-class objects that helps to decompose the interactive system for improving the object reusability. However, runtime adaptation is not supported when the context changes.

Egoki system [20] provides adaptive UI services in ubiquitous environments to users that have physical, sensory, and cognitive disabilities. It uses the model-driven approach for the generation of adaptive UI. However, they have some issue in models' creation and presentation with final UI and risk management measures to all the processes concerned in a digital health and wellness framework.

CEDAR [3] propose a model-driven approach for the adaptive user interface that can be easily integrated with a legacy system. They used a role-based UI simplification (RBUIS) method having a minimal feature-set and an optimal layout functionality to end users. The adaptive behavior of CEDAR system increased the usability. For the evaluation of CEDAR studio, they integration with open-source ERP system so called OFBiz.

In most of the above-mentioned proposed architectures have no support of user feedback. In addition, the integration with a legacy system is very difficult except CEDAR [3], its evaluation required to build new prototype.

Different adaptation techniques have been used, related to UI features, such as layout optimization, content, navigation, and modality [3]. Still there are gaps and limitations in existing adaptation techniques, such as they focus on design time features minimization according to role rather than at runtime [3]. Most of them are theoretically based on UI features set selection. For example, different versions of UI are designed for different contexts. Several free and commercial software have used fixed role-based tailored UI, such as ERP and Moodle. Most of them used pre-identified UI feature set based on context at design time. However, they lack runtime feature selection methodology, which is essential for contextual changes. Similarly, the existing literature focus on the layout optimization, for example, SUPPLE [19], which automatically generate UI on the basis of user profile, preferences, tasks, and ability. It considers the user motor, vision ability, along with device use and task performed by the user for adapting the UI at runtime. It is very difficult to apply this method to large-scale application due to the human involvement at different levels at the design-stage. Additionally, it supports adaptation at a different aspect i.e. user with disabilities, which cannot be extended due to the specialized nature of adaptation algorithms.

MyUI [42] is another study that presents infrastructure for increasing the accessibility of information by providing adaptive UI. MyUI used multimodal design patterns for generating the adaptive UI according to the user preferences. Due to the multimodal design patterns, it provides transparency for both designers and developers with the share-ability feature. However, the adaptation rules are designed at the development time. Whenever a new rule is to be added, the system needs to be redeployed, which is an expensive task.

Roam framework [16] provides environment for developers to create adaptive UI having responsive design feature. This toolkit has two main approaches to generate adaptive UI for the target device. In the first approach, it has used multiple device-depended UI, which is created at the design time. The selection of UI is made at runtime on the basis of the target device. In the second approach, a single UI design (i.e., universal design) is set according to the target device, at runtime, which is device independent. Unlike model-driven approaches, it uses the toolkit for UI creation at design time rather than runtime.

Like Roam framework, [44] XMobile has proposed an environment for the creation of adaptive UI, which uses multiple device-dependent UI variation based on the device characteristics. They have used a model-driven approach, however the code generated from the model is produced at design time rather than runtime.

In the literature, several commercial and academic open source tools are presented for the development of model-driven UI. These tools and software have used different user interface description language (UIDL) [23]. These UIDLs describes different aspects of a UI focusing on multi-platform, multi-context, device independence, and content. Usually based on XML, because XML is easily extensible, very expressive, declarative and can be used by normal users and naive developers. UIDLs can be differentiated on the basis of models, methodology, tools, supported languages, platforms, and concepts. Teresa XML [40] is aUIDL based on Concur Task Tree Environment (CTTE) [37] tool for modeling and analyzing the task modeling, which is based on the Concur Task Tree (CTT) notations. Where Model-based language for Interactive Applications (MARIA) [41] is an extension of Teresa XML that provides the authoring environment based on Maria XML which is compatible with the Cameleon Reference Framework [7]. It supports non-static behaviors, events, interactive web applications, and multi-target UIs. Grafi XML exploited Usi XML which is another UIDL for automatic generation of UI of different devices according to the contexts [32,35]. It comprises different abstraction levels models, such as task model, abstract UI model, concrete UI model, and transformation model. Some other software such as WiSel focused on a framework for supporting Intelligent Agile Runtime Adaptation by integrating adaptive and adaptable approach [34]. However, the user interface markup language (UIML) [25] is best suited for our proposed A-UI/UX-A tool due to mapping of different resources with the UI elements. It is pioneer in the user interface markup languages and its implementation is dependent on vendor. UIML is an XML-based language which supports device, modality independent method for a UI specification. It interconnects UI appearance and interaction with the application logic. Most of adaptive UI system used the ontological models for storing the information for tailoring the UI [3,15,20]. The Table 18.1 shows the comparison of our proposed AUI-UXA with the existing work.

Our proposed model-based system is designed by taking these limitations into account i.e. our system generates the UI at runtime, does not need to redeploy the system, and with the help of authoring tools new rules are added without effecting the running system. Additionally, the adaptation on UI is made when the context is change, which is observed by implicit and explicit (user feedback) ways and then evaluate the context and user experience.

Table 16.1 Comparison of our proposed AUI-UXA with the existing work

Legend
- ● Completely
- ◑ Partially
- O Does not
- ○ Not Specified

	Multimodal data source	Directed and indirect adaptation	Modeling approach	Context			Supporting Tool	Adaptation Aspects			User Feedback on Adaptation
				User	Platform	Environment		Presentation	Navigation	Content	
3-Layer Architecture	◑	◑	◑	●	●	●		○	○	○	◑
CAMELEON-RT	●	●	○	◑	◑	◑	●	○	○	○	O
CEDAR	●	●	●	●	●	●	●	◑	●	●	●
Malai	◑	●	◑	O	●	O	●	●	●	◑	O
TRIPLET	◑	◑	●	●	●	●	○	●	●	●	◑
Egoki system	◑	◑	●	●	●	O	O	●	●	●	◑
SUPPLE	◑	●	●	●	●	O	●	●	◑	O	O
MyUI	●	◑	●	●	●	●	●	●	●	◑	◑
Roam framework	○	◑	●	O	●	O	○	●	O	O	O
XMobile	○	◑	●	O	●	O	◑	●	◑	O	○
AUI-UXA	●	●	●	●	●	●	●	●	●	●	●

16.3 Mining Minds platform and UI/UX: an overview

Mining Minds (MM) [8–10] is a novel platform that provides a collection of services, by monitoring the user's daily routines and providing personalized wellness support services. The MM platform is built on a five layers architecture that uses the concept of curation at different levels in different layers. The curation concept is applied at data level in the data curation layer (DCL) [6], information level in the information curation layer (ICL) [11,45], knowledge level in the knowledge curation layer (KCL), and service level in the service curation layer (SCL) [4].The services are delivered through the support of supporting layer (SL) and personalized at the interface level by using the proposed concept of adaptive UI. Figure 16.1 shows how these layers are interconnected in the MM platform. MM platform acquires data from heterogeneous data source (various sensors, SNS, survey) via DCL [6].

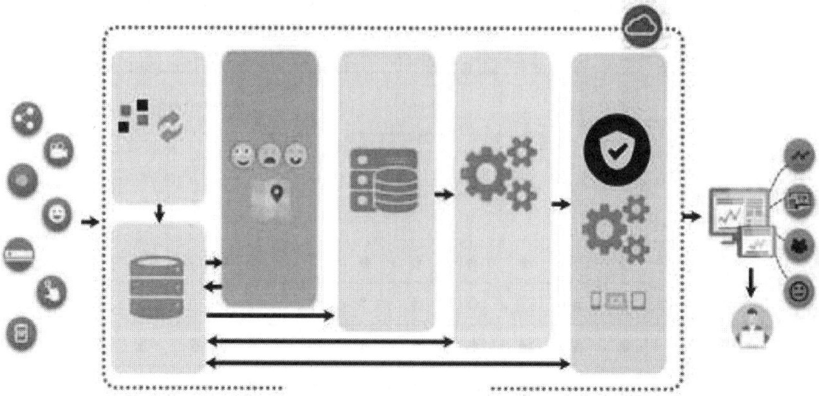

Figure 16.1 Mining Minds Platform

The acquired multimodal data is used in ICL to find the low-level and high-level contextual information. The contextual information describes the user context, user behavior, and user mental and social states. ICL sends the inferred information to DCL for storage in user lifelog, which is a relational data model. The KCL uses two approaches for knowledge creation: data driven and expert driven. The domain expert uses the knowledge-authoring tool [5] for the creation of wellbeing rules utilizing the insights of inferred information recognized by the ICL. The SCL layer uses the created rules and user's current context information in the multimodal hybrid reasoner [4] for the generation of personalized recommendation. The SL is responsible for the adaptive UI generation, service content presentation, information visualization and privacy and security related issues.

Data acquisition and synchronization (DAS) component in DCL is a REST base service that collects real-time data from multimodal data sources e.g. smart watch, mobile phone, camera, Kinect, and SNS. After acquiring the data, the synchronization is done based on the time stamp of the device, and queued based on event for mining of low level context (LLC) and high level context (HLC) [11,45] that consumed by SCL and SL for personalization of services in the form of adaptive UI. LLC is responsible for converting the multimodal data obtaining from user interaction into the classified data such as physical activities (e.g. running, walking, standing, and busing, etc.), user emotions, location, and weather information while HLC is responsible for the identification of user context by combining semantically the recognized LLC. Both LLC and HLC play important role in forming the adaptive UI from recognized context. For example, based on user recognized context (e.g. walking, running), UI adapt to simplified version such as bigger font-size and Icons etc.

The key role of SL is empowering the overall MM functionality via human behavior quantification, personalized user interface based on implicit and explicit feedback analysis for improving the positive experience via A-UI/UX-A tool [26], and privacy and security [1]. The analyzed feed-back data use to enhanced the adaptation aspects such as presentation, navigation, and content. All these types of feed-back are devised to help measuring user interest level and devotion of users to the services delivered through Mining Minds. Considering user capability, mood, way of interaction, A-UI/UX-A tool allows the end-user app UI adopted accordingly. This adaptation aligned the UI based on context and user experience with respect to presentation, navigation, and content. Initially, the user interaction data collects from the interaction between the user and the application to evaluate the user's ability to understand and use the system, e.g. estimating the magnitude of a specific usability issue, of knowing how well users are actually using an application, Then, measures the satisfaction level based on the analysis of the collected data. The key focus of this chapter is on the design and development of A-UI/UX-A tool for MM platform, which can be easily adapted for any interactive system to provide adaptive user interfaces.

16.4 Framework for Adaptive User Interface

Motivations for adaptive user interface is to increase positive user experience in the term of accessibility and user satisfaction. To achieve the stated goal, [26] has proposed an initial adaptive UI/UX authoring tool that dynamically adapts UI based on the user context and experience, which is evaluated automatically. The proposed A-UI/UX-A tool has used a model-based approach, tailored with the UI, which is based on the context-of-use. This chapter is an extension of the same work [26] that extends reference architecture, adaptation techniques with detailed empirical and statistical evaluation. Generally, the context-of-use consists of user, platform, and environment [7,14], as shown in Figure 16.2.

The proposed A-UI/UX-A tool evaluates context-of-use, and user experience via context monitoring and feedback. The user feedback is collected through various ways, ranging from implicit feedback to explicit feedback. The implicit feedback is acquired from the user behavioral responses, which are collected automatically when user start interaction with the system, while the explicit feedback is acquired through questionnaires. From the evaluation of user response along with the context-of-use, the adaptation aspects are inferred in the term of functionality, navigation, content, and presentation of UI for provisioning personalized services to the end user. All these types of feedback are considered to evaluate the level of interest and devotion of users to the services.

The detailed methodology of the proposed idea of adaptive user interfaces in the context of MM in specific and every other adaptive UI design in general is explained in the next section.

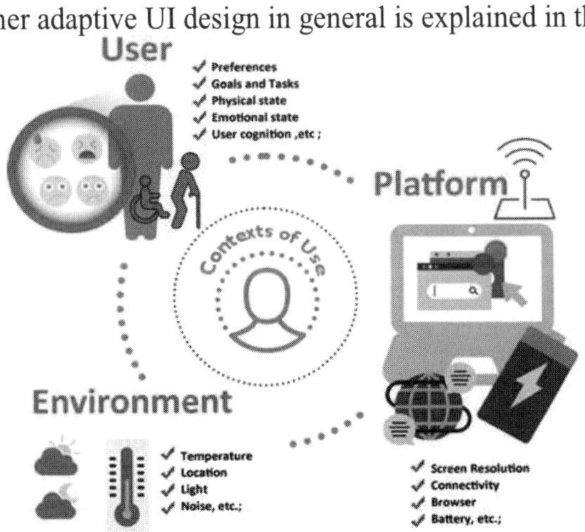

Figure 16.2 The Context-of-use for adaptive UI

16.5 Methods for adaptation of user interface

This section introduces the proposed system methodology in the form of an A-UI/UX-A tool, which is based on the evaluation of context and user experience. The construction of proposed system is divided into two processes: (i) offline process for model's creation and adaptation rules generation and (ii) online process for adaptive UI generation.

16.5.1 Models creation and adaptation rules generation

To build A-UI/UX-A tool for adapting UI, the methodology comprises the development of different models and the creation of adaptation rules in the offline phase. These models and rules are the baseline requirements for the adaptive UI generation. The A-UI/UX-A tool has been used for modeling these models. The models main classes shown in the Figure 16.3. The detail description of these models is given below.

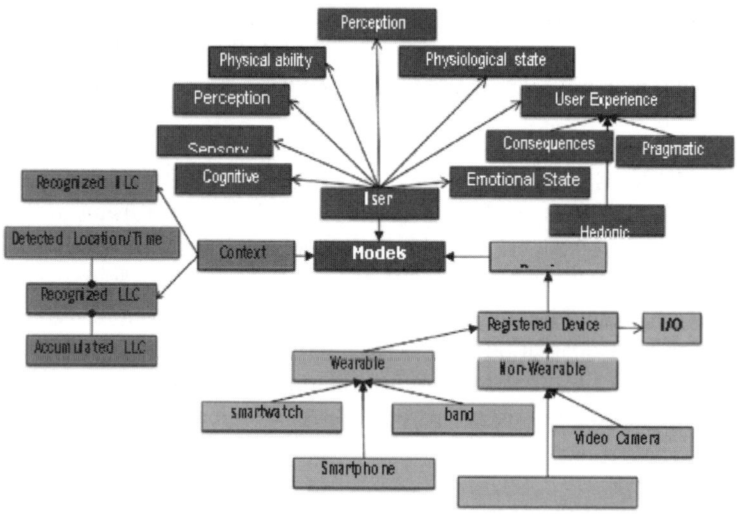

Figure 16.3 Models for user, context, and device

16.5.1.1 User Model

The user model stores information related to user cognition, physical characteristics, sensory, and user experience (UX). The general user model ontology (GUMO) [24] model is used with additional classes and subclasses required for the adaptive UI creations. User cognition is all about the user attention, learning ability, concentration, and user perceptions. Physical characteristics are modeled as user mobility and abilities or disabilities that effect the user interaction with the system, such as hand or finger precision. User sensory information are modeled as user sight, hearing, and touch sensitivity that also have direct impact on user interaction with the system. The user positive and negative emotions are modeled as user experience information. The UX is all about how the user feels about any artifact before and after the usage [30]. The UX constructs was mainly divide into products perceived hedonic quality, pragmatic quality, goodness and beauty [30]. We added new construct, such as emotional state because the current constructs are not enough to model the UX. UX is used to check the level of satisfaction of user interface adaptation after changing the UI according to user context.

16.5.1.2 Context Model

Context model is used to adapt the system based on the current situations. It stores information about the contextual factors such as light, noise level, and event occurrences in the environment. The context information is classified as follows.

– *Physical context:* The environmental variables, such as light and noise level, temperature and weather information are included as physical context, which are collected through the environmental sensors.
– *Time and location context:* The temporal and location information are the essential elements of any context model and we model them together to enable the system for answering questions, such as where the user is right now or where he/she was at a particular time.

16.5.1.3 Device Model

Device model stores information about different characteristics of the devices, such as screen resolution and their abilities of displaying content. These characteristics are essential for the efficient adaptation of a UI. For example, smart phone and tablet require different adaptations at the user interface. Additionally, the user preferred input modality is also required for the UI adaptation. The device characteristics are mainly divided into two types:

– *Hardware:* All hardware related features are modeled as input/output capabilities (e.g., mouse, keyboard, HUD, HMD, touch, sensory input, eye-gauze), interaction modalities (e.g., graphics, speech, haptics, gesture, EEG, ECG), memory, battery, connectivity and so on.
– *Software*: Software related information, installed on the device are modeled as operating system platform, web browser and supporting markup languages and so on.

16.5.1.4 Adaptation rules generation using rule authoring tool

The A-UI/UX-A tool is web-based that provide a way to create the adaptation rules in intuitive way. In rule authoring tool, the concepts are selected from model hierarchy, that associated with the contextual dimension (user, platform and environment). The user can create rules in the form of Conditions-Actions [22] starting either from trigger or from actions. Each rule has two parts: condition part, and action part as follows:

IF (Condition Part) Do (Action Part)

The Condition Part has event(s) that describes the occurrence of actions of the rule. It can be either one condition or more, concatenated using Boolean operators for the executions of action(s). In the action part, there might be one or more actions associated to the same condition part when the rule triggered. Below, there is a partial list of adaptation rules supported by the MM Platform shown in Table 18.2. For each rule, we use a rule name with a brief explanation and the three key parts, i.e., event, condition, and action.

Table 16.2 A partial list of the adaptation rules used in the generation of adaptive UI on the basis of context

RuleID	Rule name	Descriptions	Event	Condition	Action
R1	Noisy environment	For noisy environment, the UI should be in only-graphical mode	The environment becomes noisy	The graphical and vocal modality used by application for user interaction	The application changes to the only-graphical modality
R2	Light Level	The environment light intensity is high or low, then the application switch to night or day mood accordingly for the greater information accessibility	Based on light sensor lux values	The light level is too low	The user interface changed to a night mood
R3	Color Blind	If the user is colorblind then change the application color to black and white	onRender	The user is a colorblind	Change the foreground color to black and background color to white
R4	Low Vision	If the user has low vision by checking then increases the UI size accordingly	The size of the text of the UI is smaller than 16px	The user has low vision	Increase the size of the text of the UI to 16px
R5	Cognitive	If the user has cognitive problem then simplify the UI	The application contains too many different interaction elements for performing different tasks	the user has a cognitive disability	Split the UI into simplified UI having multi-steps to achieve the desire goal

16.5.2 Adaptive UI generation

The whole adaptation process is pictorially represented in Figure 16.4. In the offline phase of adaptive UI design, all the relevant models are built and the adaptation rules are generated using rule authoring tool. The Created rules subscribed as event in context evaluator. This process is termed as real-time monitoring of the user's context and reasoning. In the monitoring process, the information required for the reasoner to adapt the UI behavior, is obtained using implicit and explicit strategies. The real adaptive behavior data preparation process starts from user interaction with the system. The monitoring module is responsible for data collection while user is interacting with the system through different sensors and trackers (e.g., facial, vocal, eye, and analytics). We also consider the user feedback as a self-reported data. The evaluator component evaluates the acquired information and decides whether adaptation is required on UI or not.

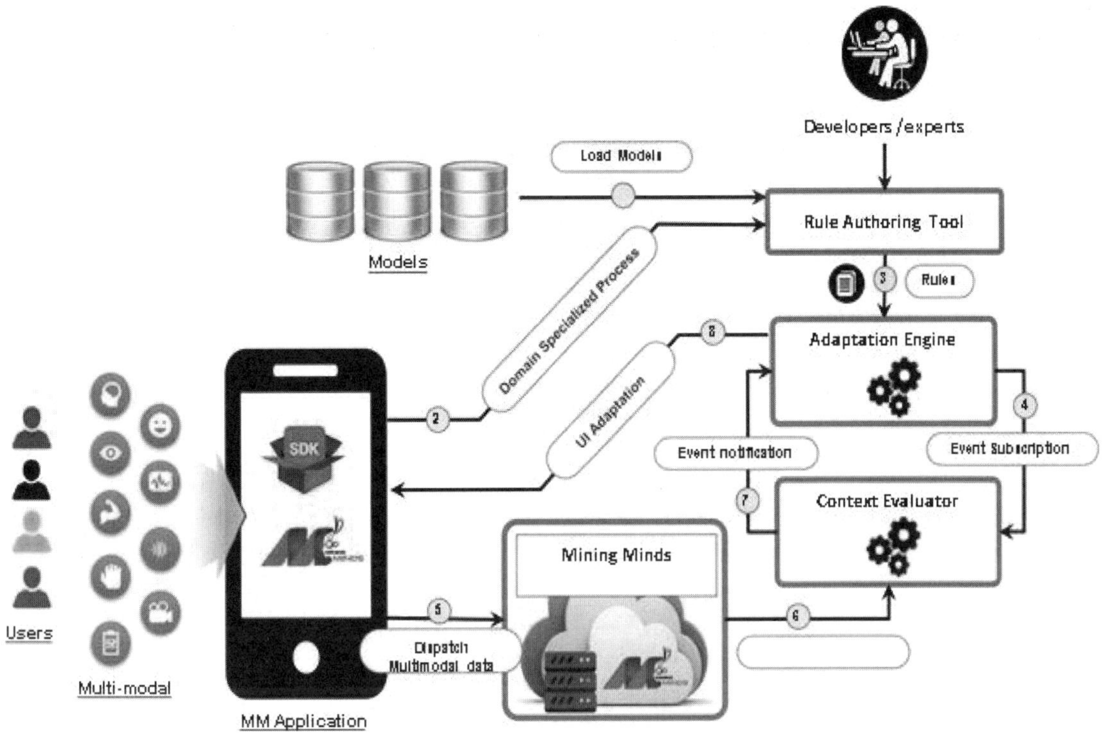

Figure 16.4 Adaptive behavior data flow

If any adaptation is needed, UI is adapted accordingly, otherwise ignored. The adaptation on user interface is made when the context is changed, which is monitored by the context monitor, and sent the context information to the context evaluator. The context evaluator makes decision about the adaptation on UI by checking the current states of the system according to the context-of-use. Based on the decision made by context evaluator the adaptation engine invoked. All the data and model that are required based on current situation by the adaptation engine are loaded along with the adaptation rules. Adaptation engine preforms reasoning using reasoning module called reasoner. Reasoner possess a pattern matcher that uses a forward chaining mechanism, by checking the conditions of selected rule loaded in the reasoner. The rule added in the resultant result of the pattern matcher, if all conditions of rule are satisfied. The resultant rules list is passed to the conflict resolver. The conflict resolver acts as a trade-off between multiple adaptations aspects in the given situation because the resultant list of pattern matcher might be many rules that might have conflict. After that, the result generator fires the final rules and sends to the adaptation engine to generate the UI by the genera- tor engine module in the form of content, presentation and navigation adaptation aspects at the target device.

16.6 Implementation, experiments and evaluation

16.6.1 Use-Case Scenario

To validate the proposed adaptive UI methodology, we considered a wellness application scenario from a real-world health and wellness platform, so called Mining Minds (MM). The MM platform is to provide wellness recommendation to different age users having different characteristics, using different devices under different context-of-use. An application on the top MM platform is previously developed and we designed the application UI to validate the proposed method- ology from the operability and accessibility perspectives. The initial UI design of the MM application is shown in Figure 16.5.

The main sections of the MM application UI are: list view of generated recommendation based on user activities, social sharing, archive, user activities graphs, user feedback invoking by users on recommendations and over- all application features, and prompt feedback invoking by UX evaluator based on user app usage behavior. These are the defaults controls and elements of the MM application to validate the proposed model-based adaptive UI methods, consider the following real-world scenario shown in Figure 16.6.

16.6.1.1 Scenario

John is 31-year-old, overweight person with a visual impairment. He installed the MM application and use it for getting physical activity recommendation to control his body weight. As John has special conditions, therefore the UI of MM application is adapted according to his special characteristics. The adaptation process for this scenario is described below.

1. John's characteristics such as his preferences, visual impairment, and cognition information are collected during his registration in Mining Minds application and stored in the user model.

2. After registrations, the user gets login to use MM application for the accessing wellness services.

3. As user has a low vision, the context evaluator infers the UI needs to be changed. It provides a flag to the reasoner to start reasoning for the corresponding adaptation.

4. In the adaptation engine, the reasoner is invoked to fire the appropriate rule (Rule 4) for the required adaptation according to the current situation.

5. The action of adaptation engine is get effective and the adaptation takes place (i.e., bigger fonts, icons size, and simple UI) for the generation of adaptive UI.

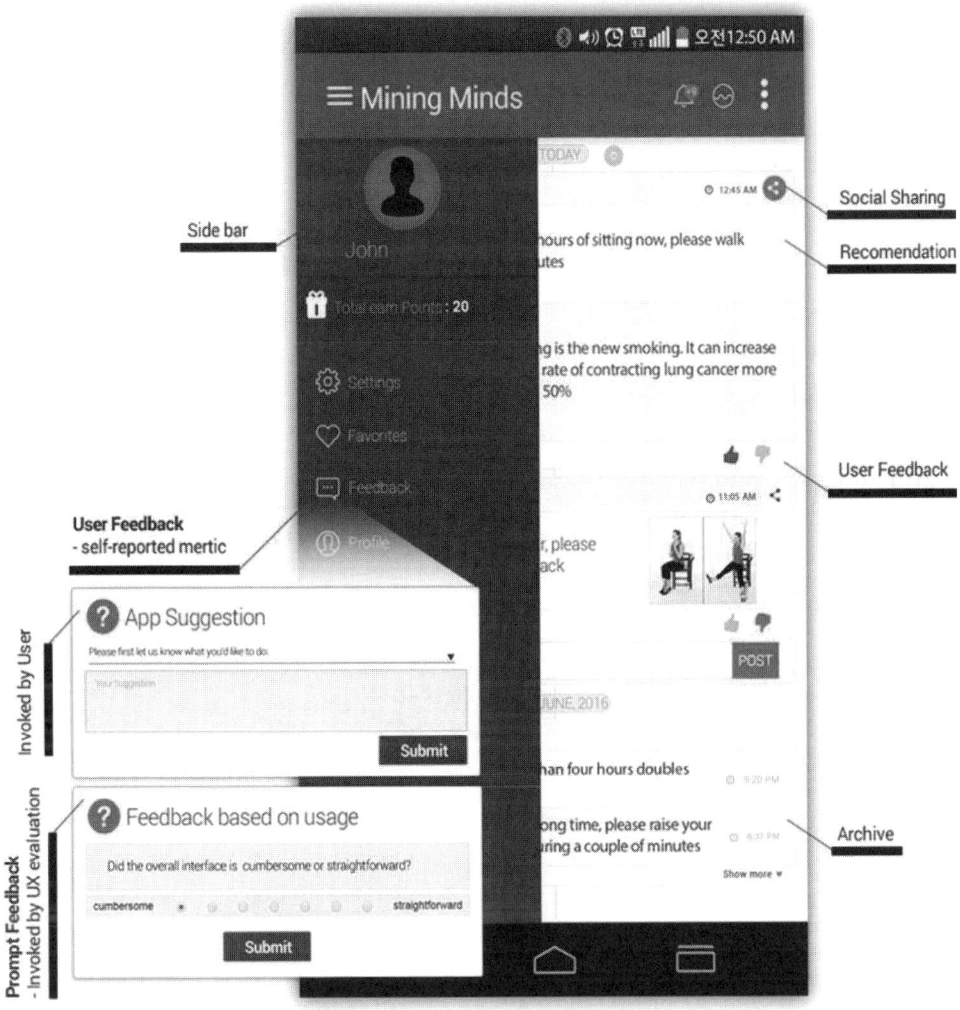

Figure 16.5 Mining minds platform application dashboard

16.6.2 Implementation

To execute the proposed methodology of adaptive UI, we developed the adaptive UI engine so a so-called A-UI/UX-A tool. The tool is developed in the laravel PHP Framework [43] as a web application along with other additional libraries as follow.

1. Protégé editor is used for model's creation.

2. Pallet reasoner and OWL API are used for accessing the model ontologies and do inferencing using Semantic Web Rule Language (SWRL) rules.

3. Easyrdf, a PHP library, is used for data accessing and storage from/to Resource Description Framework (RDF).

4. For the xml documents creation, parsing, and manipulation, a laravel-parser is used.

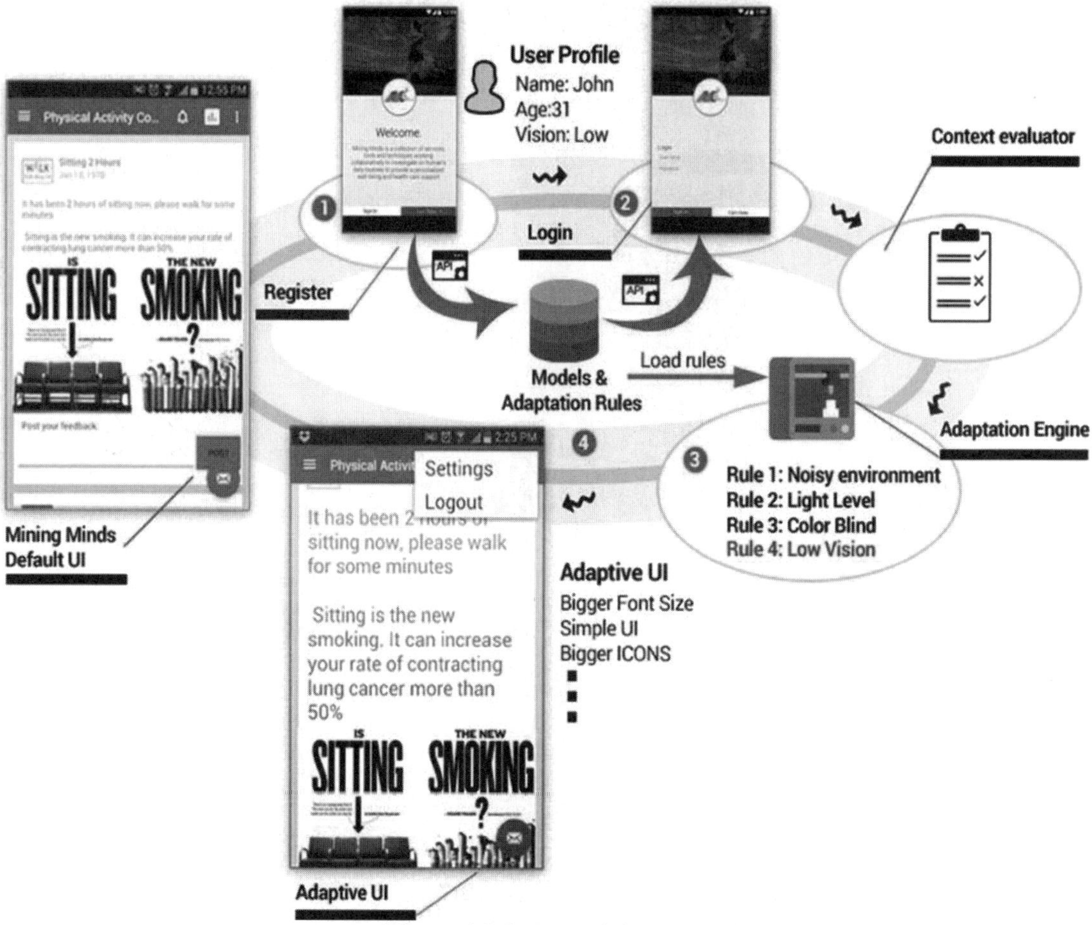

Figure 16.6 Low vision scenario

All the ontological models, used in A-UI/UX-A tool, are developed using OWL in Protégé editor and SWRL rules are used for inferencing over the pre-adaptation rules. The final user interfaces are web-based UIs, which are designed using HTML, JavaScript (JQuery, and AngularJs framework). The rationale of using these techniques and technologies is to support interactivity and extraction of user's behaviors from the UI.

16.7 Experiments and Evaluation

We performed user-based evaluation for adaptive user inter- faces that are automatically generated using the proposed model-based adaptive UI methodology using the developed A-UI/UX-A tool. For the evaluation, we address the following research questions:

RQ1 How the adaptive UI behavior improves the efficiency?

RQ2 How the adaptive UI behavior improves the user satisfaction?

RQ3 How adaptive UI improves the positive user experience (UX)?

16.7.1 User recruitment

In the evaluation of adaptive user interface of MM application, 32 participants (MM users) were used for evaluation purpose and their profile information are shown in Table 18.3. Participants are from different countries and observed different cultures. The participants were from Pakistan, Vietnam, China, Korea, Egypt, Spain, Yemen, Ecuador, Guatemala, Bangladesh, India, Iran, and Australia. Each of the users had different demographics, such as age, gender, vision impairment, education, and wellness applications expertise etc. The participants were provided with initial training of the MM application usage. The participants are briefly addressed regarding the purpose of the research and got their willing- ness. The participants had personal computing devices like smart phone, laptop and desktop, and tablets and had access to internet on these devices 24/7. These participants were already using wellness application and health conscious.

16.7.2 Type of Experiments and Evaluation Criteria

We performed three types of experiments. These includes Perceived Usability, User Satisfaction, and User Experience Assessment. For the perceived usability, we used the Sysem Usability Scale (SUS) [13], which is one of the most commonly used measures in literature. SUS questionnaire performed more accurately than computer system usability questionnaire (CSUQ) and Post Study System Usability Questionnaire (PSSUQ) when sample size greater than 8. The user subjective satisfaction is assessed by using the criteria of Questionnaire for User Interaction Satisfaction [39], which measures the overall system satisfaction in term of nine specific UI factors. The user experience assessment, called User Experience Questionnaire (UEQ) [29] is used. The UEQ allow a rapid assessment of the user experience by getting user express feelings, impressions, and attitudes after using a product. It measures both classical usability aspects as well as user experience aspects. It has been used by different companies for the evaluation their products and is a good measure, therefore we have also adopted it in our study.

16.7.3 Evaluation process

For the user evaluation of the proposed methodology, the real-world application A-UI/UX-A tool, developed as a part of mining minds platform, was given to all the participants to use it for a period of one month. After full use of the application, the participants were asked to fill-out the questionnaires (SUS, QUIS, and UEQ) to find out the A-UI/UX-A tool perceived usability, user satisfaction, and user experience. The results of each of the experiments are given in the subsequent sections.

16.7.4 Perceived usability and efficiency results

The average SUS score is 89.7, which is ranked as B+ means that MM application is higher perceived usability.

16.7.5 User satisfaction

In many cases, the efficiency is less important than how satisfied the users are while they are experiencing the product. Therefore, for the user satisfaction measurement, we used the

Questionnaire for User Interaction Satisfaction (QUIS), Figure 16.7 shows the means values for each scale.

The mean response for the questions was 5.833 with SD = 1.048, which means that the overall user satisfaction of MM application is above the average. The confidence intervals for the scale means are smaller that estimate higher is the precision, more trust the results and shows how consistent the participants judged the A-UI/UX-A tool. The alpha-coefficient values are higher than 0.7 for all the scales except terminology and system information. This may be due to the users misinterpretation of the terminology and system information.

Table 16.3 Personal profile information of the volunteers who participated in the evaluation of mining minds platform (n = 32)

Age (years)	No. of users	% of users	Mean (SD)
18–24	10	31.25	29.125 (6.8)
25–34	13	40.625	
35–44	9	28.125	
Gender			
Male	25	78.125	
Female	7	21.875	
Health Status			
Normal	12	37.5	
Hypertension	10	31.25	
Obesity	10	31.25	
Activity Level			
Normal	13	40.625	
Active	10	31.25	
Sedentary	9	28.125	
Disabilities			
Vision	17	53.125	
Limb	7	21.875	
Hearing	4	12.5	
No	4	12.5	
Education			
Under graduation	19	59.375	
Graduation	8	25	
Post-graduation	5	15.625	
Computation Expertise			
Expert	27	84.375	
Intermediate	4	12.5	
Novice	1	3.125	
Ethnicity, culture			
East Asia	12	37.5	
South Asia	11	34.375	
Australia	4	12.5	
Middle East	3	9.375	
Europer	2	6.25	
Upper limb Usage			
Right hand	16	50	

Both	11	34.375	
Left hand	5	15.625	

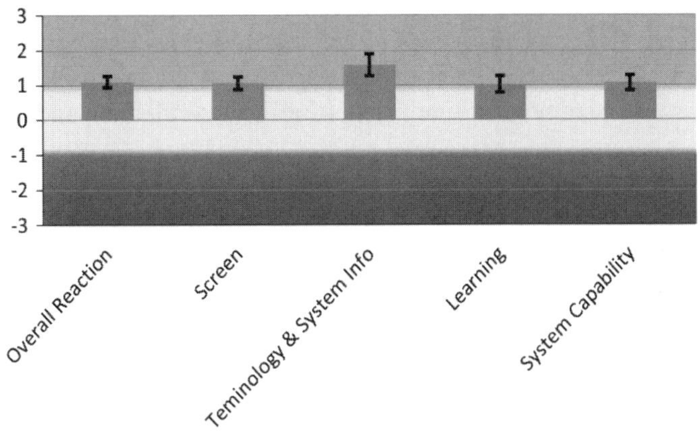

Figure 16.7 User interaction satisfaction (QUIS) scores for each factor

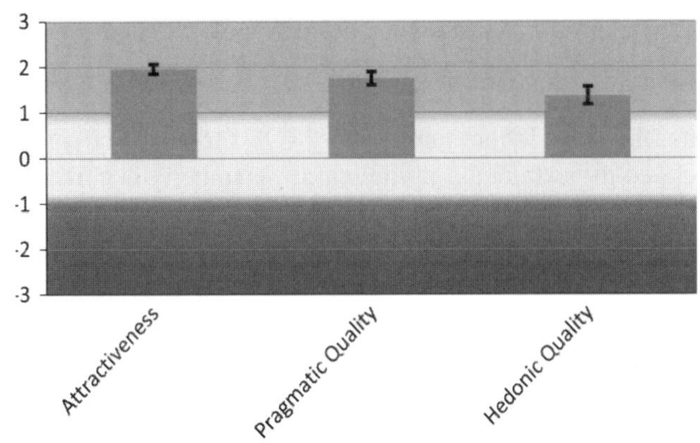

Figure 18.8 The UEQ pragmatic and hedonic quality score

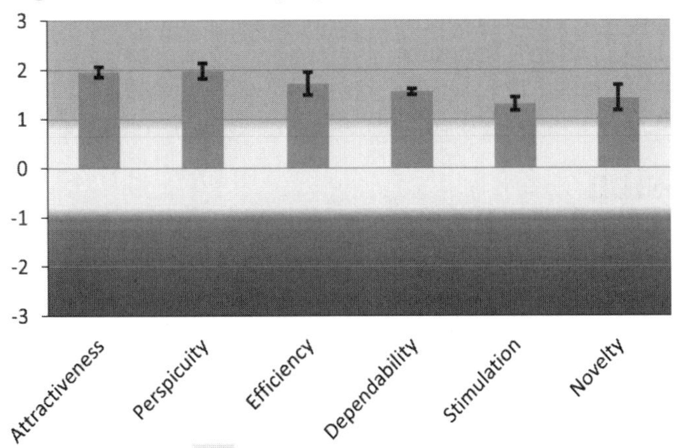

Figure 16.9 UEQ resultant scores for six dimensions scales

16.7.6 User Experience Assessment

For the user experience assessment, the participants were asked to fill the UEQ questionnaire. UEQ is the widely used questionnaire for the subjectivity measurement of the user experience of any interactive system. They provide a tool in the form of excel sheet for capturing the user experience of users, while they are interacting with the product. It consists of six-dimension scales such as attractiveness, perspicuity, efficiency, dependability, stimulation, and novelty.

The scales of questionnaire are grouped into the pragmatic quality (perspicuity, efficiency, and dependability) and hedonic quality (stimulation, originality). The pragmatic quality is related to the task, while the hedonic quality is represented as non-task related aspects. Figure 16.8 shows the pragmatic and hedonic quality aspects of MM application along with the application attractiveness.

The results show that all the scales have quite good results including the hedonic and pragmatic aspect of the MM application. In Figure 16.9, the smaller confidence interval indicates that the measurements are accurate. The value of Cronbachs alpha-coefficient of attractiveness is higher than 0.7, which shows that users like the adaptive UI generated by the A- UI/UX-A tool. The value of Cronbachs alpha-coefficient for novelty is low, which means that it does not play an important role in adaptive UI.

Table 18.4 represents the correlation among the UX factors. The evaluation depicts that attractiveness is correlated to perspicuity, stimulation; perspicuity is correlated to efficiency and dependability; dependability is correlated to stimulation and novelty; and Stimulation is correlated to novelty.

The UEQ also provide a benchmark that contains data collected from 4818 participants of 163 products evaluation. The benchmark easily gives insight of a comparative analysis that a product satisfactory user experience to be successful in the market. In Figure 16.10, the comparison results for the evaluated MM application are relatively good as compared to benchmark data.

The Kendalls correlation is shown Table 18.5, which depicts that there is agreement among the participants for all UEQ factors. The value above 0.7 is considered excellent in its agreement, which is the case for 4 factors: Attractiveness, Perspicuity, Efficiency, and Novelty. The minimum level of agreement is shown in the Stimulation and Dependability factors.

16.8 Discussion

The evaluation results obtained from user-based evaluation, out of 32 participants, there were 3 participants which were not able to use the application for maximum of 5 days. On average all the participants use the application more than 27 days. From the results achieved, we concluded that the adaptive UIs generated by A-UI/UX-A tool for all users having impairments have positive user experience because the accessibility of all services functionality are increased.

The user-based evaluation results show that performance of the UI improved system functionality. UI is adapted according to the user ability and requirements. The SUS evaluation scored greater than 89% which ranked it as B+. It means that the user's efficiency increased with the adaptability behavior of the UI. It is noted that the adaptive accuracy of UI has significant impact on user performance.

The hypothesis regarding the user satisfaction is evaluated through QUIS with alpha coefficient score which is more than 0.7. It means that users are more satisfied with the adaptive ability of the MM application. However, frequent adaptation which causes change in UI, annoying some of the hypertensive users. It disturbs their learning ability and cause the negative impact on overall reaction. The user experience in terms of hedonic and pragmatic quality is evaluated through UEQ. The evaluation represents that hedonic quality is little low than pragmatic quality. It is because the occasional diminish of UI representation due to adaptive UI behavior. However, A-UI/UX-A have some issues to be considered.

Table 16.4 Correlation of UX factors/scales

	Attractiveness	Perspicuity	Efficiency	Dependability	Stimulation	Novelty
Attractiveness	1	0.1598701	0.525075	0.214811376	0.49154268	−0.2987
Perspicuity		1	0.246627	0.091777454	−0.47288	−0.197
Efficiency			1	0.054750579	−0.4114699	−0.5516
Dependability				1	0.20404049	0.65361
Stimulation					1	0.01932
Novelty						1

Significant with $p < 0.05$

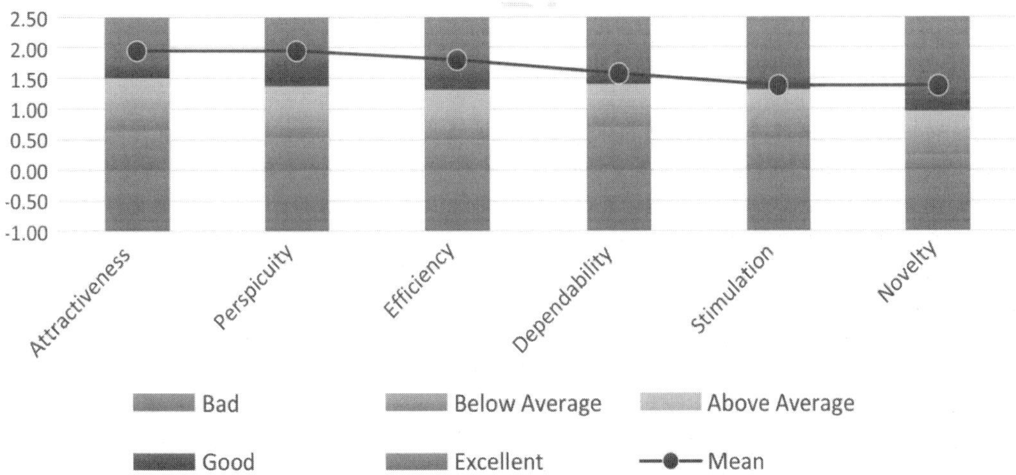

Figure 16.10 UEQ resultant scores for six dimensions scales with benchmark data

Table 18.5 Kendall's W of UEQ factors	
Attractiveness	0.771
Perspicuity	0.855
Efficiency	0.836
Dependability	0.556
Stimulation	0.453
Novelty	0.753

– Issue with the final UI presentation the analysis of user revealed problem with the final user interface presentation such as UI elements adjustment and alignment, which sometimes break the UI design and functions. Automatically generated user interfaces are generally perceived less aesthetic appeal as compared to create by a designer. User interfaces created by a designer reflects the creativity and are well aligned with application. Furthermore, recurrent adaptations diminish the consistency in the UI, and reduce the learning rate. For example, frequent changes in the UI may frustrate and confuse some users.

– Issue with model and adaptation rule creation Indeed, model-driven user interface begins with model's creation, which required expertise even the system provide graphical user interface for creating such models. Although, we provide A-UI/UX-A tool, the designer can create models and adaptation rules that can manage the adaptation in user interface based on the user context. However, the creation of complex rules is difficult to manage.

16.9 Summary

The proposed model-based system is designed by taking the limitations of existing system into account. The existing systems are not capable of generating UI at runtime, require the redeployment of the system, and new rules are not added without effecting the running system. In addition, these systems lack in modeling approach, considering multimodal data sources, user feedback and content base adaptation. While our proposed methodology comprehends multimodal data for context identification; support direct and indirect adaptation; converting generalized context model into specialized domain context through authoring tool while considering the environment, platform and user; and focusing the content along with presentation and navigation in adaptation aspects. Last but not least, the adaptation on UI is made when the context is change, which is observed by implicit and explicit (user feedback) ways and then evaluate the context and user experience. It considers the dynamics of the UI associated with the user in the form of context-of-use. It helps in improving the information accessibility, usability, user experience of system. The efficiency of the proposed methodology with respect to adaptive UI ranked as B+ which is considered as quite acceptable in term of usability. The QUIS questionnaires are used to evaluate the overall user satisfaction of the proposed methodology. The obtained alpha score is higher than 0.7 for all the scale except terminology and system information due to misinterpretation. The user experience assessment is evaluated through widely used UEQ questionnaire for the subjectivity measurement of the user experience of any interactive system in six dimensions e.g. attractiveness, perspicuity, efficiency, dependability, stimulation, and novelty. The results show that hedonic quality is lower than pragmatic quality due to occasional diminish of UI representation. Adaptive UI representation generation is generally perceived less aesthetic as compared to create by a designer. Designer created User interfaces reflects the creativity and are well aligned with application. Furthermore, recurrent adaptations decrease the consistency in the UI, and reduce the learning ability.

Currently the rule authoring is able to manage basic level adaptation rule. In future, we will improve the rule-authoring tool for management of complex adaptation rules and as well a final UI presentation issue. The authoring tool can be enhanced for application users to add specialized rules, based on personalized context. In addition to user-based evaluation, we will enhance evaluation through physiological measurements to remove subjectivity in evaluating user experience.

Source Code

For source code, please contact us at:

The contents of this chapter have been previously published in the following article:

Hussain, Jamil, et al. "Model-based adaptive user interface based on context and user experience evaluation." Journal on Multimodal User Interfaces 12.1 (2018): 1-16.

References

[1] Ahmad M, Amin MB, Hussain S, Kang BH, Cheong T, Lee S (2016) Health fog: a novel framework for health and wellness applications. J Supercomput 72(10):3677–3695

[2] Akiki PA, Bandara AK, Yu Y (2014) Adaptive model-driven user interface development systems. ACM Comput Surv CSUR 47(1):9

[3] Akiki PA, Bandara AK, Yu Y (2016) Engineering adaptive model- driven user interfaces. IEEE Trans Softw Eng 42(12):1118–1147

[4] Ali R, Afzal M, Hussain M, Ali M, Siddiqi MH, Lee S, Kang BH (2016) Multimodal hybrid reasoning methodology for personalized wellbeing services. Comput Biol Med 69:10–28

[5] Ali T, Lee S (2016) Wellness concepts model use and effectiveness in intelligent knowledge authoring environment. In: International conference on smart homes and health telematics. Springer, pp 271–282

[6] Amin MB, Banos O, Khan WA, Muhammad Bilal HS, Gong J, Bui DM, Cho SH, Hussain S, Ali T, Akhtar U et al (2016) On curating multimodal sensory data for health and wellness platforms. Sensors 16(7):980

[7] Balme L, Demeure A, Barralon N, Coutaz J, Calvary G (2004) Cameleon-rt: a software architecture reference model for dis- tributed, migratable, and plastic user interfaces. In: European symposium on ambient intelligence. Springer, pp 291–302

[8] Banos O, Bilal Amin M, Ali Khan W, Afzal M, Hussain M, Kang BH, Lee S (2016) The mining minds digital health and wellness framework. Biomed Eng Online 15(1):165–186. https://doi.org/10. 1186/s12938-016-0179-9

[9] Banos O, Bilal-Amin M, Ali-Khan W, Afzel M, Ahmad M, Ali M, Ali T, Ali R, Bilal M, Han M, Hussain J, Hussain M, Hussain S, Hur TH, Bang JH, Huynh-The T, Idris M, Kang DW, Park SB, Siddiqui M, Vui LB, Fahim M, Khattak AM, Kang BH, Lee S (2015) An innovative platform for person-centric health and well- ness support. In: Proceedings of the international work-conference on bioinformatics and biomedical engineering (IWBBIO 2015)

[10] Banos O, Bilal-Amin M, Ali-Khan W, Afzel M, Ali T, Kang BH, Lee S (2015) The mining minds platform: a novel person-centered digital health and wellness framework. In: Proceedings of the 9th international conference on pervasive computing technologies for healthcare (PervasiveHealth 2015)

[11] Banos O, Villalonga C, Bang JH, Hur TH, Kang D, Park SB, Hyunh-The T, Vui LB, Amin MB, Razzaq MA, Ali Khan W, Hong CS, Lee S (2016) Human behavior analysis by means of multimodal context mining. Sensors 16(8):1–19

[12] Blouin A, Beaudoux O (2010) Improving modularity and usabil- ity of interactive systems with malai. In: Proceedings of the 2nd ACM SIGCHI symposium on engineering interactive computing systems. ACM, pp 115–124
[13] Brooke J et al (1996) Sus: a quick and dirty usability scale. Usability Eval Ind 189(194):4–7
[14] Calvary G, Coutaz J, Thevenin D, Limbourg Q, Bouillon L, Vander- donckt J (2003) A unifying reference framework for multi-target user interfaces. Interact Comput 15(3):289–308
[15] Castillejo E, Almeida A, López-de Ipiña D (2014) Ontology-based model for supporting dynamic and adaptive user interfaces. Int J Hum Comput Interact 30(10):771–786
[16] Chu H, Song H, Wong C, Kurakake S, Katagiri M (2004) Roam, a seamless application framework. J Syst Softw 69(3):209–226
[17] Coutaz J (2010) User interface plasticity: Model driven engineering to the limit! In: Proceedings of the 2nd ACM SIGCHI symposium on engineering interactive computing systems. ACM, pp 1–8
[18] Daniel AO, Yinka A, Frank I, Adesina S (2013) Culture-based adaptive web design Int J Sci Eng Res 4(2)
[19] Gajos KZ, Weld DS, Wobbrock JO (2010) Automatically gen- erating personalized user interfaces with supple. Artif Intell 174(12):910–950
[20] Gamecho B, Minón R, Aizpurua A, Cearreta I, Arrue M, Garay- Vitoria N, Abascal J (2015) Automatic generation of tailored accessible user interfaces for ubiquitous services. IEEE Trans Hum Mach Syst 45(5):612–623
[21] Ghiani G, Manca M, Paternò F (2015) Authoring context- dependent cross-device user interfaces based on trigger/action rules. In: Proceedings of the 14th international conference on mobile and ubiquitous multimedia. ACM, pp 313–322
[22] Ghiani G, Manca M, Paternò F, Santoro C (2017) Personalization of context-dependent applications through trigger-action rules. ACM Trans Comput Hum Interact TOCHI 24(2):14
[23] Guerrero-Garcia J, Gonzalez-Calleros JM, Vanderdonckt J, Munoz-Arteaga J (2009) A theoretical survey of user interface description languages: preliminary results. In: Web congress, 2009. LA-WEB'09. Latin American. IEEE, pp 36–43
[24] Heckmann D, Schwartz T, Brandherm B, Schmitz M, von Wilamowitz-Moellendorff M (2005) GUMO—the general user model ontology. In: International conference on user modeling. Springer, pp 428–432
[25] Helms J, Schaefer R, Luyten K, Vermeulen J, Abrams M, Coyette A, Vanderdonckt J (2009) Human-centered engineer- ing of interactive systems with the user interface markup lan- guage. Hum Cent Softw Eng 139–171. https://doi.org/10.1007/ 978-1-84800-907-3_7
[26] Hussain J, Khan WA, Afzal M, Hussain M, Kang BH, Lee S (2014) Adaptive user interface and user experience based authoring tool for recommendation systems. In: International conference on ubiq- uitous computing and ambient intelligence. Springer, pp 136–142
[27] Jorritsma W, Cnossen F, van Ooijen PM (2015) Adaptive support for user interface customization: a study in radiology. Int J Hum Comput Stud 77:1–9
[28] Langley P (1997) Machine learning for adaptive user interfaces. In: Annual conference on artificial intelligence. Springer, pp 53–62

[29] Laugwitz B, Held T, Schrepp M (2008) Construction and evaluation of a user experience questionnaire. In: Symposium of the Austrian HCI and usability engineering group. Springer, pp 63–76
[30] Law ELC, van Schaik P (2010) Modelling user experience-an agenda for research and practice. Interact Comput 22(5):313–322
[31] Lehmann G, Rieger A, Blumendorf M, Albayrak S (2010) A 3-layer architecture for smart environment models. In: 2010 8th IEEE inter- national conference on pervasive computing and communications workshops (PERCOM workshops). IEEE, pp 636–641
[32] Limbourg Q, Vanderdonckt J, Michotte B, Bouillon L, López- Jaquero V (2004) USIXML: a language supporting multi-path development of user interfaces. In: International workshop on design, specification, and verification of interactive systems. Springer, pp 200–220
[33] Meixner G, Paterno F, Vanderdonckt J (2011) Past, present, and future of model-based user interface development. i-com 10(3):2– 11
[34] Mezhoudi N, Khaddam I, Vanderdonckt J (2015) Wisel: a mixed initiative approach for widget selection. In: Proceedings of the 2015 conference on research in adaptive and convergent systems. ACM, pp 349–356
[35] Michotte B, Vanderdonckt J (2008) GrafiXML, a multi-target user interface builder based on Usixml. In: Fourth international confer- ence on autonomic and autonomous systems (ICAS'08), pp 15–22. https://doi.org/10.1109/ICAS.2008.29
[36] Miñón R, Paternò F, Arrue M (2013) An environment for design- ing and sharing adaptation rules for accessible applications. In: Proceedings of the 5th ACM SIGCHI symposium on engineering interactive computing systems. ACM, pp 43–48
[37] Mori G, Paternò F, Santoro C (2002) CTTE: support for develop- ing and analyzing task models for interactive system design. IEEE Trans Softw Eng 28(8):797–813
[38] Motti VG, Vanderdonckt J (2013) A computational framework for context-aware adaptation of user interfaces. In: 2013 IEEE seventh international conference on research challenges in information sci- ence (RCIS). IEEE, pp 1–12
[39] Norman KL, Shneiderman B, Harper B, Slaughter L (1998) Ques- tionnaire for user interaction satisfaction. University of Maryland (Norman, 1989) Disponível em
[40] Paternò F, Santoro C (2003) A unified method for designing interac- tive systems adaptable to mobile and stationary platforms. Interact Comput 15(3):349–366
[41] Paterno F, Santoro C, Spano LD (2009) Maria: a universal, declar- ative, multiple abstraction-level language for service-oriented applications in ubiquitous environments. ACM Trans Comput Hum Interact TOCHI 16(4):19
[42] Peissner M, Häbe D, Janssen D, Sellner T (2012) MyUI: generat- ing accessible user interfaces from multimodal design patterns. In: Proceedings of the 4th ACM SIGCHI symposium on engineering interactive computing systems. ACM, pp 81–90
[43] Surguy M (2013) History of Laravel PHP framework, Elo- quence emerging. Maxoffsky. http://maxoffsky.com/codeblog/ history-of-laravel-php-framework-eloquence-emerging
[44] Viana W, Andrade RM (2008) XMobile: a MB-UID environment for semi-automatic generation of adaptive applications for mobile devices. J Syst Softw 81(3):382–394
[45] Villalonga C, Banos O, Khan WA, Ali T, Razzaq MA, Lee S, Pomares H, Rojas I (2015) High-level context inference for human behavior identification. In: International workshop on ambient assisted living. Springer, pp 164–175

Part VII

Appendix

Appendix - I

Requirements Engineering

17.1 Mining Minds Terms and Definitions

Term	Definition
DCL	Data Curation Layer
ICL	Information Curation Layer
KCL	Knowledge Curation Layer
SCL	Service Curation Layer
SL	Supporting Layer
Lifelog	Information associated to the user's life-events over time
Lifelog schema	Lifelog schema represents the structure and associated semantics of user profile and lifelog data.
User profile	Information describing the user characteristics (i.e., age, gender, etc.)
Data source	User devices sending the required data, i.e., smartphone, video camera
Raw sensory data	Numerical values describing a physical phenomenon such as human body motion (e.g., acceleration)
Sensory metadata	Information that describes, at least, the source of data (e.g., video), the user to which the raw sensory data belongs (e.g., user ID) and the time in which the raw sensory data was registered (e.g., timestamp)
Sensory data	Raw sensory data plus sensory metadata
SNS data	Data from social networks (i.e., twitter, Facebook)
Context	General concept to refer either to low-level context and/or high-level context
Situation	An abnormal status of a subject caused by unhealthy behaviors
Rule verification and validation	Verification ensures that rule created is consistent with requirements and validation ensures that the rule created is correctly working on real data
Unresolved case	A new case for which the existing knowledge is insufficient to solve
Recommendation	An actionable statement provided to the subject for healthy habit induction
Fact	An informative statement provided to the subject for education
Reasoning	The process of producing recommendations
Context	General concept to refer either to low-level context and/or high-level context
Low-level context	Information describing the user activities (e.g., sitting), user locations (e.g., restaurant) and user emotions (e.g., happy)
High-level context	Information describing the situation of the user (e.g., lunch)

Production Rule	Production rule is ultimate and shareable rule which is used in reasoning to produce recommendation.
Domain Expert	Domain expert is an actor who will interact with system to create knowledge base.
Verification and Validation	Verification ensures that rule created is consistent with requirements and validation ensures that the rule created is correctly working on real data
Schema	Schema represents the structure and associated semantics of user profile and lifelog data.
RBR	Rule Base Reasoning
Case	A case is collection of data/information that represent a complete state of a subject in a particular time
CBR	Case Base Reasoning
Hybrid Reasoning	A combined reasoning of RBR and CBR
Unresolved Case	A new case for which the existing knowledge is insufficient to solve
Production Knowledge	The knowledge is in production environment and is ready for execution
Recommendation	An actionable statement provided to the subject for healthy habit induction
Fact	An informative statement provided to the subject for education
	A target that a subject is intending to achieve
Achievement	The measurement of the subject status so far towards achieving the goal
Interpreted Recommendation	The recommendation passed through the process of interpretations
Environmental Variables	Environment variables represent the factors related to environment rather than user such as weather, time, season etc.
Service	An outcome of the system in which a subject is interested such as recommendation, facts, alerts, notifications.
Self-report	A method which involves asking a participant about their feelings, attitudes, beliefs and so on
User Capabilities	User cognitive, perceptual and physical characteristics
Context of use	Environmental variables and low-level context (location)
Device Characteristics	Screen size, resolution, memory, and battery
UI Adaptation	The changes in user interface
Observational Data	User interaction data with the user interface
User Experience	User perception, satisfaction about the user interfaces
User Profile	User related data that do not change frequently

17.2 Data Curation Layer

17.2.1 Functional Requirements

ID	Description
DCL-FR-01	The platform shall read the raw sensory data of the user from his/her data source
DCL-FR-02	The platform shall provide permanent persistence to the user generated raw sensory data
DCL-FR-03	The platform shall provide raw sensory data for context determination of the user
DCL-FR-04	The platform shall maintain user profile data
DCL-FR-05	The platform shall maintain user timeline as a lifelog of daily behaviors
DCL-FR-06	The platform shall provide read, write, delete, and update access to the subscribers of lifelog data
DCL-FR-07	The platform shall provide read access to the subscribers of raw sensory data
DCL-FR-08	The platform shall monitor the lifelog of a user for notify-able situations
DCL-FR-09	The platform shall persist user feedback regarding generated recommendations and identified context
DCL-FR-10	The platform shall manipulate the value of the factors from lifelog and questionnaires related to nutrition, physical activity and diseases.
DCL-FR-11	The platform shall use the questionnaire responses for the factors manipulation when the registration age is less than seven days.
DCL-FR-12	The platform shall use the lifelog for the factors manipulation when the registration age is greater than seven days.
DCL-FR-13	The platform shall identify the risk status associated with the manipulated factors.
DCL-FR-14	The platform shall provide the risk factor's vector for the recommendation generation and adaptive questionnaires.
DCL-FR-15	The platform shall use factor's value to manipulate the index for the healthy behavior identification.
DCL-FR-16	The platform shall provide the details of the healthy behavior index on the basis of the every factors' status on the basis of the week.

17.2.2 Non-Functional Requirements

ID	Description
DCL-NFR-01	The platform shall read the raw sensory data of the user from his/her personal device in real-time with delay no later than 3 seconds
DCL-NFR-02	The platform shall provide raw sensory data for low level activities determination in real-time with delay no later than 3 seconds
DCL-NFR-03	The platform shall only read the raw sensory data from verified personal device
DCL-NFR-04	The platform shall maintain the consistency, integrity, and reliability of raw sensory data in non-volatile storage

17.3 Information Curation Layer

17.3.1 Functional Requirement

ID	Description
ICL-FR-01	The platform shall provide each low-level context recognizer with the appropriate raw sensory data for recognition
ICL-FR-02	The platform shall identify the user's low-level context
ICL-FR-03	The platform shall identify the user's high-level context
ICL-FR-04	The platform shall provide low-level context information for the generation of the lifelog
ICL-FR-05	The platform shall provide high-level context information for the generation of the lifelog

17.3.2 Non-Functional Requirements

ID	Description
ICL-NFR-01	Overall low-level context recognition accuracy of the platform shall be be greater than or equal to 85%
ICL-NFR-02	Overall high-level context inference accuracy of the platform shall be greater than or equal to 80%

17.4 Knowledge Curation Layer

17.4.1 Functional Requirement

ID	Description
KCL-FR-01	The data-driven knowledge acquisition shall know schema detail of lifelog and user profile data in order to load the data and extract feature model.
KCL-FR-02	The data-driven knowledge acquisition shall load all related data specified as feature model from Data Curation Layer (DCL). The loaded lifelog and user profile data will be used for classification model creation.
KCL-FR-03	The expert-driven knowledge acquisition shall share the production rules with Service Curation Layer (SCL) for final reasoning.
KCL-FR-04	The expert-driven environment shall create "Situations" and share its configuration with SCL and DCL. Furthermore, all associated rules with "Situation" shall be provided to SCL.

17.4.2 Non-Functional Requirements

ID	Description
KCL-NFR-01	The layer shall persist only verified and validated rules into knowledge base.
KCL-NFR-02	The layer shall ensure consistency of distributed copies of knowledge base.

17.5 Service Curation Layer

17.5.1 Functional Requirement

ID	Description
SCL-FR-01	The layer shall receive the service request from user application, third party application, or mining mind platform generated events
SCL -FR-02	The layer shall retrieve data from intermediate database (user profile, lifelog, and environmental variables)
SCL -FR-03	The layer shall retrieve production knowledge from knowledge base
SCL -FR-04	The layer shall identify the unresolved user requests and notify the corresponding layer for missing knowledge
SCL -FR-05	The layer shall deliver the results to the service requester and to corresponding layer of mining mind for persistence
SCL -FR-06	The layer shall generate goal-based recommendation
SCL -FR-07	The layer shall personalize the recommendation based on location and weather information.
SCL -FR-08	The layer shall provide take care of user preference-based recommendation through continuous feedback from the user.

17.5.2 Non-Functional Requirements

ID	Description
SCL -NFR-01	The service request shall include the user identification required to prepare the data request
SCL -NFR-02	The user application and host layer of the services shall connect to the internet

17.6 Supporting Layer

17.6.1 Functional Requirements

ID	Description
SL-FR-01	The platform shall retrieve the user profile information, context of use and device information for adaptation of the user interface
SL -FR-02	The platform shall collect the user data such as user feedback and user observational data for the enhancement of user interface
SL -FR-03	The platform shall utilize the user profile data, lifelog and raw sensory data for analytics

17.6.2 Non-Functional Requirements

ID	Description
SL-NFR-01	The platform shall provide user interface that is easy to use and intuitive

Appendix - II

Use Cases & Design

18.1 Data Curation Layer

18.1.1 Use Case List

ID	Name
DCL-UC-01	Receive sensory and environmental data from data source
DCL-UC-02	Receive video data stream from data source
DCL-UC-03	Synchronize heterogeneous user data
DCL-UC-04	Send data for context determination
DCL-UC-05	Receive context data
DCL-UC-06	Retrieve Lifelog Information
DCL-UC-07	Persist Lifelog Information
DCL-UC-08	Map Instances
DCL-UC-09	Validate Instances
DCL-UC-10	Situation configuration
DCL-UC-11	LLM configuration for target variables
DCL-UC-12	LLM for situation detection
DCL-UC-13	Retrieve sensory data from non-volatile storage for intermediate data generation (offline)
DCL-UC-14	Retrieve sensory data from non-volatile storage (online)
DCL-UC-15	Persist sensory data in non-volatile storage
DCL-UC-16	Manipulate Behavior factors
DCL-UC-17	Identify Risky factors
DCL-UC-18	Identify Healthy Behavior Index (HBI)
DCL-UC-19	Generate detail of HBI week wise

18.1.2 Use Case Diagram

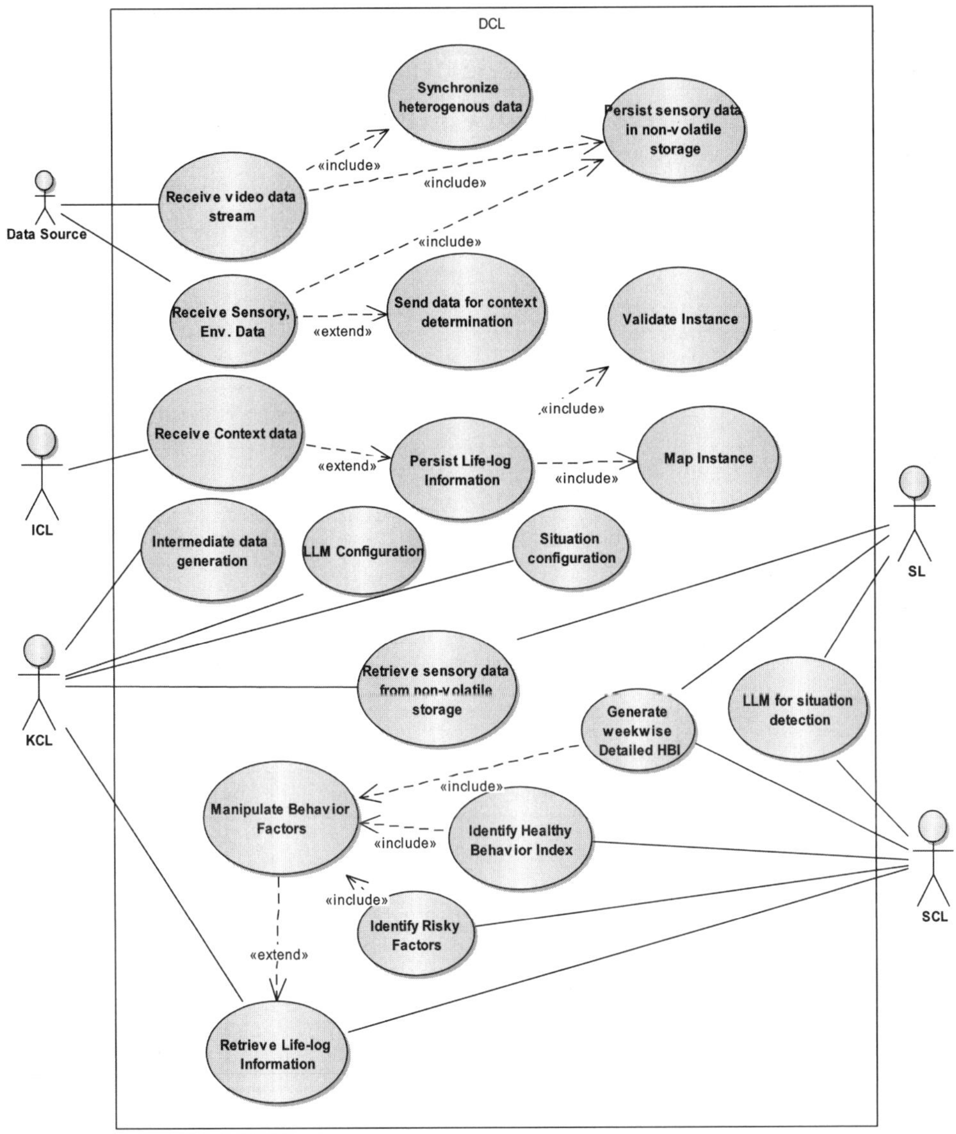

18.1.3 Use Case Description

Use Case ID:	DCL-UC-01		
Use Case Name:	Receive sensory and environmental data from data source		
Created By:	Bilal Amin	Last Updated By:	Bilal Amin
Date Created:	15 July 2015	Last Revision Date:	20 Dec 2016
Actors:	Data source		

Description:	User sensory data and environmental is received and buffered from data source in real time
Trigger:	User activity of at least 3 seconds
Pre-conditions:	User is a registered client of MM platform
Post-conditions:	Sensory and environmental data is persisted in the buffer
Normal Flow:	1. Sensory and environmental data is received by a data acquisition component 2. Data source is authenticated, and contents of the data are verified 3. Data is temporary buffered for context determination
Alternative Flows:	N/A
Exceptions:	2a. In step 2 of the normal flow, if the user is detected to be un-authorized or contents are un-verifiable Data acquisition component destroys the data
Includes:	N/A
Frequency of Use:	Very frequent: every 3 second
NFR ID:	DCL-NFR-01, DCL-NFR-03
Assumptions:	Communication contract is defined between data source and data acquisition component
Notes and Issues:	N/A
Sequence Diagram:	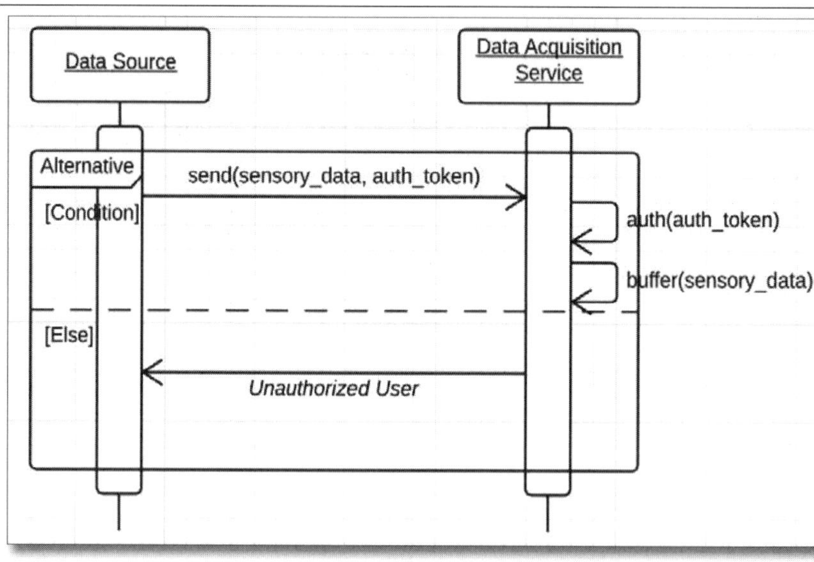

Use Case ID:	**DCL-UC-02**		
Use Case Name:	Receive video data stream from data source		
Created By:	Bilal Amin	**Last Updated By:**	Bilal Amin
Date Created:	15 July 2015	**Last Revision Date:**	20 Dec 2016
Actors:	Data source		
Description:	User video data stream is received and buffered from data source in real time		
Trigger:	Video camera is streaming user feed		

Pre-conditions:	User is a registered client of MM platform
Post-conditions:	User video data stream is persisted in the video stream buffer
Normal Flow:	1. Video data stream is received by a data acquisition component 2. Data source is authenticated, and contents of the data stream are verified 3. Video data stream is temporary buffered for context determination
Alternative Flows:	N/A
Exceptions:	2a. In step 2 of the normal flow, if the user is detected to be un-authorized or contents are un-verifiable Data acquisition component destroys the data
Includes:	N/A
Frequency of Use:	Less frequent: If video streaming-based data source is available
NFR ID:	DCL-NFR-03
Assumptions:	Video data streaming communication contract is defined between data source and data acquisition component
Notes and Issues:	N/A
Sequence Diagram:	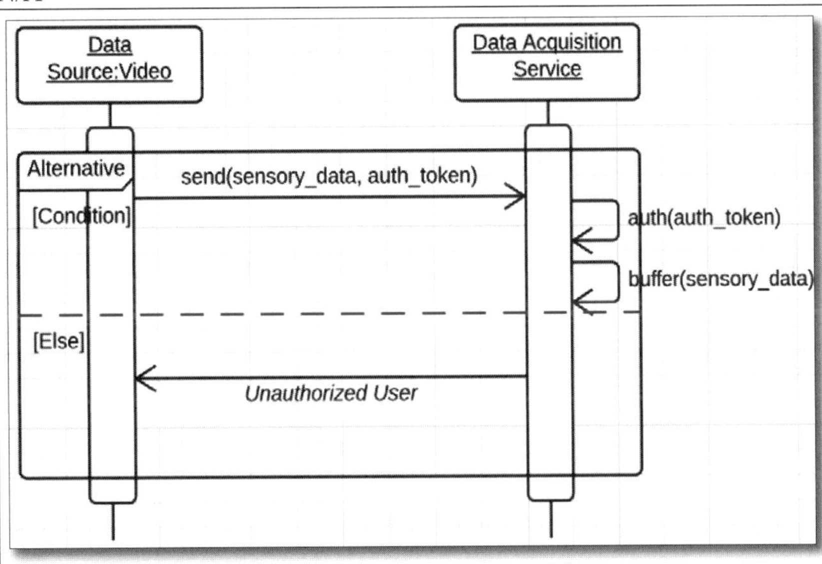

Use Case ID:	**DCL-UC-03**		
Use Case Name:	Synchronize heterogeneous user data		
Created By:	Bilal Amin	**Last Updated By:**	Bilal Amin
Date Created:	15 July 2015	**Last Revision Date:**	20 Dec 2016
Actors:	DCL		
Description:	User video data stream is synchronized with the corresponding sensory data		
Trigger:	Video camera is streaming user feed		
Pre-conditions:	Video data stream is persisted in the video stream buffer		
Post-conditions:	Video data stream is synchronized with its corresponding sensory data		

Normal Flow:	1. Time stamp and user id of video data stream is read from the video stream buffer 2. Sensory data is searched and retrieved from buffer based on the time stamp and user id 3. Retrieved sensory data is concatenated with the video stream data and stored back in the sensory data buffer for context determination
Alternative Flows:	2a. In step 2 of the normal flow, if the sensory data is not found Data acquisition component deletes the video data stream from the video data stream buffer
Exceptions:	N/A
Includes:	N/A
Frequency of Use:	Less frequent: If video streaming-based data source is available
NFR ID:	DCL-NFR-02
Assumptions:	Video data streaming communication contract is defined between data source and data acquisition component
Notes and Issues:	N/A
Sequence Diagram:	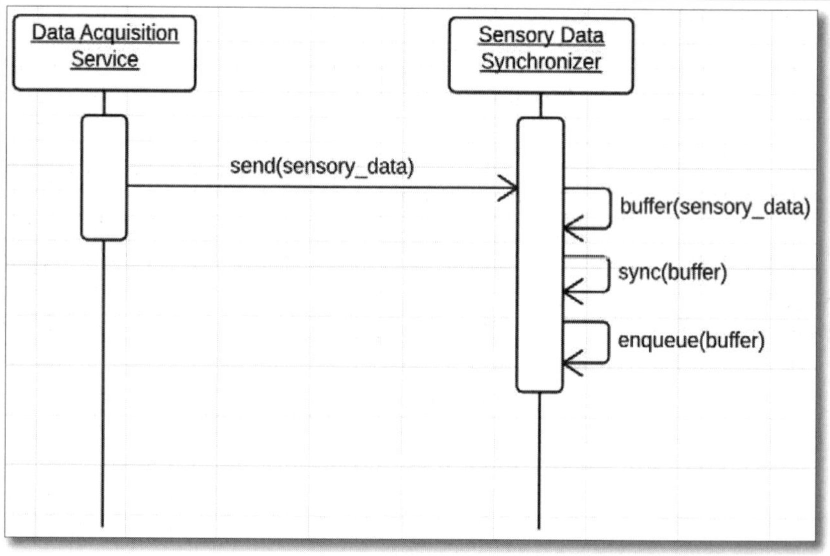

Use Case ID:	**DCL-UC-04**		
Use Case Name:	Send data for context determination		
Created By:	Bilal Amin	**Last Updated By:**	Bilal Amin
Date Created:	15 July 2015	**Last Revision Date:**	20 Dec 2016
Actors:	Context sender		
Description:	Sensory data buffer is sent to ICL for context determination		
Trigger:	Sensory data is available for context determination		
Pre-conditions:	Sensory data is persisted in the buffer		
Post-conditions:	Sensory data is sent for context determination		
Normal Flow:	1. Context sender reads sensory data from the sensory data buffer 2. Context sender creates communication object by serialization		

	3. Communication object is sent to the ICL server
Alternative Flows:	N/A
Exceptions:	N/A
Includes:	N/A
Frequency of Use:	Frequent: whenever context need to be determined
NFR ID:	N/A
Assumptions:	N/A
Notes and Issues:	N/A

Sequence Diagram:

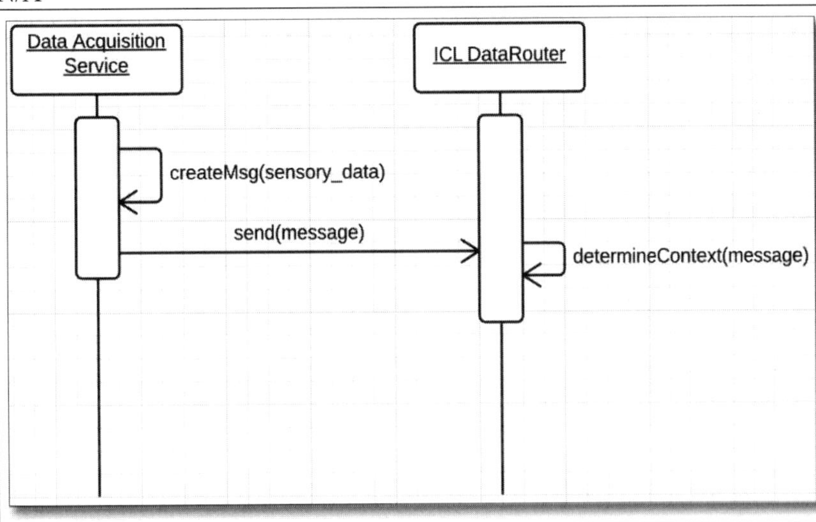

Use Case ID:	**DCL-UC-05**		
Use Case Name:	Receive context data		
Created By:	Bilal Amin	**Last Updated By:**	Bilal Amin
Date Created:	15 July 2015	**Last Revision Date:**	20 Dec 2016
Actors:	ICL server		
Description:	After the determination by ICL, context is received by context receiver component and forwarded for non-volatile storage		
Trigger:	New context or change in previous context is determined by ICL		
Pre-conditions:	Context data is available		
Post-conditions:	Context data is sent for non-volatile storage		
Normal Flow:	1. Context receiver receives context object 2. Context receiver de-serializes context object 3. Context object is sent for non-volatile persistence (async) 4. Context object is sent for lifelog mapping		
Alternative Flows:	N/A		
Exceptions:	N/A		
Includes:	N/A		
Frequency of Use:	Frequent: whenever context is determined		
NFR ID:	DCL-NFR-02		
Assumptions:	N/A		

Notes and Issues:	N/A
Sequence Diagram:	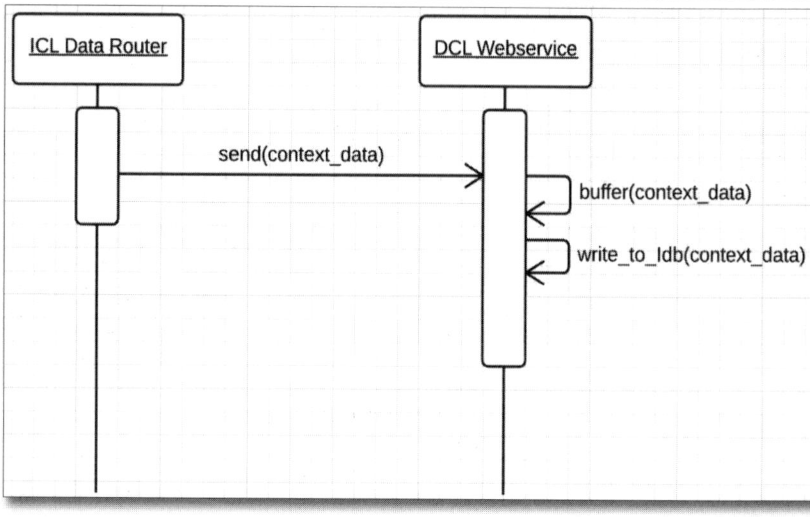

Use Case ID:	DCL-UC-06		
Use Case Name:	Retrieve Lifelog Information		
Created By:	Taqdir Ali	Last Updated By:	Taqdir Ali
Date Created:	15 July 2015	Last Revision Date:	20 Dec 2016
Actors:	SCL, KCL, SL		
Description:	Each actor needs information from lifelog for further processing. All actors shall request their related and desired Lifelog information from physical storage.		
Trigger:	On request of an actor to access required information		
Pre-conditions:	The actor shall be authorized with full access on the Lifelog data.		
Post-conditions:	Provide the required data to layer		
Normal Flow:	1. Actor sends request for desired Lifelog information. 2. The desired request shall be checked for information existence. If request is valid 3. Prepare the query for desired information based on request 4. Load the requested information from physical storage 5. Send back the loaded information to the actor		
Alternative Flows:	2b. The desired data is not existing in the schema, invalid request Acknowledge the actor with exception of invalid request.		
Exceptions:	N/A		
Includes:	N/A		
Frequency of Use:	Whenever Lifelog information is required.		
NFR ID:	N/A		
Assumptions:	N/A		
Notes and Issues:	N/A		

Sequence Diagram:	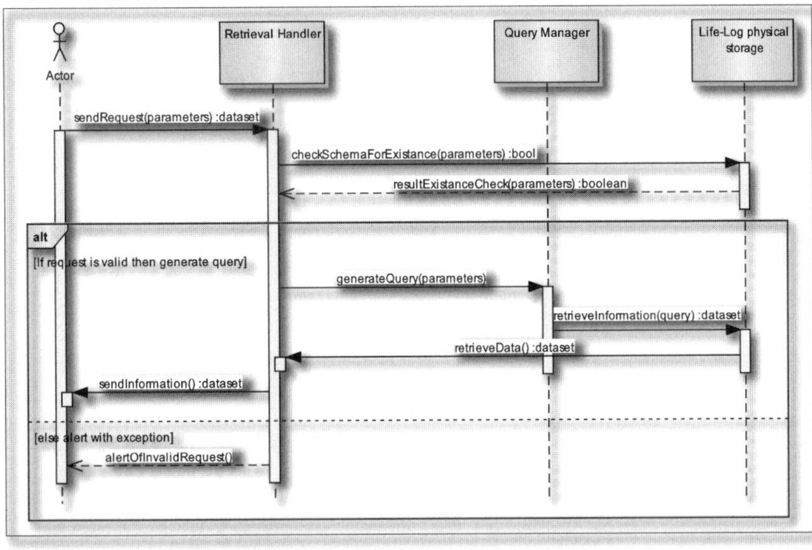

Use Case ID:	DCL-UC-07		
Use Case Name:	Persist Lifelog Information		
Created By:	Taqdir Ali	**Last Updated By:**	Taqdir Ali
Date Created:	15 July 2015	**Last Revision Date:**	20 Dec 2016
Actors:	ICL		
Description:	Each actor performed some specific operations on incoming data from external resources or on already existing information in Lifelog repository. In both cases the information shall be updated and stored in Lifelog repository.		
Trigger:	On request of an actor to persist required information		
Pre-conditions:	The actor shall be authorized with full access on the Lifelog data.		
Post-conditions:	Successfully stored the created Lifelog information		
Normal Flow:	1. Actor sends request to persist new generated Lifelog information. 2. Passes the new created information to check the appropriate hierarchical structure. 3. The appropriate selected hierarchical structure with input information passes to find the information instances. 4. Check the consistency among the records and their relationship. 5. Store the validated and structured information into physical storage		
Alternative Flows:	N/A		
Exceptions:	N/A		
Includes:	Map Instances, Validate Instances, save information to physical storage.		
Frequency of Use:	Whenever new information is generated.		
NFR ID:	N/A		
Assumptions:	N/A		
Notes and Issues:	Capability to process multiple actor's requests for storage.		

Sequence Diagram:

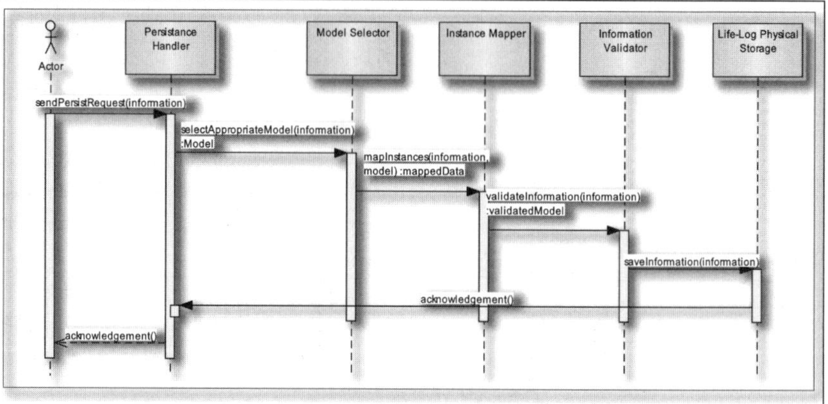

Use Case ID:	DCL-UC-08		
Use Case Name:	Map Instances		
Created By:	Taqdir Ali	**Last Updated By:**	Taqdir Ali
Date Created:	15 July 2015	**Last Revision Date:**	20 Dec 2016
Actors:	DCL, ICL, SCL, SL, and Lifelog physical storage		
Description:	The information produced by each actor shall be mapped against the hierarchical structure of storage.		
Trigger:	On request of an actor to persist required information		
Pre-conditions:	The actor shall be authorized with full access on the Lifelog data.		
Post-conditions:	Successfully mapped the instances with correct Lifelog information schema		
Normal Flow:	1. Actor sends request to persist new generated information. 2. System searches each information records against hierarchical structure. 3. System finds appropriate classes of the instances 4. System extracts attributes in the instances. 5. Find the relationship among the information records. 6. Pass the annotated information for validation.		
Alternative Flows:	N/A		
Exceptions:	N/A		
Includes:	N/A		
Frequency of Use:	Whenever new information is persisted.		
NFR ID:	N/A		
Assumptions:	N/A		
Notes and Issues:	Capability to process multiple actors' requests for storage.		

Sequence Diagram:	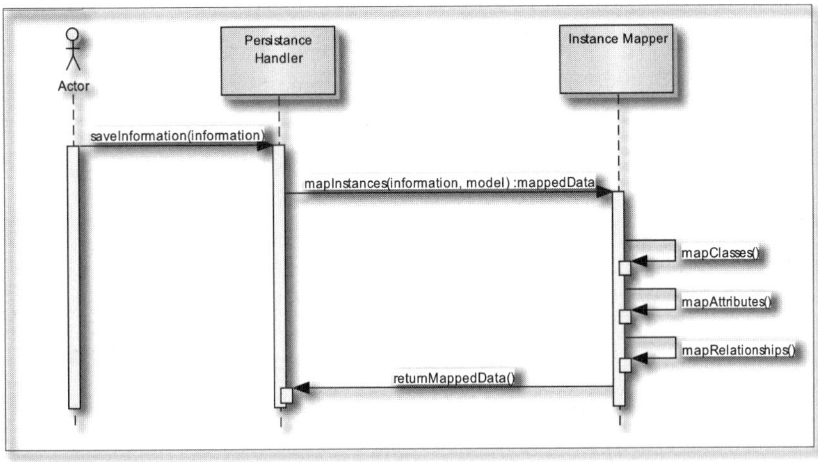

Use Case ID:	DCL-UC-09		
Use Case Name:	Validate Instances		
Created By:	Taqdir Ali	**Last Updated By:**	Taqdir Ali
Date Created:	15 July 2015	**Last Revision Date:**	20 Dec 2016
Actors:	DCL, ICL, SCL, SL, and Lifelog physical storage		
Description:	The mapped information in previous use case shall be checked for consistency among the existing information.		
Trigger:	On request of an actor to persist required information		
Pre-conditions:	The actor shall be authorized with full access on the Lifelog data.		
Post-conditions:	Successfully validate the instances with correct Lifelog information schema		
Normal Flow:	1. Actor send request to persist new generated information. 2. DCL passes the mapped information for validation of information and their relationships. 3. The system checks the information according to the specific location in the hierarchy. 4. The system checks and builds the relationship among concepts. 5. The verified information shall be passed for persistence.		
Alternative Flows:	N/A		
Exceptions:	N/A		
Includes:	N/A		
Frequency of Use:	Whenever new information is persisted.		
NFR ID:	N/A		
Assumptions:	N/A		
Notes and Issues:	Capability to process multiple actors' requests for storage.		

Sequence Diagram:	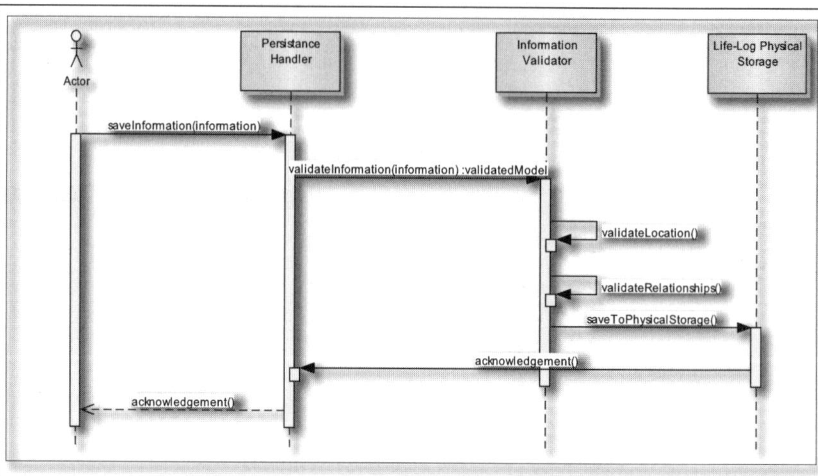

Use Case ID:	DCL-UC-10		
Use Case Name:	Situation Configuration		
Created By:	Bilal Ali	**Last Updated By:**	Bilal Ali
Date Created:	15 July 2015	**Last Revision Date:**	20 Dec 2016
Actors:	KCL		
Description:	Situation is determined by experts and is communicated to DCL for monitoring the Lifelog.		
Trigger:	Creation of new rule to capture a situation.		
Pre-conditions:	KCL and DCL should agree on common representation of sharing information of Situation configuration		
Post-conditions:	Situation is stored against a specific category. Situation is available for monitoring the Lifelog.		
Normal Flow:	1. KCL connects to DCL and send the newly created situation in common configuration format. 2. DCL evaluates the format of received situation configuration. 3. DCL responds with acknowledgement message. 4. Situation will be parsed into components. 5. Parsed components are updated in persistent storage as per categories.		
Alternative Flows:	N/A		
Exceptions:	Format of situation is not according the agreement.		
Includes:	N/A		
Frequency of Use:	Invoked per situation creation by the expert.		
NFR ID:	N/A		
Assumptions:	Well defined schema is available to store situation persistently		
Notes and Issues:	Standardize situation format is a challenging task		

Sequence Diagram:	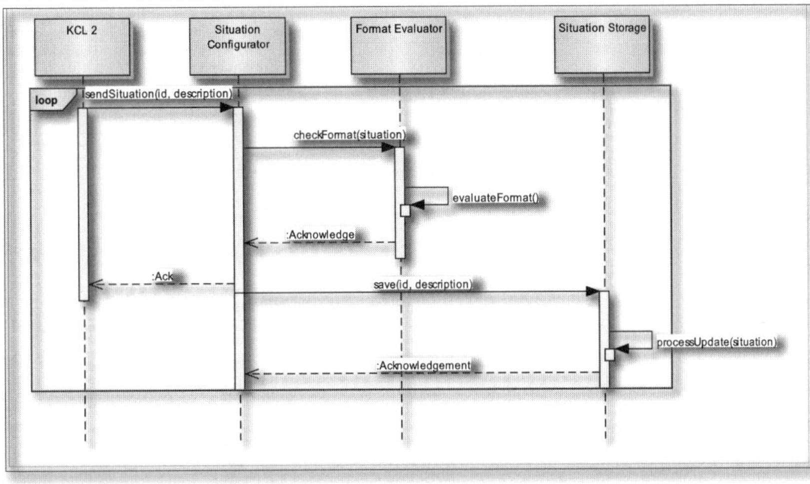

Use Case ID:	DCL-UC-11		
Use Case Name:	LLM Configuration for target Variables		
Created By:	Bilal Ali	**Last Updated By:**	Bilal Ali
Date Created:	15 July 2015	**Last Revision Date:**	20 Dec 2016
Actors:	KCL, Experts		
Description:	Configure the Lifelog monitor for the screening of the target variable from Lifelog data.		
Trigger:	On start of user's monitored activity		
Pre-conditions:	Expert defines target variable in common configuration format. Access to Lifelog.		
Post-conditions:	Targeted log is retrieved from Lifelog data as per target variable requirements.		
Normal Flow:	1. KCL will share the target variables in common configured format created by expert. 2. Lifelog monitor is configured based on the shared target variable. 3. Lifelog monitor retrieve log data from Lifelog against the target variables.		
Alternative Flows:	N/A		
Exceptions:	N/A		
Includes:	N/A		
Frequency of Use:	On update of common configuration format.		
NFR ID:	N/A		
Assumptions:	N/A		
Notes and Issues:	Real time accommodation of update in common configuration format is challenging task.		

Sequence Diagram:	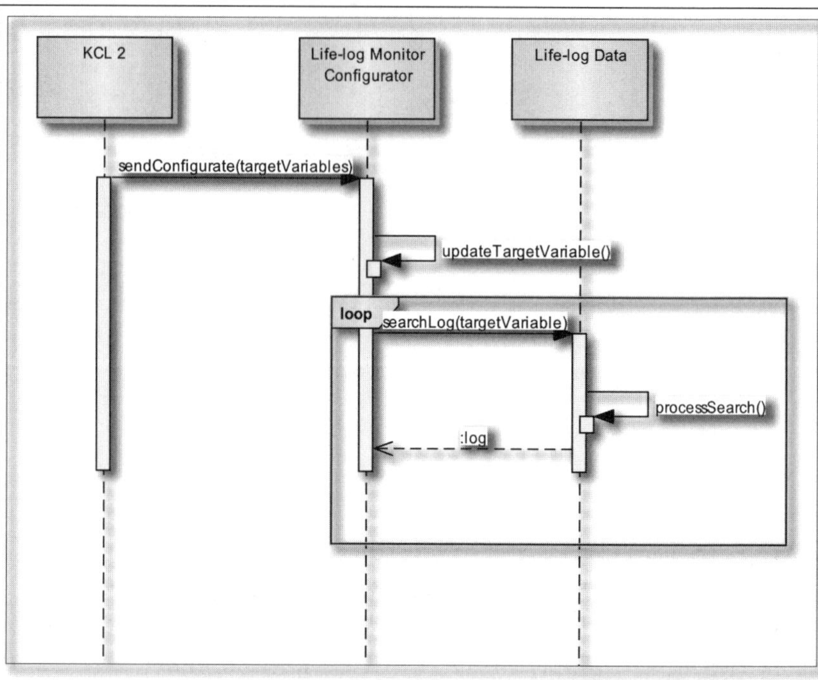

Use Case ID:	DCL-UC-12		
Use Case Name:	LLM for Situation Detection		
Created By:	Bilal Ali	**Last Updated By:**	Bilal Ali
Date Created:	15 July 2015	**Last Revision Date:**	20 Dec 2016
Actors:	Lifelog Data, SCL, ICL		
Description:	Identification of the existence of a condition in user activities to highlight the alarming situation as per experts' understanding.		
Trigger:	On start of user's monitored activity		
Pre-conditions:	1. Activity is identified. 2. Situation is configured. 3. Access to Lifelog.		
Post-conditions:	Alarming situation is detected and triggered the SCL with situation and user.		
Normal Flow:	1. ICL recognizes activity and sends to Lifelog. 2. Lifelog monitor identify the target activity. 3. Retrieve associated situation with the activity. 4. Continuous access that activity log. 5. Aggregate the interval/duration of activity. 6. Remove the irregularity in activity as per situation. 7. Evaluate the duration of activity against the situation. 8. If situation condition meets then send message to SCL to inform about the occurrence of a situation along with user information. 9. If situation condition does not occur, don't send message to SCL.		
Alternative Flows:	N/A		
Exceptions:	N/A		

Includes:	N/A
Frequency of Use:	For every activity with configured situation.
NFR ID:	N/A
Assumptions:	N/A
Notes and Issues:	Management of irregularity in activity is a challenging task.
Sequence Diagram:	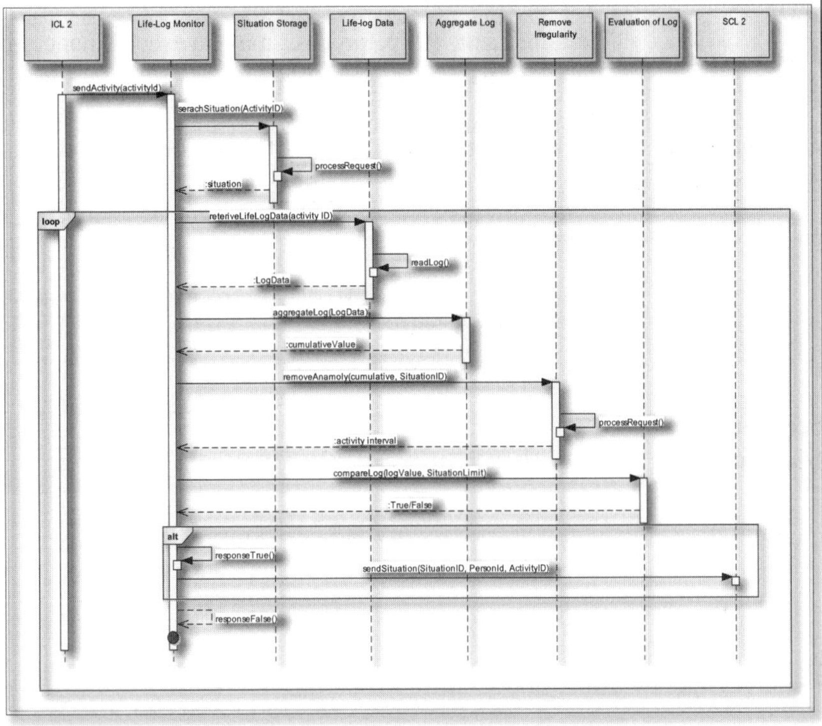

Use Case ID:	DCL-UC-13		
Use Case Name:	Retrieve sensory data from non-volatile storage for intermediate data generation (offline)		
Created By:	Usman	**Last Updated By:**	Bilal Amin
Date Created:	15 July 2015	**Last Revision Date:**	20 Dec 2016
Actors:	KCL		
Description:	Raw data in HDFS is retrieved based on the request from KCL and converted to relational format and stored in IDB.		
Trigger:	KCL requests the data		
Pre-conditions:	1. Relational IDB schema has already been described and shared 2. The data exists in HDFS		
Post-conditions:	1. The data has been transformed and exported to IDB 2. The KCL is informed		
Normal Flow:	1. SCL receives requests from KCL and creates a NoSQL query 2. NoSQL query is executed using Apache Hive on HDFS to retrieve the data		

	3. Retrieved data is processed and transformed to relational format based on IDB schema 4. Transformed data is exported to IDB
Alternative Flows:	N/A
Exceptions:	N/A
Includes:	N/A
Frequency of Use:	Less frequent, offline process, may be executed once or on change in the IDB schema
NFR ID:	N/A
Assumptions:	NoSQL query results are easy to transform to relational format
Notes and Issues:	N/A
Sequence Diagram:	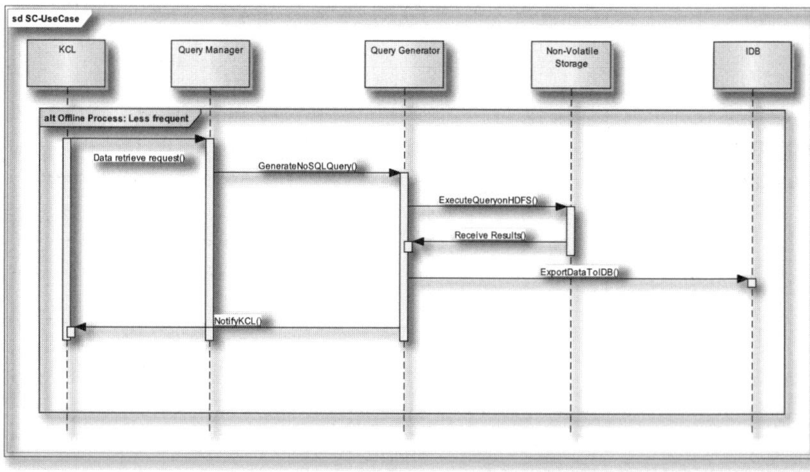

Use Case ID:	DCL-UC-14		
Use Case Name:	Retrieve sensory data from non-volatile storage (online)		
Created By:	Usman	Last Updated By:	Bilal Amin
Date Created:	15 July 2015	Last Revision Date:	20 Dec 2016
Actors:	SL		
Description:	Raw sensory data in HDFS is retrieved and provided to analytics component of SL in an online process		
Trigger:	Request for data from descriptive analytics is received		
Pre-conditions:	Raw sensory exists and persisted in HDFS (non-volatile storage)		
Post-conditions:	1. Required data is retrieved from HDFS 2. Data is cached locally in SCL 3. Required data is communicated to descriptive analytics in SL directly (online)		
Normal Flow:	1. Descriptive analytics in SL requests data from SCL 2. SCL receives the request and maintains its log. 3. SCL transforms request to a MapReduce Job. 4. MapReduce job is executed on HDFS and results are retrieved. 5. Retrieved results are cached locally in volatile storage		

	6. Results are forwarded directly to descriptive analytics
Alternative Flows:	1. Descriptive analytics requests data from SCL 2. SCL receives the request and examines it for duplicity (a request coming more than one time) 3. Duplicate request results are directly forwarded from the cached results to descriptive analytics 4. First time requests follow the normal flow.
Exceptions:	N/A
Includes:	N/A
Frequency of Use:	Frequent requests from descriptive analytics in SL
NFR ID:	N/A
Assumptions:	Request format contract already defined between SL(descriptive analytics) and DCL (SCL)
Notes and Issues:	N/A
Sequence Diagram:	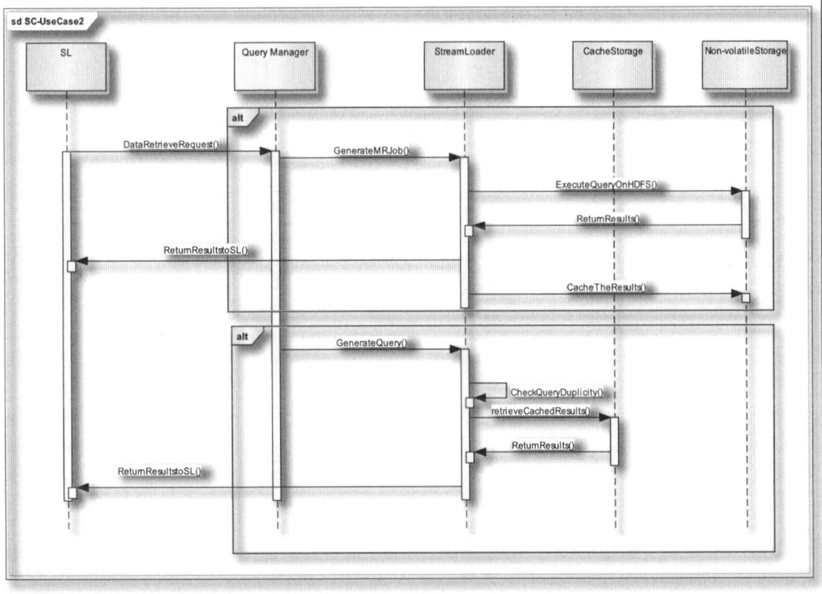

Use Case ID:	DCL-UC-15		
Use Case Name:	Persist sensory data in non-volatile storage		
FR ID:			
Created By:	Usman	**Last Updated By:**	Bilal Amin
Date Created:	15 July 2015	**Last Revision Date:**	20 Dec 2016
Actors:	DCL		
Description:	Receive and persist raw sensory data from DCL in to HDFS		
Trigger:	DCL request to upload data, every 3 seconds		
Pre-conditions:	1. Data storage structure, directory structure in HDFS defined 2. File formats and data formats in HDFS known 3. Raw sensory data is received from DCL		

	4. Big Data server is already running
Post-conditions:	1. Raw sensory data is persisted in HDFS non-volatile storage 2. Data is available for processing and access by SL and KCL
Normal Flow:	1. Big Data server listening for data requests from DCL 2. DCL connects and sends data to SCL 3. SCL uploads received data to HDFS
Alternative Flows:	N/A
Exceptions:	N/A
Includes:	N/A
Frequency of Use:	Very frequent, every 3 seconds
NFR ID:	N/A
Assumptions:	Data format and specifications already defined between DCL and SCL
Notes and Issues:	N/A
Sequence Diagram:	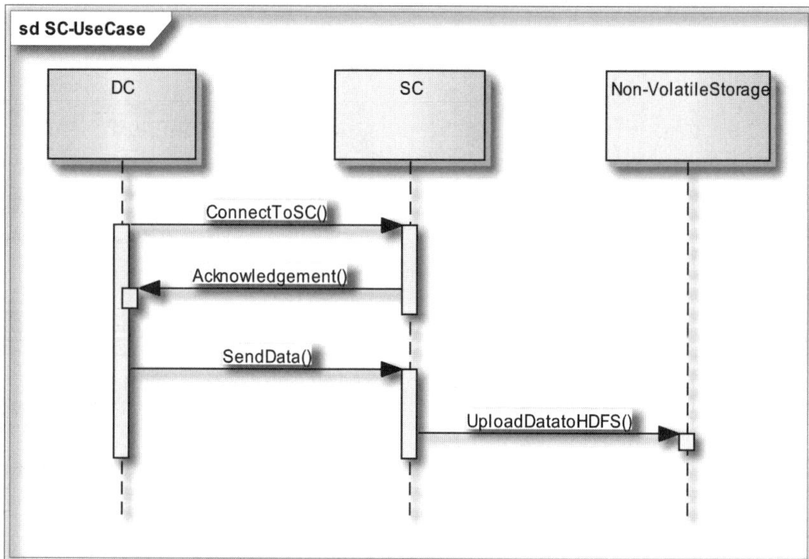

Use Case ID:	DCL-UC-16		
Use Case Name:	Manipulate Behavior Factor		
Created By:	Bilal Ali	**Last Updated By:**	Bilal Amin
Date Created:	2 July 2018	**Last Revision Date:**	2 July 2018
Actors:	SCL		
Description:	User lifelog and questionnaires responses are used to manipulate the factors which are related to dietary behavior, physical activities and diseases.		
Trigger:	SCL triggers it when it need to give recommendations and generate adaptive questionnaires.		
Pre-conditions:	User has filled the questionnaire and lifelog is maintained		
Post-conditions:	All factors are manipulated and healthy behavior index		
Normal Flow:	1. Receive request from SCL.		

	2. Calculate the registration age of the user. 3. For qualitative factors assess the latest responses of the questionnaires. 4. For qualitative factors accumulate the lifelog values week wise. 5. Map each factor with assigned range defined by expert. 6. Build factor vector and accumulate the factors with assigned proportion.
Alternative Flows:	N/A
Exceptions:	2a. In step 2 of the normal flow, if the user age is zero or data is unavailable the system not recognized exception must occur.
Includes:	N/A
Frequency of Use:	Depending on report generation for each user.
NFR ID:	N/A
Assumptions:	User provides the responses of all the allocated questions and lifelog is maintained over time.
Notes and Issues:	N/A
Sequence Diagram:	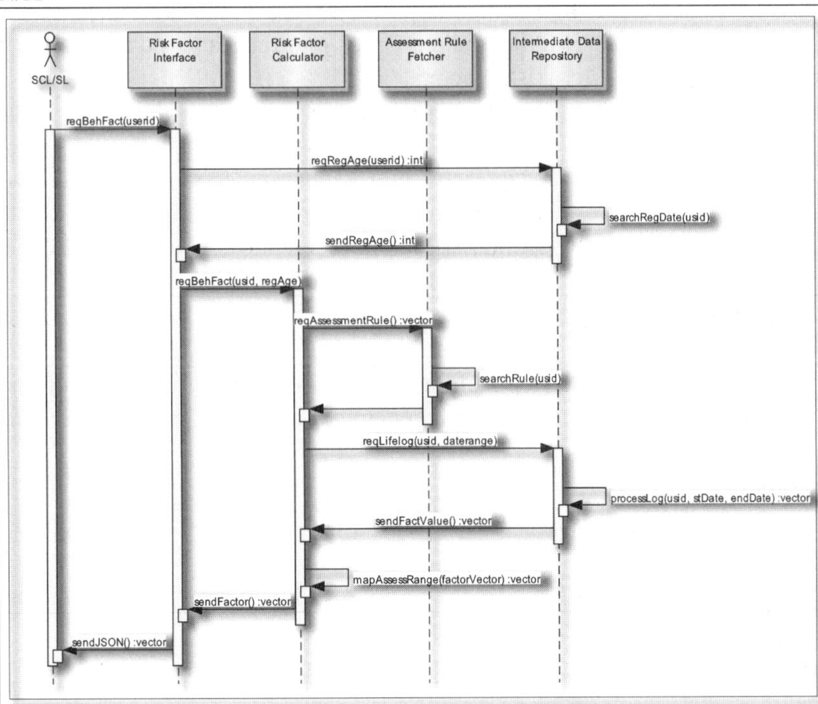

Use Case ID:	DCL-UC-17		
Use Case Name:	Identify Risk Factors		
Created By:	Bilal Ali	**Last Updated By:**	Bilal Amin
Date Created:	2 July 2018	**Last Revision Date:**	2 July 2018
Actors:	SCL		
Description:	User lifelog and questionnaires responses are used to manipulate the factors which are linked to find out the risky values on the basis of the rules defined by expert		
Trigger:	SCL triggers it when it need to give recommendations for dinning time and generate monthly questionnaires.		
Pre-conditions:	User has filled the questionnaire and lifelog is maintained		
Post-conditions:	Personalized Risky factors vector is available to generate recommendations		
Normal Flow:	1. Receive request from SCL. 2. Calculate the registration age of the user. 3. Identify the registration status of the user. 4. For qualitative factors assess the latest responses of the questionnaires. 5. Map the responses into ranges for identification of the categories for risky factors. 6. For qualitative factors accumulate the lifelog values on the basis of the portion of the day passes. 7. Map each factor with assigned range defined by expert to identify the risky factor values. 8. Build risk factors vector and convert it into JSON to communicate with SCL in common communication format.		
Alternative Flows:	N/A		
Exceptions:	2a. In step 2 of the normal flow, if the user age is zero or data is unavailable the system should generate user not recognized exception.		
Includes:	N/A		
Frequency of Use:	At-least 3 times a day depending on report generation for each user.		
NFR ID:	N/A		
Assumptions:	User provides the responses of all the allocated questions and lifelog is maintained over time.		
Notes and Issues:	N/A		

Sequence Diagram:

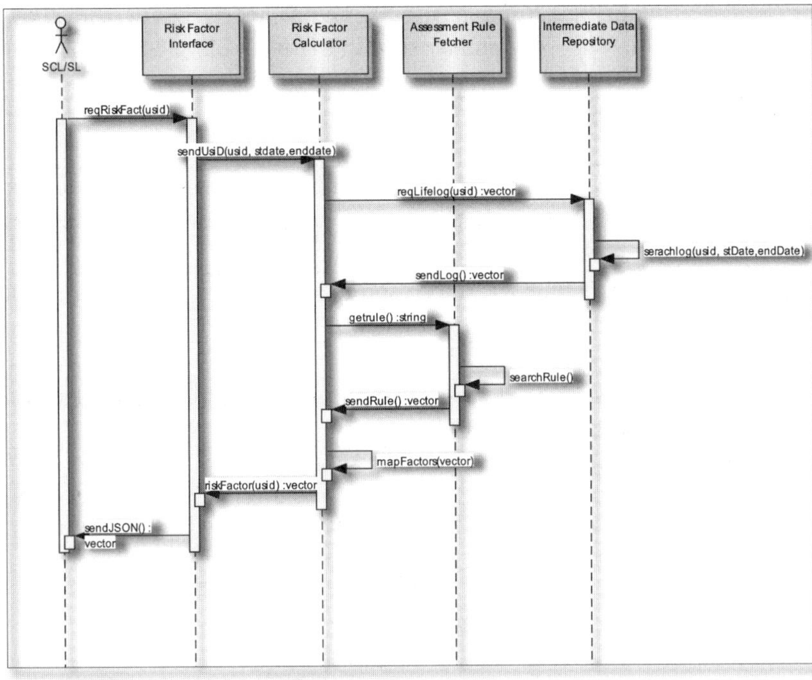

Use Case ID:	DCL-UC-18		
Use Case Name:	Identify Healthy Behavior Index (HBI)		
Created By:	Bilal Ali	**Last Updated By:**	Bilal Amin
Date Created:	2 July 2018	**Last Revision Date:**	2 July 2018
Actors:	SCL, SL		
Description:	User lifelog and questionnaires responses are used to recognize the behavior status of the user in-term of the healthy dieting, physical activity, smoking and alcohol consumption.		
Trigger:	SCL, SL can trigger it when they need to generate the progress report for the evaluation of user behavior.		
Pre-conditions:	User has filled the questionnaire and lifelog is maintained		
Post-conditions:	Healthy behavior index week wise is available to represent the behavior status.		
Normal Flow:	1. Receive request from SCL. 2. Identify the total number of weeks from lifelog. 3. For qualitative factors assess the latest responses of the questionnaire week-wise. 4. Quantify the qualitative factor and map to a single value from the ranges defined by the expert. 5. Accumulate the qualitative factors from the lifelog values week wise and map it to single value from the ranges defined by the expert. 6. Accumulate the values of the contributing factors on the basis of the weightage and convert it into a single value.		

	7. Build healthy behavior index vector and convert it into JSON to communicate with SL and SCL in common communication format.
Alternative Flows:	N/A
Exceptions:	2a. In step 2 of the normal flow, if the user age is zero or data is unavailable the system should generate user not recognized exception.
Includes:	N/A
Frequency of Use:	Any time when user and expert generate request to evaluate the change in behavior.
NFR ID:	N/A
Assumptions:	User provides the responses of all the allocated questions and lifelog is maintained over time.
Notes and Issues:	N/A
Sequence Diagram:	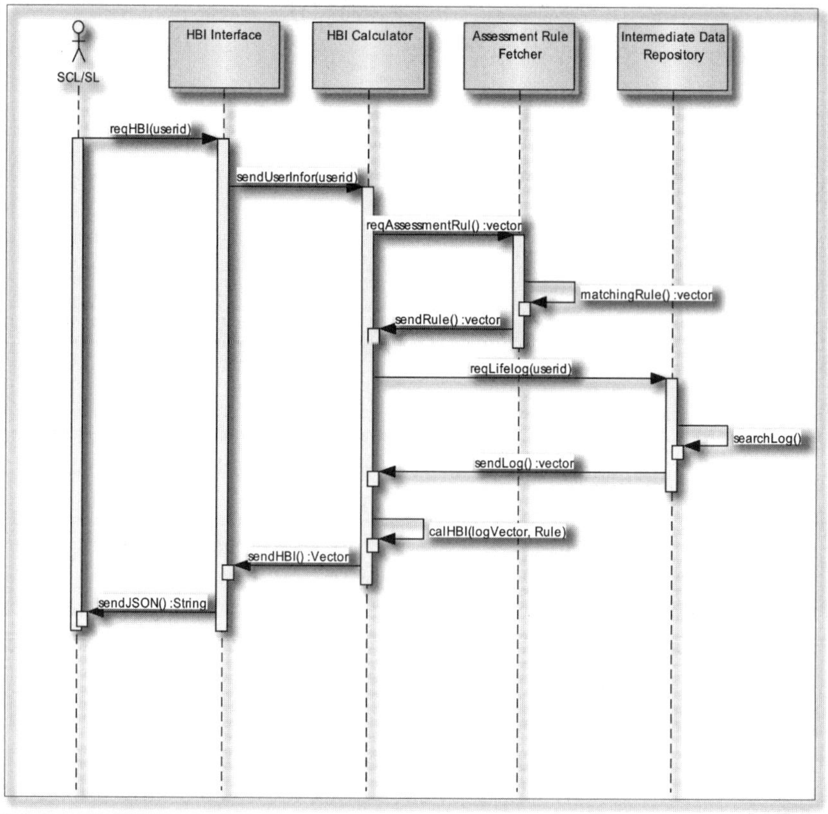

Use Case ID:	DCL-UC-19		
Use Case Name:	Generate detail of HBI week-wise		
Created By:	Bilal Ali	**Last Updated By:**	Bilal Amin
Date Created:	2 July 2018	**Last Revision Date:**	2 July 2018
Actors:	SCL, SL		

Description:	User lifelog and questionnaires responses are used to recognize the behavior status of the user in-term of the dietary factors, physical activity, smoking and alcohol consumption in a specified week.
Trigger:	SCL, SL can trigger it when they need to generate the detail progress report for factors related to behavior which can affect the health of a person.
Pre-conditions:	User has filled the questionnaire and lifelog is maintained
Post-conditions:	Contributing factors status in a week is available to represent the status.
Normal Flow:	1. Receive request from SCL and SL. 2. Receive the week number. 3. For qualitative factors assess the latest responses of the questionnaires in the week number. 4. Quantify the qualitative factor and map to a single value from the ranges defined by the expert in that week. 5. Accumulate the qualitative factors from the lifelog values in that week and map it to single value from the ranges defined by the expert. 6. Build healthy behavior factor vector and convert it into JSON to communicate with SL and SCL in common communication format.
Alternative Flows:	N/A
Exceptions:	2a. In step 2 of the normal flow, if the required week has no information in lifelog then the system should generate week not registered exception.
Includes:	N/A
Frequency of Use:	Any time when user and expert generate request to visualize the factors value to identify the change in behavior.
NFR ID:	N/A
Assumptions:	User provides the responses of all the allocated questions and lifelog is maintained over time.
Notes and Issues:	N/A

Sequence Diagram:

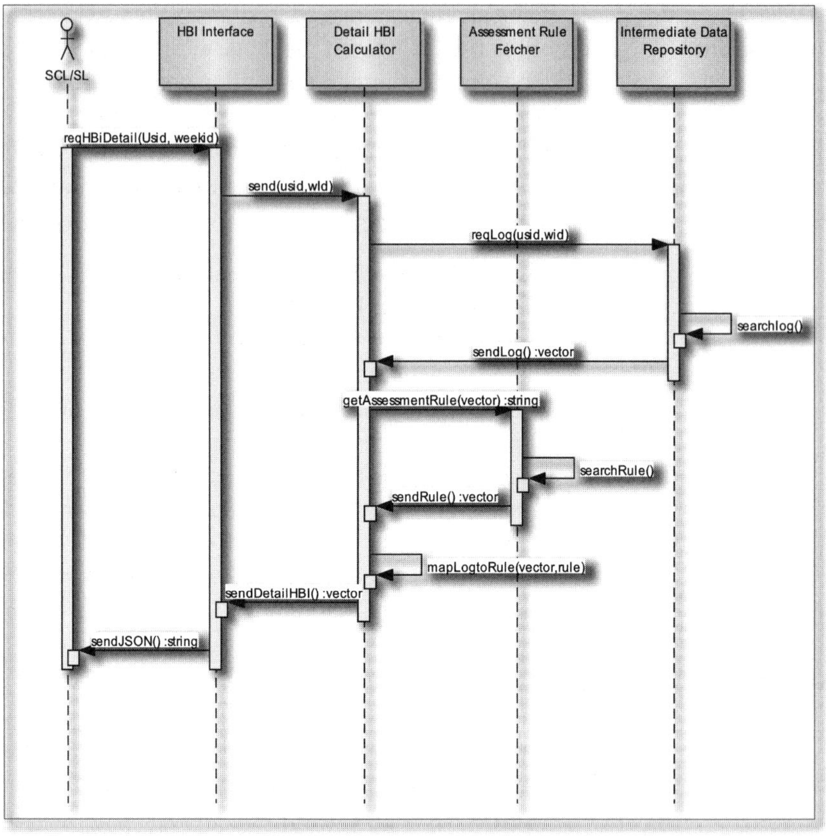

18.2 Information Curation Layer

18.2.1 Use Case List

ID	Name
ICL-UC-01	Derive optimal low-level context recognizer
ICL-UC-02	Create low-level context recognizers
ICL-UC-03	Route sensory data for the low-level context identification
ICL-UC-04	Recognize user low-level context
ICL-UC-05	Recognize user activity based on inertial raw sensory data
ICL-UC-06	Recognize user activity based on video raw sensory data
ICL-UC-07	Recognize user location based on geo-positioning raw sensory data
ICL-UC-08	Recognize user emotion based on audio raw sensory data
ICL-UC-09	Recognize user emotion based on video raw sensory data
ICL-UC-10	Recognize food based on tag data
ICL-UC-11	Unify low-level contexts
ICL-UC-12	Notify new low-level context
ICL-UC-13	Create unclassified high-level context instance
ICL-UC-14	Classify high-level context instance
ICL-UC-15	Notify new high-level context
ICL-UC-16	Load context ontology model
ICL-UC-17	Store context instance
ICL-UC-18	Retrieve context instance
ICL-UC-19	Evolve Ontology
ICL-UC-20	High Level Physical Activity Context
ICL-UC-21	High Level Nutrition Context
ICL-UC-22	High Level Clinical Context

18.2.2 Use Case Diagram

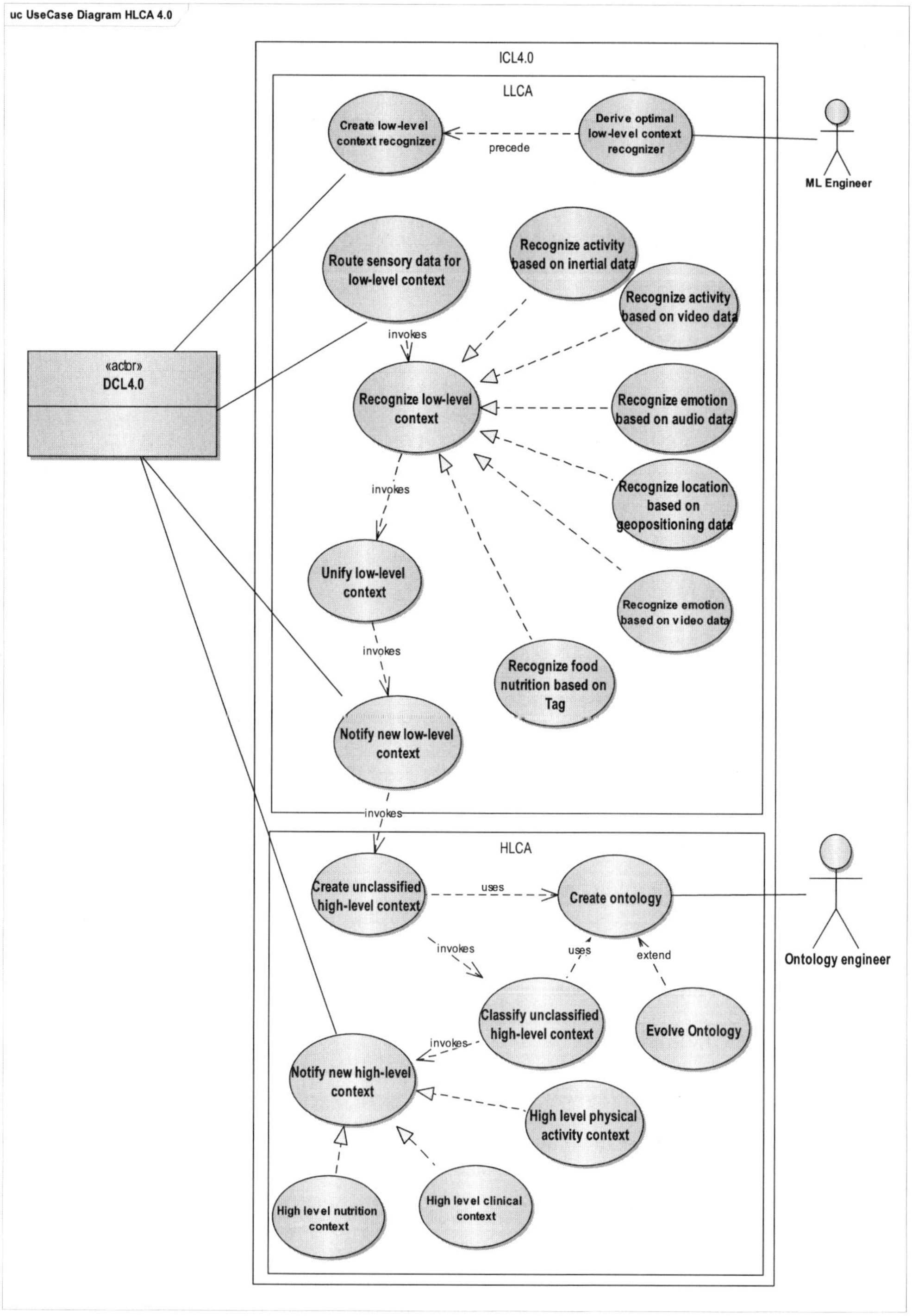

18.2.3 Use Case Description

Use Case ID:	**ICL-UC-01**		
Use Case Name:	Derive optimal low-level context recognizer		
Created By:	Oresti Banos	**Last Updated By:**	Jaehun Bang
Date Created:	22 July 2015	**Last Revision Date:**	02 July 2018
Actors:	Engineer		
Description:	Create an optimal recognition model through the evaluation of multiple recognition model candidates (offline process).		
Trigger:	Engineer initiates the process for creating an optimal recognition model		
Pre-conditions:	A human expert or engineer sets up the experimental setup for the evaluation process		
Post-conditions:	• The optimal recognition model among considered is delivered to the expert • A recognizer descriptor containing the characteristics of the optimal model is stored		
Normal Flow:	1. Load dataset 2. For each combination of preprocessing methods, segmentation methods, feature sets, feature selection methods, and classification methods, the dataset is preprocessed (e.g., filtered) 3. The preprocessed dataset is segmented (e.g., partitioned into windows) 4. Features (e.g., mean, variance) are extracted from each segment of the dataset 5. The best features are selected 6. Cross validation is applied to the selected features 7. The feature set is split into training and testing 8. The classifier is trained using the training features 9. The classifier is tested in order to determine the model performance 10. The model performance is stored 11. Once the model performance has been calculated for all the possible combinations, the optimal model is selected 12. A recognizer descriptor is generated according to the characteristics of the model (e.g., median filtering, 3 sec window size, etc.) 13. The generated recognizer descriptor is stored		
Alternative Flows:	N/A		
Exceptions:	N/A		
Includes:	N/A		
Frequency of Use:	Infrequent		
NFR ID:	MM-NFR-05		
Assumptions:	N/A		
Notes and Issues:	Matlab and Weka tools will be used for this task. A multimodal dataset must be collected for the training and evaluation of the candidate's models.		

Sequence Diagram:	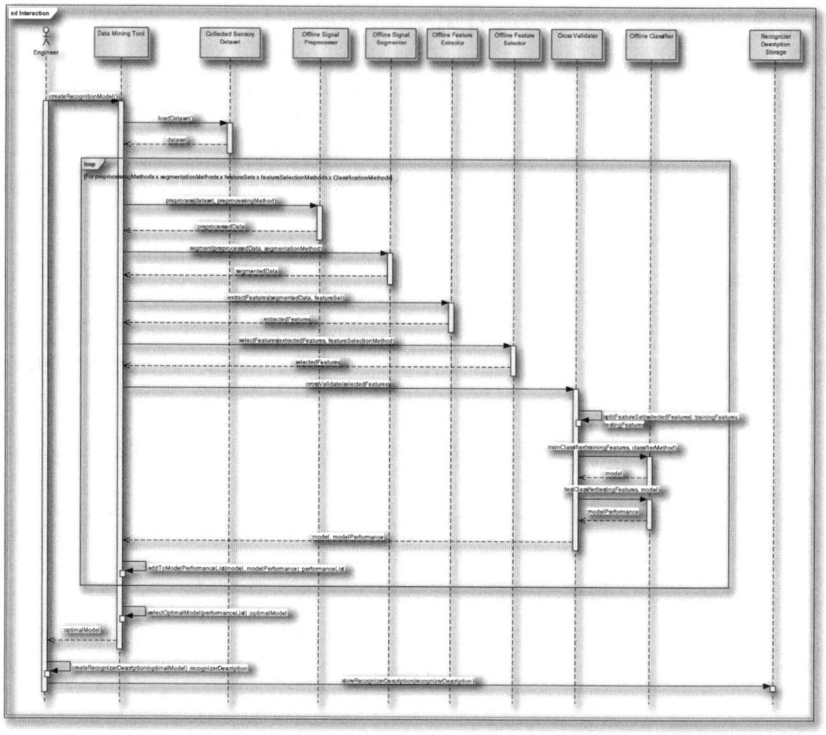

Use Case ID:	**ICL-UC-02**		
Use Case Name:	Create low-level context recognizers		
Created By:	Oresti Banos	**Last Updated By:**	Jaehun Bang
Date Created:	22 July 2015	**Last Revision Date:**	02 July 2018
Actors:	DCL 3		
Description:	Sensory data is received from DCL 3 and it is distributed to the corresponding low-level context recognizer based on the data type(s).		
Trigger:	Receive userID and part of the user profile information send by DCL 3 to ICL4		
Pre-conditions:	DCL 3 sends the userID and part of the user profile information to ICL 4 whenever a new user is registered in the platform		
Post-conditions:	Low-level context recognizers are generated for the new user for all context types		
Normal Flow:	1. Receive UserID and (part of the) user profile information 2. Load the recognizer descriptions containing the low-level context model types (e.g., emotion recognizer) and characteristics (e.g., median filtering, 3 sec window size, etc.) 3. Create a new recognizer for each recognizer description 4. Create a recognizer identifier for the generated recognizer 5. Save the recognizer identifier in a persistent storage		
Alternative Flows:	N/A		

Exceptions:	N/A
Includes:	N/A
Frequency of Use:	Less frequent
NFR ID:	N/A
Assumptions:	• DCL 3 will send the required user profile information together with the userID only the first time a user is registered • No user profile updates are considered in this version
Notes and Issues:	N/A
Sequence Diagram:	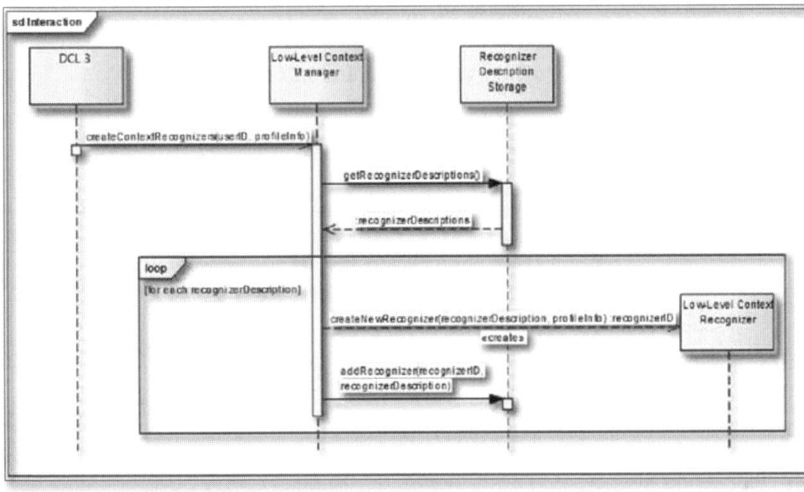

Use Case ID:	**ICL-UC-03**		
Use Case Name:	Route sensory data for the low-level context identification		
Created By:	Tae Ho Hur	**Last Updated By:**	Taeho Hur
Date Created:	06 Dec 2015	**Last Revision Date:**	04 July 2018
Actors:	Sensor Devices		
Description:	Sensory data is received, and it is distributed to the corresponding low-level context recognizer based on the data type(s).		
Trigger:	Receive sensory data send by each sensor device		
Pre-conditions:	Device sends sensory data, i.e., raw sensory data plus sensory metadata (e.g., data type, time stamp, device ID, device type, and user ID)		
Post-conditions:	The adequate raw sensory data is sent to each low-level context recognizer in order to perform the recognition process		
Normal Flow:	1. Receive sensory data 2. Get the user identifier to which the sensory data belongs 3. Load the low-level context recognizers identifiers for the given user 4. For each low-level context recognizer identifier, get the sensory data type(s) it requires 5. Match the received sensory data with the sensory data type(s) required by the low-level context recognizer		

	6. Create a copy with the compatible data required by the low-level context recognizer 7. Distribute the data to the corresponding low-level context recognizer
Alternative Flows:	N/A
Exceptions:	5a. If no compatible data types are identified for the given low-level context recognizer 1. Go to step 3
Includes:	N/A
Frequency of Use:	Very frequent
Assumptions:	• There is an established communication between Sensor Devices and the Sensory Data Router module • Incoming sensory data is already preprocessed (i.e., without missing samples and with synchronized streams)
Notes and Issues:	N/A
Sequence Diagram:	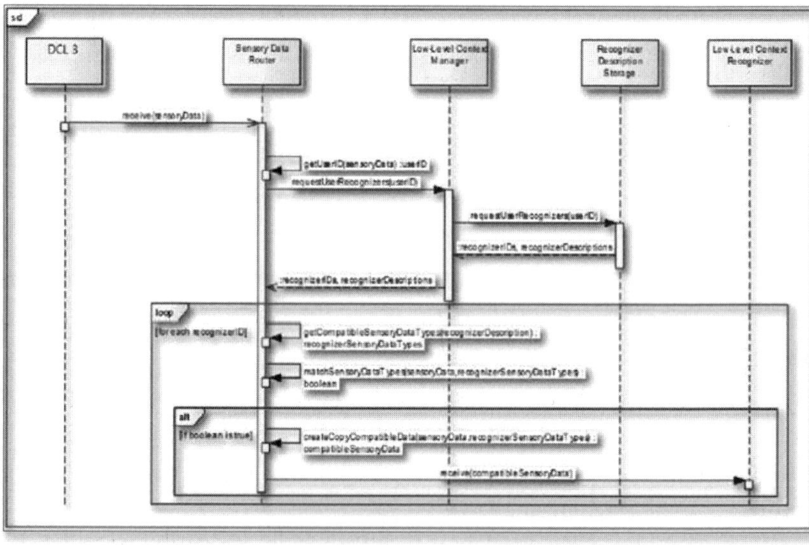

Use Case ID:	**ICL-UC-04**		
Use Case Name:	Recognize user low-level context		
Created By:	Oresti Banos	**Last Updated By:**	Oresti Banos
Date Created:	14 July 2015	**Last Revision Date:**	02 July 2018
Actors:	Sensory Data Router, Low-Level Context Unifier		
Description:	The low-level context associated to a given user is identified based on the received compatible sensory data. The low-level context recognition may be of diverse nature depending upon the data types, thus this use case defines an abstract representation of the process to be followed.		
Trigger:	Receive compatible sensory data		
Pre-conditions:	Compatible sensory data is sent to a given low-level context recognizer		
Post-conditions:	The recognized low-level context instance is provided to the Low-Level Context Unifier		

<table>
<tr><td>Normal Flow:</td><td>1. Compatible sensory data is received by a given low-level context recognizer
2. The raw sensory data is extracted from the sensory data
3. The low-level context label is recognized
4. The sensory metadata is extracted from the sensory data
5. A low-level context instance is generated by combining the low-level context label and the sensory metadata
6. The generated low-level context instance is provided to the Low-Level Context Unifier</td></tr>
<tr><td>Alternative Flows:</td><td>N/A</td></tr>
<tr><td>Exceptions:</td><td>N/A</td></tr>
<tr><td>Includes:</td><td>N/A</td></tr>
<tr><td>Frequency of Use:</td><td>Frequent: at every reception of sensory data</td></tr>
<tr><td>NFR ID:</td><td>MM-NFR-05</td></tr>
<tr><td>Assumptions:</td><td>Only compatible sensory data is received by each corresponding low-level context recognizer</td></tr>
<tr><td>Notes and Issues:</td><td>N/A</td></tr>
<tr><td>Sequence Diagram:</td><td>
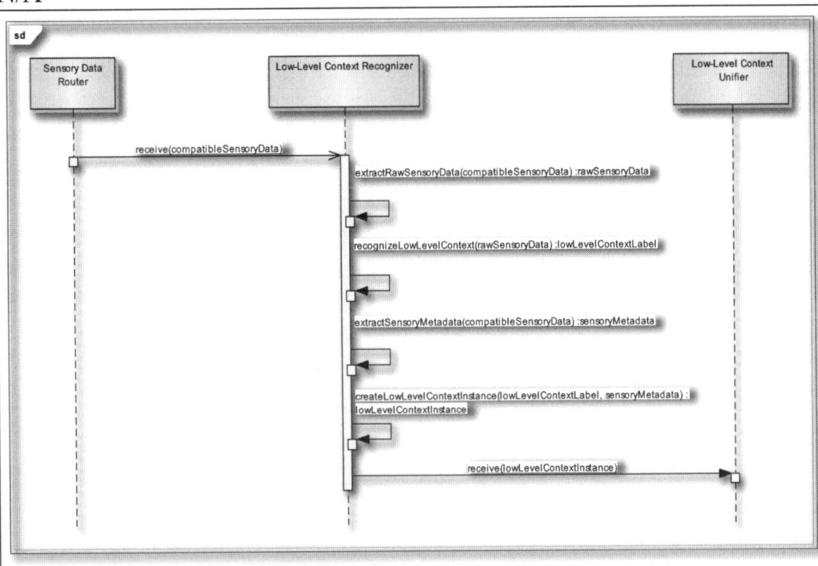

</td></tr>
</table>

<table>
<tr><td>Use Case ID:</td><td colspan="3">ICL-UC-05</td></tr>
<tr><td>Use Case Name:</td><td colspan="3">Recognize user activity based on inertial raw sensory data</td></tr>
<tr><td>Created By:</td><td>Taeho Hur</td><td>Last Updated By:</td><td>Taeho Hur</td></tr>
<tr><td>Date Created:</td><td>09 March 2017</td><td>Last Revision Date:</td><td>02 July 2018</td></tr>
<tr><td>Actors:</td><td colspan="3">ICL-UC-04</td></tr>
<tr><td>Description:</td><td colspan="3">Identification of the user physical activity (e.g., “sitting”) based on the processing of the body-motion raw sensory data collected from an inertial sensor. The body-motion raw sensory data consists of triaxial acceleration, triaxial rate of turn and triaxial magnetic field data.</td></tr>
</table>

Trigger:	Request for the recognition of the user activity based on a given inertial raw sensory data
Pre-conditions:	Raw sensory data is extracted from compatible sensory data (inertial sensory data)
Post-conditions:	A label corresponding to the recognized activity is generated
Normal Flow:	1. Inertial raw sensory data is received for analysis 2. The raw sensory data is preprocessed (e.g., filtered) 3. The preprocessed raw sensory data is segmented (e.g., partitioned into windows) 4. Features (e.g., mean, variance) are extracted from each segment of raw sensory data 5. The extracted features are classified 6. A label identifying the corresponding user activity is generated 7. Decision fusion of activities is made based on majority voting 8. Final activity is chosen
Alternative Flows:	N/A
Exceptions:	N/A
Includes:	N/A
Frequency of Use:	Frequent: at every reception of inertial raw sensory data
NFR ID:	MM-NFR-05
Assumptions:	The raw sensory data is of the nature required by the inertial activity recognizer
Notes and Issues:	N/A
Sequence Diagram:	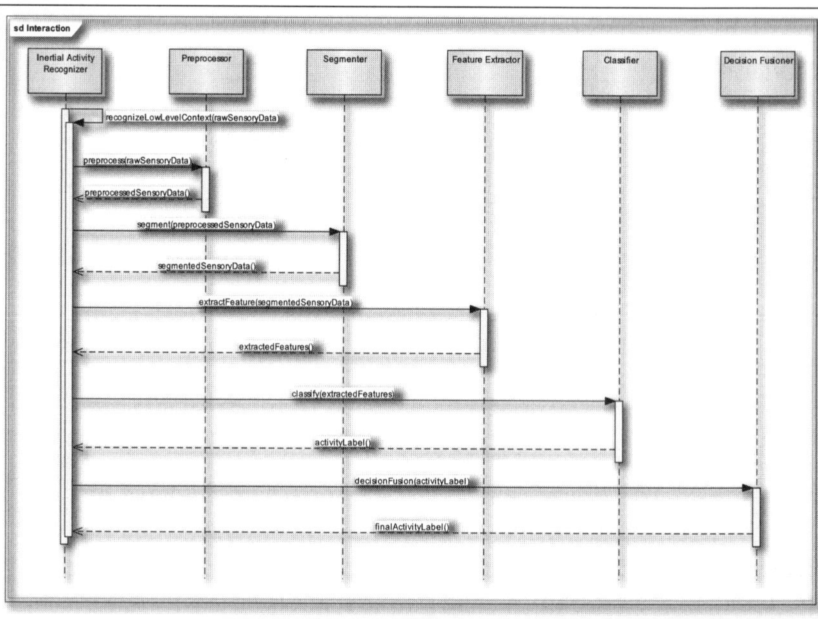

Use Case ID:	**ICL-UC-06**		
Use Case Name:	Recognize user activity based on video raw sensory data		
Created By:	Oresti Banos	**Last Updated By:**	Oresti Banos

<table>
<tr><td>Date Created:</td><td>17 July 2015</td><td>Last Revision Date:</td><td>02 July 2018</td></tr>
<tr><td>Actors:</td><td colspan="3">ICL-UC-04</td></tr>
<tr><td>Description:</td><td colspan="3">Identification of the user physical activity (e.g., “standing”) based on the processing of the body-motion raw sensory data collected through a video camera. The body-motion raw sensory data consists of RGB and depth video.</td></tr>
<tr><td>Trigger:</td><td colspan="3">Request for the recognition of the user activity based on a given video raw sensory data</td></tr>
<tr><td>Pre-conditions:</td><td colspan="3">Raw sensory data is extracted from compatible sensory data (video sensory data)</td></tr>
<tr><td>Post-conditions:</td><td colspan="3">A label corresponding to the recognized activity is generated</td></tr>
<tr><td>Normal Flow:</td><td colspan="3">1. Video raw sensory data is received for analysis
2. The raw sensory data is preprocessed (e.g., filtered)
3. The preprocessed raw sensory data is segmented (e.g., partitioned into windows)
4. Features (e.g., SIFT, HOG) are extracted from each segment of raw sensory data
5. The extracted features are classified
6. A label identifying the corresponding user activity is generated</td></tr>
<tr><td>Alternative Flows:</td><td colspan="3">N/A</td></tr>
<tr><td>Exceptions:</td><td colspan="3">N/A</td></tr>
<tr><td>Includes:</td><td colspan="3">N/A</td></tr>
<tr><td>Frequency of Use:</td><td colspan="3">Frequent: at every reception of video raw sensory data</td></tr>
<tr><td>NFR ID:</td><td colspan="3">MM-NFR-05</td></tr>
<tr><td>Assumptions:</td><td colspan="3">The raw sensory data is of the nature required by the video activity recognizer</td></tr>
<tr><td>Notes and Issues:</td><td colspan="3">N/A</td></tr>
<tr><td>Sequence Diagram:</td><td colspan="3">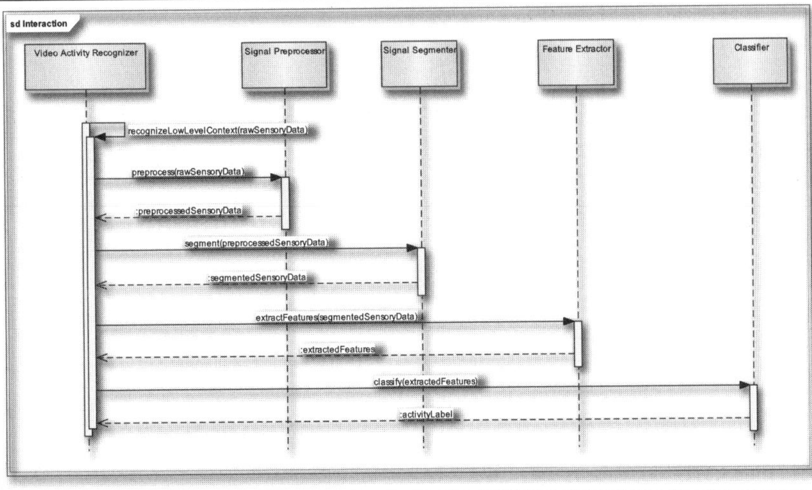
</td></tr>
</table>

Use Case ID:	**ICL-UC-07**
Use Case Name:	Recognize user location based on geo-positioning raw sensory data

Created By:	Oresti Banos	**Last Updated By:**	Oresti Banos
Date Created:	17 July 2015	**Last Revision Date:**	02 July 2018
Actors:	ICL-UC-04		
Description:	Identification of the user location (e.g., "restaurant") based on the processing of the geo-positioning raw sensory data collected from a portable GPS sensor. The body-motion raw sensory data consists of latitude, longitude and speed data.		
Trigger:	Request for the recognition of the user location based on a given geo-positioning raw sensory data		
Pre-conditions:	Raw sensory data is extracted from compatible sensory data (geo-positioning sensory data)		
Post-conditions:	A label corresponding to the recognized location is generated		
Normal Flow:	1. Geo-positioning raw sensory data is received for analysis 2. The geo-positioning raw sensory data is compared with the predefined map coordinates 3. A label identifying the corresponding user location is generated		
Alternative Flows:	N/A		
Exceptions:	N/A		
Includes:	N/A		
Frequency of Use:	Frequent: at every reception of geo-positioning raw sensory data		
NFR ID:	MM-NFR-05		
Assumptions:	The raw sensory data is of the nature required by the geo-positioning location recognizer		
Notes and Issues:	N/A		
Sequence Diagram:	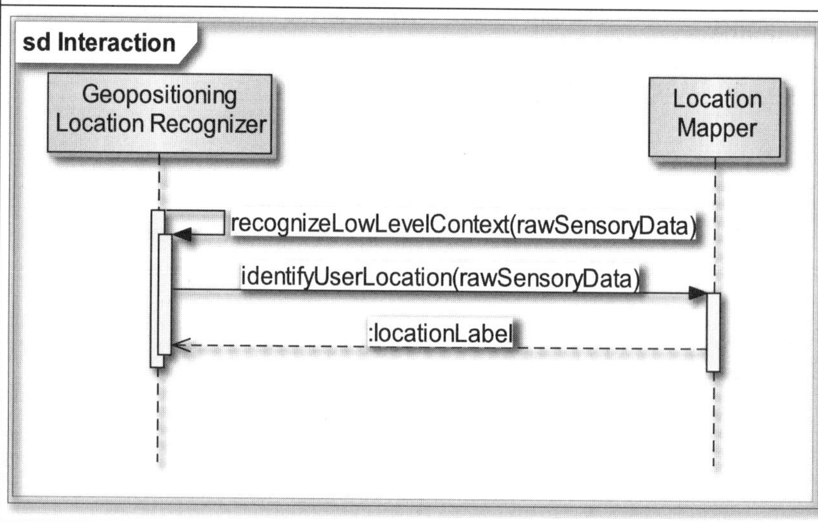		

Use Case ID:	**ICL-UC-08**		
Use Case Name:	Recognize user emotion based on audio raw sensory data		
Created By:	Oresti Banos	**Last Updated By:**	Jaehun Bang
Date Created:	17 July 2015	**Last Revision Date:**	02 July 2018

Actors:	ICL-UC-04
Description:	Identification of the user emotional state (e.g., “happy”) based on the processing of the audio raw sensory data collected from a microphone sensor. The audio raw sensory data consists of the user voice data.
Trigger:	Request for the recognition of the user emotion based on a given audio raw sensory data
Pre-conditions:	Raw sensory data is extracted from compatible sensory data (audio sensory data)
Post-conditions:	A label corresponding to the recognized emotion is generated
Normal Flow:	1. Audio raw sensory data is received for analysis 2. The raw sensory data is preprocessed (e.g., filtered) 3. The preprocessed raw sensory data is segmented (e.g., partitioned into windows) 4. Features (e.g., LPC, MFCC) are extracted from each segment of raw sensory data 5. The extracted features are classified 6. A label identifying the corresponding user emotion is generated
Alternative Flows:	N/A
Exceptions:	N/A
Includes:	N/A
Frequency of Use:	Frequent: at every reception of inertial raw sensory data
Assumptions:	The raw sensory data is of the nature required by the audio emotion recognizer
Notes and Issues:	N/A
Sequence Diagram:	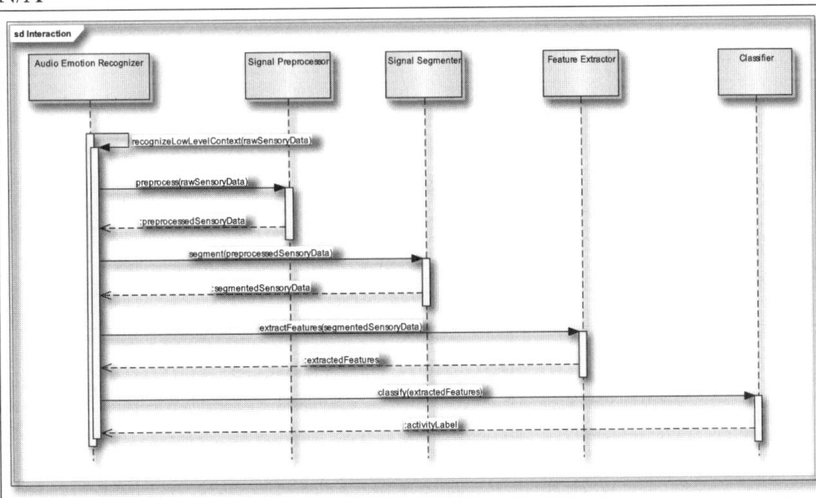

Use Case ID:	ICL-UC-09		
Use Case Name:	Recognize user emotion based on video raw sensory data		
Created By:	Jaehun Bang	Last Updated By:	Jaehun Bang
Date Created:	9 March 2017	Last Revision Date:	02 July 2018
Actors:	ICL-UC-04		

Description:	Identification of the user emotional state (e.g., "happy") based on the processing of the video raw sensory data collected from a camera sensor. The video raw sensory data consists of the user facial data.
Trigger:	Request for the recognition of the user emotion based on a given video raw sensory data
Pre-conditions:	Raw sensory data is extracted from compatible sensory data (video sensory data)
Post-conditions:	A label corresponding to the recognized emotion is generated
Normal Flow:	1. Video raw sensory data is received for analysis 2. The raw sensory data is preprocessed (e.g., filtered and face detection) 3. The preprocessed raw sensory data is segmented (e.g., partitioned into face area) 4. Features (e.g., face factor statistical features) are extracted from each segment of raw sensory data 5. The extracted features are classified 6. A label identifying the corresponding user emotion is generated
Alternative Flows:	N/A
Exceptions:	N/A
Includes:	N/A
Frequency of Use:	Frequent: at every reception of inertial raw sensory data
NFR ID:	MM-NFR-05
Assumptions:	The raw sensory data is of the nature required by the video emotion recognizer
Notes and Issues:	N/A
Sequence Diagram:	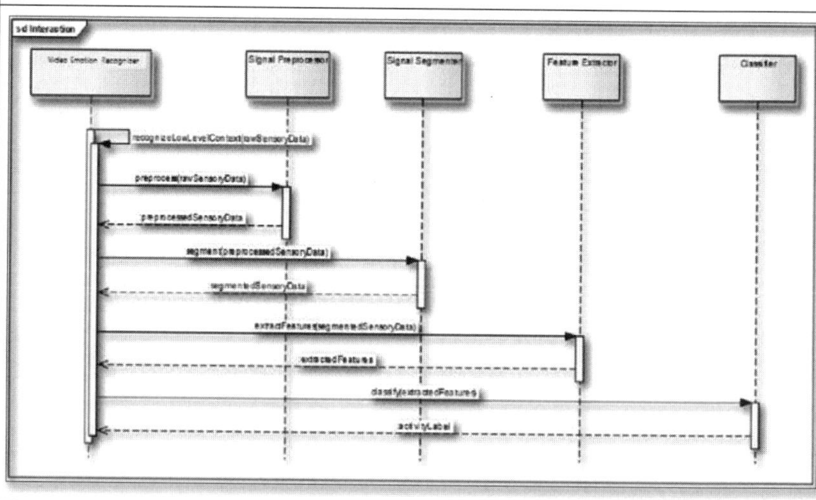

Use Case ID:	**ICL-UC-10**		
Use Case Name:	Recognize food based on tag data		
Created By:	Taeho Hur	**Last Updated By:**	Taeho Hur
Date Created:	9 March 2017	**Last Revision Date:**	02 July 2018
Actors:	ICL-UC-04		

Description:	User selects the category of the intaken food (e.g., "grain") from the food DB list from the app. The related nutrition information (e.g, "protein") shall be sent to the HLCA.
Trigger:	User selects the food category tag
Pre-conditions:	User is going to have a meal/snack
Post-conditions:	Nutrition information is retrieved based on the selected food
Normal Flow:	1. User selects the food to intake from the app 2. The selected food item is parsed and conclude the food category 3. The category is mapped to the food DB 4. According nutrition information is retrieved
Alternative Flows:	N/A
Exceptions:	N/A
Includes:	N/A
Frequency of Use:	Episodic: Only when the user has a meal
NFR ID:	MM-NFR-05
Assumptions:	User is having a meal
Notes and Issues:	N/A

Sequence Diagram:

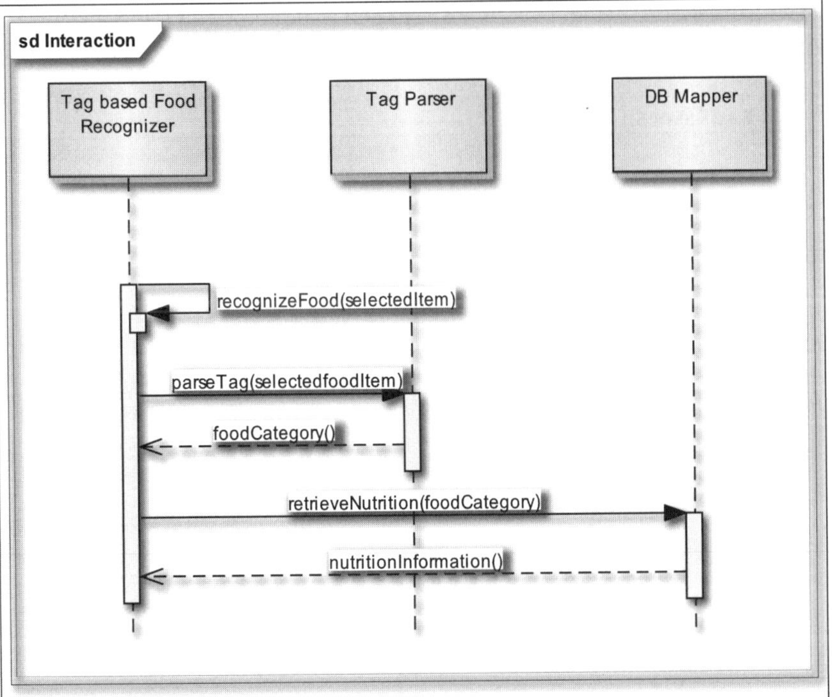

Use Case ID:	**ICL-UC-11**		
Use Case Name:	Unify low-level contexts		
FR ID:	MM-FR-11		
Created By:	Oresti Banos	**Last Updated By:**	Oresti Banos
Date Created:	20 July 2015	**Last Revision Date:**	02 July 2018
Actors:	Low-Level Context Recognizer, Low-Level Context Notifier		

Description:	Aggregation of multiple low-level context instances of the same context type (e.g., activity) corresponding to a similar period of time
Trigger:	Receive low-level context instance
Pre-conditions:	Low-level context instances are received from different recognizers of the same context type
Post-conditions:	A single low-level context instance is served for notification
Normal Flow:	1. A low-level context instance is received 2. Search for other low-level context instances of the same type valid at the same time 3. Fuse the identified low-level context instances into a unified low-level context instance 4. Serve the unified low-level context instance for notification
Alternative Flows:	N/A
Exceptions:	N/A
Includes:	N/A
Frequency of Use:	Frequent: at every reception of a low-level context label
NFR ID:	MM-NFR-05
Assumptions:	Identical labels are used to describe the same low-level context for each recognizer of the same context type (e.g., inertial activity recognizer, video activity recognizer)
Notes and Issues:	N/A
Sequence Diagram:	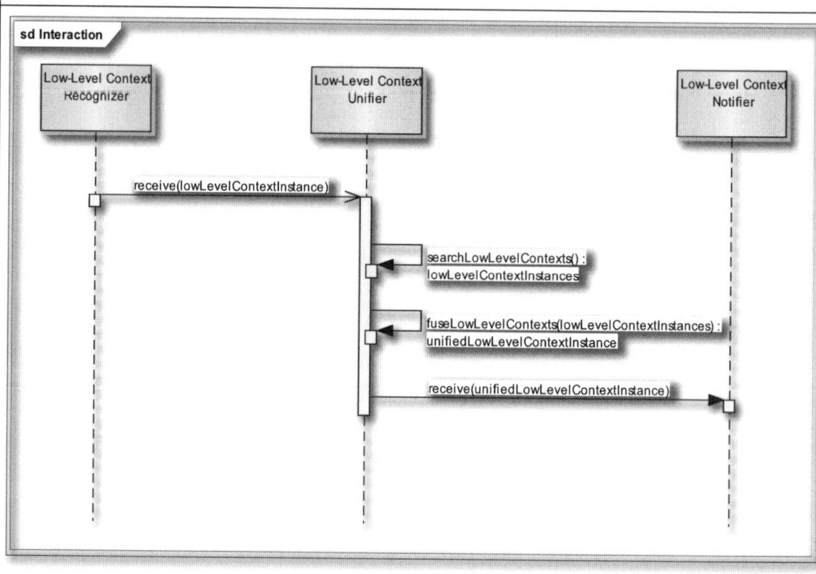

Use Case ID:	**ICL-UC-12**		
Use Case Name:	Notify new low-level context		
Created By:	Oresti Banos	**Last Updated By:**	Oresti Banos
Date Created:	14 July 2015	**Last Revision Date:**	02 July 2018
Actors:	Low-Level Context Unifier, High-Level Context Builder, DCL		

Description:	Serve the newly recognized low-level context for the identification of high-level context and also communicate it to DCL for persistence.
Trigger:	New low-level context is identified
Pre-conditions:	A unified low-level context instance is received
Post-conditions:	• The unified low-level context instance is served for the identification of the high-level context(s) • The unified low-level context instance is sent to DCL 3
Normal Flow:	1. A low-level context instance is received from the low level context unifier 2. The received instance is compared with the last low-level context instance 3. The new low-level context instance is served for the identification of the high-level context 4. The new low-level context instance is sent to DCL 3
Alternative Flows:	3a. If the received instance contains the same low-level context type as the previous one 1. Finalize
Exceptions:	N/A
Includes:	N/A
Frequency of Use:	Frequent: at every reception of a low-level context instance
NFR ID:	N/A
Assumptions:	N/A
Notes and Issues:	N/A
Sequence Diagram:	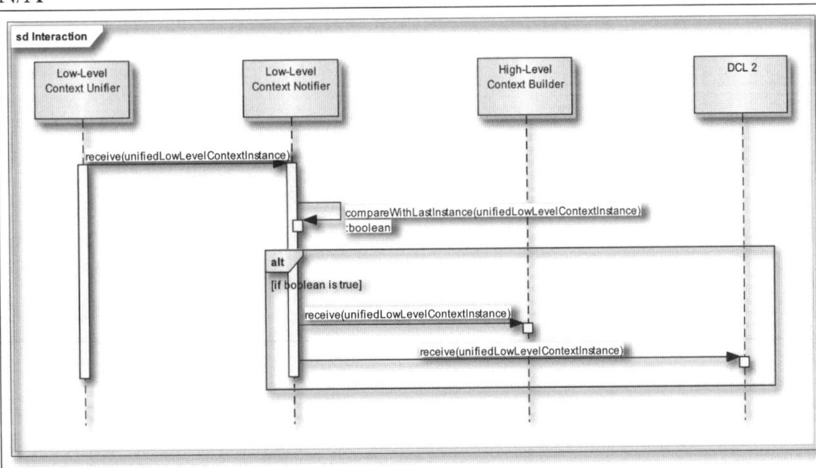

Use Case ID:	**ICL-UC-13**		
Use Case Name:	Create unclassified high-level context instance		
Created By:	Claudia Villalonga	**Last Updated By:**	Claudia Villalonga
Date Created:	14 July 2015	**Last Revision Date:**	02 July 2018

Actors:	Low-Level Context Notifier, Context Ontology Manager, High-Level Context Reasoner
Description:	Build a high-level context instance based on the identified low-level contexts
Trigger:	Receive low-level context instance (label plus metadata)
Pre-conditions:	A new low-level context instance is served to the high-level context builder
Post-conditions:	The unclassified high-level context instance is created
Normal Flow:	1. Map low-level context instance into ontological format 2. Store low-level context instance (ICL4-SUC-17) 3. Search for other low-level context instances of different type valid at the same time 4. 3.1. Create a request for other low-level context instances of different type that are valid at the same time 5. 3.2. Retrieve matching context instances (ICL4-SUC-18) 6. Create new unclassified high-level context instance which links to the available low-level context instance(s) 7. Assert on the unclassified high-level context instance that the missing low-level context instances do not exist 8. Serve the unclassified high-level context instance for classification
Alternative Flows:	N/A
Exceptions:	N/A
Includes:	N/A
Frequency of Use:	Less Frequent: whenever a new low-level context is recognized
NFR ID:	N/A
Assumptions:	Low-level contexts are interpretable
Notes and Issues:	N/A
Sequence Diagram:	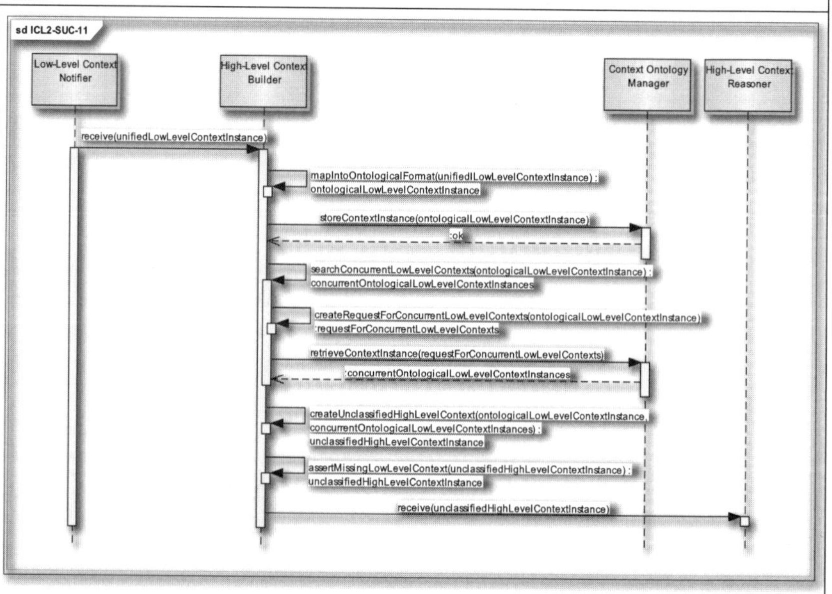

Use Case ID:	ICL-UC-14		
Use Case Name:	Classify high-level context instance		
FR ID:	MM-FR-12		
Created By:	Claudia Villalonga	Last Updated By:	Claudia Villalonga
Date Created:	14 July 2015	Last Revision Date:	01 July 2018
Actors:	High-Level Context Builder, High-Level Context Notifier		
Description:	Classify the unclassified high-level context instance into one of the high-level context categories		
Trigger:	Creation of unclassified high-level context instance		
Pre-conditions:	The unclassified high-level context instance is created		
Post-conditions:	The classified high-level context instance is served for notification		
Normal Flow:	1. Verify the consistency of unclassified high-level context instance 2. Reason on the unclassified high-level context instance to identify the context type to which it belongs 3. Serve the classified high-level context for notification		
Alternative Flows:	1a. If the unclassified high-level context instance is not valid 1. Communicate unidentified context		
Exceptions:	N/A		
Includes:	N/A		
Frequency of Use:	Less Frequent: whenever an unclassified high-level context instance is created		
Assumptions:	Low-level contexts and high-level contexts are interpretable		
Notes and Issues:	N/A		

Sequence Diagram:

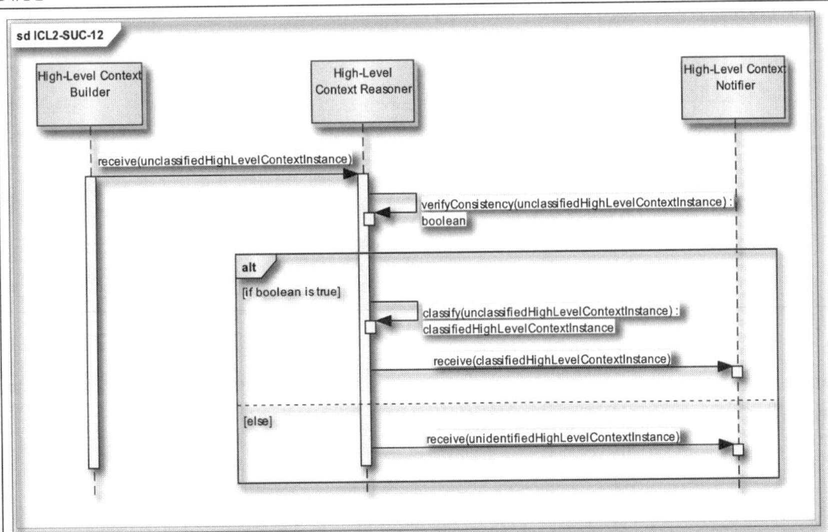

Use Case ID:	ICL-UC-15
Use Case Name:	Notify new high-level context
FR ID:	MM-FR-14

<table>
<tr><td>Created By:</td><td>Oresti Banos</td><td>Last Updated By:</td><td>Claudia Villalonga</td></tr>
<tr><td>Date Created:</td><td>14 July 2015</td><td>Last Revision Date:</td><td>01 July 2018</td></tr>
<tr><td>Actors:</td><td colspan="3">High-Level Context Reasoner, DCL</td></tr>
<tr><td>Description:</td><td colspan="3">Communicate the newly recognized high-level context to DCL for persistence.</td></tr>
<tr><td>Trigger:</td><td colspan="3">High-level context is identified</td></tr>
<tr><td>Pre-conditions:</td><td colspan="3">A high-level context instance is received</td></tr>
<tr><td>Post-conditions:</td><td colspan="3">The new high-level context instance is sent to DCL</td></tr>
<tr><td>Normal Flow:</td><td colspan="3">1. A high-level context instance is received from the high-level context classifier
2. Search for the last high-level context instance
3. 2.1. Create a request for the last high-level context instance
4. 2.2. Retrieve the matching context instance (ICL4-SUC-18)
5. Store high-level context instance (ICL4-SUC-17)
6. Compare the high-level context instance with the last high-level context instance
7. The new high-level context instance is sent to DCL 3</td></tr>
<tr><td>Alternative Flows:</td><td colspan="3">5a. If the received instance contains the same high-level context type as the previous one
1. Finalize</td></tr>
<tr><td>Exceptions:</td><td colspan="3">N/A</td></tr>
<tr><td>Includes:</td><td colspan="3">N/A</td></tr>
<tr><td>Frequency of Use:</td><td colspan="3">Less frequent: at every reception of a high-level context instance</td></tr>
<tr><td>NFR ID:</td><td colspan="3">N/A</td></tr>
<tr><td>Assumptions:</td><td colspan="3">N/A</td></tr>
<tr><td>Notes and Issues:</td><td colspan="3">N/A</td></tr>
<tr><td>Sequence Diagram:</td><td colspan="3">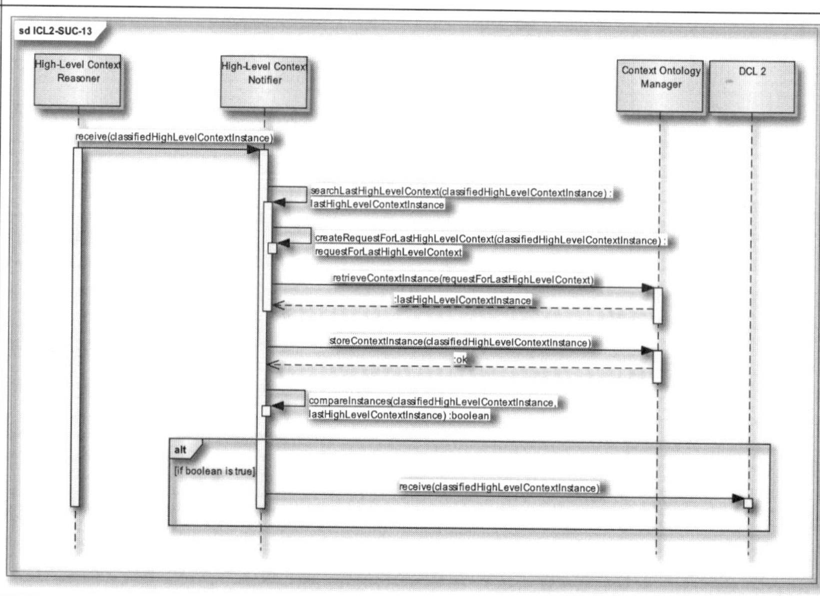
</td></tr>
</table>

<table>
<tr><td>Use Case ID:</td><td colspan="3">ICL-UC-16</td></tr>
<tr><td>Use Case Name:</td><td colspan="3">Load context ontology model</td></tr>
<tr><td>Created By:</td><td>Claudia Villalonga</td><td>Last Updated By:</td><td>Claudia Villalonga</td></tr>
<tr><td>Date Created:</td><td>31 August 2015</td><td>Last Revision Date:</td><td>01 July 2018</td></tr>
<tr><td>Actors:</td><td colspan="3">Ontology Engineer</td></tr>
<tr><td>Description:</td><td colspan="3">Load and store a context ontology model that describes high-level context and its relations to low-level context into the system in order to eN/Able the recognition of high-level context</td></tr>
<tr><td>Trigger:</td><td colspan="3">The ontology engineer who has created a context ontology model loads it through the interface</td></tr>
<tr><td>Pre-conditions:</td><td colspan="3">A context ontology model that describes high-level context and its relations to low-level context has been created</td></tr>
<tr><td>Post-conditions:</td><td colspan="3">The context ontology model is stored and available for the recognition of high-level context</td></tr>
<tr><td>Normal Flow:</td><td colspan="3">1. A context ontology model is received
2. The context ontology model is analyzed for its consistency and validity
3. The context ontology is stored in order to provide persistence
4. Success is notified</td></tr>
<tr><td>Alternative Flows:</td><td colspan="3">2a. If the context ontology model is not valid or inconsistent
1. Error is notified
3a. If there is an error during storage
1. Repeat step 3</td></tr>
<tr><td>Exceptions:</td><td colspan="3">N/A</td></tr>
<tr><td>Includes:</td><td colspan="3">N/A</td></tr>
<tr><td>Frequency of Use:</td><td colspan="3">Infrequent</td></tr>
<tr><td>NFR ID:</td><td colspan="3">N/A</td></tr>
<tr><td>Assumptions:</td><td colspan="3">N/A</td></tr>
<tr><td>Notes and Issues:</td><td colspan="3">N/A</td></tr>
</table>

Sequence Diagram:

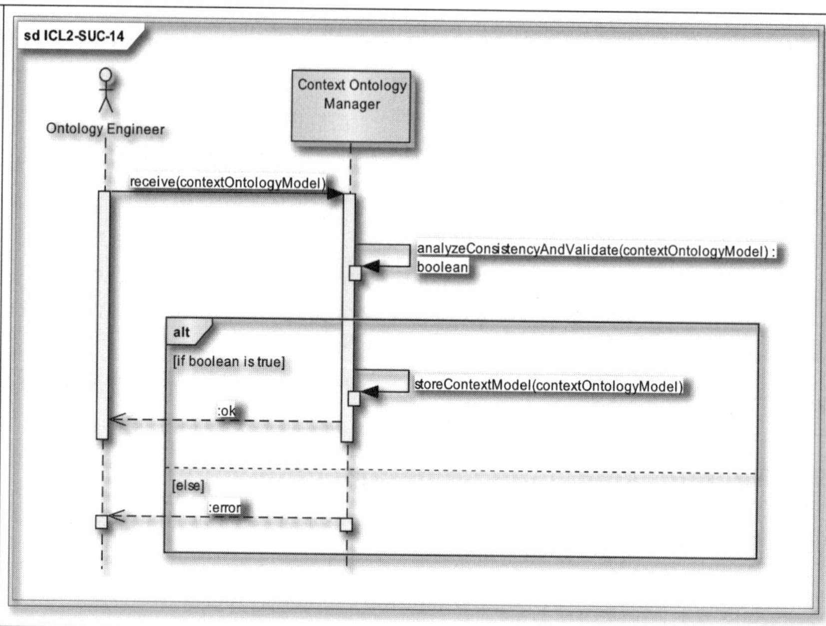

Use Case ID:	**ICL-UC-17**		
Use Case Name:	Store context instance		
Created By:	Claudia Villalonga	**Last Updated By:**	Claudia Villalonga
Date Created:	31 August 2015	**Last Revision Date:**	01 July 2018
Actors:	High-Level Context Builder and High-Level Context Notifier		
Description:	Persist a context instance (high-level context instance or low-level context instance) into the system		
Trigger:	A new context instance has been created or identified		
Pre-conditions:	A new context instance is received		
Post-conditions:	The context instance is stored		
Normal Flow:	1. Receive context instance 2. Validate the context instance 3. Store the context instance 4. Notify success		
Alternative Flows:	2a. If the context instance is not valid 1. Error is notified 3a. If there is an error during storage 1. Repeat step 3		
Exceptions:	N/A		
Includes:	N/A		
Frequency of Use:	Less Frequent: whenever a new low-level context instance is created, a new high-level context instance is created, or a high-level context instance is classified		
NFR ID:	N/A		

Assumptions:	N/A
Notes and Issues:	N/A
Sequence Diagram:	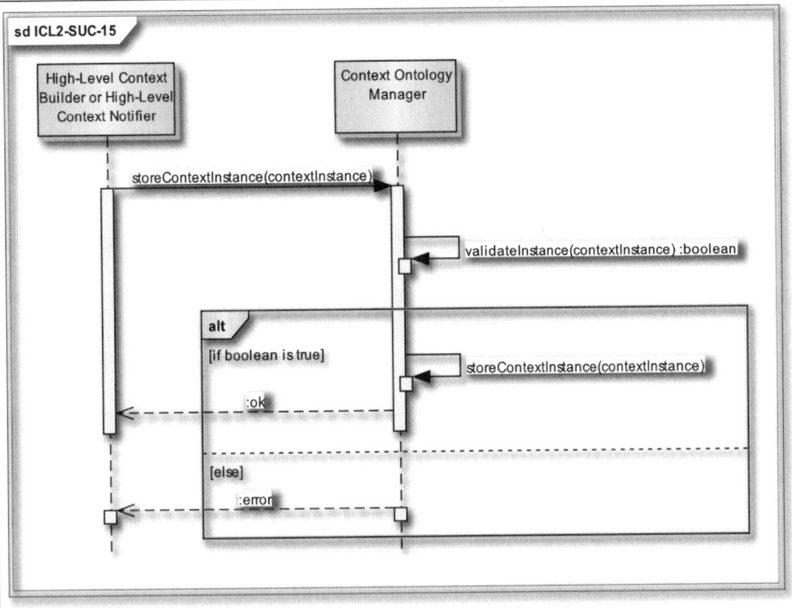

Use Case ID:	**ICL-UC-18**		
Use Case Name:	Retrieve context instance		
Created By:	Claudia Villalonga	**Last Updated By:**	Claudia Villalonga
Date Created:	31 August 2015	**Last Revision Date:**	01 July 2018
Actors:	High-Level Context Builder and High-Level Context Notifier		
Description:	Provide context instances (high-level context instances or low-level context instances) that match a given request		
Trigger:	A requester retrieves context instances		
Pre-conditions:	A request for context instances is received		
Post-conditions:	Matching context instances are provided to the requester		
Normal Flow:	1. Receive a request for a specific context 2. Validate the request 3. Generate the query associated to the request 4. Match the query to the stored context instances 5. Return the matching context instances		
Alternative Flows:	2a. If the request for context is not valid 1. Return error message		
Exceptions:	N/A		
Includes:	N/A		
Frequency of Use:	Less frequent: whenever context instances are required in order to generate a new high-level context instance or to verify the high-level context		
NFR ID:	N/A		

Assumptions:	N/A
Notes and Issues:	N/A
Sequence Diagram:	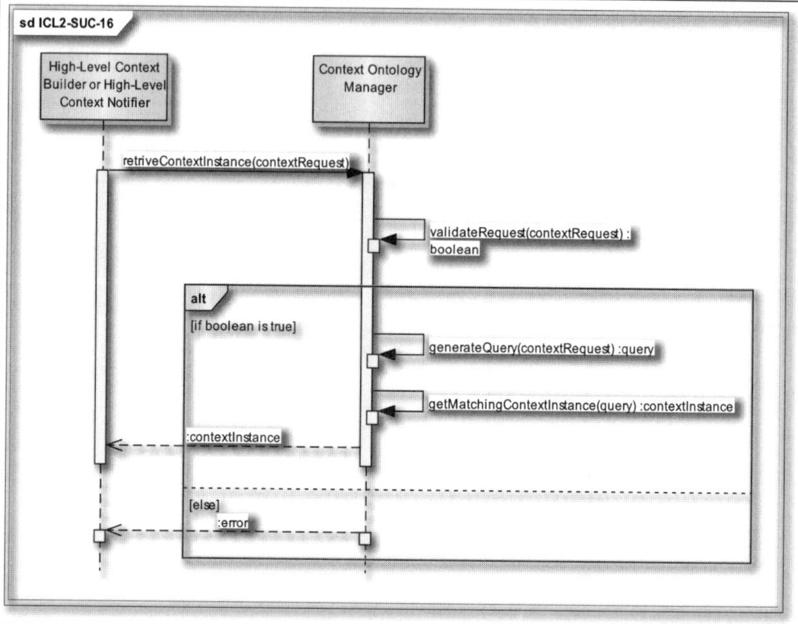

Use Case ID:	**ICL-UC-19**		
Use Case Name:	Evolve Ontology		
Created By:	Wajahat Ali Khan	**Last Updated By:**	Muhammad Asif Razzaq
Date Created:	18 Mar 2016	**Last Revision Date:**	01 July 2018
Actors:	Ontology Engineer		
Description:	Evolving the already created context ontology based on the clinical service. The low level and high level clinical related contexts are modelled in the context ontology that only included physical activities and nutrition related low level and high-level entities.		
Trigger:	The ontology engineer who has created a context ontology model loads it through the interface		
Pre-conditions:	A context ontology model that describes high-level context and its relations to low-level context has been created with physical activities, nutrition and clinical information related resources		
Post-conditions:	The modified or evolved context ontology model is stored and available for the recognition of high-level context		
Normal Flow:	1. Ontology engineer defines the low level clinical concepts in addition to the low level physical activities, and nutrition concepts 2. Ontology engineer defines the high level clinical concepts in addition to the high level physical activities and nutrition concepts 3. The constraints are defined on the new concepts added to the ontology 4. Consistency of the ontology is checked with reasoner		

<table>
<tr><td></td><td>5. The modified context ontology is stored for persistence
6. Success is notified</td></tr>
<tr><td>Alternative Flows:</td><td>4a. If the context ontology model is not valid or inconsistent
a. Error is notified
b. Check step 1,2,3</td></tr>
<tr><td>Exceptions:</td><td>N/A</td></tr>
<tr><td>Includes:</td><td>N/A</td></tr>
<tr><td>Frequency of Use:</td><td>Infrequent</td></tr>
<tr><td>NFR ID:</td><td>N/A</td></tr>
<tr><td>Assumptions:</td><td>Context Ontology based on physical activities and nutrition service already exists</td></tr>
<tr><td>Notes and Issues:</td><td>N/A</td></tr>
<tr><td>Sequence Diagram:</td><td>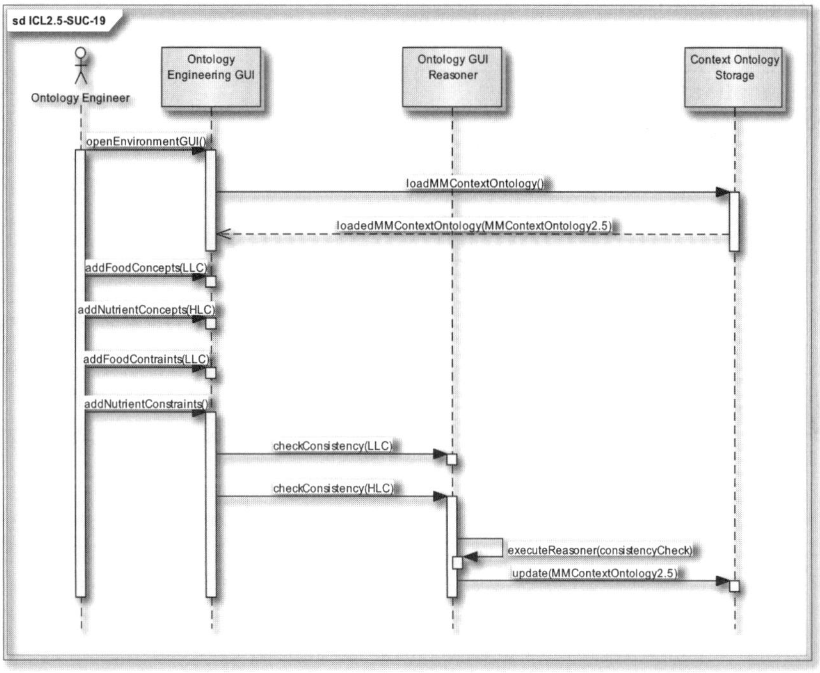
</td></tr>
</table>

Use Case ID:	**18.2.4ICL-UC-20**		
Use Case Name:	High level physical activity context		
Created By:	Wajahat Ali Khan	**Last Updated By:**	Wajahat Ali Khan
Date Created:	18 March 2016	**Last Revision Date:**	18 June 2018
Actors:	High-Level Context Reasoner		
Description:	A classified high level physical activity context is recognized by the reasoner from the unclassified high level context.		
Trigger:	High-level context is identified		
Pre-conditions:	An unclassified high-level physical activity context instance is received		

Post-conditions:	The new high-level physical activity context instance is forwarded to Notify DCL
Normal Flow:	1. A high-level physical activity context instance is processed by high-level context classifier 2. Reasoning is performed by the reasoner to find out classified high level physical activity context 3. The classified high level physical activity context is provided to Notify DCL
Alternative Flows:	N/A
Exceptions:	N/A
Includes:	N/A
Frequency of Use:	Less frequent: at every reception of a unclassified high-level physical activity context instance
NFR ID:	N/A
Assumptions:	N/A
Notes and Issues:	N/A
Sequence Diagram:	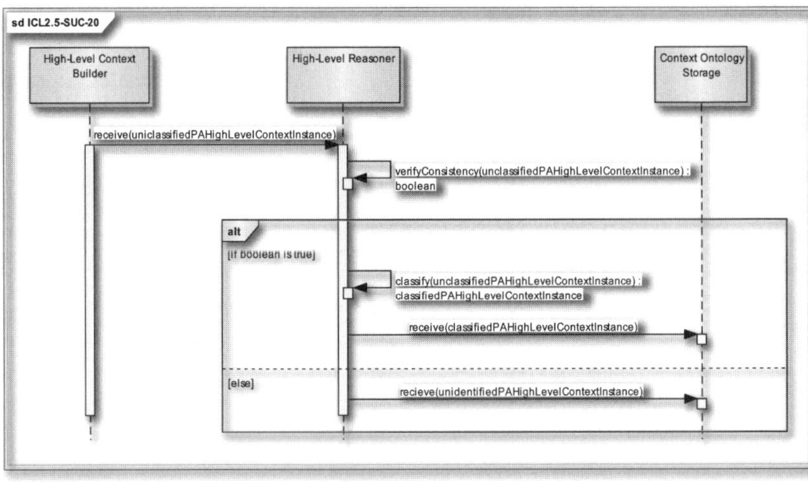

Use Case ID:	**ICL4-SUC-21**		
Use Case Name:	High level nutrition context		
Created By:	Wajahat Ali Khan	**Last Updated By:**	Wajahat Ali Khan
Date Created:	18 March 2016	**Last Revision Date:**	18 June 2018
Actors:	High-Level Context Reasoner		
Description:	A classified high-level nutrition context is recognized by the reasoner from the unclassified high-level context.		
Trigger:	High-level context is identified		
Pre-conditions:	An unclassified high-level nutrition context instance is received		
Post-conditions:	The new high-level nutrition context instance is forwarded to Notify DCL		
Normal Flow:	1. A high-level nutrition context instance is processed by high-level context classifier		

	2. Reasoning is performed by the reasoner to find out classified high level nutrition context 3. The classified high-level nutrition context is provided to Notify DCL
Alternative Flows:	N/A
Exceptions:	N/A
Includes:	N/A
Frequency of Use:	Less frequent: at every reception of an unclassified high-level nutrition context instance
NFR ID:	N/A
Assumptions:	N/A
Notes and Issues:	N/A
Sequence Diagram:	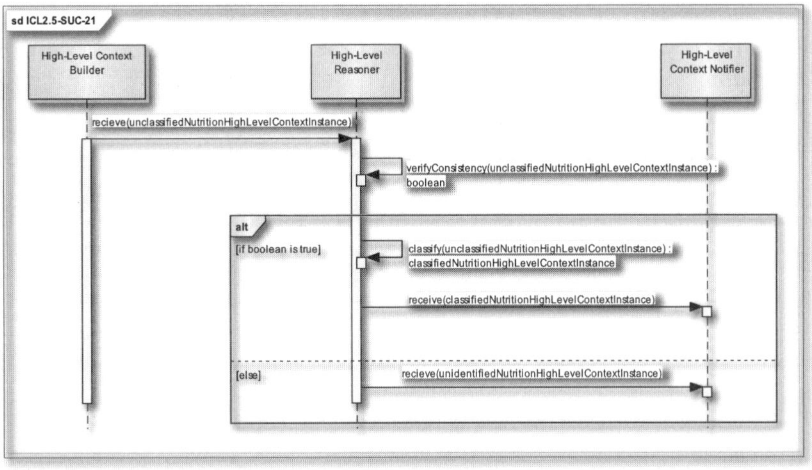

Use Case ID:	**ICL-UC-22**		
Use Case Name:	High level clinical context		
Created By:	Muhammad Asif Razzaq	**Last Updated By:**	Muhammad Asif Razzaq
Date Created:	10 March 2017	**Last Revision Date:**	10 March 2017
Actors:	High-Level Context Reasoner		
Description:	A classified high level clinical context is recognized by the reasoner from the unclassified high-level context.		
Trigger:	High-level context is identified		
Pre-conditions:	An unclassified high-level clinical context instance is received		
Post-conditions:	The new high-level clinical context instance is forwarded to Notify DCL		
Normal Flow:	1. A high-level clinical context instance is processed by high-level context classifier 2. Reasoning is performed by the reasoner to find out classified high level clinical context 3. The classified high level clinical context is provided to Notify DCL		
Alternative Flows:	N/A		
Exceptions:	N/A		

Includes:	N/A
Frequency of Use:	Less frequent: at every reception of a unclassified high-level clinical context instance
NFR ID:	N/A
Assumptions:	N/A
Notes and Issues:	N/A
Sequence Diagram:	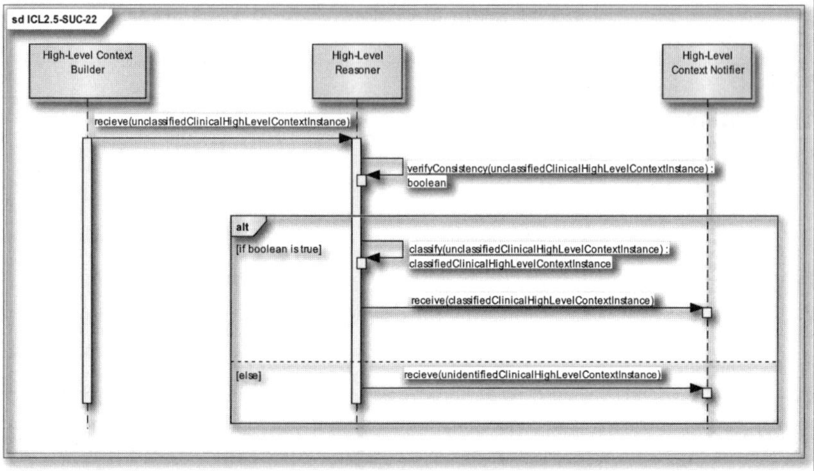

18.3 Knowledge Curation Layer

18.3.1 Use Case List

ID	Description
KCL-UC-01	Select valid combinations of features from lifelog and user profile schema to build feature model for yielding correct classification model.
KCL-UC-02	Apply preprocessing methods on retrieved lifelog and user profile data to prepare the data for classification model learning.
KCL-UC-03	Expert generate guidelines to utilize their practices to create rules in the knowledge bases.
KCL-UC-04	System validate the guidelines in tree structure to maintain the rules.
KCL-UC-05	User profile and lifelog schema is needed to be known before feature modeling and creation of classification model.
KCL-UC-06	Retrieve user profile and lifelog data for creation of classification model.
KCL-UC-07	Extract meta-features of classification datasets.
KCL-UC-08	Evaluate performance of decision tree algorithms (i.e, f-measure)
KCL-UC-09	Create automatic algorithm recommendation model (AARM) from offline datasets. AARM will be used as recommendation model for algorithm selection.
KCL-UC-10	Create rules to enhance the knowledge base of the system to generate recommendations in easy manner.
KCL-UC-11	Rule validation avoid the duplication of rules in the knowledge base and enhance the maintainability of knowledge base.
KCL-UC-12	It integrates AARM dataset in Mining Minds Data Driven knowledge acquisition approach for recommendation of automatic algorithm on given dataset.
KCL-UC-13	It generates classification model from user profile lifelog data that can be explored by model learning mechanism with the help of learning method as well as processed data.
KCL-UC-14	The integrated AARM shall automatically recommend appropriate classification algorithm. Or domain expert can select any algorithm from available set of decision tree algorithms.
KCL-UC-15	Domain model is used in creation of rule. It manages the domain model for creating rule.
KCL-UC-16	It transforms the rules or guidelines into executable knowledge representation.
KCL-UC-17	It creates situation event and index the rule based on situation event.
KCL-UC-18	Compute features priorities to help the domain expert for selecting appropriate features from available schema.

18.3.2 Use Case Diagram

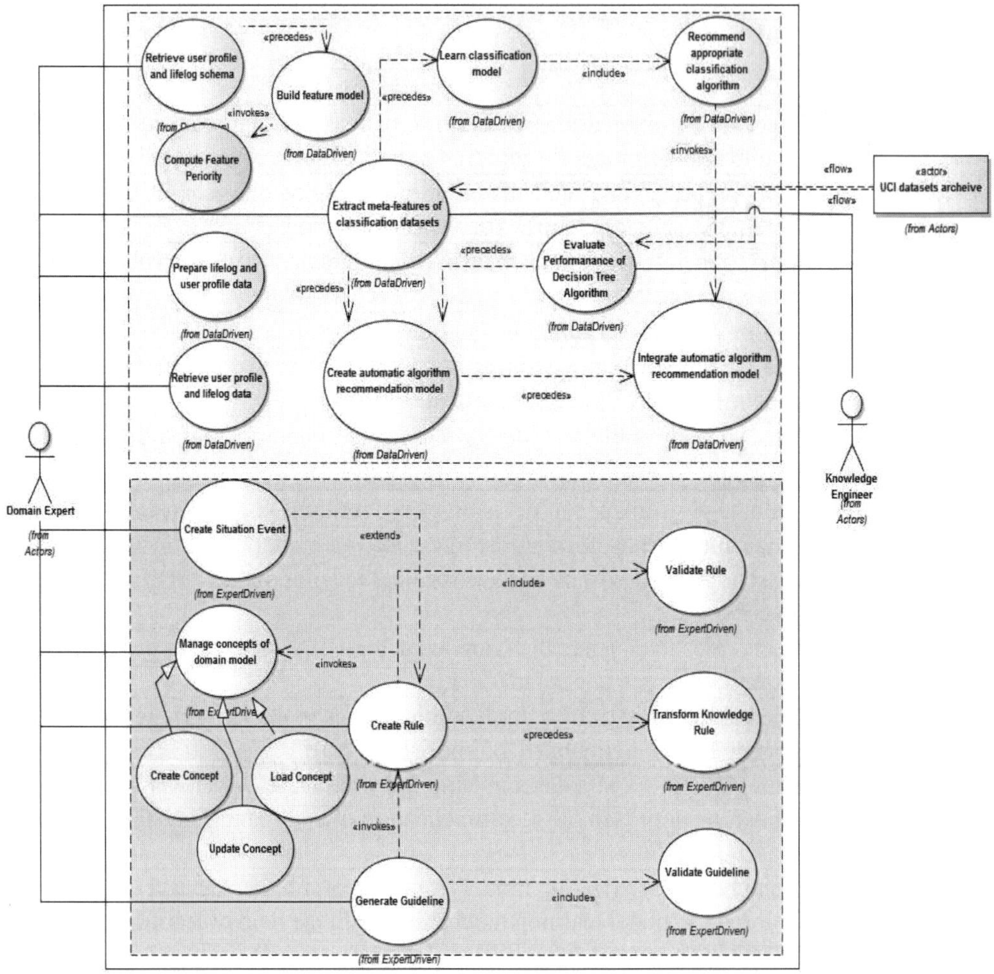

18.3.3 Use Case Description

Use Case ID:	**KCL-UC-01**		
Use Case Name:	Build feature model		
Created By:	Maqbool Ali	**Last Updated By:**	Maqbool Ali
Date Created:	11-07-2015	**Last Revision Date:**	03-07-2018
Actors:	Domain Expert		
Description:	A feature model defines the valid combinations of features in a domain that enables capturing feature variability and interdependencies. For building feature model and its reusability, domain expert uses selected domain schema (i.e. lifelog and user		

	profile schema) and selects the related features for final feature model.
Trigger:	Prior to classification model creation needed for required domain
Preconditions:	• System has retrieved the schema from DCL. • Domain expert has selected domain under consideration (e.g. nutrition).
Postconditions:	System will build the feature model
Normal Flow:	1. Domain expert retrieves the schema from schema storage. 2. System loads and plots the schema 3. Domain expert builds the feature models as follows: a. Select the required features for corresponding domain b. Verify the consistency of the selected features (such as concept hierarchy) c. Save the feature model 4. System creates the feature model based on selected features and visualizes it in hierarchical form 5. Domain expert reviews the feature model and confirms it for saving into repository 6. System persists the feature model into repository.
Alternative Flows:	N/A
Exceptions:	
Includes:	N/A
Frequency of Use:	When new service is required and mining mind have sufficient data for classification model creation
Special Requirements:	N/A
Assumptions:	Initially we assume that feature model is valid
Notes and Issues:	One possible candidate representation for feature model is XML.
Sequence Diagram:	

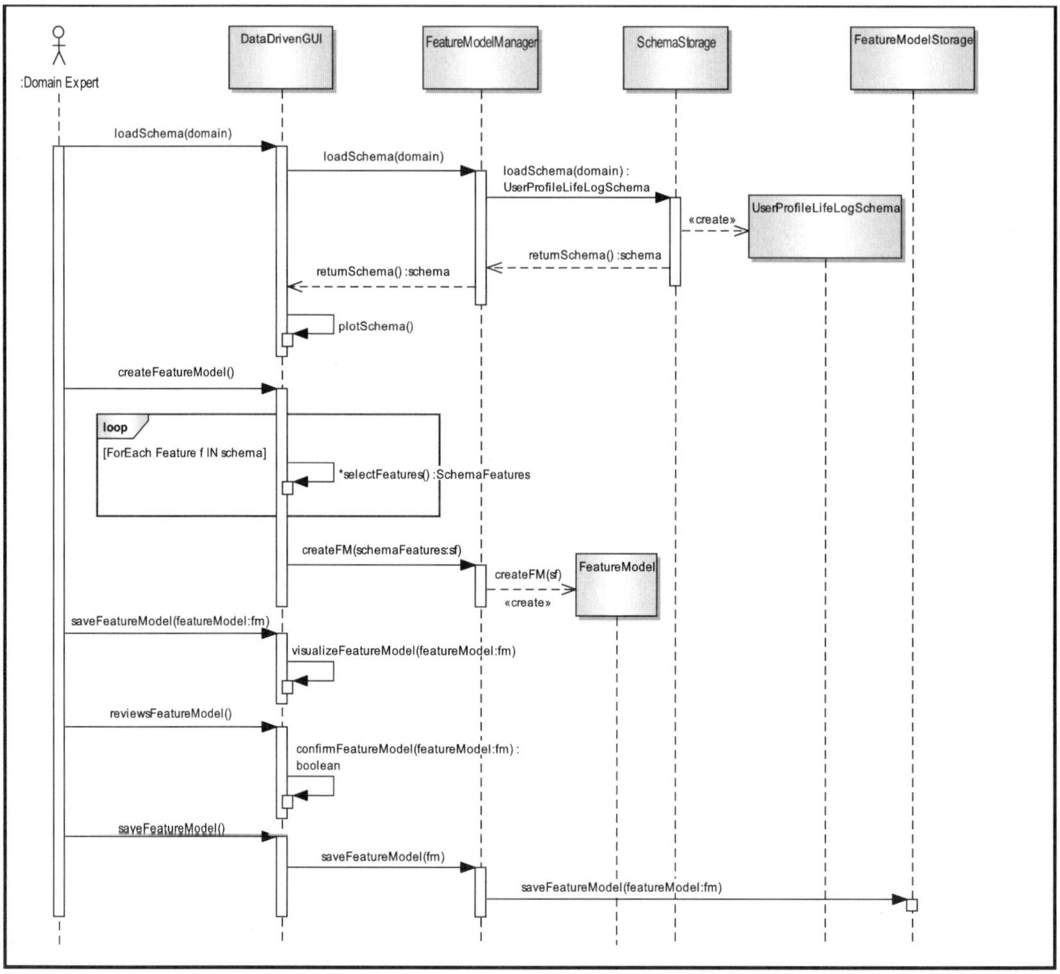

Use Case ID:	**KCL-UC-02**		
Use Case Name:	Prepare lifelog and user profile data		
Created By:	Maqbool Ali	**Last Updated By:**	Maqbool Ali
Date Created:	10-07-2015	**Last Revision Date:**	03-07-2018
Actors:	Domain Expert		
Description:	It is important to pre-process the data (i.e. lifelog and user profile data) to generate models with high accuracy. '*Prepare lifelog and user profile data*' use case apply various pre-processing techniques such as missing value handling, outlier detection, transformation, and features selections to convert unprocessed data into processed data.		
Trigger:	Prior to classification model creation needed for high accuracy of model learning		

<table>
<tr><td>Preconditions:</td><td><ul><li>System has retrieved the data from DCL, which is unprocessed data.</li></ul></td></tr>
<tr><td>Postconditions:</td><td>System will prepare and store the data</td></tr>
<tr><td>Normal Flow:</td><td><ol>
<li>Domain expert loads the unprocessed data</li>
<li>System displays the retrieved data</li>
<li>For each attribute:<ol type="a">
<li>Domain expert identifies the missing values and select appropriate method from following options for missing value replacement.<ul><li>Default value</li><li>Mean</li><li>Mode</li></ul></li>
<li>System replaces the missing values using selected method.</li></ol></li>
<li>For each attribute:<ol type="a">
<li>Domain expert apply outlier detection method such as interquartile range and scatterplot.</li>
<li>System display the outliers</li>
<li>Domain expert select appropriate method from following options for outlier replacement.<ul><li>Mean</li><li>Mode</li></ul></li>
<li>System replace the outlier using selected method.</li></ol></li>
<li>For each attribute:<ol type="a">
<li>Domain expert identifies, normalizes the non-transformed values, and updates the dataset.</li>
<li>System modifies the values set and update the dataset</li></ol></li>
<li>Domain expert applies the attributes filtration techniques (i.e ranking)</li>
<li>System computes the ranks for all attributes and displays to expert</li>
</ol></td></tr>
</table>

	8. Domain expert select the highly ranked attributes (i.e. rank value >= 0.8) 9. System filters the attributes based on selected attributes and displays to domain expert 10. Domain expert saves the processed data into repository 11. System persists the processed data into repository
Alternative Flows:	N/A
Exceptions:	N/A
Includes:	N/A
Frequency of Use:	When new service is required, and mining mind have sufficient data for classification model creation
Special Requirements:	N/A
Assumptions:	N/A
Notes and Issues:	• An **outlier** is any value that is numerically distant from most of the other data points in a set of data. It can be detected by histograms, scatterplots, or interquartile range techniques. • **Data transformation** is the process to convert and normalize the data from one format to another. It can be done by Log, square root, or arcsine transformation techniques.
Sequence Diagram:	

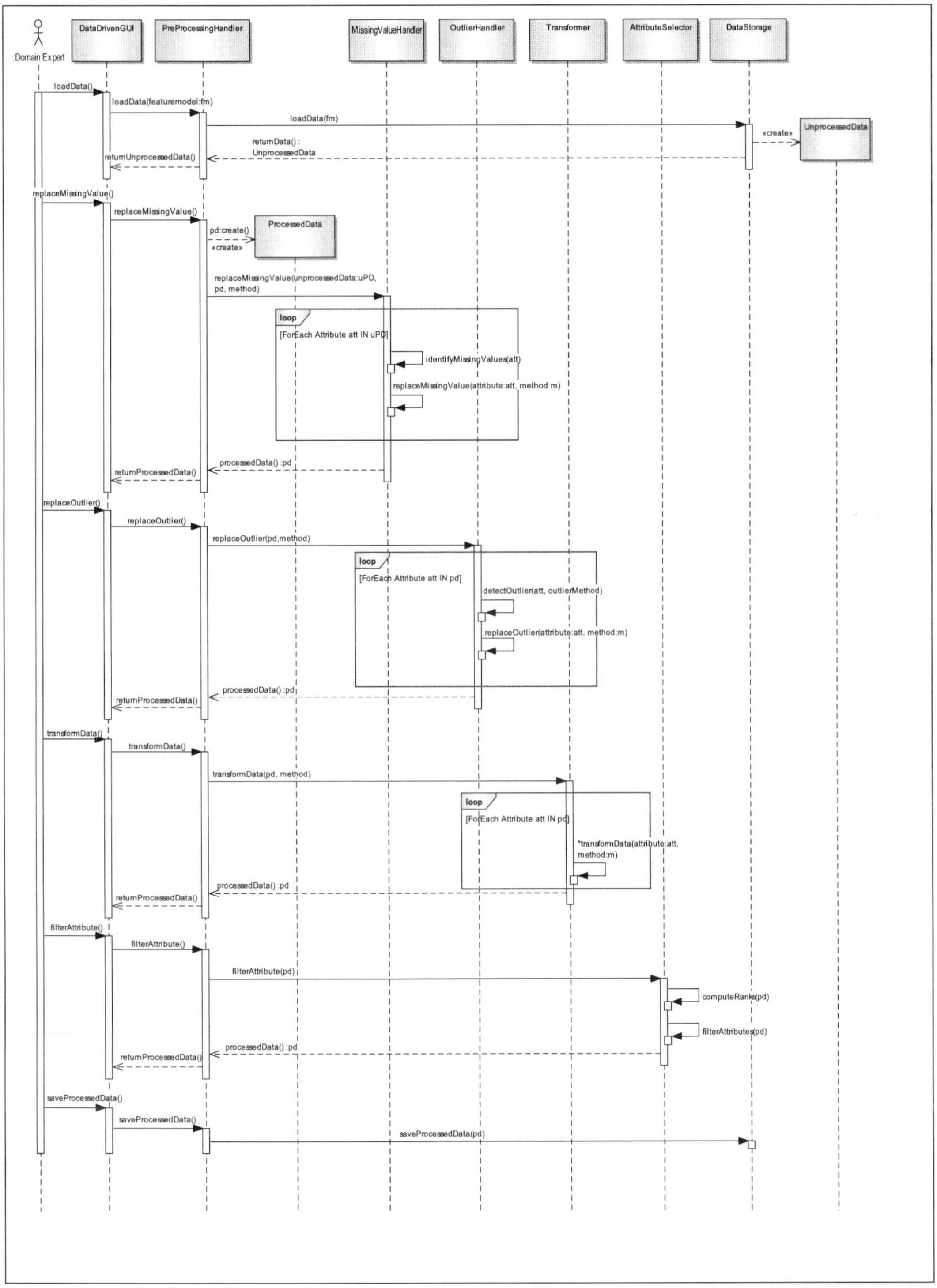
:Domain Expert
DataDrivenGUI
PreProcessingHandler
MissingValueHandler
OutlierHandler
Transformer
AttributeSelector
DataStorage
UnprocessedData
ProcessedData
loadData()
loadData(featuremodel:fm)
loadData(fm)
«create»
returnData() : UnprocessedData
returnUnprocessedData()
replaceMissingValue()
replaceMissingValue()
pd:create()
«create»
replaceMissingValue(unprocessedData:uPD, pd, method)
loop
[ForEach Attribute att IN uPD]
identifyMissingValues(att)
replaceMissingValue(attribute:att, method m)
processedData() :pd
returnProcessedData()
replaceOutlier()
replaceOutlier()
replaceOutlier(pd,method)
loop
[ForEach Attribute att IN pd]
detectOutlier(att, outlierMethod)
replaceOutlier(attribute:att, method:m)
processedData() :pd
returnProcessedData()
transformData()
transformData()
transformData(pd, method)
loop
[ForEach Attribute att IN pd]
*transformData(attribute:att, method:m)
processedData() :pd
returnProcessedData()
filterAttribute()
filterAttribute()
filterAttribute(pd)
computeRanks(pd)
filterAttributes(pd)
processedData() :pd
returnProcessedData()
saveProcessedData()
saveProcessedData()
saveProcessedData(pd)

<table>
<tr><td>Use Case ID:</td><td colspan="3">KCL-UC-03</td></tr>
<tr><td></td><td colspan="3"></td></tr>
<tr><td>Use Case Name:</td><td colspan="3">Generate Guideline</td></tr>
<tr><td>Created By:</td><td>Taqdir Ali and Maqbool Hussain</td><td>Last Updated By:</td><td>Taqdir Ali, Maqbool Hussain</td></tr>
<tr><td>Date Created:</td><td>11-07-2015</td><td>Last Revision Date:</td><td>15-07-2015</td></tr>
<tr><td>Actors:</td><td colspan="3">Domain Expert</td></tr>
<tr><td>Description:</td><td colspan="3">Guidelines are the combination of one or multiple rules in form of decision tree. The tree format guidelines are understandable to the domain experts and it can easily interpret and execute by computer.</td></tr>
<tr><td>Trigger:</td><td colspan="3">Whenever domain expert wants to generate new guideline or update the existing one.</td></tr>
<tr><td>Preconditions:</td><td colspan="3">1. The domain expert shall be authenticated with full access on the guideline management.
2. Domain expert shall have existing guidelines as reference for generating guideline tree.</td></tr>
<tr><td>Postconditions:</td><td colspan="3">• The expert shall generate guidelines to acquire their knowledge into the system.</td></tr>
<tr><td>Normal Flow:</td><td colspan="3">1. Domain expert opens the guidelines editor.
2. System displays new guideline tree form and load the wellness model.
3. Domain expert selects/drags tree node into editor form.
4. System display the node and open the corresponding properties window, which includes;
a. Loads wellness model tree.
b. Displays operators, relationships and node type (conditional, conclusion or both) artifacts.
5. Domain expert selects concepts for the node using any of the following methods and confirm to save the node.
a. Using wellness model, dragging concepts and facts into node conditional or conclusion part.</td></tr>
</table>

	b. Using auto pop-up Intelli-sense window to select concepts and facts into conditional or conclusion part. 6. System saves the tree node and displays as part of the guideline tree. 7. Domain expert add other nodes to guideline tree by using step repeating step 3 on ward. After completion, (s)he saves the guideline tree. 8. System validates the guideline tree using "KCL-UC-04" and save into guideline repository.
Alternative Flows:	2a. System loads existing guideline tree for modification (modifying existing or adding new node). a. Domain expert selects existing node in guideline tree or drag new node to appropriate place in guideline tree. b. To modify node, step 3 onward will be invoked in Normal Flow.
Exceptions:	N/A
Includes:	Validate Guideline
Frequency of Use:	Whenever domain expert wants to create new guideline tree or update existing guideline tree.
Special Requirements:	N/A
Assumptions:	N/A
Notes and Issues:	• Guidelines tree created will base on existing guidelines of corresponding domain and domain expert shall interpret textual guidelines into tree format. • Appropriate modelling of guideline is challenging task.
Sequence Diagram:	

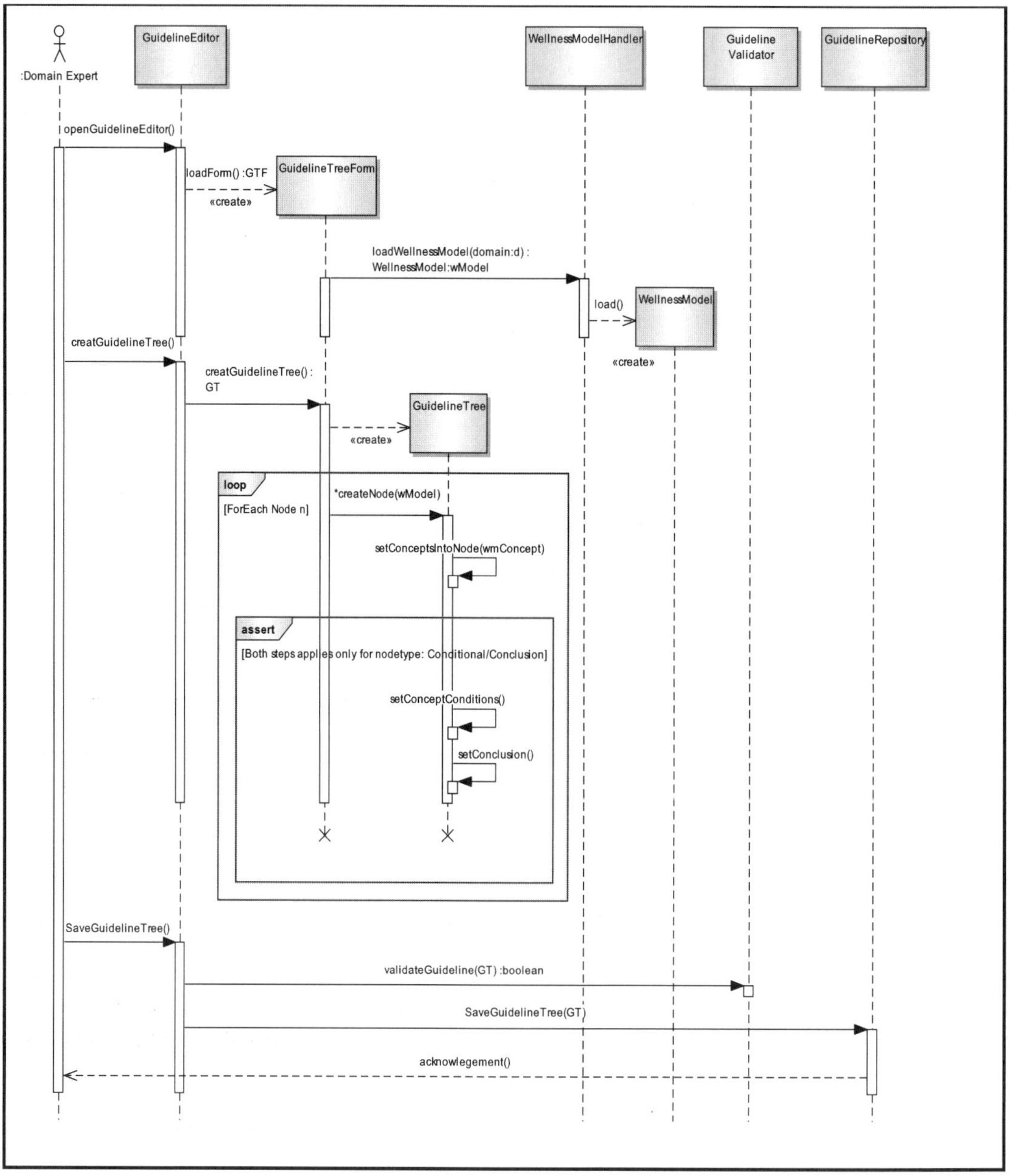

Use Case ID:	KCL-UC-04		
Use Case Name:	Validate Guideline		
Created By:	Taqdir Ali and Maqbool Hussain	Last Updated By:	Taqdir Ali, Maqbool Hussain
Date Created:	11-07-2015	Last Revision Date:	15-07-2015

Actors:	Domain Expert
Description:	Guidelines have different facts and conclusions in form of nodes related with different relationships. The guidelines tree shall be validated for the possible duplication.
Trigger:	Whenever domain expert wants to generate new guideline or update the existing one.
Preconditions:	1. System shall be running 2. The domain expert shall be authenticated with full access on the guideline management.
Postconditions:	• Validated guideline tree
Normal Flow:	1. Domain Expert save the new guideline or update the existing guideline. 2. The system validate guideline for inconsistency and duplication as follows. a. Fetch the existing guidelines and process each node and relationship b. Guideline Tree is approved for having no inconsistency and duplication of new nodes and relationships of the facts and conclusion with the existing guidelines. c. Guideline Tree is stored into guidelines repository. d. Acknowledge the expert to save guideline successfully.
Alternative Flows:	2b. Guideline Tree is found having inconsistency or duplication with existing guideline tree a. The system produces alert the inconsistency or duplication in guideline tree b. Domain expert review the alert message and correct the guideline tree. c. Step 1 and Step 2 of normal flow is executed.
Exceptions:	N/A
Includes:	N/A

Frequency of Use:	Whenever domain expert wants to create new guideline or update existing guideline.
Special Requirements:	N/A
Assumptions:	N/A
Notes and Issues:	Appropriate modelling of guideline and validation is challenging task.

Sequence Diagram:

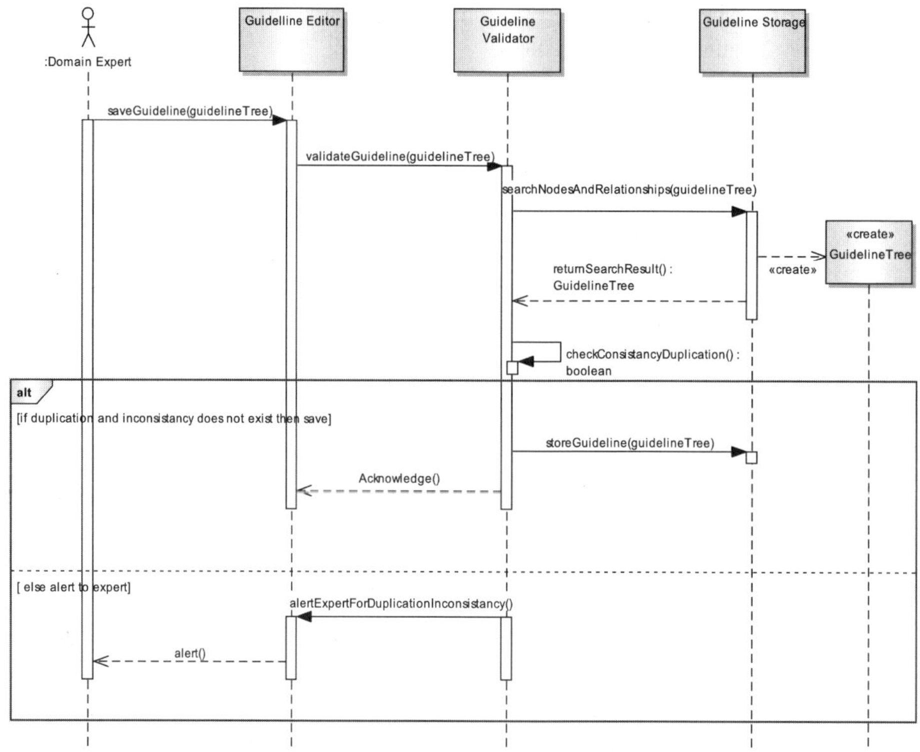

Use Case ID:	**KCL-UC-05**		
Use Case Name:	Retrieve user profile and lifelog schema		
Created By:	Maqbool Ali	**Last Updated By:**	Maqbool Ali
Date Created:	10-07-2015	**Last Revision Date:**	03-07-2018
Actors:	Domain Expert, DCL		
Description:	User profile and lifelog schema retrieval help domain expert to view all available features for building feature model.		
Trigger:	Prior to classification model creation needed for required domain		

Preconditions:	• System has access through service interface to retrieve user profile and lifelog schema from DCL • System and DCL has agreement on common schema representation format • DCL has capability to share user profile and lifelog schema in secure environment.
Postconditions:	System will receive user profile and lifelog schema conform to its representation scheme.
Normal Flow:	1. Domain expert selects the domain and sends requests to DCL for user profile and lifelog schema. 2. DCL shares the user profile and lifelog schema 3. System receives the user profile and lifelog schema 4. Domain expert uses the system and performs the following tasks; a. Verifies the conformance of received schema b. Plots the verified schema c. Saves the verified schema 5. System saves the verified schema
Alternative Flows:	N/A
Exceptions:	1a. System unable to connect to DCL a. System connection is failed during retrieving user profile and lifelog schema b. System hold and will retry after some time to connect to DCL and retrieve the user profile and lifelog schema 4a. System unable to verify lifelog schema conformance a. System fail to conform the schema representation from DCL b. System will send message to DCL about incompatible schema format
Includes:	N/A
Frequency of Use:	When new service is required, and mining mind have sufficient data for classification model creation

Special Requirements:	N/A
Assumptions:	N/A
Notes and Issues:	If DCL is unable to send user profile and lifelog schema in required format, then alternate strategy has to be considered.

Sequence Diagram:

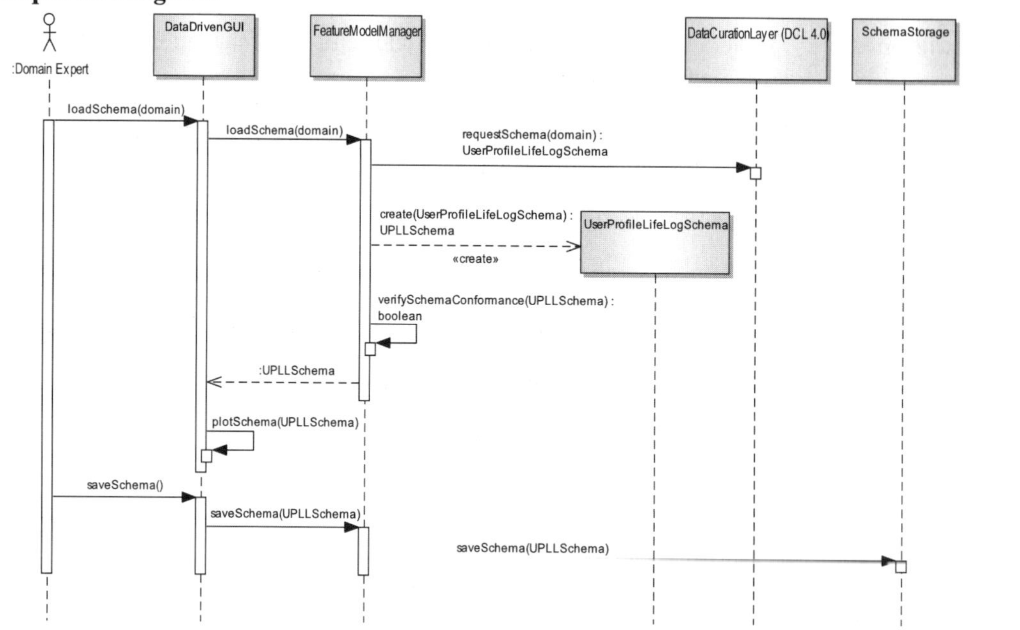

Use Case ID:	**KCL-UC-06**		
Use Case Name:	Retrieve user profile and lifelog data		
Created By:	Maqbool Ali	**Last Updated By:**	Maqbool Ali
Date Created:	10-07-2015	**Last Revision Date:**	03-07-2018
Actors:	Domain Expert, DCL		
Description:	User profile and lifelog data has hidden knowledge that can be explored after loading from data storage		
Trigger:	Prior to classification model creation needed for required data		
Preconditions:	• System has access through service interface to retrieve user profile and lifelog data from DCL		

	• DCL has capability to share user profile and lifelog data in secure environment. • System has already loaded the previously imported user profile and lifelog schema
Postconditions:	System will receive user profile and lifelog data based on selected schema
Normal Flow:	1. Domain expert loads the feature model for selected domain 2. System loads the corresponding feature model 3. Domain expert sends request to DCL for user profile and lifelog data based on loaded feature model 4. DCL shares the user profile and lifelog data 5. System receives the user profile and lifelog data 6. Domain expert uses the system and performs the following tasks; o Verifies the user profile and lifelog data o Saves the data after verification. 7. System saves the verified data
Alternative Flows:	
Exceptions:	3a. System unable to connect to DCL a. System connection is failed during retrieving user profile and lifelog data b. System hold and will retry after some time to connect to DCL and retrieve the user profile and lifelog data 6a. System receives irrelevant data a. System detects the irrelevant data sent by DCL. b. System request again DCL to make sure that data received is according to feature selected.
Includes:	
Frequency of Use:	When new service is required and mining mind have sufficient data for classification model creation

Special Requirements:	N/A
Assumptions:	N/A
Notes and Issues:	If DCL is unable to send data based on dynamic feature selection from schema, then alternate strategy has to be considered.

Sequence Diagram:

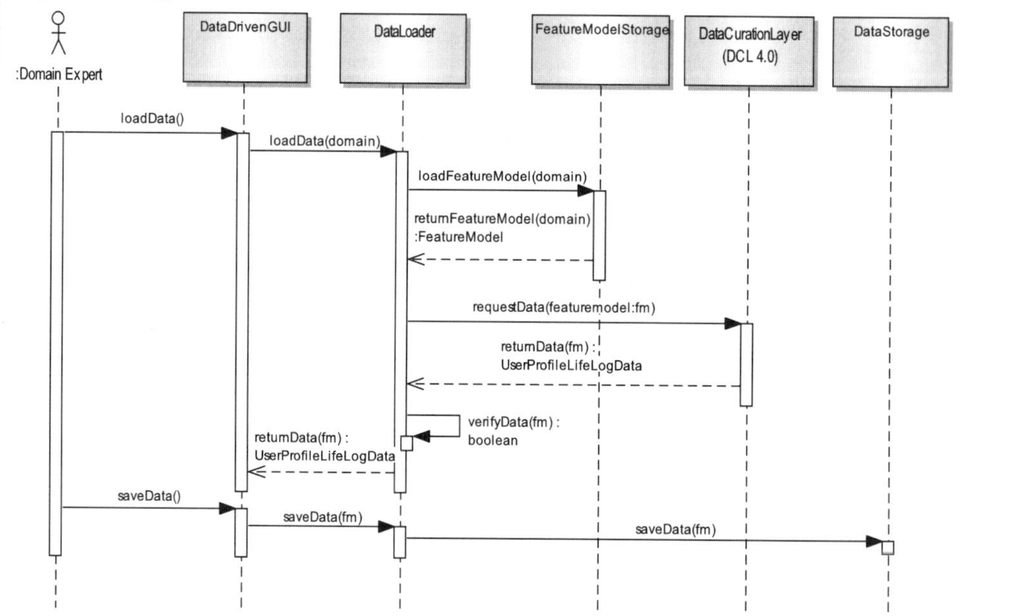

Use Case ID:	**KCL-UC-07**		
Use Case Name:	Extract meta-features of classification datasets		
Created By:	Rahman Ali	**Last Updated By:**	Maqbool Hussain
Date Created:	16-07-2015	**Last Revision Date:**	20-07-2015
Actors:	Knowledge Engineer/Domain Expert, UCI archive		
Description:	Datasets have simple, statistical, information theory and landmarking meta-features that can best describe nature of a dataset. These features can best used for building an algorithm selection model.		
Trigger:	In the offline process, when the algorithm selection model is build, and in the online process, when an appropriate algorithm is needed to be identified for a new query dataset		
Preconditions:	UCI archive datasets are available and are in refined format		

<table>
<tr><td>Postconditions:</td><td>The meta-features are ready for being used in building algorithm selection model.</td></tr>
<tr><td>Normal Flow:</td><td>1. Knowledge Engineer selects one dataset from UCI archive.
2. System retrieves selected dataset.
3. Knowledge Engineer provides dataset to meta-feature extractor for extracting meta-features.
4. System extracts following meta-features set for selected dataset.
a. basic meta-features
b. statistical meta-features
c. information theory meta-features
d. extract landmark features
5. Knowledge Engineer reviews the extracted meta-features and saves it into meta-features base (MFB).
6. System saves meta-features into a MFB.
7. Knowledge Engineer repeats step 1-6 for each intended dataset.</td></tr>
<tr><td>Alternative Flows:</td><td>1a. Meta-feature extraction for online dataset
a. Domain Expert provides new dataset used for classification model creation.
b. Step 3-4 of Normal Flow is executed for Domain expert interactions with system.</td></tr>
<tr><td>Exceptions:</td><td>N/A</td></tr>
<tr><td>Includes:</td><td>N/A</td></tr>
<tr><td>Frequency of Use:</td><td>Frequently, whenever a new dataset arrives as a query dataset.</td></tr>
<tr><td>Special Requirements:</td><td>Minimum availability of classification datasets > 60 for a reasonable accuracy</td></tr>
<tr><td>Assumptions:</td><td>• The archived datasets are available and are in refined .raff format
• The meta-feature space is defined in advance</td></tr>
<tr><td>Notes and Issues:</td><td>Meta-feature extraction is time consuming task for offline process as we have to take into account more than 60 datasets.</td></tr>
<tr><td colspan="2">Sequence Diagram:</td></tr>
</table>

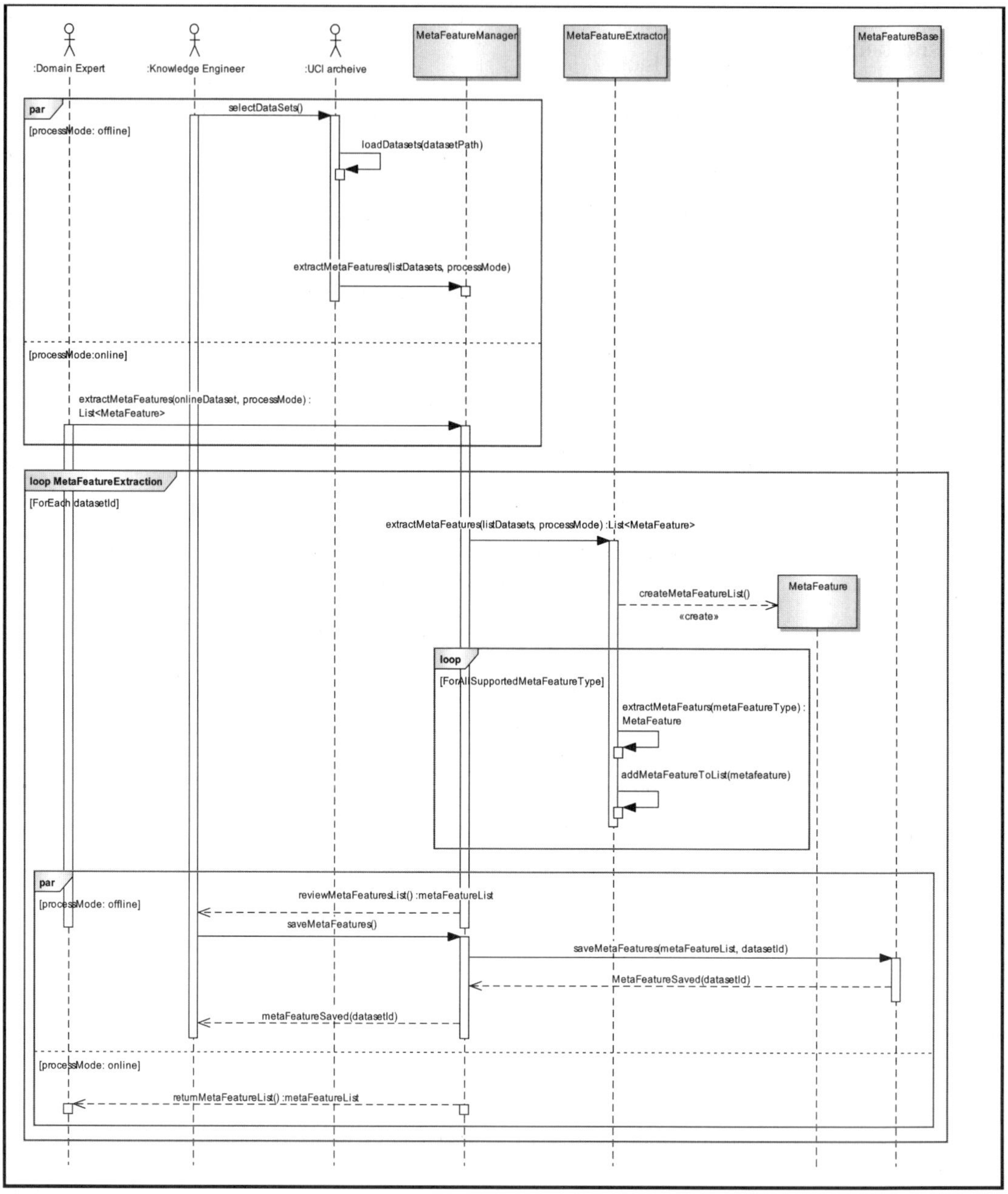

Use Case ID:	**KCL-UC-08**		
Use Case Name:	Evaluate performance of decision tree algorithm		
Created By:	Rahman Ali	**Last Updated By:**	Maqbool Hussain
Date Created:	16-07-2015	**Last Revision Date:**	20-07-2015

Actors:	Knowledge Engineer, UCI archive
Description:	Different algorithms have different performance score for the same dataset. To build an algorithm selection model, performance score of each algorithm needs to evaluate for choosing an appropriate one.
Trigger:	In the offline process, when the algorithm selection model is to build the first time.
Preconditions:	• UCI archive datasets are available and are in .arff format • The algorithm to be considered is specified in advanced (Decision Tree algorithms implemented in Weka) • The evaluation metric is specified (F-measure)
Postconditions:	All datasets records in Meta-Feature Base (MFB) will be assigned with optimal decision tree algorithm class label.
Normal Flow:	1. Knowledge Engineer selects UCI archive dataset, mentioned in MFB, for finding optimal decision tree algorithm. 2. System (Weka) loads selected datasets. 3. Knowledge Engineer setups experiment; a. Enlists all the decision tree algorithms available in system (Weka) b. Configure significance test (alpha=0.5) c. Configure algorithms comparison metric (f-measure) 4. System runs experiment and produces detailed f-score for all selected algorithms. 5. Knowledge Engineer performs following tasks; a. Records evaluation matrix. b. Chooses algorithm with the highest f-score. c. Assigns chosen algorithm as class label in MFB. d. Step 1-5 are repeated for other non-labeled datasets in MFB. e. After finishing labeling all records in MFB, saves the updated MFB as training dataset for algorithm selection (TDAS). 6. System saves the updated records in MFB as final TDAS.
Alternative Flows:	N/A

Exceptions:	N/A
Includes:	N/A
Frequency of Use:	• Rarely, once enough new datasets are added to the system
Special Requirements:	N/A
Assumptions:	• The decision tree-based algorithms are implemented in Weka.
Notes and Issues:	Evaluating performance of decision tree algorithms over a large number (min 60) classification dataset is a computationally complex task. For minimum 60 datasets and at least 5 decision tree algorithms, a minimum of 300 experiments are required. Moreover, 60 additional significance test experiments are needed. On average, each experiment takes times in minutes ranging from 2 minutes to 30 minutes, depending on the complexity of the dataset.

Sequence Diagram:

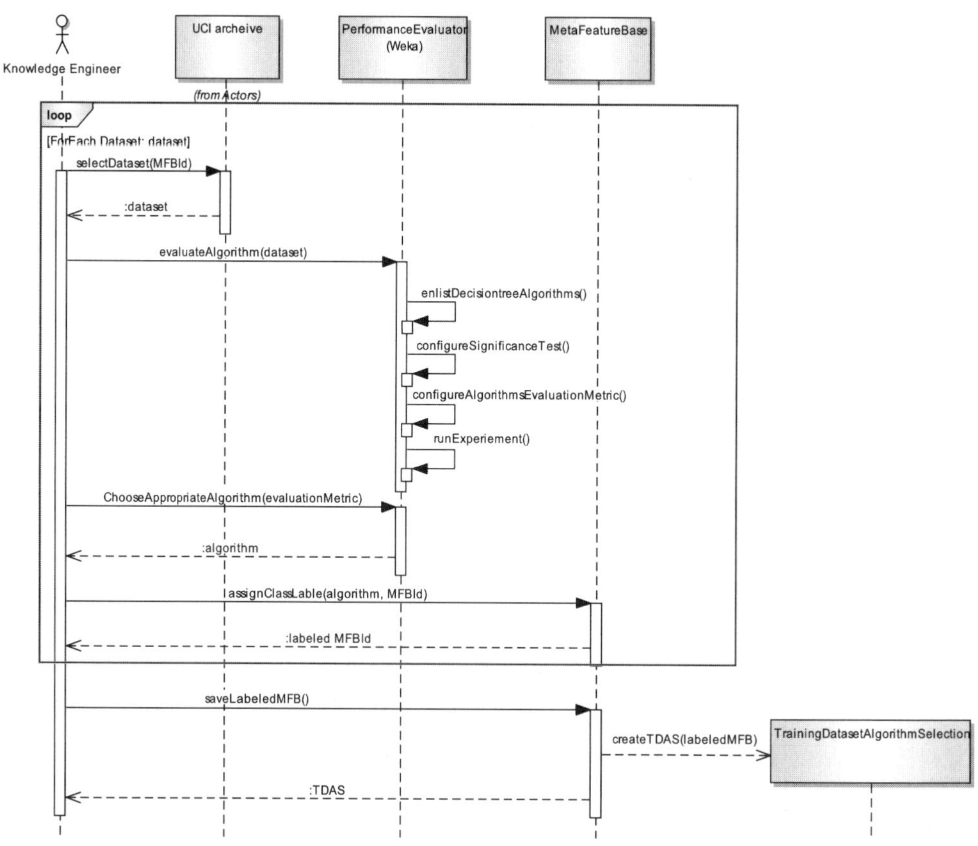

<table>
<tr><td>Use Case ID:</td><td colspan="3">KCL-UC-09</td></tr>
<tr><td>Use Case Name:</td><td colspan="3">Create automatic algorithm recommendation model</td></tr>
<tr><td>Created By:</td><td>Rahman Ali</td><td>Last Updated By:</td><td>Maqbool Hussain</td></tr>
<tr><td>Date Created:</td><td>10-07-2015</td><td>Last Revision Date:</td><td>22-07-2015</td></tr>
<tr><td>Actors:</td><td colspan="3">Knowledge Engineer/Domain Expert</td></tr>
<tr><td>Description:</td><td colspan="3">An automatic algorithm selection model enables knowledge engineer to automatically select appropriate algorithm for building classification model for his new dataset</td></tr>
<tr><td>Trigger:</td><td colspan="3">When the training dataset comprising datasets meta-features and algorithms performance evaluation are made available.</td></tr>
<tr><td>Preconditions:</td><td colspan="3">The datasets meta-features and algorithms performance training datasets is made available.</td></tr>
<tr><td>Postconditions:</td><td colspan="3">The automatic algorithm recommendation model (AARM) is ready to integrate in Mining Minds for real time algorithm selection.</td></tr>
<tr><td>Normal Flow:</td><td colspan="3">1. Knowledge Engineer selects TDAS.
2. System (Weka) loads TDAS.
3. Knowledge Engineer performs preprocessing of the TDAS (i.e., discretization, and features selection).
4. System refines the datasets with appropriate features.
5. Knowledge Engineer select an algorithm from decision tree (DT) or Rules learner (RL) for building AARM.
6. System executes selected algorithm on TDAS and produces evaluation matrix.
7. Knowledge Engineer records performs following tasks;
a. Records evaluation matrix and repeats step 5-6 till all algorithms finished.
b. Knowledge Engineer selects the appropriate algorithm.
8. System builds AARM model using the selected algorithm.
9. Knowledge Engineer saves AARM.
10. System saves the AARM into AARM storage.</td></tr>
<tr><td>Alternative Flows:</td><td colspan="3">N/A</td></tr>
</table>

Exceptions:	N/A
Includes:	N/A
Frequency of Use:	Rarely, when TDAS is updated with new datasets or algorithms
Special Requirements:	Availability of records > 60 for minimum acceptable accuracy
Assumptions:	N/A
Notes and Issues:	N/A

Sequence Diagram:

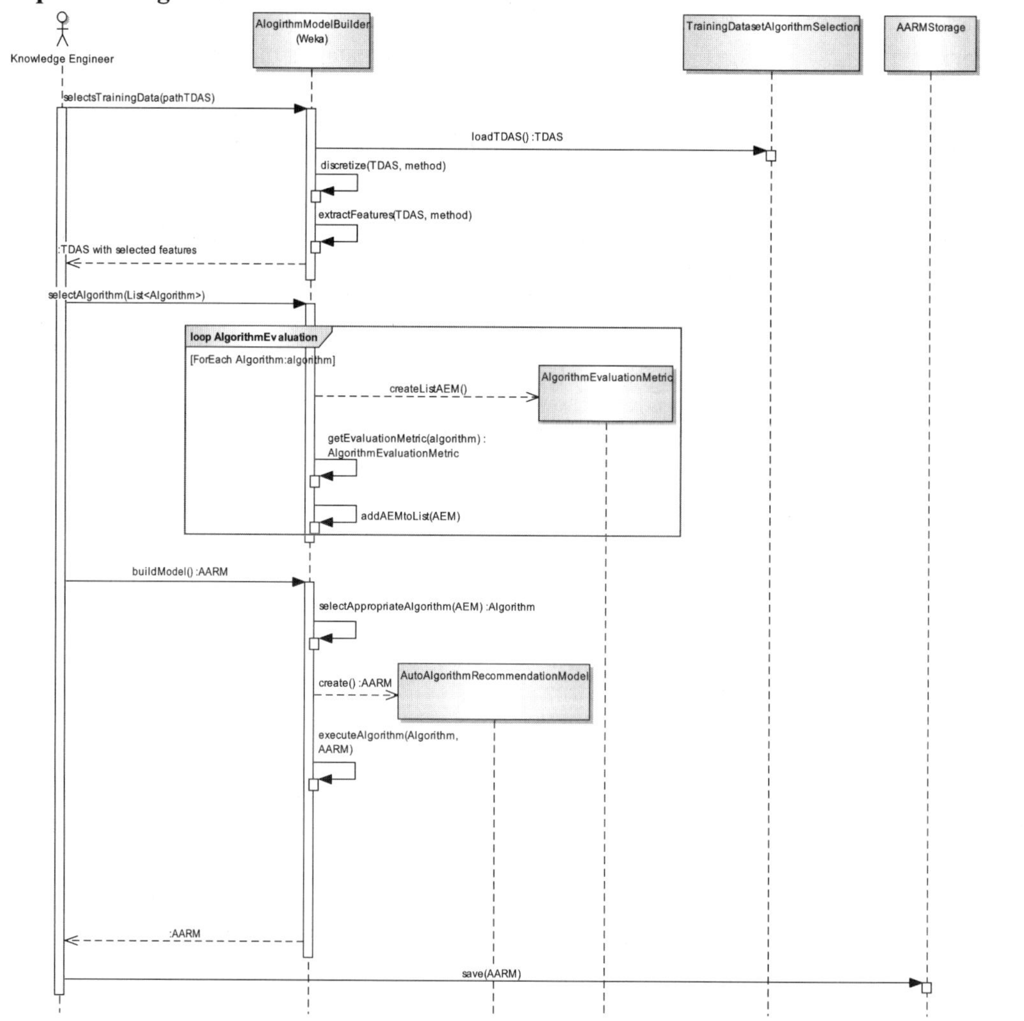

<table>
<tr><td>Use Case ID:</td><td colspan="3">KCL-UC-10</td></tr>
<tr><td>Use Case Name:</td><td colspan="3">Create Rule</td></tr>
<tr><td>Created By:</td><td>Taqdir Ali</td><td>Last Updated By:</td><td>Maqbool Hussain</td></tr>
<tr><td>Date Created:</td><td>11-07-2015</td><td>Last Revision Date:</td><td>29-07-2015</td></tr>
<tr><td>Actors:</td><td colspan="3">Domain Expert</td></tr>
<tr><td>Description:</td><td colspan="3">Knowledge bases need to enhance with up-to-date knowledge for correct recommendation. The expert shall create rules in the knowledge base to transform their practices into executable knowledge in form of rules.</td></tr>
<tr><td>Trigger:</td><td colspan="3">Domain experts trigger it for rule creation/updating when needed.</td></tr>
<tr><td>Preconditions:</td><td colspan="3">• The domain expert shall be authenticated with full access of rule management in the knowledge base.</td></tr>
<tr><td>Postconditions:</td><td colspan="3">The correct rule shall be saved into the knowledge base.</td></tr>
<tr><td>Normal Flow:</td><td colspan="3">1. Domain expert opens the rule editor.
2. System loads wellness domain model in form of concepts tree.
3. Domain expert selects concepts for the rule conditions and conclusion using any of the following methods;
o Using wellness model, dragging concepts and facts into conditional or conclusion part of the rule editor.
o Using auto pop-up Intelli-sense window to select concepts and facts into conditional or conclusion part of the rule editor.
4. System checks the existing rules to add/update the rule
o Add new facts of the rule in condition.
o Add new conclusion according to rule facts.
5. Step 3-4 will be repeated for each new/updated concept added to rule, and domain expert finally saves the rule.
6. System save rule as follows;
o The system validates the rule using “KCL-UC-11”.
o The system stores the validated rule into the knowledge base</td></tr>
</table>

Alternative Flows:	6a. System founds the rule is already exists in rule repository o Domain expert review the existing facts and conclusion. o Step 5-6 will be followed to change the rule.
Exceptions:	N/A
Includes:	Validate Rule
Frequency of Use:	Whenever domain expert wants to add rule or edit the existing rule.
Special Requirements:	N/A
Assumptions:	N/A
Notes and Issues:	• If knowledge base does not exist in system, the administrator shall build the knowledge base first and configure with system. • After investigation, we may use unify representation for rules and guidelines.
Sequence Diagram:	

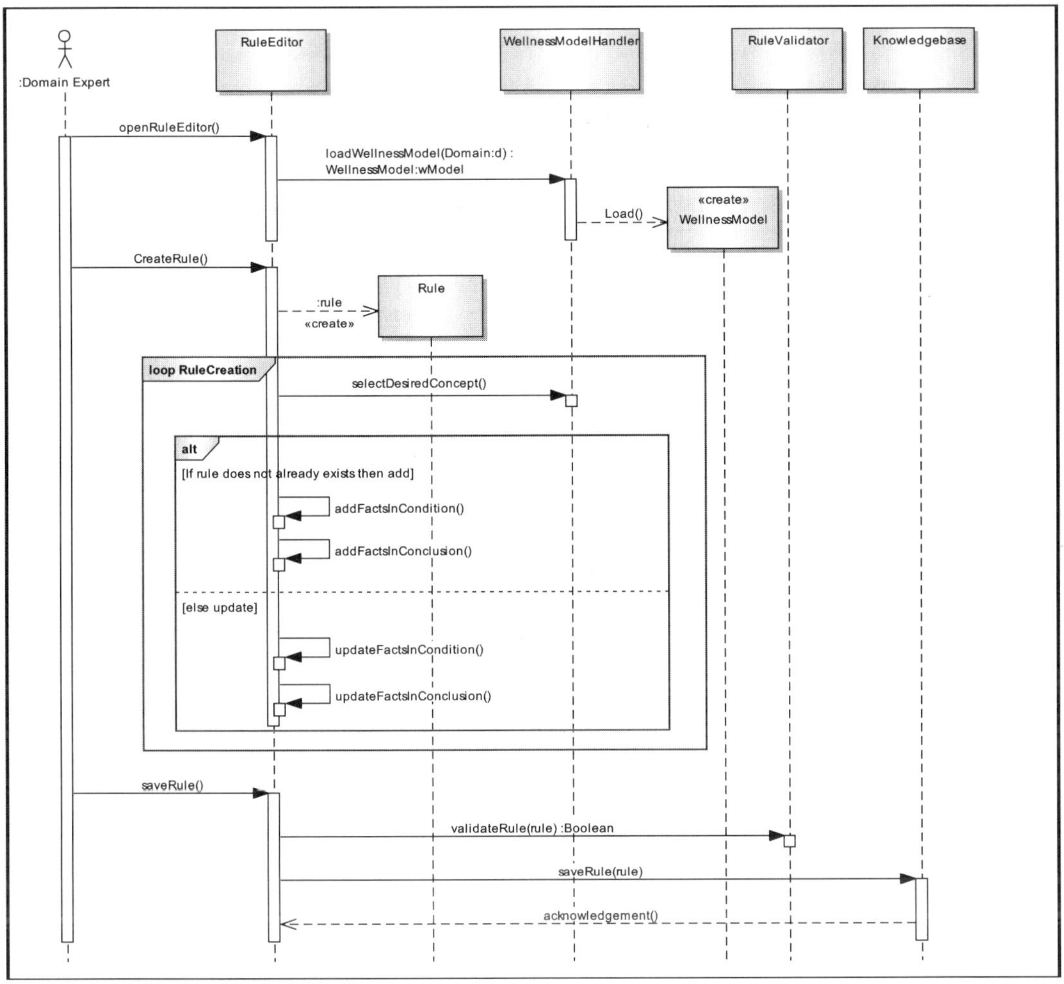

Use Case ID:	**KCL-UC-11**		
Use Case Name:	Validate Rule		
Created By:	Taqdir Ali	**Last Updated By:**	Maqbool Hussain
Date Created:	11-07-2015	**Last Revision Date:**	29-07-2015
Actors:	Domain Expert		
Description:	In new rules creation and editing existing rules, duplication and inconsistency may occur. The validation is needed to validate and find the duplication and inconsistency among the rules.		
Trigger:	• When new rule is going to create.		

	• When existing rule is going to update
Preconditions:	The rule creation and editing process completed by physician successfully.
Postconditions:	The validated rule shall be saved into knowledge base.
Normal Flow:	1. Domain expert saves the created rule. 2. System validate rule for inconsistency and duplication as follows a. Fetch the facts and conclusion of existing rules. b. The new or updated rule approved for having no inconsistency and duplication. c. Created rule stores into the rules repository. d. Acknowledge the expert to save the rule successfully.
Alternative Flows:	2b. The created rule is found having inconsistency or duplication with existing rules in the rules repository a. The system produces alert the inconsistency or duplication of the rule with existing rules in repository. b. Domain expert review the alert message and correct the created rule. c. Step 1 and Step 2 of normal flow is executed.
Exceptions:	N/A
Includes:	N/A
Frequency of Use:	Whenever domain expert want to save the rule
Special Requirements:	N/A
Assumptions:	N/A
Notes and Issues:	Finding duplication using facts of condition and conclusion in existing rules is challenging task.
Sequence Diagram:	

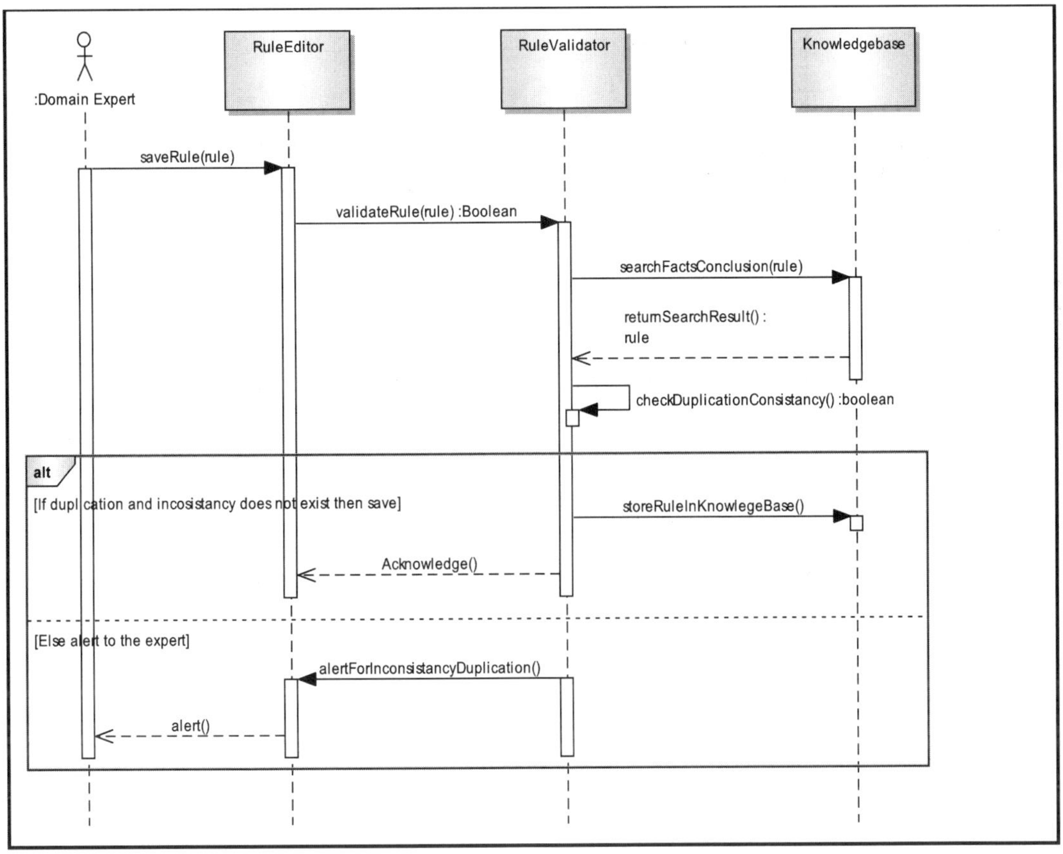

Use Case ID:	KCL-UC-12		
Use Case Name:	Integrate automatic algorithm recommendation model		
Created By:	Rahman Ali	Last Updated By:	Maqbool Hussain
Date Created:	10-07-2015	Last Revision Date:	28-07-2015
Actors:	Knowledge Engineer		
Description:	For real time recommendation of classification algorithm for a new dataset, AARM need to be integrated in Mining Minds Data Driven knowledge acquisition approach.		
Trigger:	When AARM is built.		
Preconditions:	• AARM is available • Data driven approach has a unified interface to support AARM as plugin		

	• Data driven has unified interface for accessing Meta-Feature Extractor.
Postconditions:	AARM is plugged into data driven environment and readily available for real time recommendation of appropriate classification algorithm.
Normal Flow:	1. Knowledge engineer selects AARM and performs the following tasks; • Analyses number of rules in the AARM • Analyses condition attributes used in each rule of AARM • Transforms rules into executable classes (using any IDE of Java). 2. Knowledge engineer integrates the executable AARM into data driven as follows; a. Write integration code (following unified interface) into data driven source code b. Update possible configuration for newly added AARM plugin. c. Update possible configuration for accessing Meta-Feature Extractor. 3. Knowledge Engineer compile the AARM as integral part with data driven code. 4. Knowledge engineer tests AARM with sample dataset.
Alternative Flows:	N/A
Exceptions:	N/A
Includes:	N/A
Frequency of Use:	Rarely, once the AARM is updated
Special Requirements:	AARM has acceptable accuracy (60%)
Assumptions:	AARM is created
Notes and Issues:	N/A
Sequence Diagram:	

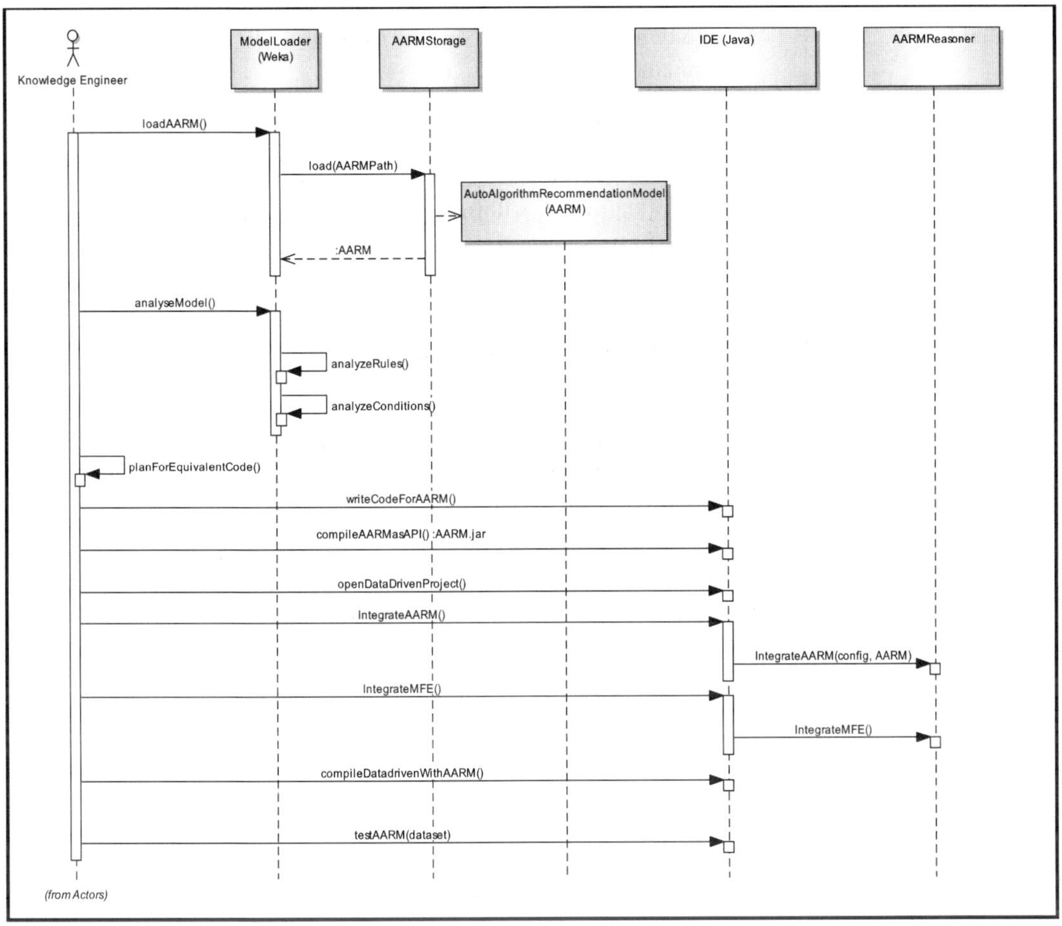

Use Case ID:	**KCL-UC-13**		
Use Case Name:	Learn classification model		
Created By:	Maqbool Ali	**Last Updated By:**	Maqbool Ali
Date Created:	10-07-2015	**Last Revision Date:**	03-07-2018
Actors:	Domain Expert		
Description:	An expert wants to see hidden knowledge from user profile lifelog data that can be explored by model learning mechanism with the help of learning method as well as processed data.		
Trigger:	Learn model required to explore hidden knowledge		
Preconditions:	• System has loaded the prepared user profile lifelog data		
Postconditions:	System will build the classification model (decision tree)		

Normal Flow:	1. Domain expert loads the user profile lifelog processed data for selected domain 2. System loads the corresponding processed data 3. Domain expert invokes the "Recommend appropriate classification algorithm" use case by providing processed data to load the appropriate learning algorithm 4. System loads the appropriate decision tree learning algorithm 5. Domain expert select the algorithm tuning parameters of selected algorithm for further improving the results 6. System applies the tuning parameters on selected algorithm and computes the learning accuracy after learning the user profile lifelog processed data 7. Repeat the step 5-6 until required learning accuracy is achieved. 8. Domain expert finalizes the classification model with acceptable accuracy and saves the model. 9. System saves the decision tree learning model.
Alternative Flows:	N/A
Exceptions:	N/A
Includes:	KCL-UC-14 (Recommend appropriate classification algorithm)
Frequency of Use:	When new service is required, and mining mind have sufficient data for classification model creation
Special Requirements:	N/A
Assumptions:	N/A
Notes and Issues:	Acceptable Accuracy: Depends on criticality of the domain. For example, classification model for clinical domain needs high accuracy, while for the case of nutrition domain, high accuracy is not critical.
Sequence Diagram:	

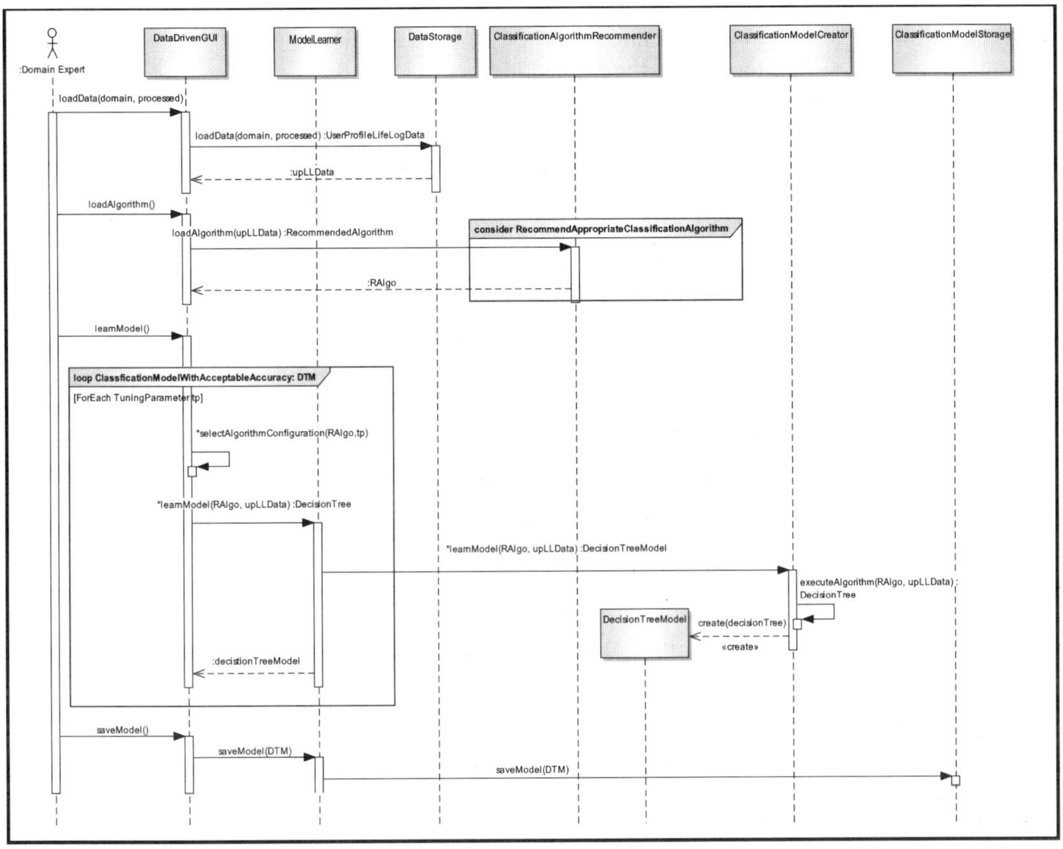

Use Case ID:	KCL-UC-14		
Use Case Name:	Recommend appropriate classification algorithm		
Created By:	Rahman Ali	Last Updated By:	Rahman Ali
Date Created:	16-07-2015	Last Revision Date:	27-07-2015
Actors:	Domain expert		
Description:	For building classification model for the user new dataset, AARM shall automatically recommend appropriate classification algorithm.		
Trigger:	When domain expert wants to build a classification model.		
Preconditions:	• AARM is plugged into the data driven environment • Meta-features extractor is plugged into the data driven environment • New dataset is stored in local machine, structured in .arff file format		

Postconditions:	The recommended appropriate classification algorithm can be used for building classification model
Normal Flow:	1. Domain expert loads new dataset (.arff file) from the data driven datasets storage using data driven environment. 2. System extracts meta-features of the new dataset by including KCL-UC-07 (alternate flow) 3. Domain experts provides meta-features to system for recommending appropriate classification algorithm 4. System performs meta-reasoning over integrated AARM using the following steps; a. Starts matching each meta-feature value of the new dataset with condition attributes of each rule b. If matched, fires the rule, recommend right hand side of the rule as the appropriate algorithm c. Else, display a message "could not recommend"
Alternative Flows:	1a. 4c(a) If AARM not available or have no acceptable recommendation accuracy, use Weka experimenter.
Exceptions:	N/A
Includes:	KCL-UC-07 (alternate flow)
Frequency of Use:	Frequently, when domain expert needs to select appropriate algorithm for his/her dataset
Special Requirements:	N/A
Assumptions:	N/A
Notes and Issues:	N/A
Sequence Diagram:	

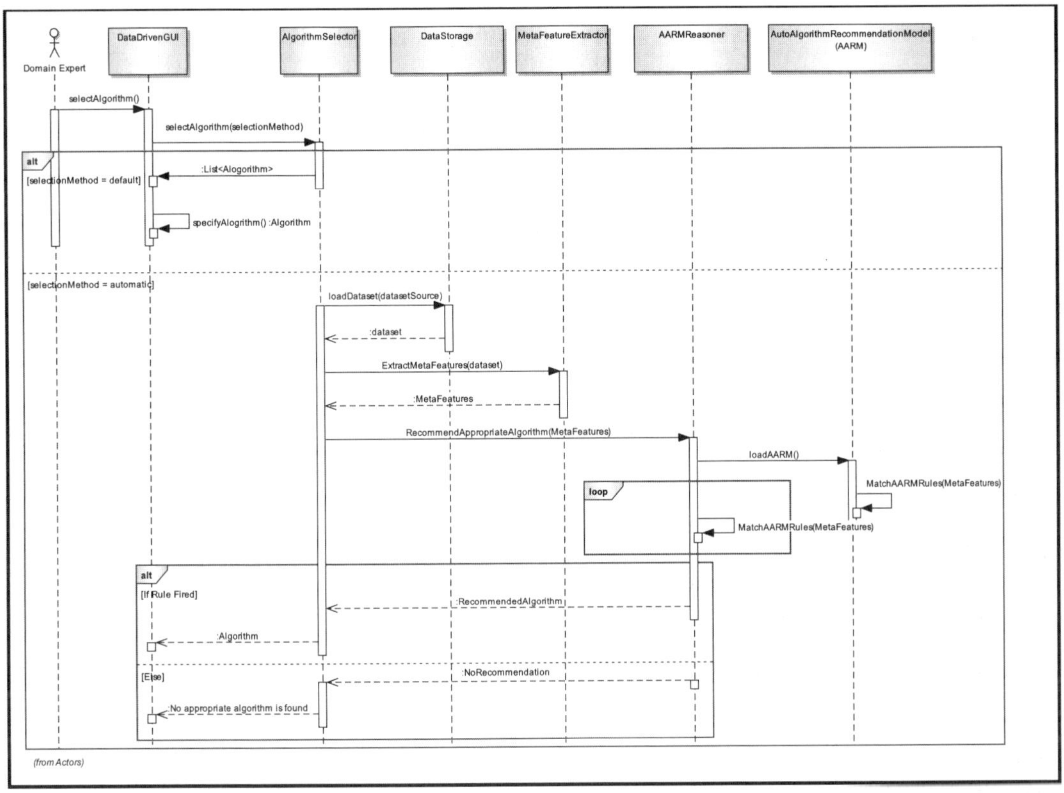

Use Case ID:	**KCL-UC-15**		
Use Case Name:	Manage concepts of domain model		
Created By:	Taqdir Ali	**Last Updated By:**	Taqdir Ali, Maqbool Hussain
Date Created:	27-07-2015	**Last Revision Date:**	27-07-2015
Actors:	Domain Expert		
Description:	The concepts of wellness domain shall be used in creation of rules and generation of guidelines in tree format. The domain expert shall easily select the required concepts from wellness domain model.		
Trigger:	Domain Model will be loaded during rule creation or guideline creation.		
Preconditions:	The expert be authenticated with full access of concepts management in domain model		
Postconditions:	The right concept shall be added or edited at the right location in wellness model		

Normal Flow:	1. Domain expert creates rule (using KCL-UC-10) or creates guideline (using KCL-UC-03). 2. System loads domain model for corresponding domain. 3. Domain expert selects concepts from loaded domain model. 4. System associate domain concept to part of rule or guideline tree. 5. Domain expert assigns value to selected concept. 6. System assigns corresponding value to selected concept and show it in rule or guideline tree. 7. Step 4-6 are repeated till rule or guideline is finished.
Alternative Flows:	N/A
Exceptions:	N/A
Includes:	N/A
Frequency of Use:	Whenever domain expert wants to add or edit the concepts in wellness model
Special Requirements:	N/A
Assumptions:	Wellness model repository in the system is exist.
Notes and Issues:	If wellness model storage does not exist in system, the administrator shall build the wellness model storage first and configure with system.
Sequence Diagram:	

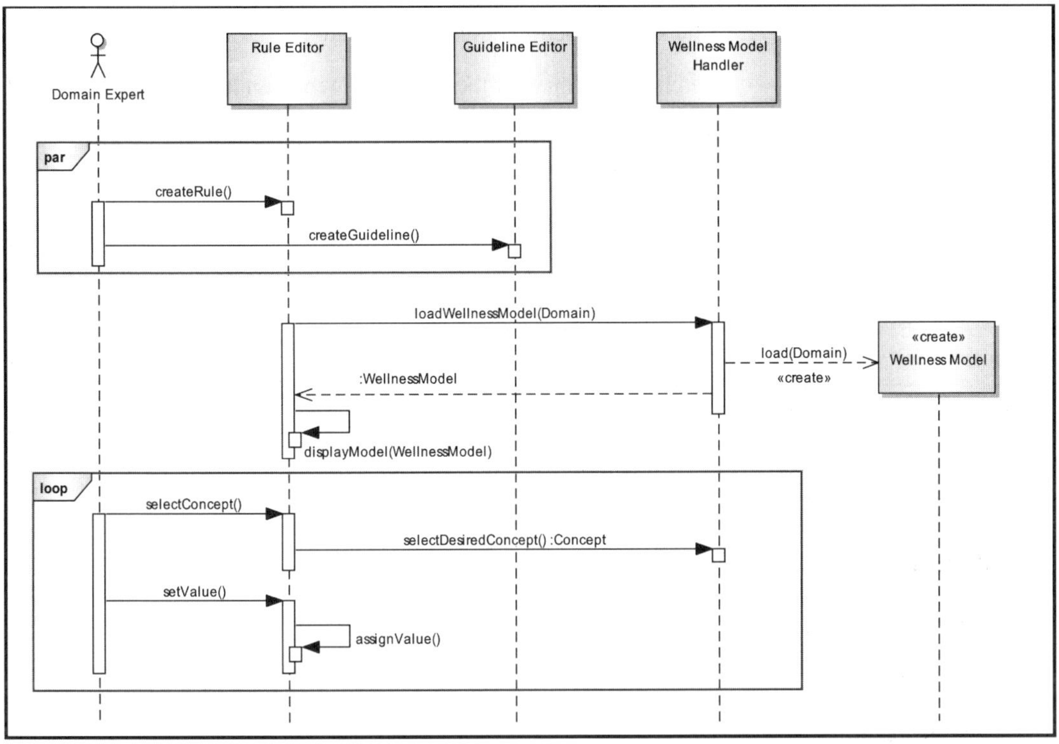

Use Case ID:	**KCL-UC-16**		
Use Case Name:	Transform Knowledge Rule		
Created By:	Taqdir Ali and Maqbool Hussain	**Last Updated By:**	Maqbool Hussain
Date Created:	27-07-2015	**Last Revision Date:**	27-07-2015
Actors:	Domain Expert		
Description:	The new created rules are needed to transform to some computer interpretable, executable format for execution as well as to shareable, standard format for maintenance and sharing with other organizations.		
Trigger:	Whenever domain expert wants to store the created or updated rule.		
Preconditions:	The expert created rule successfully and the system validated the rule.		
Postconditions:	System shall transform the created and validated rule into appropriate representation.		
Normal Flow:	1. Domain expert save the new created rule or update the existing rule.		

	2. The system identifies the appropriate representation model 3. Fetch the artifacts of the identified representation model 4. Transforms the rule into the artifacts and syntax of the identified representation model. 5. The rule in the representation model is stored into the repository.
Alternative Flows:	N/A
Exceptions:	N/A
Includes:	N/A
Frequency of Use:	Whenever domain expert wants to save rule
Special Requirements:	N/A
Assumptions:	N/A
Notes and Issues:	Appropriate representation configuration is challenging task.

Sequence Diagram:

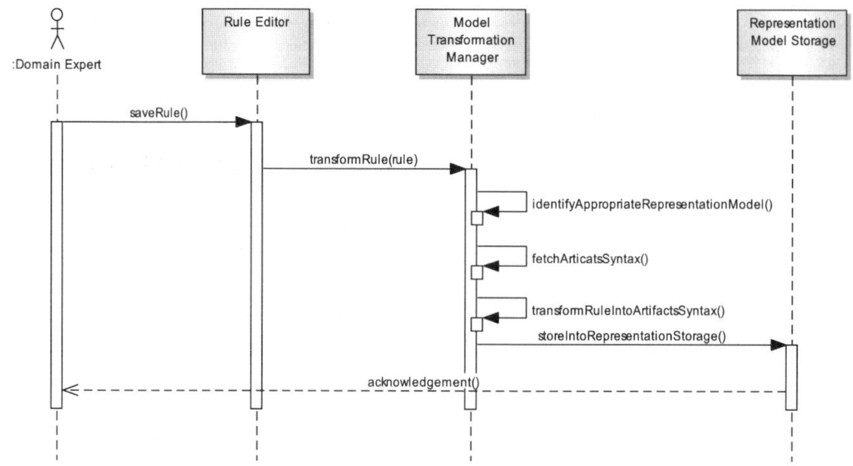

Use Case ID:	**KCL-UC-17**		
Use Case Name:	Create Situation Event		
Created By:	Maqbool Hussain	**Last Updated By:**	Maqbool Hussain
Date Created:	29-07-2015	**Last Revision Date:**	29-07-2015

Actors:	Domain Expert
Description:	Situation Event is important features of mining mind which includes set of associated recommendation rules. Situation event is created, and the rule is indexed in knowledgebase based on situation event.
Trigger:	Whenever domain expert wants to store the created or updated rule.
Preconditions:	The rule has salient features based on which the rule can be indexed.
Postconditions:	• Rule is saved into knowledgebase • Rule is indexed based on the created situation event
Normal Flow:	1. Domain expert start creating rule; a. Performs steps 1-5 in KCL-UC-10. b. Selects salient features (indicating as event) from conditions of the rule. 2. The system performs following actions; a. Create situation event with salient features. b. Saves the situation event and assign index (generate if situation event is not existing in knowledgebase index). c. Index the created rule with situation event. 3. Domain expert saves the rule by performing steps 5-6 in KCL-UC-10. 4. System saves the rule and index of the rule.
Alternative Flows:	N/A
Exceptions:	N/A
Extends:	Create Rule (KCL-UC-10)
Frequency of Use:	Whenever domain expert wants to save rule
Special Requirements:	N/A
Assumptions:	N/A
Notes and Issues:	
Sequence Diagram:	

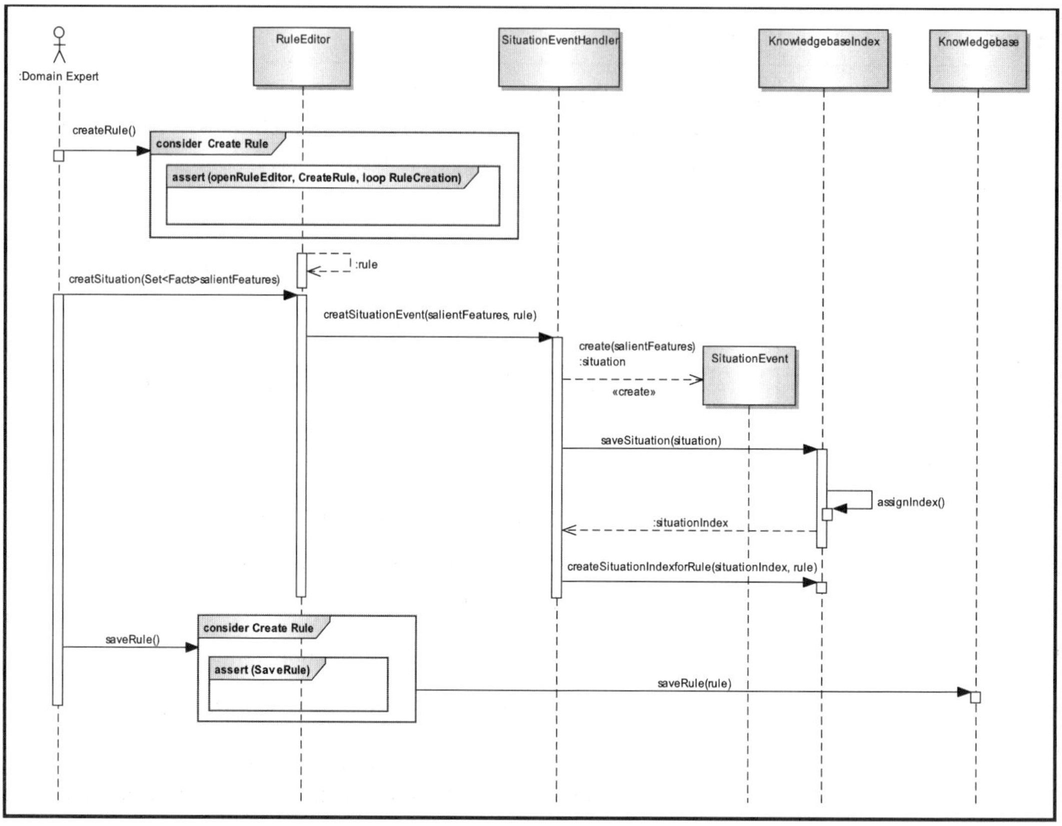

Use Case ID:	KCL-UC-18		
Use Case Name:	Compute features priorities		
Created By:	Maqbool Ali	**Last Updated By:**	Maqbool Ali
Date Created:	01-07-2018	**Last Revision Date:**	03-07-2018
Actors:	Domain Expert, DCL		
Description:	Features priorities computation help domain expert for selecting appropriate features from available schema		
Trigger:	Prior to data preprocessing needed for required data		
Preconditions:	• KCL has access through service interface to retrieve user profile lifelog data from DCL • KCL and DCL has agreement on common data representation format		
Postconditions:	KCL will display the features priorities list		

Normal Flow:	1. KCL connects to DCL via unified service interface and sends request for user profile lifelog data based on selected features of schema and features conditions. 2. DCL sends the required data to KCL. 3. KCL receives user profile lifelog data 4. KCL computes the features priorities 5. KCL displays the features priorities list
Alternative Flows:	N/A
Exceptions:	2a. KCL unable to connect to DCL a. KCL connection is failed during retrieving user profile lifelog data b. KCL hold and will retry after some time to connect to DCL and retrieve the user profile lifelog data 3a. KCL unable to verify lifelog data conformance a. KCL fail to conform the data representation from DCL b. KCL will send message to DCL about incompatible data format
Includes:	N/A
Frequency of Use:	When new service is required, and mining mind have sufficient data for classification model creation
Special Requirements:	N/A
Assumptions:	N/A
Notes and Issues:	If DCL is unable to send data, then alternate strategy has to be considered.

Sequence Diagram:

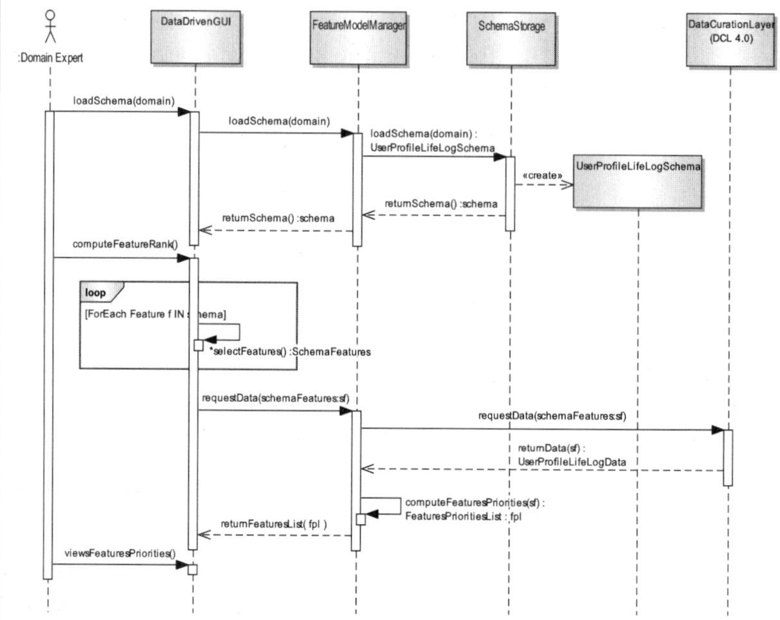

Use Case ID:	**KCL-UC-19**		
Use Case Name:	Validate Rule		
Created By:	Taqdir Ali	**Last Updated By:**	Taqdir Ali
Date Created:	04-03-2017	**Last Revision Date:**	05-03-2017
Actors:	Domain Expert		
Description:	In new rules creation and editing existing rules, duplication and inconsistency may occur. The validation is needed to validate and find the duplication and inconsistency among the rules.		
Trigger:	• When new rule is going to create. • When existing rule is going to update		
Preconditions:	The rule creation and editing process completed by physician successfully.		
Postconditions:	The validated rule shall be saved into knowledge base.		
Normal Flow:	3. Domain expert saves the created rule. 4. System validate rule for inconsistency and duplication as follows		

	a. Fetch the facts and conclusion of existing rules. b. The new or updated rule approved for having no inconsistency and duplication. c. Created rule stores into the rules repository. d. Acknowledge the expert to save the rule successfully.
Alternative Flows:	3b. The created rule is found having inconsistency or duplication with existing rules in the rules repository a. The system produces alert the inconsistency or duplication of the rule with existing rules in repository. b. Domain expert review the alert message and correct the created rule. c. Step 1 and Step 2 of normal flow is executed.
Exceptions:	N/A
Includes:	1. Extract conditions 2. Test cases generation
Frequency of Use:	Whenever domain expert wants to save the rule
Special Requirements:	N/A
Assumptions:	N/A
Notes and Issues:	Finding duplication using facts of condition and conclusion in existing rules is challenging task.
Sequence Diagram:	

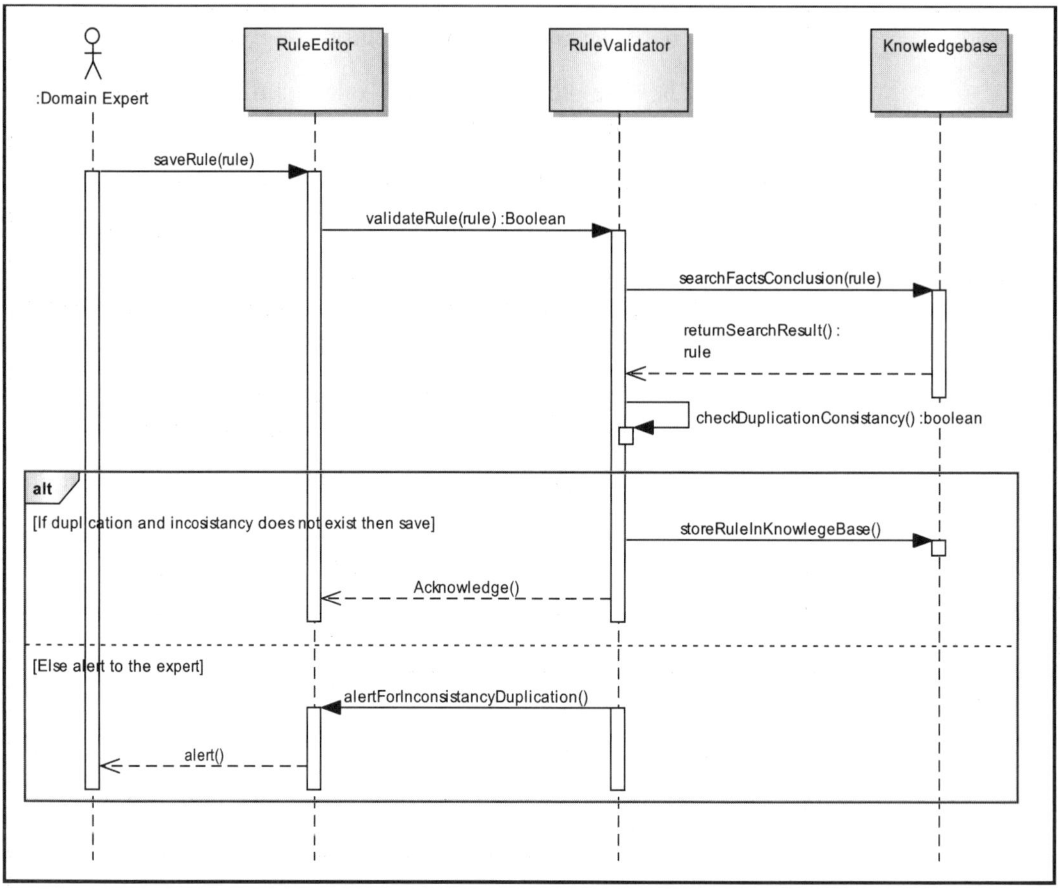

Use Case ID:	KCL-UC-20		
Use Case Name:	Extract conditions		
Created By:	Taqdir Ali	**Last Updated By:**	Taqdir Ali
Date Created:	04-03-2017	**Last Revision Date:**	05-03-2017
Actors:	Domain Expert		
Description:	Whenever the rule is validated, the test cases are generated, the test cases depends on conditions of the rule. Therefore, all the facts and conditions are needed to extract from rules.		
Trigger:	• When new rule is going to validate. • When existing rule is going to validate.		
Preconditions:	The rule creation and editing process completed by physician successfully.		

Postconditions:	Multiple pairs of facts and conditions are extracted.
Normal Flow:	1. System fetch the rule, which is being to be added or updated 2. System shall identify the logical operators in the rule. 3. System splits the rule based on the identified logical operators 4. In splat conditions, find the type of keys and their values. a. If type is discrete then execute non-interval test case generation.
Alternative Flows:	4b. If type is interval, then a. Execute interval case generator
Exceptions:	N/A
Includes:	N/A
Frequency of Use:	Whenever domain expert wants to validate the rule
Special Requirements:	N/A
Assumptions:	N/A
Notes and Issues:	Finding duplication using facts of condition and conclusion in existing rules is challenging task.

Sequence Diagram:

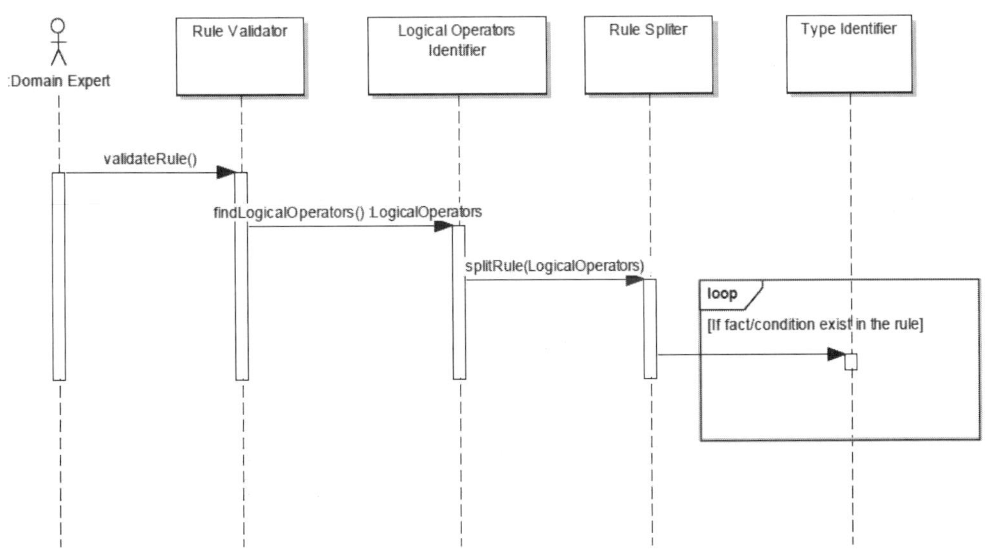

Use Case ID:	KCL-UC-21		
Use Case Name:	Test cases generation		
Created By:	Taqdir Ali	Last Updated By:	Taqdir Ali
Date Created:	04-03-2017	Last Revision Date:	05-03-2017
Actors:	Domain Expert		
Description:	Whenever the rule is validated, the test cases are generated, the new created rule or existing modified rule is checking for duplications and conflict using the generated test cases.		
Trigger:	• When new rule is going to validate. • When existing rule is going to validate.		
Preconditions:	The rule conditions and facts are identified and extracted successfully.		
Postconditions:	Multiple test cases shall generate after successful process.		
Normal Flow:	1. If type of extracted condition or fact is discrete a. System shall fetch the possible values from wellness model b. Generate matched test cases with respect to the extracted condition. c. Generate unmatched conditions with respect to the extracted condition. d. Store the generated test cases with corresponding conditions in test case base.		
Alternative Flows:	1. (b) If type of extracted condition or fact is interval a. System finds the type of interval b. If interval is single side infinite interval or exact value interval, then generate following 3 test cases. i. Generate case for X-1 ii. Generate case for X iii. Generate Case for X+1 c. If interval is double sided finite interval, then generate		

	following 6 test cases. i. Generate case for X-1 ii. Generate case for X iii. Generate Case for X+1 iv. Generate case for Y-1 v. Generate case for Y vi. Generate Case for Y+1
Exceptions:	N/A
Includes:	N/A
Frequency of Use:	Whenever domain expert wants to validate the rule
Special Requirements:	N/A
Assumptions:	N/A
Notes and Issues:	Finding duplication using facts of condition and conclusion in existing rules is challenging task.
Sequence Diagram:	

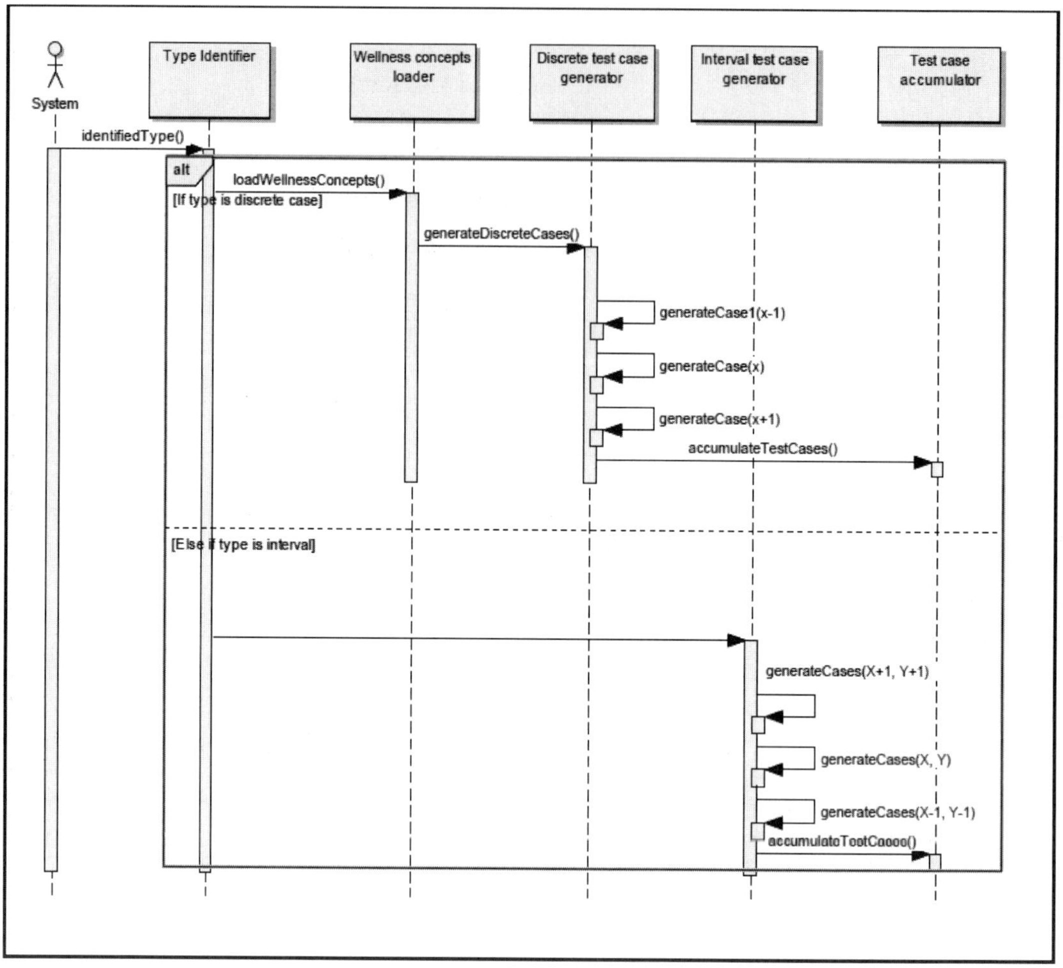

Use Case ID:	**KCL-UC-22**		
Use Case Name:	Evaluate rule		
Created By:	Taqdir Ali	**Last Updated By:**	Taqdir Ali
Date Created:	04-03-2017	**Last Revision Date:**	05-03-2017
Actors:	Domain Expert		
Description:	Whenever the rule is to be validated, the new created or existing modified rule is needed to test with respect to generated test cases, then evaluate the rule with those test cases		
Trigger:	• When new rule is going to validate. • When existing rule is going to validate.		

Preconditions:	The test cases are successfully generated and executed for rule which is going to evaluate.
Postconditions:	Find the duplicate and conflicted rules based on executed test cases.
Normal Flow:	1. Domain experts views all the auto generated test cases on viewer. 2. Domain expert selects the test cases to execute and test on the created rule 3. Domain experts executes the selected test cases 4. The system gives results of executed test cases based on the included use case "check and resolve anomalies".
Alternative Flows:	N/A
Exceptions:	N/A
Includes:	N/A
Frequency of Use:	Whenever domain expert want to validate the rule
Special Requirements:	N/A
Assumptions:	N/A
Notes and Issues:	Finding duplication using facts of condition and conclusion in existing rules is challenging task.
Sequence Diagram:	

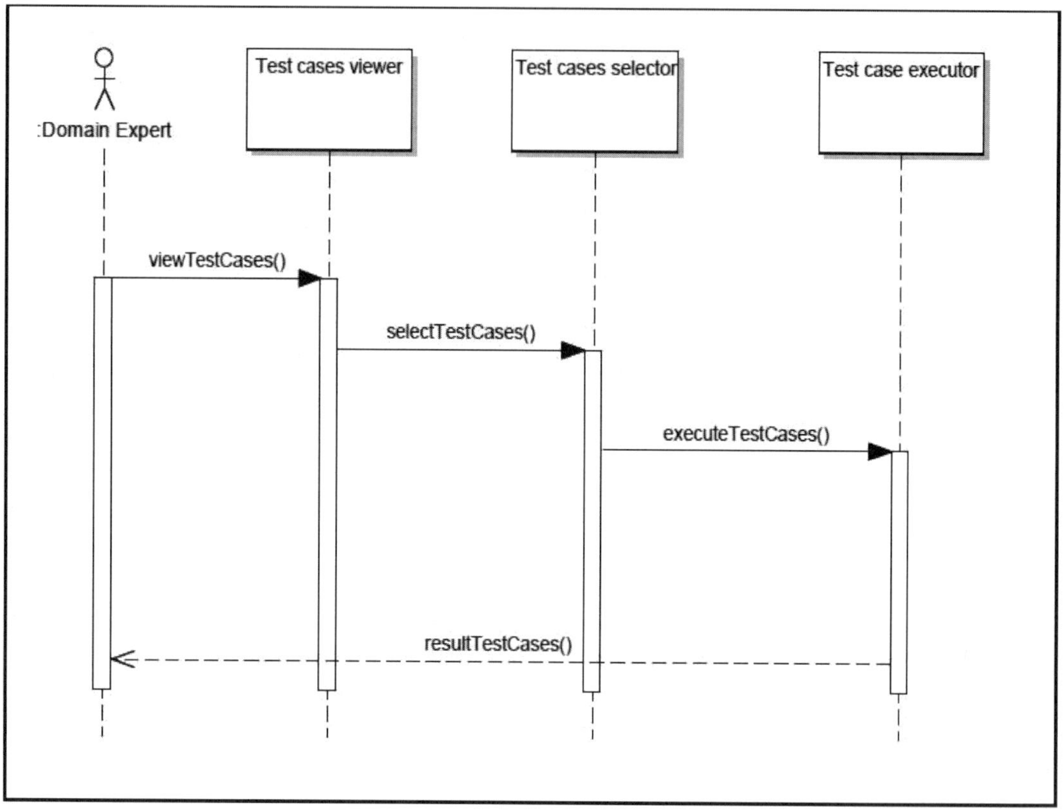

Use Case ID:	KCL-UC-23		
Use Case Name:	Check and resolve anomalies		
Created By:	Taqdir Ali	Last Updated By:	Taqdir Ali
Date Created:	04-03-2017	Last Revision Date:	05-03-2017
Actors:	Domain Expert		
Description:	Whenever the rule is to be validated, the executed test cases checks and identifies the anomalies in form of duplicate and conflict. The domain experts identified and resolve those anomalies.		
Trigger:	• When new rule is going to validate. • When existing rule is going to validate.		
Preconditions:	The test cases are successfully generated and executed for rule which is going to evaluate.		
Postconditions:	Find and resolve the duplicate and conflicted rules based on executed test cases.		

Normal Flow:	1. System shows the results of execution of test cases on the creation rule or modification rule. 2. Domain experts views the result messages on result viewer for finding duplication and conflict 3. If duplicate rules exist a. Discard the new created rule. 4. If conflict exists in the created rule a. Find the conflicting attributes and facts in the rule. b. Resolve the conflict and gives the priority to rules 5. Store the rules into the knowledge base.
Alternative Flows:	3 (a) If there is no duplicate a. Check the rule for conflict. 4 (a) If there is no conflict a. Store the rule into the knowledge base
Exceptions:	N/A
Includes:	N/A
Frequency of Use:	Whenever domain expert wants to validate the rule
Special Requirements:	N/A
Assumptions:	N/A
Notes and Issues:	Finding duplication using facts of condition and conclusion in existing rules is challenging task.
Sequence Diagram:	

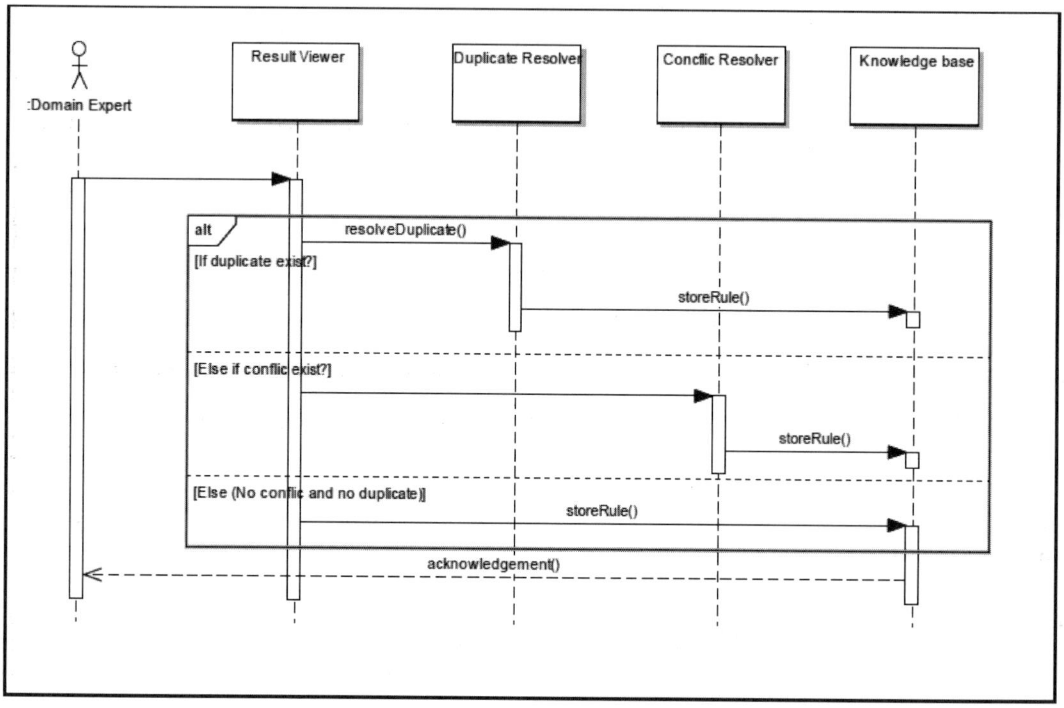
:Domain Expert
Result Viewer
Duplicate Resolver
Concflic Resolver
Knowledge base
alt
resolveDuplicate()
[If duplicate exist?]
storeRule()
[Else if conflic exist?]
storeRule()
[Else (No conflic and no duplicate)]
storeRule()
acknowledgement()

18.4 Service Curation Layer

18.4.1 Use Case List

ID	Description
SCL-UC-01	Load data for building recommendation
SCL-UC-02	Prepare data for building recommendation
SCL-UC-03	Load Rules
SCL-UC-04	Build Recommendation
SCL-UC-05	Receive Production Knowledge
SCL-UC-06	Report Unresolved Case
SCL-UC-07	Load data for interpreting recommendation
SCL-UC-08	Prepare data for interpreting recommendation
SCL-UC-09	Interpret Context
SCL-UC-10	Interpret Content
SCL-UC-11	Explain recommendations
SCL-UC-12	Prepare Results
SCL-UC-13	Receive service request
SCL-UC-14	Handle Data
SCL-UC-15	Deliver service results
SCL-UC-16	Goal-based recommendation Generation
SLC-UC-17	Provide Educational Support for user awareness
SCL-UC-18	Location- and weather-based Personalized recommendation
SCL-UC-19	User Preference-based refined recommendations
SCL-UC-20	Provide Alternative Recommendation
SCL-UC-21	Retrieve risk factors
SCL-UC-22	Retrieve risk assessment
SCL-UC-23	Adaptive education
SCL-UC-24	Adaptive physical and nutrition recommendation
SCL-UC-25	Question/Answer recommendation

18.4.2 Use Case Diagram

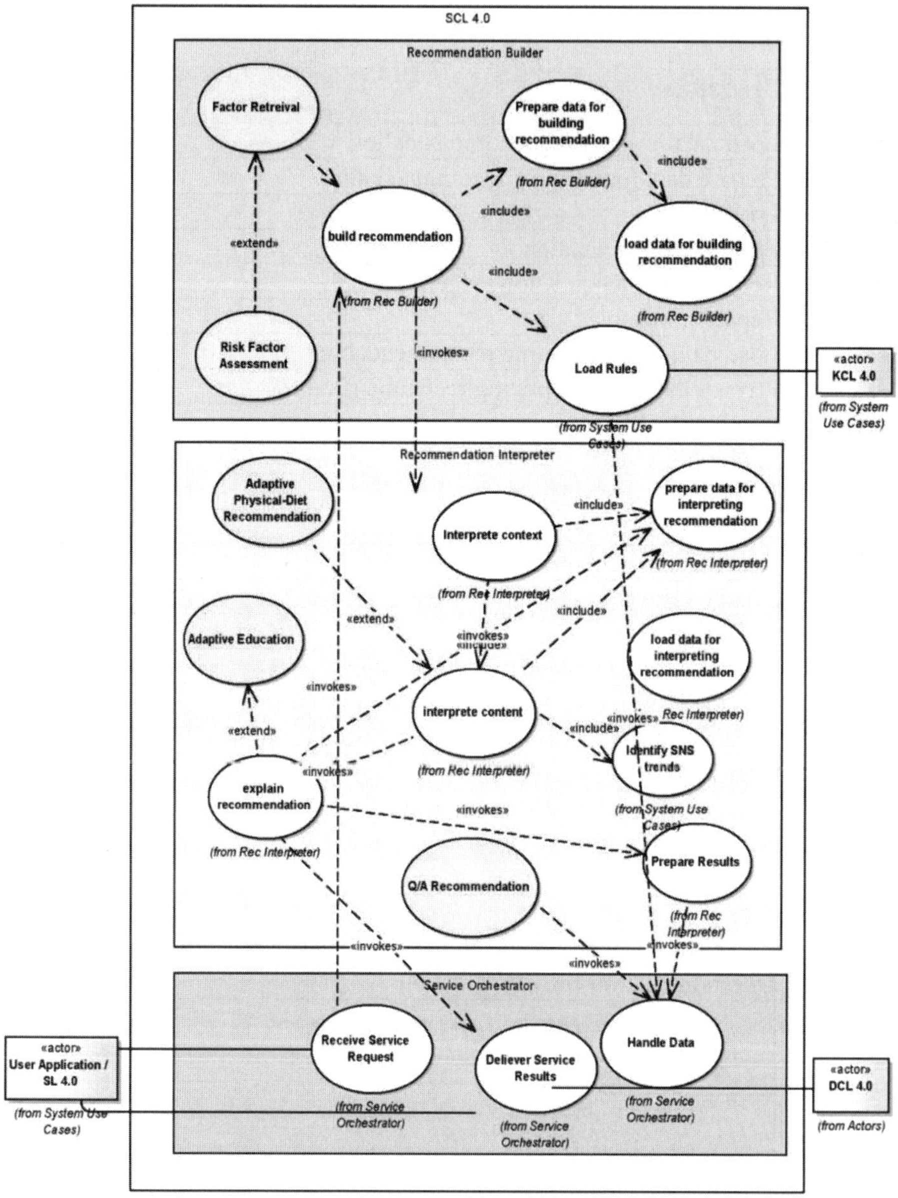

18.4.3 Use Case Description

Use Case ID:	**SCL-UC-01**		
Use Case Name:	Load data for building recommendation		
Created By:	Rahman Ali	**Last Updated By:**	Rahman Ali
Date Created:	July 14, 2015	**Last Revision Date:**	July 28, 2015
Actors:	SCL-UC-02 (Prepare Data)		
Description:	Retrieving user profile and lifelog data is required for reasoning to generate recommendation. This data is retrieved using Data Handler of the Service Orchestrator.		
Trigger:	Triggered when a new service request is received from the user application or DCL.		
Preconditions:	User profile and lifelog data is available in user lifelog.		
Postconditions:	User profile and lifelog data is successfully retrieved and prepared for reasoner to process.		
Normal Flow:	1. Data Preparator sends request for loading data 2. Data Loader receives the request and performs the following tasks; a. Analyses the request and user for the appropriate data loading b. Prepare separate requests for user lifelog data 3. Data Loader sends analyses request to Data Handler 4. Data Handler provides the data to Data Loader		
Alternative Flows:	N/A		
Exceptions:	N/A		
Includes:	N/A		
Frequency of Use:	Very frequent; repeated for every service request		
Special Requirements:	N/A		
Assumptions:	Service Orchestrator knows the required data for each registered service.		
Notes and Issues:	N/A		
Sequence Diagram			

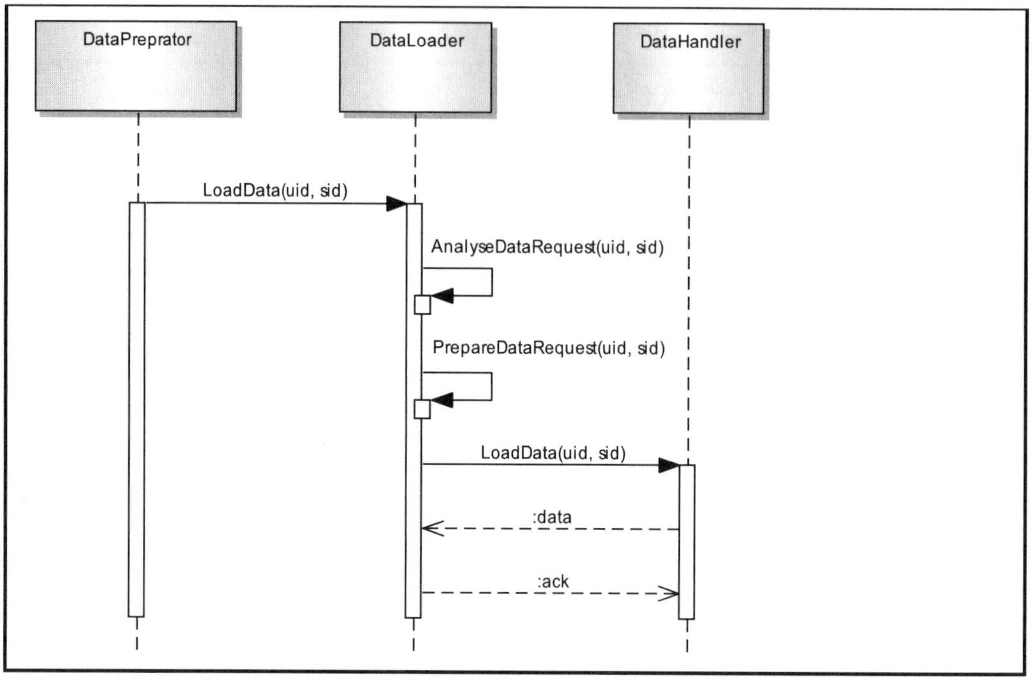

Use Case ID:	SCL-UC-02		
Use Case Name:	Prepare data for building recommendation		
Created By:	Rahman Ali	Last Updated By:	Rahman Ali
Date Created:	July 14, 2015	Last Revision Date:	July 28, 2015
Actors:	SCL-UC-04 (Build Recommendation)		
Description:	Knowledge based reasoning requires prepared data to execute the rules during the reasoning process.		
Trigger:	Triggered when new service request is made for generating recommendations		
Preconditions:	User profile and lifelog data is loaded into RB 2		
Postconditions:	User prepared data is readily available for reasoner to process.		
Normal Flow:	1. Recommendation Builder sends data preparation request to Data Preparator along with the loaded data 2. Data Preparator prepares profile data 3. Data Preparator prepares lifelog data 4. Data Preparator returns prepared data to Recommendation Builder		

Alternative Flows:	N/A
Exceptions:	N/A
Includes:	SCL-UC-01
Frequency of Use:	Very frequent; for every service request
Special Requirements:	N/A
Assumptions:	N/A
Notes and Issues:	N/A

Sequence Diagram

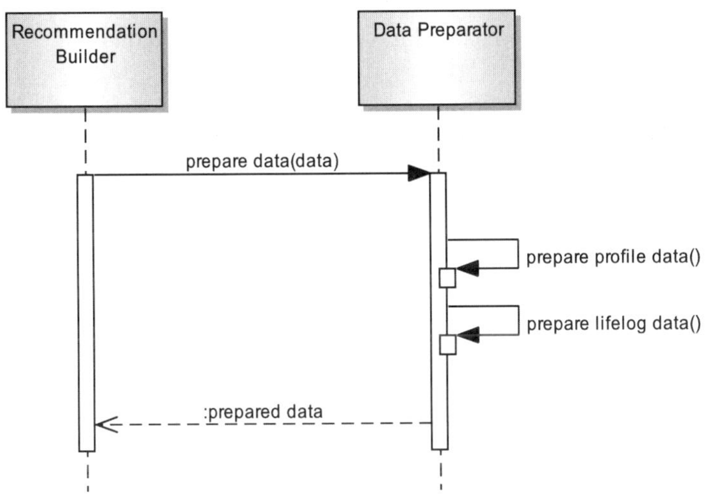

Use Case ID:	**SCL-UC-03**		
Use Case Name:	Load Rules		
Created By:	Rahman Ali	**Last Updated By:**	Rahman Ali
Date Created:	July 28, 2015	**Last Revision Date:**	July 28, 2015
Actors:	SCL-UC-04 (Build Recommendation)		
Description:	Rule-based reasoned needs knowledge rules to perform reasoning using the prepared data to generate recommendations for the service request.		
Trigger:	At the time when new service request arrives for recommendation.		

Preconditions:	• Updated knowledge is available in Production Knowledge Base. • KCL and RB 2 agree on common format of production rules.
Postconditions:	The reasoned is ready to execute the rules and generate recommendations.
Normal Flow:	1. Recommendation Builders send knowledge load request to Rule Loader 2. Rule Loader sends request to Production Knowledge Base 3. System performs the following tasks; a. Analyses the request knowledge b. Search production knowledge base for the requested rules c. Loads the rules d. Provides the rules back to Recommendation Builder
Alternative Flows:	N/A
Exceptions:	N/A
Includes:	N/A
Frequency of Use:	Frequent: when reasoner is invoked for new service generation.
Special Requirements:	N/A
Assumptions:	N/A
Notes and Issues:	N/A
Sequence Diagram	

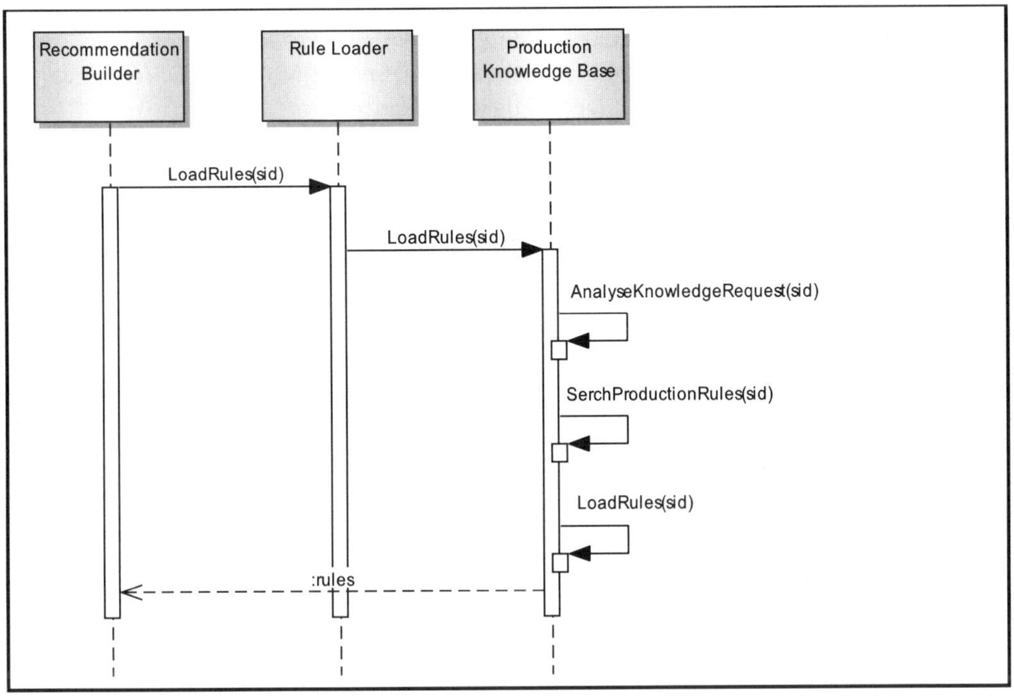

Use Case ID:	SCL-UC-04		
Use Case Name:	Build recommendations		
Created By:	Rahman Ali	Last Updated By:	Rahman Ali
Date Created:	July 15, 2015	Last Revision Date:	July 15, 2015
Actors:	SCL-UC-13 (Request Handler), SCL-UC-04, SCL-UC-02, SCL-UC-01, SCL-UC-03, SCL-UC-09 (Interpret Context)		
Description:	RBR performs rule-based reasoning to generate recommendations using the production rules and prepared data.		
Trigger:	At the time when new service request arrives for recommendation.		
Preconditions:	Knowledge is available in Production Knowledge Base.		
Postconditions:	The recommendation is reported to RI 2, if reasoning is successful, otherwise the new case is provided to Unified Knowledge Interface along with the missing rule message.		
Normal Flow:	1. Request Handler invokes recommendation builder for recommendation 2. Recommendation Builder load prepared data		

	3. Recommendation Builder retrieves loaded rules 4. Recommendation Builder performs rule-based reasoning on the prepared data and loaded rules 5. Recommendation Builder generates recommendation and perform the following tasks; a. Prepare recommendation b. Provides recommendations to Context Interpreter for interpretation
Alternative Flows:	5a. The system could not find rule to execute a. Recommendation Builder sends message along with Unresolved Case to Case Notifier
Exceptions:	N/A
Includes:	SCL-UC-02, SCL-UC-03
Frequency of Use:	Frequent: when recommendation builder is invoked for generating recommendation.
Special Requirements:	N/A
Assumptions:	KCL and RB 2 agree on common format of production rules.
Notes and Issues:	N/A
Sequence Diagram	

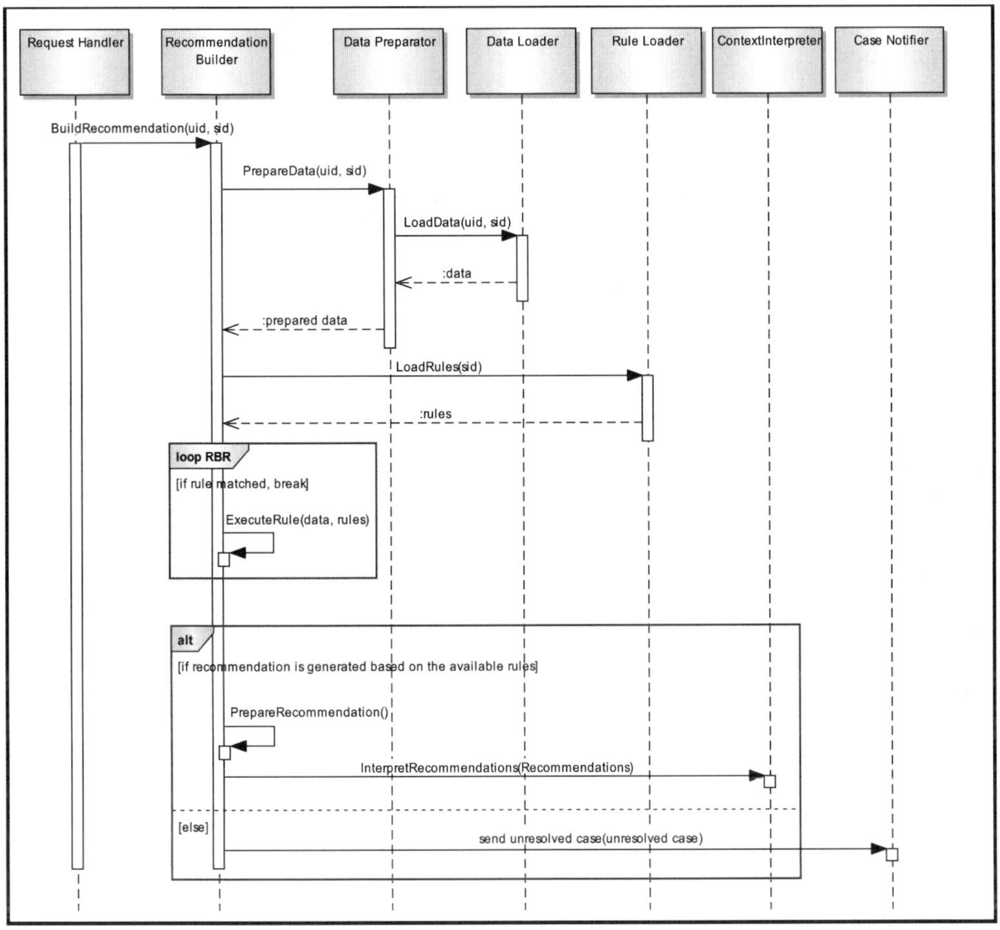

Use Case ID:	**SCL-UC-05**		
Use Case Name:	Receive Production Knowledge		
Created By:	Muhammad Afzal	**Last Updated By:**	Rahman Ali, Muhammad Afzal
Date Created:	July 5, 2015	**Last Revision Date:**	July 28, 2015
Actors:	KCL		
Description:	The knowledge is originated by KCL and is transfer to SCL 2 to keep a local copy of the production knowledge.		
Trigger:	At knowledge creation/update time		
Preconditions:	SCL 2 and KCL has a common representation agreement		

Postconditions:	The SCL 2 copy of knowledge is updated and is synchronized with KCL
Normal Flow:	1. KCL interrupt Knowledge Handler for new knowledge 2. Knowledge Handler verifies the knowledge 3. Knowledge Handler make a local of the received knowledge in the Production Knowledge Base 4. Knowledge is persisted in Production Knowledge Base 5. KCL is acknowledged of the knowledge receipt
Alternative Flows:	N/A
Exceptions:	N/A
Includes:	N/A
Frequency of Use:	Less frequent: at knowledge creation/update time
Special Requirements:	N/A
Assumptions:	N/A
Notes and Issues:	N/A

Sequence Diagram

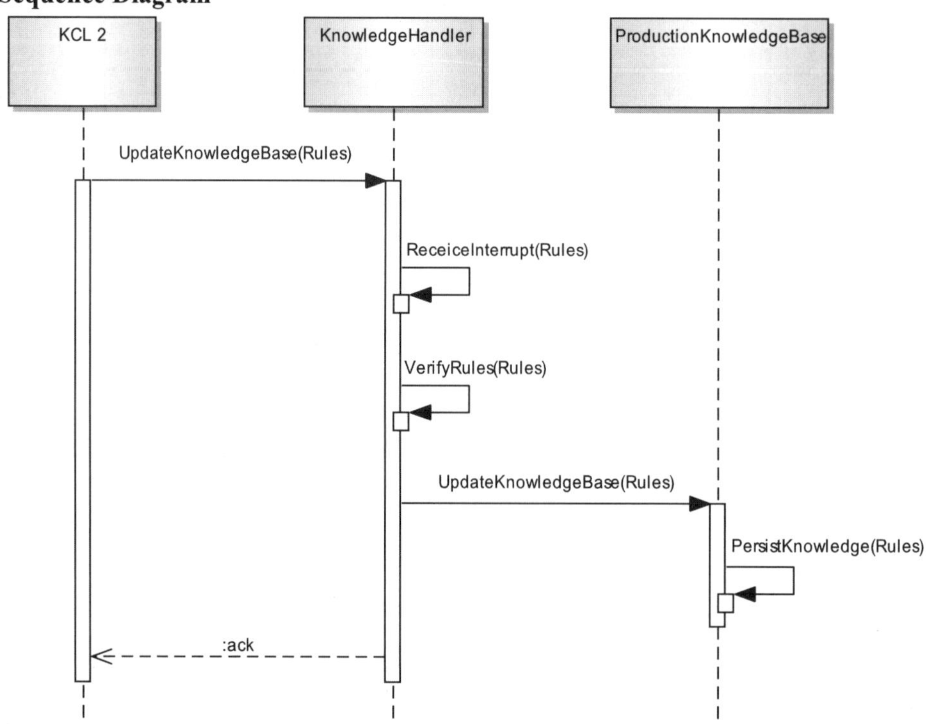

<table>
<tr><td>Use Case ID:</td><td colspan="3">SCL-UC-06</td></tr>
<tr><td>Use Case Name:</td><td colspan="3">Report unresolved case</td></tr>
<tr><td>Created By:</td><td>Muhammad Afzal</td><td>Last Updated By:</td><td>Rahman Ali,
Muhammad Afzal</td></tr>
<tr><td>Date Created:</td><td>July 5, 2015</td><td>Last Revision Date:</td><td>July 28, 2015</td></tr>
<tr><td>Actors:</td><td colspan="3">SCL-UC-04 (Build Recommendation), KCL</td></tr>
<tr><td>Description:</td><td colspan="3">Notifying KCL that reasoner is incapable to generate recommendation for the service request. KCL may be able to acquire new knowledge for such service request to handle in future.</td></tr>
<tr><td>Trigger:</td><td colspan="3">At the time when reasoner is not capable to generate recommendation because of insufficient knowledge in the KB.</td></tr>
<tr><td>Preconditions:</td><td colspan="3">Reasoner has completed the reasoning process</td></tr>
<tr><td>Postconditions:</td><td colspan="3">The message with reason is successfully reported to KCL</td></tr>
<tr><td>Normal Flow:</td><td colspan="3">1. Recommendation Builder notify unresolved case as new case prepare the report
2. Case Notifier analyses the new case
3. Case Notifier prepare the new case report
4. Case Notifier sends new case report to KCL
5. KCL acknowledges the new case receipt</td></tr>
<tr><td>Alternative Flows:</td><td colspan="3">N/A</td></tr>
<tr><td>Exceptions:</td><td colspan="3">N/A</td></tr>
<tr><td>Includes:</td><td colspan="3">N/A</td></tr>
<tr><td>Frequency of Use:</td><td colspan="3">Less frequent: when reasoner detects new case not handled with existing knowledge.</td></tr>
<tr><td>Special Requirements:</td><td colspan="3">N/A</td></tr>
<tr><td>Assumptions:</td><td colspan="3">N/A</td></tr>
<tr><td>Notes and Issues:</td><td colspan="3">N/A</td></tr>
<tr><td colspan="4">Sequence Diagram</td></tr>
</table>

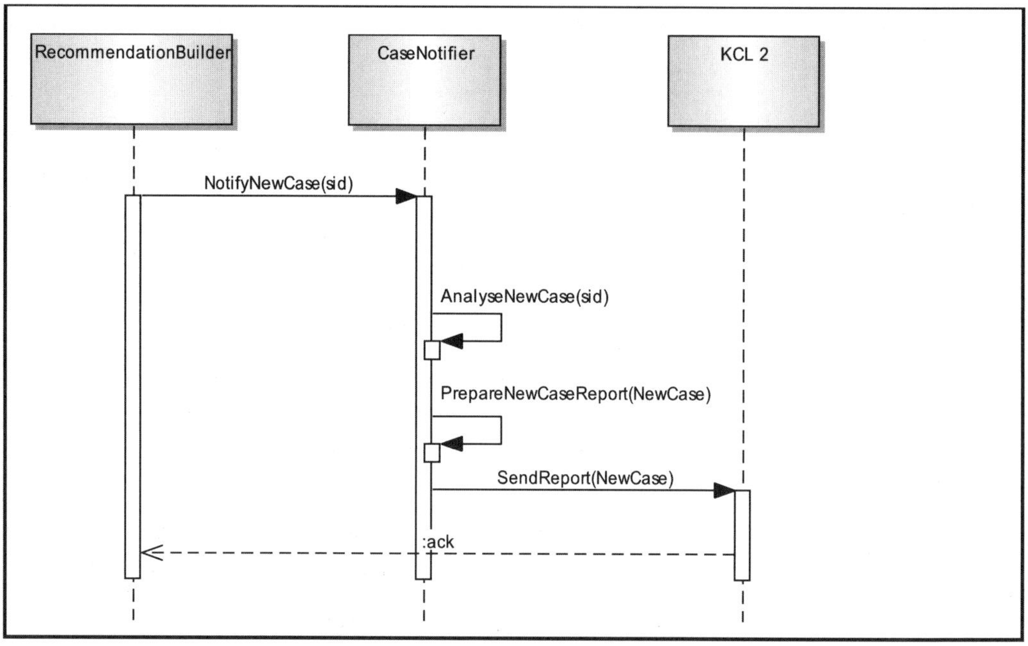

Use Case ID:	**SCL-UC-07**		
Use Case Name:	Load data for interpreting recommendations		
Created By:	Muhammad Afzal	**Last Updated By:**	Rahman Ali, Muhammad Afzal
Date Created:	July 15, 2015	**Last Revision Date:**	July 28, 2015
Actors:	Data Preparer		
Description:	The data is loaded from DCL through Service Orchestrator in order to interpret the recommendations		
Trigger:	After recommendation is built		
Preconditions:	• Recommendation are built • User profile is stored in lifelog • Context is recognized		
Postconditions:	The user profile, lifelog, and environmental variable data is available for preparation.		
Normal Flow:	1. Data Loader receives interrupt from Data Preparer 2. Data loader prepare data request 3. Data loader send request to Data Handler 4. Data loader receives data from Data Handler		

Alternative Flows:	N/A
Exceptions:	N/A
Includes:	N/A
Frequency of Use:	Very frequent; at every service request
Special Requirements:	N/A
Assumptions:	N/A
Notes and Issues:	N/A

Sequence Diagram

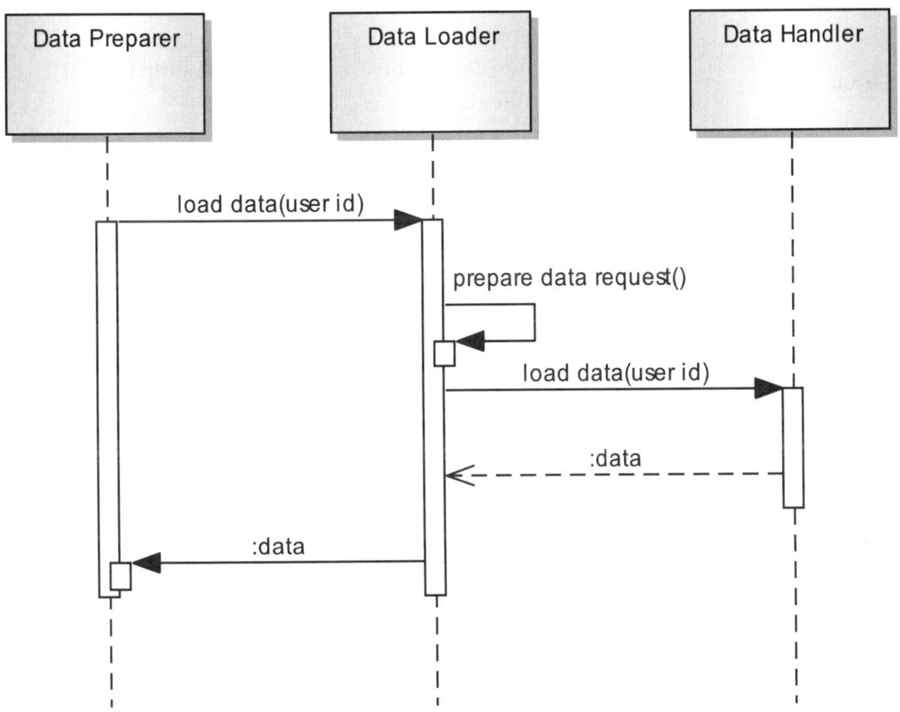

Use Case ID:	**SCL-UC-08**		
Use Case Name:	Prepare data for interpreting recommendations		
Created By:	Muhammad Afzal	**Last Updated By:**	Rahman Ali, Muhammad Afzal
Date Created:	July 15, 2015	**Last Revision Date:**	July 28, 2015
Actors:	Context Interpreter		

Description:	The loaded data is prepared for interpretations according to different functions such as lifelog for contextual interpretations, user profile for content interpretations, and environmental variables for explanations.
Trigger:	After loading data for interpretations
Preconditions:	• Recommendation are built • Data is loaded
Postconditions:	The user profile, lifelog, and environmental variable data is prepared and is available for interpretations
Normal Flow:	1. Context Interpreter sends data to Data Preparer for preparations 2. Data Preparer prepares lifelog data 3. Content Interpreter sends request to Data Preparer for preparing profile data 4. Data Preparer prepares profile data 5. Data Preparer prepares environmental variable data for the Explanation Generator
Alternative Flows:	N/A
Exceptions:	N/A
Includes:	SCL-UC-07
Frequency of Use:	Very frequent: at every service request
Special Requirements:	N/A
Assumptions:	N/A
Sequence Diagram	

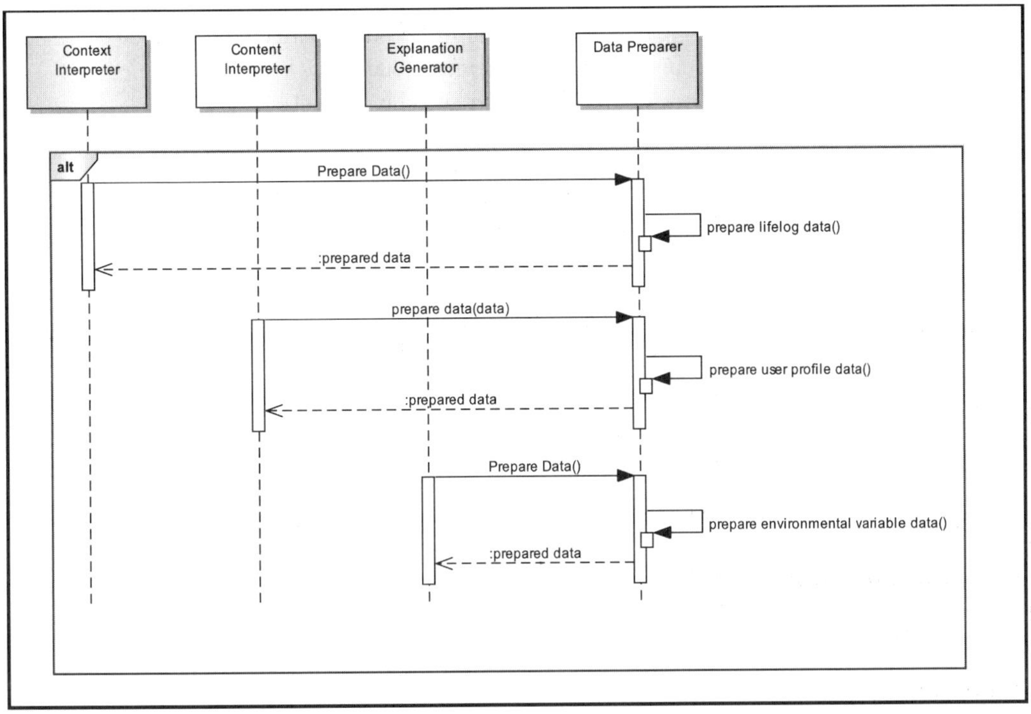

Use Case ID:	**SCL-UC-09**		
Use Case Name:	Interpret context		
Created By:	Muhammad Afzal	**Last Updated By:**	Rahman Ali, Muhammad Afzal
Date Created:	July 15, 2015	**Last Revision Date:**	July 28, 2015
Actors:	Build Recommendation		
Description:	The loaded data is prepared for interpretations according to different functions such as lifelog for contextual interpretations, user profile for content interpretations, and environmental variables for explanations.		
Trigger:	After loading data for interpretations		
Preconditions:	Recommendation are built, and data is loaded		
Postconditions:	The user profile, lifelog, and environmental variable data is prepared and is available for interpretations		
Normal Flow:	1. Context Interpreter receives request for from Recommendation Interpreter for context interpretation		

	2. Context Interpreter load and prepare data lifelog data (contextual data) for interpretations. 3. Context interpreter select a context 4. Context interpreter interprets the context 5. Repeat 2-4 until all applicable contexts interpreted 6. Context Interpreter receives the interpreted context 7. Context Interpreter sends the recommendations to content interpreter for interpreting the contents
Alternative Flows:	7a. if user is not available then the process is halt and message is sent to Recommendation Builder.
Exceptions:	N/A
Includes:	SCL-UC-08
Frequency of Use:	Very frequent; at every service request
Special Requirements:	N/A
Assumptions:	N/A
Notes and Issues:	N/A

Sequence Diagram

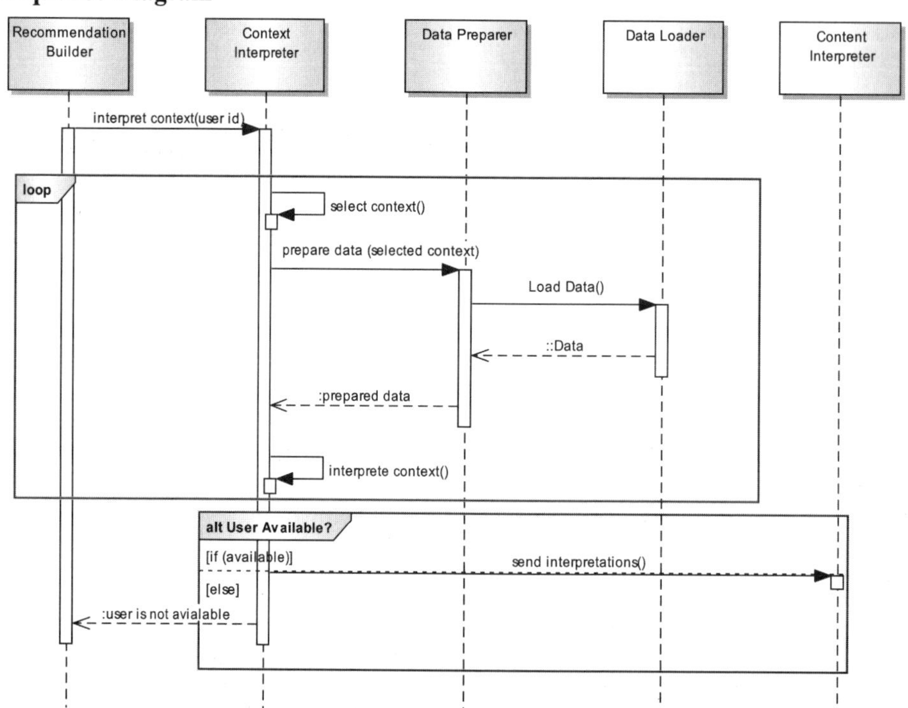

Use Case ID:	SCL-UC-10		
Use Case Name:	Interpret contents		
Created By:	Muhammad Afzal	Last Updated By:	Rahman Ali
Date Created:	July 15, 2015	Last Revision Date:	July 28, 2015
Actors:	Interpret Context		
Description:	The recommended contents of recommendations are difficult for user to understand. These contents need to be interpreted with support of multimedia contents.		
Trigger:	After interpretation of the context		
Preconditions:	Recommendations are generated, and context is interpreted		
Postconditions:	Recommendations are ready for explanation		
Normal Flow:	1. Context Interpreter sends the contextually interpreted recommendations to the content filterer. 2. Content interpreter perform the following tasks; a. Select appropriate filter b. Applies the filter 3. Step 2 is repeated for all filters 4. Content interpreter selects the appropriate format 5. Content interpreter adds the relevant url 6. Content interpreter forwards the format and filtered contents to explanation generator		
Alternative Flows:	N/A		
Exceptions:	N/A		
Includes:	SCL-UC-08		
Frequency of Use:	Very frequent: when recommendation are generated		
Special Requirements:	The format should be defined in advanced based on the user special conditions		
Assumptions:	N/A		
Notes and Issues:	N/A		
Sequence Diagram			

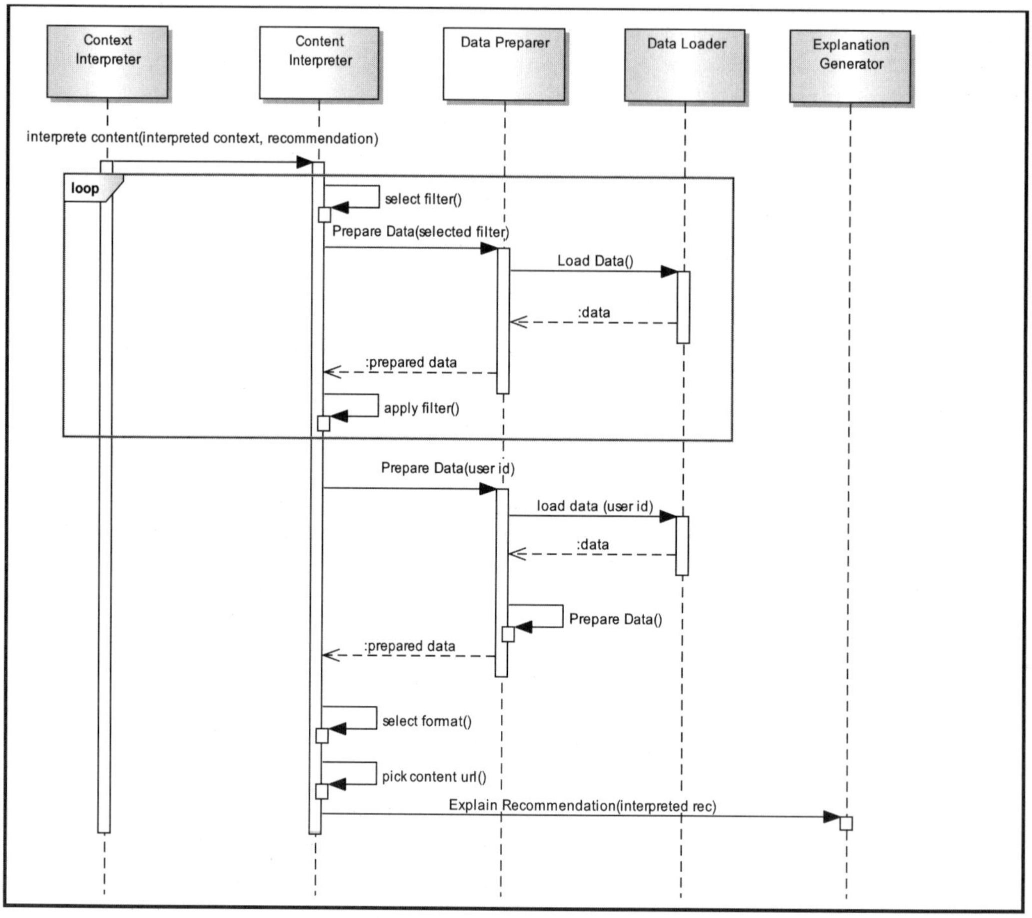
Context Interpreter
Content Interpreter
Data Preparer
Data Loader
Explanation Generator
interprete content(interpreted context, recommendation)
loop
select filter()
Prepare Data(selected filter)
Load Data()
:data
:prepared data
apply filter()
Prepare Data(user id)
load data (user id)
:data
Prepare Data()
:prepared data
select format()
pick content url()
Explain Recommendation(interpreted rec)

Use Case ID:	SCL-UC-11		
Use Case Name:	Explain Recommendations		
Created By:	Muhammad Afzal	**Last Updated By:**	Rahman Ali
Date Created:	July 15, 2015	**Last Revision Date:**	July 20, 2015
Actors:	Interpret content		
Description:	Usually user don't understand the contents of recommendations. To make them understandable the interpreted recommendations needs to be explained based on the user understandability.		
Trigger:	When contents are interpreted		
Preconditions:	Recommendations are interpreted		
Postconditions:	Recommendations are ready to deliver to the user		
Normal Flow:	1. Explanation generator receives the interpreted recommendations from content interpreter. 2. Explanation generator performs the following tasks; a. Select environment variable b. Generate explanation 3. Explanation Generator sends explained recommendation to educational support handler 4. Educational support handler performs the following tasks a. generate query b. locate resource c. link resource d. send resource link to interpreter 5. System sends explanation and educational resource links to result preparer.		
Alternative Flows:	N/A		
Exceptions:	N/A		
Includes:	SCL-UC-08		
Frequency of Use:	Very frequent: when recommendations are interpreted		
Special Requirements:	N/A		
Assumptions:	N/A		
Notes and Issues:	N/A		
Sequence Diagram			

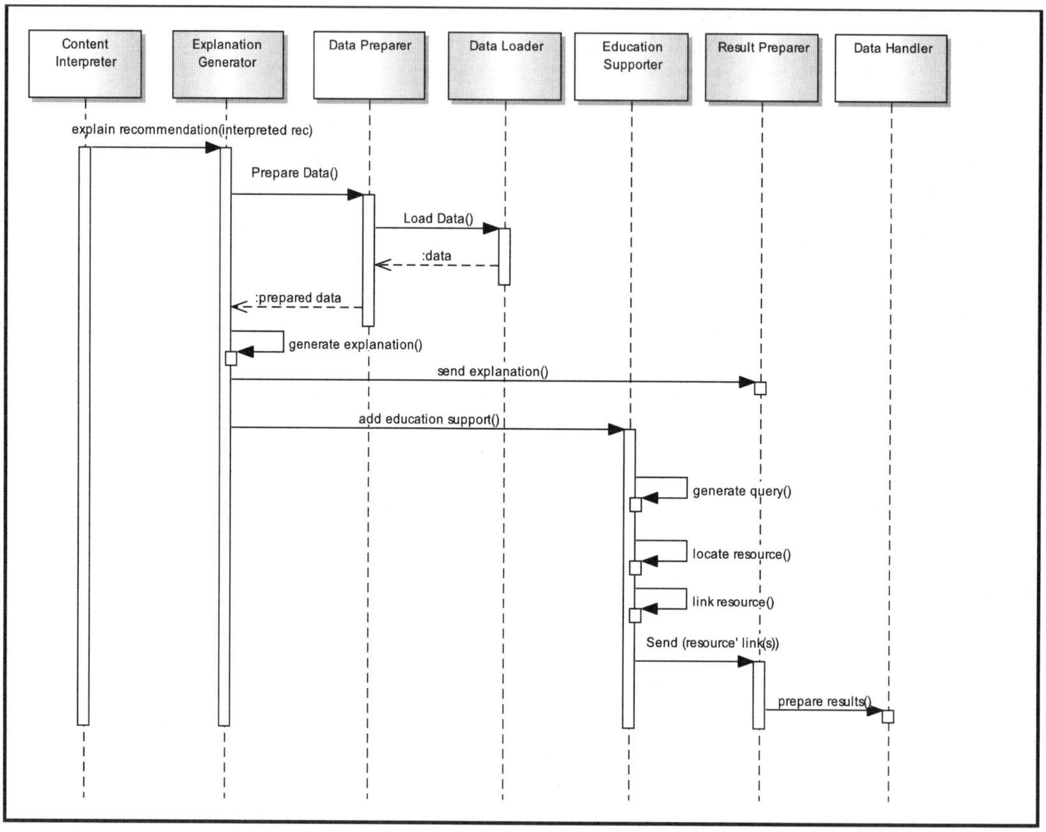

Use Case ID:	SCL-UC-12		
Use Case Name:	Prepare Results		
Created By:	Muhammad Afzal	**Last Updated By:**	Rahman Ali, Muhammad Afzal
Date Created:	July 5, 2015	**Last Revision Date:**	July 20, 2015
Actors:	Explain Recommendation (SCL-UC-11), Interpret Contents (SCL-UC-10)		
Description:	This use case prepares the results accumulated from explanation generator and content interpreter and forwards to results handler of service orchestrator.		
Trigger:	When recommendation is interpreted and explained		
Preconditions:	The recommendation is interpreted and explained		
Postconditions:	The results are forwarded to service orchestrator.		

Normal Flow:	1. Result Preparer receives outputs from content interpreter and/or explanation generator as well as education support. 2. Result Preparer combines the received results 3. Result Preparer sends the results to result handler of service orchestrator
Alternative Flows:	N/A
Exceptions:	N/A
Includes:	N/A
Frequency of Use:	Frequent
Special Requirements:	N/A
Assumptions:	N/A
Notes and Issues:	N/A

Sequence Diagram

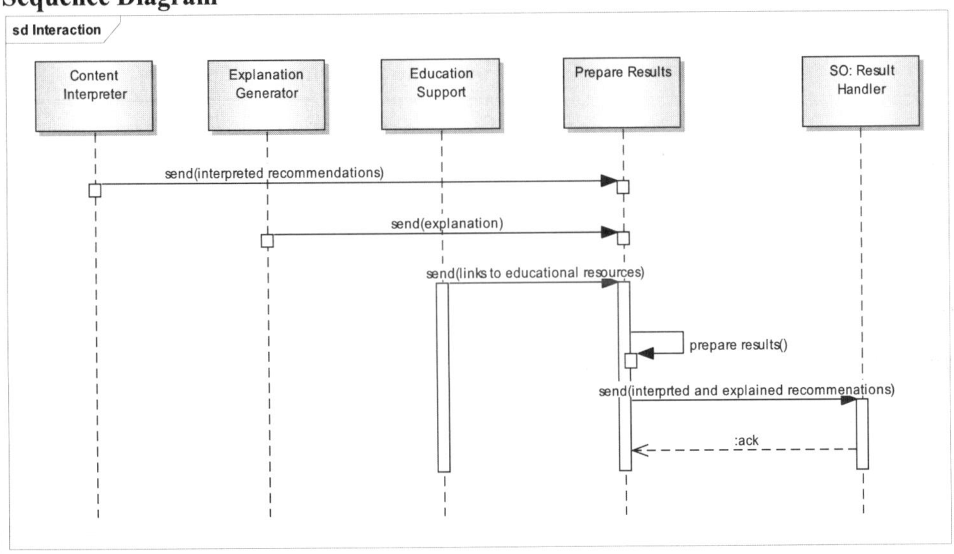

Use Case ID:	**SCL-UC-13**		
Use Case Name:	Receive service request		
Created By:	Muhammad Afzal	**Last Updated By:**	Rahman Ali, Muhammad Afzal
Date Created:	July 5, 2015	**Last Revision Date:**	July 20, 2015
Actors:	User Application / SL		

Description:	Service orchestrator receives request from user application, or DCL for recommendation. Orchestrator parses the request and invokes required service of Mining Mind for responding.
Trigger:	At the time of a request from the user application, or from mining mind generated events.
Preconditions:	• User is registered with Mining Minds • Service is registered as mining Minds valid service • Service-data binding is specified in advance
Postconditions:	The request is received, and recommendations are generated
Normal Flow:	1. Service orchestrator receives the service request from user application 2. System parses the request a. Search for the registered service b. Identifies the service type c. Identifies data requirements of the service d. Identifies the appropriate handling module 3. Service Orchestrator passes the request to recommendation builder of SCL 2 to build the recommendation
Alternative Flows:	1.a Event handler of service orchestrator receives the request as an interrupt from DCL, whenever a situation occurs 4.a Step 2-4 of the normal flow are executed.
Exceptions:	N/A
Includes:	N/A
Frequency of Use:	Very frequent: at every service request
Special Requirements:	N/A
Assumptions:	Service orchestrator and DCL agreed on service contract.
Notes and Issues:	
Sequence Diagram	

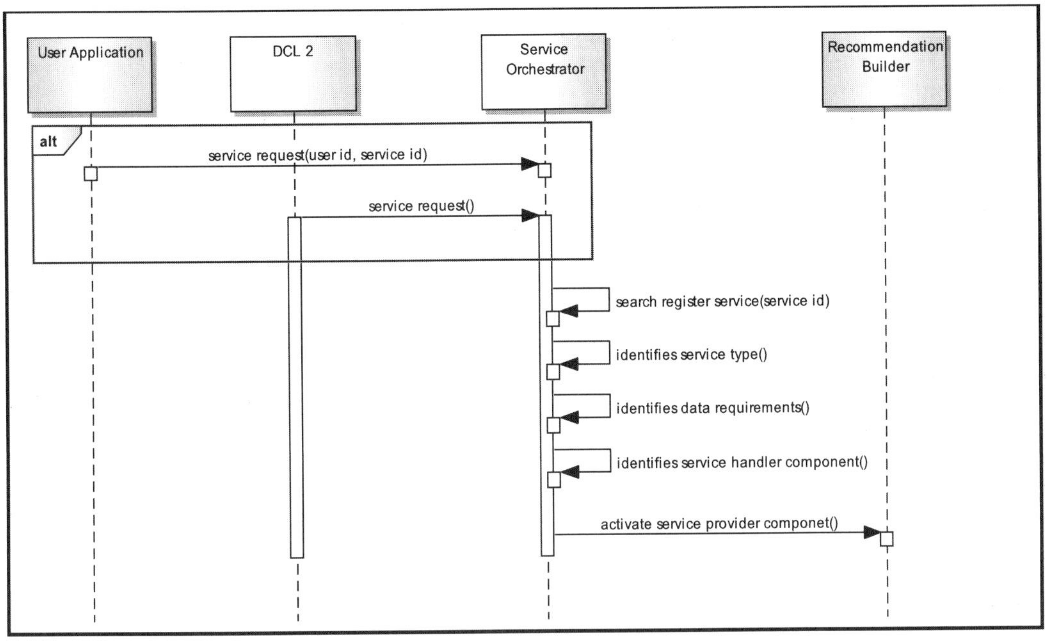

Use Case ID:	SCL-UC-14		
Use Case Name:	Handle Data		
Created By:	Muhammad Afzal	Last Updated By:	Muhammad Afzal
Date Created:	July 28, 2015	Last Revision Date:	July 28, 2015
Actors:	DCL		
Description:	This use case receives data request from recommendation builder and recommendation interpreter. It makes request from DCL to get the data for requester.		
Trigger:	At data request time		
Preconditions:	Service Request has been received to service orchestrator		
Postconditions:	Data has been provided to requester		
Normal Flow:	1. Data Handler in Service Orchestrator received data loading request from recommendation builder 2. Prepare data request 3. Retrieve data from DCL 4. Send data to RB: Data Loader		
Alternative Flows:	1a. Data Handler in Service Orchestrator received data loading request from recommendation interpreter Step 2-3 of normal flow		

	4a. Send data to RI: Data Loader
Exceptions:	N/A
Includes:	N/A
Frequency of Use:	Very Frequent: At every service request
Special Requirements:	N/A
Assumptions:	N/A
Notes and Issues:	N/A

Sequence Diagram

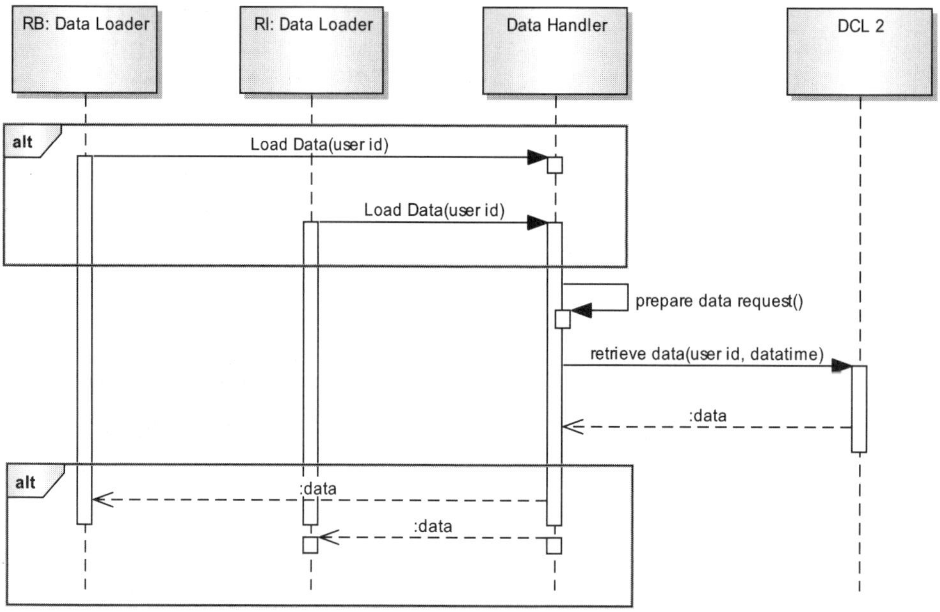

Use Case ID:	**SCL-UC-15**		
Use Case Name:	Deliver service results		
Created By:	Muhammad Afzal	**Last Updated By:**	Rahman Ali, Muhammad Afzal
Date Created:	July 5, 2015	**Last Revision Date:**	July 20, 2015
Actors:	Application / SL		

Description:	It is required to send request response to the service requester in the form of recommendation. Service orchestrator delivers the interpreted recommendation to user.
Trigger:	At the time of completion of interpretations
Preconditions:	Recommendations are generated and interpreted
Postconditions:	Service results are successfully delivered to the requester and DCL for persistence
Normal Flow:	1. Service orchestrator receives results from recommendation interpreter 2. System perform the following tasks; a. Prepares the response message b. Associate recommendations with service meta-data 3. Service Orchestrator sends recommendations to DCL for persistence 4. Service Orchestrator receives acknowledgement of storage 5. Service Orchestrator sends interpreted recommendations to SL 6. Service Orchestrator receives acknowledgement of receipt
Alternative Flows:	N/A
Exceptions:	N/A
Includes:	N/A
Frequency of Use:	Very frequent: at every service request completion
Special Requirements:	N/A
Assumptions:	Service orchestrator agreed on service contract with DCL and user application.
Notes and Issues:	N/A
Sequence Diagram	

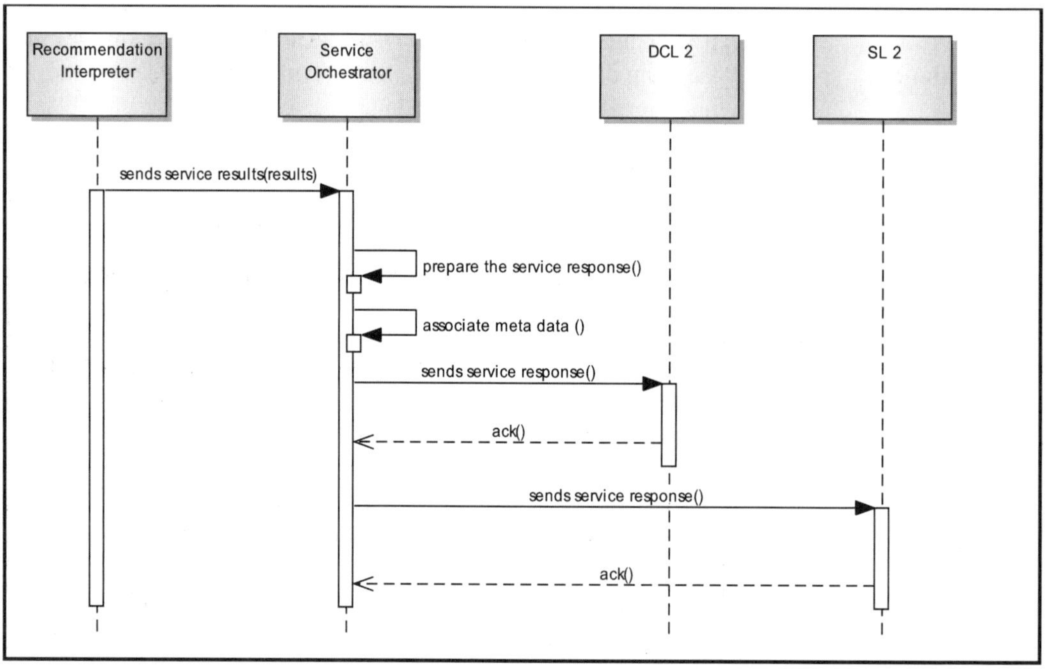

Use Case ID:	**SCL-UC-16**		
Use Case Name:	Goal-based recommendation Generation		
Created By:	Muhammad Sadiq	**Last Updated By:**	Muhammad Sadiq
Date Created:	March 16, 2017	**Last Revision Date:**	March 16, 2017
Actors:	DCL, Service Orchestrator, Recommendation Interpreter		
Description:	Goal Based recommender generates goal-based recommendation based on the user values		
Trigger:	DCL/User invokes goal-based recommender through service orchestrator for goal based personalized recommendation generation		
Preconditions:	Prepares request		
Postconditions:	Goal based recommendation is ready to be sent		
Normal Flow:	1. User characteristic information e.g. height, weight etc. is received 2. Goal Based Reasoner computes user BMI 3. Computed BMI is compared with Standard BMI 4. The difference of computed and standard BMI is generated 5. Categorize user based on the computed BMI difference		

	6. Generate recommendation based on respective BMI status 7. Return recommended goal and associated information to service orchestrator 8. Service orchestrator sends the recommendation to RI for personalization of the recommendation 9. RI personalizes the generated recommendation and sends it back to service orchestrator 10. Service orchestrator return the generated personalized goal-based recommendation to DCL
Alternative Flows:	N/A
Exceptions:	N/A
Includes:	
Frequency of Use:	Depending on situation.
Special Requirements:	N/A
Assumptions:	KCL 3.0 and RB 2 agree on common format of production rules.
Notes and Issues:	N/A

Sequence Diagram

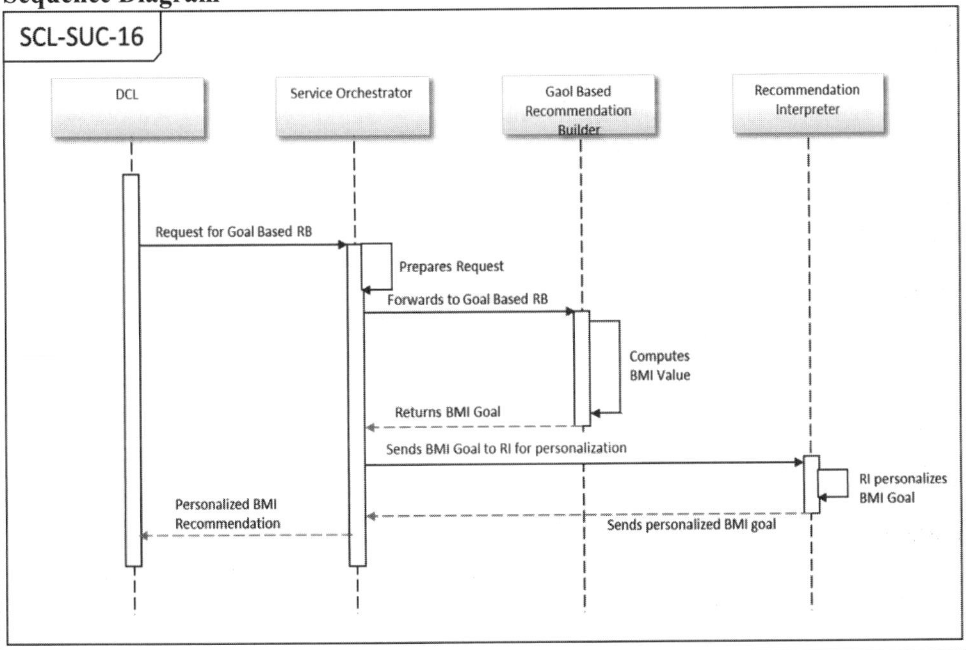

<table>
<tr><td>Use Case ID:</td><td colspan="3">SCL-UC-17</td></tr>
<tr><td>Use Case Name:</td><td colspan="3">Provide Educational Support for user awareness</td></tr>
<tr><td>Created By:</td><td>Imran Ali</td><td>Last Updated By:</td><td>Imran Ali</td></tr>
<tr><td>Date Created:</td><td>March 16, 2017</td><td>Last Revision Date:</td><td>March 16, 2017</td></tr>
<tr><td>Actors:</td><td colspan="3">Build Recommendation (SCL-UC-4)</td></tr>
<tr><td>Description:</td><td colspan="3">Provide educational support to the user for first 4 weeks of the subscription period. Educational support consists of audio/visual aids and informative web resources</td></tr>
<tr><td>Trigger:</td><td colspan="3">After loading data for interpretations</td></tr>
<tr><td>Preconditions:</td><td colspan="3">Recommendation are built and data is loaded</td></tr>
<tr><td>Postconditions:</td><td colspan="3">The user profile, lifelog, and environmental variable data is prepared and is available for interpretations</td></tr>
<tr><td>Normal Flow:</td><td colspan="3">1. Recommendation Interpreter receives request from Recommendation Builder
2. Recommendation Interpreter extracts users information from lifelog
3. Recommendation Interpreter evaluates the matching educational contents for the target user audience
4. Recommendation Interpreter prepares the required educational contents
5. Recommendation Interpreter sends the required educational content unit to result preparer</td></tr>
<tr><td>Alternative Flows:</td><td colspan="3">N/A</td></tr>
<tr><td>Exceptions:</td><td colspan="3">N/A</td></tr>
<tr><td>Includes:</td><td colspan="3">SCL-UC-08</td></tr>
<tr><td>Frequency of Use:</td><td colspan="3">Thrice a day: Time-based</td></tr>
<tr><td>Special Requirements:</td><td colspan="3">N/A</td></tr>
<tr><td>Assumptions:</td><td colspan="3">Service Orchestrator knows the required data for each registered service.</td></tr>
<tr><td>Notes and Issues:</td><td colspan="3">N/A</td></tr>
<tr><td colspan="4">Sequence Diagram</td></tr>
</table>

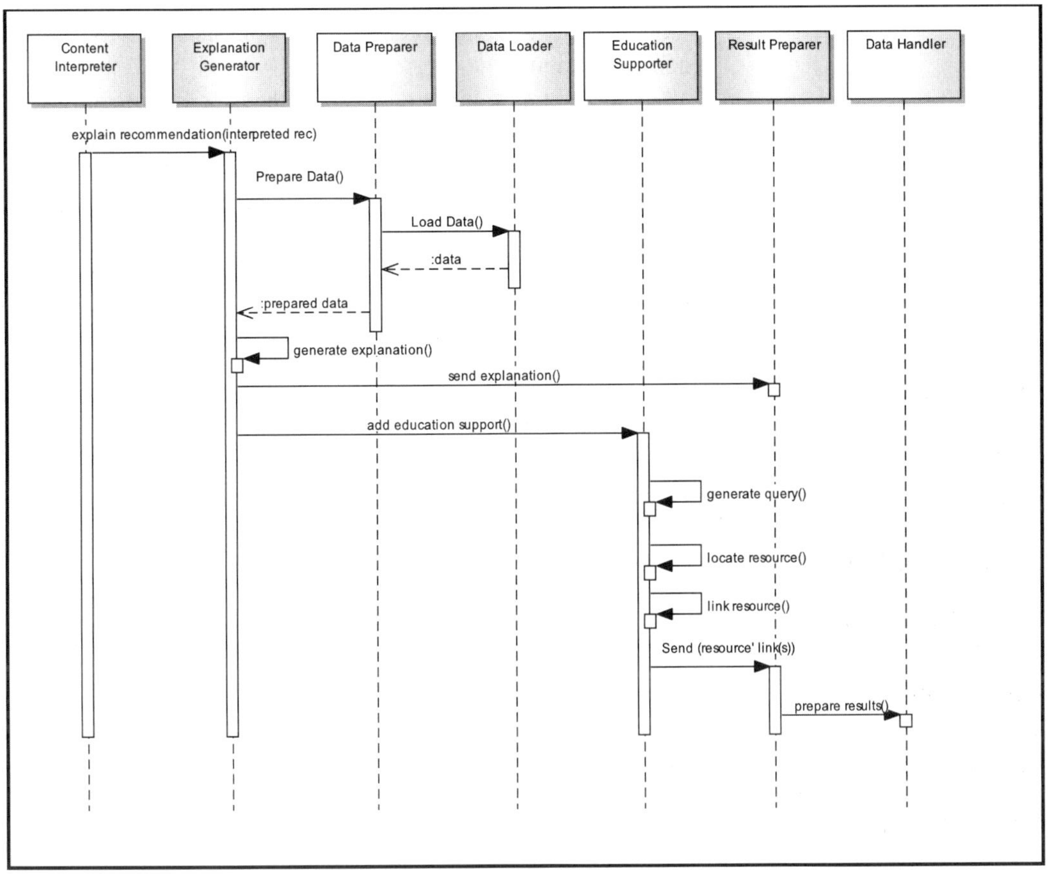

Use Case ID:	SCL-UC-18		
Use Case Name:	Location- and weather-based Personalized recommendation		
Created By:	Imran Ali	Last Updated By:	Imran Ali
Date Created:	March 16, 2017	Last Revision Date:	March 16, 2017
Actors:	Build Recommendation (SCL-UC-4)		
Description:	Interpret recommendations for environmental contexts and provide the required information in an structured form to SL		
Trigger:	After loading data for interpretations		
Preconditions:	Recommendation are built, and data is loaded		
Postconditions:	The user profile, lifelog, and environmental variable data is prepared and is available for interpretations		

Normal Flow:	1. Recommendation Interpreter receives physical activity-based recommendation 2. Recommendation Interpreter assess the user interpretability 3. In case of availability Recommendation Interpreter evaluates the contextual viability of the recommendation 4. Recommendation Interpreter sends the recommendation for education support 5. Recommendation Interpreter prepares educational unit for the target user is prepared 6. Final recommendation package is sent to Result Preparer
Alternative Flows:	N/A
Exceptions:	N/A
Includes:	SCL-UC-08
Frequency of Use:	Very frequent; at every service request
Special Requirements:	N/A
Assumptions:	Service Orchestrator knows the required data for each registered service.
Notes and Issues:	N/A
Sequence Diagram	

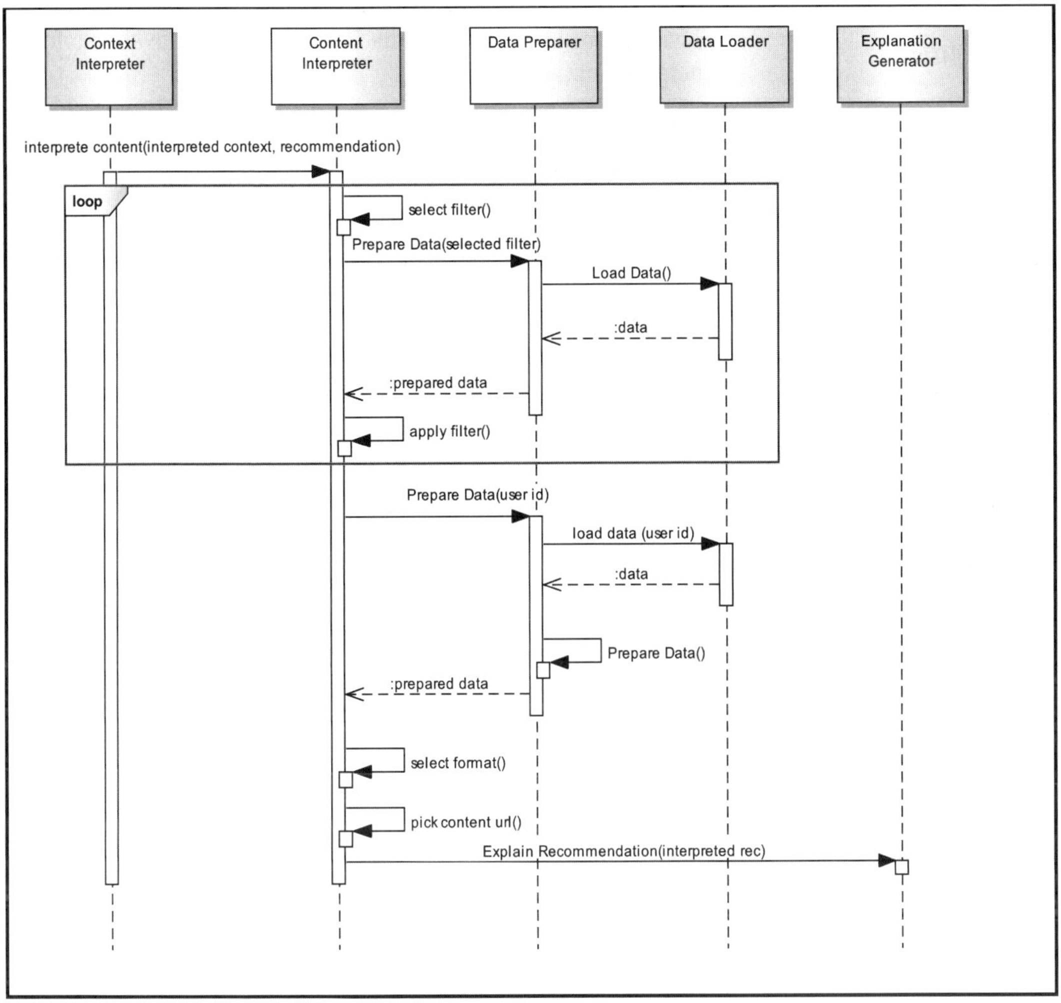

Use Case ID:	**SCL-UC-19**		
Use Case Name:	User Preference-based refined recommendations		
Created By:	Imran Ali	**Last Updated By:**	Imran Ali
Date Created:	March 16, 2017	**Last Revision Date:**	March 16, 2017
Actors:	Build Recommendation (SCL-UC-4)		
Description:	Interpret Recommendations based on User's Preferences for Food-based Recommendation		
Trigger:	After loading data for interpretations		
Preconditions:	Recommendation are built, and data is loaded		

Postconditions:	The user profile and lifelog data is prepared and is available for interpretations
Normal Flow:	1. Recommendation Interpreter receives food-based recommendation 2. Recommendation Interpreter evaluates the targeted user group 3. Recommendation Interpreter retrieves preferences of the user 4. Recommendation Interpreter matches user preferences with the targeted food-categorizes (menu-sets) 5. Recommendation Interpreter finalizes the menu-set selection 6. Final recommendation package is sent to Result Preparer
Alternative Flows:	N/A
Exceptions:	N/A
Includes:	SCL-UC-08
Frequency of Use:	Very frequent; at every service request
Special Requirements:	N/A
Assumptions:	Service Orchestrator knows the required data for each registered service.
Notes and Issucs:	N/A

Sequence Diagram

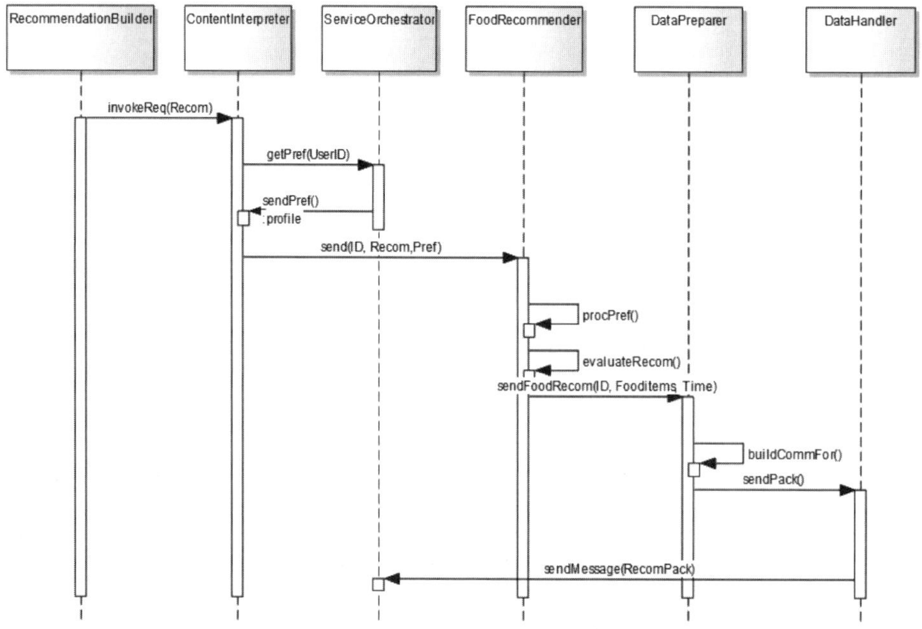

<table>
<tr><td>**Use Case ID:**</td><td colspan="3">**SCL-UC-20**</td></tr>
<tr><td>**Use Case Name:**</td><td colspan="3">Provide Alternative Recommendation</td></tr>
<tr><td>**Created By:**</td><td>Imran Ali</td><td>**Last Updated By:**</td><td>Imran Ali</td></tr>
<tr><td>**Date Created:**</td><td>March 16, 2017</td><td>**Last Revision Date:**</td><td>March 16, 2017</td></tr>
<tr><td>**Actors:**</td><td colspan="3">Build Recommendation (SCL-UC-4)</td></tr>
<tr><td>**Description:**</td><td colspan="3">Interpret Recommendation for special condition. An alternative recommendation is generated when the provided recommendation is not deemed viable for the user</td></tr>
<tr><td>**Trigger:**</td><td colspan="3">After loading data for interpretations</td></tr>
<tr><td>**Preconditions:**</td><td colspan="3">Recommendation are built, and data is loaded</td></tr>
<tr><td>**Postconditions:**</td><td colspan="3">The user profile, lifelog, and environmental variable data is prepared and is available for interpretations</td></tr>
<tr><td>**Normal Flow:**</td><td colspan="3">1. Recommendation Interpreter receives physical activity-based recommendation
2. Recommendation Interpreter evaluates the availability of thc uscr
3. Recommendation Interpreter evaluates the special user conditions
4. Recommendation Interpreter decides of the need for alternative recommendation
5. Educational contents are prepared for the final recommendation
6. Final recommendation package is sent to Result Preparer</td></tr>
<tr><td>**Alternative Flows:**</td><td colspan="3">1.1 Stall recommendation is user is not available</td></tr>
<tr><td>**Exceptions:**</td><td colspan="3">N/A</td></tr>
<tr><td>**Includes:**</td><td colspan="3">SCL-UC-08</td></tr>
<tr><td>**Frequency of Use:**</td><td colspan="3">Very frequent; at every service request</td></tr>
<tr><td>**Special Requirements:**</td><td colspan="3">N/A</td></tr>
<tr><td>**Assumptions:**</td><td colspan="3">Service Orchestrator knows the required data for each registered service.</td></tr>
<tr><td>**Notes and Issues:**</td><td colspan="3">N/A</td></tr>
<tr><td colspan="4">**Sequence Diagram**</td></tr>
</table>

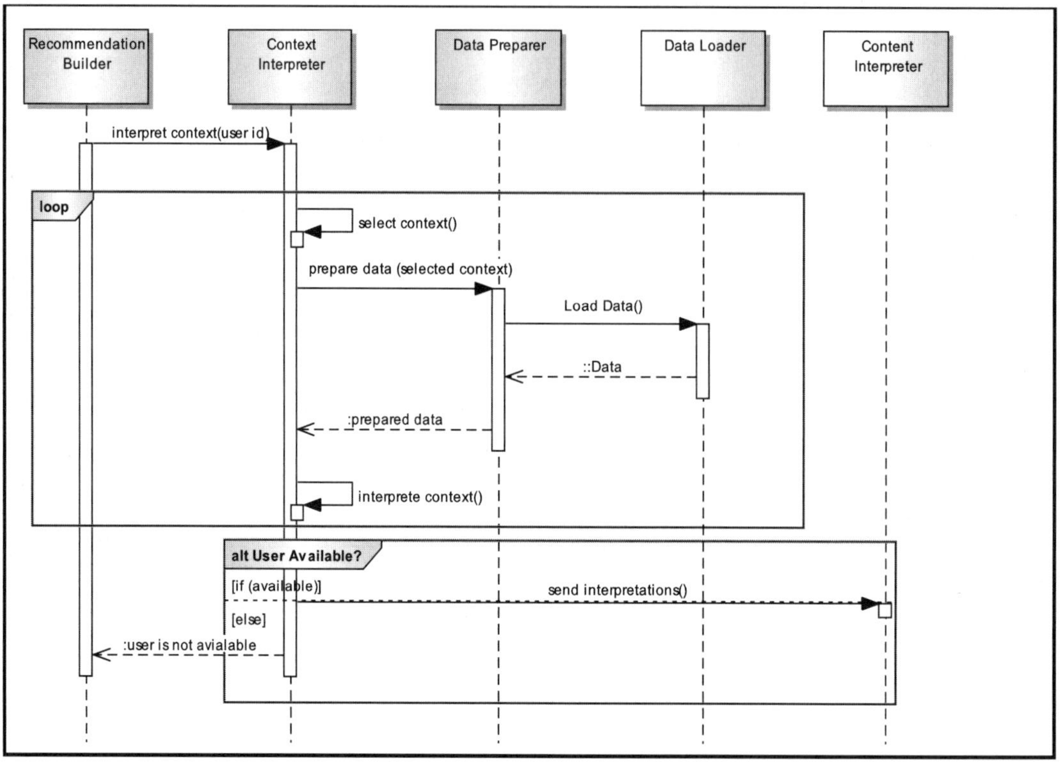
Recommendation Builder
Context Interpreter
Data Preparer
Data Loader
Content Interpreter
interpret context(user id)
loop
select context()
prepare data (selected context)
Load Data()
::Data
:prepared data
interprete context()
alt User Available?
[if (available)]
send interpretations()
[else]
:user is not avialable

18.5 Supporting Layer

18.5.1 Use Case List

ID	Description
SL-UC-01	User registration
SL-UC-02	Retrieve capabilities for user interface adaptation
SL-UC-03	Mapping the user capability information into model
SL-UC-04	Adapt user interface based on user profile, context and device
SL-UC-05	User capabilities collection
SL-UC-06	Self-reporting user experience measurement
SL-UC-07	Collect and analyze observational data
SL-UC-08	Acquire Recommendations for displaying to end user
SL-UC-09	Feedback Collection
SL-UC-10	Retrieve capabilities for context-based services
SL-UC-11	Map Request to Query
SL-UC-12	Transform Data
SL-UC-13	Classify Data
SL-UC-14	Analyze Data
SL-UC-15	Display Analytics
SL-UC-16	Take Expert Input
SL-UC-17	Display Adaptive Questions

18.5.2 Use Case Diagram

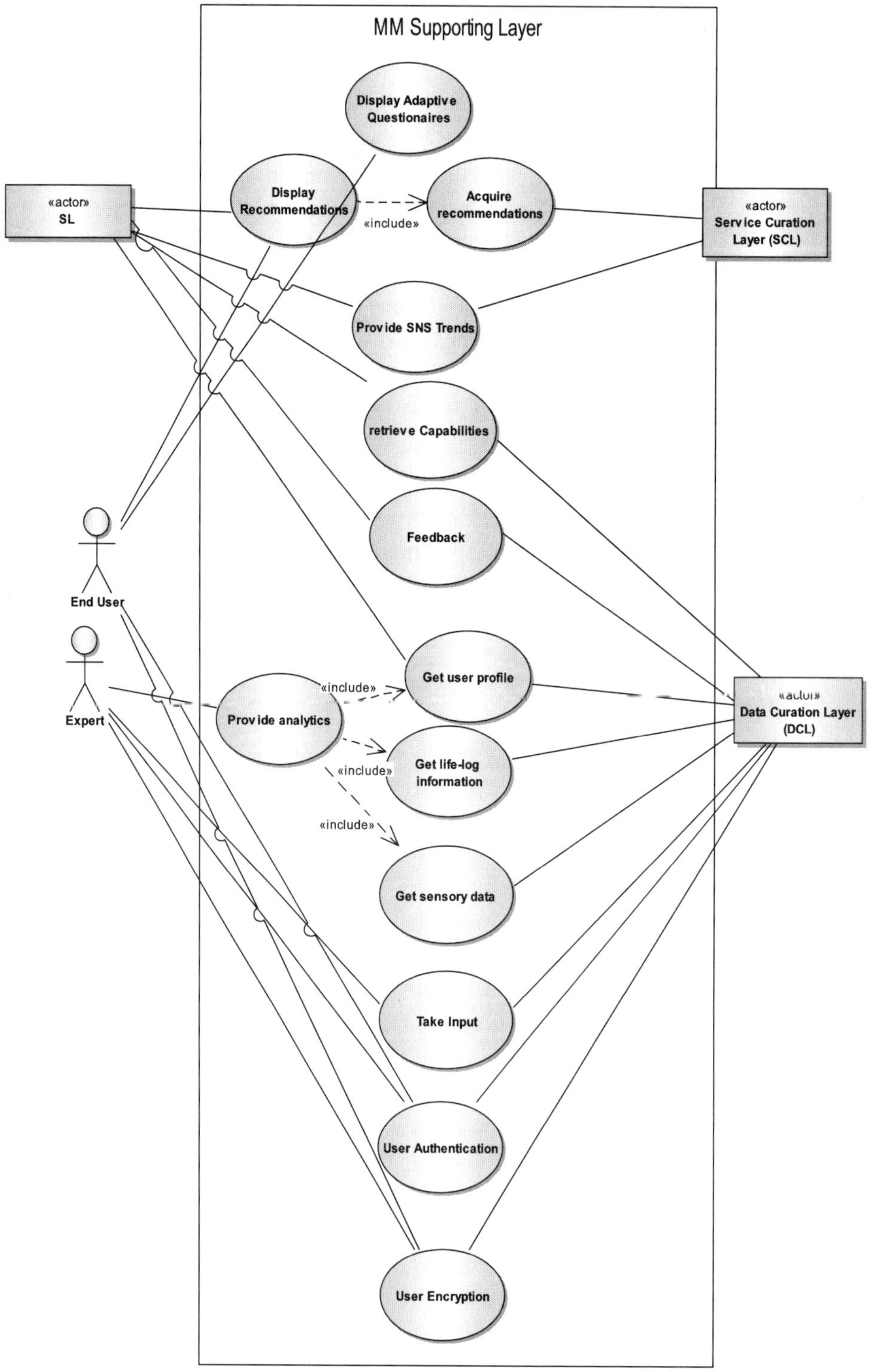

18.5.3 Use Case Description

<table>
<tr><td>Use Case ID:</td><td colspan="3">SL-UC-01</td></tr>
<tr><td>Use Case Name:</td><td colspan="3">User registration</td></tr>
<tr><td>Created By:</td><td>Jamil Hussain</td><td>Last Updated By:</td><td>Anees Ul Hassan</td></tr>
<tr><td>Date Created:</td><td>14 July 2015</td><td>Last Revision Date:</td><td>01 July 2018</td></tr>
<tr><td>Actors:</td><td colspan="3">Primary: End-user
Secondary: DCL</td></tr>
<tr><td>Description:</td><td colspan="3">This use case is for the user registration. A user must register with the MM app before they are able to use it. Registration primarily consists of entering an email address for verification and creating a password. All basic demographics, account, activity level, user interest information, and personalized map information shall be collect from user and persist in DCL.</td></tr>
<tr><td>Trigger:</td><td colspan="3">End user</td></tr>
<tr><td>Preconditions:</td><td colspan="3">The non-register user asked the application to register to it.</td></tr>
<tr><td>Postconditions:</td><td colspan="3">The user successfully registered to the application and can access its functionality</td></tr>
<tr><td>Normal Flow:</td><td colspan="3">1. The user starts registration of the new account by pressing the “Sig up” button on the application first screen.
2. Then Terms & Conditions page displayed
3. The application will display the multi-step registration form with empty fields for the account and user profile.
4. The user annotates the map for personalization by selecting different locations of his interest.
5. Validate User Input
• The application will automatically validate all the user input for all the required fields
• The user cannot proceed until providing the correct data.
6. The user can press “Submit” button and the new account data will be persisted to the DCL.</td></tr>
<tr><td>Alternative Flows:</td><td colspan="3">2a. In step 2. If the user Agree with Terms & Conditions
• User is allowed to the next step by click on agreed term & condition checkbox.
2b. In step 2. If user not agree with terms & conditions, then
• User is redirect to the first screen.

3a. in step 3. Display Validation Error</td></tr>
</table>

	• If the validation failed, then the validation icon will be displayed nearby the wrong field and there will be validation message.
Exceptions:	N/A
Includes:	N/A
Frequency of Use:	When user first time use the system [low]
Special Requirements:	N/A
Assumptions:	N/A
Notes and Issues:	N/A
Sequence Diagram	

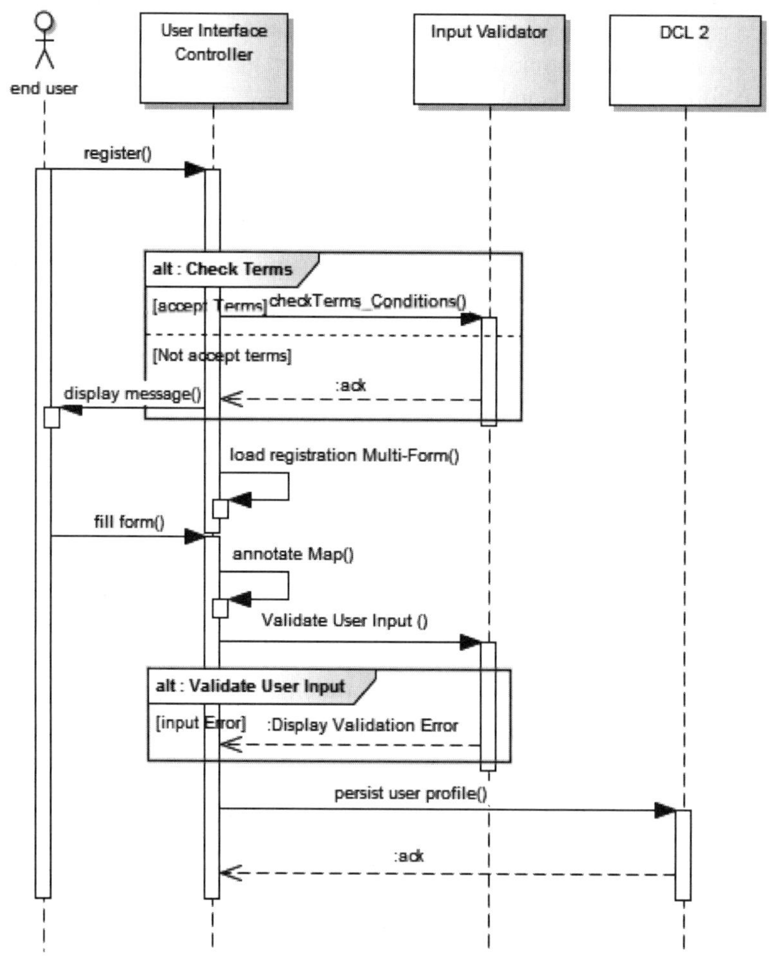

Use Case ID:	SL-UC-02		
Use Case Name:	Retrieve capabilities for user interface adaptation		
Created By:	Jamil Hussain	Last Updated By:	Anees Ul Hassan
Date Created:	14 July 2015	Last Revision Date:	01 July 2018
Actors:	DCL		
Description:	This use case focuses on the retrieval of the capabilities for user interface adaptation. The capabilities include user profile information, context information and device information. It is utilized for adaptation based on changes or observational data.		
Trigger:			
Preconditions:	The DCL provide the access to required information		
Postconditions:	All required capabilities are successfully collected.		
Normal Flow:	1. SL generates request for user, device, and context information collection from DCL 2. This information is utilized for the adaptation of the user interfaces 3. The adaptation is based on changes in user profile, context information or collected observational data		
Alternative Flows:	N/A		
Exceptions:	If there is not capabilities information, then the default user interfaces will be displayed.		
Includes:	N/A		
Frequency of Use:	Always when the application is running [High]		
Special Requirements:	N/A		
Assumptions:	The capabilities information should be available with the DCL.		
Notes and Issues:	N/A		
Sequence Diagram			

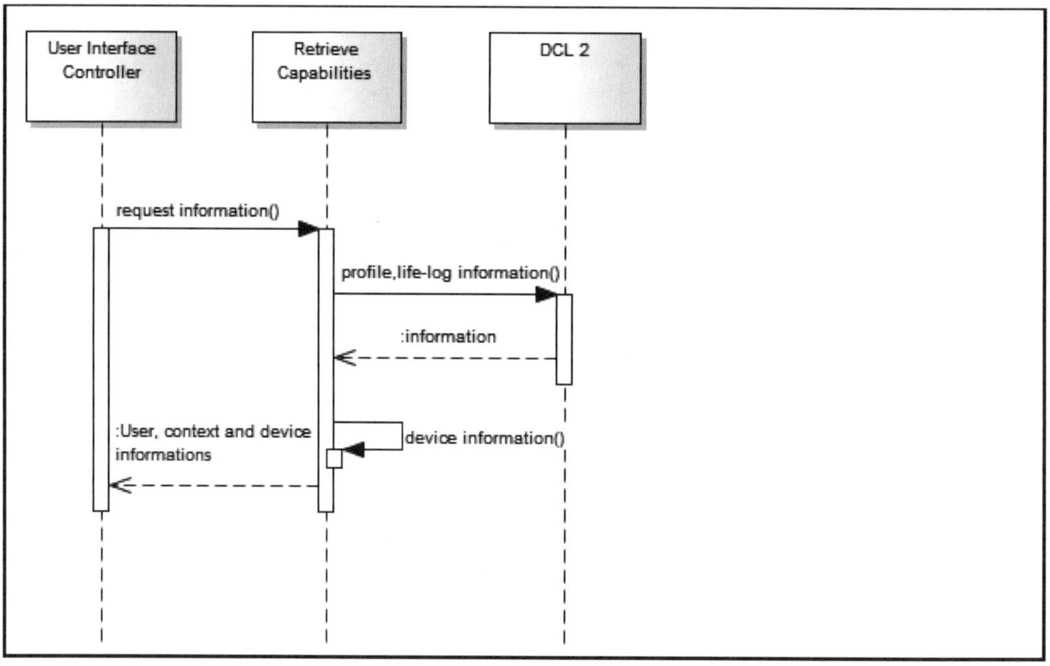

Use Case ID:	**SL-UC-03**		
Use Case Name:	Mapping the user capability information into model		
Created By:	Jamil Hussain	**Last Updated By:**	Anees Ul Hassan
Date Created:	14 July 2015	**Last Revision Date:**	01 July 2018
Actors:	DCL		
Description:	The collected capabilities information from DCL.0 shall be mapped against the hierarchical structure of the model		
Trigger:	SL initiate communication with DCL.		
Pre-conditions:	1. User is a registered client of MM platform 2. Updated user profile must be available		
Post-conditions:	1. User profile and environmental variables are received by UI/UX 2. All collected variables are successfully mapped and validated		
Normal Flow:	1. UI/UX send request to DCL.0 for environmental variables (e.g., temperature, weather, time, noise, light level etc.) and user profile variables (e.g. uid, name, age, perceptual information) 2. DCL sent back the requested variables. 3. The semantic modeler maps the data to model		

	4. The mapped information is persisted in model.
Alternative Flows:	N/A
Exceptions:	
Includes:	**SL-UCS-01**
Frequency of Use:	Always when the application is running [High]
Assumptions:	N/A
Notes and Issues:	N/A
Sequence Diagram	

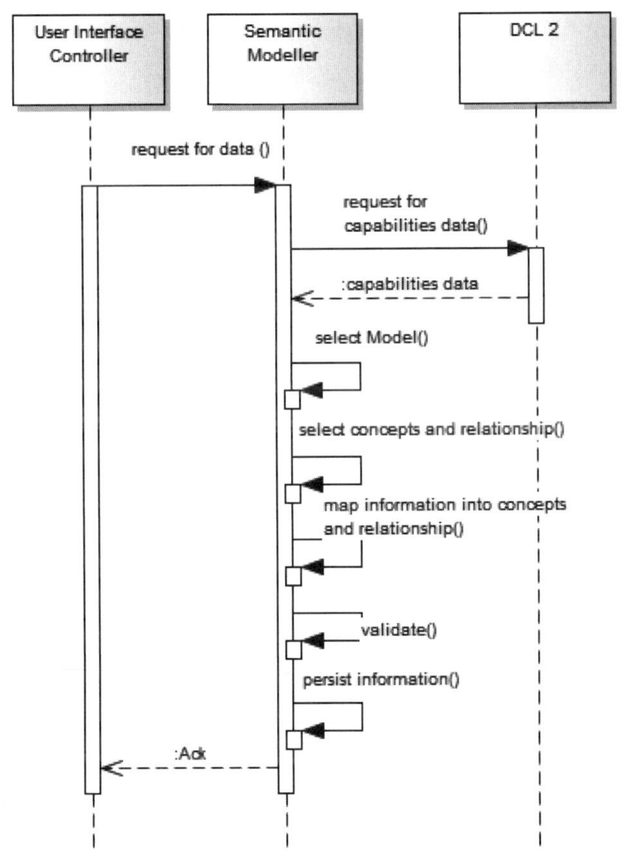

<table>
<tr><td>Use Case ID:</td><td colspan="3">SL-UC-04</td></tr>
<tr><td>Use Case Name:</td><td colspan="3">Adapt user interface based on user profile, context and device</td></tr>
<tr><td>Created By:</td><td>Jamil Hussain</td><td>Last Updated By:</td><td>Anees Ul Hassan</td></tr>
<tr><td>Date Created:</td><td>14 July 2015</td><td>Last Revision Date:</td><td>01 July 2018</td></tr>
<tr><td>Actors:</td><td colspan="3">DCL, end user</td></tr>
<tr><td>Description:</td><td colspan="3">The collected information of user profile, context of use and device characteristics from DCL results in adaption of the user interface</td></tr>
<tr><td>Trigger:</td><td colspan="3">End user start interacting with user interface</td></tr>
<tr><td>Pre-conditions:</td><td colspan="3">• The user profile and context of use and device data has been collected by UI/UX Authoring tool</td></tr>
<tr><td>Post-conditions:</td><td colspan="3">• Adaptive UI rendered/generated based on collected information</td></tr>
<tr><td>Normal Flow:</td><td colspan="3">1. User request for personalize user interface to UI/UX.
2. UI/UX send request to adaptation engine for generating the personalized user interface based on user, context and device information.
3. Adaptation engine perform reasoning based on pre-defined adaption and navigations rules.
4. Reasoner recommend the user interface components and its styles to generate the UI.
5. Then personalized generated UI is displayed to end user.</td></tr>
<tr><td>Alternative Flows:</td><td colspan="3">N/A</td></tr>
<tr><td>Exceptions:</td><td colspan="3">N/A</td></tr>
<tr><td>Includes:</td><td colspan="3">N/A</td></tr>
<tr><td>Frequency of Use:</td><td colspan="3">When user interact with the system</td></tr>
<tr><td>Assumptions:</td><td colspan="3">N/A</td></tr>
<tr><td>Notes and Issues:</td><td colspan="3">N/A</td></tr>
<tr><td>Sequence Diagram</td><td colspan="3"></td></tr>
</table>

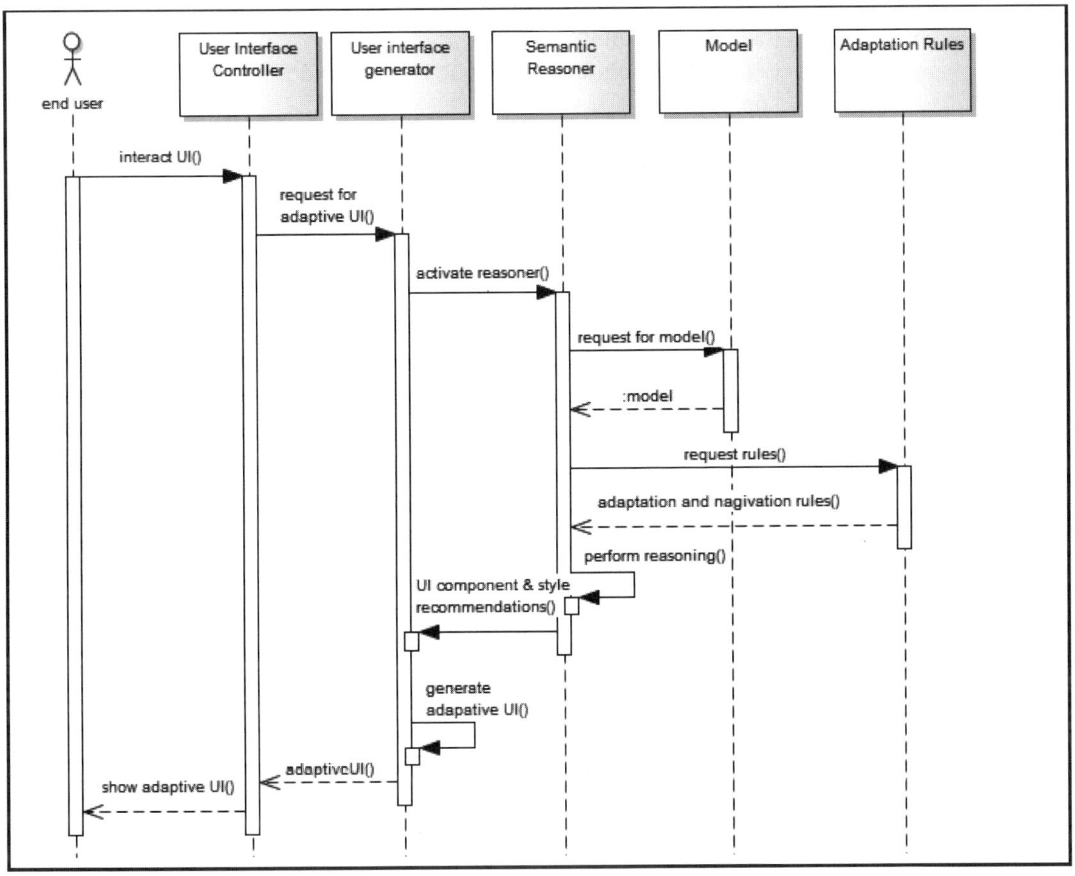

Use Case ID:	**SL-UC-05**		
Use Case Name:	User capabilities collection		
Created By:	Jamil Hussain	**Last Updated By:**	Anees Ul Hassan
Date Created:	14 July 2015	**Last Revision Date:**	01 July 2018
Actors:	End user, DCL		
Description:	The UI/UX collects the user capabilities information's by analyzing the user perception such as user visual and color perception		
Trigger:	User uses the tools for collection		
Pre-conditions:	• Perception collection tools are installed		
Post-conditions:	• User perceptual information successfully collected and update information in user profile DCL		
Normal Flow:	1. User select the tools for color and visual perception and interact		

	with it accordingly. 2. Tools acquire its interaction data in order to find the user perceptions 3. User experience calculate its final value. 4. Final values are stored in user profile DCL.
Alternative Flows:	
Exceptions:	N/A
Includes:	N/A
Frequency of Use:	When user interact with the system
Special Requirements:	
Assumptions:	Service contract between SL and DCL is defined
Notes and Issues:	N/A
Sequence Diagram	

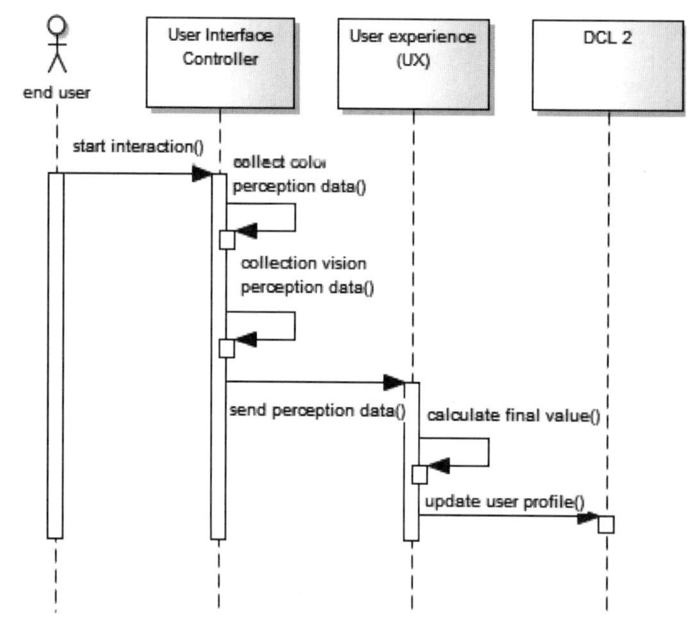

Use Case ID:	**SL-UC-06**		
Use Case Name:	Self-reporting user experience measurement		
Created By:	Jamil Hussain	**Last Updated By:**	Anees Ul Hassan
Date Created:	14 July 2015	**Last Revision Date:**	01 July 2018
Actors:	End user, DCL		
Description:	The UI/UX shall collect feedback about how users feel about the system during or after use by self-reporting method.		
Trigger:	End user		
Pre-conditions:	• Self-reporting questionnaire already exist		
Post-conditions:	• The feedback is successfully collected		
Normal Flow:	1. The end user provide feedback using the questionnaire. 2. The feedback is sent to user experience in order to evaluate the user response. 3. user experience variables such as usability, pleasure, beauty are calculated based on filled questions 4. The UI/UX update the calculated variables values in user profile by sending request to DCL		
Alternative Flows:	N/A		
Exceptions:	N/A		
Includes:	N/A		
Frequency of Use:	When user interact with the system		
Special Requirements:	N/A		
Assumptions:	N/A		
Notes and Issues:	N/A		
Sequence Diagram			

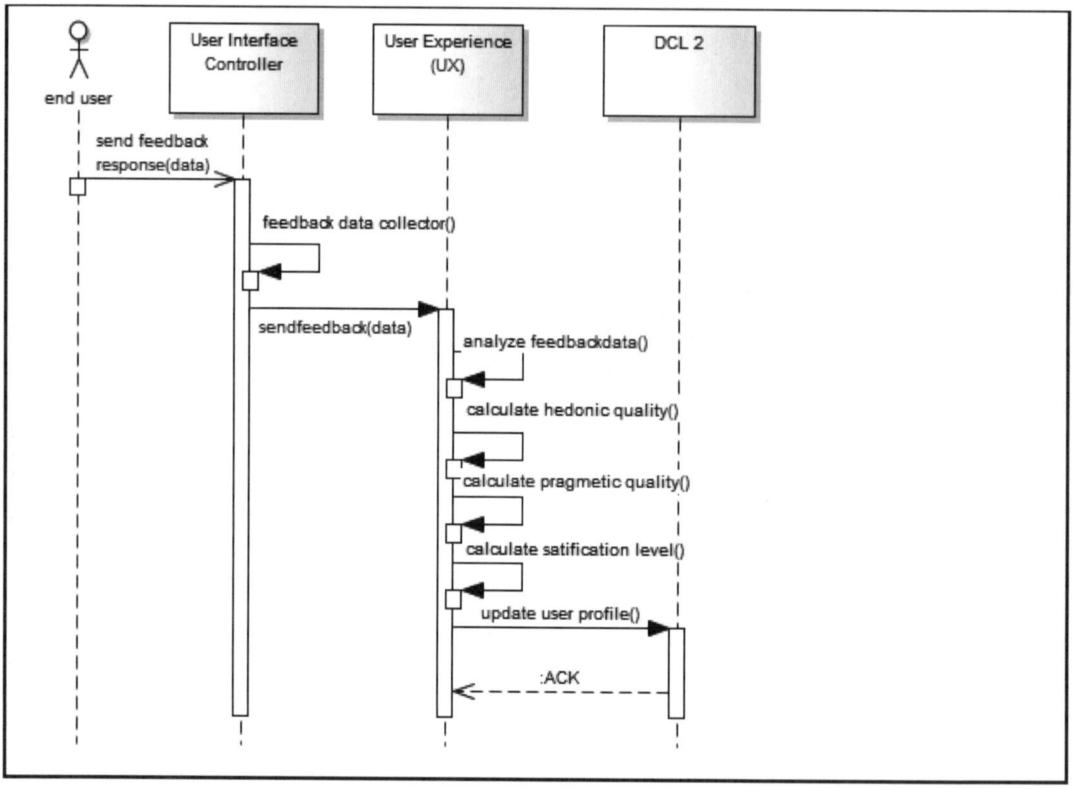

Use Case ID:	**SL-UC-07**		
Use Case Name:	Collect and analyze observational data		
Created By:	Jamil Hussain	**Last Updated By:**	Anees Ul Hassan
Date Created:	14 July 2015	**Last Revision Date:**	01 July 2018
Actors:	End user, DCL		
Description:	The UI/UX shall identify areas of improvement and maximize the user interaction by analyzing the user interaction with app.		
Trigger:	Initiated by end user		
Pre-conditions:	• Analytics tracker is already installed		
Post-conditions:	• Observational data are successful collected and analyzed for user experience measurement		
Normal Flow:	1. Analytics collector collect the user interaction data such as user ID, event, session, screen, crashes & exceptions, and user timings 2. The collected data is stored locally before being dispatched 3. Data is dispatched for user experience measurement from the app		

	for every 30 minutes 4. the pragmatic quality such as usability-(e.g. performance, issues) are calculated in order to find the user experience (UX) 5. UX quality variables are sent to DCL2 for storage/updating in user profile.
Alternative Flows:	N/A
Exceptions:	N/A
Includes:	N/A
Frequency of Use:	Frequent, request by SL
Special Requirements:	N/A
Assumptions:	Service contract between DCL and SL is defined
Notes and Issues:	N/A
Sequence Diagram	

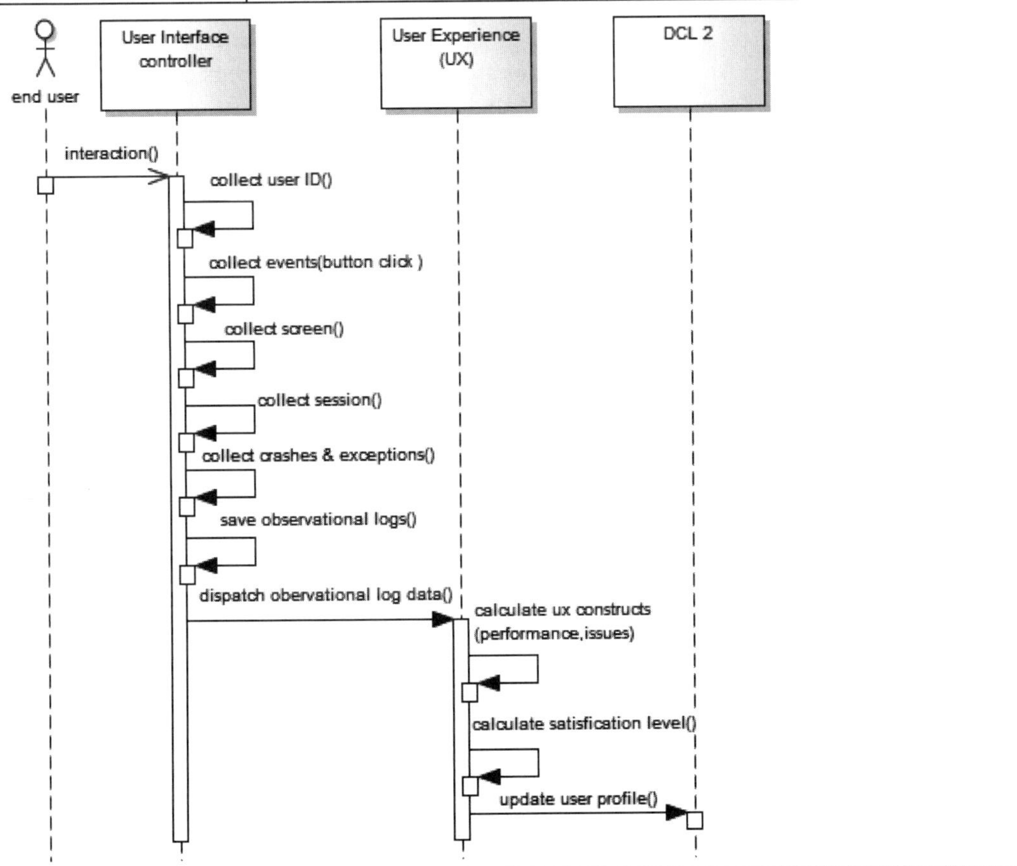

<table>
<tr><td>Use Case ID:</td><td colspan="3">SL-UCS-08</td></tr>
<tr><td>Use Case Name:</td><td colspan="3">Acquire Recommendations for displaying to end user</td></tr>
<tr><td>Created By:</td><td>Jamil Hussain</td><td>Last Updated By:</td><td>Anees Ul Hassan</td></tr>
<tr><td>Date Created:</td><td>14 July 2015</td><td>Last Revision Date:</td><td>01 July 2018</td></tr>
<tr><td>Actors:</td><td colspan="3">Primary: End-user
Secondary: SCL, DCL</td></tr>
<tr><td>Description:</td><td colspan="3">This use case collects the recommendations generated by SCL and displays it on the user interface for the end users. The provided recommendations are displayed according to user capabilities, context of use, and device characteristics. This information is obtained from the DCL.</td></tr>
<tr><td>Trigger:</td><td colspan="3">SCL push the recommendations to the App or end-user send request for recommendations</td></tr>
<tr><td>Preconditions:</td><td colspan="3">End-user subscribes to particular services</td></tr>
<tr><td>Postconditions:</td><td colspan="3">All recommendations are successfully displayed according to user capabilities, context, and device characteristics.</td></tr>
<tr><td>Normal Flow:</td><td colspan="3">1. SCL generate the recommendations and provide it to user interface
2. The SCL recommendations are acquired by the SL
3. SL investigates the user capabilities, context of use, and device characteristics by obtaining from DCL
4. The recommendation is displayed in graphical user interface based on collected capabilities of user, context and device information.</td></tr>
<tr><td>Alternative Flows:</td><td colspan="3">2a. In step 2. The SCL recommendations are acquired by the SL
1. user request for recommendations (pull method)

2b. In step 2. The SCL recommendations are acquired by the SL
1. SL push recommendations to App based on situations</td></tr>
<tr><td>Exceptions:</td><td colspan="3">N/A</td></tr>
<tr><td>Includes:</td><td colspan="3">N/A</td></tr>
<tr><td>Frequency of Use:</td><td colspan="3">Whenever the recommendations are generated by SCL [Medium]</td></tr>
<tr><td>Special Requirements:</td><td colspan="3">N/A</td></tr>
<tr><td>Assumptions:</td><td colspan="3">The user profile data and context information should exist in the DCL</td></tr>
<tr><td>Notes and Issues:</td><td colspan="3">N/A</td></tr>
<tr><td>Sequence Diagram</td><td colspan="3"></td></tr>
</table>

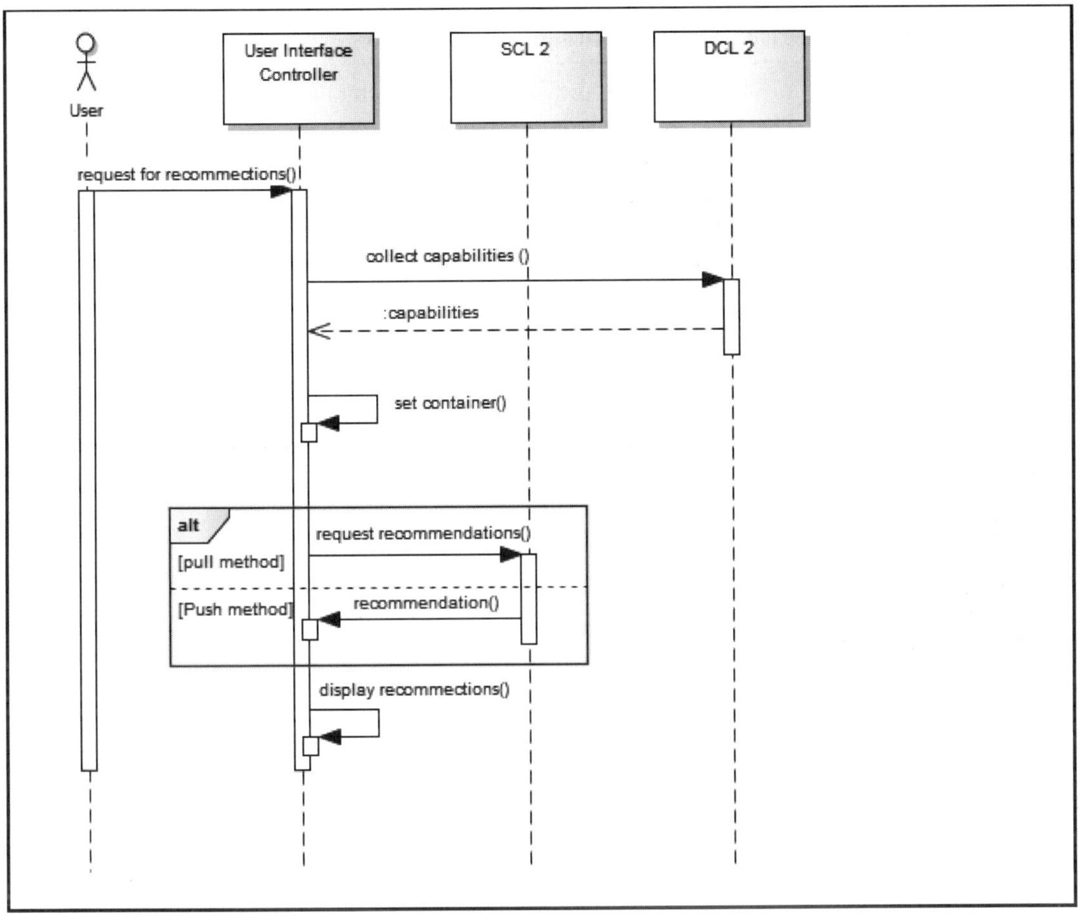

Use Case ID:	SL-UCS-09		
Use Case Name:	Feedback Collection		
Created By:	Jamil Hussain	Last Updated By:	Anees Ul Hassan
Date Created:	March 09 2017	Last Revision Date:	01 July 2018
Actors:	Primary: End-user Secondary: DCL 3		
Description:	The UI/UX shall collect feedback about how users feel about recommendations and additional questionnaires in a predefined time period		
Trigger:	End user		
Preconditions:	Self-reporting questionnaire already exist		

Postconditions:	The feedback is successfully collected
Normal Flow:	1. The end user provide feedback using the questionnaires and feedback about recommendation. 2. The DCL stores the feedback in the lifelog for user preferences in the case of feedback. 3. The questionnaires are stored in the lifelog for further analysis from the expert
Alternative Flows:	NA
Exceptions:	N/A
Includes:	N/A
Frequency of Use:	Every 3 weeks
Special Requirements:	N/A
Assumptions:	The feedback data is saved in DCL
Notes and Issues:	N/A
Sequence Diagram	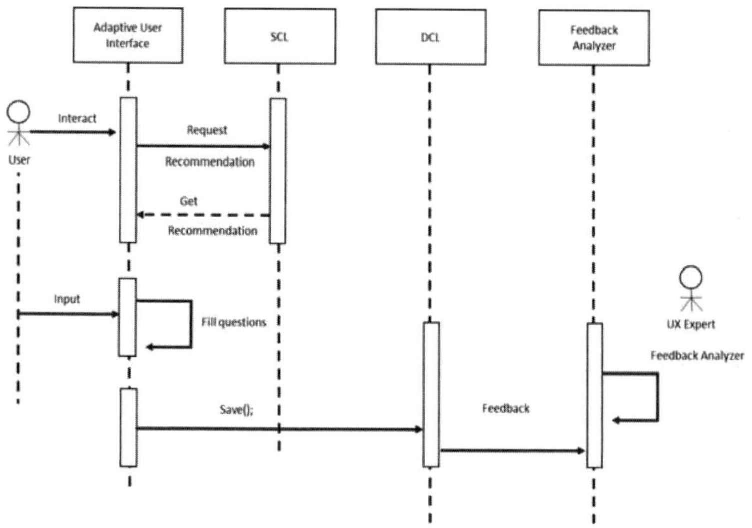

Use Case ID:	SL-UC-10		
Use Case Name:	Retrieve capabilities for context-based services		
Created By:	Jamil Hussain	Last Updated By:	Anees Ul Hassan
Date Created:	March 09 2017	Last Revision Date:	01 July 2018
Actors:	DCL, SCL		
Description:	The UI/UX shall collect feedback about how users feel about recommendations and additional questionnaires in a predefined time period		
Trigger:	End user		
Preconditions:	Self-reporting questionnaire already exist		
Postconditions:	The feedback is successfully collected		
Normal Flow:	1. The end user provide feedback using the questionnaires and feedback about recommendation. 2. The DCL stores the feedback in the lifelog for user preferences in the case of feedback. 3. The questionnaires are stored in the lifelog for further analysis from the expert		
Alternative Flows:	NA		
Exceptions:	N/A		
Includes:	N/A		
Frequency of Use:	Every 3 weeks		
Special Requirements:	N/A		
Assumptions:	The feedback data is saved in DCL		
Notes and Issues:	N/A		
Sequence Diagram			

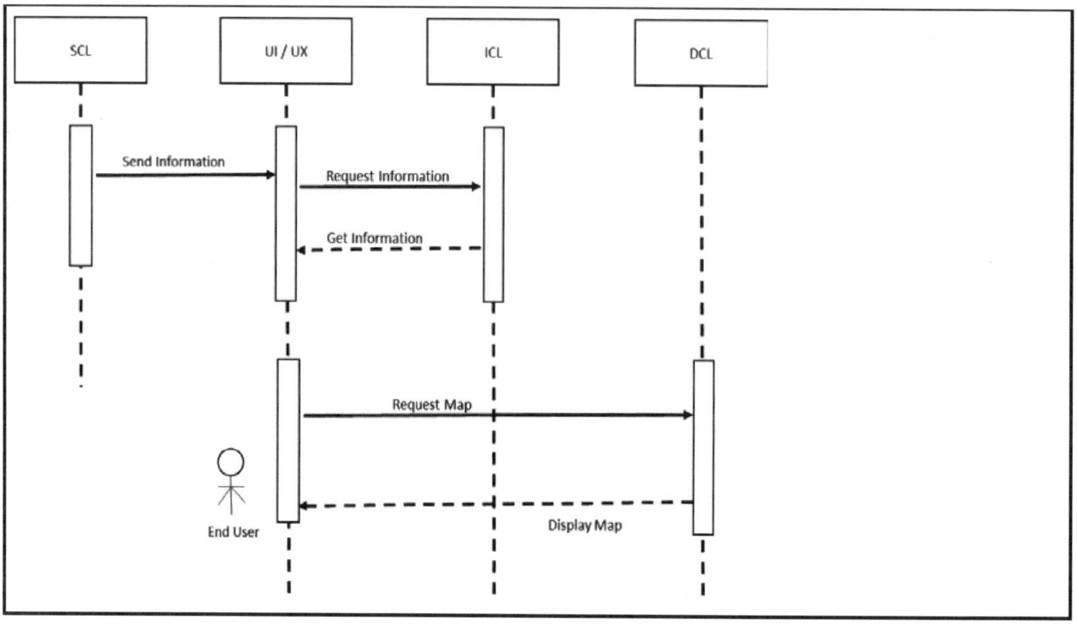

Use Case ID:	SL-UC-11		
Use Case Name:	Map Request to Query		
Created By:	Shujaat Hussain	Last Updated By:	Shujaat Hussain
Date Created:	14 July 2015	Last Revision Date:	01 July 2018
Actors:	Primary: Expert		
Description:	This use case focuses on mapping the expert request to the query library for data store interface.		
Trigger:	The request from the expert panel for analytics		
Preconditions:	A predefined query library for retrieving the big data		
Postconditions:	The query is sent to the data store interface and the data is fetched.		
Normal Flow:	1. The expert requests the analytics for a specific context. 2. The parameters of the request is extracted and sent to query manager. 3. The query manager matches the parameters with the predefined queries in the query library. 4. The Query is selected and tuned according to the duration of the data to be extracted.		

Alternative Flows:	4a. In step 4 of the normal flow, if there is a more tuning done than the query 1. The query is saved in the library for future calls.
Exceptions:	N/A
Includes:	N/A
Frequency of Use:	This use case can be used by the domain expert about 5-10 times based on the volume of data. [Low]
Special Requirements:	N/A
Assumptions:	For this use case the assumption is a query library.
Notes and Issues:	1. How many queries are there in the query library?
Sequence Diagram	

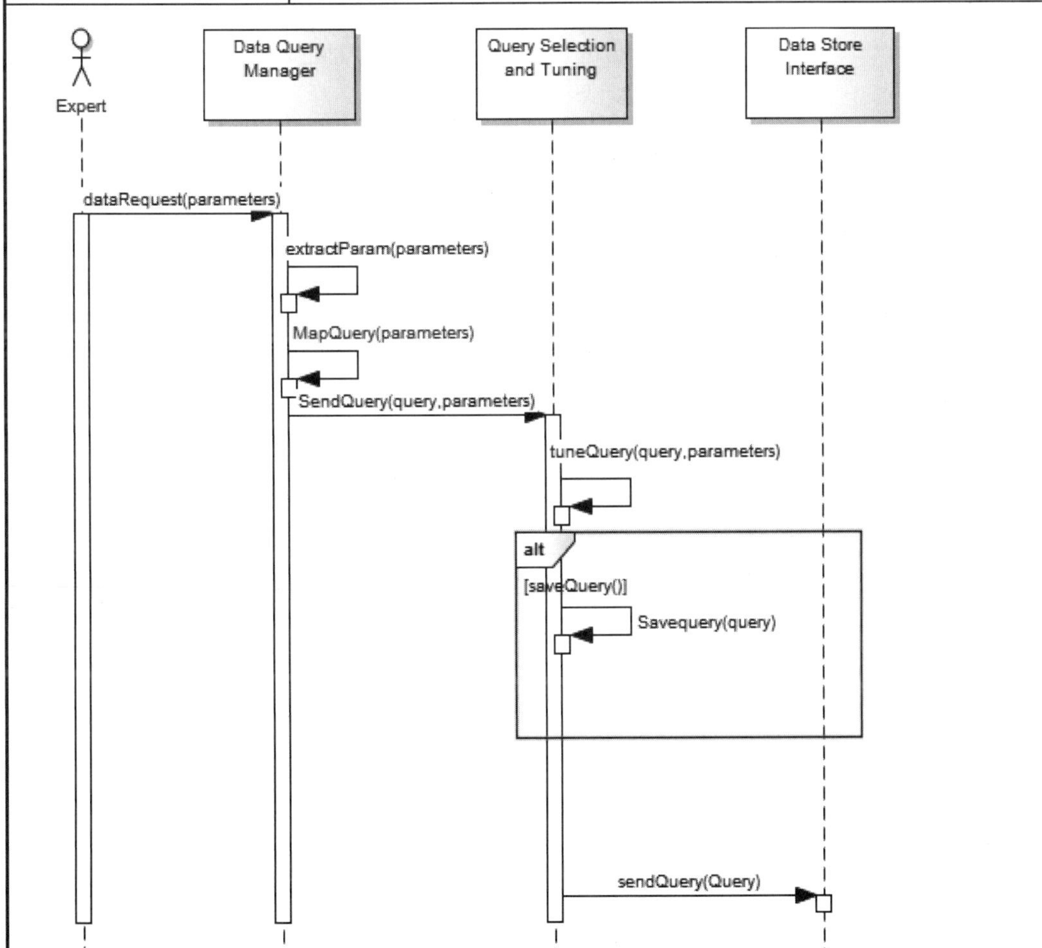

Use Case ID:	SL-UC-12		
Use Case Name:	Transform Data		
Created By:	Shujaat Hussain	Last Updated By:	Shujaat Hussain
Date Created:	14 July 2015	Last Revision Date:	01 July 2018
Actors:	Primary: Expert		
Description:	The mapping query is transformed to specific model structure for trend analysis.		
Trigger:	The data store interface initiates the data transformation process		
Preconditions:	The data is sent from the data store interface.		
Postconditions:	The transformed data is sent to trend analyzer.		
Normal Flow:	1. The unstructured data from the big data repository is sent to the data integration component. 2. The data is transformed in an object model or a table depending on the requirements. 3. The social network data is than additionally integrated which is retrieved through a web service. 4. The transformed data is then checked for compliance with the model template.		
Alternative Flows:	2a. In step 2 of the normal flow, if the data is retrieved from the lifelog then it is sent directly to the integration component.		
Exceptions:	If the transformed data does not pass the compliance check, step 2 is started again.		
Includes:	N/A		
Frequency of Use:	This use case is used when the data comes from the big data and requires social data integration. [Low]		
Special Requirements:	N/A		
Assumptions:			
Notes and Issues:	1. How many models can the data be transformed in?		
Sequence Diagram			

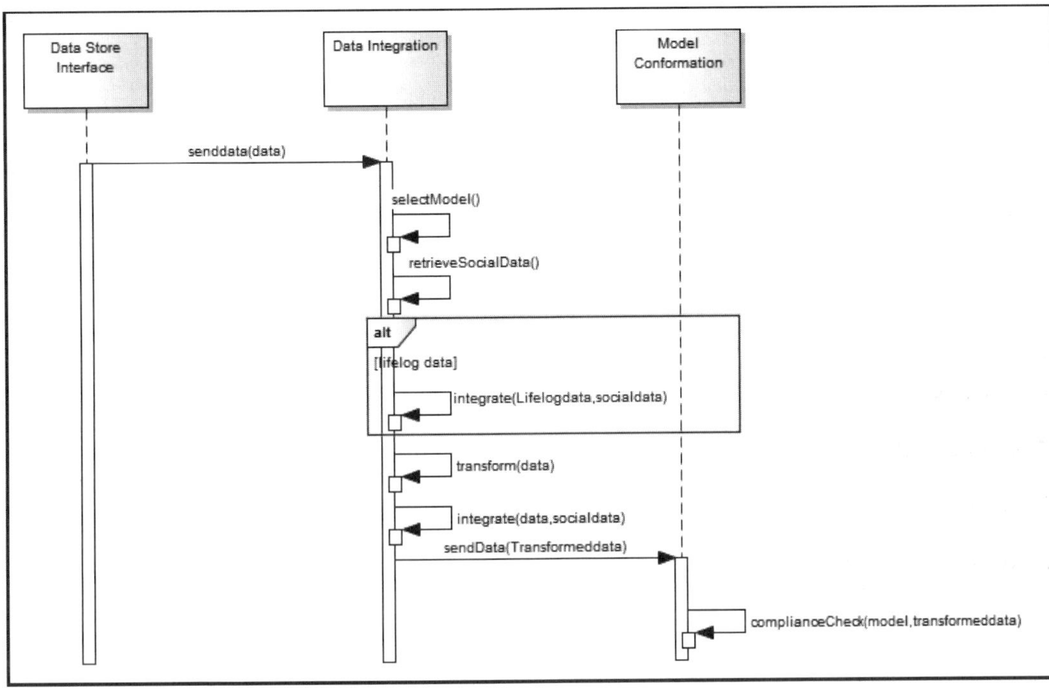

Use Case ID:	SL-UCS-13		
Use Case Name:	Classify Data		
Created By:	Shujaat Hussain	Last Updated By:	Shujaat Hussain
Date Created:	14 July 2015	Last Revision Date:	01 July 2018
Actors:	Primary: Expert		
Description:	The transformed data is further classified and clustered to identify and analyze trends.		
Trigger:	The transformed data is sent for trend analysis.		
Preconditions:	The data is structured into a particular model.		
Postconditions:	The data is classified into temporal, numerical and textual categories		
Normal Flow:	1. The model is passed for the classification. 2. Metadata is extracted from the model. 3. The data is categorized based on the extracted metadata. 4. The temporal, numerical and textual data is extracted from the transformed data.		

Alternative Flows:	
Exceptions:	1. There is no temporal data to be classified. 2. There is no numerical data to be classified. 3. There is no textual data to be classified.
Includes:	
Frequency of Use:	This use case is used when the transformed data comes from model transformation module. [Low]
Special Requirements:	NA
Assumptions:	NA
Notes and Issues:	NA
Sequence Diagram	NA

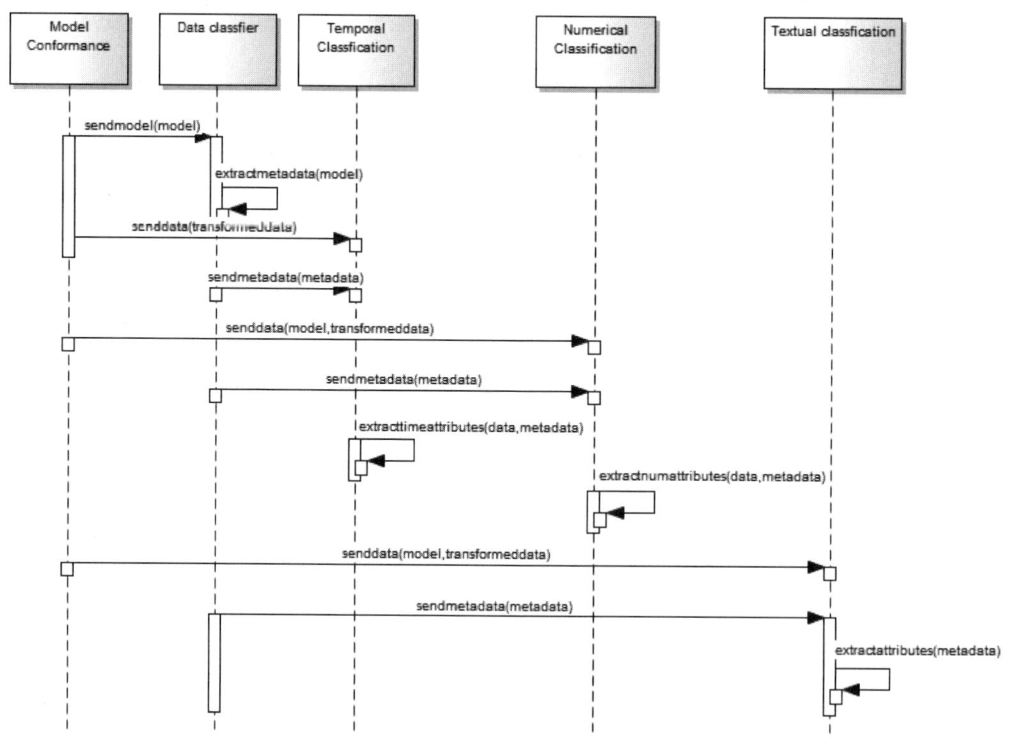

Use Case ID:	SL-UC-14		
Use Case Name:	Analyze Data		
Created By:	Shujaat Hussain	Last Updated By:	Shujaat Hussain
Date Created:	14 July 2015	Last Revision Date:	01 July 2018
Actors:	Primary: Expert		
Description:	The classified data is analyzed through association and clustering techniques for visualization and analytics.		
Trigger:	The classified data is passed to association clustering for finding analytics and trends.		
Preconditions:	The numerical, temporal and textual data is classified separately so that association could be applied.		
Postconditions:	The association is done with the data for analytics and data to be plotted is sent for visualization.		
Normal Flow:	1. The data classifier passes the data for association clustering. 2. The temporal and numerical data is analyzed for clustering. 3. The data is clustered into a group for graph plotting. 4. The textual data is associated with each other to create analytics based on the textual attribute and their corresponding facts.		
Alternative Flows:			
Exceptions:	1. Clustering could not be done due to multiple outliers.		
Includes:			
Frequency of Use:	This use case is used when the classified data is sent for grouping and association. [Low]		
Special Requirements:	NA		
Assumptions:	NA		
Notes and Issues:	NA		
Sequence Diagram	NA		

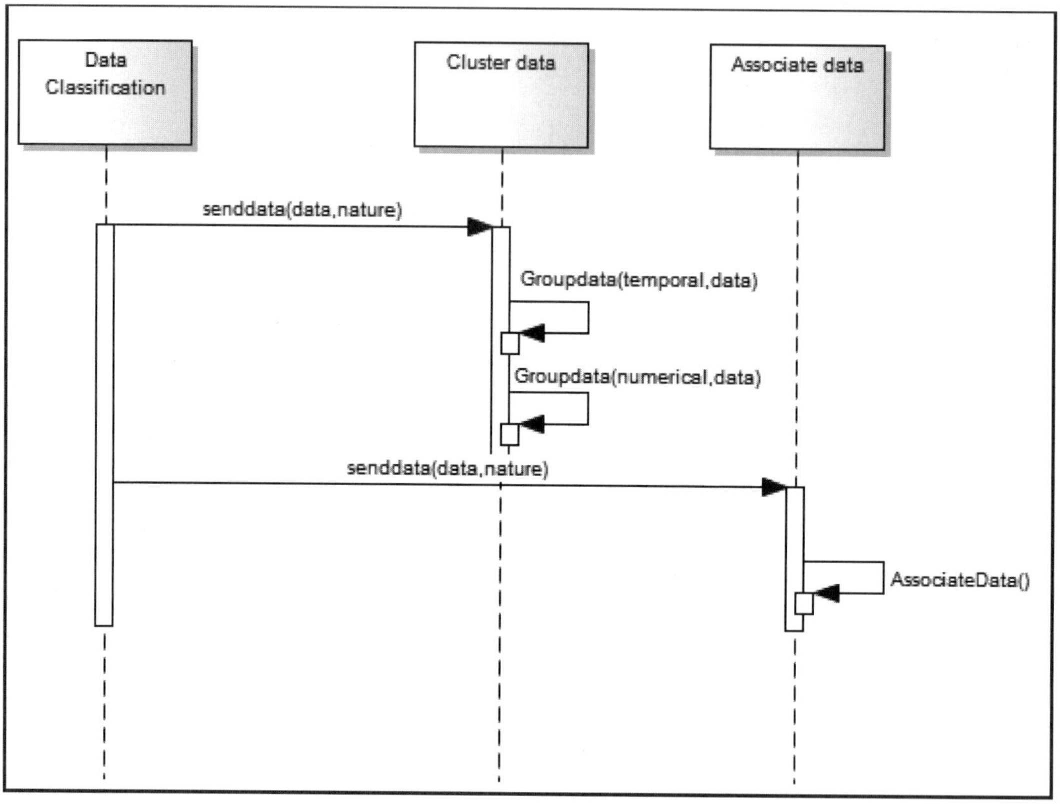

Use Case ID:	SL-UC-15		
Use Case Name:	Display Analytics		
Created By:	Shujaat Hussain	Last Updated By:	Shujaat Hussain
Date Created:	14 July 2015	Last Revision Date:	01 July 2018
Actors:	Primary: Expert		
Description:	The grouped data and relevant analytics is passed to visualization enabler so that the graphs are plotted and displayed.		
Trigger:	The trend analyzer sends the data for graph visualization and plotting.		
Preconditions:	The data is sent to visualization enabler distinguishable by their attributes and association.		
Postconditions:	The analytics and relevant visualization is sent to the user interface.		
Normal Flow:	1. The data is categorized according to the graph templates for visualization.		

	2. The scales are defined for the grouped data to be plotted on the coordinates. 3. The association text and the relevant facts about the data is also attached to the graph as analytics.
Alternative Flows:	NA
Exceptions:	NA
Includes:	NA
Frequency of Use:	This use case is used when the grouped data is sent for display in graph and analytics form. [Low]
Special Requirements:	NA
Assumptions:	NA
Notes and Issues:	NA
Sequence Diagram	

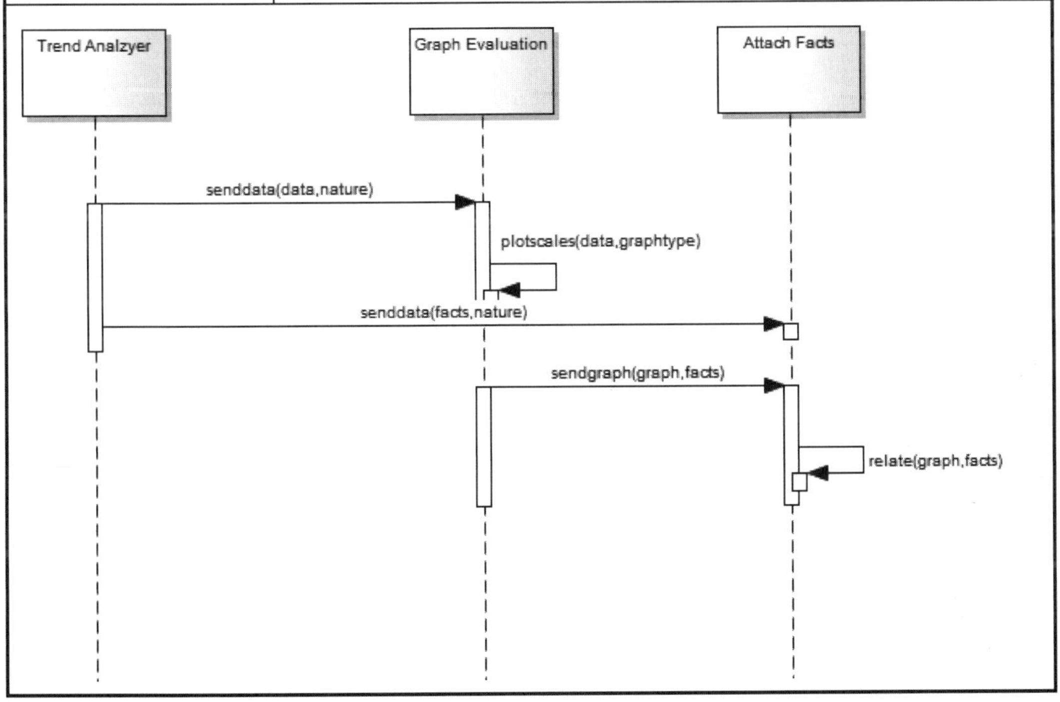

Use Case ID:	SL-UC-16		
Use Case Name:	Take Expert Input		
Created By:	Shujaat Hussain	Last Updated By:	Shujaat Hussain
Date Created:	14 July 2015	Last Revision Date:	01 July 2018
Actors:	Primary: Expert		
Description:	This use case focuses on taking expert input on activity and nutrition for the user's analytics		
Trigger:	The request from the expert panel for input		
Preconditions:	The user meal and activity information is stored		
Postconditions:	The query is sent to the data store interface and the data is stored.		
Normal Flow:	1. The expert requests the input panel for a specific user. 2. The parameters of the request is extracted and sent to query manager. 3. The query manager matches the parameters with the predefined queries in the query library. 4. The interface is shown for expert to input activity and meal information 5. It is stored in the lifelog		
Alternative Flows:	4a. In step 4 of the normal flow, if there is a more tuning done than the query 1. The query is saved in the library for future calls.		
Exceptions:	NA		
Includes:	NA		
Frequency of Use:	NA		
Special Requirements:	NA		
Assumptions:	NA		
Notes and Issues:	NA		
Sequence Diagram			

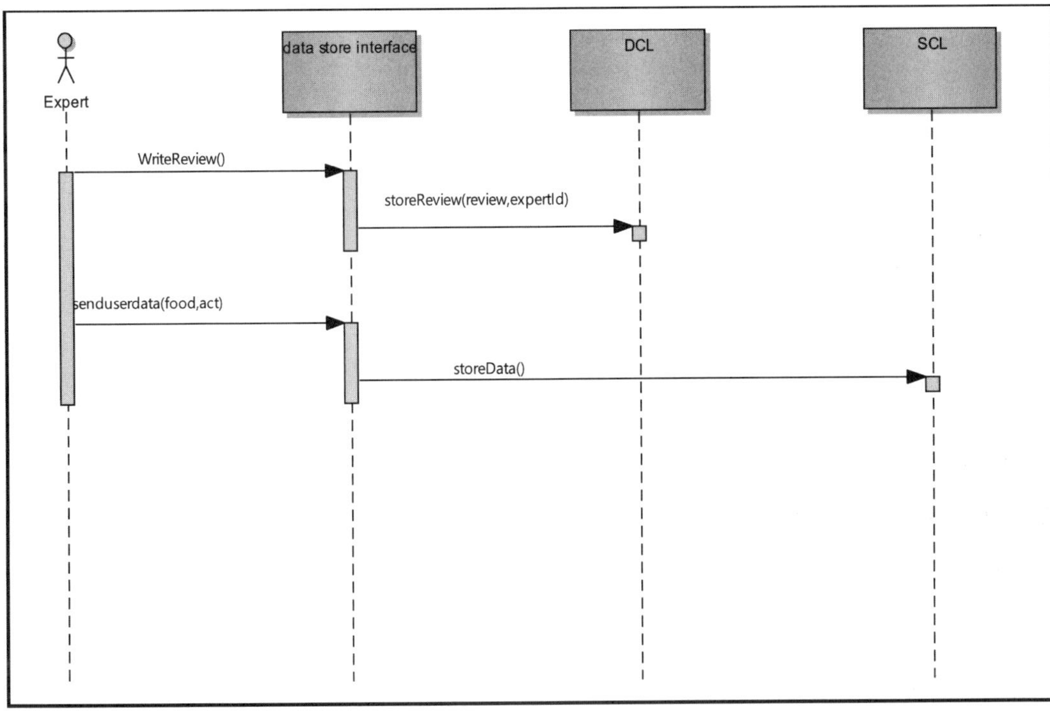

Use Case ID:	SL-UC-17		
Use Case Name:	Display Adaptive Questionnaires		
Created By:	Shujaat Hussain	Last Updated By:	Shujaat Hussain
Date Created:	26 October 2017	Last Revision Date:	01 July 2018
Actors:	Primary: User		
Description:	This use case focuses on displaying questions adaptively depending on the user situation.		
Trigger:	The request from the user after a stage is completed for questions		
Preconditions:	The situation is analyzed to identify the questions.		
Postconditions:	The questions are displayed to the user		
Normal Flow:	1. The user requests questions after completing the stage. 2. The parameters of the request is extracted and sent to query manager according to the user situation. 3. The query manager matches the parameters with the predefined		

	queries in the query library. 4. The questions are shown to the user with respect to the stage and situation
Alternative Flows:	4a. In step 4 of the normal flow, if there is a more tuning done than the query 2. The query is saved in the library for future calls.
Exceptions:	NA
Includes:	NA
Frequency of Use:	NA
Special Requirements:	NA
Assumptions:	NA
Notes and Issues:	NA
Sequence Diagram	

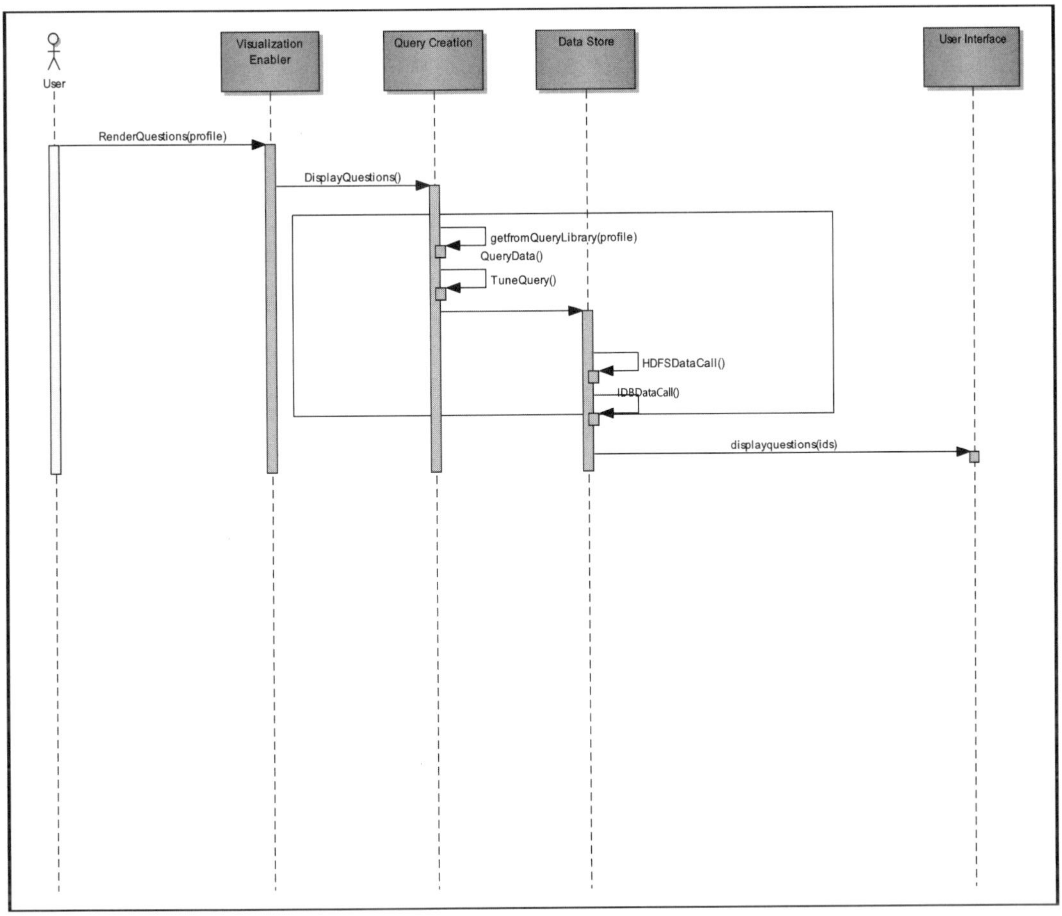
User
Visualization Enabler
Query Creation
Data Store
User Interface
RenderQuestions(profile)
DisplayQuestions()
getfromQueryLibrary(profile)
QueryData()
TuneQuery()
HDFSDataCall()
IDBDataCall()
displayquestions(ids)